MW00789301

AIRPORT GARAGE
ENTS
HENLYS
MILITARY POLICE
MILITARY POLICE
7
9X9019

D-DAY
THEN AND NOW

Volume 1

It is easier to let the mind wander back among things done, when to speculate upon and calculate the unknown ahead needs so much effort.

LIEUTENANT-GENERAL SIR FREDERICK MORGAN
Chief-of-Staff to the Supreme Allied Commander
and chief planner of Operation 'Overlord'

D-DAY
THEN AND NOW

Volume 1

Credits

© *After The Battle* 1995
ISBN: 0 900913 84 3
Printed in Great Britain
Edited and designed by Winston G. Ramsey

PUBLISHERS
Battle of Britain Prints International Ltd,
Church House, Church Street, London E15 3JA
An *After the Battle* publication

PRINTERS
Plaistow Press Ltd,
Church House, Church Street, London E15 3JA

FRONT COVER
On the evening of D–1, General Eisenhower visited units of the 101st Airborne Division on their airfields near Newbury, Berkshire. At Greenham Common, he is pictured speaking with Lieutenant Wallace Strobel, 502nd Parachute Infantry Regiment (see page 295). The label '23' denotes the number of the stick with which Strobel was to drop. From a painting by George A. Campbell.

REAR COVER
Troops board their LSI (Landing Ship, Infantry) at Dartmouth on June 2, the name of the port on the River Dart being visible along the quayside of the South Embankment. (US Army)

FRONTISPIECE
Men of the 6th Airborne Division admire the message chalked on their Horsa glider. (Imperial War Museum)

FRONT ENDPAPER
Typical pre-D-Day scene in Britain: MPs lead a convoy along 'a highway near London'. These GMC CCKW-353 2½-ton 6×6 cargo trucks are negotiating the roundabout junction of the Great South-West Road (the A30) and the Bath Road (A4) at Hounslow on March 7, 1944. (US Army)

REAR ENDPAPER
British troops who have advanced inland from Sword, watch the arrival of reinforcements for the 6th Airborne Division on the evening of D-Day. The location is most probably Beauvais Farm, north of the 'Hillman' strong point (see page 560). (Imperial War Museum)

EXTRACTS
Acknowledgement is given to the following authors and their publishers for permission to quote from published works:

PRELUDE by General George C. Marshall from the *Biennial Report of the Chief of Staff of the United States Army to the Secretary of War, July 1, 1943, to June 30, 1945.*
OPERATION 'OVERLORD' and OK, LET'S GO? from *Crusade in Europe* by Dwight D. Eisenhower. Copyright 1948 by Doubleday, a division of Bantam Doubleday Dell Publishing Group, Inc. Used by permission of Doubleday, a division of Bantam Doubleday Dell Publishing Group, Inc.
SUPREME HEADQUARTERS ALLIED EXPEDITIONARY FORCE from *Eisenhower's Six Great Decisions* by Walter B. Smith published by Longmans, London, 1956.
GERMAN DEFENCES from *The Fatal Decisions* published by Michael Joseph, London, 1956.
ULTRA from *Ultra in the West* by Ralph Bennett, published by Hutchinson, 1989.
COMMAND DECISIONS reprinted with the permission of Simon & Schuster Inc. from *With Prejudice* by Lord Tedder. Copyright © 1966 by The Lord Tedder. Originally published by Cassell and Co., Ltd, London.
PLANS AND PREPARATIONS from *Normandy to the Baltic* by Field Marshal The Viscount Montgomery of Alamein published by BAOR, 1946, by permission of A. P. Watt Ltd, and *The Memoirs of Field-Marshal Montgomery* by the same author published by Collins, London, 1958.
AIR OPERATIONS FOR D-DAY by Air Chief Marshal Sir Trafford Leigh Mallory from the Fourth Supplement to *The London Gazette*, HMSO, December 31, 1946.
OPERATION NEPTUNE by Admiral Sir Bertram Ramsay from the Supplement to *The London Gazette*, HMSO, October 28, 1947.
6th AIRBORNE DIVISION from *With the 6th Airborne Division in Normandy* by R. N. Gale published by Sampson, Low, Marston & Company Ltd, 1948.
82nd AIRBORNE DIVISION reprinted from *Soldier: The Memoirs of Matthew B. Ridgway* by General Matthew B. Ridgway as told to Harold H. Martin. Copyright © 1956 by Matthew B. Ridgway and Harold H. Martin. Copyright © 1956 by Curtis Publishing Company. Copyright renewed 1984. Reprinted by permission of HarperCollins Publishers, Inc.
101st AIRBORNE DIVISION reprinted from *Swords and Plowshares* by Maxwell D. Taylor, by permission of W. W. Norton & Company, Inc. Copyright © 1972 by Maxwell D. Taylor.
The Editor is indebted to Major General C. A. Ramsay, CB, OBE, for granting permission to include extracts from his father's diary for 1944 published as *The Year of D-Day* by the University of Hull Press, 1994.

ACKNOWLEDGEMENTS
The Editor is indebted to many individuals and organisations for their assistance:
Paul Almasy; Lieutenant-Colonel D. A. Armitage, Museum of Army Flying; R. R. Aspinall, The Museum of London; Roger Bell; Maria Blyzinsky, National Maritime Museum; P. J. Bottrill, Area Librarian, South Devon; Phillip N. Bradley; Keith Braybrooke; David Buxton; Roger Day; Steve Casely; Peter Chamberlain; Terry Charman, Imperial War Museum; Lieutenant-Colonel M-J. P. Chilcott; M. J. Conroy; Major R. K. Cross; Lieutenant-General Sir Napier Crookenden; Maureen Dale, AEA Technology; Brian L. Davis; S. Dawson, Royal Engineers Library; Gerard M. Devlin; Leonard Dry; Harrie Dijkhuizen; J. R. Elliott, Area Librarian, West Devon; David Fletcher, The Tank Museum, Bovington; Roger Freeman; Ray Funnel, RAF Museum, Hendon; Gwenaël Garçon, Hotel George V, Paris; Frank Gillard; Laurie Goldstraw; Arlette Gondrée-Pritchett; Christine Grant, COMNAVACTUK; Dr Colin Greaves, West Sussex Institute of Higher Education; A. G. Gueymard; David O. Hale; Douglas Harper; Guy Hartcup; Max Hastings, *The Daily Telegraph*; Major Winfried Heinemann, Militärgeschichtliches Forschungsamt, Freiburg; Jan Heitmann; Jan Hey; Chris Hobson, RAF Staff College, Bracknell; Hans Houterman; Gary Howard; Roy Howard; D. J. Hubbard, Exeter County Council; Gillian Hughes; Roy Humphreys; Richard James; Paul Kemp, Imperial War Museum; Alan King, Central Library, Portsmouth; Bill King; Brad King, Imperial War Museum; Norman Kirby; George E. Koskimaki; the late Mari Laurent; George Laws; James Layerzapf, Dwight D. Eisenhower Library; D. Leavy; David List; Bob Lock, School of Infantry, Warminster; Peter G. de Lotz; Herr von Lutzau, Volksbund Deutsche Kriegsgräberfürsorge; Alistair Macdonald; Wilbert Mahoney, US National Archives; John Major, The University of Hull; Commander N. I. C. Manger RN, HMS *Osprey*; Armand Martin, Musée de la Guerre des Ondes, Tourcoing; Yolanda Mausbridge, Rank Hovis; Tamara McAvie of COMNAVACTUK; Major M. J. Menage, School of Infantry, Warminster; Hubert Meyer; Lieutenant-Colonel Terence Miller; Barry Murphy, Commonwealth War Graves Commission; Michael Ockenden; Dr C. A. Olford and E. A. Tiller; Bernard Paich, Heimdal; Richard Ponman, Cabinet Office, Historical Section; Seimon Pugh-Jones; Major John Porter-Wright, School of Infantry, Warminster; Alan Reeves; Clive Richards, RAF Museum; P. G. Rowe Esq, Atomic Weapons Establishment, Aldermaston; Hans Sakkers ; P. A. Sanderson Esq, EODTIC; Derek R. Sansom, Ford Motor Company; Andy Saunders; Mme J. Scheepers, Hotel Prince de Galles, Paris; Jack Schlegel; Lieutenant-Colonel Chris Sexton; Kathleen A. Struss, Dwight D. Eisenhower Library; Denis Sweeting; Stephen Sykes; Michael J. Teevens; Father Gerard Thuring, Groesbeek Liberation Museum; Ian Toler; Alan Tomkins; Janet Thomson, Tewkesbury Library; Michel De Trez; Bart Vanderveen; Jean-Bernard Valognes; Henri Vasselin; Robert Voskuil; Chris Webb, Airborne Forces Museum; Henry Wills; Michael J. Winey, US Army Military History Institute; Marion Wollaston, Port of Tilbury Ltd.

PHOTOGRAPHS
Copyright is indicated for all original illustrations where known. Present-day photographs are the copyright of *After the Battle* magazine unless otherwise stated.

AEA Technology: 220 middle right, 248 middle right.
Aerofilms: 59 top right.
101st Airborne Division: 305 top left.
M. P. Almassy: 230 top left.
Archives du Val D'Oise: 51 bottom.
Elisa Blacker: 155 top left, top right.
Phillip Bradley: 306 middle right, bottom right.
Keith Braybrooke: 142 middle right, 143 top.
Charles E. Brown: 219 top.
Commonwealth War Graves Commission: 259 bottom.
CS(Photography) 231 top right.
Bundesarchiv: 34 top, 35 top left, top right, 37 top, bottom right, 42 top right, 43 top, bottom left, 44 top, middle left, bottom left, 45 top left, bottom left, 46 bottom left, centre right, 47 bottom left, bottom right, 48 top, bottom left, bottom right, 49 top right, 51 top right, 52 top left, bottom left, 53 top, bottom left, bottom right, 54 bottom left, 56 top left, bottom left, 57 top left, middle right, bottom, 58 top right, 66 top, 67 bottom left, 265 top, 266 bottom left, 267 bottom left.
George A. Campbell: 165 top.
Canadian National Archives: 205 top, 206 top left.
Centre de Recherches et d'Etudes Historiques de la Seconde Guerre Mondiale, Brussels: 49 top.
Lieutenant Colonel M-J P. Chilcott: 236 bottom right, 237 top left.
Commonwealth War Graves Commission: 259 bottom.
The Daily Telegraph: 157 middle right, 295 bottom left.
Ray Delvert: 225 top, 227 top.
Dwight D. Eisenhower Library: 8, 163 bottom right.
ECP Armées, Paris: 47 top and middle, 55 bottom left, 246 middle left, 300 top, bottom right.
Edinburgh City Library: 260 top.
Exeter City Council: 226 middle.
FOSF Photographic Unit: 179 top right, bottom.
Alan French: 86 bottom.
James M. Gavin: 261 top right, bottom right, 262 top right, bottom left, 264 middle right.
Frank Gleeson: 246 bottom right.
Arlette Gondrée-Pritchett: 245 bottom left.
Malcolm Gray: 75 bottom right.
Forrest Guth: 306 middle left, bottom left, 307 top left, top right, 310 top left.
C. W. F. Holmes: 21 top left, top right.
HMS *Dryad*: 160 bottom.
HMS *Nelson*: 160 top, 162 top.
HMSO: 172 top.
Hulton Picture Company: 16 top left, second left.
IGN Paris: 113 bottom right, 150 top right, bottom right, 154 bottom right, 235 bottom, 275 bottom right.
***Illustrated*:** 9 bottom right.
Imperial War Museum: 6 top, bottom, 15 bottom left, 16 bottom right, 31 bottom left, bottom right, 76 top, 77 top left, middle right, 80 bottom right, 83 top right, 84 bottom right, 85 top right, 92 middle, 93 top, bottom left, bottom right, 94 top, 95 top left, top right, bottom left, 96 top, bottom left, 97 bottom left, bottom right, 98 top left, middle, 99 top, 100 top, bottom right, 101 top left, top right, bottom, 102 top left, top right, 103 top right, bottom right, 114 top left, bottom left, 115 top right, bottom left, 117 top left, middle, 118 top left, bottom left, 119 top left, middle left, bottom left,120 top left, 121 top left, top right, bottom left, bottom right, 122 top left, middle right, bottom left, 123 top, bottom left, 124 bottom left, 129 top, 135 top right, 137 top, 138 top left, top right, middle right, bottom right, 140 top, 145 top right, bottom right, 146 bottom right, 147 top, 152 top, middle right, bottom left, bottom right, 153 top, bottom left, bottom right, 157 top left, 161 top left, 168 top, 169 top left, top right, bottom right, 174 bottom right, 176 top right, 177 top, bottom right, 178 top, bottom right, 179 top right, 181 top left, middle right, 184 middle, bottom left, bottom right, 191 bottom left, 192 top bottom left, bottom right, 193 top, middle left, bottom left, bottom right, 195 middle left, middle right, middle right, 208 top, 212 centre, 214 top, bottom left, 218 top, bottom, 220 top, 221 top, 222 top left, top right, middle right, bottom left, bottom right, 223 top right, bottom, 225 bottom right, 227 bottom right, 228 top, 229 top left, middle left, 233 top, 244 top left, middle left, 245 top left, 246 top left, 247 top left, bottom left, 248 top, bottom, 249 top right, top left, middle right, bottom, 259 top, 288 top right, bottom left, 292 top right, 310 bottom.
Keele University: 235 top right, 267 top right.
Laing Photographic Services: 80 top right.
London Transport Mueum: 141 top left.
Frank Martin: 231 top right.
Guy Maugrain: 241 centre left.
Robert Mead: 81 top right, bottom left.
Bill Miller: 245 bottom left.
Mirror Syndication International: 244 bottom.
Museum of London: 97 top right, 197 top left, bottom left, 198 top, 199 middle left.
National Monuments Record Centre: 237 bottom right.
US National Archives: 7 top, 46 top right, 156 top, 158 top left, 159 top left, bottom right, 189 top right, 190 top, 302 middle, 303 middle left, 306 top right.
Office of the Chief of Military History (US): 146 top.
Ordnance Survey: 226 bottom left, 237 bottom left, 285 top left.
Norman Ottaway: 285 top right.
William H. Parkhill: 298 bottom left, bottom right.
Port of Tilbury Ltd: 197 top right.
Portsmouth Publishing & Printing Ltd: 128 top, 133 bottom.
Press Association: 231 bottom.
Public Record Office: 59 bottom left, 60 middle, 61 top right, 67 top left, top right, 68 top right, bottom left, bottom right, 69 top right, bottom left, bottom right, 70 top left, bottom right, 71 top left, top right, bottom right.
RAF: 27 top, 29 bottom right.
RAF Northwood: 77 bottom.
RAF Staff Collsge, Bracknell: 78 bottom.
Hans Sakkers: 45 top right, 46 top left, 54 top left, 55 top right.
St Paul's School: 88 top, 89 top right, bottom, 90 top right, bottom left, 110 top left, top right, middle, bottom right, 111 top left.
Jack Schlegel: 267 bottom right.
Science Museum: 58 top left, bottom left.
Southampton City Heritage Services: 130 top left, 131 top.
Studio Goron: 269 bottom left, bottom right.
Sunday Mirror: 244 bottom left.
Tangmere Military Aviation Museum: 86 top left.
Michel De Trez: 261 top left, 264 top left, 310 top right.
440th Troop Carrier Group: 289 top.
US Army: 9 top, 10 bottom left, bottom right,11 top left. top middle, top right, 14 top left, bottom left, 15 top left, top right, 19 top left, 20 top, bottom middle, 21 bottom left, bottom right, 26 top, bottom left, 28 top, 30 top left, top middle, top right, 31 top left, top middle, top right, 33 bottom, 63, top left, 64 top right, bottom left, 79 top left, 81 top left, 82 top left, 87 bottom right, 88 bottom left, 116 top, 141 middle, 142 top left, bottom left, 260 middle, 266 top, 268 top, bottom right, 283 top left, bottom left, 311 top right, bottom, 312 top, 313 top right.
US Navy: 131 bottom left, 187 top, 189 bottom right, 210 top, bottom left, 211 top, middle right, 272 top left, middle, bottom left, 273 bottom left, 303 bottom left.
US Signal Corps: 10 top, 13 bottom left, 18 top left, top right, 19 middle right, 125 top, 180 top, bottom, 182 top, 183 top right, 188 top left, bottom left, bottom right, 200 top right, 201 top, bottom left, 202 top, bottom left, 203 top right, bottom left, 209 top, 270 bottom left, 271 top left, middle right, 273 top, 274 top, bottom right, 275 top, 277 top right, 278 top left, middle, 279 top right, 280 top left, bottom left, 281 top left, middle right, 282 top, 285 bottom left, 286 top, bottom left, bottom right, 289 bottom, 290 top, middle right, bottom right, 291 top, 292 top left, 295 top, 297 bottom left, 303 top, 304 top right, 305 bottom left, 309 top, 312 bottom left, 313 middle, 314 top left, middle, bottom left.
Nigel West: 62 bottom left, bottom right.
Henry Wills: 214 bottom right, 216 top left.

Contents

Volume 1

Volume 2

In November 1943, two top-level conferences were held to map out the future course of the war. *Above:* In Cairo, the 'Sextant' conference was attended by President Franklin D. Roosevelt and Prime Minister Winston Churchill and their staffs from November 23–26. No firm decisions were made, although the Allied Commander-in-Chief in the Mediterranean, General Dwight D. Eisenhower, pressed emphatically for continuing support for the Italian campaign and he stressed the 'vital importance of continuing the maximum possible operations in an established theater since much time was invariably lost when the scene of action was changed, necessitating as it did the arduous task of building up a fresh base'.

Below: The scene of action then shifted to Teheran in Persia where the Big Three Conference opened on November 28. Churchill and Roosevelt were meeting Marshal Josef Stalin for the first time, and the Soviet leader stated that the Red Army was depending upon the opening of the 'Second Front' in 1944. He was told that 'Overlord' (the liberation of North-West Europe) was scheduled for 'some time in May', the final official communiqué announcing that 'our military staffs have joined in our round table discussions, and have concerted our plans for the destruction of the German forces. We have reached complete agreement as to the scope and timing of the operations which will be undertaken from the east, west and south.'

Prelude

By General George C. Marshall
CHIEF-OF-STAFF, UNITED STATES ARMY

In November and December 1943, the Combined Chiefs-of-Staff had met with President Roosevelt and Prime Minister Churchill at the 'Sextant' Conference in Cairo and then with the President, Prime Minister, Marshal Stalin and his military adviser at Teheran. By that time, it was clear how the defeat of Germany could be brought about — but the Allies were beset by innumerable specific problems of implementing the desired strategy.

The greatest of these by far was the critical shortage of landing craft. Those available for the top priority Operation 'Overlord' in Normandy still seemed insufficient and there were many other vital operations that had to be undertaken if we were to maintain the initiative on the global battlefronts. Even though an attack in the south of France was considered essential to the success of 'Overlord', the Combined Chiefs-of-Staff had previously directed that 68 landing ships be returned from the Mediterranean Theater to the United Kingdom beginning January 15, 1944 to meet the requirements of the cross-Channel assault as then planned.

Despite these additional ships, it became evident that there would not be sufficient landing craft in Great Britain by the invasion target date to provide a sufficient margin of safety for the hazardous amphibious assault. Therefore, upon their return to Cairo from Teheran, the Combined Chiefs resolved that more strenuous measures must be taken to permit a broadening of the initial landing in Normandy. The Mediterranean Theater could be bled no further. Only sufficient resources were left there for an assault force of two divisions for southern France, and military intelligence indicated that while this force could probably overcome anticipated German resistance on the Riviera coast, the rapid development of the operation northward up the Rhône valley would not permit further reduction.

The remaining possible source for additional landing ships was in the shipyards of Great Britain and the United States. Such an increase in time for 'Overlord' would require a miracle of production since these shipyards were already overcrowded and working at furious speed to maintain the heavy existing schedule of landing craft production, as well as that for the construction of destroyers and destroyer escorts urgently required to combat the German submarines.

An added complication at this time was the possibility that Turkey might enter the war on the side of the United Nations, exposing herself to attack by Bulgaria. The possibility of operations to support her in the eastern Mediterranean had to be considered.

At the same time, there was grave concern over the situation then obtaining in Asia. The Generalissimo, Chiang Kai-shek, met with President Roosevelt, Prime Minister Churchill, and their military advisers at Cairo, and all were convinced that a determined effort must be made to re-establish surface communication with our Chinese allies in 1944. Agreement was reached for Operation 'Capital' in which the forces of Admiral Mountbatten and General Stilwell were given the mission of investing northern and central Burma. It was realised that the success of these operations could be made much more certain by an amphibious landing in the Bay of Bengal, but there were not sufficient landing craft to ensure the success of our European offensive and at the same time undertake a landing on the shores of Burma.

Victory in this global war depended on the successful execution of 'Overlord'. That must not fail. Yet, the Japanese could not be permitted meanwhile to entrench in their stolen empire, and China must not be allowed to fall victim to further Japanese assaults. Allied resources were searched through again and again, and strategy reconsidered in the light of the deficiencies. These conclusions seemed inescapable: France must be invaded in 1944, to shorten the war by facilitating the advance westward of the Soviet forces. At the same, time German technological advances such as the development of atomic explosives made it imperative that we attack before these terrible weapons could be turned against us. In addition, the pressure on the Japanese in the Pacific must not be relaxed. Communications with China must be reopened. Resources were allocated accordingly. The balance was extremely delicate but we had to go ahead.

From the President to Marshal Stalin

The immediate appointment of General Eisenhower to command of Overlord operation has been decided upon.

Roosevelt

Cairo, Dec. 7. 43

Dear Eisenhower, I thought you might like to have this as a memento. It was written very hurriedly by me as the final meeting broke up yesterday, the President signing it immediately.

G.C.M.

At Teheran, Stalin had pressed the question as to the identity of the Allied commander for 'Overlord', but the answer was sidestepped by Roosevelt saying that he and Churchill would make the final decision when they returned for further talks in Cairo. It had already been agreed at the Quebec conference the previous August that the final choice would be the President's responsibility, the two contenders being either General Marshall, his Chief-of-Staff in Washington, aged 63, or General Eisenhower, ten years his junior. The former deserved command of 'Overlord' as he had already been closely concerned with its planning, but Eisenhower, on the other hand, had already proved himself with a string of victories in the Mediterranean, confirming that a unified Allied command was not only possible but eminently successful in battle. Roosevelt deliberated for several days, finally reaching his decision on the evening of December 6, telling Marshall, who was travelling with the President: 'I don't think I could sleep at night with you out of the country'. According to Marshall, the President asked him to write down a message to be transmitted to Marshal Stalin, Roosevelt adding the word 'immediate' before signing it. After it had been sent, Marshall retrieved the piece of paper and added a postscript before passing it for delivery to Eisenhower in Algiers. Today, the original is held by the Eisenhower Library in Abilene, Kansas.

Operation 'Overlord'

By General Dwight D. Eisenhower
SUPREME COMMANDER, ALLIED EXPEDITIONARY FORCE

In early December, I had received word that the President would return to the United States through our area. I went to Tunis to meet him. During the remainder of the afternoon, we made arrangements to conduct the President to Malta and to Sicily.

A few hours before his arrival, I received a somewhat garbled radiogram from General Marshall that discussed some administrative details incident to my forthcoming change in assignment. When he wrote the message, General Marshall apparently assumed that I had already received specific information concerning the new assignment through staff channels. But, lacking such information, I was unable to deduce his meaning with certainty. The President arrived in mid-afternoon and was scarcely seated in the automobile when he cleared up the matter with one short sentence. He said: 'Well, Ike, you are going to command "Overlord".'

Because I had to discuss with him, at once, details of his next day's plans, we had no opportunity, at that moment, to talk further about the new assignment; but I did manage to say: 'Mr. President, I realize that such an appointment involved difficult decisions. I hope you will not be disappointed.'

During his visit, the President on several occasions discussed matters in connection with my imminent transfer to London. He was quite concerned with two points that did not seem particularly important to me. The first of these was the timing of the announcement. It was finally decided that the President would do this from Washington; in the meantime, my change in assignment would be a closely-guarded secret. The second point was my title as commander of 'Overlord'. He toyed with the word 'supreme' in his conversation but made no decision at the moment. He merely said that he must devise some designation that would imply the importance the Allies attached to the new venture.

A few days after the President's departure, I received from General Marshall a scrap of paper that is still one of my most cherished mementos of World War II.

The new Supreme Commander meets the press. Three days after Eisenhower arrived in London in January 1944, pictures were taken in his old office in Grosvenor Square, last used by him in 1942 prior to Operation 'Torch', although *Illustrated* went to press with an old photograph.

General Dwight D. Eisenhower, 53 years old when appointed Supreme Commander for Operation 'Overlord', graduated from West Point in 1915, his first assignment being with the 19th Infantry Regiment. After the war, he commanded tank corps troops at Fort Dix, New Jersey, and at Fort Benning, Georgia. From 1919 to 1922, he served in various tank battalions until he moved to the Panama Canal Zone where he served as executive officer at Camp Gaillard. In 1925, he attended the Command and General Staff School at Fort Leavenworth, graduating as an honor student in June 1926. A brief tour with the 24th Division followed. In 1927, and again in 1928, he was on duty with the American Battle Monuments Commission in Washington and France. From November 1929 to February 1933, he was Assistant Executive, Office of the Assistant Secretary of War, and from then until September 1935 he worked in the office of the Chief-of-Staff (General Douglas MacArthur). He served as assistant to the military adviser of the Philippine Islands from September 1935 to 1940 when he was assigned to the 15th Infantry Regiment. In November that year, he became Chief-of-Staff of the 3rd Division, in March 1941 Chief-of-Staff of the IX Corps, and in June 1941 Chief-of-Staff of the Third Army. He joined the War Plans Division of the War Department in December 1941 and became chief of the division in the following February. On June 25, 1942, he was named commanding general of the European Theater of Operations (ETO) and in November 1942 he commanded the Allied landings in North Africa (Operation 'Torch') and in the same month became Commander-in-Chief Allied Forces in North Africa. As commander of Allied Forces in the Mediterranean, he directed operations in Tunisia, Sicily, and Italy until December 1943. His appointment as chief of Supreme Headquarters, Allied Expeditionary Force (SHAEF), was announced on Sunday, January 16, and he was introduced to the press the following Tuesday.

The honour and confidence implied by my selection for this critical post were, of course, tremendous, and of this I was well aware and appreciative. Nevertheless, there is always some degree of emotional let-down when a military commander in war is removed from one task to enter upon another. By the nature of his work he has become so intimately tied up with close friends and assistants and with innumerable intricate problems that he feels almost a resentful shock at facing again the problem of building up organizations, staffs, and plans necessary for the conduct of another operation.

Our Mediterranean experiences had reaffirmed the truth that unity, co-ordination and co-operation are the keys to successful operations. War is waged in three elements but there is no separate land, air, or naval war. Unless all assets in all elements are efficiently combined and co-ordinated against a properly-selected, common objective, their maximum potential power cannot be realized. Physical targets may be separated by the breadth of a continent or an ocean, but their destruction must contribute in maximum degree to the furtherance of the combined plan of operation. That is what co-ordination means.

Not only would I need commanders who understood this truth, but I must have those who appreciated the importance of morale and had demonstrated a capacity to develop and maintain it. Morale is the greatest single factor in successful war. Endurable comparisons with the enemy in other essential factors — leadership, discipline, technique, numbers, equipment, mobility, supply, and maintenance — are prerequisite to the existence of morale. It breeds most readily upon success; but under good leaders it will be maintained among troops even during extended periods of adversity. A human understanding and a natural ability to mingle with all men on a basis of equality are more important than any degree of technical skill.

I was happy to secure Air Chief Marshal Sir Arthur Tedder as my deputy for 'Overlord'. In the Mediterranean he had won the respect and admiration of all his associates not only as a brilliant airman but as a staunch supporter of the 'allied' principle as practised in that command. Authority was also granted to take along my Chief-of-Staff, Lieutenant General Walter B. Smith, without whose services it would have been difficult to organize a staff for the conduct of a great allied operation.

Left: **Air Chief Marshal Sir Arthur W. Tedder, 53, served as British air commander in the Middle East in 1942, and from February 1943 until the end of the year as Commander-in-Chief, Mediterranean Allied Air Forces, which included RAF Middle East, RAF Malta Air Command, and the North-West African Air Forces. In January 1944, he was appointed Deputy Supreme Commander, SHAEF.**

Right: **Lieutenant General Walter Bedell Smith, 48, became Secretary, General Staff, in September 1941, and in February 1942 was named US secretary of the Combined Chiefs-of-Staff. General Eisenhower chose him in September 1942 to be Chief-of-Staff of the European Theater of Operations and later he became Chief-of-Staff of the Allied forces in North Africa and of the Mediterranean theatre. At the end of 1943, he was appointed Chief-of-Staff of SHAEF.**

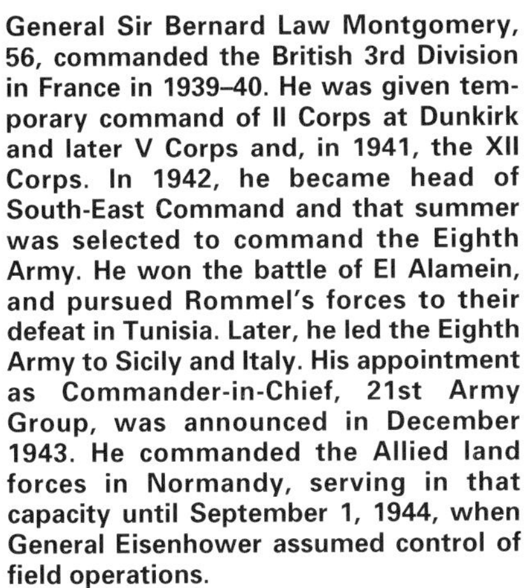

General Sir Bernard Law Montgomery, 56, commanded the British 3rd Division in France in 1939–40. He was given temporary command of II Corps at Dunkirk and later V Corps and, in 1941, the XII Corps. In 1942, he became head of South-East Command and that summer was selected to command the Eighth Army. He won the battle of El Alamein, and pursued Rommel's forces to their defeat in Tunisia. Later, he led the Eighth Army to Sicily and Italy. His appointment as Commander-in-Chief, 21st Army Group, was announced in December 1943. He commanded the Allied land forces in Normandy, serving in that capacity until September 1, 1944, when General Eisenhower assumed control of field operations.

Admiral Bertram H. Ramsay had retired in 1938 after 42 years' service with the Royal Navy. He saw action in the First World War as commander of the destroyer *Broke*, and ended his service with three years as Chief-of-Staff, Home Fleet. He was recalled to duty in 1939 as Flag Officer Commanding, Dover, and in that post organised the naval forces for the evacuation of Dunkirk. Later, he helped plan the 'Torch' operation, commanded a task force in the Sicilian invasion, and became British naval commander in the Mediterranean. He was selected to be the Allied Naval Commander-in-Chief, Expeditionary Force (ANCXF) in October 1943, aged 60, and served in that post until his death in a plane crash on January 2, 1945.

Lieutenant General Omar N. Bradley, 50, was an assistant secretary of the General Staff in the US War Department in 1940 and in February 1941 was given command of the Infantry School at Fort Benning. Later, he commanded the 82nd Division, followed by the 28th Division. In February 1943, he went to North Africa to act as an observer for General Eisenhower, becoming deputy commander of II Corps under General Patton, and then commander when Patton was given the task of planning the Sicilian campaign. He fought with the corps in Tunisia and Sicily. In September 1943, he was selected to head the US First Army in the invasion of north-west Europe as well as a US army group headquarters — the 1st (later 12th) Army Group.

I at first understood that originally either General Sir Harold Alexander or General Sir Bernard L. Montgomery was available for the command of the British forces in the new venture. At that time, I expressed a preference for Alexander, primarily because I had been so closely associated with him and had developed for him an admiration and friendship which have grown with the years. I regarded Alexander as Britain's outstanding soldier in the field of strategy. He was, moreover, a friendly and companionable type; Americans instinctively liked him.

The Prime Minister finally decided, however, that Alexander should not be spared from the Italian operation, which would have an important effect upon the one we were to undertake the following summer, and from which he still hoped for almost decisive results. Consequently, General Montgomery was assigned to command the British forces in the new operation, a choice acceptable to me. General Montgomery had no superior in two most important characteristics. He quickly developed among British enlisted men an intense devotion and admiration — the greatest personal asset a commander can possess. Montgomery's other outstanding characteristic was his tactical ability in what might be called the 'prepared' battle. In the study of enemy positions and situations and in the combining of his own armor, artillery, air, and infantry to secure tactical success against the enemy, he was careful, meticulous, and certain.

I was particularly pleased to secure the services of Admiral Sir Bertram H. Ramsay as the naval commander-in-chief. Admiral Sir Andrew Cunningham had left us some weeks earlier to become First Sea Lord of the Admiralty, but Admiral Ramsay was a most competent commander of courage, resourcefulness, and tremendous energy. Moreover, all of us knew him to be helpful and companionable, even though we sometimes laughed among ourselves at the care with which he guarded, in British tradition and practice, the 'senior service' position of the British Navy.

I foresaw some possibility of friction in advancing General Omar N. Bradley to the highest American ground command in 'Overlord' because I was also planning to use Patton in that operation, provided he concurred in the new arrangement, which would involve a reversal of the relative positions the two men had held in the successful Sicilian campaign. Both were my intimate friends of many years' standing and I knew that each would loyally accept any assigned duty. I was hopeful, however, that Patton, who for certain types of action was the outstanding soldier our country has produced, would whole-heartedly support the plan I had in mind. I had a frank talk with him and was gratified to find that he thoroughly agreed that the rôle for which he personally was ideally suited was that of an army commander.

My high opinion of Bradley, dating from our days at West Point, had increased during our months together in the Mediterranean. At my request, he had come to Africa in February 1943, as a major general to assist me in a rôle that we called 'Eyes and Ears'. He was authorized and expected to go where and when he pleased in the American zone to observe and report to me on anything he felt worthy of my attention. He was especially suited to act in such an intimate capacity, not only by reason of our long friendship, but because of his ability and reputation as a sound, painstaking, and broadly-educated soldier. He was a keen judge of men and their capabilities and was absolutely fair and just in his dealings with them. Added to this, he was emotionally stable and possessed a grasp of larger issues that clearly marked him for high office. I looked forward to renewal of our close association in the cross-Channel operation.

I also desired to take General Carl Spaatz to England. By agreement reached in Cairo, the American strategic bombers in the Mediterranean and in England were to be combined under Spaatz's single operational command, a circumstance that made it more than ever necessary that he should be in the UK, where the principal effort was to be mounted.

DIRECTIVE TO SUPREME COMMANDER, ALLIED EXPEDITIONARY FORCE

1. You are hereby designated as Supreme Allied Commander of the forces placed under your orders for operations for the liberation of Europe from the Germans. Your title will be Supreme Commander, Allied Expeditionary Force.

2. *Task.* You will enter the Continent of Europe and, in conjunction with the other United Nations, undertake operations aimed at the heart of Germany and the destruction of her armed forces. The date for entering the Continent is the month of May, 1944. After adequate Channel ports have been secured, exploitation will be directed towards securing an area that will facilitate both ground and air operations against the enemy.

3. Notwithstanding the target date above, you will be prepared at any time to take immediate advantage of favorable circumstances, such as withdrawal by the enemy on your front, to effect a re-entry into the Continent with such forces as you have available at the time; a general plan for this operation when approved will be furnished for your assistance.

4. *Command.* You are responsible to the Combined Chiefs-of-Staff and will exercise command generally in accordance with the diagram at Appendix A. Direct communication with the United States and British Chiefs-of-Staff is authorized in the interest of facilitating your operations and for arranging necessary logistic support.

5. *Logistics.* In the United Kingdom the responsibility for logistics organization, concentration, movement and supply of forces to meet the requirements of your plan will rest with British Service Ministries so far as British Forces are concerned. So far as United States Forces are concerned, this responsibility will rest with the United States War and Navy Departments. You will be responsible for the co-ordination of logistical arrangements on the Continent. You will also be responsible for co-ordinating the requirements of British and United States Forces under your command.

6. *Co-ordination of operation of other Forces and Agencies.* In preparation for your assault on enemy-occupied Europe, Sea and Air Forces, agencies of sabotage, subversion, and propaganda, acting under a variety of authorities, are now in action. You may recommend any variation in these activities which may seem to you desirable.

7. *Relationship to United Nations Forces in other areas.* Responsibility will rest with the Combined Chiefs-of-Staff for supplying information relating to operations of the forces of the USSR for your guidance in timing your operations. It is understood that the Soviet forces will launch an offensive at about the same time as OVERLORD with the object of preventing the German forces from transferring from the Eastern to the Western front. The Allied Commander-in-Chief, Mediterranean Theater, will conduct operations designed to assist your operation, including the launching of an attack against the south of France at about the same time as OVERLORD. The scope and timing of his operations will be decided by the Combined Chief-of-Staff. You will establish contact with him and submit to the Combined Chiefs-of-Staff your views and recommendations regarding operations from the Mediterranean in support of your attack from the United Kingdom. A copy of his directive is furnished for your guidance. The Combined Chiefs-of-Staff will place under your command the forces operating in Southern France as soon as you are in a position to assume such command. You will submit timely recommendations compatible with this regard.

8. *Relationship with Allied Governments — the re-establishment of Civil Governments and Liberated Allied Territories and the administration of enemy territories.* Further instructions will be issued to you on these subjects at a later date.

February 12, 1944

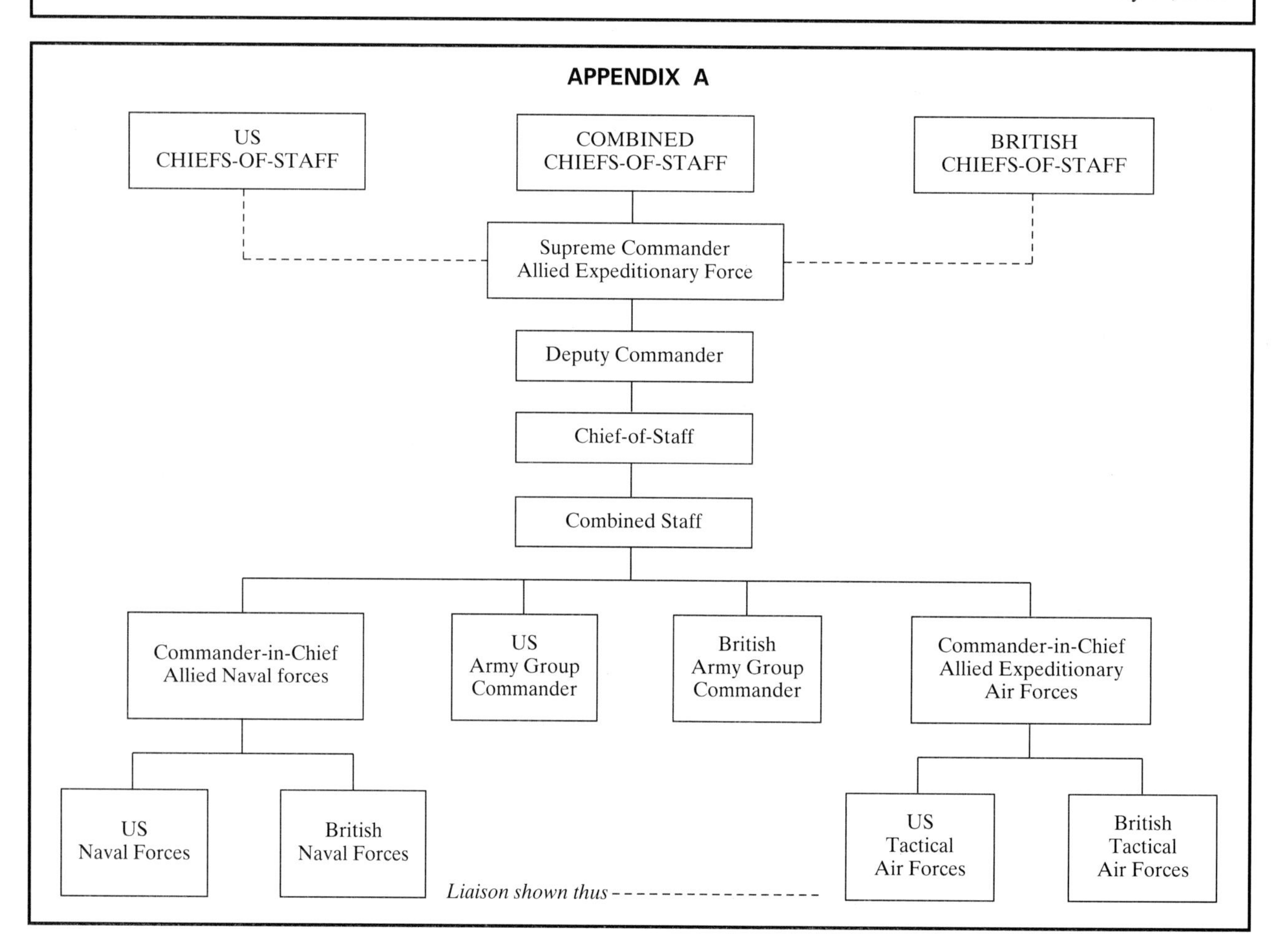

Left: **It was a bombed and battered London which greeted Eisenhower when he returned to what was officially the headquarters of the European Theater of Operations, United States Army (ETOUSA). His office was on the corner of the first (US second) floor of the building on the left.** *Right:* **Today, No. 20 houses the HQ for US Naval Forces in Europe, Eisenhower's office on the '1st Deck' having been converted into an operations planning office. In April 1948, Grosvenor Square, which had become known during the war as 'Eisenhower Platz', was re-landscaped prior to the erection of the Roosevelt Memorial, but it was to be another 40 years before the General himself was honoured with the unveiling of his statue in January 1989. In April 1994, Prime Minister John Major dedicated the square as a permanent D-Day Garden of Remembrance.**

On Christmas Eve, we listened to the radio, having learned that President Roosevelt was to make a significant speech. During that talk he made the first public announcement of my transfer to command of 'Overlord' and included in the statement the designation of the title I was to assume. The title was Supreme Commander, Allied Expeditionary Forces.

I left the United States on January 13 to undertake the organization of the mightiest fighting force that the two Western Allies could muster. As on my first arrival in London in June 1942, I found headquarters staffs concentrated in the heart of the city, but this time I determined I would not be defeated in my plan to find a suitable site somewhere in the countryside. I found one, and there were protests and gloomy predictions. Once concentrated in the Bushy Park area, however, we quickly developed a family relationship that far more than made up for minor inconveniences, due to distance from the seat of Britain's administrative organization. My headquarters was officially called Supreme Headquarters, Allied Expeditionary Force, and taking the initials from the name, SHAEF was born.

It was important that a long-term strategic concept of the operation — of which the amphibious assault would be merely the opening phase — should develop early. The directive from the Combined Chiefs-of-Staff was very simple, merely instructing us to land on the coast of France and thereafter to destroy the German ground forces. Its significant paragraph read: 'You will enter the Continent of Europe and, in conjunction with the other Allied Nations, undertake operations aimed at the heart of Germany and the destruction of her armed forces.'

The timing of the operation was a difficult matter to decide. At Teheran, the President and the Prime Minister had promised Generalissimo Stalin that the attack would start in May but we were given to understand that any date selected in that period of the year would fulfil the commitments made by our two political leaders.

In order to obtain the maximum length of good campaigning weather, the earlier the attack could be launched the better. Another factor in favour of an early attack was the continuing and frantic efforts of the German to strengthen his coastal defences. Because of the weather conditions in the Channel, May was the earliest date that a landing attempt could be successfully undertaken and the first favourable combination of tides and sunrise occurred early in the month. Thus early May was the original and tentatively-selected target date.

Five days after Eisenhower arrived in London, the capital suffered its first serious air raid since 1941 as the Luftwaffe launched Operation 'Steinbock' in retaliation against the RAF/USAAF attacks which were laying waste much of the Third Reich. The Germans claimed nearly 450 sorties on the night of Friday, January 21/22, although the bombing was widely scattered. *Left:* **Nevertheless, the attack led to the introduction of white accessories for American military police, to make them more visible in the black-out, modelled here on January 30 by Private Louis H. Kotha, Pfc Fred O. Guidry and Pfc Horace Thibodeaux outside the blast-protected entrance to No. 20.** *Right:* **The blue plaque records that General Eisenhower's headquarters were located here from June–November 1942 and again from January–March 1944.**

Left: **Lieutenant-General Sir Frederick E. Morgan, 49, served in France in 1940 with the 1st Armoured Division. In May 1942, he was appointed to command the I Corps District, which included Lincolnshire and the East Riding of Yorkshire. In October that year, he was made commander of I Corps and placed under General Eisenhower. He was given the task of preparing a subsidiary landing in the western Mediterranean either to reinforce the initial landings or to deal with a German thrust through Spain. When neither operation proved necessary, he was directed to plan the invasion of Sardinia. When this was abandoned, he began planning the invasion of Sicily although this project was later given to the armies in North Africa. In the spring of 1943, he became Chief-of-Staff to the Supreme Allied Commander (COSSAC) and as such directed planning for the invasion of north-west Europe at Allied Forces Headquarters (AFHQ) in Norfolk House in the south-eastern corner of St James's Square** ***(right).*** **When the Supreme Commander was appointed and Eisenhower chose General Smith to be the SHAEF Chief-of-Staff, General Morgan agreed to serve as Smith's deputy.**

Two considerations, one of them decisive in character, combined to postpone the target date from May to June. The first and important one was our insistence that the attack be on a larger scale than that originally planned by the staff assembled in London under Lieutenant-General Sir Frederick Morgan. He had in the months preceding my arrival accomplished a mass of detailed planning, accumulation of data, and gathering of supply that made D-Day possible. My ideas were supported by General Morgan personally but he had been compelled to develop his plan on

Left: **Eisenhower leaves Norfolk House on Friday, January 21, after the first full meeting with his commanders. General Montgomery had already spent three weeks examining the plans for 'Overlord' and strongly recommended that the planned assault by three divisions (all that Morgan had been allowed) be increased to five with a two-division follow-up, the 'minimum . . . to make a proper success of the operation'.** *Right:* **From the outside, Norfolk House presents the same face today as it did in 1944, save for the repaired windows and the addition of two commemorative plaques.**

Left: **Air Chief Marshal Sir Trafford Leigh-Mallory, 51, was present at the meeting in his capacity of Allied Air Commander-in-Chief. He had seen service in the Royal Flying Corps in the First World War and had been awarded the Distinguished Service Order in 1919. In 1937, he became Air Officer Commanding-in-Chief, No. 12 Group, and from November 1942 to December 1943 he served as AOC Fighter Command. As Allied Air C-in-C, he was to command the tactical air forces in support of the Allied Expeditionary Force (AEF).**

Right: **However, Lieutenant General Carl Spaatz, commander of the US Eighth and Fifteenth Air Forces, whose co-operation was essential, was a notable absentee from the meeting, although he was now based in the UK as the commander of the United States Strategic Air Forces in Europe (USSAFE).**

the basis of a fixed number of ships, landing craft, and other resources. Consequently, he had no recourse except to work out an attack along a three-division front, whereas I insisted on five and informed the Combined Chiefs-of-Staff that we had to have the additional landing craft and other gear essential to the larger operation, even if this meant delaying the assault by a month. To this the Combined Chiefs agreed.

Another factor that made the later date a desirable one was the degree of dependence we were placing upon the preparatory effort of the air force. An early attack would provide the air force with only a minimum opportunity for pin-point bombing of critical transportation centres in France, whereas the improved weather anticipated for the month of May would give them much more time and better opportunity to impede the movement of German reserves and demolish German defences along the coastline. The virtual destruction of critical points on the main roads and railroads leading into the selected battle area was a critical feature of the battle plan. Nevertheless, acceptance of the later date was disappointing. We wanted all the summer weather we could get for the European campaign.

Along with the general plan of operations we thoroughly considered means of deceiving the enemy as to the point and timing of attack. Our purpose was to convince him that we intended to strike directly across the Channel at its narrowest point, against the stronghold of Calais. In many ways great advantages would have accrued to us could we have successfully attacked in this region. Not only were the beaches the best along the coast, they were closest to the British ports and to the German border. The enemy, fully appreciating these facts, kept strong forces in the area and fortified that particular section of coastline more strongly than any other.

SUPREME HEADQUARTERS
ALLIED EXPEDITIONARY FORCE — COPY NO. 31

31 January 1945

Wing Commander Dodds
Air Ministry
King Charles St.
Whitehall

RESTRICTED
(Not for Publication)

PICTORIAL INVITATION

Dear Sir:

Arrangements have been made for a pictorial session at which photographs and silent newsreels may be made of certain members of the Supreme Command. Because of the many duties confronting these high officers, this will be the only photographic and film session scheduled for some time to come.

This numbered letter will serve as a pass for one photographer for your associated newspapers or one cameraman from your organization It is necessary that those selected be either accredited to the British, United States or Canadian forces, or have other official authority satisfactory to the security Officer.

Arrangements are as follows:

1. All photographic or newsreel correspondents will assemble at the Public Relations Office, ETOUSA, 28 Grosvenor Square (Pictorial Office, Ground Floor) at 0900 hours, Tuesday, 1 February 1944.

a. Here, they will be briefed, and checked by the Security Officers from the Supreme Hq., A.E.F., asked to sign a "Facility Visit" certificate, ensuring policy check on the photographs and newsreels, in addition to the routine censorship. A Censor will be present to anticipate any "Stops".

2. All Photographic and newsreel correspondents will then be conducted in buses to the location which must be regarded as "SECRET". Upon completion of the entire mission, the correspondents will be returned in one body to 28 Grosvenor Square to take their own transportation from there.

3. One location will be announced where photographers can be passed quickly for policy supervision: newsreel arrangements will be similarly made All newsreel coverage must be silent. Color Photographs may be made

4. Arrangements have been made for advance scrutiny by newsreel representatives and electrical pre-arrangements have also been made.

5. Please direct any further questions to CAPTAIN HERBERT BREGSTEIN, PICTORIAL OFFICER, PRO, ETOUSA

FOR THE ASS. C/S P & PW Division,

ERNEST DUPUY
Colonel, F.A.

By the end of the first day-long conference, important fundamental issues had been agreed in that the assault must be widened with five divisions landing simultaneously; port facilities were essential on 'the far shore', and that the tactical advantage must be seized as early as possible after the landing. A cable setting out the criteria for the revised plan, which would require an additional 47 large tank-carrying ships (LSTs), 144 tank landing craft (LCTs), 72 large infantry craft (LCI(L)s), 5 cruisers and 24 destroyers, was despatched to the Combined Chiefs-of-Staff in Washington on January 23. A reply was received by Eisenhower on January 31 authorising the enlarged assault, although it failed to specify which other operations planned in the Mediterranean and Pacific would have to be robbed to provide the additional ships required. The same day that the Combined Chiefs' cable was received in London, invitations were sent out to the press for a photo session with 'certain members of the Supreme Command'. The location of the 'shoot' was not given as it 'must be regarded as secret'. *Below:* **The initial rendezvous was to be the Public Relations Office of ETOUSA at 28 Grosvenor Square, demolished in 1957 to make way for the new American Embassy.**

One of the photographers who was present on February 1 has left us his impressions: 'Twenty minutes before time, a taxi driver set me down at the rendezvous. Glancing at my shiny metal tripod and camera bag, he called after me, "Don't let Monty catch you snooping around with them secret weapons or he'll be after you!" A white helmeted and gloved US service policeman curtly waved the jovial one on, for taxis were queuing up behind us. As the driver shot away he called, "I ask yer! White helmets!" Hurrying indoors, I was ushered into a large gloomy room where a staff of US officers checked up on my credentials and those of my colleagues. Soon, the place was filled to capacity with the representatives of the world's press, many of them in uniform. The officers in charge of affairs allowed us to talk for a while, and then called us to attention; this was an historic event which demanded organisation. One, who acted as spokesman, addressed us in this vein. "Boys!" said he, "here are your instructions." Like very good boys we listened smugly while "instructions" were solemnly read out. They were designed to cover our every movement during the next hour. My uniformed colleagues resigned themselves to being "briefed" and "disciplined".'

'When it was all over, we were split into three parties of twenty and hurried out of the building to board three covered wagons. Since we knew the generals were waiting for us within easy walking distance, we questioned the need of transport and, after the convoy had been moving for two minutes, called out to tell the driver that he was heading the wrong way. His reply was "Nerts". Then he ran us around the houses for a while before pulling up at Supreme HQ. A nice touch of "security" that, we thought, designed to fox any snoopers who might happen to be standing around. Leaping down from the covered wagons, we hustled into headquarters and were conducted to the conference room. Losing our newly-gained sense of discipline, we dashed to grab a good shooting position; it was every man for himself. The room was hot, for it had been fitted up with special studio lighting. At one end, tables were arranged as an open square. Behind, on the wall, hung huge maps of Europe, containing nothing to interest you or me. The officers arranged us. We were drawn up in three waves, one behind the other — still cameras, colour cameras, movie cameras. Suddenly, there came the sound of men springing to attention. The Supreme Commander had entered the room, followed by his staff. They walked to the table, arranged themselves round it, sat down and looked at the cameras.'

'We had been warned that on no account must we address them personally, but after a few cameras had clicked on the invasion chiefs staring straight ahead, we ignored our mentors and called out for a little natural action. For two minutes, we shot. Then, at a signal, we moved aside for the colour cameramen. Then the third wave of newsreel men moved into position. Now cine-men like action on their film (so does everyone else!), so all 60 of us got busy at once. The three waves merge into one, the "boys" are happy, so are the Supreme Staff, who relax and try to help us secure worth-while pictures.'

The location of 'Supreme Headquarters' has meant many things to post-war caption writers, and the location of the photographic session has been previously stated as taking place at a variety of places until we carried out detailed research early in 1994. The interior of Norfolk House was totally gutted and a new central lift shaft installed during refurbishment of the building in 1977-80, at which time the panelling from the boardroom, formerly the preserve of the British Aluminium Company, on the sixth (US seventh) floor was stripped out. In 1945, General Eisenhower had set down in writing the fact that the boardroom 'will always occupy a place in British and American history' yet none of the organisations in Britain or the United States contacted by the project manager were interested in preserving the panelling, which subsequently 'disappeared' from the building site. With the aid of original plans of the building (see *After the Battle* No. 84), we were able to take the comparison in what is now the accounts section of Lamco Paper Sales Ltd.

As yet, Eisenhower had not received a formal 'directive' from the Combined Chiefs confirming his appointment and defining his precise task and the extent of his powers. This finally arrived on February 14 after more than five weeks of haggling behind the scenes in an effort to reconcile British and American points of view. Like all political communiqués, words are carefully chosen to please all parties, the initial British draft specifying that Eisenhower obtain a lodgement area in France from which 'further offensive action *can* be aimed at the heart of Germany'. This the Americans rejected, rephrasing the sentence: 'striking at the heart of Germany'. In the end, the final version (reproduced on page 12) was less specific which, as far as Eisenhower was concerned, was all to the good as it allowed him more leeway. On the other hand, it failed to give him overall authority over the strategic air forces (RAF Bomber Command and the US Eighth Army Air Force) which was to cause much argument in the future. On Friday, February 25, Eisenhower got out of the office for the day, having left by train the previous evening with Tedder, Montgomery and Bradley for an inspection tour in the West Country. (That night, a German air raid resulted in a bomb hitting St James's Square, blasting the front of Norfolk House — the patched-up windows being evident in the picture on page 14.) Here, the commanders are pictured during their visit to the US 3rd Armored Division, the 'Spearhead' division being in the vanguard in the US First Army breakout from the Normandy bridgehead. Major General Leroy H. Watson, the divisional commander, wears the belted raincoat.

The defences were so strong that none of us believed that a successful assault from the sea could be made except at such terrific cost that the whole expedition might find itself helpless to accomplish anything of a positive character, after it got ashore. But we counted upon the enemy believing that we would be tempted into this operation, and the wide variety of measures we took for convincing him were given extraordinary credence by his intelligence division.

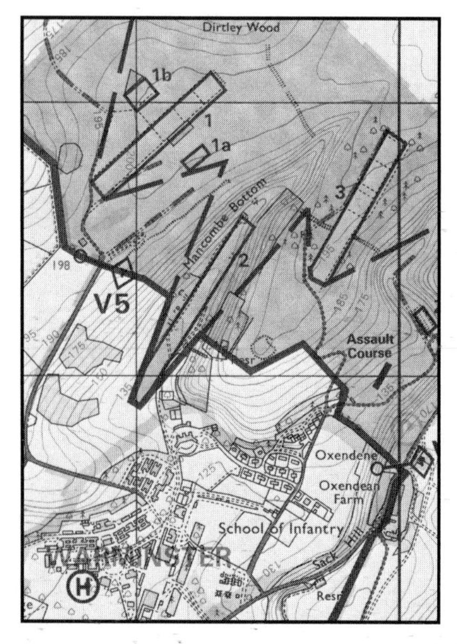

Major Mike Menage, the Range Safety Officer at the School of Infantry at Warminster, Wiltshire, established that the photographs had been taken on what is now No. 2 Small-arms Range. However, the odd thing is that there is little over 50 yards between the party and the steep side of Mancombe Bottom, and the Sherman M4A1 is actually pointing its 75mm gun *across* the valley, not down it. David Fletcher of Bovington Tank Museum thinks that the picture shows a demonstration of external fire control on a pellet range. For this, a modified airgun, lined up with the main armament, was fired instead. This would explain why everyone is looking intently at a spot just a few yards away.

Left: **This frequently-used picture of Eisenhower presenting the commander of the 21st Army Group with an M1 carbine is always reproduced with the shoulder imposing on the right cropped out to give a more balanced picture. Also, the location is never stated, just 'somewhere in England'.** *Right:* **It was, in fact, taken on the same day at Warminster, the tank hangar in the background surviving unchanged enabling us to pinpoint the exact spot where the parade took place.**

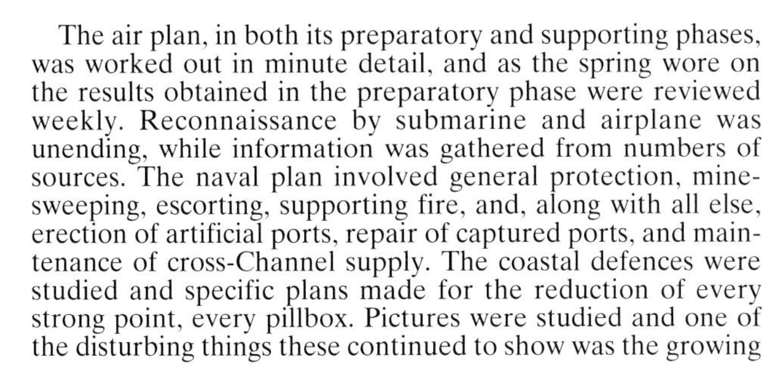

The air plan, in both its preparatory and supporting phases, was worked out in minute detail, and as the spring wore on the results obtained in the preparatory phase were reviewed weekly. Reconnaissance by submarine and airplane was unending, while information was gathered from numbers of sources. The naval plan involved general protection, mine-sweeping, escorting, supporting fire, and, along with all else, erection of artificial ports, repair of captured ports, and maintenance of cross-Channel supply. The coastal defences were studied and specific plans made for the reduction of every strong point, every pillbox. Pictures were studied and one of the disturbing things these continued to show was the growing profusion of beach obstacles, most of them under water at high tide. Embarkation plans for troops, equipment, and supplies were voluminous, and exact in detail. Routes to ports, timings of departures and arrivals, locations, protection and camouflage of temporary camps, and a thousand related matters, were all carefully predetermined and, so far as feasible, tested in advance.

Senior commanders used every possible moment in visiting and inspecting troops. Records left by a staff officer show that in four months, from February 1 to June 1, I visited 26 divisions, 24 airfields, five ships of war, and numerous depots, shops, hospitals, and other important installations.

Right: **On March 11, the Supreme Commander visited No. 100 Officer Cadet Training Unit at Sandhurst Academy near Camberley in Surrey. Before reviewing the passing-out parade, Eisenhower addressed the cadets. He retraced the history of previous successful alliances between Britain and the United States which he believed was largely due to common values. 'You young men have this war to win', he told them. 'It is small unit leadership that is going to win the ground battle and that battle must be won before that enemy of ours is finally crushed. It is up to you men to give your units — whether it is a tank crew, platoon, or becomes a company — leadership, every hour of the day, every day of the week. You must know every single one of your men. It is not enough that you are the best soldier in that unit, that you are the strongest, the toughest, the most durable and the best equipped technically. You must be their leader, their father, their mentor even if you are half their age. You must understand their problems. You must keep them out of trouble. If they get in trouble, you must be the one to go to their rescue. That cultivation of human understanding between you and your men is the one art that you must yet master and you must master it quickly. Then you will be doing your duty and you will be worthy of the traditions of this great school and of your great country. To each one of you I wish Godspeed and Good Luck. If I could have my wish as I stand here today, feeling honored as I do in the tribute paid me, I would say this: If I could only meet you all somewhere east of the Rhine and renew the acquaintanceship of this pleasant morning. Good Luck.'**

Fifty years later, cadets of today prepare for the Sovereign's Parade.

Supreme Headquarters, Allied Expeditionary Force

By Lieutenant General Walter Bedell Smith
CHIEF-OF-STAFF, ALLIED EXPEDITIONARY FORCE

When General Eisenhower was appointed Supreme Commander of the Allied Expeditionary Force to cross the Channel and destroy the German armies in western Europe, we were still at our headquarters in North Africa. The appointment was confirmed by President Roosevelt himself on December 7, 1943. I was to continue as his chief-of-staff.

But planning for 'Overlord', code-name for the European operation, was already well started under the direction of Lieutenant-General Sir Frederick E. Morgan. At the Casablanca Conference held in in January 1943, General Morgan was appointed Chief-of-Staff to the Supreme Allied Commander, though it was another 11 months before a supreme commander was selected. The initials of the new designation spelled out COSSAC, and COSSAC became the code-name of the headquarters in London which went into business at Norfolk House in St James's Square.

In North Africa, General Eisenhower had just time for a brief study of the COSSAC plan before a hurried trip home to confer with General Marshall and the Combined Chiefs-of-Staff in Washington. While he approved the general strategy and the area selected for assault, he felt the three divisions COSSAC had allotted for the landings, with two more in the immediate follow-up, were not enough to storm the beaches against the formidable defenses the Germans had prepared.

'I'd like to assault with 12 divisions if I could', he told General Montgomery, who was to command all ground forces in the initial phase. He was resigned to the fact that the shortage of landing craft, which had plagued him so gravely during the Salerno landings, would never permit an assault with 12 divisions. 'But I must have at least five', he insisted. 'Five divisions in the first assault and two to follow up.'

He thought, too, that for five divisions, the beaches chosen were too narrow. Since General Montgomery and I were to precede him to London, he directed us to study the 'Overlord' plan in detail and do our best to work out these changes.

I flew to England in early January and went directly to the headquarters of General Morgan, an old friend from the planning days of the North African expedition who would remain as Deputy Chief-of-Staff when I took over

Top: **Mission accomplished in 306 days! Back in January 1944, General Smith (seen here admiring the two gold pens used to sign the German surrender at SHAEF headquarters in Reims in 1945) could hardly have foreseen the outstanding success achieved within a year from landing in France. Also in the picture is his deputy, General Sir Frederick Morgan (left rear), Eisenhower's naval aide Captain Harry C. Butcher (looking worried in the background), Deputy Supreme Commander Tedder, and Admiral Harold M. Burrough, Naval C-in-C, who took over after Admiral Ramsay was killed in January 1945. The rôle of a chief-of-staff is largely unsung, yet he is the man behind the commanding general whose duty it is to ensure the smooth running of the administration. Eisenhower described Smith as 'a godsend, a master of detail, with clear comprehension of the main issues'.** *Left:* **It is fitting, therefore, that to General Smith was given the final accolade in signing the surrender document.**

When General Smith arrived in London in early January 1944, he went straight to see General Morgan at Allied Force Headquarters in Norfolk House. Having been used for the planning of the invasion of North Africa in 1942, throughout the following year it served as the nerve centre during forward planning for the forthcoming assault on north-west Europe. After the successful conclusion of the war, however, the government was very reluctant to relinquish its hold over the building and the British Aluminium Company was not able to regain possession until 1950. By then, it was in a sorry state and, combined with the later decline of the company's fortunes in the 1970s, British Aluminium had to sell the lease to UK Provident who began the major rebuild in 1977. The work involved the total gutting of the interior and the addition of a seventh floor.

for General Eisenhower. He showed me the 'Overlord' preparations, and my first reaction was one of absolute astonishment. Not only had great strides been made, but I was amazed at the courage and imagination shown by the War Cabinet and all the planning agencies. Bold and novel measures had been improvised to overcome the obstacles we should encounter in the invasion and build-up of men and supplies in France. On the following morning, General Montgomery met the air and naval commanders and the COSSAC staff. Then the general review of plans began.

The exhaustive requirements of staff planning for an operation like 'Overlord' are almost unbelievable. It is the job of the staff to keep the commander constantly up-to-date on everything which may conceivably affect his overall decisions. This includes not only the situation of his own forces but an estimate of the enemy's capabilities and probable intentions as well. The staff develops plans for all operations. In preparing 'Overlord', the staff at Supreme Headquarters issued directives on which detailed plans were submitted by ground, air, and naval commanders to cover their responsibilities in every campaign. These were not only the tactical plans of maneuver but also supply plans listing the weapons, ammunition, and equipment needed and charting their flow to the men at the front. All these plans were assembled, studied, and criticised by the staff at Supreme Headquarters till they were in such shape that the complete master plan could be submitted to General Eisenhower for his decision.

The responsibility of a staff chief and his principal assistants is to direct the planning, coordinate the planning of

While COSSAC did not have a formation insignia, General Morgan set the wheels in motion for the creation of a suitable emblem for SHAEF. In the autumn of 1943, he appointed a committee to oversee the matter which, in turn, asked the Royal College of Heralds to submit a design. Butcher explains that this was not acceptable, so Colonel Norman Lack, assisted by an ATS girl, Corporal Doreen Goodall, produced a revised version incorporating a flaming sword based on the one on the US 2nd Division Memorial in Washington. The final design was approved by Eisenhower on December 20, 1943, and by March 1944 it was in general use. Its correct heraldic interpretation was described as: 'Upon a field of heraldic sable [black], representing the darkness of Nazi oppression, is shown the sword of liberation in the form of a crusader's sword, the flames arising from the hilt and leaping up the blade. This represents avenging justice by which the enemy power will be broken in Nazi-dominated Europe. Above the sword is a rainbow, emblematic of hope, containing all the colours of which the National Flags of the Allies are composed. The heraldic chief of azure above the rainbow is emblematic of a state of peace and tranquillity, the restoration of which to the enslaved people is the objective of the United Nations.'

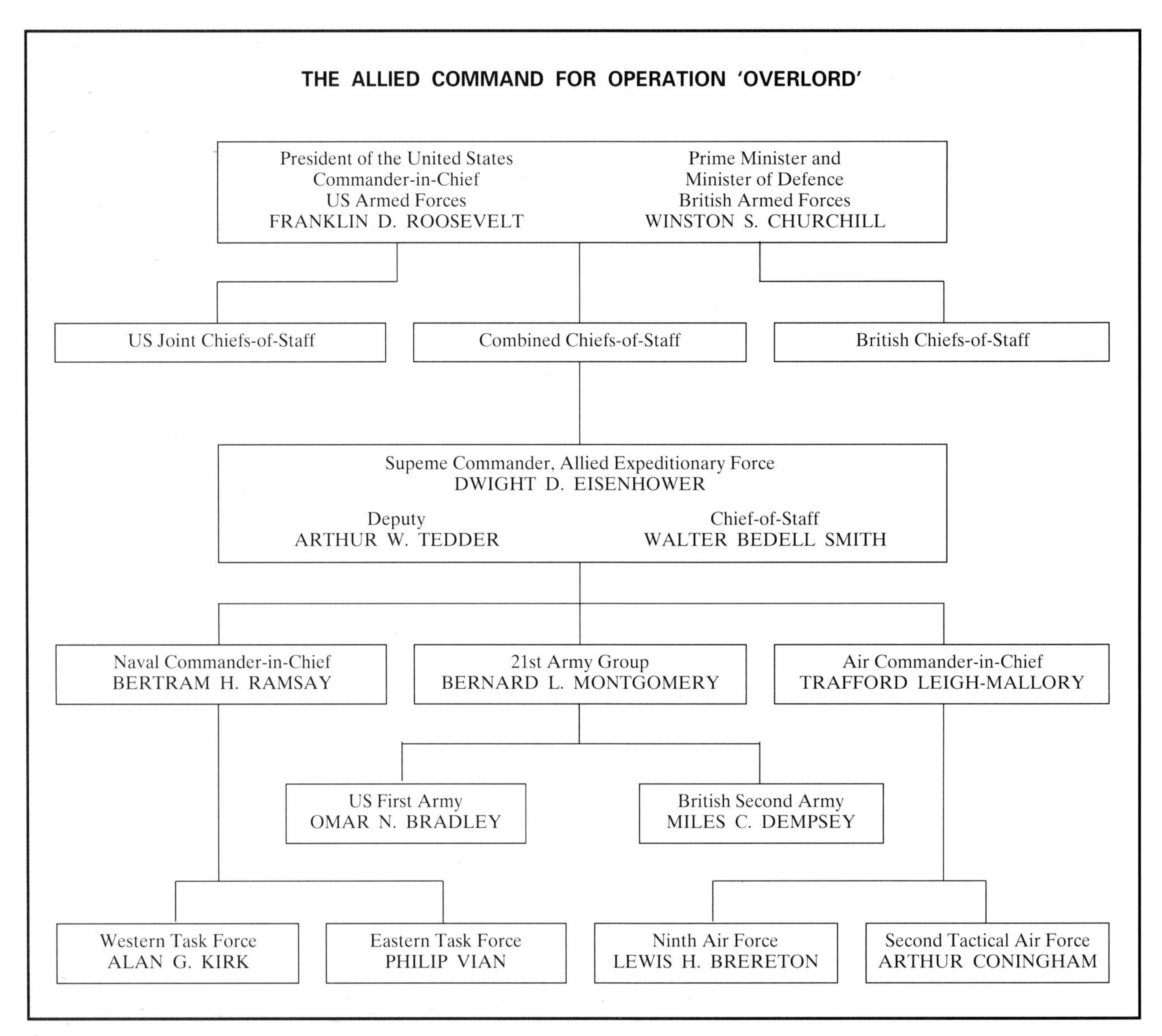

subordinate headquarters, and to make such decisions as are possible without the personal intervention of the Supreme Commander. Such decisions are made in his name and by his delegated authority. Where really important decisions were involved, the problems had to be presented to General Eisenhower. He made literally thousands of decisions in the days between January and June and I think it should be established just how utterly the military system makes this matter of decision the responsibility of one man — the commander. Only thus can be made clear the awful responsibility which one man accepts when he occupies the position of supreme commander in a major theater of war, where the victory is to be achieved.

In the military system, the chain of command is absolute. Each commander in that chain is responsible as an individual for his own decisions. In turn, he is responsible to the next higher commander. General Eisenhower, as Supreme Commander of the Allied Expeditionary Force, was responsible for each decision his subordinates made. This, in turn, indicates how carefully the high commander must weigh the choice of his division, corps, and army commanders, since, if a subordinate commander fails, it is the Supreme Commander who is at fault for having placed him in a position of command.

During a D-Day broadcast, Major George Fielding Eliot said '. . . the present American Army is the most capably commanded army which the United States has ever placed in the field at the outset of a war. . . . Every American general who now commands a division, a corps or an army of American troops, has now been put through this hard and unforgiving mill of trial. Those who have failed in any degree have been relegated to non-combat duties or to the retired list.'

The same could have been said of our British contingent, with even more force because of their years of trial by combat.

General Eisenhower's 'commander' was the Combined Chiefs-of-Staff whose headquarters was in Washington. I was intimately familiar with the functioning of this command group since I was appointed its first American secretary when it was brought into being in Washington shortly after the Pearl Harbor attack. The Combined Chiefs-of-Staff exercised over-all command of British and American operations in all theaters of war. They, in turn, were responsible only to the heads of government — to President Roosevelt in the United States, to Prime Minister Churchill in the United Kingdom.

General Eisenhower's directive to command 'Overlord' was issued by the Combined Chiefs-of-Staff. Though the appointment had been made in December 1943, it was on Lincoln's Birthday, February 12, 1944, that the directive was issued [see page 12]. A directive establishes the broad latitude given to a commander within which he is authorized to establish his own policies. The directive fixes responsibility on the individual commander. It is left to him to decide how it is to be carried out.

The wording of this directive fixed on one man the responsibility for its execution. With the assistance of a staff who acted as an extension of his mind, it was General Eisenhower's burden to weigh recommendations and then make his decisions. They were never easy. Ground, air, and naval commanders were all strong men, with strong opinions reinforced by demonstrated professional ability. When I was a young officer, I once heard it said that the loneliest post in the world was that of a commander of a fleet about to go into battle. Yet, I have never known a lonelier decision than General Eisenhower was forced to make when he ordered the invasion to proceed. The drama of the unique responsibility which he carried that early morning makes a scene which will never leave my memory. The commanders who surrounded him could only express opinions, yet they were the highest tactical commanders of the forces which would make the assault. Theirs was the responsibility of carrying out the order which he alone could give, and, when his decision was announced, they would have no course but to carry it out with all their heart and skill.

A staff at this high level is also composed of men who have demonstrated outstanding professional ability, and they are entitled, indeed required, to give their honest estimates of the course which should be followed. Their views may differ from the one which the commander appears to favor. In advance of the final decision, it is the duty of a staff officer to express freely this difference of view. Once the decision is made, he accepts it completely, as though it were his own.

Staff work in war is exacting business. If judgment is faulty in any major particular, the issue on the battlefield is in peril. If the staff overlooks any detail in the enemy's situation or its own armies' needs, a promising victory may be turned into a bitter defeat. A staff lives constantly by Ben Franklin's maxim: 'For want of a nail the shoe was lost, for want of a shoe the horse was lost, for want of a horse the rider was lost.' For want of good staff work the war could be lost.

During my first days in London, I began to develop the staff at Supreme Headquarters along the lines General Eisenhower wanted. It was to be a fully-integrated Allied staff like the one which had planned and directed our operations in the Mediterranean. Nationality was completely disregarded. Already, under General Morgan, the staff was about evenly divided between American and British officers, but the uniform a man wore had been no consideration in his selection. I proposed to keep it that way. As time went on, a few officers were relieved — not many — and replaced by others who seemed more imaginative or better suited to produce under pressure the results we must have. In deference to the nationality of the Supreme Commander, we substituted American for British staff methods. This caused minor confusion at first, but our British officers soon became accustomed to American procedure and liked it.

With a soldier's impatience of cities when operations are to be planned, one of General Eisenhower's first orders was to move the staff out of London. General Spaatz made room for us at his headquarters, Bushy Park, near Kingston-on-Thames, and we completed the move in early March. Not entirely in secrecy as it developed. The late Lord Haw-Haw wished us well in our new surroundings a few days after we were installed.

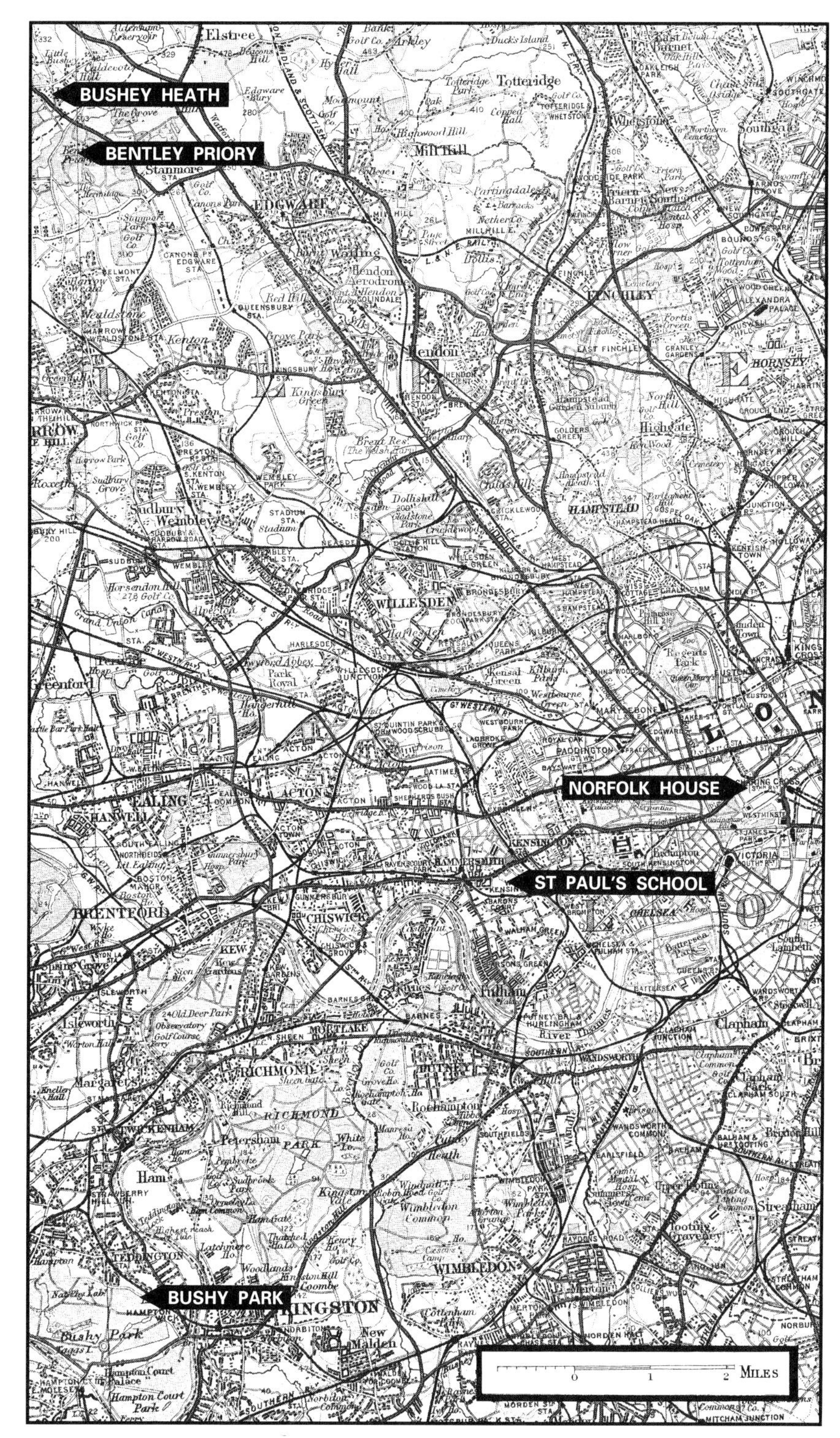

Because of the vital importance of close liaison between air and ground forces for the coming invasion, when appointed Allied Air Commander-in-Chief back in November, Air Chief Marshal Sir Trafford Leigh-Mallory declared that it would be essential that the headquarters of the Supreme Commander should be located not far away from his own air headquarters already in being at Bentley Priory at Stanmore with its good communications, tried and tested since the earliest days of the Battle of Britain. He proposed that one of the groups of government buildings just down the road in Bushey Heath be chosen. However, according to General Morgan, when the decision was made by General Smith to relocate, he, Morgan, was temporarily incapacitated in hospital. In his absence, Leigh-Mallory's strong views that the two headquarters must be close together — even within walking distance — were not passed on, and instead Smith was shown the Eighth Air Force HQ at Bushy Park, Teddington, part of which was about to be moved to the disbanded VIII Bomber Command complex at High Wycombe, Buckinghamshire. Smith considered that Bushy Park would be ideal for their purpose and, by the time the full significance of the error had sunk in, it was too late to make a change. Leigh-Mallory was furious and made an official complaint to Eisenhower in his post-'Overlord' despatch. Even Smith was forced to concede his mistake: 'My God!', he exclaimed, 'I've married the wrong woman!'

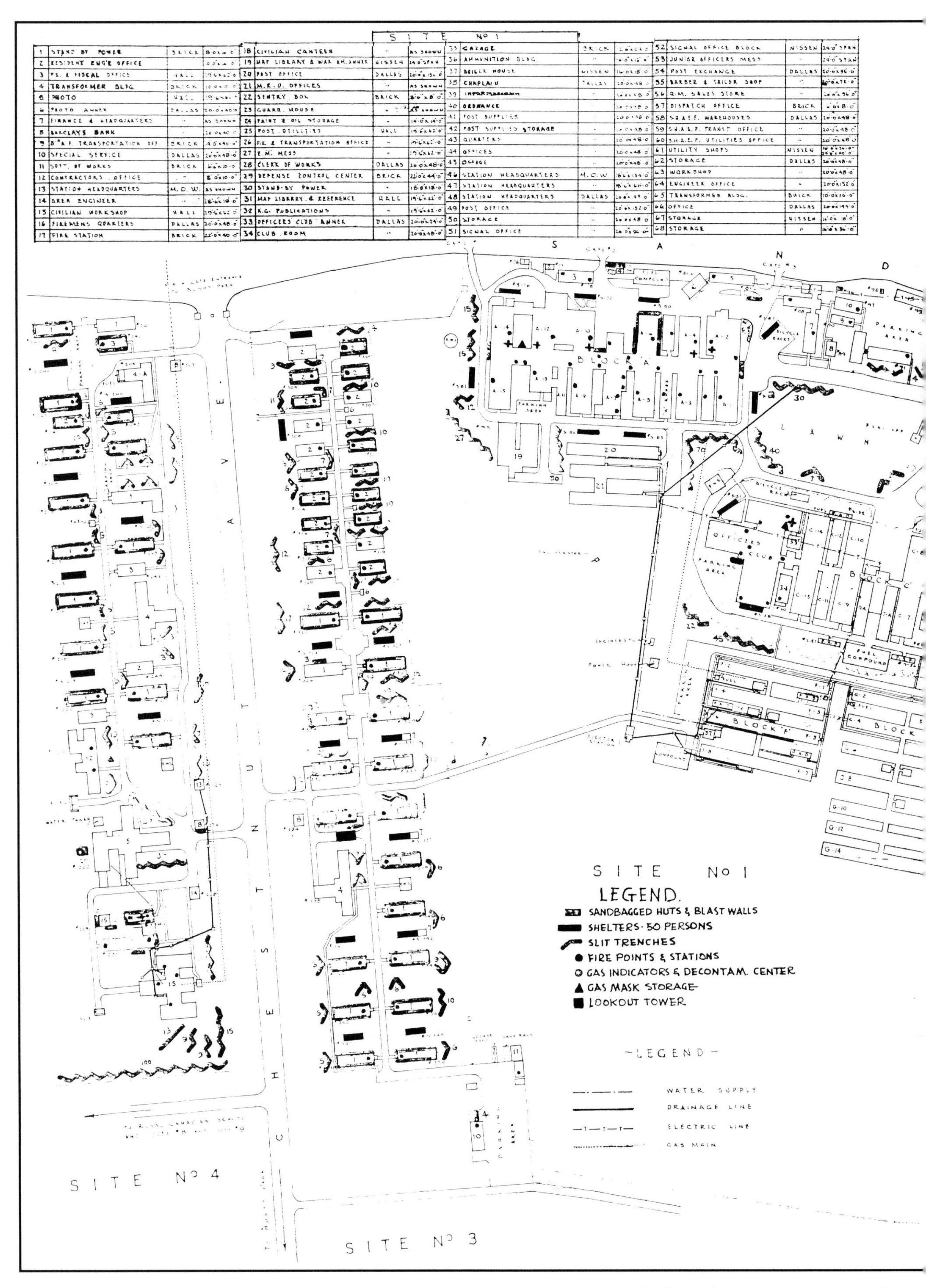

SITE No 1

No.	Building	Type	Size
1	STAND BY POWER	BRICK	8·0x·0
2	RESIDENT ENG'R OFFICE		10·0x·0
3	P.X. & FISCAL OFFICE	HALL	19·6x62·0
4	TRANSFORMER BLDG	BRICK	10·0x10·0
5	PHOTO	HALL	19·6x62·0
6	PHOTO ANNEX	DALLAS	20·0x40·0
7	FINANCE & HEADQUARTERS	"	AS SHOWN
8	BARCLAYS BANK	"	20·0x40·0
9	8th A.F. TRANSPORTATION OFF.	BRICK	14·0x40·0
10	SPECIAL SERVICE	DALLAS	20·0x48·0
11	SUPT. OF WORKS	BRICK	6·6x10·0
12	CONTRACTORS OFFICE	"	8·0x10·0
13	STATION HEADQUARTERS	M.O.W.	AS SHOWN
14	AREA ENGINEER	"	18·6x18·0
15	CIVILIAN WORKSHOP	HALL	19·6x62·0
16	FIREMENS QUARTERS	DALLAS	20·0x48·0
17	FIRE STATION	BRICK	22·0x40·0
18	CIVILIAN CANTEEN	"	AS SHOWN
19	MAP LIBRARY & WAR RM. ANNEX	NISSEN	24·0 SPAN
20	POST OFFICE	DALLAS	20·0x15·0
21	M.R.U. OFFICES	"	AS SHOWN
22	SENTRY BOX	BRICK	8·0x8·0
23	GUARD HOUSE	"	AS SHOWN
24	PAINT & OIL STORAGE	"	14·0x14·0
25	POST UTILITIES	HALL	19·6x62·0
26	P.X. & TRANSPORTATION OFFICE	"	19·6x62·0
27	E.M. MESS	"	19·6x62·0
28	CLERK OF WORKS	DALLAS	20·0x48·0
29	DEFENSE CONTROL CENTER	BRICK	22·0x44·0
30	STAND-BY POWER	"	18·0x18·0
31	MAP LIBRARY & REFERENCE	HALL	19·6x62·0
32	A.G. PUBLICATIONS	"	19·6x62·0
33	OFFICERS CLUB ANNEX	DALLAS	20·0x24·0
34	CLUB ROOM	"	20·0x48·0
35	GARAGE	BRICK	20·0x24·0
36	AMMUNITION BLDG.	"	16·0x16·0
37	BOILER HOUSE	NISSEN	16·0x18·0
38	CHAPLAIN	DALLAS	20·0x48·0
39	INFORMATION	"	20·0x48·0
40	ORDNANCE		20·0x48·0
41	POST SUPPLIES		20·0x48·0
42	POST SUPPLIES STORAGE	"	20·0x48·0
43	QUARTERS	"	20·0x48·0
44	OFFICES	"	20·0x48·0
45	OFFICE	"	20·0x48·0
46	STATION HEADQUARTERS	M.O.W.	18·6x154·0
47	STATION HEADQUARTERS	"	18·6x60·0
48	STATION HEADQUARTERS	DALLAS	20·0x49·0
49	POST OFFICE	"	20·0x152·0
50	STORAGE	"	20·0x48·0
51	SIGNAL OFFICE	"	20·0x96·0
52	SIGNAL OFFICE BLOCK	NISSEN	24·0 SPAN
53	JUNIOR OFFICERS MESS	"	24·0 SPAN
54	POST EXCHANGE	DALLAS	20·0x96·0
55	BARBER & TAILOR SHOP	"	20·0x72·0
56	Q.M. SALES STORE	"	20·0x96·0
57	DISPATCH OFFICE	BRICK	6·0x8·0
58	S.H.A.E.F. WAREHOUSES	DALLAS	20·0x48·0
59	S.H.A.E.F. TRANSP. OFFICE	"	20·0x48·0
60	S.H.A.E.F. UTILITIES OFFICE	"	20·0x48·0
61	UTILITY SHOPS	NISSEN	16·0x36·0 / 24·0x40·0
62	STORAGE	DALLAS	20·0x48·0
63	WORKSHOP	"	20·0x48·0
64	ENGINEER OFFICE	"	20·0x152·0
65	TRANSFORMER BLDG.	BRICK	10·0x10·0
66	OFFICE	DALLAS	20·0x144·0
67	STORAGE	NISSEN	16·0x18·0
68	STORAGE	"	16·0x36·0

The Eighth Air Force headquarters complex in Bushy Park had been named Camp Griffiss on its inauguration in February 1943 in honour of Lieutenant Colonel Townsend Griffiss, the first American airman to lose his life in Europe during the Second World War, who had been shot down in a civilian aircraft in February the previous year.

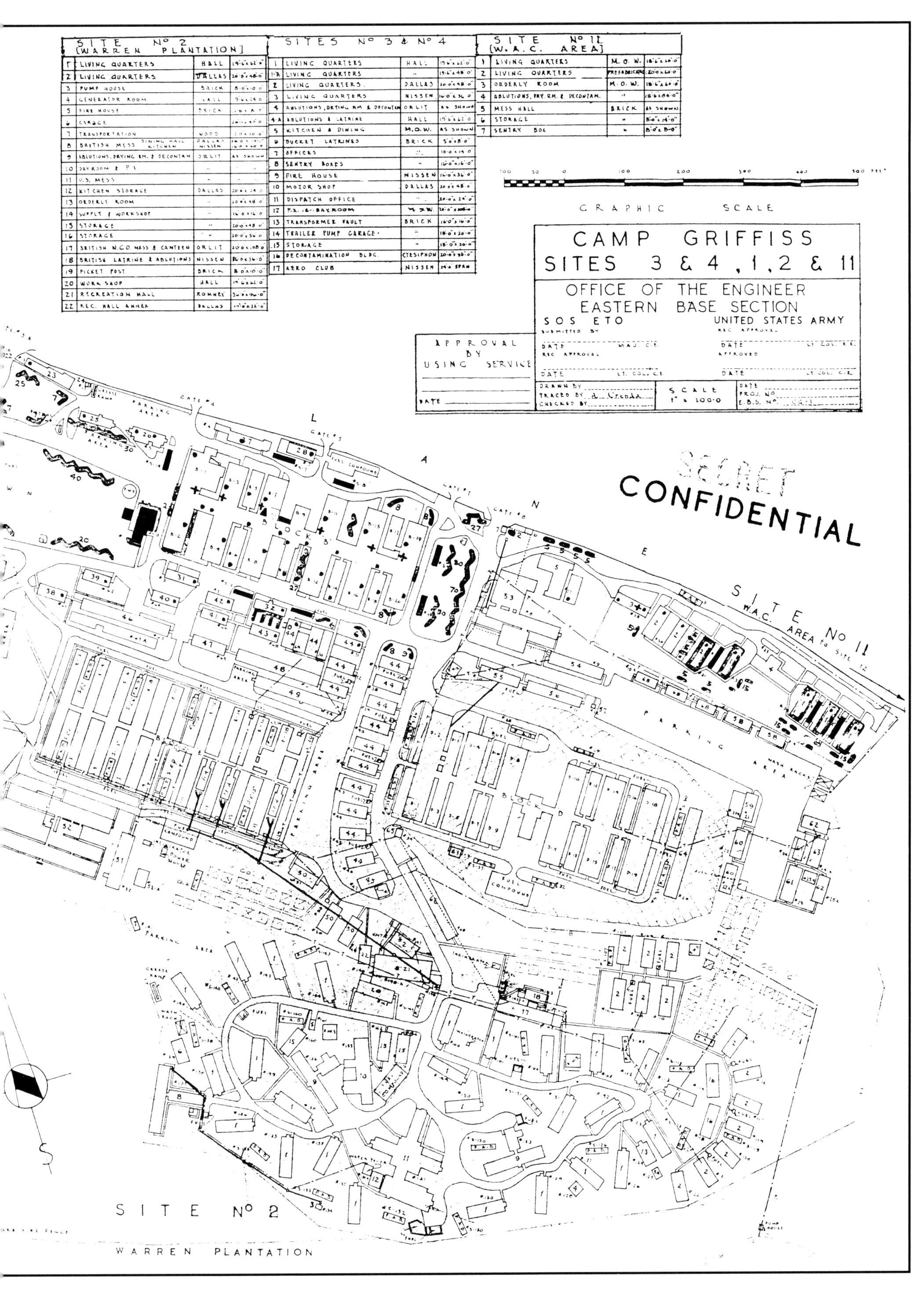

The headquarters had been code-named 'Widewing' by the air force and the name was retained when SHAEF took over. They occupied Blocks 'C' and 'D' with overspill accommodation being provided in Blocks 'E' and 'F'. By the time all the arrangements had been made, SHAEF moved in over the weekend of March 4-5, about a month later than planned.

From one central command building — Norfolk House — which had served the planning stage of 'Overlord' so well, accommodating unified staffs from the naval, air and land forces, now, for the more important operational phase, each was separated. This led to the splitting and duplication of personnel as representatives of the various commands now had to maintain a presence at Bushy Park as well as Norfolk House which was still retained as a rear HQ. On March 27, at an award ceremony held on the lawned parade area in front of the camouflaged Block 'C', Field-Marshal Sir Alan Brooke, Chief of the Imperial General Staff, decorated seven American officers for distinguished service in North Africa. Lieutenant General George S. Patton, recently in Eisenhower's bad books for hitting a soldier in Sicily, commander of the US Third Army, looks particularly pleased with himself as he is awarded the Order of the Bath.

Shuttling between Bushy Park and conferences in London, the advancing spring required a never-ending series of decisions by the Supreme Commander, some minor but others reached only after the most grave deliberation.

Major General Manton S. Eddy had commanded Task Force 'A' for 'Torch', and then led the 9th Infantry Division in Tunisia and Sicily. He was to lead the 9th into Normandy and, later, further enhance his reputation as the commander of US XV Corps.

Exactly 50 years later, on Sunday. March 27, 1994, we re-staged the award ceremony as part of our tribute to the events of 1944. We even got the timing right as evidenced by the shadows.

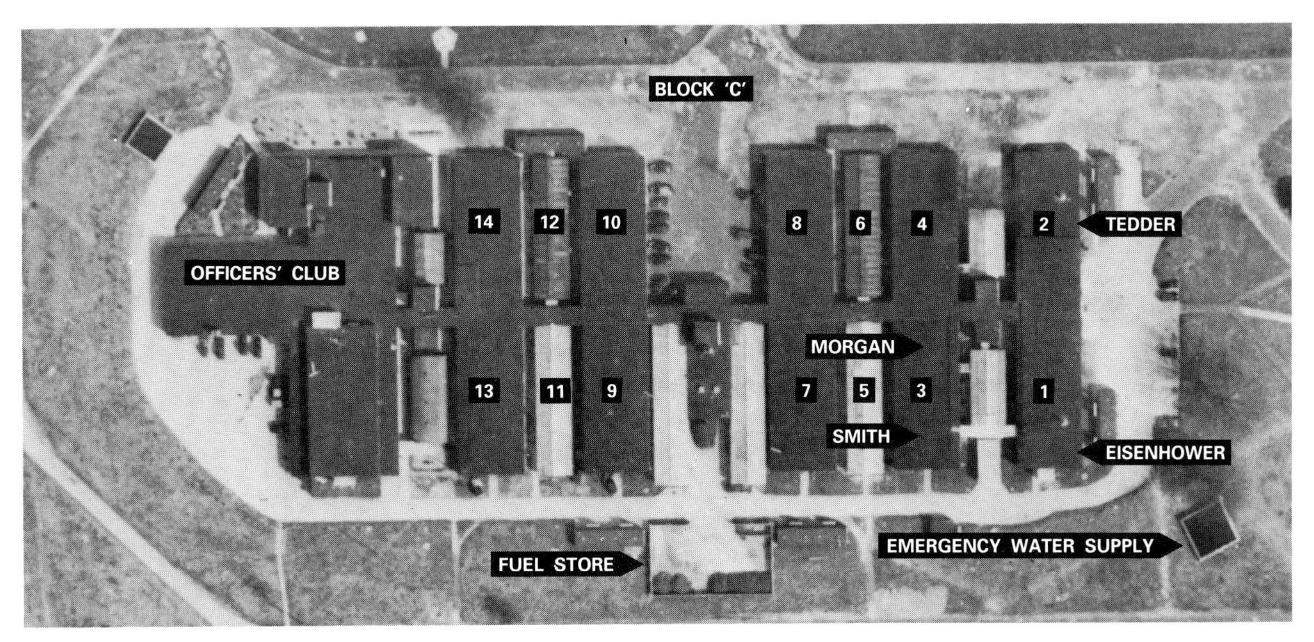

SHAEF's tenure at Bushy Park was short — barely six months — for no sooner had Eisenhower moved in than plans were being made to set up both an Advance Command Post and Forward HQ at Portsmouth before the Main HQ moved to France in September. By February 1945, the only American occupants were the US Group for the Control Commission for the occupation of Germany. However, in 1948, the US Air Force returned when 'Widewing' became the headquarters of the 3rd Air Division. For seven months during the Berlin Airlift, the USAF shared the base with RAF Transport Command which had moved in when US forces left in 1945. This enlargement of the main SHAEF Block 'C' is from the picture taken by the RAF on April 14, 1947. Note the covered passageway between the offices of Eisenhower and Smith: this was damaged by a near miss from a V1 on July 1, 1944. Final closure of the base, then including a beautifully-appointed American boarding school with extensive sports facilities and a 400-seat theatre, came in 1962 against much opposition from the local authorities who wished to preserve the amenities for the benefit of the local population. Matters came to a climax in September with hunreds protesting at the imminent demolition of the school, its theatre and hospital. A protest march on the 30th (a Sunday) was simply met by a deafening silence from the Minister of Public Buildings and Works. During that winter, the facilities began to decay from lack of use, and vandals added to the deterioration, hastening the inevitable end. The open days held on Armed Forces Day by the USAF during the 1950s made a feature of the 'Eisenhower Room' in C1 wing, yet it is only when such historic places have passed from our sight that people really come to realise what has been lost. In March 1994 — 50 years after SHAEF moved in — moves were made to redress the balance.

General Eisenhower's office lay at the southern end of Wing 1 of Block 'C' and Tony Molloy, project manager for the 50th anniversary event scheduled to be held in the park on May 30, had two ideas for commemorating the occasion. A memorial was already in existence on the front lawn, unveiled by General Ira C. Eaker on August 20, 1945, but this only recorded the use of Bushy Park by the USAAF. Tony felt strongly that its occupation by SHAEF had been overlooked, and his plan was to re-concrete the floor of Eisenhower's office and mark it with a suitable plaque. On March 4, 1994, exactly 50 years from the day when SHAEF moved in, trenches were cut across the site, the exact position occupied by the office being determined by the architect, Don Wilson, from scaling up the aerial photograph at the top of this page.

Above: **On April 12, 1944, an award ceremony was held in front of Block 'C' for British officers being decorated for meritorious service by the Supreme Commander.**

Below: **On May 30, 1994, we took this comparison as men of the Royal Canadian Air Force, Army and Navy marched across the old SHAEF parade ground.**

Left: **All the old wartime entrances, which cut through the brick wall bordering the park on its northern side along Sandy Lane, had been sealed up when the Americans left, so the second part of Tony Molloy's commemoration plan was to cut a 'SHAEF Gate' at the exact point where the original main entrance (No. 3A) once lay.**

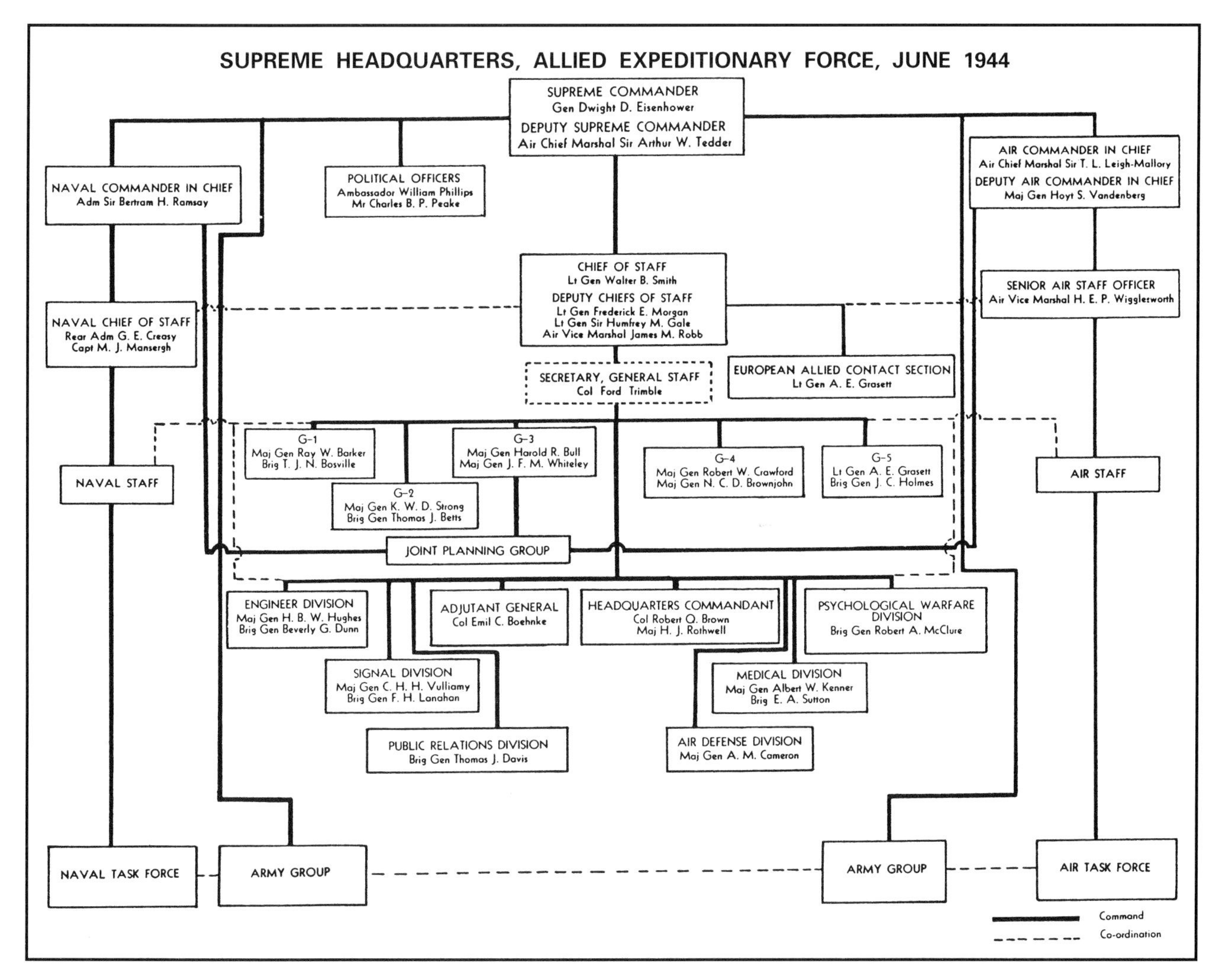

For those who are unfamiliar with the military establishment, I think it may be useful to give a brief summary of the purpose and duties of the staff which functions for a high commander in war under the general direction of a chief-of-staff. Its broad mission is to draw up strategic plans, provide information on the disposition and capabilities of the enemy forces, allocate the troop units to the operation, and estimate the supplies necessary to bring the commander victory in the field. It is the duty of the staff to anticipate all foreseeable problems which the armies may meet and to recommend solutions. Its ultimate purpose is to free the commander from countless details of administration and organization and thus leave his mind clear to consider only the great purpose which he has been designated to carry out and to make the major decisions which he alone can make.

The general staff is divided functionally into several sections, each headed by a general officer who has the title of Assistant Chief-of-Staff, followed by the designation of his section. The four basic sections are abbreviated G-1, G-2, G-3, and G-4 (there may be others). The first of these, G-1, deals with personnel. It formulates the policies which govern the handling of the soldier as an individual, including, among other things, his morale and general welfare, his assignment, and his replacement if incapacitated.

In August 1943, General Morgan's plan for 'Overlord' had been accepted by the 'Quadrant' conference in Quebec, at which point COSSAC as a planning agency became the operational body charged with putting the plan into effect. Brigadier-General Ray W. Barker was Morgan's deputy, and he streamlined the original organisation and introduced the American 'G' system, Barker being appointed to the position of G-1 on the formation of SHAEF.

'Widewing' had its own airstrip for liaison aircraft, located on the southern side of the park. Blocks 'C' and 'D' are camouflaged in this picture taken on August 7, 1944.

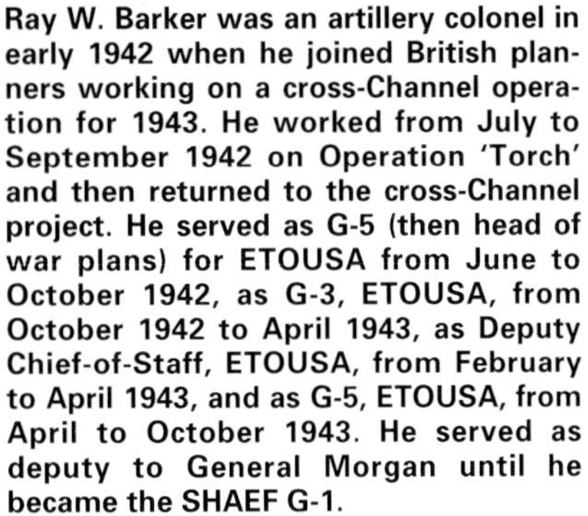

Ray W. Barker was an artillery colonel in early 1942 when he joined British planners working on a cross-Channel operation for 1943. He worked from July to September 1942 on Operation 'Torch' and then returned to the cross-Channel project. He served as G-5 (then head of war plans) for ETOUSA from June to October 1942, as G-3, ETOUSA, from October 1942 to April 1943, as Deputy Chief-of-Staff, ETOUSA, from February to April 1943, and as G-5, ETOUSA, from April to October 1943. He served as deputy to General Morgan until he became the SHAEF G-1.

Major-General Kenneth W. D. Strong served as assistant military attaché in Berlin shortly before the outbreak of war in 1939, and in the first one and a half years of the war as head of the German Section at the War Office. Later, he commanded a battalion and then became chief of intelligence of Home Forces. In February 1943, he was appointed G-2 of Allied Force Headquarters in the Mediterranean and in this capacity he helped General Smith in armistice negotiations with the Italians. In the spring of 1944, he became G-2 of SHAEF.

Major General Harold R. Bull was serving as Secretary, General Staff, of the War Department in 1939. In 1941, he became G-3 of the War Department, and went from this post to head the Replacement School Command, Army Ground Forces. In the summer of 1943, General Marshall sent him to North Africa as a special observer. On his return, he became the commanding general of III Corps, holding this post from June to September 1943. In the latter month, he was sent to London where he became deputy G-3 of COSSAC. In February 1944, he was appointed G-3, SHAEF.

G-2 is Intelligence. It collects and evaluates from many sources every obtainable scrap of information about the enemy. It seeks to learn where his forces are located, the extent of his defenses at every point of the territory he holds. It traces the movements of enemy divisions in and out of the line and evaluates from this and other information what these shifts may mean. When our troops began moving across the Channel on D-Day, the location of every German division in north-west France was pinpointed on the tactical commanders' battle maps. In our war room at SHAEF, we had marked in the disposition of every enemy unit in all of Europe. From this information we could immediately trace the movement of reinforcements to the battle area. It is an interesting fact that during the critical fighting in Normandy only one German division arrived on our front as a surprise.

Just ten days before the invasion, Intelligence brought news that three German divisions had been moved to the base of the Cotentin Peninsula, almost at the spot where our 82nd Airborne Division was scheduled to drop. As a result, the drop zone was moved nearer Utah Beach and north of the zone of the 101st Airborne. The 82nd was given the mission of seizing the roadhead at Ste Mère-Eglise to protect the beach against a possible counter-attack by enemy troops on the Cotentin peninsula. On June 5, just after General Bradley had gone aboard Admiral Kirk's flagship *Augusta* for the invasion, we were able to get word to one of his officers still in Plymouth that the excellent German 352nd Infantry Division had moved to the area of Omaha Beach. It was too late for General Bradley to warn the assault troops, since radio silence had to be observed throughout the invasion fleet. And, before it was cut to pieces, the 352nd gave all too good an account of itself against the American 1st and 29th Divisions the following day.

The G-3 section of the staff is concerned with preparation of the battle plans and the assignment of the major units which are to carry them out. Working from a directive which states the objectives to be gained, it is the mission of the Assistant Chief-of-Staff, G-3, to develop the tactics and to make assignments of units from the troops available. His plans must always depend on the supplies of every nature which the troops will require in the field.

G-4 deals with supply and transport. For such an enormous undertaking as Operation 'Overlord' the extent and intricacy of this phase of the planning were almost beyond belief. Everything that a soldier requires for success in battle must be furnished to him. There must be food to feed him, ammunition for the weapon he uses, medical supplies if he is wounded, transport to carry him to the point of contact with the enemy. And transport means gasoline — thousands and hundreds of thousands of gallons once troops are on the move. To meet this need, our engineers planned to lay pipelines on the Channel floor, and the first of these, stretching 70 miles from Sandown Bay on the Isle of Wight to Nacqueville [near Cherbourg], went into operation on August 12, before we broke out of the lodgement area in Normandy.

For such an amphibious operation as 'Overlord', all the vessels which carry troops and supplies are 'combat-loaded', another problem which calls for the most minute planning on the part of G-4. The technique had been developed for the North African operation when ships were combat-loaded in both Great Britain and the United States for the assault. The purpose is to establish the priority of weapons, supplies and transport as the troops will need them from the moment they are set down on a hostile shore. This priority is then followed on the vessels transporting each unit of troops so that the required matériel will be ready to hand when it is called for. The rule is that what will be needed first is last to be loaded on the ship. And while the routine seems simple, each officer who takes part in the invasion feels that his own effort requires a priority over some other need.

How complex these needs can be is indicated by some of the priorities assigned to the American First Army which was to strike Omaha and Utah beaches in the D-Day dawn. Something over 55,000 American troops were to land on the beaches that day. The basic needs were easy enough to write down — food, ammunition, transport. But in addition there were 120-foot steel span

Major General Robert W. Crawford was district engineer in New Orleans in 1939 when he was called to the War Plans Division in Washington working on overseas supplies and munitions. By July 1942, he was head of a combat command of the 8th Armored Division before becoming Commanding General, Services of Supply, US Army Forces in the Middle East. In July 1943, he was deputy commander and later Chief-of-Staff of Services of Supply, and G-4 in ETOUSA. In November 1943, he became deputy G-4 of COSSAC, and on the activation of SHAEF, its G-4.

Lieutenant-General Sir A. E. Grasett, a Canadian-born officer, was stationed in China in 1938-41. He returned to the United Kingdom in 1941 to command a division, and from 1941 to 1943 a corps. He next served as chief of the Liaison Branch of the War Office and, after the organisation of Supreme Headquarters, became chief of the European Allied Contact Section. In April 1944, he was appointed chief of the G-5 division which had the responsibility of looking after civil affairs, a task which included setting up missions to deal with relations with the various occupied countries.

Brigadier General Robert A. McClure, US Military Attaché in London in 1941 and military attaché to the eight governments-in-exile in the United Kingdom, became G-2 of ETOUSA under General Eisenhower early in 1942. From November 1942 to November 1943, he headed the Public Relations, Psychological Warfare and Censorship Section at AFHQ. In November 1943, he was sent to COSSAC to organise a similar section. In February 1944, he became G-6 of SHAEF. When that division was split on April 13, he was appointed chief of the Psychological Warfare Division of SHAEF.

bridges which Intelligence had pointed out would be necessary to carry transport over rivers and flooded areas. There were sulpha pills. If a bulldozer, needed immediately at one of the beaches, was not available when required, lives and time would be lost. There was fresh drinking water — more than 300,000 gallons for the first three days ashore. Everything had to be anticipated by G-4, and the staff at SHAEF had to check all these plans, confirm them, and ask the Supreme Commander to approve them, too. Supporting and working with the general staff is the special staff, groups of technical experts each headed, as in the case of the general staff, by a senior officer whose title is descriptive of his function. The Surgeon General, the Chief of Engineers, the Quartermaster General, and the Chief of Ordnance are examples among others. At the headquarters of a theater of operations the special staff is, relatively, quite large since its various sections must cover all of the activities and responsibilities of the theater.

The Supreme Commander was provided with an armoured train — or rather two specially-converted LNER coaches (Nos. 1591 and 1592) — for use as a mobile command headquarters. He had used the same carriages, code-named *Bayonet*, in 1942.

Here, he alights at Newmarket station after inspecting American air force bases on April 11. Today, the two coaches can be seen preserved at the National Railroad Museum, Green Bay, Wisconsin, which acquired them in 1967.

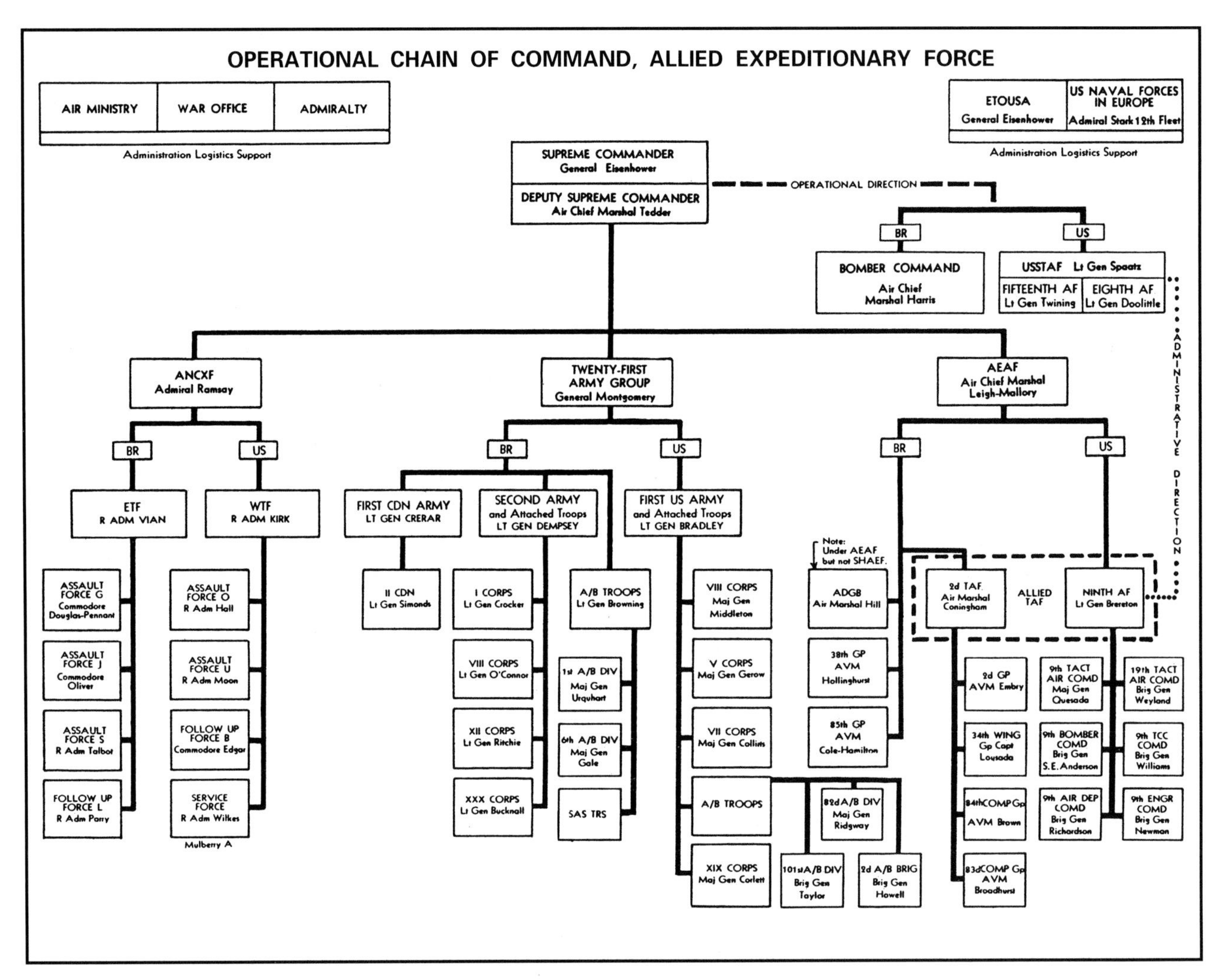

At Supreme Headquarters, the personnel of the three arms, Army, Navy, and Air, were integrated for all practical purposes and they lived and worked together.

Most of the detailed plans were not made at SHAEF itself. Reporting to the staff at Supreme Headquarters were the subordinate staffs of the commanders of the three combat arms — air, ground, and sea. These staffs carried on the tactical planning for the assault, the gaining of a bridgehead, and the build-up in the lodgement area which would precede our breakthrough onto the plains of Normandy. General Eisenhower himself would take over tactical command of the ground forces once we were established on the Continent. In the preliminary phases, command was held by General Montgomery as commander of the 21st Army Group. General Bradley's First Army was part of this force during the invasion. His headquarters was at Bristol, where his staff prepared the plans for pressing the war at the western end of the invasion line and taking the port of Cherbourg. But because General Bradley was also to command an American army group after the breakthrough, separated from Montgomery and reporting directly to General Eisenhower as overall tactical commander, he had established a separate headquarters and staff for this higher command which reported to SHAEF.

The US First Army, for the time being, was under command of General Montgomery, but the American 12th Army Group was always to be separate from Montgomery's 21st Army Group.

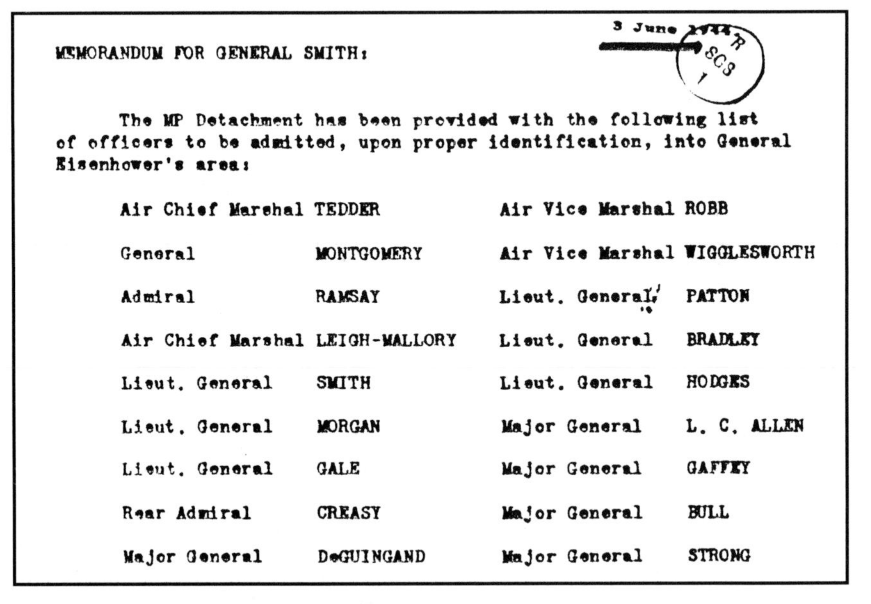

3 June 1944

MEMORANDUM FOR GENERAL SMITH:

The MP Detachment has been provided with the following list of officers to be admitted, upon proper identification, into General Eisenhower's area:

Air Chief Marshal	TEDDER	Air Vice Marshal	ROBB
General	MONTGOMERY	Air Vice Marshal	WIGGLESWORTH
Admiral	RAMSAY	Lieut. General	PATTON
Air Chief Marshal	LEIGH-MALLORY	Lieut. General	BRADLEY
Lieut. General	SMITH	Lieut. General	HODGES
Lieut. General	MORGAN	Major General	L. C. ALLEN
Lieut. General	GALE	Major General	GAFFEY
Rear Admiral	CREASY	Major General	BULL
Major General	DeGUINGAND	Major General	STRONG

On March 3 — even before 'Widewing' was operational — Major General Bull sounded out General Smith as to the Supreme Commander's wishes for his Advance Command Post, to which he would move just before 'Neptune' was set in motion. Eisenhower rejected the idea of using *Bayonet*, preferring the option of a tented camp close to Admiral Ramsay's headquarters in Southwick House, some five miles north of Portsmouth. Major R. E. Baker, the SHAEF General Staff Assistant Secretary, drew up this list for the approval of General Smith of those persons who would be permitted to enter the Advance CP which was code-named 'Sharpener'.

Once more, I feel I must digress briefly for those who are not familiar with military terms to discuss the chain of command in Operation 'Overlord' and to explain some of the terms involved.

As Supreme Commander, General Eisenhower was in direct command of the forces dedicated to the conquest of Hitler's armies. Under him was a deputy supreme commander, Air Chief Marshal Tedder. The Supreme Headquarters staff reported to them. In the next echelon stood the Commander in Chief, Allied Naval Forces (Admiral Ramsay), the United States Army Group Commander (General Bradley), the British Army Group Commander (General Montgomery), and the Commander in Chief, Allied Expeditionary Air Forces (Air Chief Marshal Leigh-Mallory). Arrayed below these headquarters were the British and American naval and air commanders.

If the terms here are somewhat technical, let me start with a division which, in World War II, comprised about 17,000 men. The next higher echelon is a corps, composed of two or more divisions and various corps troops. For the invasion of Normandy, the Americans employed two corps, composed of two divisions each. The British also employed two corps, comprising both British and Canadian troops. Next above corps headquarters there is the army, composed of two or more corps. General Bradley's First Army, originally comprised of four divisions for the assault, had re-established command over all the other divisions which came across the Normandy beaches of his American area during the build-up.

It seems incredible, considering the hazards, how successful we were in keeping the enemy from learning where we intended to strike. But the special precautions were thorough. In effect, all the exits from England to the outside world were sealed off. Civilian travel between Great Britain and Ireland was halted on February 9. This seemed a necessary measure, since neutral Eire had plenty of Axis agents working quite openly. Beginning on April 1, visitors were excluded from the coastal areas in southern England. A ten-mile strip was placed off-limits to all who had no official business in the area. In the middle of April, the British government placed restrictions on the activities of diplomatic missions. Diplomats and couriers were forbidden to leave or enter the United Kingdom. And diplomatic mail, ordinarily free from inspection, was censored. Beginning May 25, all mail from American personnel to the United States or elsewhere was subjected to a ten-day delay.

In those last days of May, the staff at SHAEF was watching the completion of its five months of ceaseless effort to mount the invasion force. The final great moves were under way. One of the most intricate pieces of planning was now put in execution when the schedules prepared by the combined Army and Navy headquarters began to send troops to the ports in southern England. It was a marvel of inspired timing which brought these thousands of soldiers and their mass of transport to the Channel without attracting undue attention.

Then it was June, and we were with General Eisenhower at the forward command post he had established near Portsmouth. Whatever happened now, we knew that everything was ready. The agonizing threats of shortages in vital landing craft and matériel had been met. For these next few days, our principal enemy was the weather. If General Eisenhower made the decision to go, it would start a mighty offensive that would halt only when Hitler's forces were destroyed and our Allied armies stood victorious in the heart of the Reich.

A suitable site was selected in a wooded enclave in Sawyer's Wood less than a mile from the house. Here, a collection of tents and mobile trailers had been made ready by April 27, this picture being taken of the site by the 7th Photo Group (US Eighth Air Force) from 12,000 feet on April 21. A track was prepared from the metalled road leading along the edge of the field to the south of Southwick House so that Eisenhower could enter the park via its rear entrance (see page 102).

German Defences

By Oberst Bodo Zimmermann

ERSTER STABSOFFIZIER, OBERBEFEHLSHABER WEST

I remember clearly a March morning in 1943 at St Germain-en-Laye, the headquarters of the Oberbefehlshaber West (OB West) [Commander-in-Chief West], just outside Paris. Von Rundstedt's office was in a small villa, and I was his Erster Generalstabsoffizier [First Operations Officer] or Ia.

It was a lovely spring day and the Generalfeldmarschall was as spruce and youthful as ever when I entered his office. No matter what the circumstances, von Rundstedt always managed to look as neat as a new pin. But this morning his manner was one of deep depression. His first words told me why.

'Stalingrad', he said, 'has fallen. Now what?'

Top: **Le Tréport in the département of the Somme, February 1944. As far as the Allies were concerned, having established that Normandy offered the best all-round option for a landing in France, they could concentrate all their efforts on the minute study of a 50-mile stretch of coastline. The Germans, on the other hand, had to be prepared to repel an attack anywhere from Denmark to Spain, a distance of some 600 miles. It was realised — on both sides — that ports were the key to sustaining a landing and, after the assault on Dieppe in 1942, their defences were strengthened even further.** *Above:* **This is Le Tréport today from almost exactly the same vantage point on the southern headland, the Calvaire des Terrasses.**

Generalfeldmarschall Gerd von Rundstedt, 69, left, seen here being visited at his headquarters at St Germain by Generaloberst Heinz Guderian, the Inspector-General of Armoured Forces, in April 1944. In the First World War, von Rundstedt had served as Chief-of-Staff of various division and corps headquarters, and he had retired in 1938 but, in June 1939, was recalled to command Heeresgruppe Süd (Army Group South) in the Polish campaign. After a very short term as Oberbefehlshaber Ost (Commander-in-Chief East) in occupied Poland, he was redesignated as C-in-C of Heeresgruppe A and transferred to the Western Front. In May 1940, his forces broke through the Ardennes and advanced to the Channel coast. In October 1940, he was designated Oberbefehlshaber West (OB West), a position he held until the transfer of his headquarters to the east in the spring of 1941. During the Russian campaign, von Rundstedt commanded Heeresgruppe Süd from June until December 1941, when at his own request he was relieved of command because of ill-health. In March 1942, he was re-assigned as OB West until he was relieved early in July 1944. Von Rundstedt was to return to his former position on September 5, 1944 and to remain OB West until his final relief on March 19, 1945, only to be taken prisoner on May 1.

Like his predecessor in the West, Generalfeldmarschall Erwin von Witzleben, von Rundstedt was at all times aware that the eventual battle against the British and Americans in France could be, perhaps was being, lost on the Eastern Front before ever the Anglo-Saxon armies set foot on the Continent. The men, the guns and the tanks which would be needed to repel the probable invasion were being consumed in the vast holocaust raging at the other end of Europe. This had already been true in 1942; it was to become more so during 1943, the year in which the RAF and USAAF gained supremacy over Generalfeldmarschall Hugo Sperrle's Luftflotte 3 [3rd Air Fleet], a state of affairs for which Reichsmarschall Hermann Göring's laziness and inefficiency were at least partly to blame.

The heavy fighting in Africa and later in Sicily and Italy provided a secondary though by no means insignificant drain on Germany's resources, already affected by the mounting weight of the enemy's bomber offensive.

Such, then, were very briefly the external circumstances in which von Rundstedt attempted to organise the defence of France and the Low Countries against the coming invasion.

Until our French researcher, Jean Paul Pallud, visited St Germain-en-Laye on the western outskirts of Paris in 1993, the location of von Rundstedt's villa had been lost to history. However, using photographs of the period, and his detective's nose, he found the correct one on the Rue Alexandre Dumas.

Left: The Villa David is now the office of the Claude Debussy School. *Right:* Jean Paul, right, stands in for Guderian as Colonel Henri de Rolland of the local tourist office impersonates von Rundstedt. We are indebted to the school's director, André Orsini, for allowing us into his private quarters.

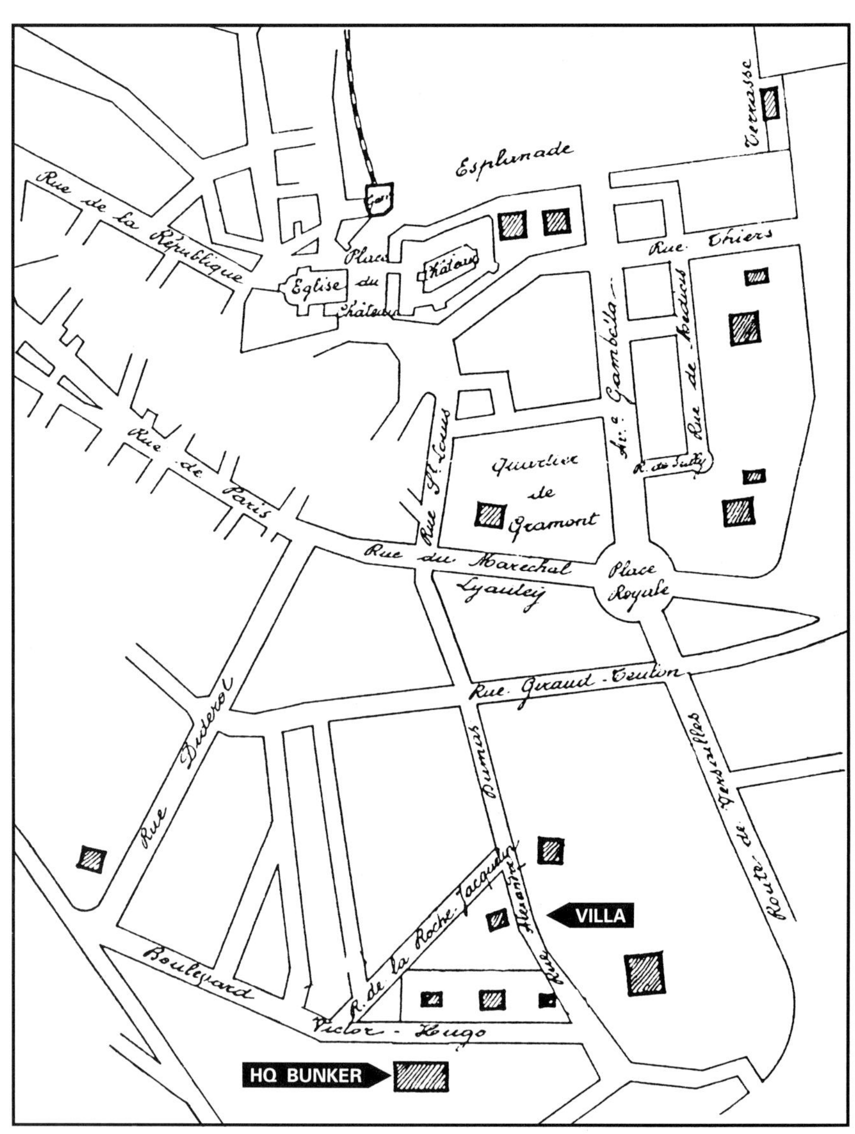

Jean Paul subsequently found this sketch plan in French Army archives produced at the end of the war illustrating the OB West bunker complex at St Germain. Unlike the Allied Supreme Commander, the Oberbefehlshaber West was provided with several large bomb-proof bunkers for his headquarters. ***Above left:*** **Basement entrance from the Villa David to the underground air raid shelter, constructed beneath the garden, which still contains its wood panelling and air ventilation equipment in pristine condition.** ***Below:*** **The massive HQ bunker, now located on private ground just off Boulevard Victor-Hugo.**

VON RUNDSTEDT AT ST GERMAIN

I recall two characteristic anecdotes concerning the OB West during these months of preparing and waiting.

As the tempo of the Allied air attacks increased, his staff grew worried for the field-marshal's personal safety, though he himself took no notice of the raids. While he was absent from his headquarters, an air raid shelter was rapidly built in the garden of his house at St Germain and most effectively camouflaged, but when the old gentleman saw it he declared quite categorically that nothing would ever induce him 'to set foot inside the thing'. However, one evening, Allied bombers dropped marker flares over St Germain and it seemed likely that a rain of bombs would follow. I therefore ordered von Rundstedt's son, who was acting as his aide-de-camp, to take his father to the shelter. After meeting considerable opposition, the young Rundstedt succeeded eventually in carrying out this order. As it happened, the bombers hit a neighbouring suburb. I was much occupied on the telephone, and I forgot all about the Commander-in-Chief. An hour later my telephone rang. It was the field-marshal who simply asked, in his usual courteous fashion: 'Zimmerman, can I please come out now?'

The calm before the storm. The German High Command in the West relax in the garden of OB West's Villa David. Identifiable in this picture are von Rundstedt [1]; his Chief-of-Staff, Günther Blumentritt [2]; Guderian [3] and our author Bodo Zimmermann [4]. Born in November 1886, Zimmermann joined the Reichsheer as a cadet in 1906, serving in the First World War as a leutnant with Infanterie-Regiment 145. He retired with the rank of major in April 1920 but was recalled to the General Staff with his old rank in 1939. December that year found him appointed the Erster Generalstabsoffizier (First Operations Officer, often seen abbreviated in German documents to 'Ia') with the 1. Armee and, from October 1940, with Heeresgruppe D. He was promoted Oberst in December 1942 and in the spring of 1944 was posted to von Rundstedt's OB West HQ with the same appointment.

Another story about the raids was one he himself told with a smile in our officers' mess. It was his custom each day to take a walk through the streets of St Germain, alone and armed only with his walking-stick. The air raid sirens howled. The field-marshal, as usual, took no notice. Nor did an elderly French housewife whom he passed, her shopping basket on her arm.

'But, Madame', von Rundstedt enquired, 'are you not frightened of the bombs?'

The old lady replied: 'Why should I be afraid, mon maréchal? They won't bomb St Germain. It has no military importance, for nothing ever happens here.'

Right: **Oberst Zimmermann (left) with two staff officers and Leutnant Dr Hans-Gerd von Rundstedt, seated on the right, who served as his father's aide-de-camp**

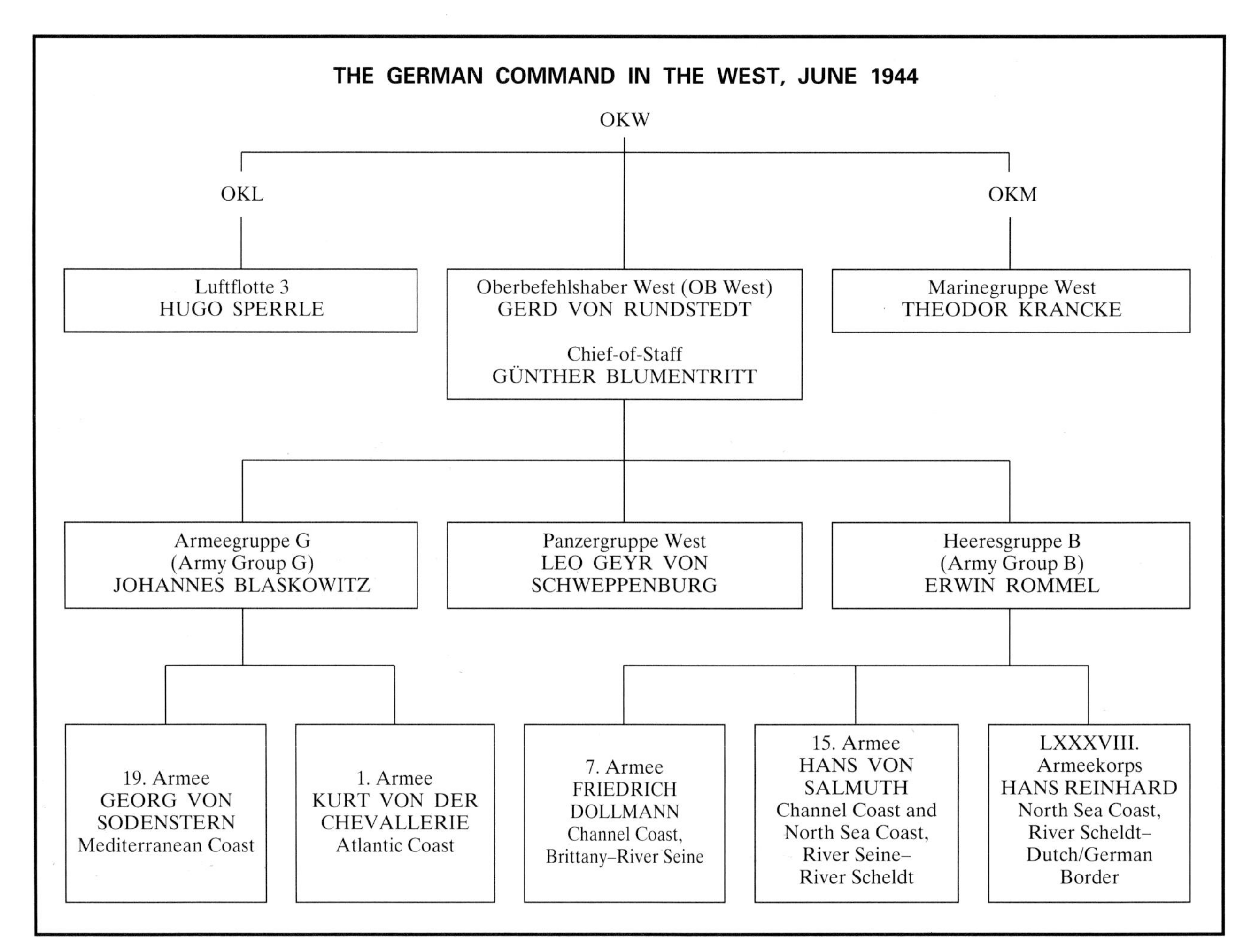

The most serious weakness of the German defence in the West was the lack of any unified command — there was no supreme commander in the Allied sense (excluding, of course, Hitler) and von Rundstedt did not have authority over the air and naval forces. Panzergruppe West, created on January 24, 1944, served to concentrate all armoured formations in the west under one command. The LXXXVIII. Armeekorps was officially under the Wehrmachtbefehlshaber in den Niederlanden (Commander of Armed Forces in the Netherlands), General der Flieger Friedrich Christiansen, but in practice Rommel's orders went direct to corps commander, Reinhard.

THE WESTERN FRONT

The army in the West was spread in a great bow, with most of its forces disposed on or close to the coast. The bow stretched from Holland, along the Channel and Biscay coasts, to the Pyrenees, then along the Mediterranean to Toulon. Part of the Italian Fourth Army, which was also under von Rundstedt, manned defensive positions from Toulon to the Italian frontier. Many German troops, including units of the field army as well as of the navy and the air force, were locked up in the so-called 'fortresses', which included exposed islands as well as fortified bases. In the Channel Isles alone, for example, there were some 30–40,000 men consisting of one reinforced infantry division, one anti-aircraft brigade, numerous heavy naval batteries, engineers and construction workers of the Organisation Todt. This large body of troops held this isolated position, where the problems of supply were already so great that an entire year's stocks were accumulated, on Hitler's direct orders. There could be no question of von Rundstedt's evacuating this or any other area of his enormous front.

It was a front of over 600 miles, as the crow flies, and much longer if one measured the coastline of the mainland and islands. Such a vast line could not, of course, be 'held' with the troops available. Nor indeed were there enough divisions in the West during 1943 to meet a large-scale invasion at any point.

In addition to the troops stretched out along the coast, there were insignificant units of elder men in the rear areas under the Military Commanders of France and Belgium: the Militärbefehlshaber in Frankreich, General der Infanterie Karl-Heinrich von Stülpnagel, and the Militärbefehlshaber in Belgien und Nord-Frankreich, General der Infanterie Alexander Freiherr von Falkenhausen. These could not be regarded as a reserve. Indeed, there was at this time no sort of flexible, strong, mobile reserve in the West. Whenever such a reserve began to be built up in 1943, the units were invariably taken away to fight in Russia or Italy, particularly Russia. It would be no exaggeration to say that the western army was steadily drained of all its able-bodied manpower and supplies for the Eastern Front.

As a result, organisational and tactical dispositions in the West were a mere patchwork. Commanders, troops and equipment were second-rate. From 1943 on, the basis of the western army consisted of over-age men armed with over-age weapons. Neither the one nor the other were a match, even physically, for the demands of the coming battle.

THE ATLANTIC WALL

To conceal the real weakness of Germany's western defences, Hitler ordered the building of fortifications along the coast, with greatest intensity along the Channel, during 1942. Gigantic concrete structures sprang up, but of course it was impossible to complete these strong fortifications everywhere, let alone arm this 'Atlantic Wall'. The French Mediterranean coast, which we only occupied in November of 1942, was not fortified at all. Owing to supply shortages, most of the weapons for the Atlantic Wall, down to mines and even barbed wire, were taken from the old West Wall along the Franco-German frontier.

It was the policy of the Oberkommando der Wehrmacht (OKW) [High Command of the Armed Forces] to transfer exhausted, often decimated, divisions from the Eastern Front to the West for rest and rehabilitation. As soon as these divisions had been reformed and re-equipped, they returned to Russia. Thus, our order of battle, which frequently showed numerous divisions which were in fact only skeletons, was quite misleading. And the draining of combat troops continued. A typical example of this was the arrival of the Russians.

By order of the OKW, 20 of the best-equipped battalions were transferred from the West, with their heavy weapons, to the Eastern Front. In return, von Rundstedt was promised 60 battalions of the so-called 'Eastern volunteers', mostly former Russian prisoners-of-war, ill-trained and ill-equipped. What earthly use could such troops be against the enemy's tremendous weight or technical skill? What reason was there to believe that these 'volunteers' would even pretend to fight against their Western allies? It was all quite insane.

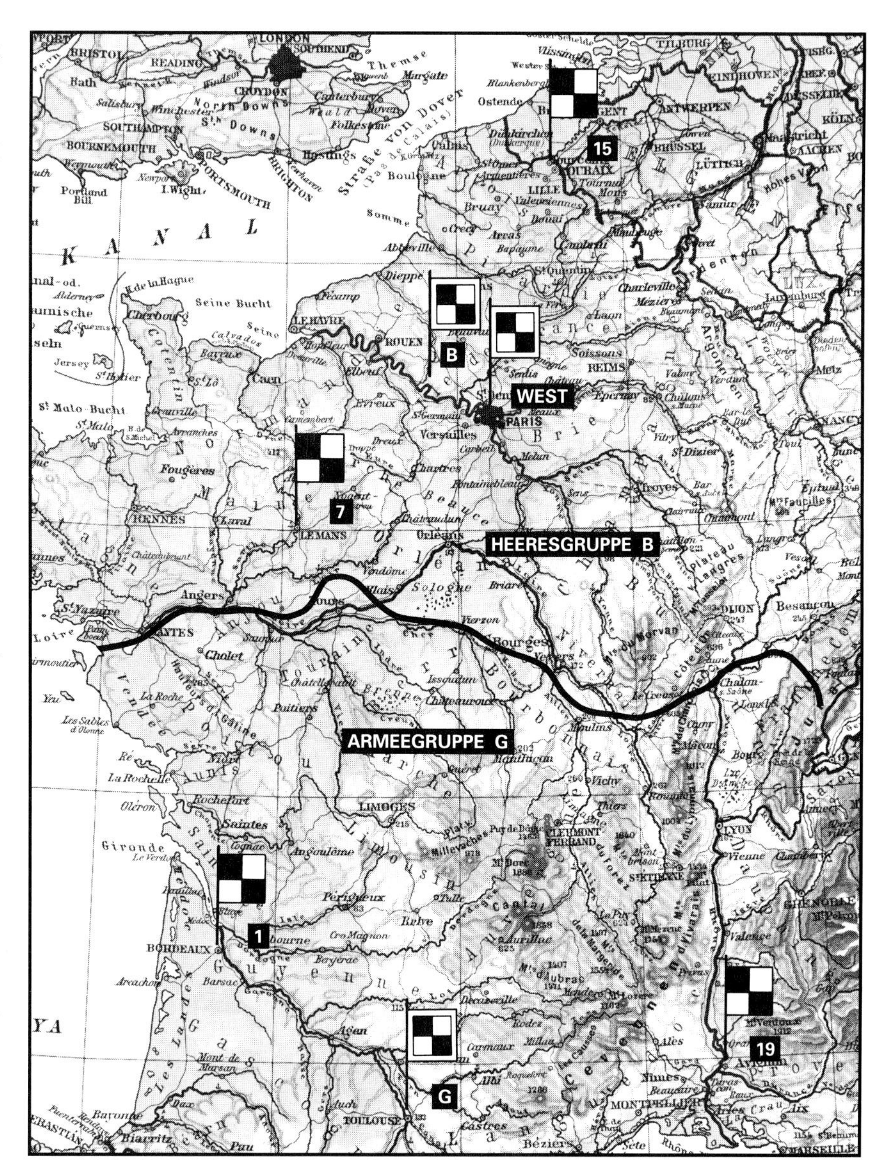

Generalfeldmarschall von Rundstedt, the OB West, controlled two army groups, Heeresgruppe B under Generalfeldmarschall Rommel and Armeegruppe G under Generaloberst Johannes Blaskowitz. North of an east-west boundary line across France was Heeresgruppe B, with headquarters in La Roche-Guyon. Rommel controlled the LXXXVIII. Armeekorps of Generalleutnant Hans Reinhard which occupied the Netherlands, the 15. Armee of Generaloberst Hans von Salmuth (headquarters in Tourcoing), which defended the Channel coast from Antwerp to the Orne river, and the 7. Armee of Generaloberst Friedrich Dollmann (HQ in Le Mans) which covered north-west France between the Orne and Loire rivers. South of the dividing line was Armeegruppe G with its headquarters in Toulouse. Created late in April, the headquarters still lacked many of the normal communication and support units necessary for command and control. Its inferior status was recognised by its designation, 'Armeegruppe'. Blaskowitz's headquarters was not to achieve the full status of Heeresgruppe until September. Generaloberst Blaskowitz commanded the 1. Armee of General der Infanterie Kurt von der Chevallerie (HQ in Bordeaux) which defended the Atlantic coast of France from the Loire to the Spanish border, and the 19. Armee of General der Infanterie Georg von Sodenstern (HQ in Avignon) which was responsible for the Mediterranean coast of France.

During the spring of 1943, von Rundstedt attempted to report to Hitler on the actual situation as it then existed in the West. It was time wasted. The interview on the Obersalzberg, which lasted for three hours, consisted of a two-hour monologue by Hitler giving his views on the Eastern Front, followed by a tea-hour during which the discussion of official matters was forbidden. Von Rundstedt's mounting fury, as he shifted in his chair, can be easily imagined. All he could do was, later, to utter some caustic comments on his supreme commander and order that a detailed report on the whole subject of coastal defences in the West be prepared for despatch to the OKW.

Throughout the year, interference in France from the RAF and USAAF increased in volume and efficiency. This affected German administration, industry, railway construction and finally the railways themselves. The building of defences along the Channel grew more and more difficult. Nor was this facilitated by a typical administrative 'mix-up', which resulted in the transfer of thousands of construction workers from the building of defences to the building of launching sites for the hush-hush V-weapons. This was done without informing von Rundstedt. His anger when he discovered that the workers had been stolen from behind his back is surely comprehensible.

Meanwhile, in the late summer of 1943, a basic order, entitled 'Führerweisung Nr. 51' (Führer Directive No. 51), was issued. This stated that the Western theatre would be the decisive defence area. The point of main effort, or 'Schwerpunkt', of Germany's defence would henceforth be the Channel. In support of this policy, the bulk of the new heavy weapons production together with the necessary munitions and supplies would be sent to von Rundstedt. Not content with this reasonable strategic directive, Hitler also gave operational instructions to OB West. Directive No. 51 laid down that the enemy must not be allowed to maintain a foothold on the coast, but must be thrown back into the sea at once. The coast must be held in all circumstances, and all withdrawal was forbidden.

Von Rundstedt's reply, which reached the OKW in the autumn, was the detailed report which he had ordered to be prepared after his abortive interview with Hitler earlier in the year. In its effect at supreme headquarters, it was something of a bombshell.

The report stated that most of the German soldiers in the West were too old. Officers with artificial limbs were not infrequent. A battalion had been formed of men suffering from ear complaints. Later, a division, the 70. Infanterie-Division, was created for men with poor stomachs who needed special diet. (The division was to fight bravely on Walcheren Island, despite the fact that many of the troops were in constant pain.) As for mobility, most of the units in the West were insufficiently flexible or even completely inflexible and therefore tactically of only limited value. There was a severe lack of heavy weapons and particularly of tanks — repeated crises in the East had nullified the expectations of reinforcements contained in Führer Directive No. 51. Only a very few parachute and panzer divisions formed an exception to this depressing picture and could be regarded as theoretically fit for operations.

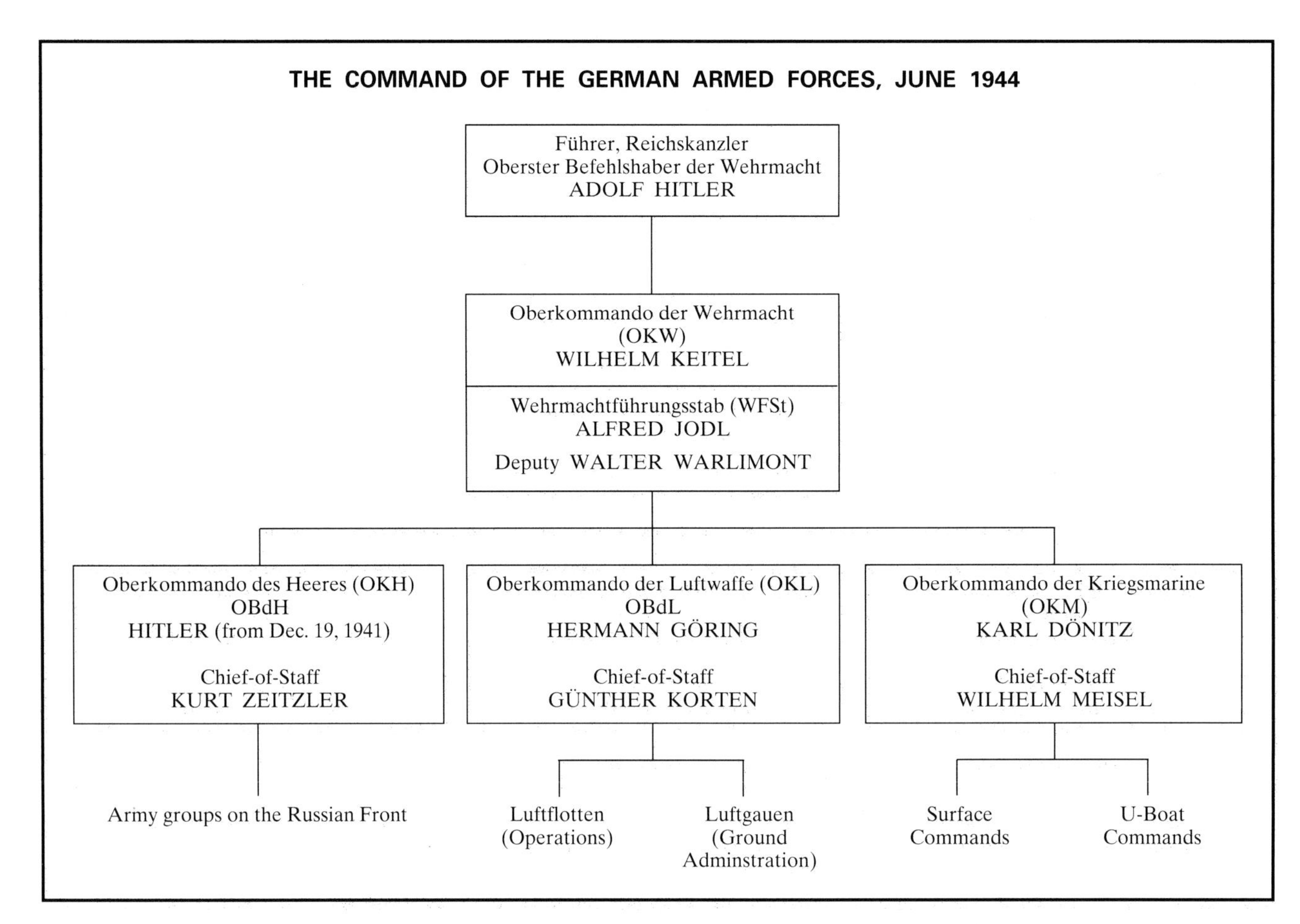

Having lost his foothold in Africa in May 1943, and being forced into a retreat on the Eastern Front two months later; with Italy capitulating in September and the Battle of the Atlantic all but lost, by October, Hitler knew that an Allied invasion of France was now a very real threat, creating the dreaded 'Two-Front War' which he had always declared he would avoid. On November 3, he issued his 51st directive of the war setting out his plans to counter the invasion.

The Führer

Führerhauptquartier,
November 3, 1943
27 copies

Directive No. 51

The hard and costly struggle against Bolshevism during the last two and a half years, which has involved the bulk of our military strength in the East, has demanded extreme exertions. The greatness of the danger and the general situation demanded it. But the situation has since changed. The danger in the East remains, but a greater danger now appears in the West: an Anglo-Saxon landing! In the East, the vast extent of the territory makes it possible for us to lose ground, even on a large scale, without a fatal blow being dealt to the nervous system of Germany.

It is very different in the West! Should the enemy succeed in breaching our defences here on a wide front, the immediate consequences would be unpredictable. Everything indicates that the enemy will launch an offensive against the Western front of Europe, at the latest in the spring, perhaps even earlier.

I can therefore no longer take responsibility for further weakening the West, in favour of other theatres of war. I have therefore decided to reinforce its defences, particularly those places from which the long-range bombardment of England will begin. For it is here that the enemy must and will attack, and it is here — unless all indications are misleading — that the decisive battle against the landing forces will be fought.

Holding and diversionary attacks are to be expected on other fronts. A large-scale attack on Denmark is also not out of the question. From a naval point of view, such an attack would be more difficult to deliver, nor could it be as effectively supported by air, but if successful, its political and operational repercussions would be very great.

At the beginning of the battle, the whole offensive strength of the enemy is bound to be thrown against our forces holding the coastline. Only by intensive construction, which means straining our available manpower and materials at home and in the occupied territories to the limit, can we strengthen our coastal defences in the short time which probably remains.

The ground weapons which will shortly reach Denmark and the occupied areas in the West (heavy anti-tank guns, immobile tanks to be sunk in emplacements, coastal artillery, artillery against landing troops, mines, etc.) will be concentrated at strong points in the most threatened areas on the coast. Because of this, we must face the fact that the defences of less threatened sectors cannot be improved in the near future.

Should the enemy, by assembling all his forces, succeed in landing, he must be met with a counter-attack delivered with all our weight. The problem will be by the rapid concentration of adequate forces and material, and by intensive training, to form the large units available to us into an offensive reserve of high fighting quality, attacking power, and mobility, whose counter-attack will prevent the enemy from exploiting the landing, and throw him back into the sea.

Moreover, careful and detailed emergency plans must be drawn up so that everything we have in Germany, and in the coastal areas which have not been attacked, and which is in any way capable of action, is hurled immediately against the invading enemy.

The Luftwaffe and Kriegsmarine must go into action against the heavy attacks which we must expect by air and sea with all the forces at their disposal, regardless of the losses.

I therefore order as follows:

A. *Heer* [Army]

1. The Chief of the Army General Staff and the Inspector-General of Armoured Forces will submit to me without delay a plan for the distribution, within the next three months, of weapons, tanks, self-propelled guns, motor vehicles, and ammunition on the Western Front and in Denmark, in accordance with the requirements of the new situation.

The plan will rest on the following basic principles:

(a) All panzer and panzergrenadier divisions in the West will be assured of adequate mobility, and each will be equipped with 93 PzKpfw IV tanks or self-propelled guns, and with strong anti-tank weapons by the end of December 1943.

Six days later he was haranguing the Party faithful on the 20th anniversary of the 'putsch' in Munich's Löwenbräukeller.

The 20. Feld-Division (L) will be converted into an effective mobile offensive formation by the allocation of self-propelled artillery before the end of 1943.

SS-Panzergrenadier-Division 'Hitlerjugend', 21. Panzer-Division, and the infantry and reserve divisions stationed in Jutland will be brought up to full armed strength with speed.

(b) There will be a further reinforcement with PzKpfw IVs, self-propelled guns and heavy anti-tank guns of a panzer division in reserve in the West and in Denmark, and of the self-propelled artillery training unit in Denmark.

(c) A monthly allocation of a hundred Pak 40 and Pak 43 heavy anti-tank guns (of which half will be mobile), for the months of November and December, in addition to the heavy anti-tank guns, will be made to the newly raised formations in the West.

(d) An increased allocation of weapons (including about 1,000 machine guns) will be made to improve the equipment of ground forces engaged in coastal defence in the West and in Denmark, and to co-ordinate the equipment of units which are to be withdrawn from sectors not under attack.

(e) A liberal supply of short-range anti-tank weapons will be granted to formations stationed in threatened areas.

(f) The fire-power in artillery and anti-tank guns of formations stationed in Denmark, and on the coasts of occupied territories in the West, will be increased, and Army artillery will be strengthened.

2. No units or formations stationed in the West and in Denmark, nor any of the newly raised self-propelled armoured artillery or anti-tank units in the West, will be withdrawn to other fronts without my approval.

The Chief of the Army General Staff and the Inspector-General of Armoured Forces will report to me, through the High Command of the Armed Forces (Operations Staff), when the equipment of armoured units, self-propelled artillery units, and light anti-tank units and companies is complete.

3. Commander-in-Chief West will decide which additional formations from sectors of the front that have not been under attack can be moved up and made capable of an offensive role, by a time-table of exercises in the field and similar training measures. In this connexion, I insist that areas unlikely to be threatened should be ruthlessly stripped of all except the smallest forces essential for guard duties. In areas from which these reserves are drawn, units will be formed from security and emergency forces for duties of surveillance and protection. Our labour units employed on construction will open the lines of communication which will probably be destroyed by the enemy, employing for this the help of the local population on an extensive scale.

4. The Commander of German troops in Denmark will adopt the measures outlined in paragraph 3 for the area under his command.

The Chief of Army Equipment and Commander of the Replacement Army will raise battle groups of regimental strength in the Home Defence Area from training depots, troops under instruction, army schools, training battalions and recuperative establishments. These will form security and engineer-construction battalions, and will be ready, on receipt of special orders, to move within 48 hours of being called up.

In addition, all further personnel available will be incorporated in infantry units and equipped with such weapons as are available, so that they may immediately replace the heavy casualties to be expected.

B. *Luftwaffe*

In view of the new situation, the offensive and defensive power of formations of the Air Force stationed in the West and in Denmark will be increased. Plans will be drawn up to ensure that all forces available and suitable for defensive operations will be taken from flying units and mobile anti-aircraft artillery units engaged in home defence, from schools and training units in the Home Defence Area, and will be employed in the West, and if necessary in Denmark.

Ground establishments in southern Norway, Denmark, north-western Germany, and the West will be organised and supplied so that, by the largest possible degree of decentralization, our own units are not exposed to enemy bombing at the beginning of large-scale operations, and the weight of the enemy attack will be effectively broken up. This applies particularly to our fighter forces, whose ability to go into action must be increased by the establishment of a number of emergency airfields. Particular attention will be paid to good camouflage. Here also, I expect all possible forces to be made available for action regardless of the circumstances, by stripping less threatened areas of their troops.

C. *Kriegsmarine*

The Navy will draw up plans for bringing into action naval forces capable of attacking the enemy landing fleet with all their strength. Coastal defences under construction will be completed with all possible speed, and the establishment of additional coastal batteries and the laying of further obstacles on the flanks will be considered.

Preparations will be made for the employment of all ranks capable of fighting, from schools, training establishments, and other land establishments, so that they may be deployed with the least possible delay, if only on security duties, in the battle area where enemy landings have taken place.

In the naval plans for strengthening defences in the West, special attention will be given to defence against enemy landings in Norway or Denmark. In this connexion, I attach particular importance to plans for using large numbers of submarines in the northern sea areas. A temporary diminution of submarine forces in the Atlantic must be accepted.

D. *SS.*

The Reichsführer-SS will test the preparedness of units of the Waffen-SS and police for operational, security, and guard duties. Preparations will be made to raise battle-trained formations for operational and security duties from training, reserve, and recuperative establishments, and from schools and other units in the Home Defence Area.

E. Commanders-in-Chief of the branches of the Armed Forces, the Reichsführer-SS, the Chief of the Army General Staff, the Commander-in-Chief West, the Chief of Army Equipment and Commanding General of Replacement Army, the Inspector-General of Armoured Forces, and the commander of German troops in Denmark will report to me by November 15 the steps taken, and those which they propose to take.

I expect all staffs concerned to exert every effort during the time which still remains in preparation for the expected decisive battle in the West.

All those responsible will ensure that time and manpower are not wasted in dealing with questions of jurisdiction, but that they are employed in increasing our powers of defence and attack.

ADOLF HITLER

Nor was this the end. There was no strategic reserve whatever in the West, though such a reserve was supposed to intervene rapidly and effectively at the point of main effort as soon as the invasion had begun. The Luftwaffe was so weak that it could not hope to curb the operations of the RAF and the USAAF. The Kriegsmarine consisted of a few motor launches and a couple of torpedo flotillas. Submarines could not operate properly in the Channel owing to its shallowness.

This report made a great impression on Hitler and once again promises of reinforcements were sent to us. The reinforcements themselves, however, only arrived in small numbers or not at all as crisis after crisis necessitated their transfer to the East. As for the Luftwaffe, Hitler promised that powerful groups of bombers and fighters would be switched to France as soon as the invasion began. Even Hitler should have known that by then it would be too late. Indeed, perhaps he did know: perhaps these 'orders' were only another example of his powers of self-deception.

Thus did 1943 pass in France, while across the Channel the British and American forces were being built up for the gigantic operation which would undoubtedly decide the outcome of the war and which von Rundstedt anticipated for the spring of the following year. Nor did the OB West cherish any illusions concerning the violence with which the blow would be struck and the tremendous technical virtuosity with which it would be backed. Allied landings in Sicily and at Salerno had shown how little the bravery and sacrifice of Kesselring's men had availed against the enemy's naval gunnery and air supremacy. And we could well anticipate that this would be nothing when compared to what was being made ready for us.

On the southern front, following the collapse of the Fascist administration and defection of Italy, Hitler was receiving conflicting advice from his two commanders in Italy, Generalfeldmarschall Albert Kesselring (Luftwaffe), the Oberbefehlshaber Süd, and Generalfeldmarschall Erwin Rommel (Army), commanding Heeresgruppe B in northern Italy. Initially, Hitler was going to make Rommel the theatre commander, but he subsequently changed his mind and left Kesselring in charge while giving Rommel a new task: inspecting the coastal defences of the Atlantic Wall and improving them to withstand an Allied assault. Rommel had served as an infantry officer in World War I and in August 1939 had been assigned to command the Führerhauptquartier (Hitler's headquarters), a position he held until February 1940. He then participated in the French campaign as commander of the 7. Panzer-Division, and in February 1941 was assigned to command the Afrika Korps assisting the Italians in North Africa. Rommel remained in Africa from September 1941 until March 1943, commanding first Panzergruppe Afrika and, later, Panzerarmee Afrika. Although Rommel was disappointed with his new, uninspiring mission, far from the limelight, his support for Hitler was unshaken, writing after hearing the Löwenbrau speech: 'What power he radiates . . . what faith and confidence he inspires in his people'. Rommel arrived in France on December 14 and immediately began planning his initial inspection tour which would begin in Denmark and work its way south. On the 19th, he arrived at the George V in Paris to confer with his new chief, von Rundstedt. Here he is pictured entering the hotel which was used by OB West as a convenient location for conferences, followed by Generalleutnant Alfred Gause, his Chief-of-Staff since May 1943, who was succeeded on April 15, 1944 by Generalleutnant Hans Speidel.

ROMMEL

Towards the end of 1943, Hitler assigned Rommel the task of inspecting the coastal defences in the West, from Denmark to the Spanish frontier. He had no troops, save his highly-competent staff. OKW, however, expected valuable help from Rommel's initiative, experience and sound technical knowledge. In addition, it was hoped that his presence in the West would be useful as a propaganda weapon.

Below: **Still one of the most influential hotels in Paris, the George V (on the Avenue George V) is used by world leaders and has hosted a variety of important conferences since the days of OB West.**

Watched by Rommel, von Rundstedt and Gause, Oberst Zimmermann points out a salient point on a map which has been heavily obliterated on the original negative by the German press censor.

I recall his first conference with von Rundstedt, in Paris, shortly before Christmas. Von Rundstedt outlined the situation briefly and sceptically, speaking of the poor quality of the troops, the dangerous weakness of the Luftwaffe, the almost total absence of naval craft and stressing particularly the main defect of our defensive organisation, namely the complete lack of a powerful central reserve. He ended with the words: 'It all looks very black to me.'

Afterwards, the two field-marshals lunched together. A few senior staff officers, of whom I was one, were present. We expected one or other of the field-marshals to open the conversation, but neither showed any inclination to do so. Both were apparently preoccupied with their thoughts which, after their discussion, can only have been of a most sombre hue. It was a strange, silent meal which will never be forgotten by any man who was present.

The interior of the prestigious George 'Sank' has been considerably modernised since the war, yet Suite 142 on the first floor remains recognisable. The Ionic columns have been removed, but the double doors and windows have survived.

By December 22, Rommel had reached the Pas-de-Calais — the vital stretch of coastline closest to Britain. By various ploys and deceptions, the Allies were already trying to persuade the Germans to accept the idea that the invasion would take place in this sector and, although several heavy batteries were sited to cover the approaches, the beaches were still devoid of landing obstructions. *Above:* Here, Rommel is being filmed on the beach at Wissant with Cap Blanc-Nez in the background. *Below:* This Type 631 bunker at the northern end of the beach housed a 4.7cm fortress anti-tank gun 36(t). *Below right:* Today it lies hidden behind the holiday chalet.

Further down the road at Framzelle, he inspected the Grosser Kurfürst (The Great Elector) battery consisting of four 28cm (11-inch) guns in naval-type turrets sited a mile inland from

Cap Gris-Nez. This is the range-finder which was located in the battery command post area close to the cliff-top. *Right:* Today, the cliff has collapsed, throwing the BCP into the sea.

Over the Christmas period, which Rommel spent at his headquarters located in the château which once belonged to Madame de Pompadour at Fontainebleau, he prepared his first report for Hitler which he submitted on December 31. 'The focus of the enemy landing operation will probably be directed against the 15. Armee sector, largely because it is from this sector that much of our long-range attack [the V1] on England and central London will be launched. With difficult sea conditions, it is likely that the enemy's main concern will be to get the quickest possible possession of a port or ports capable of handling large ships. Furthermore, he will probably endeavour to capture the area from which our long-range attack is coming as quickly as possible. It is most likely that the enemy will make his main effort against the sector between Boulogne and the Somme estuary and on either side of Calais, where he would have the best support from his long-range artillery, the shortest sea route for the assault and for bringing up supplies, and the most favourable conditions for the use of his air arm. As for his airborne forces, we can expect him to use the bulk of them to open up our coastal front from the rear and take quick possession of the area from which our long-range missiles will be coming.' *Left:* Rommel was featured on the cover of 'Our Army' magazine and, although uncaptioned as to the location, Hans Sakkers of Koudekerke on Walcheren who has made a detailed study of Rommel's Atlantic Wall inspection tours (published in his excellent book *Generalfeldmarschall Rommel*), recognised it as the windmill at nearby Westkapelle, visited on January 4. *Top right:* Later that day, he inspected the HQ of the 712. Infanterie-Division located in a school at Oostburg. Its entrance has since been remodelled *(above)*.

Rommel told Hitler that he thought 'the landing will probably be preceded by very heavy attacks from the air and be made under cover of a smoke-screen and of intense fire from numerous warships, with simultaneous heavy-bomber attacks. In addition to the seaborne landing, airborne troops will probably be dropped close behind the coastal defences in the main attack sectors, in order to break up the defences from the rear and create a major bridgehead in the shortest possible time.' German air defence in the West was the responsibility of Luftflotte III, the main day-fighter force comprising Fliegerdivision 4 with 71 serviceable machines, and Fliegerdivision 5 with 48. On January 5, Rommel visited JG26, based at St Omer/Wizernes, the 'Schlageter' Geschwader being led by its diminutive, yet renowned, commander, Oberstleutnant Josef 'Pips' Priller.

His visit to Les Petites Dalles on March 14 *(right)* must have been tinged with nostalgia — did the cameraman deliberately take an almost exact comparison of the day in June 1940 *(above)* when Rommel's 7. Panzer-Division reached the coast at this very spot? How things had changed since the day he triumphantly wrote after their victorious advance across France: 'We climbed out of our vehicles and walked down to the water's edge until the water lapped over our boots.' (See *Blitzkrieg in the West Then and Now*.)

His report continued: 'On the coast, our defence line, thin as it is at present, will suffer severely from the enemy bombing and artillery bombardment and it seems very doubtful whether, after this battering, it will be capable of beating off the enemy, whose forces will be approaching over a wide front, in hundreds of armoured assault craft and landing craft and under cover of darkness or fog. But if the landing is not beaten off, our thinly held and shallow front will soon be pierced and contact will be established with the airborne troops behind. We know from experience that the British soldier is quick to consolidate his gains and then holds on tenaciously with excellent support from his superior air arm and naval guns.' On April 19, Rommel was back in Holland. *Above:* Stützpunkt 'Hötzendorf' was a two-gun casemated position just inland from Westkapelle and housed a batterie of Reserve-Regiment 5 of 165. Reserve-Division. Rommel could not have been very pleased with what he found on his inspection as Hauptmann Schmersow (left), the CO of Reserve-Artillerie-Abteilung 61, was relieved of his command after the visit!

That same day, the party inspected the beach at Flushing (Vlissingen) in front of Nos. 246-260 Scheldt Boulevard.

In the course of the winter, it was decided at OKW to give Rommel a command in the West. Hitler's first idea was that Rommel should command a large mobile force intended to counter-attack and defeat the invading forces at the earliest opportunity. There were, however, no suitable formations available. Rommel, with von Rundstedt's approval, was therefore given command of Heeresgruppe B [Army Group B], which covered the invasion front. His command included the divisions in Holland, the 15. Armee [Fifteenth Army] along the Channel, and the 7. Armee [Seventh Army] in Normandy and Brittany. Rommel, when carrying out his inspection, had realised that only the Channel sector had a certain defensive strength. Now, he was in a position to do more than merely make recommendations, and he set to work with all the great energy of which he was capable.

In a later report, he wrote: 'Since the end of January, the construction of foreshore obstacles has been in progress along the whole of the Atlantic coast and, at the more important points, is now steadily approaching completion. It will be asked why the work was not started earlier, for that would have enabled a far stronger barrier to be built. The answer is that this form of obstacle was not thought of earlier. There is even an advantage in having begun the work so late, for the enemy will have to adapt himself at the last moment to this new form of defence, which is certain to take a heavy toll of his landing craft. The object of these new underwater obstructions is not only to halt the enemy's approach which will be made in hundreds of landing boats and ships, in amphibious vehicles and in waterproofed and underwater tanks, all under cover of darkness or artificial fog — but also to destroy his landing equipment and troops.'

This later progress report written by Rommel further explained that 'they consist of a wide variety of obstacles armed by mines or shells. Every effort will be made to have them installed in depth and make them effective at all states of the tide. Recent Anglo-American invasion exercises have been timed for the landing to be made two hours after low tide, after artillery and bombers have previously attempted to destroy dummy foreshore obstacles. We all know how difficult it is to destroy barbed wire obstructions by artillery fire. How much more difficult, then, will it be to do enough damage to a wide and deep belt of such stoutly-constructed obstacles as to make a trouble-free landing possible across them? The more time the enemy gives us, the stronger will be the obstacles, and we may sooner or later expect all battalions to be in a position to report that their barriers are dense, deep and armed, i.e. supplied with thousands of mines and shells . . . '

Throughout the spring, the defences were intensively strengthened. Two innovations for which Rommel was responsible were the erection of the so-called 'Rommel Asparagus', which was the planting with posts of areas previously considered suitable for the landing of gliders, and the sowing of the beaches with underwater obstacles and mines. Of course, these feverish preparations became known to the Allies through their air reconnaissance; indeed, the underwater obstacles caused them to alter their plan and land at low instead of at high tide. It was hoped that they would be sufficiently worried to make them postpone their invasion, if only for a few months, for the objective of both Rommel and von Rundstedt now was to gain time. With this end in view, attempts were made to mislead the Allies by scattering staffs, disguised as the headquarters of panzer divisions and corps, across France. These dummy staffs could not, however, hope to confuse the enemy for long. There were too many French and British agents in France for the trick to work for more than a month or two.

However, Rommel's energy and drive had a very animating effect on the troops. Their morale certainly improved, though he worked them so hard that by the summer signs of fatigue were beginning to appear.

'I come now to security against airborne troops. It is possible that the enemy will commit everything he has, at the outset of his attack, in order to gain a quick victory and secure a wide foothold at some point along the coast. The enemy powers dispose of a large number of very powerful and highly-trained airborne formations. We must therefore be prepared for these forces to be used against the coastal defence zones, either in a sudden surprise attack or after a short but intense aerial bombardment. Parachute troops could be dropped in very large numbers, by moonlight or at dawn or dusk, either along the coast or a few miles inland. Or airborne troops at divisional strength with load-carrying gliders could land behind our coastal front and attempt to break through the defences from the rear. Hence the important thing is to ensure that all territory which might conceivably be used for landing airborne troops is treated in such a manner that enemy aircraft and gliders will break up while landing, and the enemy as a result suffer severe losses in men and matériel — in addition to those caused by the quick opening of our defensive fire. All divisions will take the necessary steps, as early as possible, to have the area between the land and sea fronts thoroughly staked out.'

Within three months, Rommel's ceaseless activity had transformed the defences, and it is doubtful if 'Neptune' would have succeeded had he been charged with the task six months earlier. As it was, his original plans for a 1,000-metre-deep minefield strip along the coast at a density of 10 mines per metre, had only just begun but, of the planned 20 million mines required, 1½ million had already been laid with a further 2½ million put in place by June. Rommel explained that 'if the enemy should ever set foot on land, an attack through the minefields against the defence works sited within them will present him with a task of immense difficulty. He will have to fight his way through the zone of death in the defensive fire of the whole of our artillery. And not only on the coast, for numerous and extensive minefields will also exist round our positions in the rear areas.' Nominally, Rommel was still subordinate to von Rundstedt, but in reality his energy and drive meant that he was now the dominant personality in the West.

Back in December, von Rundstedt had recommended that Rommel's position be formalised with his appointment as commander of Heeresgruppe B covering the 7. Armee and 15. Armee in France and also those forces in the Netherlands. The new army group was brought into being on January 15 but its subordination to OB West was blurred by the fact that Rommel was responsible for the tactical command of operations. As a field-marshal, he also had the right to go over von Rundstedt's head direct to Hitler. *Left:* **During his hectic schedule, a lunchtime halt on the Calais-Dunkirk road on April 18. With Rommel are Generalleutnant Hans Speidel, the new Chief-of-Staff of Heeresgruppe B, Vizeadmiral Friedrich Ruge, his naval liaison officer, and his adjutant, Hauptmann Hellmuth Lang.** *Right:* **The following day, Rommel looked pleased during an inspection at Breskens: left, Kapitän zur See Frank Aschmann, naval commander in southern Holland; right, General der Infanterie Werner von und zu Gilsa of LXXXIX. Armeekorps.**

COASTAL DEFENCES IN NORMANDY

The Channel sector — by which is meant the coastal sector between the mouths of the Seine and of the Scheldt — had always been regarded as the most likely point of assault, being the part of the coast which is nearest to England. This assumption had been strengthened by Führer Directive No. 51. Priority in the deployment of troops and the building of defences had therefore been assigned to this sector. As these defences increased, the relative neglect of Normandy became more and more obvious. This was noticed by a commission of inspection which visited the West on behalf of the OKW in January 1944.

In Normandy, the coastal defences were, in general, undermanned, because the sectors assigned to the coastal divisions were too wide. The Kriegsmarine was largely to blame for this. Naval intelligence had declared that the coast between the Seine and the Cotentin peninsula was unsuitable for the landing of large bodies of troops: the western Cotentin was clearly quite out of the question as an assault area, while the eastern Cotentin was believed adequately covered by the powerful fortress of Cherbourg. This last and traditional assumption, which was held until the actual invasion proved it incorrect, had also led to an optimistic overestimate of the terrain which the fortress could command. Its land front was a good 25 miles too long, and when the time came the fortress proved untenable by its garrison.

From April 1944, evidence began to accumulate that Normandy might be the scene of the coming invasion. This

On February 23, Hitler had left his Eastern Front headquarters at Rastenburg to allow uninterrupted work to proceed on the reinforcement of the 'Wolfschanze' bunkers. Temporarily, therefore, the Führerhauptquartier was transferred to Hitler's mountain retreat on the Obersalzberg, and it was to the Berghof that he summoned his leading field-marshals, including Rommel and von Rundstedt, on March 19. The following day, Hitler expounded his views on the current situation in the West. Rommel had a private audience with Hitler, requesting an extension of his authority in that all armoured units in the West be put under his command and that he be given control 'as far as work on the coastal defences was concerned', over the 1. and 19. Armees. Realistically, this would have eliminated von Rundstedt from effective command and his protest, supported by the OKW, led Hitler to only agree partly to Rommel's request. Three panzer divisions were assigned to him as Heeresgruppe B reserves, while four divisions — three panzer and one panzergrenadier — were set aside as a central mobile reserve under the direct command of the OKW. The compromise did little to resolve either von Rundstedt's concept of defence or Rommel's own defensive theories, and the disposition of the forces satisfied neither viewpoint. Meanwhile, the great guessing game continued. Rommel considered the most threatened area for the assault was between Boulogne and the Somme estuary, whereas Hitler favoured the Cherbourg and Brest peninsulas. *Above:* **Rommel had visited Normandy at the end of January. Kapitän zur See Walter Hennecke, the naval commander for Normandy, points out a particular feature in his sector.**

It is evident that an Anglo-American landing in the West will and must come. How and where it will come no one knows. Equally, no kind of speculation on the subject is possible. Whatever concentrations of shipping may exist, they cannot and must not be taken as any evidence, or any indication, that the choice has fallen on any one sector of the long Western Front from Norway to the Bay of Biscay, or on the Mediterranean — either the south coast of France, the Italian coast or the Balkans. Such concentrations can be moved or transferred, at any time, under cover of bad visibility, and will obviously serve as feints. At no place along our long front is a landing impossible, except, perhaps, where the coast is broken by cliffs. The most suitable and hence the most threatened areas are the two west coast peninsulas, Cherbourg and Brest, which are very tempting and offer the best possibilities for the formation of a bridgehead, which would then be enlarged systematically by the mass use of air forces and heavy weapons of all kinds.

By far the most important thing for the enemy will be to gain a port for landings on the largest possible scale. This alone gives a wholly special importance to the west coast ports and orders have therefore been issued designating them 'Fortresses', in which the Commandant alone will be responsible for the training and operations of all three services. He has the task of doing everything possible to make the fortress impregnable. He is personally responsible for ensuring that the fortress is held to the last round of ammunition, the last tin of rations, until every last possibility of defence has been exhausted.

The enemy's entire landing operation must under no circumstances be allowed to last longer than a matter of hours or, at the most, days, with the Dieppe attempt as a model. Once the landing has been defeated, it will under no circumstances be repeated by the enemy. Quite apart from the heavy casualties he would suffer, months would be needed to prepare for a renewed attempt. Nor is this the only factor which would deter the Anglo-Americans from trying again. There would also be the crushing blow to their morale which a miscarried invasion would give. It would, for one thing, prevent the re-election of Roosevelt in America and, with luck, he would finish up somewhere in jail.

In England, too, war-weariness would assert itself even more greatly than hitherto and Churchill, in view of his age and his illness, and with his influence now on the wane, would no longer be in a position to carry through a new landing operation. We could counter the numerical strength of the enemy — about 50 to 60 divisions — within a very short time, by forces of equal strength. The destruction of the enemy's landing attempt means more than a purely local decision on the Western Front. It is the sole decisive factor in the whole conduct of the war and hence in its final result.

The 45 divisions which we now have in Europe, excluding the Eastern Front, are needed in the East, and will and must be transferred there so as to effect a fundamental change in that situation as soon as the decision in the West has been reached. Thus, on every single man fighting on the Western Front, as representing the decisive front of the war, depends the outcome of the war and with it the fate of the Reich. This realisation of the decisive importance of each individual's effort must at all costs become part and parcel of the thought process of every officer and man.

ADOLF HITLER, MARCH 20, 1944

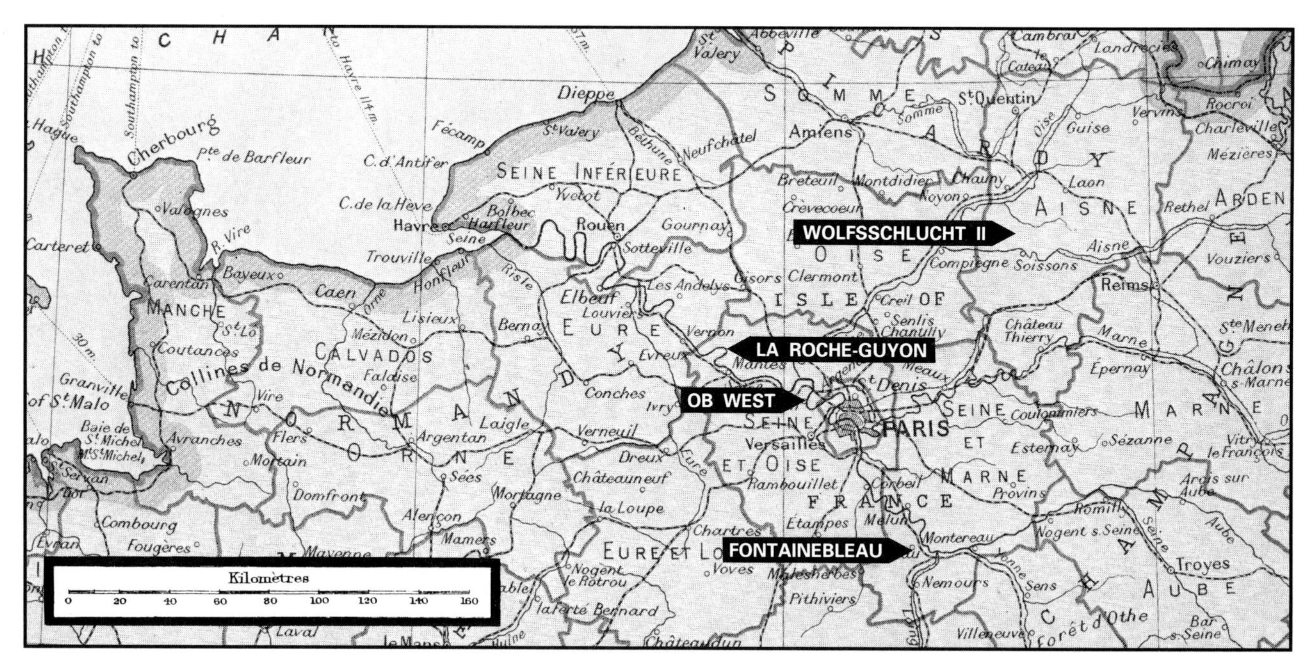

On March 10, Rommel moved his headquarters from Fontainebleau to La Roche-Guyon, on the River Seine near Vernon, and closer to the supposed landing area. The new location was also more accessible to the OB West headquarters at St Germain.

evidence was, however, never conclusive, and the Channel sector remained the principal defensive area. No troops were allowed to be withdrawn from there to defend Normandy. But Hitler, who shared this presentiment concerning Normandy, ordered that the 91. Luftlande-Division [91st Airlanding Division] and Fallschirmjäger-Regiment 6 [6th Parachute Regiment] be stationed in the area which seemed most likely to be threatened by parachute or glider-borne troops. Incidentally, despite their names, this division and regiment were intended to fight as normal infantry.

There were three divisions holding the critical stretch of the Norman coast. From east to west these were the 716., 352. and 709. Infanterie-Divisions. The latter was also responsible for the defence of Cherbourg. One regiment of the 243. Infanterie-Division was located in north-western Normandy, its other two, together with the 91. Luftlande-Division and Fallschirmjäger-Regiment 6, being stationed near the base of the Cotentin peninsula as defence against airborne landings. The west coast of the peninsula, because of its formation and the very high tides prevalent there, was not regarded as a danger point and was guarded by a single brigade, mostly bicyclists, called the schnelle Brigade 30 [30th Mobile Brigade]. At the request of the OB West, the Militärbefehlshaber in France, General von Stülpnagel, transferred a garrison regiment, Grenadier-Regiment 1057, to Normandy. This unit was poorly equipped and had few heavy weapons. The three coastal divisions in the area which saw the assault held sectors averaging 25 miles in breadth, with relatively few fortified strong points.

The only immediate reserve available to Rommel as commander of Heeresgruppe B was the 21. Panzer-Division in the area east of the Orne. The bulk of this division was assembled in the Caen area, though part of its armoured infantry had been moved closer to the coast as a security measure.

HITLER'S WESTERN STRATEGY

There can be no doubt that Hitler's entire attitude towards German strategy in the West had, since 1942, been based on one conviction: namely that the battle in the East would not be brought to a quick conclusion and that its developments would be increasingly felt in the West.

At that time, no matter how unfavourably the Eastern battle might go, we still possessed sufficient Russian territory to make any direct threat to Germany herself a remote danger.

In the West, however, the distances between the Channel and the Ruhr were so short that a successful mass invasion of the former must quickly bring the leading enemy troops to Germany's most vital industrial area. From a spatial point of view, the peril in the West was therefore greater than in the East. Hence Hitler's basic theory that the enemy must be defeated on the beaches and thrown back into the sea at once. Hence the building of the Atlantic Wall. As the months of 1944 passed, this thesis was reinforced by one simple consideration. Owing to heavy losses in Russia there were only inadequate mobile forces available in the West to fight a battle of manoeuvre. There was therefore no choice but to adhere to Hitler's theory of rigid, linear defence.

Hitler also had a requirement for a forward battle HQ for use when the invasion of Fortress Europe took place, and a suitable site had been selected in 1943, 15 kilometres north-east of Soissons. Several reinforced concrete bunkers were constructed close to the railway track at Margival where a nearby railway tunnel would provide a ready-made shelter for the Führer's train. The complex was code-named 'Wolfsschlucht 2' or 'W2' to differentiate it from Hitler's 1940 headquarters in France which had also been called 'Wolfsschlucht' (Wolf's Lair). In the event, Hitler only made a fleeting visit to Margival — on June 17 to confer with Rommel and von Rundstedt. Today, the Führerbunker lies within a military training area although it is visible from the trackside.

Meanwhile, the big question, unresolved at this time, was the basic strategy to be adopted to repel invasion. Von Rundstedt had created Panzergruppe West, under General der Panzertruppen Leo Freiherr Geyr von Schweppenburg, to command and co-ordinate the armoured forces in a major counter-attack against the main Allied assault. Rommel's experience in North Africa, however, had taught him the folly of using massed armour in a situation where the enemy had air superiority. Thus, he had concentrated on improving the fixed defences, believing, as did Hitler, that the outcome of the battle would be determined on the beaches within the first 48 hours. General von Geyr held totally opposing views as he felt the major threat would come from an airborne landing inside France and he had deployed his forces with that in mind. Any idea of co-operation between the two commanders was out of the question and Rommel pressed for Panzergruppe West to be placed under his command.

Although the compromise which had been put forward gave Rommel the 2., 21. and 116. Panzer-Divisions to be used as Heeresgruppe B reserves, their training and organisation was to remain with General von Geyr so it really solved nothing. At the end of April, Rommel called a meeting at his HQ in the castle at La Roche-Guyon to try to settle the issue once and for all. L–R: Speidel, Rommel, Guderian and Geyr confer on April 28 in the Grand Salon.

AIR SITUATION IN THE WEST

The increasing weight of air attack, both by day and by night, revealed the relative impotence of the Luftwaffe. The French and Belgian rail networks, as well as the Luftwaffe's own installations, were the main objectives. Troop movements by train became more and more difficult, until at last the reinforcement of the coast had to be carried out almost entirely by road. When the Seine and Loire bridges were methodically destroyed, even road movement grew difficult and very slow. Meanwhile, the bases of the Luftwaffe had been pushed back from the coast to the Paris area. These raids were so widespread that a study of the areas attacked gave little if any indication as to the point against which the invasion would be launched.

Our own extremely-spasmodic air reconnaissance over southern and south-eastern England was hardly more enlightening. In fact, the German command remained completely in the dark concerning the future target area, which might be anywhere along the Channel or in Normandy. The greatest advantage that the Allies enjoyed was that, in view of our lack of a clear intelligence picture, we must be prepared for an assault at almost any point along this extended coast; but, when that assault came, it would be in a relatively small sector with concentrated technical power and with the best-equipped and best-trained forces at the disposal of the enemy. This knowledge led to repeated alarms, particularly during those nights when tide and weather conditions made a landing feasible.

The castle at La Roche-Guyon had been in the ownership of the La-Rochefoucauld family since 1829 and the Count continued to live there when it was taken over for Rommel's headquarters. In April 1994, it was opened to the public for the first time. The meeting took place in that part of the château called the Corps de Logis which dates back to the 16th century. The Grand Salon is one of the rooms which can be visited today.

Nevertheless, the major armoured divisions in OB West's sector — the 1. SS-Panzer, 12. SS-Panzer, 17. SS-Panzer-grenadier and the Panzer-Lehr — were being retained under the direct command of the Oberkommando der Wehrmacht (OKW) as a centralised reserve. Rommel tried hard to get them released to him but General von Geyr's arguments also had their supporters in Armed Forces High Command. Rommel wrote to Generaloberst Alfred Jodl, the chief of the OKW Operations Staff, on April 23 to try to get a change of heart: 'If, in spite of the enemy's air superiority, we succeed in getting a large part of our mobile force into action in the threatened coast defence sectors in the first few hours, I am convinced that the enemy attack on the coast will collapse completely on its first day. Very little damage has so far been done by the heavy enemy bombing to our reinforced concrete installations, although our field positions, dugouts and communication trenches have in many places been completely obliterated. This shows how important it is to get concrete over all our positions, even those, such as artillery, anti-aircraft and reserve positions, which are located behind the front.' To thrash out the issues involved, a top-level conference was called by OB West for 12 noon on Monday, May 8. We had initially thought that the meeting had been held in the usual Paris venue for such meetings — the George V — but when *After the Battle* European Editor, Karel Margry, visited the hotel to take the comparisons, none of the rooms corresponded to the panelled conference room. It was only when he matched the shot *(left)* of Rommel arriving with Speidel and Lang that Karel realised that they were not entering the George V but the hotel next door — the Prince de Galles. *Right:* A reverse comparison is more meaningful in this case as it shows the relationship between the two hotels.

Rommel and Speidel exchange pleasantries in the hotel lobby with Generaloberst Johannes Blaskowitz. He had been the commander of the 1. Armee since October 1940 although his command had technically ceased five days before the meeting. His new appointment as commander of Armeegruppe G was not due to take effect until two days hence, but as General der Infanterie Georg von Sodenstern of 19. Armee was not present, it could be that Blaskowitz's presence was more as a representative of the armies in the south not under Heeres-gruppe B, rather than as commander-to-be of Armeegruppe G.

OUR KNOWLEDGE OF THE ENEMY

By the spring of 1944, we believed that some 75 Allied divisions were assembled in Britain. Of these, 65, including six airborne divisions, were considered suitable for use in the invasion. They were believed to consist of 20 to 25 American and 40 to 45 British divisions.

From April 1944, Allied landing exercises, carried out in co-operation with airborne troops, increased along the coasts of England. Since March, high-quality formations had been returning to Great Britain from the Mediterranean: these included the US 1st and 9th Infantry Divisions, the British 51st Highland Division, 1st Airborne and 1st and 7th Armoured Divisions, in addition to a special American engineer assault brigade.

The landing tonnage available in British harbours was estimated to be enough for the transfer across the Channel of 20 divisions in a single flight. In addition, there were believed to be a further 45 divisions, trained and ready

Above: **The meeting took place in the basement suite, now the Salon Ascot** ***(below)*** **under the chairmanship of von Rundstedt. He is flanked (L–R) by General von Geyr, Blaskowitz, Generalfeldmarschall Hugo Sperrle (commander of Luftflotte 3), Rommel and Admiral Theodor Krancke (commanding Marinegruppe West).**

Left: **The respective chiefs-of-staff sat opposite.** *Right:* **This shot would appear to have been taken after the formal discussion was over. The participants have split into three cliques: in the background, Rommel, Blaskowitz and von Rundstedt; then Sperrle and Krancke with the chiefs-of-staff; then Geyr in a separate group in the foreground.**

After all the talking was over, the conference came up with no new solution and, as far as the armoured reserve was concerned, Rommel still had his hands tied behind his back. The next day, he was back travelling along the Normandy coast.

This is the four-gun battery (15cm) sited on the cliff-top at Longues-sur-Mer. It remains one of the most impressive of all the big gun casemates in the Normandy sector and the only one where the guns are still in situ.

My only real anxiety concerns the mobile forces. Contrary to what was decided at the conference on March 21, they have so far not been placed under my command. Some of them are dispersed over a large area well inland, which means that they will arrive too late to play any part in the battle for the coast. With the heavy enemy air superiority we can expect, any large-scale movement of motorised forces to the coast will be exposed to air attacks of tremendous weight and long duration. But without rapid assistance from the armoured divisions and mobile units, our coast divisions will be hard put to it to counter attacks coming simultaneously from the sea and from airborne troops inland. Their land front is too thinly held for that. The dispositions of both combat and reserve forces should be such as to ensure that the minimum possible movement will be required to counter an attack at any of the most likely points, whether in the Low Countries, in the Channel area proper, in Normandy or in Brittany, and to ensure that the greater part of the enemy troops, sea and airborne, will be destroyed by our fire during their approach.

Contrary to myself, General Geyr von Schweppenburg, who may well know the British in peacetime but has never yet met them in battle, sees the greatest danger in an operational airborne landing deep inside France, and so wishes to be in a position to mount a quick counter-operation. His forces have been located mainly with that end in view. Furthermore, he does not wish to take his armoured divisions to an area behind the land front of the coastal defences, where the enemy could make an airborne landing. I, on the other hand, see the greatest danger in the enemy using every weapon he has, especially airborne troops, to break through our coastal defences over a wide front, and thus gain a foothold on the Continent. To my mind, so long as we hold the coast, an enemy airborne landing of an operational nature must, sooner or later, finish up in the destruction of the troops who have landed. In our experience, moreover, enemy airborne forces have in the past always been wiped out wherever the landing has been made in areas held by our troops. I believe airborne troops can be destroyed in this way at far less cost in bloodshed than by mounting an attack from outside against an already landed enemy, who could have large numbers of anti-tank guns ready for action within a few minutes, and could then be supported by his bomber formations. I have disagreed very violently with General von Geyr over this question and will only be able to execute my ideas if he is put under Army Group command early enough.

GENERALFELDMARSCHALL ERWIN ROMMEL,
APRIL 23, 1944

The following day, Rommel inspected the heavy gun positions in the Cherbourg Peninsula. This is the 21cm K39/41 battery at St Marcouf where only two of the four guns were protected by concrete casemates. The other two were under construction but repeated air attacks had disrupted the work.

Rommel must have known that he now had very little time left: in fact, he had less than four weeks. His anxiety now focussed on Normandy and, over the next few days, he concentrated on visiting the divisional headquarters of the various units in the area. He saw Generalleutnant Karl-Wilhelm von Schlieben of the 709. Infanterie-Division on May 10.

for combat, available in the United States. They could be shipped direct to the invasion area and unloaded as soon as a bridgehead had been formed.

In the air, we anticipated that we would be outnumbered in the ratio of 50 to 1. Our naval forces were, as already stated, virtually non-existent. Therefore, all that von Rundstedt could muster against this massive force poised to strike anywhere along the French coast was a single, immobile, defensive system consisting of ground troops without air support.

Two days later, he met with Fritz Bayerlein, formerly Chief-of-Staff of the Afrika-Korps, who had recently returned from Hungary with his Panzer-Lehr-Division. There they had taken part in the occupation of the country of an ally showing signs of wavering, and paraded through Budapest on March 26. In a private meeting at La Roche-Guyon, Rommel confided his thoughts to his old colleague who later recalled the conversation. 'Our friends from the East cannot imagine what they're in for here. It's not a matter of fanatical hordes to be driven forward in masses against our line, with no regard for casualties and little recourse to tactical craft; here we are facing an enemy who applies all his native intelligence to the use of his many technical resources; who spares no expenditure of matériel and whose every operation goes its course as though it had been the subject of repeated rehearsal. Dash and doggedness alone no longer make a soldier, Bayerlein. He must have sufficient intelligence to enable him to get the most out of his fighting machine. And that's something the Anglo-Americans can do — we found that out in Africa. You have no idea how difficult it is to convince these people [at OKW]. At one time, they looked on mobile warfare as something to keep clear of at all costs, but now that our freedom of manoeuvre in the West is gone, they're all crazy after it. Whereas, in fact, it's obvious that if the enemy once gets his foot in, he'll put every anti-tank gun and tank he can into the bridgehead and let us beat our heads against it, as he did at Medenine. To break through such a front you have to attack slowly and methodically, under cover of massed artillery, but we, of course, thanks to the Allied air forces, will have nothing there in time. The day of the dashing cut-and-thrust tank attack of the early war years is past and gone — and that goes for the East too, a fact which may, perhaps, by this time have gradually sunk in.'

Rommel now considered that Normandy, with its relatively weak defences and small garrison, was particularly vulnerable, and he pressed for the immediate transfer from the OKW reserve of the Panzer-Lehr to Avranches; the 12. SS-Panzer-Division forward to the Cherbourg peninsula, as well as other units to the Normandy area. Although his request fell on deaf ears, quite independently Hitler, possibly acting on an appreciation by Admiral Krancke of the pattern of Allied bombing attacks, also began to see the vulnerability of Normandy, and on May 6 reinforcement began with the move of Fallschirmjäger-Regiment 6, followed by Panzer-Abteilung 206 and an assault battalion from 7. Armee. The 91. Luftlande-Division, then en route for Nantes, was also diverted to La Haye-du-Puits. Meanwhile, Rommel continued his unit inspections and on May 13 saw Generalleutnant Heinrich Freiherr von Lüttwitz of 2. Panzer. The division was based in the Amiens area, this Sdkfz 250 *(left)* being pictured leaving the Friant Barracks on the Avenue du Général Foy *(above)*.

In quick succession, Rommel visited the 85. Infanterie-Division (Generalleutnant Kurt Chill) at Abbeville; the 348. Infanterie-Division (Generalleutnant Paul Seyffardt) near Cayeux; the 344. Infanterie-Division (Generalleutnant Felix Schwalbe) at Mahon-Plage; the 326. Infanterie-Division (Generalleutnant Viktor von Drabich-Waechter) at Enquin; the 49. Infanterie-Division (Generalleutnant Sigfrid Macholz) at Montreuil; the 331. Infanterie-Division (Generalmajor Heinz Furbach) behind Boulogne, and the 182. Reserve-Division (Generalleutnant Richard Baltzer) at Halfaut, before returning to Normandy. *Left:* On May 17, he saw Generalleutnant Wilhelm Falley of the 91. Luftlande-Division in his HQ in the château in the hamlet of Bernaville, about six kilometres to the west of Ste Mère-Eglise, now owned by the Communauté du Bon Sauveur *(right).*

WEATHER AND TIDE

Needless to say, tides, weather and wind were a source of constant preoccupation to us and to the Kriegsmarine along the entire coast. The system was that if these looked likely to favour an assault in the early hours at any particular point, the troops stationed there would be alerted. The total number of dawn alerts which therefore were ordered at one spot or another was well-nigh astronomic. The strain on the men, who were already carrying out training exercises and building defences at high pressure, was considerable, possibly even excessive.

During June 4-5, the weather situation was considered unfavourable for a landing on the Normandy coast, an opinion which was shared by the naval experts. The commander of the 7. Armee, Generaloberst Friedrich Dollmann (who later died of a heart attack during the Normandy battle), therefore ordered a temporary relaxation of 'alert' conditions, and summoned his senior officers to Rennes on the 5th for a map exercise.

On June 5, wind velocity in eastern Normandy was Force 5, direction east-south-east, and the force of the sea was between 4 and 5. German naval craft, attempting to put to sea for minelaying operations, were forced back into harbour, when the stormy conditions threatened to overturn the heavily-laden vessels. The moon was nearly full.

Thus, despite the fact that low tide in eastern Normandy was due between 5 a.m. and 6 a.m. on the 6th, there seemed no prospect of an immediate assault against this sector of the coast.

On May 30, a demonstration of new weaponry was held by the 21. Panzer-Division at Lion-sur-Mer, already designated Sword area on the Allied invasion maps. Present were (left) Generaloberst Hans von Salmuth (commander of 15. Armee); Rommel; General der Infanterie Walter Buhle (Chief of the OKW Army Staff) and General der Pioniere Alfred Jacob (Chief Engineer of OKH). Behind, between Rommel and Buhle, is Generaloberst Friedrich Dollmann of 7. Armee and, between Buhle and Jacob, General der Artillerie Erich Marcks of LXXXIV. Armeekorps. *Right:* The demonstration was held almost on the junction of Peter and Queen sectors, soon to be assaulted by the British 3rd Division.

Four pieces of equipment were demonstrated: a rocket-launcher, and three versions of multi-barrelled grenade-launchers. *Above left:* The rocket device, known as the R-Vielfachwerfer (24 fin-stabilised rockets) was mounted on a Zugkraftwagen S303(f) — a captured French Somua MCL chassis — and resembled the Soviet Katyusha, more familiarly known by the euphemism 'Stalin's Organ'. General der Panzertruppen Adolf Kuntzen, of LXXXI. Armeekorps (right), views the launcher. *Above right:* It stood on the corner of the Rue de la Heve, facing the promenade. *Right:* The rockets explode across the sea. Amazingly, the villa has survived both the battle and the intervening 50 years.

Still lacking adequate forces, and the overall authority he needed to react with speed at the appropriate hour, Rommel's responsibility for repelling the invasion was equal to that of his old adversary of the North African campaign, now in charge of the Allied Expeditionary Force across the Channel. However, while Montgomery knew exactly where and when the hammer would strike, Rommel did not. 'The most decisive battle of the war, and the fate of the German people itself, is at stake', he wrote. 'Failing a tight command in one single hand of all the forces available for defence; failing the early engagement of all our mobile forces in the battle for the coast, victory will be in grave doubt. If I am to wait until the enemy landing has actually taken place before I can demand, through normal channels, the command and dispatch of the mobile forces, delays will be inevitable. This will mean that they will probably arrive far too late to intervene successfully in the battle for the coast and prevent the enemy landing. A second Nettuno, a highly undesirable situation for us, could result . . . '

Ultra

By Major Ralph Bennett

Left: **The Enigma coding machine, developed by a German, Arthur Scherbius, in the 1920s, was marketed by Chiffriermaschinen Aktiengesellschaft in Berlin. It was adopted by the Wehrmacht and was used by German forces in its developed forms throughout the war.** *Right:* **One can be seen in operation in the foreground of General Heinz Guderian's command vehicle pictured on the Western Front in June 1940.**

Both sides set up a command structure for the invasion during the winter of 1943-44. General Eisenhower was appointed Supreme Allied Commander on December 6 and arrived in England on January 15, by which time General Montgomery, commanding 21st Army Group (which was to control the invading armies), was already at work examining and criticising the draft plans for the operation. Special Liaison Units (SLUs) were established at both headquarters (which until now had been kept abreast of Ultra information by the three service ministries), and the first signal was dispatched to Supreme Headquarters Allied Expeditionary Force (SHAEF) on January 26, giving the not very momentous news that I/KG30 had flown from Istres to Piacenza on the previous day, i.e. that some 35 German bombers had moved from the south of France to the Italian front.

On the other side, von Rundstedt had been Oberbefehlshaber West since May 1942. Rommel was transferred from the command of Heeresgruppe B (Army Group B) in Italy on November 5, 1943 to examine the state of the western defences and report directly to Hitler on them. He was assigned a special staff for the purpose, and Ultra identified it on March 2 when a situation report on the Russian front was sent to 'Staff Rommel' via OB West.

Six weeks earlier, this special staff had already been formally rechristened with the name of Rommel's old Italian command and put in charge of coastal

The successful deciphering of German messages encoded on the Enigma machine stands as one of the supreme achievements of the Second World War, especially when one considers the number of permutations possible. The scrambler at the top of the machine consisted of five different, lettered rotors, of which any three could be used in varying order, giving 60 possible wheel alternatives. A fixed drum, on the left, held 26 pin terminals through which electric current was 'turned around' to flow back through the rotors. The three rotors alone (a fourth was added later) would give 26x26x26 combinations, i.e. 17,576 successive positions, before returning again to their starting positions. This gave 60x17,576 or 1,054,560 possible ways of setting up the scrambler unit. In addition, the plug board at the front, with a jack for each letter, gave a choice of cross-plugging to vary the normal path of the electric current through the rotors. Using 13 connections, the possible number of combinations increased to 8,000,000,000,000 and, by leaving four letters unplugged, the variations rose to 200,000,000,000,000. Thus, the problem for the code-breaker tackling Enigma was, to say the least, rather daunting. The remarkable achievement of cracking Enigma-produced messages — code-named 'Ultra' by the Allies — remained a closely-guarded secret long after the war was over. This total security clamp-down — in part a voluntary ban by all those in the know but strictly enforced in Britain by the Defence Press and Broadcasting Committee — totally inhibited the 'Overlord' commanders from mentioning 'the Ultra secret' in their immediate post-war accounts which form the core of this book. Even Churchill, in his six-volume history of the war, covered up the fact that transcripts of decoded messages were provided to him daily by enigmatically referring to his 'secret source'. His personal copies of Ultra were only finally declassified in May 1994.

'The Ultra secret' was first revealed in the book of that name, published in 1974, written by Frederick Winterbotham. He had been senior air staff officer to General Menzies, head of the Secret Service (SIS, otherwise MI6). In this capacity, he had connexions with SIS's war station, the Government Code and Cypher School at Bletchley Park, a large, secluded country estate in Buckinghamshire. GC&CS was to expand far beyond its boundaries to house an organisation which employed over 10,000 by the war's end when it was renamed the Government Communications Headquarters (GCHQ). All the personnel had signed the Official Secrets Act but, faced with the fait accompli of Winterbotham's unauthorised disclosure, the British government stated in 1978 that former employees could henceforth 'acknowledge having worked as interceptors, cypher breakers, distributors or users of this material'.

defence, but Ultra's first glimpses of Heeresgruppe B in the west did not come until mid-March when the senior signals officer of Heeresgruppe B was asked to say where one of his subordinates was to be posted, and the extremely-cautious comment which was agreed with MI14 and appended to the signal reads oddly today: 'No mention of Army Group B since December and no location since it left North Italy. But suggest former connection with Rommel may have been maintained.'

By March 21, Heeresgruppe B's headquarters had been tentatively located in the St Quentin area. The armoured striking force, Panzergruppe West, turned up for the first time in a mention of its signals section on March 6. The four armies in von Rundstedt's command were well known. In the north, Heeresgruppe B controlled 7. Armee on the western sector of the Channel coast and 15. Armee on the eastern. Farther south, Armeegruppe G was established in May to control 1. Armee on the Atlantic coast and 19. Armee on the Mediterranean.

Behind these arrangements for assaulting and defending German-occupied Europe lay the organisation of the High Command on both sides. The German was the neater and the more logical or, rather, it had been so until December 1941 when Hitler dismissed Generalfeldmarschall von Brauchitsch from the post of Oberbefehlshaber des Heeres (Supreme Commander of the Army) and appointed himself instead (thus giving himself two places in the hierarchy of command at different levels) and deprived OKH (Supreme Command of the Army) of strategic control over all theatres but the Russian. The apparently-superior merits of the German system were enough to convince Hitler even as late as September 1944 that the whole world envied Germany her OKW (Armed Forces High Command), but in fact the Allied system worked far more smoothly and far more efficiently.

Hitler's interference wrecked the very real advantages which the German system might have possessed. But, even on paper, the simplicity and comprehensiveness of the OKW was never reproduced in the command arrangements for the western or any other theatre of war — whereas, paradoxically, the Allies secured to themselves the benefits of unified command in every theatre although, in the nature of the case, they could not attain it in Washington or London. Eisenhower was given authority over all three services of both nations, but von Rundstedt had none over the Kriegsmarine or the Luftwaffe in the West, and only limited power over the SS troops in his armies and he had to tolerate the occasional interference of Dönitz, Göring and Himmler as well as Hitler's control over his strategic reserve. Finally, the demands of a war on three fronts, and the severe industrial damage inflicted by the RAF and USAAF, kept von Rundstedt short of men and equipment.

INTERCEPT OPERATOR'S ADDITIONS

a. Frequency: 4760 Kilocycles
b. Time of Interception: 11.10

UNENCIPHERED PREAMBLE

1. *Call Signs:* P7J to SF9 and 5KQ
2. *Time of Origin:* 10.30
3. *Number of letters:* 114
4. *Single or Multi-part:* Part 2 of 4 parts
5. *Discriminant:* QXT
6. *Indicator Setting:* VIN

ENCIPHERED TEXT

```
W Q S E U   P M P I Z   T L J J U   W Q E H G   L R B I D
F E W B O   J I E P D   J A Z H T   T B J R O   A H H Y O
J Y G S F   H Y K T N   T D B P H   U L K O H   U N T I M
O F A R L   B P A P M   X K Z Z X   D T S X L   Q W H V L
R A G U Z   Z T S G G   Y I J V
```

Restrictions still remained on disclosing the actual techniques used as these were undoubtedly still valid and, more importantly, GCHQ wanted to preserve an even greater secret: that it was only the Germans' *misuse* of the Enigma machine which had made it possible to decipher intercepts. In 1982, Gordon Welchman's book, *The Hut Six Story*, revealed that 'the machine would have been impregnable if it had been used properly'. He explained that some German operators, when setting up, took short cuts which reduced the security of the coded message, enabling the keys to be broken. 'A few minor security measures', wrote Welchman, 'could have defeated us completely.' The whole system hinged on the extensive use of radio by the Germans to send messages between units and commands. These Morse-coded signals were picked up by listening stations in Britain and written down as shown in this example. The first part was in clear text to give the operator on the receiving end the three letters necessary to set his own machine to correspond with that of the sender.

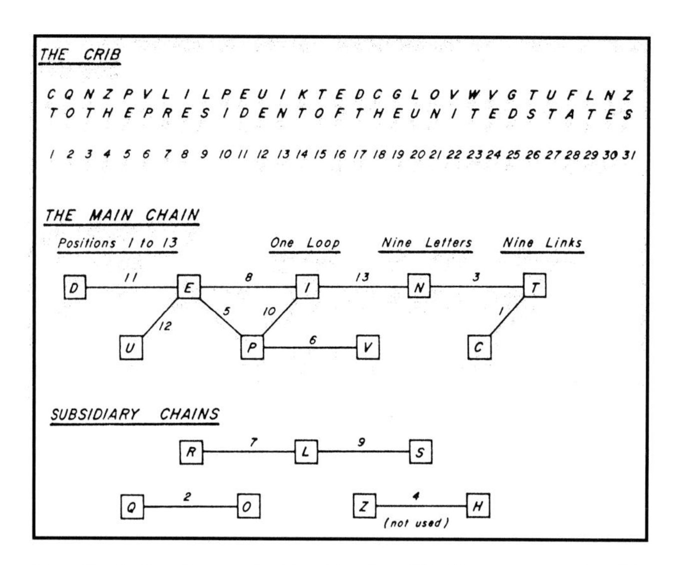

One 'technique' revealed by Gordon Welchman was that his Hut 6 (in reality an extensive, purpose-built office block) at Bletchley Park produced a 'crib' which was a guestimate as to how the German operator might have set up his Enigma.

This was then used as a 'menu' to configure the huge electro-mechanical computers (called 'bombes') which were fitted with rows of revolving drums to process the coded message and try to duplicate the settings on the Enigma rotors.

GERMAN PREPARATIONS AND ALLIED DECEPTION

'Where will they land, and in what strength?' 'How strong will the opposition be, and where are its resources concentrated?' — these were the questions uppermost in the minds of the rival leaders during the spring and early summer. Ultra provided a good deal of information under both heads, but it could not draw a complete picture either of what the Germans expected or of how they had disposed their troops. It could do neither of these things, so long as the enemy relied — as he could until the middle of June — on telephones and teleprinters in preference to the slower business of encoding and decoding wireless messages. But there was a compensating advantage, and it went some way towards levelling the balance. During these same months, the cryptographers managed to break a number of isolated days' traffic in hitherto impregnable Army keys. It was so difficult to do this that they were sometimes held up for a week or more, but the effort was abundantly worthwhile.

In an appreciation of invasion prospects, drawn up on October 28, 1943, von Rundstedt pointed to the Channel coast, the French Riviera and the Bay of Biscay as the probable assault areas, perhaps in some combination. This was quickly followed on November 3 by Hitler's Directive No. 51, which laid it down that Germany was now in more danger from the west than from the east, and added that the forces stationed there should not be reduced but that more tanks and guns should be allotted to the western theatre of war. However, the directive was quite unspecific about the point at which the blow to be expected 'at latest in the spring' would fall. Both of these, it has been asserted, became known through Ultra: however, the evidence to confirm this cannot be consulted, since both date back to a time before signals were sent to field commanders in the West.

REF. CX/MSS/T.74/89 VL 4789/PK/BI/SB/ZU/KQ/CO/SH

MED ZZ/WEST Z

TWO JU £ JU OF FIRST GRUPPE KING THREE NOUGHT, ONE OF SECOND GRUPPE KING THREE NOUGHT LANDED PIACENZA £ PIACENZA BETWEEN NOUGHT ONE FOUR FIVE AND NOUGHT THREE HOURS TWENTYFIFTH. XX

((VL 4789 £ 4789 PK 46 £ 46 BI 57 £ 57 SB 25 £25 ZU 19 £ 19 KQ 21 £ 21 CO 38 £ 38 SH 1 £ 1))

(FAIR INDICATIONS ISTRES £ ISTRES) INFORMED.

(COMMENT, FIRST AND SECOND GRUPPEN LEFT ITALY £ ITALY FOR WESTERN EUROPE £ EUROPE LAST DECEMBER £ DECEMBER)

PNL/RFB/JEM 260031Z/1/44.

Once a message had been decoded it was, of course, still in German. This was passed to Hut 3 — another large, single-storey office complex — staffed by intelligence officers, one of whom was our author Ralph Bennett. Before the war, he had been an historian at Magdalene College, Cambridge, but by 1944 he was one of over a thousand Hut 3 specialists translating and disseminating the decodes to those approved to see them. This is the form in which Ultra was sent out. The three sets of initials at the bottom indicate, respectively, the air, military or naval advisor who drafted it (in this case Peter Labouchere); the duty officer who approved it for transmission (Ralph Bennett), and the typist. Each series of signals bore a two-letter prefix, 'VL' signifying that it was issued between January 26 and March 29, 1944, a new prefix being assigned once the numbering reached 9999. The double brackets which enclose this coding within the text, as well as giving the organisations which were to receive it, e.g. 'SH' stands for SHAEF, were a coding device used for security reasons. Single brackets enclose agreed phraseology concerning uncertain words, for example (fair indications Istres). The '£' sign indicates the repetition of a word or number. The word 'Comment' separates a summarised translation of the German original from Hut 3's comment upon it.

The first invasion news to appear in these signals was a rhetorical order promulgated to the troops in Italy by Hitler on January 28: the Allies' invasion year, he said, had already begun at Anzio, the landings which were designed to tie down German troops as far away from the Channel as possible, and the battle for Rome would soon flare up. 'Fanatical determination therefore required . . . holy hatred of enemy conducting a merciless campaign of extermination . . . destruction of European civilisation . . . enemy to be made to realise that German fighting spirit was unbroken and that the great invasion of 1944 would be stifled in the blood of its soldiers.'

After this, there was silence on the subject until March, when a succession of reports showed how difficult the German command was finding it to determine whether any one point on the European coastline from Norway to Spain was more threatened than another, and to decide where the Mediterranean figured in Allied plans. OKM (Supreme Command of the Navy) believed on March 5 that there might be as many as six British divisions in Scotland ready for an operation 'of limited scope' in central or southern Norway, and clung to its opinion well into May. ('Fortitude North', the deception plan, was in fact suggesting this, and the heavy-water plant at Rjukan in Norway had been blown up on February 20.) Fremde Heere West (Foreign Armies West) — the intelligence department of OKH responsible for estimating the strength and order of battle of the British and American armies — could not be more precise about the assault area than 'somewhere between the Pas-de-Calais and the Loire valley' on March 20, but von Rundstedt received from Kesselring on the same day a description of the Allies' assault procedures and their use of new types of landing craft. A long appreciation from OB West next day said that prepar-

REF. 32.
REF. CX/MSS/T125/26 VL 8693

MED ZZ
WEST Z

((VL 8693 £ 8693 PK 75 £ 75 LM 78 £ 78

SB 29 £ 29 SHA 39 £ 39 AG 9 £ 9.%

ARMY GROUP BAKER REPEAT BAKER SENIOR SIGNALS OFFICER)) ASKED ON EIGHTH BY CHARLIE IN CHARLIE SOUTHWEST ~~IS~~ TO NAME DESTINATION FOR ELEMENT OF PANZER ARMY SIGNALS REGIMENT FIVE, READY TO BE LOADED FROM TWENTIETH. COMMENT AGREED WITH MIKE ITEM ONE FOUR COLON NO £ NO MENTION SINCE DECEMBER LAST OF ARMY GROUP BAKER AND NO £ NO LOCATION SINCE IT LEFT NORTH ITALY £ NORTH ITALY. NEVERTHELESS SUGGEST FORMER CONNECTION WITH ROMMEL £ ROMMEL MAY PROVE TO HAVE BEEN MAINTAINED

GELO/HDD/DJM 171711Z/3/44

Single letters within the text were always spelt with their phonetic equivalent, 'Army Group Baker' standing for 'Heeresgruppe B'. The time and date line translates as '17 March 1944' at '1711' hours, 'Z' indicating Zebra time, i.e. Greenwich Mean Time, in military terminology. Central European Time had been imposed on France after the occupation and had advanced on April 3, 1944 to GMT plus 2 hours.

leader of the Yugoslav partisans, is attempting to hold open "an invasion corridor" for the Allies message. This view of Tito's strategy is based on documents seized after the battle of to "Aftonbladet's" Berlin correspondent. A popular legend among the people of Yugoslavia, says the and a detachment of guerrillas have, accordingly, presented Tito with such a horse.

EISENHOWER TAKES OVER AS INVASION C.-IN-C.

PM Back to Health in Morocco

Has Talks with Gen. de Gaulle

Daily Mail Special Correspondent
ALGIERS, Sunday.

Saw Roosevelt on Way Here

SUPREME Headquarters of the Allied Expeditionary Force — the army to invade Europe—issued its first communiqué last night. It stated that General Dwight Eisenhower has taken over his post in Britain as the Supreme Commander-in-Chief.

The announcement marks the final phase of the vast preparation for the offensive operations planned from this country.

On his journey from the Mediterranean to Britain General Eisenhower had a conference with Mr. Churchill and spent several days in the United States, where he had conferences with President Roosevelt and General George Marshall, the United States Chief of Staff.

Already many of the leading figures who will conduct the great campaign for the liberation of Europe—the commanders of the various Allied forces—have assembled at Supreme Headquarters.

General Eisenhower will begin his conferences with General Montgomery, the commander of the British group of armies, and other Allied staff officers at once. But his

15 Killed in Train Collision

30 Injured: Crash in Station

FIFTEEN people were killed and 30 injured in a train collision at Ilford, Essex, yesterday.

A statement by the L.N.E.R. Company said that the 2.40 p.m. Norwich to Liverpool-street (London) train ran into the rear of the 2.38 p.m. train from Yarmouth to Liverpool-street.

One of the trains is stated to have been standing at the platform when the other hit the rear coach, which was lifted into the air and became perched on the engine of the second train.

The serious casualties were taken to the King George Hospital.

American and British soldiers waiting on the platform helped in demolition work. Glass and wood-

Through in North

100,000 GERMAN DEAD IN 3 WEEKS

THERE was more good news from Russia last night. The Moscow communiqué reported a new break-through on the Nevel front west of Novo-Sokolniki, on a front eight miles wide and five miles deep.

It was also officially stated that 100,000 Germans have been killed and 7,000 prisoners taken in the fighting on the First Ukrainian Front between December 24 and January 13.

The break-through at Novo-Sokolniki was achieved after three days' fighting. Red Army troops have occupied more than 40 places, including the railway station of Natva, and the railway line Novo-Sokolniki-Dno has been cut.

Novo-Sokolniki, at the southern end of the Northern Russian front, is 25 miles north of Nevel and 10 miles west of Vel'ki Luki, held by the Russians.

Cutting of the railway to Dno junction, 100 miles farther north, means that one rail route to the Leningrad sector has been lost by the Germans.

Of the fighting in White Russia, the communiqué said: "West and north-west of Kalinkovichi our troops fought their way forward and occupied several inhabited localities, including the large localities of Novoselki, Yakimovichi, and Klinsk.

RAIL TOWN TAKEN

"West and south-west of Sarny there was fighting of local importance, in the course of which our troops occupied the town and large railway station of Kostopol (14 miles north of Rovno on the Sarny-Rovno railway) as well as other

Soviet Gains on All Front

'5th' STORM TROCCHIO

Win 1,400ft. Peak

ALLIED FORCE H.Q., Sunday.

IT was officially announced here to-night that United States troops of the Fifth Army have captured Mount Trocchio, the 1,400ft. "concrete castle" barring the way to Cassino, only three miles away.

Mount Trocchio is the last mountain barrier standing directly before Cassino, still in German hands. Its capture followed an all-out Allied attack which began at 6.30 a.m. yesterday, and was taken after United States forces had battled up the steep mountain slopes from the south-west and south-east.

Dozens of concrete pillboxes had been built by the German defenders into the mountain-side.—*B.U.P.*

Details of the fighting—BACK Page.

Canadians' New C.-in-C. in Italy

In the run-up to D-Day, as well as providing information about the more straightforward issues like the movement of men and machines, Ultra gave an insight as to how far the Germans had been taken in by Allied deception plans. The overall strategic deception, code-named 'Bodyguard' and finalised on January 23, 1944, was to try to persuade the German High Command that Scandinavia, Italy and the Balkans were the main Allied targets, although the plan was a lost cause even before it had been drawn up Hitler was already convinced that the main threat lay in the west; his directive of the previous November even narrowing down the area to the Channel coast. Moreover, in the week before 'Bodyguard' was finalised, headlines in the press publicised the appointment of Eisenhower as commander for the 'invasion of Europe'.

ations were complete but that agents reported that the invasion had been postponed; an attack on the south-west of France was possible and this, OKH concluded a week later, might be synchronised with landings from England.

April brought nothing but a proclamation from Dönitz on the 17th along much the same lines as Hitler's of January 28. A large-scale landing was to be expected at any moment; its success or failure would decide the issue of the war and the fate of the German people. 'Throw yourselves recklessly into the fight . . . any man who fails to do so will be destroyed in shame and ignominy.'

The fullest information yet came in a lengthy appreciation from von Rundstedt on May 8 decoded a week later. Agents had forecast a number of different landing dates, he said, but most of them were in the first half of May; Allied preparations were complete and more than 20 divisions would be landed in the first wave. This was four times the number of divisions then preparing for the first day of the assault, and was therefore a valuable indication of the state of German intelligence. Von Rundstedt was nearer the mark when locating the main concentration between Southampton and Portsmouth, but could not narrow the assault area down more closely than somewhere between the Scheldt and the tip of Brittany, most probably 'between Boulogne and Normandy'. It would be essential for the Allies to capture large ports like Le Havre and Cherbourg; they were modifying their landing techniques to cope with the new outer beach obstacles and would attack 'not only on the

On the other hand, the *tactical* deception plan approved by Eisenhower on January 23 was an outstanding success. Split into two parts, 'Fortitude North' attempted to convince the Germans that the Fourth Army — a fictional formation — in Scotland was to mount an assault against Norway in conjunction with the Soviets. 'Fortitude South' implied that once the Norwegian landing had succeeded, a second assault would be mounted in mid-July across the Channel at the Pas-de-Calais, aimed at Antwerp and Brussels. However, once the landings in Normandy — scheduled for June 1 — had actually taken place, 'Fortitude South' would switch to phase two: that the Normandy landings were a feint intended to draw German reserves away from the Pas-de-Calais where the main assault was yet to take place. It was an ingenious plan but the real credit for its success was never disclosed in any of the 'Overlord' commanders' writings. In 1972, Lieutenant-Colonel T. A. Robertson was publicly identified as the man who had masterminded MI5's outstanding wartime success which became known as the 'Double Cross System' — that the British Security Services had controlled more than 40 German agents who were feeding false information to the Abwehr. 'TAR' Robertson (left) with one of his agents TATE (Wulf Schmidt) (centre) and MI5 radio operator Russell Lee in the Cambridgeshire village of Willingham near where TATE had landed by parachute. (See *After the Battle* No. 74.) In 1944, TATE was notionally 'moved' to Wye in Kent, ostensibly having taken agricultural work to report on troop movements (fictitious) facing the Pas-de-Calais.

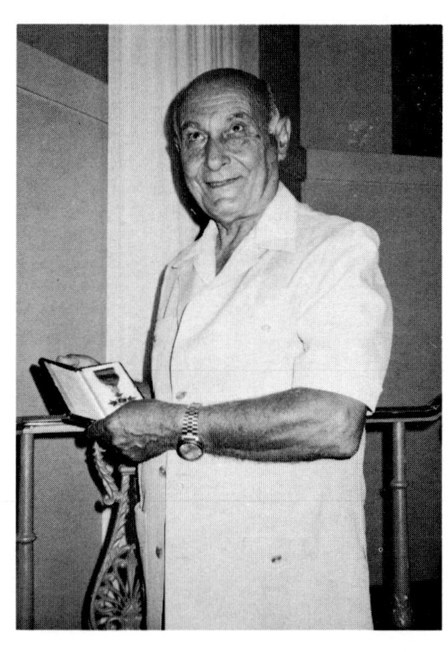

However, the 'jewel in the crown' as far as Operation 'Fortitude' was concerned was agent GARBO. If ever a claim could be made for one person to have changed the course of the war, that could be truthfully said of Juan Pujol. He had been recruited by the Abwehr in Spain, but by the time he arrived in Britain in April 1942 he had become an MI5 double agent. His case officer was Cyril Mills and, over the course of the next two years, a fictitious network of 27 sub-agents was set up, all positioned in localities from where credible intelligence could realistically have been gathered for passing back to GARBO's Abwehr controller, Karl-Erich Kühlenthal. Ultra revealed that the information transmitted to Madrid was sent on to Berlin, evidence of the value placed on GARBO's network being signalled to him by Kühlenthal: 'Your activity and that of your informants gave us a perfect idea of what is taking place over there. These reports . . . have an incalculable value . . . ' Juan Pujol was decorated by both sides for his services, but it was not until the 40th anniversary of D-Day that the full story was revealed and GARBO, previously believed to be dead, was re-united with his former case officer, Cyril Mills (right), at the Special Forces Club. *Right:* GARBO had been awarded an MBE in 1944 by Sir David Petrie, Director-General of MI5, but it was not gazetted for security reasons. In 1984, it was decided to extend a more formal presentation at Buckingham Palace.

The principal feature of 'Fortitude South' was to try to convince the Germans that the main Pas-de-Calais attack would be made by the US 1st Army Group (also written as First US Army Group — hence the abbreviation FUSAG). FUSAG had been established in October 1943 as the follow-up formation which would move to France once a lodgement area had been secured. As many of its divisions were already camped in south-east England, their locations, if leaked to the Germans, would substantiate the idea that they were positioned ready to cross the Channel at its narrowest point for the main assault which was yet to take place. The US First Army commander, Lieutenant General Bradley, was also commander of the 1st Army Group with a headquarters based in Bryanston Square, London. Bradley's office was located at No. 20.

incoming tide before dawn' but also later. The main assault would take place as soon as there was a series of fine days, but commando raids on the southern French coast might occur at any time. On the same day, Luftflotte 3, the senior air command in the west, made the best forecast so far picked up by Ultra — the landings would be between Le Havre and Cherbourg — and this was decoded at once; three weeks later, Luftflotte 3 wrongly thought they might be as far east as Dieppe.

It was just as important to deceive the enemy about date as about place. Operation 'Fortitude' sought to persuade the enemy that the United States 1st Army Group (FUSAG — which

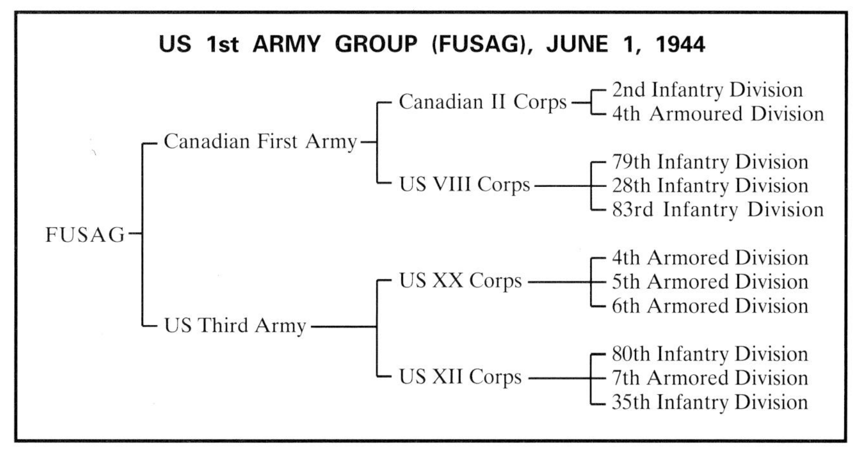

If the Germans were to be made to believe that FUSAG posed the main threat, once General Bradley moved to Normandy with the First Army their suspicions were bound to be aroused. Instead, therefore, the name of the US Third Army commander, Lieutenant General George S. Patton, whose recent arrival in the UK had been widely publicised, was put forward by the double agents as the FUSAG commander. It was an ideal solution as Patton was not due to cross to France with the Third Army for at least a month after D-Day, by which time it was assumed that the Germans would have rumbled the trick. Patton's first public appearance was at the Ruskin Rooms in Knutsford, some four miles from his real headquarters at Poever Hall in Cheshire. He had been invited by the local Women's Voluntary Service chairman, Mrs M. Constantine-Smith, to say a few words at the opening of a Welcome Club. Still smarting from a recent dressing-down received from Eisenhower over the hitting of a soldier in Sicily, Patton was obviously mindful that he must be on his best behaviour, and he only agreed to speak providing his remarks were off the record. In the event, the American press misquoted him, implying that he had insulted the Russians. It was not true, a fact we confirmed when interviewing Mrs Constantine-Smith in 1975 *(right)*, but the resulting furore nearly put paid to the carefully-laid FUSAG deception plan.

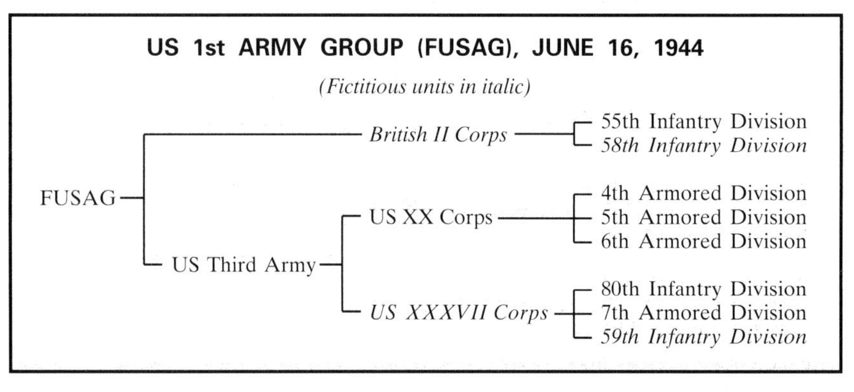

Although Patton had done no wrong, that was not the way it was seen in Washington and there was an outcry in the American press. However, Eisenhower needed Patton — as much for his talent as a commander as for his notional command of FUSAG — and by May 3 the matter had been smoothed over. After D-Day, as 1st Army Group formations were transferred to Normandy, they had to be replaced by fictitious units and, when Patton flew to France at the beginning of July, a replacement commander for FUSAG also had to be found. Ultra decodes indicated that the Germans still believed the disinformation being fed to them, so it was considered worthwhile continuing with the subterfuge.

eventually had no real existence at all) under General Patton would land in the Pas-de-Calais during July and that this, not the Normandy landing, would be the chief invasion effort. The object, of course, was to ensure that German troops and armour were retained north of the Seine for as long as possible, and so to prevent the reinforcement of the German forces in Normandy until the invaders were too strong to be dislodged. Some indication that the deception was proving successful came when FUSAG first appeared in Enigma traffic on January 9, 1944 and again on March 23, and when Patton was mentioned in this context in late March; evidence that its (entirely imaginary) threat to 15. Armee in Calais and the Netherlands was still being taken seriously persisted until late July.

In his dealings with Washington, Eisenhower emphasised 'the great importance of maintaining as long as humanly possible the Allied threat to the Pas-de-Calais area which has already paid enormous dividends', and he stressed to General Marshall that he needed someone credible to replace Patton. There was also an additional problem in that General Bradley now needed to move his 1st Army Group headquarters to Normandy to be ready when he took over as an army group commander, but at the same time FUSAG was needed in Britain to maintain the deception. The solution was to rename the 1st Army Group the 12th Army Group, but deliberately to include a phrase in the General Order for the benefit of the German High Command stating that the transfer included all units 'except those specifically excepted', thus maintaining the concept of continuing the build-up in the UK of the assault force against the Pas-de-Calais. The officer chosen to lead the 'new' FUSAG — now almost totally denuded of genuine divisions — was the Stateside-based Chief of the Army Ground Forces, Lieutenant General Lesley J. McNair *(top right)*. On July 14, he took over with the dual responsibility of decoy commander of the 1st Army Group and also observer for SHAEF in France to assess the effectiveness of army training. General McNair had already been wounded in Tunisia while getting too close to the front line, and he was killed in an accident near St Lô on July 25 when a US bombing attack landed short, killing over 100 Americans. General McNair was buried secretly two days later in a ceremony attended only by Bradley, Patton, Lieutenant General Courtney H. Hodges, now commanding the US First Army, and Major General E. R. 'Pete' Quesada, commanding general of the Ninth Tactical Air Command, for fear that news of his death might reach the Germans and compromise the 'Fortitude' deception.

The 'Fortitude' deception was helped in varying degrees in Britain by simulated signals traffic; dummy landing craft; lighting to simulate troop concentrations, as well as direct air attacks against the Pas-de-Calais. The US 1st Army Group continued on paper with a new commander, General John L. DeWitt, until October 18, 1944, when it was finally 'deactivated'. General Bradley wrote FUSAG's epitaph: 'In devising this cover plan, we had hoped for no more than a modest delay, a week or two at the most, until we had sufficient divisions ashore to secure the Normandy landing. Even now [1951], I cannot understand why the enemy believed for so long in so transparent a hoax. For, once we had landed in Normandy, only a fool could have thought us capable of duplicating so gigantic an effort elsewhere.'

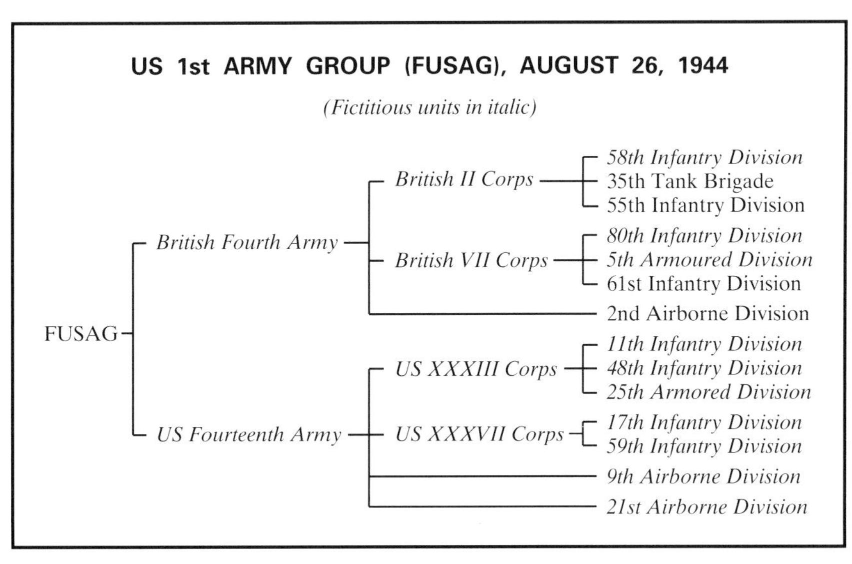

In 1943, MI5 staged Operation 'Mincemeat' to try to deceive the Germans as to Allied intentions prior to the invasion of Sicily. To this end, a dead body given a fictitious identity was planted on a Spanish beach with the hope that the spoof documents carried by the 'Royal Marine courier' would be accepted as genuine. Now, in 1944, MI5 again chose the Mediterranean to stage another ploy — Operation 'Copperhead' — to try to give the impression that the forthcoming assault would take place in that theatre. General Montgomery was already known to be one of the invasion commanders so it was thought that, if he were to appear in the Mediterranean, it would give credibility to the idea. Montgomery himself could not be spared, but a Lieutenant Clifton James, who bore a distinct likeness to the General, was recruited to become Monty's double. For a few days in May, Lieutenant James *(left)* acted out the part at Gibraltar where Spanish agents were bound to report his arrival. *Right:* In 1958, Lieutenant James re-enacted the scene for the film *I Was Monty's Double*. *Below:* The original locations used in 1944 were reused in 1958; this is the entrance to the Governor's residence in Convent Place.

Practice anti-invasion exercises were held at various points along the coast from Bruges to the mouth of the Loire; one assumed a bridgehead 50 kilometres long between Ouistreham and Isigny (just where the assault forces landed on June 6), but no particular importance was assigned to this over other areas. Fremde Heere West's last appreciation before the invasion was dated June 4 but was not decoded for ten days. It forecast June 12 as the beginning of the next danger period and deduced that a landing might take place in southern France because Montgomery and General Sir Henry Maitland Wilson, the Supreme Commander in the Mediterranean, were said to have met in North Africa (perhaps one of the very few known repercussions of the visit of an actor disguised as Montgomery to Gibraltar and Algiers on May 26 and 27), with evidence of a landing in the Balkans as well.

Panzers on the Western Front. A PzKpfw IV of the 12. SS-Panzer-Division 'Hitlerjugend' — one of the formidable armoured units in the Normandy area at the beginning of June. Information on the disposition of German forces was vital although not all could be supplied by Ultra. Most internal communications went by land-line, but when teleprinter and telephone traffic was interrupted by Allied bombing in April and May, an increasing number of signals were sent by wireless.

DIVISIONS LOCATED

Some 28 German divisions manned the coast between Amsterdam and Brest on June 6; Ultra had mentioned 15 of them at least once in a French context (not always very precise) by the end of May. From Brest along the Biscay coast to the Spanish frontier, the figures are seven and five, and on the French Riviera seven and four. By D-Day, therefore, Ultra had identified (and in a good many cases located) well over half the garrison-type divisions which would be the first line of resistance to the landings. In addition, all the army and corps commands along the coast had been identified at least once, many of them together with evidence showing what units or formations each controlled. This probably did not provide more than a hard core to other information about the tactical disposition of German troops manning the coastal defences, and it no doubt fell a good deal short of what was desirable. Thus, the 352. Infanterie-Division, a field division of good quality which moved into the Cotentin in March and right up to Omaha Beach a few days before the landings, received only a single mention in Ultra before the fighting began: this was on January 22 in an OKH order which provided the first evidence that this division existed but did nothing to locate it beyond showing that it was under OB West's command. Ultra was even less well informed about the division's right-hand neighbours in the British landing area, the 716. and 711. Infanterie-Divisions. There was no mention at all of the 716. Division in Ultra signals before D-Day and only the bare record of a fusilier battalion reaching the 711. Division on May 23.

The panzer divisions in the west were better documented. The 2. Panzer-Division was heard of in a western context in late March and firmly located at Amiens on April 20. The 9. Panzer-Division (which had refitted and absorbed the 155. Reserve-Panzer-Division) was at Nîmes in the spring and was frequently noted in the same area thereafter. On May 2, the 9. Panzer-Division and two other new armoured divisions, the 11. and 116. Panzer-Divisions, were to be equipped with motor transport during the late summer months. The 21. Panzer-Division was moving to a new location in March, which was known early in April to be Brittany and precisely located as Rennes a month later, and its composition figured in two later signals; the 116 Panzer-Division (a merging of the battered 16. Panzergrenadier-Division and the 179. Reserve-Panzer-Division) was taking over the 21. Panzer-Division's old positions on March 22 and was near Paris on April 2.

Valuable confirmation that Ultra had correctly identified and located all the armour in the west was provided by an announcement by the Generalinspekteur der Panzertruppen (Inspector-General of Armoured Forces), Generaloberst Heinz Guderian, of his itinerary for a western tour on April 20;

Peter Taghon identified the location as Gistel, Belgium, although when he photographed the junction of the N367 from Jabbeke (on the right) with the main N33 Torhout–Ostend road, he found that nothing original remained.

REF: CX/MSS/T172/24 KV 2624

WEST: ZZZ

((KV 2624 £ 2624 SH 29 £ 29 AG 1 £ 1 FU 59 £ 59 ON 92 £
92 YK 77 £ 77 OX 83 £ 83 IN TWO PARTS, PART ONE %

INFORMATION TWENTIETH TO PANZER GRUPPE WEST ON ITINERARY
FOR)) TOUR OF INSPECTION IN FRANCE £ FRANCE BY INSPECTOR
GENERAL OF PANZER TROOPS COLON TWENTYSECOND APRIL LEAVE
SALZBURG £ SALZBURG TWENTYTHIRD MAILLY LE CAMP £ MAILLY LE
CAMP. TWENTYFOURTH, MORNING (ROMAN) ONE STROKE TWO SEVEN
QUOTE AND GROSSDEUTSCHLAND £ GROSSDEUTSCHLAND UNQUOTE (COMMENT
SUGGEST (ROMAN) ONE STROKE ~~GERMENIAGHELAND~~ Grossdeutschland MEANT, COMPARE
KV £ KV ONE EIGHT NINE ONE). AFTERNOON QUOTE ABTEILUNG
SIX FIVE FOUR UNQUOTE AND (ROMAN) TWO STROKE THREE FIVE.
TWENTYFIFTH (STILL MAILLY £ MAILLY) (ROMAN) ONE SUGAR SUGAR
TOTENKOPF £ TOTENKOPF AND (ROMAN) ONE HOHENSTAUFEN,
TWENTYSIXTH PARIS £ PARIS, VISIT TO RUNDSTEDT £ RUNDSTEDT
AND ROMMEL £ ROMMEL. TWENTYEIGHTH AMIENS £ AMIENS, TWO

OCB/RFB/BMF 021140Z/5/44

Ultra's coverage of the overall picture in the West was therefore patchy. Some decodes produced a mine of intelligence of almost inestimable value like this itinerary of Generaloberst Guderian's inspection of armoured formations which listed each unit and its location. The tour went ahead following his meeting with Rommel on April 28 (see page 51).

REF. 701 VL 6997 IN FOUR
" CX/MSS/T103/54 ZZ MED PARTS PART ONE
ZZ WEST

((VL 6997 £ 6997 PK 61 £ 61 SB 39 £ 39/ C099£99 SH 99 £ 99
AG 54 £ 54 IN FOUR PARTS, PART ONE %

OKH £ OKH ORDERS TWENTYSECOND JANUARY UNDER HEADING
QUOTE BRINGING UP OF)) VOLUNTARY ASSISTANTS FOR
DIVISIONS OF TWENTYFIRST AND TWENTYSECOND WAVE UNQUOTE
(ONE) TO BE BROUGHT UP BY HQ £ HQ OF THE OST £ OST
LEGIONS (ABLE) TO CHARLIE IN CHARLIE WEST COLON FOR
THREE FOUR NINE AND THREE FIVE TWO INFANTRY DIVISIONS,
EACH ONE FIVE NOUGHT NOUGHT MEN. FOR THREE FIVE THREE
INFANTRY DIVISION ONE EIGHT NOUGHT NOUGHT MEN. ALL
FROM OST £ OST LEGIONS, (BAKER) TO CHARLIE IN CHARLIE
SOUTHWEST COLON FOR THREE SIX TWO INFANTRY DIVISION,
TWO HUNDREL FROM LEGIONS AND ONE THOUSAND MEN FROM
COSSACK £ COSSACK ERSATZ REGIMENT(S). (TWO) TO BE
BROUGHT UP BY WEHRKREIS GENERAL GOUVERNEMENT (ABLE)

GELC/HDD/KH 241919Z/2/44

However, one vital factor which totally slipped the Ultra net was the reinforcement of the Omaha area by the 352. Infanterie-Division of Generalleutnant Dietrich Kraiss. The division had been inspected by Rommel on May 9 but the only decrypt which mentioned the existence of the 352nd in OB West's sector was this old signal of January 22.

this gave a splendid insight into the distribution of the armour a month before the landings. He was first to spend three days with various SS tank units at Mailly-le-Camp near Reims before calling on von Rundstedt and Rommel in Paris on the 26th. [In the event, the meeting took place at La Roche-Guyon on the 28th.] After this, he would inspect the 2. Panzer-Division at Amiens and the 12. SS-Panzer-Division at Dreux, and take in a visit to Generaloberst Friedrich Dollmann (commanding 7. Armee) on the way westwards to the 21. Panzer-Division at Rennes and the 17. SS-Panzergrenadier-Division at Thouars. Moving south, he would next see Generaloberst Johannes Blaskowitz (just about to take over the new Armeegruppe G) and inspect the 10. Panzer-Division at Bordeaux, the 2. SS-Panzer-Division at Montauban and the 9. Panzer-Division at Nîmes, returning to Paris to call on the 116. Panzer-Division on May 8. Mailly-le-Camp was a well-known SS tank training area (it was reported in this connection from March to May) and it was heavily raided, with 400 casualties, while Guderian was on his way to Paris, possibly as a result of Ultra information.

A real plum, had it only been available a little earlier, was a long OB West return of May 19 which gave full details of the 1. SS-Panzer-Division's strength (over 20,000 men) and some information about its equipment; the section covering its tanks was missing, but the same return showed that the 2. SS-Panzer-Division, then still around Toulouse, had 55 Mark IVs and 37 Mark Vs (Panthers), with 46 and 62 respectively still to be delivered. The 1. SS-Panzer-Division had been regularly reported at Turnhout in Belgium in late April and early May. The 12. SS-Panzer-Division, also in Belgium in February, could be followed to southern Normandy in April and was still firmly located in the Evreux area right up to D-Day, while the 17. SS-Panzergrenadier-Division

A Panther of the 1. SS-Panzer-Division proceeds through Eeklo, Belgium, shortly after having arrived from the East in May.

remained consistently at Tours and westwards throughout the spring and early summer. Further south, the 2. SS-Panzer-Division was regularly reported between Bordeaux and Toulouse from February to May and the allocation of the 11. Panzer-Division (not the 10. Panzer-Division, as first intended) to the same area in early May for rest and refit was duly noted.

Towards the end of April, the Panzer-Lehr-Division figured alongside the 1. and 12. SS-Panzer-Divisions and the 17. SS-Panzergrenadier-Division (the first two equipped with two tank and six armoured infantry battalions, the third with one assault gun battalion and six lorried infantry battalions) in one of Ultra's best hauls in the west so far. On April 26, Hitler ordered that I. SS-Panzerkorps, consisting of these four divisions, was to constitute the OKW reserve in the West and was not to be moved without his prior permission.

Finally, as D-Day approached and the success of the operation might depend on weather conditions, the weather reports and forecasts which had for years been one of the least-interesting features of Enigma traffic suddenly acquired a greater potential importance. One was sent to commands with very high priority in the late evening of June 2 (illustrated below); it may conceivably have contributed a little to the pool of information at Eisenhower's headquarters and to the agonising 'To-go-or-not-to-go' debates of the next two or three days. Since they were very often received and decoded well before the period covered by the forecasts, and they were often associated with intended raids by the Luftwaffe, it was often worthwhile to give them high priority during the next few weeks to provide information on Continental conditions which were difficult for Allied weather bureaux to ascertain.

REF. CX/MSS/T169/71 KV 2388 IN TWO PARTS, PART ONE 152

ZZZ MED
ZZZ WEST

((KV 2388 £ 2388 PK 25 £ 25 LM 80 £ 80 SB 58 £ 58 CO 82 £ 82 AL 11 £ 11 SH 74 £ 74 AG 86 £ 86 FU 45 £ 45 ON 85 £ 85 YK OX 76 £ 76 ST 69 £ 69 / IN TWO PARTS PART ONE %

ORDER SIGNED JODL # JODL, OKW £ OKW OPS £ OPS STAFF))
ON TWENTYSIXTH APRIL COLON FOLLOWING DIVISIONS ARE
OKW £ OKW RESERVE AND ONLY TO BE MOVED OR EMPLOYED
WITH PRIOR PERMISSION OF OKW £ OKW. (ONE) IN THE WEST
COLON FIRST SUGAR SUGAR PANZER CORPS WITH ONE, TWELVE
AND SEVENTEEN SUGAR SUGAR PANZER DIVISIONS AND PANZER
LEHR DIVISION (WHEN BROUGHT UP). (TWO) ITALY £
ITALY COLON DIVISION GOERING £ GOERING. (THREE)
IN SOUTHEASTERN AREA COLON FOUR TWO JAEGER DIVISION,
ONE MOUNTAIN DIVISION (WHEN BROUGHT UP). (FOUR) HUNGARY
£ HUNGARY COLON SIXTEEN, EIGHTEEN SUGAR SUGAR PG £ PG
AND EIGHT SUGAR SUGAR CAVALRY DIVISIONS. (FIVE) IN

GELC/AHW/KH 292255Z/4/44

Possibly the most significant inside information of all, which was to have grave repercussions on the ability of Rommel to counter the assault: Hitler's order taking personal responsibility for the deployment of the four armoured divisions of I. SS-Panzerkorps was picked out of the ether on April 26.

REF: CX/MSS/T203/59 KV 6169 IN TWO PARTS, PART ONE

ZZZZ

104

((KV 6169 £ 6169 SH 39 £ 39 ON 32 £ 32 DL 77 £ 77 ST 89 £ 89 EF 5 £ 5 TA 74 £ 74 IN TWO PARTS, PART ONE %

WEATHER SURVEY AT ONE TWO THREE NOUGHT HOURS SECOND))
BY (STRONG INDICATIONS THREE JD £ JD). ABLE, GENERAL
SITUATION, THE LOW PRESSURE SYSTEM OVER SILESIA £ SILESIA,
CENTRAL GERMANY £ GERMANY AND JUTLAND £ JUTLAND IS
MOVING EAST. A POWERFUL WEDGE OF THE AZORES £ AZORES HIGH
PRESSURE SYSTEM IS ADVANCING EASTWARDS OVER ENGLAND £
ENGLAND AND FRANCE £ FRANCE THE WEAKENING OF THE COLD AIR SYSTEM
WHICH HAS STREAMED INTO CENTRAL AND WEST EUROPE £ EUROPE WILL
INCREASE AND LEAD TO A DISPERSAL OF CLOUDS PROCEEDING FROM
WEST TO EAST. BAKER, RAID SITUATION, TAKE OFF AND
ASSEMBLY DURING THE NIGHT UNIMPEDED. CHARLIE, DEFENCE
SITUATION, LIFTING AND DISPERSAL OF CLOUDS PROCEEDING WEST
TO EAST, CLOUD BASE OVER HOLLAND £ HOLLAND AND BELGIUM £
BELGIUM AT THE BEGINNING OF THE NIGHT (SLIGHT INDICATIONS
FROM) FIVE HUNDRED TO ONE THOUSAND METRES. UPPER
EF/HDD/GB 022241Z/6/44

REF: CX/MSS/T203/59 KV 6169 PART TWO AND FINAL

ZZZZ

105

((KV 6169 £ 6169 PART TWO AND FINAL %

LIMIT ONE FIVE NOUGHT NOUGHT TO TWO THOUSAND METRES.
VISIBILITY)) AROUND TEN KILOMETRES. THE IMPROVEMENT IN
WEATHER WILL EXTEND TO THE WESER £ WESER DURING THE
NIGHT. OVER CENTRAL AND NORTH GERMANY £ GERMANY AND IN
ALPINE £ ALPINE FOOTHILLS COMPLETE CLOUD COVER DURING
WHOLE NIGHT, BASE ONE HUNDRED TO THREE HUNDRED METRES,
FLUCTUATING MODERATE TO BAD VISIBILITY. OPS £ OPS BY
SINGLE ENGINED AIRCRAFT POSSIBLE IN SECOND HALF OF
NIGHT. OPS £ OPS BY TWIN ENGINED AIRCRAFT IN AREA OF
QUOTE THE DIVISION UNQUOTE IN ESSENTIALS UNIMPEDED.
TOWARDS CENTRAL AND NORTH GERMANY £ GERMANY OWING
VERY BAD LANDING CONDITIONS OPS £ OPS RENDERED VERY
DIFFICULT

EF/HDD
GB

D-DAY

D-Day in Hut 3 was tense with excitement, but even more with anxiety and hope. To begin with, nothing of much importance came to hand. There were several accounts of small-scale fighting in the beach-head, but situation reports were almost bound to be so far behind the swiftly-moving events they described that they could tell Allied generals nothing they did not know already. Gradually, however, the volume of traffic and the value of its content began to rise reassuringly and within two or three days we were giving western commands the same service we had been accustomed to provide to headquarters in Africa and Italy for the past three years, supplying a continuous stream of high-grade information and an occasional item of absolutely priceless significance.

There were three principal things to look out for at once: had surprise been achieved; how quickly would the armoured counter-attack force be assembled for a strike; and how soon would the French airfields be filled with fighters and bombers?

The complete tactical surprise of the landings is now so well known that it seems hardly necessary to add Ultra's confirmation. Such Ultra evidence as there had been during the last few days supported von Rundstedt's conclusion on the evening of June 5 that there was nothing to suggest an invasion in the immediate future, and this was borne out by the first messages received that night. There were several reports about the unserviceability of coastal radar stations (they had been systematically bombed to ensure surprise), one of which was received in time to be signalled just as the landing craft were making for the beaches, and the Kriegsmarine seemed reassured by the discovery that 'some of the parachutists reported were straw dummies'.

REF: CX/MSS/T206/92
(ZTPG/248701)
2

KV 6546

ZZZ

((KV 6546 £ 6546 SH 40 £ 40 AG 21 £ 21 FU 76 £ 76
ST 22 £ 22 EF 2 £ 2 TA 59 £ 59 XF 50 £ 50 %

SEA DEFENCE COMMANDANT NORMANDY £ NORMANDY)) AWARE
AT TWO THREE FIVE FIVE HOURS FIFTH THAT QUOTE SOME OF
PARACHUTISTS REPORTED WERE STRAW DUMMIES UNQUOTE

BLOCK A/HDD

060132Z/6/44

GB

One of the earliest D-Day intercepts timed at 0132 Zebra, i.e. 0332 German time — the same as in Britain which was on Double British Summer Time.

REF: CX/MSS/207/69

KV 6673 IN TWO
PARTS, PART ONE

ZZ

((KV 6673 £ 6673 PK 51 £ 51 LM 83 £ 83 SB 69 £ 69 JY 28 £
28 CO 96 £ 96 SH 95 £ 95 AG 70 £
70 FU 26 £ 26 EF 57 £ 57 ST 80 £ 80 DL 78 £ 78 TA 8 £ 8
XF 76 £ 76 IN TWO PARTS, PART ONE %

FOLLOWING ACCORDING TO OKL £ OKL ON FIFTH. AS RESULT OF
RENEWED INTERFERENCE)) WITH PRODUCTION OF AIRCRAFT FUEL BY
ALLIED ACTION, MOST ESSENTIAL REQUIREMENTS FOR TRAINING AND
CARRYING OUT PRODUCTION PLANS CAN SCARCELY BE COVERED BY
QUANTITIES OF AIRCRAFT FUEL AVAILABLE. BAKER FOUR ALLOCATIONS
ONLY POSSIBLE TO AIR OFFICERS FOR BOMBERS, FIGHTERS AND
GROUND ATTACK AND DIRECTOR GENERAL OF SUPPLY. NO £ NO OTHER
QUOTA HOLDERS CAN BE CONSIDERED IN JUNE. TO ASSURE DEFENCE
OF REICH £ REICH AND TO PREVENT GRADUAL COLLAPSE OF
READINESS FOR DEFENCE OF GAF £ GAF IN EAST, IT HAS BEEN
NECESSARY TO BREAK INTO OKW £ OKW STRATEGIC RESERVE.
EXTENDING THEREFORE EXISTING REGULATIONS

WM/RAWB/RFB
GD

062347Z/6/44

REF: CX/MSS/T207/69

KV 6673 PART TWO
AND FINAL

ZZ

101

((KV 6673 £ 6673 PART TWO AND FINAL %

(COMMENT NO £ NO DETAILS HERE), ORDERED THAT ALL UNITS))
TO ARRANGE OPERATIONS SO AS TO MANAGE /A/ AT LEAST UNTIL THE
BEGINNING OF JULY WITH PRESENT STOCKS OR SMALL ALLOCATIONS
WHICH MAY BE POSSIBLE. DATE OF ARRIVAL AND QUANTITIES OF
JULY QUOTA STILL UNDECIDED. ONLY VERY SMALL QUANTITIES
AVAILABLE FOR ADJUSTMENTS, PROVIDED ALLIED SITUATION REMAINS
UNCHANGED. IN NO £ NO CIRCUMSTANCES CAN GREATER ALLOCATIONS
BE MADE. ATTENTION AGAIN DRAWN TO EXISTING ORDERS FOR MOST
EXTREME ECONOMY MEASURES AND STRICT SUPERVISION OF
CONSUMPTION, ESPECIALLY FOR TRANSPORT, PERSONAL AND
COMMUNICATIONS FLIGHTS. SUPPLY OF GOODS WHERE POSSIBLE
AND DUTY JOURNEYS IN GENERAL (IN REICH £ REICH AT LEAST)
TO BE BY RAIL. Above addressed to first Parachute Army.

062356Z/6/44

WM/RAWB/RFB
GB

Another D-Day intercept bearing Ralph Bennett's own initials confirmed what had already been noted in earlier signals: that there was now a critical fuel shortage due to Allied air raids on Romanian oil fields and German production plants.

REF. CX/MSS/T206/121 KV 6573
(ZTPG/248727
0421/6)

ZZZ

((KV 6573 £ 6573 SH 52 £ 52 AG 30 £ 30 FU 85 £ 85
ON 97 £ 97 DL 54 £ 54 ST 40 £ 40 EF 14 £ 14 TA 68 £
68 XF 55 £ 55 %

AT NOUGHT TWO TWO ONE HOURS SIXTH SEA DEFENCE
COMMANDANT NORMANDY £ NORMANDY)) REPORTED NO £ NO
RADAR LOCATIONS IN QUOTE SEA AREA TO NORTH EASTWARD
UNQUOTE OWING TO FAILURE OF RADAR APPARATUS

BMSL/HDD 060535Z/6/44.

Confusion in the enemy camp. Three hours before touchdown and still no sign of the Allied armada then closing the Normandy coast, due to all radar installations having been put out of action by Allied air attacks.

It was early afternoon before there was any sign that the scale of the landings had been properly appreciated. By then, the naval authorities in Normandy had decided that they were facing a major invasion although the possibility of another in Norway could not be ruled out, and there were soon plenty of indications that Cherbourg, Brest and the whole Breton coast were believed threatened. This was enough to show that the enemy had been thoroughly confused by the deception plan and was uncertain about Allied intentions, but the only early hint of German views about the Pas-de-Calais, the most important 'red herring' of all, was an order for extra flak protection for the Quilleboeuf ferry over the Seine — which suggested that the threat of FUSAG to this area, on which so much effort had been spent, might not prove enough to deter von Rundstedt from reinforcing the over-stretched 7. Armee by drawing on the resources of 15. Armee farther up the coast. Twenty-four hours later, it had been made very difficult for him to do this: all the Seine crossings from Conflans to Rouen had been bombed, and north-south road traffic was only possible by going as far upstream as Paris.

Ultra knew nothing of the war-game at Rennes which kept 7. Armee's divisional generals away from their posts on invasion night (save that the 319. Infanterie-Division in the Channel Islands was temporarily under the command of a deputy when it was put on the alert at 11.21 p.m. on June 5), nor of Rommel's absence on leave in Germany, and it was late with news of the first armoured counter-stroke although it got the essentials: the failure of the 21. Panzer-Division's hasty attack and the preparation of another by I. SS-Panzerkorps. The most immediately useful item during the first hours was probably the news that already by midday on June 6 the British drive towards Caen was alarming the Luftwaffe enough to make them contemplate evacuating Carpiquet airfield west of the city, but it evidently proved impossible to take advantage of their panic.

The air story was in fact very encouraging right from D-Day onwards. Warning of three raids on the beaches and on ships lying just offshore was given before the attacks took place, one with nearly four hours to spare. A comprehensive list of moves of aircraft to the West became available early on the morning of June 7; several single items had preceded it and more followed. Together, they showed that at least seven Gruppen of fighters, one of ground-attack aircraft and one of bombers, were coming from as far away as Austria and Hungary: in many cases, routes and destinations were given, making interception possible. If all these Gruppen were up to their proper strength, this means that within 36 hours of the landings, Ultra had accounted for nearly 300 of the 400-450 aircraft with which the Germans are now known to have reinforced their western front by June 10.

REF. CX/MSS/T207/61
(ZTPG/249024) KV 6635

WEST ZZZ

((KV 6635 £ 6635 SH 77 £ 77 AG 53 £ 53 FU 9
£ 9 ST 68 £ 68 EF 39 £ 39 TA 90 £ 90 XF 66 £ 66 %

ACCORDING GRUPPE WEST AT ONE FIVE HOURS SIXTH
COLON ALLIED LANDING DEAUVILLE £ DEAUVILLE -
ST VAAST £ ST VAAST)) NOW IN PROGRESS RECOGNISABLE
AS A MAJOR OPERATION. THE PROCLAMATION BY THE
ALLIED LEADERS AND THE DISPOSITIORS OF ALLIED
FORCES 7Ø POINTED TO FURTHER MAJOR OPERATIONS,
BUT NO £ NO DETAILS AVAILABLE REGARDING THEIR
TARGETS. ALL TO BE PREPARED FOR SURPRISE ATTACKS
IN FURTHER (STRONG INDICATIONS AREAS)

FHH/RFB/DJM 061850Z/6/44

By the afternoon of D-Day, although the landings were accepted as 'major', 'further major operations' were anticipated — evidence of the success of 'Fortitude'.

REF.CX/MSS/T208/1.   KV 6735 IN TWO PARTS,
PART ONE.

ZZZZ

((KV 6735 £ 6735 PK 89 £ 89 LU 21 £ 21 SB 99 £ 99
JY 46 £ 46/SH 30 £ 30 AG 2 £ 2 FU 57 £ 57 ON 43 £
43 EF 90 £ 90 ST 9 £ 9 DL 99 £ 99 TA 38 £ 38
IN TWO PARTS, PART ONE %

ARRANGEMENTS EVENING SIXTH. SECOND GRUPPE JIG ONE))
ARRIVING FLERS £ FLERS (COMMENT, AS IN KV £ KV SIX
SIX FOUR SEVEN FOURTHLY). THIRD GRUPPE JIG TWO SEVEN
(COMMENT, SEE KV £ KV SIX SEVEN NOUGHT ONE FOR MOVE)
ARRIVING ROMILLY £ ROMILLY. FOURTH GRUPPE JIG TWO
SEVEN ARRIVING CHAMPFLEURY £ CHAMPFLEURY (COMMENT,
THIS GRUPPE AT SZOMBATHELY £ SZOMBATHELY ON THIRTY-
FIRST). SECOND GRUPPE NAN JIG TWO ARRIVING
COULOMMIERS £ COULOMMIERS (COMMENT, GRUPPE AT KOELN
BUTZWEILERHOF £ KOELN BUTZWEILERHOF ON EIGHTEENTH). STAB

GP/AHW/KH   070813Z/6/44

REF. CX/MSS/T208/1   KV 6735 PART TWO
AND FINAL.

ZZZZ

((KV 6735 £ 6735 PART TWO AND FINAL %

AND ONE NAG £ NAG THIRTEEN ARRIVING DINARD £ DINARD))
(COMMENT, OTHER ELEMENTS ALREADY THERE SEE KV £ KV
SIX SIX THREE NINE). ZEBRA ONE WITH TWO GRUPPEN
ARRIVING LORIENT £ LORIENT. (COMMENT, FIRST AND
THIRD GRUPPEN HITHERTO IN WEST AND SECOND GRUPPE
IN AUSTRIA £ AUSTRIA). SECOND GRUPPE JIG FIVE
THREE ARRIVING VANNES £ VANNES (COMMENT, THIS GRUPPE
AT OETTINGEN-NOERDLINGEN £ OETTINGEN-NOERDLINGEN
ON TWENTYEIGHTH SEE KV £ KV SIX SIX SIX TWO). THREE
ISSUES (COMMENT, OF FUEL, AMMUNITION ETCETERA, ONE
ISSUE FOR ONE OPERATION) TO BE MADE TO EACH UNIT.
%/£ SPECIAL ORDERS (COMMENT, NO £ NO DETAILS)
REGARDING ISSUE OF TWO ONE CM £ CM MORTAR SHELLS
RETAIN VALIDITY

GP/AHW/KH   070818Z/6/44

On the evening of D-Day, Luftwaffe units were switched to the battle zone. By early next morning, Ultra reported the moves and the destinations. 'J' (Jig) standing for Jagd (fighter) Geschwader; 'NJ' (Nan Jig) for Nachtjagd (night fighter); 'NAG' is Nahaufklärung (short-range reconnaissance), and 'Z' for Zerstörer (twin-engined fighters).

An order that bombing attacks on ships off the beaches were to be pressed home determinedly ('No possibility is to be left untried') gave a hint of anxiety about the rate of Allied reinforcement as early as the morning of June 7. Hitler had already lost his one fleeting chance of catching the invaders before they were ready by at first refusing to grant von Rundstedt's immediate request for two armoured divisions (the 12. SS-Panzer-Division and the Panzer-Lehr-Division) from OKW reserve north of Orleans; too late, he now released these two and three more (the 2. Panzer-Division from Amiens, the 1. and 2. SS-Panzer-Divisions from the Antwerp and Toulouse areas respectively), together with the 17. SS-Panzergrenadier-Division from south of the Loire, and the 3. Fallschirmjäger-Division and the 77. Infanterie-Division from central and northern Brittany. Ultra had discovered all this by midday on June 8, save that faulty interception obscured the number of what was evidently the 2. SS-Panzer-Division, adding for good measure a panzer brigade known to be equipped with Panther and Tiger tanks, and some particulars about a planned counter-attack out of the Cherbourg peninsula on the American right wing.

REF.CX/MSS/T209/35   KV 6933

ZZZZ

((KV 6933 £ 6933 SH 46 £ 46 AG 3 £ 3 FU 58 £ 58
ON 24 £ 24 CR EF 2 £ 2 TA 38 £ 38 %

SEVENTH ARMY INFORMED BY (STRONG INDICATIONS ARMY
GROUP BAKER) ON SEVENTH OF NEW COVERNAMES)) FOR
FOLLOWING FORMATIONS COLON ONE SUGAR SUGAR PANZER
DIVISION, UNSPECIFIED SUGAR SUGAR PANZER DIVISION,
SEVENTEEN SUGAR SUGAR PANZER DIVISION, PANZER LEHR
DIVISION, PANZER BRIGADE TEN REPEAT TEN. COMMENT,
(ABLE) ONE SUGAR SUGAR PANZER LAST LOCATED AT TURNHOUT
£ TURNHOUT %IN FIFTEEN ARMY. (BAKER) PANZER BRIGADE
STAFF TEN CONTROLS PANTHERS £ PANTHERS, KV £ KV
ONE FIVE ONE TWO, AND WAS INCLUDED IN DISTRIBUTION
LIST OF ORDERS CONCERNING DELIVERY OF TIGER £ TIGER
AND PANTHER £ PANTHER TANKS TO ROMAN ONE PANZER
REGIMENT GROSSDEUTSCHLAND £ GROSSDEUTSCHLAND AND
SUGAR SUGAR PANZER ABTEILUNG ONE NOUGHT ONE RESPECTIVELY
((KV £ KV ONE EIGHT NINE ONE))
081313Z/6/44
TNLB/RFB/KH

Right: **One of several very pertinent signals decoded relevant to June 8, this one timed at 1313Z. Other messages revealed that 17. SS-Panzergrenadier-Division had been subordinated to 7. Armee on the 7th, destination Villedieu and that 'One Sugar Sugar Panzer Corps Battle How Queen' was now just south of Tourville from 1800 hours on the 8th.**

CX/MSS/T210/140 KV 7171

ZZZ

((KV 7171 £ 7171 SH 81 £ 81 AG 29 £ 29 FU 84 £ 84 ON 33 £ 33 CR EF 34 £ 34 TA 59 £ 59 %

BATTLE HQ £ HQ OF PANZER GRUPPE)) WEST HAD MOVED TO NEW ((LOCATION BY EVENING EIGHTH))

PCP/HYD/NH 092044Z/6/44

CX/MSS/T210/177 KV 7225

ZZZZ

((KV 7225 £ 7225 SH 23 £ 23 AG 67 £ 67 FU 23 £ 23 ON 56 £ 56 ONA CR YK 12 £ 12 ZE EF 13 £ 13 ST 34 £ 34 DL 77 £ 77 TA 94 £ 94

BATTLE HEADQUARTERS PANZER)) GRUPPE WEST EVENING NINTH AT LA CAINE £ LA CAINE (TARE NINE ONE FIVE TWO)

APGP/AHW/DC 100439Z/6/44.

One of the biggest drawbacks with Ultra was the restriction placed on commanders from taking direct action as a result of the information received, in case the Germans suspected that their codes had been broken. Therefore, if a particular target was identified, it had to be overflown by Allied aircraft so that the Germans would assume that any subsequent bombing attack was as a result of aerial reconnaissance. The fact that the 'I. SS-Panzerkorps Battle HQ' was south of Tourville was interesting intelligence but little could be done about it. However, three days after D-Day, a message *(left)* was intercepted at 2044Z announcing that the Battle HQ of Panzergruppe West had moved to a new, yet unspecified, location. The following morning at 0439Z on June 10, a second signal gave the precise location: La Caine, a tiny hamlet ten kilometres south-east of Villers-Bocage. Hut 3 added the map square reference.

When the 17. SS-Panzergrenadier-Division was put under Panzergruppe West (after an hour and a half directly under 7. Armee), this mobile strike command emerged briefly but disastrously from the shadows in which, so far as Ultra was concerned, it had lurked hitherto. General Geyr von Schweppenburg, its commander, did not reach Panzergruppe West's battle headquarters until June 8; just as he did so, and received his orders, Ultra twice reported the position of the headquarters, the second time with a pinpoint location. A bombing attack — clearly the result of these signals — was mounted against this headquarters on the 10th, and so many of Geyr's staff were killed or wounded that Panzergruppe West was not operational again for more than a fortnight. The counterstroke planned for the day of the raid was halted in its tracks (it was first put off for 24 hours and handed over to I. SS-Panzerkorps to direct, but then cancelled before it started), and the OKW War Diary speaks of a 'crisis'. 'We should have been better off without wireless', commented Rommel's chief of intelligence later, but he suspected nothing at the time because a British aircraft had been observed reconnoitring the target before the raid.

It was at about this moment that the initiative passed decisively to the Allies, and Ultra may justly claim a share of the credit for bringing the change about. By making it possible to wipe out Panzergruppe West's headquarters staff, Ultra helped to paralyse the nerve-centre of the armoured striking force and to frustrate Rommel's plan for a concentrated blow to split the bridgehead in two and drive the

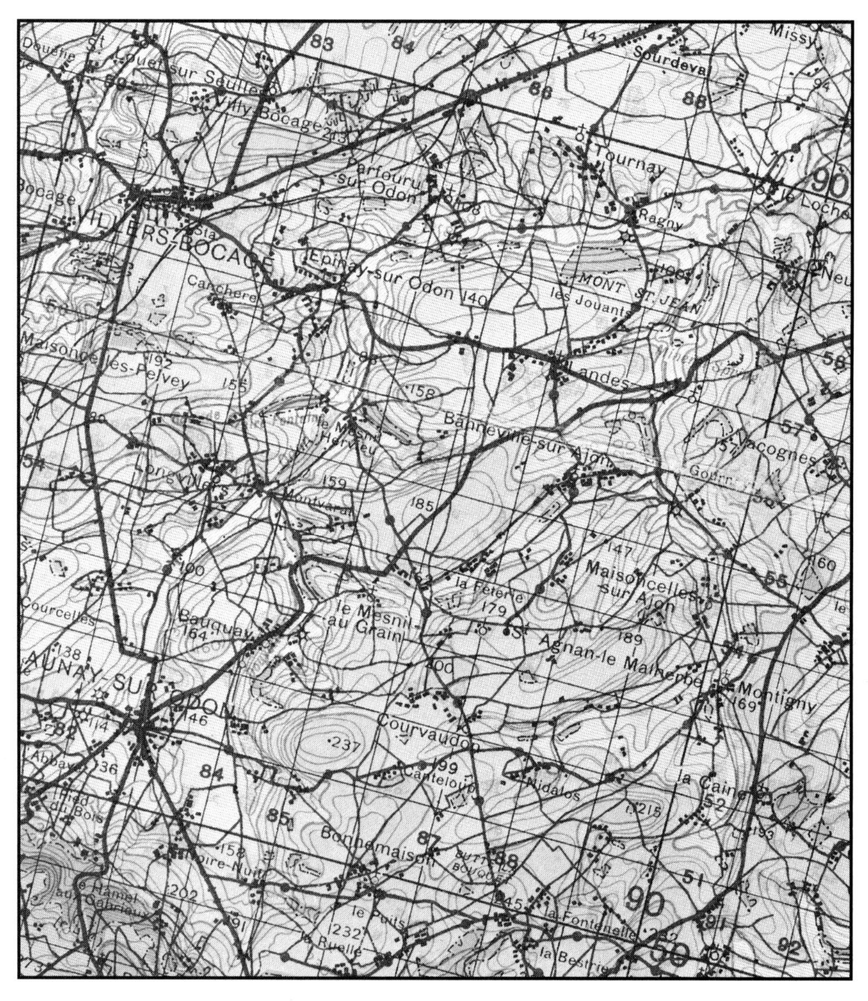

The discovery of the location of such an important German headquarters was one of Ultra's major contributions to achieving the Allied victory in Normandy. La Caine lies in map square T9152. (Extract from 1:100 000 GSGS 4249 Sheet 7F Caen-Falaise.)

La Caine — a hamlet of perhaps a dozen buildings set amidst orchards and open countryside — had already been photographed on May 30 from 26,000 feet.

invaders back into the sea. The consequence was to compound the mistake the German command had already made — that of frittering away its tanks in 'penny-packet' attacks — and to compel them to go on making the same mistake for lack of a workable alternative. Above all, it convinced both Rommel and von Rundstedt that their situation was very serious indeed.

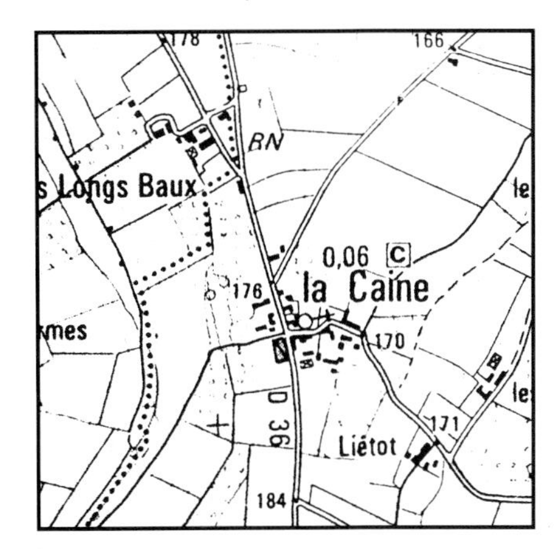

Below: **Bearing in mind over 400 bombs were dropped in the attack, as well as rocket strikes, this cover from 29,000 feet on July 6, some four weeks later, shows that only about a hundred bombs have landed in the village itself.**

The château survived remarkably intact. *Left:* **Pictured for the Bombing Analysis Unit in February 1945 and** *right:* **in 1994.**

BOMBING ANALYSIS UNIT SURVEY

1. At the request of HQ 2nd Tactical Air Force, a survey was made by the B.A.U. of the results achieved in a series of air attacks on localities believed to contain the headquarters of German military formations. The attack on LA CAINE (Map Ref. T.9152 GSGS 4250 Sheet 7/F3) proved to be the most successful of all those investigated, and it was therefore decided to carry out a more detailed investigation to obtain some evidence as to:

(i) The general accuracy of attack

(ii) The material damage inflicted on the Germans.

THE TARGET

2. The chateau at LA CAINE stands back from the main road in the centre of a small village. It has the usual out-buildings and is surrounded by trees. An orchard lies to the west of it.

3. Two days before the attack, a large formation of German troops arrived in the area, and the chateau was taken over for the headquarters. Two, and possibly three, generals were seen in the vicinity, and other officers were billeted in the village. The vehicles were parked in the orchards and under cover nearby.

4. It has been established from prisoner-of-war information, from the names of German officers killed, and from other sources, that this was the headquarters of the Panzer Group West, which later became known as the Fifth Panzer Army.

THE ATTACK

5. The attack was carried out by Mitchells and Typhoons of the 2nd Tactical Air Force on 10 June, 1944. 61 Mitchells were over the target from 2119-2121 hours and they dropped 426×500 lb. MC bombs attacking from 11-13,000 ft. The bombs dropped were fused Nose Instantaneous but some of them functioned with a slight delay. The crews reported that the target was blanketed by bombs and that there were many hits in and around the village.

6. Between 2102 and 2155 hours, 40 Typhoons attacked in three waves. One wave of 10 aircraft attacked with 80 RP [rocket projectiles]; *another, of 20 Typhoons, attacked with 128 RP, and the last 10 attacked with RP or guns.*

RESULTS

7. Fig. 1 shows a detailed plot of all the bomb craters within a quarter of a mile of the chateau. Craters at greater distances were not plotted owing to the fact that it was not possible to distinguish between bombs dropped during this attack and those dropped during subsequent attacks on other objectives in the vicinity.

8. The bombs dropped were fused Nose Instantaneous. Some, however, functioned with a delay. While only 130 craters were counted in the immediate vicinity of the chateau, it seems that some bombs detonated in the trees, since there were broken branches and fragment damage in the orchards in places fairly remote from craters. Owing, however, to the fact that six months had elapsed between the attack and the survey, it is not possible to be sure of this point. No rocket motors or other direct evidence of the RP attacks could be found.

9. Very little structural damage was found in the village, only two buildings being totally destroyed. There was, however, a large amount of blast damage to windows and roofs, and there were signs of considerable fragmentation in many areas. This type of damage is typical of 500lb bombs fused nose inst. The chateau itself had suffered little structurally. Although its windows and roofs were damaged, and its walls heavily pitted by fragments (and possibly also by gunfire), it was certainly not rendered uninhabitable by the attack.

Casualties

10. It is not known how many Germans were wounded, but it is certain that 18 of them, including the Chief-of-Staff of the Panzer Group West, were killed. They were buried in a bomb crater in the orchard. The inscription on the grave indicates that the following officers were killed: General Major Ritter und Edler von Dawans; Major i G Burgsthaler; Major i G von Waldow; Rittmeister Buchheim; Rittmeister Kuhl; S.S. Hstuf. Beck; Oblt. Fulig; Uffz. Ziedler (sic).

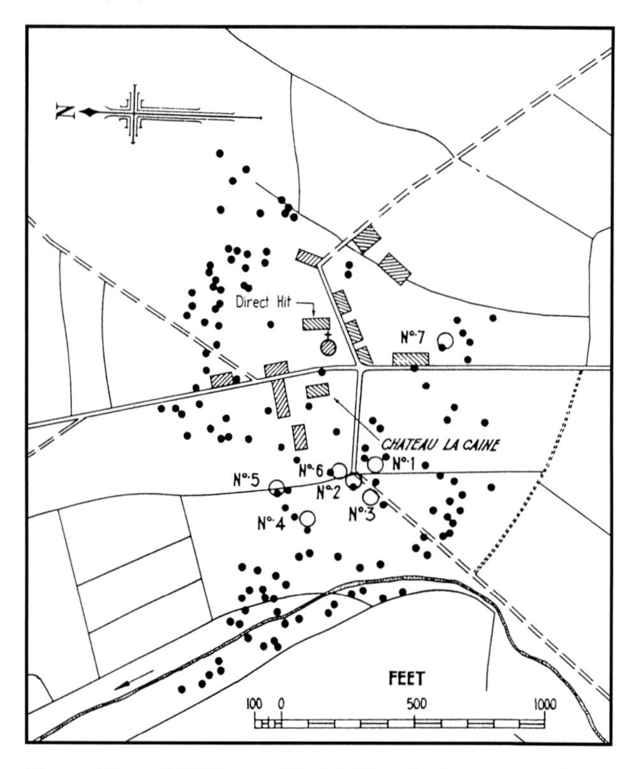

Figure 1 from BAU Report No. 24. The black spots signify HE bomb hits, the numbered circles individual incidents illustrated in the report.

It has been established from Intelligence sources that the staff positions held in the Panzer Group West by some of the officers killed were as follows: Gen. Maj. von Dawans, Chief-of-Staff; Maj. i G. Burgsthaler, Operations Officer; Maj. i G von Waldow, I.D. (Operations Training); Rittm. Kuhl, Assistant Intelligence Officer.

Damage to Vehicles

11. The following vehicles were damaged beyond repair and were abandoned by the Germans: 1 large mobile office; 1 large mobile mess; 1 large omnibus; 1 signals lorry; 1 large staff car; 2 small staff cars.

All these vehicles had been either burnt out or looted. Nearly all the damage to the vehicles was caused by fragments from bombs fused Nose Inst. It is noteworthy that a small staff car had been knocked out by a bomb fused Nose Inst. and had suffered no damage from a bomb which had fallen much nearer to it but whose fuse had functioned after a delay.

Effect of the attack on the Germans

12. The enemy left the chateau immediately after the attack, and the command of the Panzer Group West seems to have been completely disorganised. This is indicated by the following extract from the telephone log of the German 7th Army Headquarters:

'0920 hours 11 June 1944. G-3 (presumably of 7th Army) informs G-3 Army Group B that . . . the Panzer Group West has been knocked out by a direct hit on its Headquarters. Command has been given to the First Panzer Corps.'

13. It was learnt from a prisoner-of-war who had been ordered to report to the headquarters of the Panzer Group West that when he arrived at LA CAINE for duty on 11 June, 1944, the headquarters had departed. He also stated that shortly after this attack orders were received from the German High Command that in future no headquarters were to be set up in chateaux, and that they had to be established away from villages, and to have good cover from aerial observation. It seems probable that the LA CAINE attack was at least partly responsible for this order.

Incident 4. Three 500lb bombs detonated at 50ft, 90ft and 95ft from this lorry which appeared to have been used as a mobile mess vehicle.

Incident No. 5. A general's insignia was found beside this staff car struck by at least 200 bomb fragments.

The mass grave (No. 4 on plan), the inscription reading 'Es fielen am 10.6.44 für Grossdeutschland die Kameraden' followed by 17 names with one unknown: Generalmajor Ritter und Edler von Dawans, Major i.G.Burgsthaler, Major i. G. von Waldow, Rittmeister Buchheim, Rittmeister Kuhl, Oberleutnant Fuhg, Unteroffizier Ziegler, Obergefreiters Ludwig, Gunther, Thiele, and Hoppe, Gefreiters Hoeppner, Jurgensen and Lurkens, Oberschütze Kowalk and Schütze Lindemann together with SS-Hauptstürmführer Beck of the 12.SS. All the bodies were exhumed by a British graves detail and reburied at Le Mesnil-Auzouf and in 1957 the Volksbund Deutsche Kriegsgräberfürsorge moved the remains to a permanent resting place in the German War Cemetery at La Cambe (Block 30, Row 10, Graves 383-400 *above*) with Wilhelm Beck of the SS occupying a separate grave, No. 325, in Row 9 of Block 36.

Command Decisions

By Air Chief Marshal Sir Arthur W. Tedder
DEPUTY SUPREME ALLIED COMMANDER

The decision that a British airman should be Eisenhower's Deputy Supreme Commander raised complicated issues of command about which the Prime Minister, still convalescing in North Africa after his serious illness, lost no time in telegraphing to London. Both Eisenhower and his Chief-of-Staff, General Bedell Smith, spoke anxiously to Churchill about the arrangements for air command in 'Overlord'. They did not like the chain of command which put the British and the American tactical air forces under Air Chief Marshal Leigh-Mallory, the Air Commander-in-Chief, whose powers vis-à-vis the bomber commanders, Lieutenant General Spaatz and Air Chief Marshal Harris, would have to be defined. According to the Prime Minister's information, Harris had let it be known

Top: **It had already been decided that as the Supreme Commander was American, his deputy would be British. The selection of a senior RAF officer for the position was confirmation of the importance both Allied governments placed on air operations, and Air Chief Marshal Sir Arthur W. Tedder (left) was formally appointed Deputy Supreme Allied Commander on January 17, 1944. Sir Trafford Leigh-Mallory (right), who was the AOC RAF Fighter Command and held the identical rank to Tedder, had been proposed as the Allied Air Commander-in-Chief as far back as the spring of 1943. He had been unofficially acting in that position since he was designated to the rôle in August 1943 although his formal appointment did not take place until November 15. Following the agreed principle, his deputy was therefore an American, initially from January 1, 1944 Major General William O. Butler (rear), but replaced on March 25 by Major General Hoyt S. Vandenberg. This picture was taken ten days after Tedder's assumption as Eisenhower's deputy.**

The location was Bentley Priory at Stanmore, in north London, the HQ of RAF Fighter Command. Today, it is the headquarters of No. 11 Group, the organisation charged with the air defence of the United Kingdom. These are the steps leading to the garden from the terrace of the Priory itself which now serves as the Officers' Mess.

The visit on January 27 began with an inspection of the Guard of Honour provided by the RAF Regiment, Eisenhower's countenance undoubtedly reflecting the underlying mood. Things had already got off on the wrong foot, for instead of setting up his headquarters alongside the long-established one of his air commander, as Leigh-Mallory had expected, the new Supreme Commander had ill-advisedly agreed to a location 15 miles away (see page 23) which was to involve everyone in endless travelling and duplication of effort. Also, the overall command situation for air operations was far from satisfactory.

that he intended to be a real Commander-in-Chief of the Air. The post of Deputy Supreme Commander had been deliberately given to me because of the vast part the Air was to play in the battle for Europe, and Churchill insisted that I must have all the inherent powers: 'Tedder with his unique experience and close relation as Deputy to the Supreme Commander, ought to be in fact and in form the complete master of all the air operations. Everything is then quite simple. There need only be one Tactical Air Force which Leigh-Mallory can command. Spaatz will come directly under Eisenhower as his senior officer, and can be told to obey Tedder. There will be no difficulty in arranging between Tedder and Harris. I do not like the idea of Tedder being an officer without portfolio.'

In London, it was thought that these observations did not do justice to the complexity of the question. The Secretary of State for Air, Sir Archibald Sinclair, at once explained to the Prime Minister by telegram that the British tactical air force under 'Mary' Coningham would work with Montgomery's group of armies, while the American tactical air force under Brereton would also be used to support Montgomery in the initial stages of 'Overlord', but would ultimately work in the main with the American group of armies. Leigh-Mallory, as Commander-in-Chief, would be able to reinforce the one from the other, and was meanwhile in active command of both the British and American tactical air forces. Moreover, he was responsible for the air defence of Great Britain, and in the first stages of 'Overlord' would have to allocate forces between that commitment and the land battle. Leigh-Mallory must be the officer who would integrate with the operation of these tactical air forces the effort of heavy bombers which might be placed at his disposal by

With its excellent well-established procedures and communications, the underground operations room had been Air Chief Marshal Sir Hugh Dowding's command centre throughout the Battle of Britain in 1940. Then, Leigh-Mallory had been AOC of No. 12 Group, Fighter Command, covering central southern England; now, perhaps, Eisenhower is being given a lesson in history by Group Captain Ernest Stevens, the head of the Day Operations Branch.

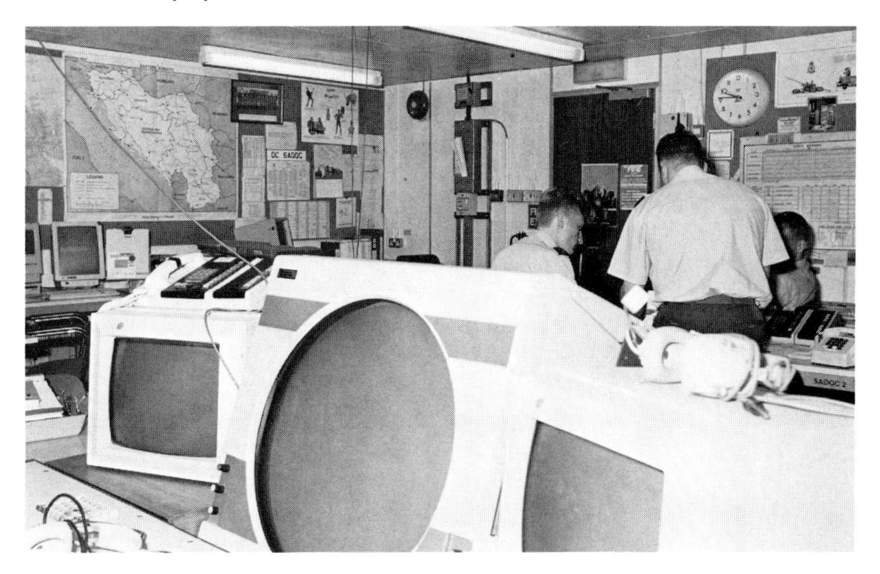

Fifty years later, higher formation displays and computer graphics have modernised the air defence systems in the reconstructed ops room, now the Standing Air Defence Operations Centre.

In his previous post, Tedder had been Air Commander-in-Chief of the Mediterranean Air Command (transformed into Mediterranean Allied Air Forces shortly before his return to the UK). In 1941, he had brought in a New Zealander, Air Marshal Arthur Coningham (right), nicknamed 'Maori', soon corrupted to 'Mary', as AOC Western Desert, a successful liaison that led to Coningham being put in charge of the Air Support Forces created to directly back up the ground forces as a 'tactical air force'. The idea was so successful that Coningham was withdrawn from Africa and, on January 21, 1944, appointed commander of the Second Tactical Air Force which had been established in June 1943 specifically for the assault on Europe.

the Chiefs-of-Staff. Sinclair was sure that it would be wrong to derogate from these responsibilities or to blur the line of definition between them and the responsibilities of Eisenhower and myself. Eisenhower would dictate strategy and policy. I should share his responsibility over the whole field of operations by land, sea, and air. The Secretary of State said that he hoped my experience and the confidence felt in my judgement by the Air Staff would ensure that liaison between the various air forces would be effective, and that differences of opinion would be resolved with goodwill: 'The Americans want to put Spaatz and Harris directly under Eisenhower. I am convinced that would be a mistake. Not even Tedder has experience of conducting the bomber offensive. Nor, if he is to be an effective deputy over the whole range of land, sea, and air, should he concentrate exclusively on air problems.'

The following day, January 8, 1944, the Chiefs-of-Staff explained to Churchill their view of the differences between command in the Mediterranean and that in the United Kingdom. Whereas in the Mediterranean Eisenhower had been supreme in all military matters, with all the forces under his command, he would while he remained in the United Kingdom be in practice a Task Force Commander. Other forces in Great Britain would further Eisenhower's plans, but would not accompany him to the Continent, and could not be placed under his sole control. Again, my position in the Mediterranean had given me centralised control of all the air forces there. This position at home was, in effect, held by Sir Charles Portal, Chief of the Air Staff, who was not only responsible for the Royal Air Force but was also the agent for the Combined Chiefs-of-Staff for the conduct of the strategic bombers until they might be placed under the Supreme Commander. Portal had already relinquished operational control of the forces commanded by Leigh-Mallory. These two officers, therefore, discharged in the UK the duties I had fulfilled in the Mediterranean.

The Chiefs-of-Staff agreed entirely with Churchill that I should not be an officer without portfolio and conceived that I should exercise authority over all three services. They realised that the existence of a Deputy Supreme Commander would make difficult Bedell Smith's position as Chief-of-Staff. This factor, they thought, explained his attitude and they reminded Churchill that I had been asked for by the Americans, not as a substitute for Leigh-Mallory, but as a deputy to Eisenhower. I should advise the Supreme Commander on the air aspects of the 'Overlord' plan, should speak in Eisenhower's name to his subordinates on air subjects, and listen to their views. The Chiefs-of-Staff, like Sinclair, did not contemplate that the strategic air forces should pass under Eisenhower's command, lock, stock and barrel.

Churchill agreed at once that this discussion concerned only the forces that had been definitely handed over. The rest would remain under the control of Portal and the Chiefs-of-Staff. Nevertheless: 'I do not know that Tedder is any great authority on war in general, and certainly not in the use of armies and fleets. He has, however, proved himself a master in the use of the Air Force, and this is the task I hoped he would have assigned to him by the Supreme Commander in the same way as Alexander was entrusted with fighting the land battles in Sicily and Italy. As Tedder is only to be a sort of floating kidney, we shall be wasting him and putting more on Leigh-Mallory than in my opinion he can carry.'

The Prime Minister said that he felt sure that Eisenhower would raise these matters as soon as he took over. He did. Eisenhower and I had many talks over the problems ahead. As far as I can remember, the point that worried him most was what his relations were going to be with Harris. Harris was by way of being something of a dictator who had very much the reputation of not taking kindly to directions from outside his own command. Eisenhower saw rocks ahead. Bomber Command had a tremendous and greatly responsible rôle to play in 'Overlord'. If Harris chose to be 'difficult' in his relationships with the Air Ministry, there might well be endless scope for friction. I did my best to reassure Eisenhower by telling him that I was quite certain that if Harris were given specific orders to carry out specific jobs, he would do them loyally. I realised that in giving such a guarantee, I was taking a chance which many people would not have risked, but, as it turned out, my estimate of Bomber Command's work, and of its commander, proved to be correct.

Coningham's Second TAF headquarters was set up in Ramslade House at Bracknell, Berkshire. Today, this building serves as the Officers' Mess for the new RAF Staff College which was built in 1969-70.

The commander of the American tactical air force for the invasion had already been selected back in July 1943 — Lieutenant General Lewis H. Brereton *(left)*, then in the Middle East with the Ninth Air Force having worked closely with Air Marshal Coningham. However, to save the logistical problem of moving a whole air force, it was largely a 'paper' transaction with only headquarters personnel moving to Britain, the combat units of the Ninth being re-assigned to the Twelfth Air Force while the Eighth Air Force in Britain was ordered to surrender the whole of the VIII Air Support Command, including its headquarters *(above)* at Sunninghill Park, near Ascot, Berkshire, to form the 'new' Ninth Air Force, as well as IX Air Service Command acquiring the Tactical Air Depot Area. On October 16, General Brereton arrived after having been briefed on his new duties in Washington.

We had to decide, and promptly, by what methods our air strength could contribute most surely to the re-establishment of the Allied armies in France. To put the matter in its broadest terms, there were two types of target for air attack: point targets and common denominators. Examples of the first category were aluminium plants, ball-bearing plants, molybdenum mines or army headquarters, points from which crucial operations were controlled, or at which vital industries could profitably be attacked. Such targets were tartly dismissed by Sir Arthur Harris as 'panaceas'. Common denominator targets were railways, canals, power plants, oil; that is, targets which were geographically dispersed, the destruction of which would cumulatively affect the whole war situation.

In an endeavour to select objectives which could be effectively dealt with, a number of new directives succeeded each other until the Casablanca Conference of 1943, out of which was developed a completely new directive: our growing bomber force was 'to secure the progressive destruction and dislocation of the German military, industrial, and economic system, and the undermining of the morale of the German people to a point where their capacity for armed resistance is fatally weakened'. This directive was nothing if not comprehensive, and allowed unlimited scope for our differences of interpretation.

The Air Plan, as developed in the summer of 1943, laid down three phases of activity. The first would be the continuation of strategic bombing of Germany, especially of the German aircraft industry; the second phase would be the bombing of targets closely linked with the invasion, especially railway centres, coastal defence installations, harbours, and airfields; the third phase would be direct assistance to the invading ground forces.

Although Leigh-Mallory had, in November, assumed control of the two tactical air forces, by January it was apparent that the scale of air effort needed before and after the 'Overlord' landings would be far beyond the capacity of these forces alone to provide. The strategic air forces must be brought in. As expected, Air Chief Marshal Harris showed himself by no means enthusiastic. Early in the New Year, he stated in writing that the only efficient support which Bomber Command could give to 'Overlord' was the intensification of attacks on industrial centres in Germany. To substitute for this process attacks on other targets such as gun emplacements, beach defences, communications or dumps, would be to 'commit the irremediable error of diverting our best weapon from the military function for which it has been equipped and trained to tasks which it cannot effectively carry out. Though this might give a specious appearance of supporting the Army, in reality it would be the greatest disservice we could do them. It would lead directly to disaster.'

This clear-cut opinion was, broadly speaking, shared by General Spaatz, who had just assumed command of the US strategic air forces in Europe.

It was at this point that Eisenhower, Montgomery, Bedell Smith and I arrived in London from the Mediterranean.

Brereton's prestigious Ninth Air Force headquarters, which had been built in 1770, burned down in 1947 just before the newly-married Princess Elizabeth and the Duke of Edinburgh were due to take up residence. The original lakeside site was completely cleared, a new high-security 'Sunninghill Park' being built in the 1980s for the Duke and Duchess of York a few hundred yards away to the north.

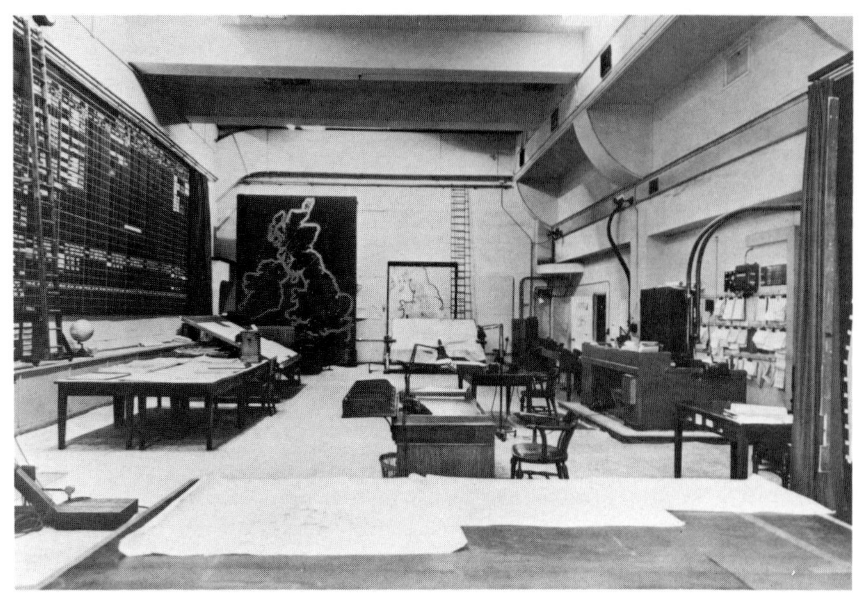

Although Leigh-Mallory was officially the Allied Air C-in-C, in reality he had only control over part of the air forces which would contribute towards 'Overlord', and even then national prerogatives and personal rivalry both played a part in reducing the effectiveness of his control. Air Chief Marshal Sir Arthur T. Harris *(left)* had commanded RAF Bomber Command since February 1942, and had his own very firm ideas of how the war should be prosecuted, believing that 'strategic' bombing alone would eventually bring victory. Harris' command of the RAF's heavy bomber force, which had not been assigned to Leigh-Mallory's control, was exercised from Bomber Command HQ, code-named 'Southdown', situated at Walter's Ash, some three miles north of High Wycombe in Buckinghamshire.

For the moment, we had to decide when we should start bombing for 'Overlord' and which targets we should attack. The new plan, based on my Mediterranean experience, was to paralyse the railways by systematic attack on railway centres, and came to be known as the Transportation Plan.

Although there were only another three months or so of the pre-'Overlord' period, the situation in London in the middle of February was confused, to say the least. The Prime Minister, the War Cabinet, and the Chiefs-of-Staff had not yet decided who was to control which portions of which air forces, let alone upon what targets these air forces should be directed. No agreed bombing policy for the pre-'Overlord' period had been decided, and neither of the bomber commanders, Harris or Spaatz, believed in the Transportation Plan. Leigh-Mallory and I were however putting our weight behind it, although earlier he had been opposed to it.

To bring the strategic bomber forces into the pre-'Overlord' operations, which Leigh-Mallory and I agreed was essential, would mark a transition in the history of Allied air-power. As bomber techniques had improved, the bomber forces had developed a rôle virtually independent of the Army, the Navy, and the other air forces. Until the last days of 1943, the strategic bombers provided the only means by which we could strike heavily at Germany itself. Now, we faced the position that unless this comparatively independent rôle were partially abandoned, 'Overlord', at least in the opinion of those responsible for its planning, could not succeed.

Meanwhile, Portal had proposed at the end of February that the practicability of attack on railway centres should be put to the test. A week later, on the night of March 6/7, the railway centre at Trappes was devastated by Bomber Command. Not for a month did this centre function again properly. Other yards were quickly attacked in succession. The results showed beyond peradventure that Harris had underestimated the skill of his crews. The Transportation Plan was shown to be feasible. Here was a development of the highest importance, and coming at exactly the right moment. Our capacity to undertake precision bombing, purchased at grim cost, now made it possible for us to advocate with confidence a programme which entirely depended on the accurate delivery of bombs. Once this was understood, the complexities became less hard to resolve. The main question would be one of timing. It was accepted by Spaatz and Harris that, immediately before and after the battle, their forces must be devoted to the success of 'Overlord'. Leigh-Mallory and I argued, on the other hand, that paralysis of the French railway system could not be achieved in a week or two. Unless we did the job properly, there would be little advantage in trying to do it at all; and if we did decide on the Transportation Plan, it must be carried out with our full resources. Even though the alternative was heavy damage to the German synthetic oil plants, that could not vitally affect the enemy's efforts in time for 'Overlord'.

On February 7, 1944, Harris received a visit from King George VI and Queen Elizabeth at the height of Bomber Command's Operation 'Pointblank' aimed at the destruction of the German fighter forces and the industry which they defended. Not until April 14 — less than two months before D-Day — did the Combined Chiefs-of-Staff direct that 'Overlord' should take priority over 'Pointblank'.

Almost in the centre of High Wycombe lay the parallel headquarters of the American strategic bombing force in Britain. When Brigadier General Ira C. Eaker arrived in Britain in February 1942 as the commander of the embryonic VIII Bomber Command, he was offered the use of a brand-new underground command bunker that the RAF had constructed beneath Daws Hill which lay behind the headquarters established in Wycombe Abbey School. ***Left:*** **This became the nerve-centre of VIII Bomber Command, code-named 'Pinetree', under Brigadier General Newton Longfellow, command passing on July 1, 1943 to Brigadier General Frank L. Anderson, seen here on the right escorting the US Secretary of War, Henry L. Stimson, on an inspection of the operations room on July 13, 1943.** ***Right:*** **The Daws Hill complex was relinquished by the Americans in 1946 but re-occupied by the 7th Air Division of the Strategic Air Command in 1951. This picture, taken 25 years later, shows the then base commander, Major Jerry McKenna, in the underground operations room, reportedly unused since 1970.**

During the first ten days of March, I saw or spoke with Portal almost every day as he struggled to reconcile the difference between Eisenhower's wish for complete control of the heavy bombers and the Prime Minister's ruling that Bomber, Fighter, and Coastal Commands could not be handed over as a whole to Eisenhower or to me. Eisenhower recognised that reservations would in practice exist upon the power of any commander, whether called 'Supreme' or not. It would always be possible for the Combined Chiefs-of-Staff to impose additional tasks, and for the British Chiefs-of-Staff to act independently in the case of an unforeseen emergency concerning the safety of Great Britain. The Supreme Commander wished to see such reservations included, and his agreement with them noted in the records; but he did not want to put them in the specific directive to the Supreme Commander. I put these arguments to the Chief of the Air Staff on March 9. He seemed willing to accept them. With Eisenhower's agreement, Portal therefore minuted to the Prime Minister on March 10 that the strategic air plan for 'Overlord' was now in my hands as Eisenhower's agent. I was dealing with Spaatz and Harris over their parts in the plan. It was Eisenhower's intention, with which Portal agreed, that the co-ordination of operations for the strategic plan should be under my control, with such reference to Eisenhower as he desired. The tactical plan around the D-Day assault involving the use of all air forces assigned to 'Overlord', including strategic bombers, coastal aircraft, and the Fleet Air Arm contingent, would be prepared and co-ordinated by Leigh-Mallory under my supervision.

It was proposed that when Portal and Eisenhower approved the air programme, the responsibility for supervising air operations out of Great Britain of all forces engaged in the programme, together with any other air forces that might be made available, should devolve upon Eisenhower. The strategic air forces were only to come under Eisenhower's direction when a plan for the air support of 'Overlord' had been approved. Even though the question was now becoming so urgent, this day still appeared to be somewhat distant.

In September 1976, three former wartime commanders came together again in High Wycombe for a combined double ceremony. Marshal of the Royal Air Force Sir Arthur Harris (centre) unveiled a commemorative plaque at Daws Hill (then in limbo since the 7563rd Air Base Squadron of the United States Air Forces in Europe left in January 1971), while General Ira Eaker (right) carried out a similar duty at the RAF base, by then the HQ of Strike Command. Also present was (left) General James Doolittle who had replaced General Eaker in January 1944 when the latter became commander of the Mediterranean Allied Air Forces.

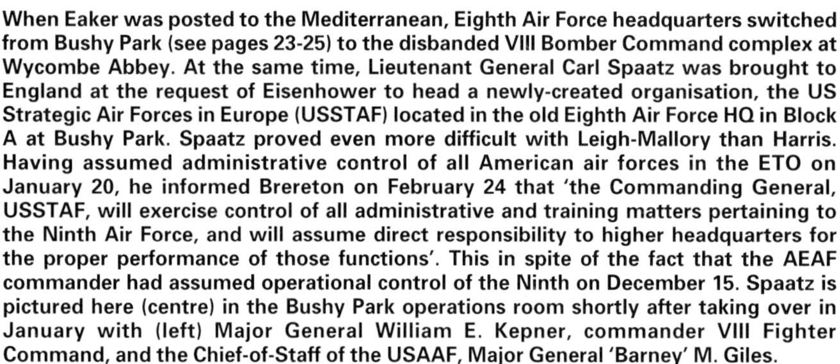

When Eaker was posted to the Mediterranean, Eighth Air Force headquarters switched from Bushy Park (see pages 23-25) to the disbanded VIII Bomber Command complex at Wycombe Abbey. At the same time, Lieutenant General Carl Spaatz was brought to England at the request of Eisenhower to head a newly-created organisation, the US Strategic Air Forces in Europe (USSTAF) located in the old Eighth Air Force HQ in Block A at Bushy Park. Spaatz proved even more difficult with Leigh-Mallory than Harris. Having assumed administrative control of all American air forces in the ETO on January 20, he informed Brereton on February 24 that 'the Commanding General, USSTAF, will exercise control of all administrative and training matters pertaining to the Ninth Air Force, and will assume direct responsibility to higher headquarters for the proper performance of those functions'. This in spite of the fact that the AEAF commander had assumed operational control of the Ninth on December 15. Spaatz is pictured here (centre) in the Bushy Park operations room shortly after taking over in January with (left) Major General William E. Kepner, commander VIII Fighter Command, and the Chief-of-Staff of the USAAF, Major General 'Barney' M. Giles.

As Eisenhower's air troubleshooter, Air Chief Marshal Tedder tried to reconcile the differences but, even if the American and British heavy bombers had been available, there was still no general agreement as to their best use. Three months were wasted in argument before some consensus appeared at a meeting held at the end of March, chaired by Marshal of the Royal Air Force Sir Charles Portal *(above)*. He had been the Chief of the Air Staff since October 1940 and had not taken sides, although favouring the destruction of the Luftwaffe as a first priority.

When the principal 'Overlord' commanders met on March 10, 1944, there appeared to be general agreement that the best methods of employing our strategic air forces in those three months before D-Day would be first the destruction of the German Air Force as laid down in 'Pointblank', and secondly the disruption of the French transportation system. Within a couple of days of that meeting, two memoranda had been circulated, one from the US Air Force and one from the Air Ministry, both of them largely occupied in erecting 'Aunt Sallies'. The case against the Transportation Plan rested on two main planks — neither of them being in accord with the facts. The first proposition was that the French and Belgian railway systems were by no means fully stretched and that their ability to repair was virtually unlimited. The second proposition was that the essential military traffic in northern France represented only a small percentage of the existing traffic, and that, therefore, only a small proportion of the railway system need be kept in working order. On the former point, there had evidently been a complete failure to appreciate the intensity, variety and far-reaching nature of the damage caused by a serious attack on an important railway centre. As for the latter point, it was stated in the American paper that military traffic in Axis Europe would not at

As far as the American tactical fighter force was concerned, there was less controversy. The IX Fighter Command was commanded by Brigadier General Elwood R. Quesada (second left), who had already achieved a formidable reputation as a fighter commander in the Middle East. By the end of November 1943, he had established his headquarters at the airfield of Middle Wallop in Hampshire. *Left:* Here he is pictured visiting the squadron commanders of the 368th Fighter Group which was based at nearby Chilbolton. *Right:* Fifty years later, the administrative area looks somewhat different, although the outlines of the Nissen (or Quonset) hutting can still be traced in the concrete.

The RAF had created the Second Tactical Air Force within Fighter Command based around the nucleus of No. 83 (Composite) Group. Other units were transferred in from Bomber Command (No. 2 Group); Army Co-operation Command (No. 38 Airborne Wing) which then ceased to exist as a separate entity; and No. 145 Photo-Reconnaissance Squadron. A totally new group, No. 84, was also formed. At the same time, the title of 'Fighter Command' was dropped and, instead, the pre-war designation 'Air Defence of Great Britain' (ADGB) was given to the eight groups that remained under its commander, Air Marshal Sir Roderic M. Hill *(left)*, appointed November 15, 1943. *Right:* On February 29, 1944, ADGB and SHAEF approved the release of pictures of the new Anglo-American tactical air chiefs taken during a conference on February 9 at Stanmore. L–R: Air Marshal Hill, Major General Butler, Air Chief Marshal Leigh-Mallory, Air Vice-Marshal Philip Wigglesworth (Senior Air Staff Officer, Allied Expeditionary Air Force), Brigadier General Auby C. Strickland (Deputy Senior Air Staff Officer), Lieutenant General Brereton (seated in the foreground), and Air Marshal Coningham (extreme right).

its maximum be more than one-fifth of the total traffic. On the American plan I felt 'that the German Air Force (which should include the bomber aircraft production) should remain as absolute first priority. I am frankly sceptical of the Oil Plan, partly because we have been led up that garden path before, partly because the targets are in difficult areas (six of them in the Ruhr, where we have been assured that the Americans could not do precision bombing on railway targets because of flak and smoke, and the most important ones in the areas south and south-west of Berlin, where penetration is most difficult), and partly because I am not sure as to the real vulnerability of the new synthetic oil plants, where the enemy has presumably taken immense precautions against an air attack by means of dispersal, protection, etc. I am even less impressed by the arguments advanced for the tank targets as a help for "Overlord".'

Portal, while refusing at this stage to take sides in the controversy, fully agreed with me that the German Air Force should remain an absolute priority. He was not at all sure that we should not find that to wipe out the German Air Force would take the whole available strategic bomber effort, and that if this could be done we should not have an 'Overlord' operation to tackle but something on the lines of a police operation, where swift mobile columns could readily penetrate and subdue a tottering Nazi empire. Even if this latter assumption were not true, Portal doubted whether the Germans could stage an effective counter-attack against 'Overlord' if their air force had been wiped out beforehand.

I felt a good deal less sanguine than did the Chief of the Air Staff about the possibility of knocking out the German Air Force in time. In any case, I was sure that any such policy was too much of a gamble. We were now approaching the end of March. D-Day was to be at the beginning of June. We could not stake everything on attacking the German Air Force at this late date.

General Montgomery asked that before D-Day the air forces should try to knock out the enemy air force, to destroy and disrupt communications so as to impose delay on enemy movement towards the landing ground, to mislead the enemy as to the real point of attack, and to assault such targets as coastal batteries and oil installations. This order of priorities accorded very much with my own views. I had by now received from the Joint Intelligence Committee a document on enemy rail movements which, if accepted, would have ruled out the dislocation which the Army commanders demanded. The paper made two main assumptions: first, that essential military movements by rail could be cut down to an extremely low figure, and second, that all other rail movement could be dispensed with indefinitely. The enemy was estimated, for no apparent reason, to possess some two months' stocks ready for intensive operations. The movement of traffic for the enemy forces in the Normandy area,

Together with Wing Commander David Asplin, President of the Mess Committee, we checked all the rooms in Bentley Priory and the most likely location for the February 9 meeting was here in the Abercorn Room, since altered by the removal of a dividing wall to create the bar for the Mess.

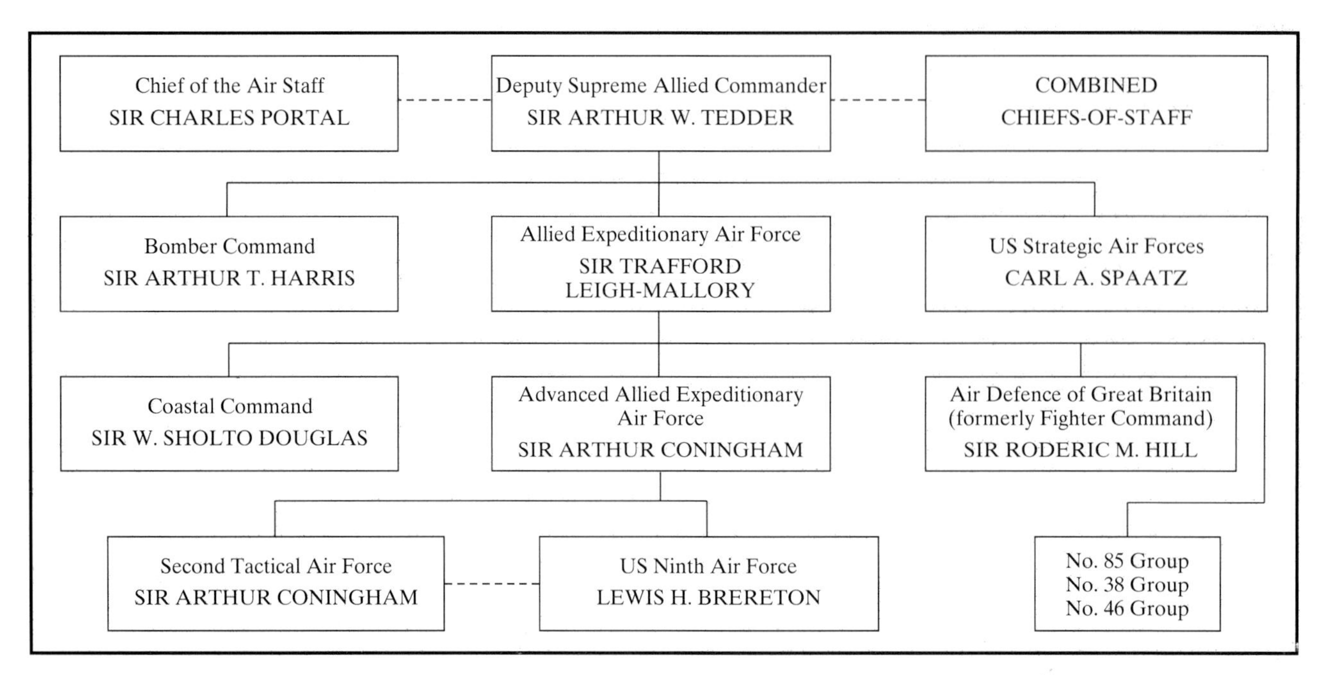

As if command of the air phase of 'Overlord' was not already complicated enough, once direction of the strategic forces passed to Eisenhower (on April 14), he instructed Tedder to act as an intermediary between Harris, Spaatz and Leigh-Mallory. Tedder felt that air operations could more easily be organised at one location, so the Air Operations Planning Staff at SHAEF was moved to Bentley Priory. However, Leigh-Mallory considered it essential that 'the air operations in immediate and direct support of the land battle should be specially co-ordinated and directed. I, therefore, decided to establish a small operational organisation to be known as Advanced Allied Expeditionary Air Force. Under my general direction, the Commander Advanced AEAF was given the task of directing and co-ordinating the planning for and operations of such forces of the Ninth Air Force and Second Tactical Air Force as were allotted to him from time to time.' Apart from his existing duties, Air Marshal Coningham was therefore appointed the commander of the Advanced AEAF 'on detachment from the Second TAF', an arrangement which introduced an additional level for the same man in the chain of command as shown above.

however, certainly did not suggest that the Germans felt able to sit back with ample stocks. We knew, from reconnaissance and from intelligence sources, that the enemy's road and rail transport was already strained. We also knew beyond doubt that the enemy hoped he might be able to keep open the three main routes from the east by manning those routes entirely with German personnel. The Joint Intelligence Committee, like the intelligence section of the Air Ministry and General Spaatz's staff, failed to appreciate how complex an organisation is a railway system, and how air-power's main characteristic, its flexibility, made it possible to retain the initiative. I was also surprised to find in this document an estimate for the German Air Force's required supplies around D-Day which was considerably less than they were already receiving. The whole basis of the figures, as I told Portal at once, seemed to me academically unrealistic. To talk of military traffic in a strictly limited way was quite misleading. Moreover: 'If the country in which an army is operating is not kept alive, it will itself become a heavy commitment on that army. Neptune area [Normandy] is not self-supporting, and I am certain the Hun cannot afford to turn off the tap. Incidentally, in all these calculations the JIC make no allowance whatever for any transverse traffic, either of military or para-military needs.'

Against such calculations we had to put concrete evidence already obtained after attacks on railway centres. A comparatively light assault on Tergnier had resulted in a seven days' delay in the movement southwards of an SS division. At Amiens, the strong attack on the night of March 15/16 brought railway working to a complete standstill. A week later, access to the marshalling yard was still barred. On the night of March 23/24, a strong attack on Creil laid both the engine sheds flat. Both lines to Paris and the lines to Beauvais were cut at least 20 times. The attack on the night of March 13/14 at Le Mans proved so effective that ten days later normal operation was still suspended and only 50 per cent of the sidings had been repaired. The attack at Trappes had caused the immobilisation of some

When Brereton heard of the new arrangement, he hit the roof. 'I am 100 per cent opposed to it', he wrote in his diary, 'because it subordinates one air force to the control of the commander of another . . . It is out of the question, as far as I am concerned, and it is my opinion that Leigh-Mallory is being continually needled by General Montgomery in this matter.' Monty, it appears, used the situation to his advantage in a classic case of divide and rule, choosing to deal with Leigh-Mallory for heavy bomber support, and direct with the AOC of No. 83 Group, Air Vice-Marshal Harry Broadhurst, on tactical matters! In the event, the HQ of the Advanced AEAF

60 locomotives, and, even at the end of March, only one half of the marshalling yard was available for traffic. At that time, nearly a month after the original attack, the standards carrying the electric cables over the main line had still not been re-erected, although the line was open for steam working. All these results had been secured by bombing of a comparatively unplanned nature.

The choice lay between Spaatz's Oil Plan and the Transportation Plan. No one could doubt that, in view of the proved ability of the American strategic forces to carry out precision bombing deep in Germany, the Oil Plan would ultimately produce grave effects on the whole German war effort. I did not think, however, that such effects would be produced in time.

On March 25 there was, I had hoped, to be the crucial meeting with the final decisions. Spaatz argued his familiar case about oil, but had to admit, when questioned by Portal, that there would be no noticeable effect until four or five months after putting the plan into action. Harris doubted whether there was time for him to complete his programme now in the short period remaining. He wanted to continue attacking cities in eastern Germany as long as the hours of darkness made it possible. He also raised the question of high casualties. Portal put the point to Churchill in a Minute a few days later: 'In the execution of this Plan, very heavy casualties among civilians living near the main railway centres in occupied territory will be unavoidable, however careful we may be over the actual bombing. Eisenhower realises this and I understand that he is going to propose that warnings should be issued to all civilians living near railway centres advising them to move. I hope you will agree that since the requirements of "Overlord" are paramount, the Plan must go ahead after due warning has been given.'

Another personality on the air scene was the AOC-in-C of Coastal Command, Air Chief Marshal Sir Sholto Douglas (left), seen here in his operations room on June 6, 1944. His HQ was sited next to the naval headquarters at Northwood, Middlesex, for close liaison with the Royal Navy. With Douglas are (L–R) Air Vice-Marshal Aubrey Ellwood, Senior Air Staff Officer, Captain Dudley 'PW' Peyton-Ward, Senior Naval Liaison Officer, and Lieutenant J. Sobieski, US Navy Liaison Officer.

At long last, a decision on the bombing plan was arrived at on a military level. Eisenhower's authority as Supreme Commander, coupled with his definite view of the most-valuable contribution which air power could make, virtually settled the matter. It was also clear that the Chief of the Air Staff now thought that the Transportation Plan offered more prospect of success than any other.

It now went before the War Cabinet with a list of more than 70 railway targets in France and Belgium. The Bomber Command estimate of high civilian casualties, perhaps between 80,000 and 160,000, caused the Cabinet on April 3 to take an adverse view. It was decided that the Defence Committee must consider the matter later that week. The Cabinet feared that to inflict death and injury upon scores of thousands of friendly civilians might bring much hatred upon the Allied air forces. The Ministers were by no means convinced that the military advantages would outweigh the obvious political drawbacks. 'The argument for concentration on these particular targets', Churchill wrote to Eisenhower, 'is very nicely balanced on military grounds.'

Eisenhower consulted me about his reply. We fully understood that the weight of argument which had been brought against the bombing of railway centres in occupied territory was, indeed, heavy, but in our view other considerations were even weightier.

Eisenhower had understood from a recent conversation with Churchill that it was intended to invite General de Gaulle to come to London soon. The Supreme Commander thought that the General should be able to explain the matter to the French nation in such a way that they would accept these bombings as a necessary sacrifice. This note went to the Prime Minister on April 5. That night, I attended the first of a series of meetings, lasting over the next month, at which the fate of the Transportation Plan was decided. We foregathered at 10.30 p.m. in the Defence Map Room, two floors below ground, in the Cabinet Offices. The Prime Minister presided. My memorandum, asking for permission to attack railway centres,

was set up at Uxbridge on May 1, using the old Battle of Britain operations room *(left)*. The Combined Control Centre, manned by a joint British-American staff with representatives from IX Fighter Command and VIII Fighter Command, was operated by the AOC of No. 11 Group. *Right:* The same operations room had also been used during the Dieppe Raid in August 1942 but, when it was restored as a museum piece in 1975, it reverted to how it had appeared at 11.30 a.m. on September 15, 1940, when Churchill watched the battle unfold while sitting up in the glass-fronted Senior Controller's box.

On April 21, while the pros and cons of the transportation bombing plan were still being fiercely debated, there came a moment of light relief when all the major players — a total of two Generals and nine assorted Air Marshals, headed by Eisenhower, Tedder, Leigh-Mallory, Brereton, Broadhurst, Coningham and Hill, gathered with 14 Group Captains, 33 Wing Commanders and others in the Officers' Mess at RAF Tangmere, in Sussex, for a celebratory dinner. The previous day, Eisenhower had inspected the squadrons of No. 84 Group stationed in the area, and also the forward air operations control centre which had been established in Bishop Otter College in Chichester (see page 155).

had been circulated in advance, together with the report on probable reactions of French and Belgian opinion. Churchill said that, even if rail communications were essential, he was not convinced that the effects which would be achieved by attacks on rail centres would justify the slaughtering of masses of friendly French allies who were burning to help us when the day came, and who showed their friendly feelings by giving unstinted help to our airmen forced down among them. He did not say that we should not bomb the railways, but that before we did so we must be convinced that the advantages counted for more than the political drawbacks.

At the War Cabinet meeting of April 27, it was agreed that the Transportation Plan should now be revised to include attacks only on railway centres where the estimated casualties did not exceed 100 to 150. Meanwhile, Churchill would telegraph to Roosevelt after seeing Eisenhower. On April 29, the Supreme Commander received from the Prime Minister a note of the conclusions reached by the Cabinet on April 27, together with a summary of the arguments which had weighed with them. These arguments ran on familiar lines. The Government did not feel sure that the Transportation Plan would actually bring great military advantages. Would it not, the Prime Minister asked, be a good thing to invite the American Air Force, perhaps in conjunction with the Directorate of Bombing Operations in the Air Ministry, to produce a plan within the next few days for employing the strategic air forces in such a way that not more than, say, a hundred French lives should be sacrificed on any target? If this plan proved to be vastly inferior to the Transportation Plan, the arguments in favour of the latter would be strengthened, and the Government could be more easily convinced that the political disadvantages must be overridden.

Eisenhower asked me to draft a reply for him. I pointed out that in deference to the strong political objections raised by the Cabinet, instructions had already been given that some of the targets should be attacked at a later stage of the operation, although this postponement affected the full efficacy of the plan. Any plan for the full use of our airpower meant civilian casualties. These had been accepted in the past when we had attacked submarine bases and factories. Railway centres had always been recognised as legitimate military targets. Although the Prime Minister's letter stated that the Transportation Plan involved the deaths of 10,000 to 15,000 Frenchmen, this estimate assumed that there would be no evacuation despite our specific warnings.

On May 3, at the last of this series of Defence Committee meetings, the Prime Minister feared propaganda to the effect that while the Russian and German armies advanced bravely despite the lack of air superiority, the British and Americans relied on ruthless employment of airpower regardless of the cost in civilian life. It might also be said that the British were the greatest offenders because they scattered their bombs over wide areas by night, whereas the Americans carried out their precision bombing by day. 'You will smear', said the Prime Minister, 'the good name of the Royal Air Force across the world.'

It was proposed that the Cabinet should communicate their views to the President and the State Department so as to ensure that the Americans accepted their share of responsibility. It was admitted that so far French reaction had been good.

After various Ministers had repeated well-known points of view, the Prime Minister said that the War Cabinet should draw up a paper for transmission to the State Department, while he would telegraph to Roosevelt. To kill some 10,000 Frenchmen before D-Day was likely to have a serious effect on European relations. On the other hand, if 'Overlord' were successful, it might, by shortening the war, save the lives of millions. It was decided that action should be taken on these lines; that I should review the railway plan to ensure that not more than 10,000 civilians were killed, and that I should report the course of the discussion and the conclusions to the Supreme Commander. This I did, while Churchill

The end of the Officers' Mess. Closed in 1970, Tangmere was demolished during the 1980s, the administrative and technical site now being largely occupied by private housing.

An Allied Expeditionary Air Force daily conference, this picture being taken in August 1944. Seated around the table, L–R: Lieutenant-Colonel D. Heathcote-Amory (AEAF), Major General R. Royce (Deputy Air C-in-C, AEAF), Air Chief Marshal Douglas, Air Chief Marshal Harris, Air Chief Marshal Leigh-Mallory, Major General Anderson, Lieutenant General Doolittle, Brigadier General F. L. Parks (First Allied Airborne Army), Air Marshal Hill. Standing, L–R: Commander L. Derek-Jones and Hilary St George Saunders (RAF historian and author of those well-known works: *The Green Beret* and *The Red Beret*).

invited Roosevelt to consider the matter from the highest political standpoint. He told the President that the War Cabinet were unanimous in their anxiety about 'these French slaughters', even on a reduced scale, and also in their doubts 'as to whether almost as good military results could not be produced by other methods. Whatever is settled between us, we are quite willing to share responsibilities with you.'

Roosevelt replied, in effect, that the military considerations must dominate. No possibility of alleviating French opinion must be overlooked, always provided that our effectiveness against the enemy was not reduced at this crucial time: 'However regrettable the attendant loss of civilian lives is, I am not prepared to impose from this distance any restriction on military action by the responsible commanders that in their opinion might militate against the success of 'Overlord' or cause additional loss of life to our Allied forces of invasion.'

As Churchill observes, this was decisive. The weight of casualties to French civilians continued to be less than had been feared, and: 'The sealing off of the Normandy battlefield from reinforcements by rail may well have been the greatest direct contribution that the bomber forces could make to 'Overlord'. The price was paid.'

Roosevelt's attitude, then, had at last decided a question which had agitated our counsels for the better part of three months. I shall never forget those meetings in the Map Room when we wrangled for hours about the Transportation Plan.

The battle won, on behalf of President Roosevelt, Eisenhower decorates the two British air commanders with the Chief Commander of the Legion of Merit, America's highest award for foreigners, at a ceremony held in Paris on November 4, 1944. Brereton (in the foreground) and Harris would end the war in their established commands, but Leigh-Mallory was not to live to see the final victory. Already earmarked as the Air Commander in South-East Asia Command, he was to leave Northolt just ten days hence for the flight to Kandy, Ceylon. His aircraft never arrived; seven months later the wreckage of his York was found amidst the melting snows of the French Alps (see *After the Battle* No. 39). His belongings and those of his wife and their eight crew-members lay scattered amongst the rocks, and there was found perhaps the most poignant item of all: a letter from the SHAEF Adjutant General, Brigadier General Thomas J. Davis, enclosing a copy of the citation for the Legion of Merit, advising that the formal certificate would be forwarded when received from the President.

Plans and Preparations

By General Sir Bernard L. Montgomery
COMMANDER, ALLIED LAND FORCES

At the end of 1943, President Roosevelt and Mr Churchill met in Cairo and subsequently went to Teheran to confer with Marshal Stalin. Following these meetings, the announcement was made of the appointment of General Eisenhower as Supreme Allied Commander for 'Overlord', and in due course I was appointed Commander-in-Chief of 21st Army Group which comprised the British and Canadian forces in the United Kingdom destined to take part in the operation.

On January 1, 1944, I handed over command of the Eighth Army and started my journey to England from the Sangro River airstrip in Italy. It was arranged that I should stop at Marrakesh to visit Mr Churchill who was recuperating there from his recent attack of pneumonia. With him I found General Eisenhower. I was shown for the first time a copy of the COSSAC plan for the invasion of France and the Prime Minister asked for my comments. In the short time available, I did no more than express the opinion that the initial assaulting forces were too weak for the task of breaking through the German coastal defences, and that the proposed frontage of assault was too narrow, having in mind the necessity to plan for rapid expansion of the bridgehead and

In July 1943, General Sir Bernard Paget (*left*), British Commander-in-Chief Home Forces, was appointed to command the 21st Army Group which comprised the British and Canadian armies to be employed in 'Overlord'. General Paget was also the chairman of the 'Combined Commanders', a planning group which included Leigh-Mallory and Ramsay, which had already been studying the possibilities for the invasion of France under Operation 'Sledgehammer' (provisional plan for a landing in 1942) and 'Roundup (a major landing in 1943 which COSSAC developed into 'Overlord' for 1944). *Top:* A convenient headquarters for the 21st Army Group had been found in west London utilising the evacuated premises of St Paul's School. *Right:* Today nothing remains to mark the site of the school in Hammersmith Road which was demolished in 1970 when St Paul's relocated to brand-new buildings on the south side of the Thames at Barnes.

In the autumn of 1943, it had been decided that the Commander-in-Chief of the 21st Army Group should be 'jointly responsible with the Allied Naval Commander-in-Chief and the Air Commander-in-Chief . . . for planning the operation (Overlord) and, when so ordered, for its execution, until such time as the Supreme Allied Commander allocated an area of responsibility to the First American Army Group'. Thus, General Paget was destined to command the Allied land forces in the initial assault phase of 'Overlord'. However, when General Eisenhower was appointed Supreme Commander, General Sir Maitland Wilson replaced him as Supreme Commander in the Mediterranean and, in turn, General Paget succeeded General Wilson as Commander-in-Chief Middle East. General Sir Bernard Montgomery was brought home from Italy, where he commanded the Eighth Army, to take over as C-in-C 21st Army Group. No doubt 'Monty' was delighted to find that his new HQ was situated at his old school which he had attended from 1902-06.

No pictures exist of Montgomery's arrival at St Paul's at the beginning of January 1944 but this shot is appropriate: the General, now a Field-Marshal, inspecting the school's Combined Cadet Force in June 1952.

for the speedy reception of the follow-up forces and subsequent build-up.

It was decided that on my arrival in England I should examine the COSSAC plan in detail, together with the Naval and Air Commanders-in-Chief, with a view to recommending any changes or modifications considered necessary to ensure the success of the operation. The Supreme Commander was on his way to the United States, but his Chief-of-Staff, General Bedell Smith, came to London bearing a letter which instructed me to act on General Eisenhower's behalf during his absence.

The Commander-in-Chief of the Allied Naval Expeditionary Force was Admiral Sir Bertram Ramsay and of the Allied Expeditionary Air Force, Air Chief Marshal Sir Trafford Leigh-Mallory. There was no parallel appointment of Commander-in-Chief of the Allied land forces, but General Eisenhower decided that I should act in that capacity for the assault, and, subsequently until the stage was reached in the development of our operations when a complete American army group could be deployed on the Continent. The assault was an operation requiring a single co-ordinated plan of action under one commander; I therefore became the overall land force commander responsible to the Supreme Commander for planning and executing the military aspect of the assault and subsequent capture of the lodgement area.

I arrived in England on January 2, 1944, and immediately started a detailed study of the COSSAC plan. I formulated my views on the measures required to convert the project into a practical proposition with reasonable chances of success, and discussed them at length with Admiral Ramsay and Air Chief Marshal Leigh-Mallory. By January 21, when the Supreme Commander held the first conference following his return from the United States, we were in agreement on a Revised Outline Plan.

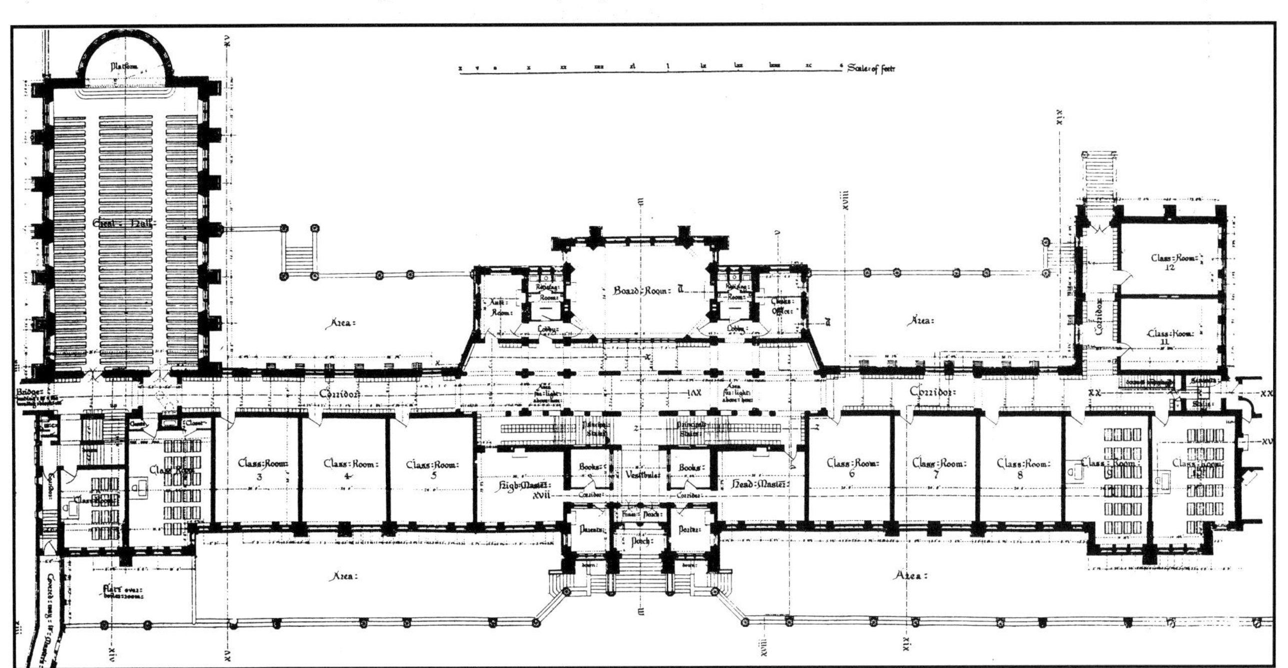

Few old boys could claim to have taken over their headmaster's study for their own office but that is exactly what Monty did. The High Master's office, on the ground floor at the centre of the south side of the school block, had officially been designated 'The Governors' Room' but had since become known as 'The Board Room'.

THE COSSAC PLAN

The object of Operation 'Overlord' was 'to mount and carry out an operation, with forces and equipment established in the United Kingdom and with target date May 1, 1944, to secure a lodgement on the Continent from which further offensive operations could be developed. The lodgement area must contain sufficient port facilities to maintain a force of some 26 to 30 divisions and enable that force to be augmented by follow-up shipments from the United States or elsewhere of additional divisions and supporting units at the rate of three to five divisions per month.'

The first problem was to decide where to deliver the assault. The Allied forces had got to smash into the German Atlantic Wall defences, gain a firm foothold, and then secure port facilities in order to build up sufficient strength and resources to carry the war into Germany.

The COSSAC plan selected the area between Grandcamp and Caen, in the Baie de la Seine, for the assault. This area was known by the code-name 'Neptune', to differentiate it from other possible sectors in which 'Overlord' might have been launched. The choice was made after exhaustive inter-service study of the 'invasion coast', which, by the factor of aircraft range for fighter cover from home bases, was limited to the sector between Flushing and Cherbourg. Consideration of the beach areas suitable for combined operations revealed that those offering the best conditions for passing vehicles and stores inland were, firstly, in the Pas-de-Calais area (between Gravelines and the River Somme) and, secondly, in the Baie de la Seine (between the River Orne and the base of the Cotentin peninsula).

Boys recall that even though it measured 40 feet × 26 feet, on first entering it appeared much larger and the newcomer usually viewed the sight with awe. We can imagine Montgomery revelling in the experience as he sat at the long table, reflecting and planning momentous events.

The Pas-de-Calais area involved a shorter distance from home bases, and thus would have enabled us to develop optimum air support and would have given a quicker turn-round for shipping; but the strongest enemy defences along the whole coast existed in this sector, which was also a focal area for hostile fighter aircraft disposed for defence. The Caen area was relatively lightly defended and afforded the great advantage of a coastline sheltered from prevailing winds.

The hinterland of the Baie de la Seine provided good terrain for airfield construction (especially south-east of Caen) and offered the choice of developing operations to secure the Seine ports or the Cherbourg-Brittany group. From the Pas-de-Calais, the rapid seizure of adequate port facilities would have been more difficult, as the alternatives were the Channel ports proper,

After the end of the war, 21st Army Group metamorphosed into the British Army of the Rhine (BAOR). Montgomery stayed in Germany as Commander-in-Chief of the British forces of occupation until June 1946 when he left to take up the top post in the War Office: Chief of the Imperial General Staff. *Left:* However, one of the Field-Marshal's (he had been promoted in September 1944) first duties when he arrived in Britain was to go back to St Paul's where, on July 4, he unveiled a carved oak plaque (designed by Eric Kennington and carved by Donald Potter) mounted above the fireplace in The Board Room. *Right:* When the school moved to Barnes, the display of the plaque, bearing in mind its wording, was not appropriate in the new building, and it was relegated to the archive where we found it in June 1994.

including Antwerp — which could be reached only after crossing a series of major river and canal obstacles — or the Seine ports, which lay some 150 miles to the south-west of the most suitable beach areas.

Obviously, the development of the full Allied potential depended on securing ports; the overriding consideration in the plan of operations once a bridgehead had been established, was the speed with which ports could be captured and opened for our shipping. Accordingly, the COSSAC plan recommended initially the seizure of Cherbourg and, subsequently, of the ports in the Brittany peninsula, including Nantes. The lodgement area therefore was to cover the Cotentin and Brittany peninsulas, and, in order to develop airfields, the area south-east of Caen. With these factors in mind, and in view of the need for space to assemble the forces required for the invasion of Germany, it was considered that the eastern flank of the lodgement area should be carried to the line of the River Eure and lower Seine, while the southern boundary was to follow the line of the Loire.

Until ports had been captured, reliance was to be placed on creating artificially sheltered berths by sinking specially-built caissons and cargo ships in the Baie de la Seine, the projects for which went by the name of Mulberry (artificial harbours) and Gooseberry (breakwaters). The COSSAC plan dismissed the possibility of the early capture of Cherbourg by assaulting the Cotentin peninsula, on the grounds that it would be easy for the enemy to block the base of the peninsula, and thus prevent further expansion of the bridgehead. The alternative — of including beaches on the eastern side of the peninsula as part of the frontage of assault — was also dismissed, as it was feared that the Carentan estuary and marshy country surrounding it would split our forces and render them liable to defeat in detail.

The operational plan of assault and subsequent development of operations was based on conjectural dispositions of enemy mobile reserve formations, on the basis of the maximum number regarded as acceptable if the project were to have a reasonable chance of success. Counting the coastal crust, it was assumed that we should encounter five enemy divisions on D-Day, and that another seven would arrive in the beach-head area by D+5. Of these 12, five would be panzer divisions.

The invasion forces were assumed to be provided with sufficient landing ships and craft to lift three assault divisions and two follow-up divisions, while two further divisions would be afloat on D-Day in ships. The anticipated air lift for airborne forces was two-thirds of one division.

The plan therefore provided for an assault on a frontage of one corps of three divisions, and, assuming optimum weather conditions, the build-up by D+5 was planned to ensure some nine divisions with a proportion of armour being available, exclusive of airborne troops. However, a study of weather conditions in the Channel in May over a number of years indicated that up to one day in four might be unsuitable for beach working. The effect of this might reduce our forces available on D+5 to only seven divisions. Subsequent build-up was to be at the rate of one division per day (again assuming favourable weather) and the bridgehead was to be developed to the general line Trouville—Alençon—Mont-St Michel by D+14, by which time it was hoped to have completed the reduction of Cherbourg. Later staff studies indicated that this timing was probably very optimistic. Meanwhile, the COSSAC plan made certain reservations: the total number of enemy first-line divisions immediately available in western Europe to reinforce Normandy was not to exceed 12, and not more than an additional 15 divisions should be moved into France from other theatres of war during the first two months after D-Day.

The COSSAC plan emphasised the vital necessity of reducing the effectiveness of the German air forces before undertaking the operation, and also the reliance which had to be placed on the untried expedient of establishing artificially sheltered waters since it would be necessary to rely on building up and maintaining our forces over the beaches for an appreciable period.

This was the plan which I first saw at Marrakesh.

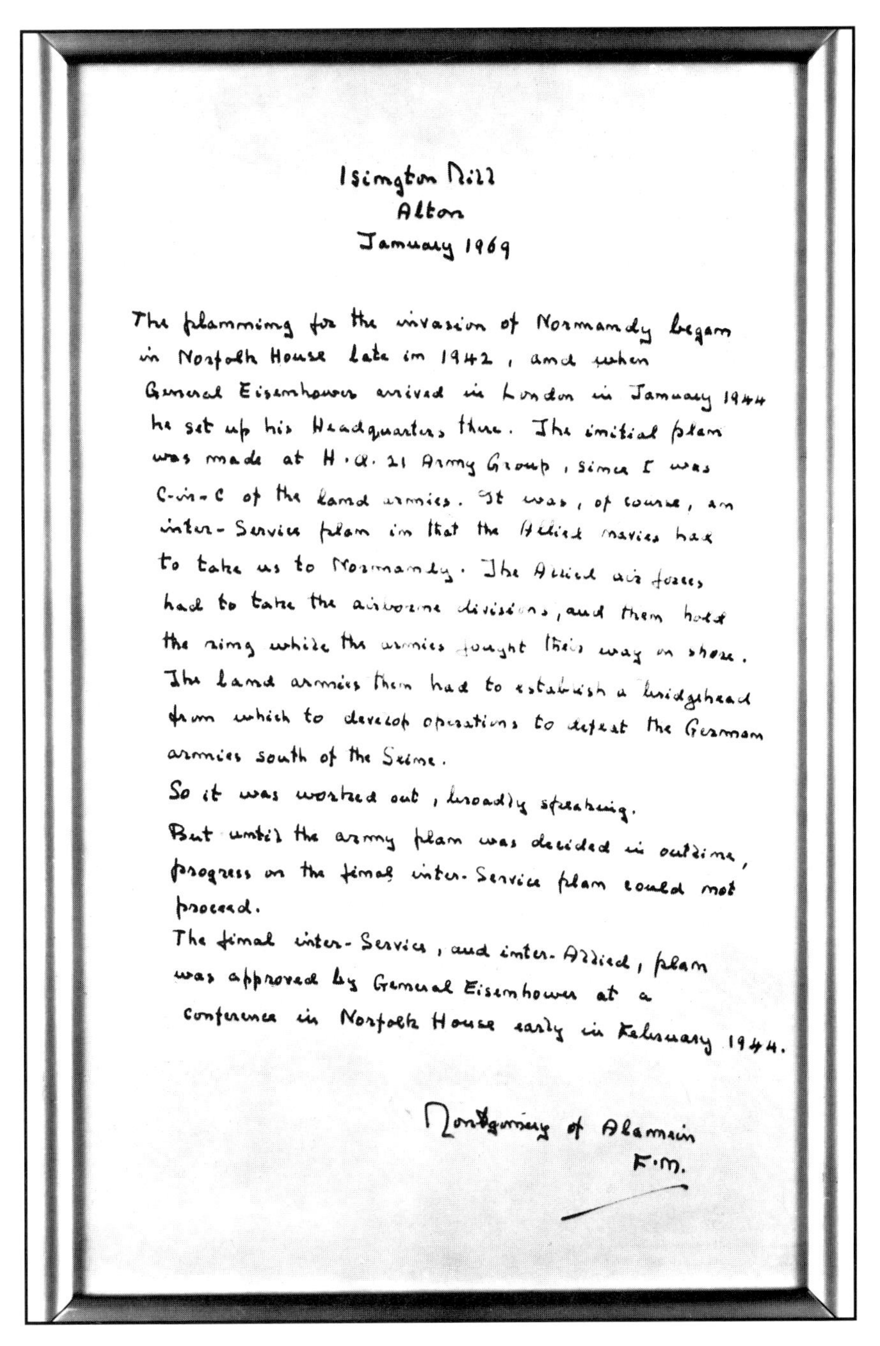

Isington Mill
Alton
January 1969

The planning for the invasion of Normandy began in Norfolk House late in 1942, and when General Eisenhower arrived in London in January 1944 he set up his Headquarters there. The initial plan was made at H.Q. 21 Army Group, since I was C-in-C of the land armies. It was, of course, an inter-Service plan in that the Allied navies had to take us to Normandy. The Allied air forces had to take the airborne divisions, and then hold the ring while the armies fought their way on shore. The land armies then had to establish a bridgehead from which to develop operations to defeat the German armies south of the Seine.

So it was worked out, broadly speaking.

But until the army plan was decided in outline, progress on the final inter-Service plan could not proceed.

The final inter-Service, and inter-Allied, plan was approved by General Eisenhower at a conference in Norfolk House early in February 1944.

Montgomery of Alamein
F.M.

In later years, Montgomery, a stickler for historical accuracy, was anxious lest the part he — and 21st Army Group HQ — played in the planning of 'Overlord' should be played down. In 1969, he sent this letter to the British Aluminium Company, who then occupied the old Allied Forces Headquarters at Norfolk House (see page 14) for them to frame for *their* board room to make sure future visitors would take note!

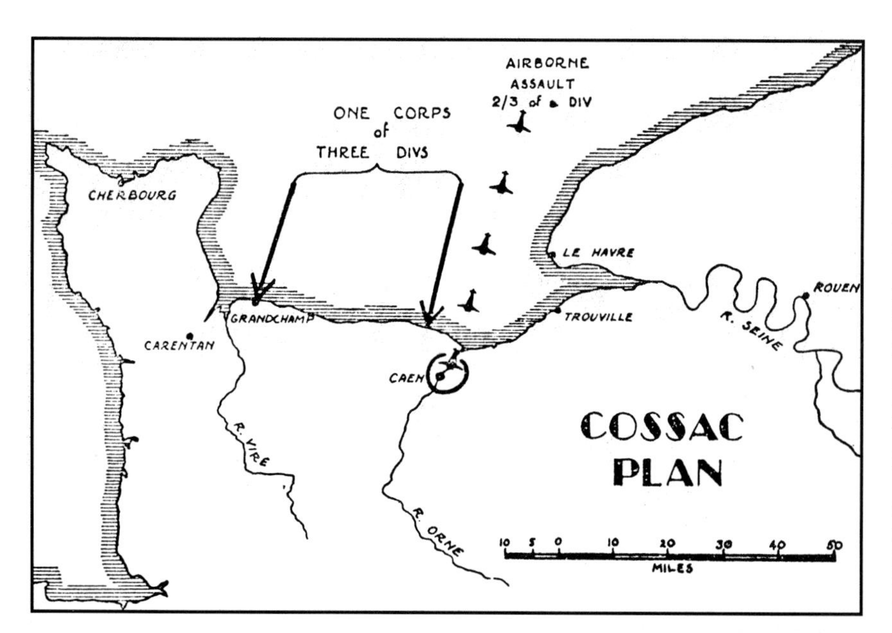

difficult and lengthy operation. I therefore recommended increasing the frontage of assault to the west, to embrace beaches on the eastern side of the Cotentin peninsula, between Varreville and the Carentan estuary. If necessary, the link-up across the estuary could be facilitated by the employment of airborne forces.

East of the River Orne, invading forces would come within range of the formidable coast defence batteries located in the Le Havre area and between Le Havre and Houlgate, and I therefore recommended that the invasion front should extend from the Varreville area to the River Orne. This frontage amounted to some 50 miles.

In deciding the degree to which the assault could be strengthened, the main factor was availability of craft and shipping but, in order to cover the front and facilitate organising the operation on a frontage of two armies, I recommended invading on a five-divisional frontage, with two divisions in the immediate follow-up, and using at least two, and if possible three, airborne divisions to be dropped prior to the actual seaborne assault.

THE REVISED PLAN

My immediate reaction was that to deliver a seaborne assault by one corps of only three divisions against the German Atlantic Wall as then constituted could hardly be considered a sound operation of war.

While accepting the suitability of the Baie de la Seine for the assault, I considered that the operation required to be mounted in greater strength and on a wider front. It was vital to secure an adequate bridgehead at the outset, so that operations could be developed from a firm and sufficiently spacious base; in any event, the area we could hope to seize and hold in the first days of the invasion would become very congested. Experience in amphibious operations had shown me that if build-up arrangements and expansion from the landing beaches are to proceed smoothly, each corps and army to be employed in forming and developing the initial bridgehead must be allotted its own sector in the assault. It is unsound to aim at passing follow-up and build-up divisions of one corps through beach-heads established by another, because confusion inevitably results together with delay in deployment at the vital time. Moreover, the relatively narrow front of assault proposed in the COSSAC plan appeared to me to give the enemy the opportunity of 'roping off' our forces quickly in a shallow covering position, in which the beaches would be under continuous artillery fire. An increased frontage would make it more difficult for the enemy to discover the extent of our operation and delay him in deciding the direction of our main axes of advance inland; at the same time, we should have greater opportunity for finding and exploiting soft spots, and greater chances of locating adequate exit routes from the beaches for our transport. The latter problem was complicated by the coastal inundations which canalised the beach exits through a number of small villages.

Recognising the vital importance of securing Cherbourg quickly, I felt that we should get a foothold in the Cotentin peninsula in the initial operation. The river lines and flooded marshy areas at the base of the peninsula might well enable the enemy to seal off our western flank even with minor forces, and thus render the capture of Cherbourg a

Major-General Sir Francis 'Freddie' de Guingand (*left*), who had served as Chief-of-Staff, Eighth Army, in 1942-43, was appointed Chief-of-Staff of 21st Army Group as part of Montgomery's need to assemble an experienced team quickly. De Guingand commented after the war that 'it was hard luck on those officers who had to make way, but then one has to be ruthless in war to be successful'. His own appointment displaced Lieutenant-General Sir William Morgan (not the COSSAC planner). 'It was bad luck on Morgan', wrote de Guingand, 'who had held the appointment for some time . . . he missed the invasion but later became Supreme Commander in the Mediterranean — the Morgan Line bears his name.' Major-General de Guingand's simple sketches (reproduced from his 1946 book *Operation Victory*, explain the basic differences between the original COSSAC plan (*above*) and the one modified by Montgomery (*below*).

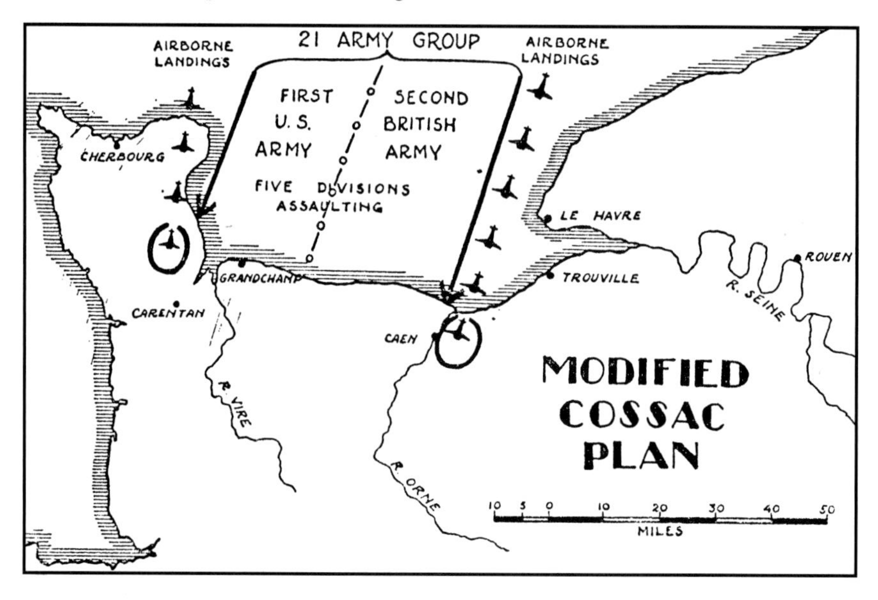

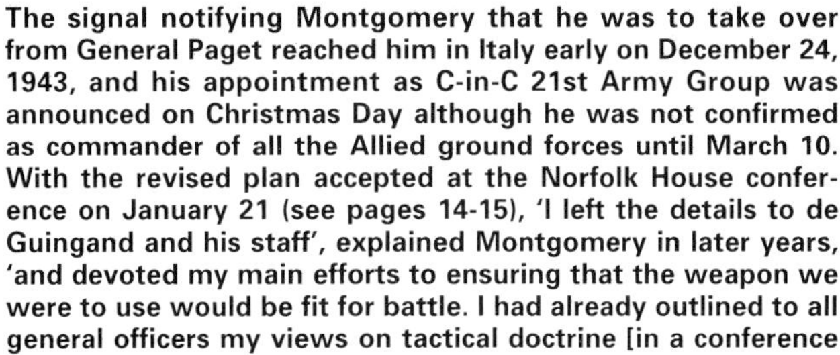

The signal notifying Montgomery that he was to take over from General Paget reached him in Italy early on December 24, 1943, and his appointment as C-in-C 21st Army Group was announced on Christmas Day although he was not confirmed as commander of all the Allied ground forces until March 10. With the revised plan accepted at the Norfolk House conference on January 21 (see pages 14-15), 'I left the details to de Guingand and his staff', explained Montgomery in later years, 'and devoted my main efforts to ensuring that the weapon we were to use would be fit for battle. I had already outlined to all general officers my views on tactical doctrine [in a conference at St Paul's on January 13], and training was proceeding accordingly. Confidence in the high command by one and all was the next essential, and was vital. I wanted to see the soldiers and, probably more important, I wanted them to see me; I wanted to speak to them and try to gain their trust and confidence.' Montgomery first visited US First Army units from January 14-20 including the 82nd Airborne Division. Then, after a break, he began again on February 1 and, during the next eight days, covered 3,000 miles using his personal train, 'Rapier', addressing over 100,000 troops of 21st Army Group. First stop was the 53rd (Welsh) Division at Sevenoaks, Kent.

General Montgomery: 'My method of inspection was characterised by informality and was, I suppose, unusual; it certainly astonished some of the generals who did not know me well. I inspected two, and often three, parades a day, each of 10,000 men or more. They were drawn up in a hollow square and I first spoke individually to the unit commanders. I then ordered the ranks to be turned inwards and walked slowly between them, in order that every man could see me; the men "stood easy" throughout so that they could lean and twist, and look at me all the time if they wished to — and most did. This inspection of the men by me, and of me by them, took some little time, but it was good value for all of us. It was essential that I gained their confidence. I had to begin with their curiosity.'

'When the appraisal was over, I stood on the bonnet of a Jeep and spoke to officers and men, quietly and very simply — using a loudspeaker or not, according to the conditions. I explained how necessary it was that we should know each other, what lay ahead and how, together, we would handle the job. I told them what the German soldier was like in battle and how he could be defeated; that if we all had confidence in the plan and in each other, the job could be done. I was their Commander-in-Chief and we had now had a good look at each other. As a result of the meeting between us, I had absolute confidence in them, and I hoped they could feel the same about me.'

We followed the route of General Montgomery early in 1994 but the passage of 50 years did not make it easy to locate some of the places chosen for the 1944 parades. Sevenoaks — the first stop on our journey — proved to be one of the most difficult. Sports fields or public parks were the usual venue but in spite of the good background detail in the Sevenoaks sequence (all four prints taken by Sergeant J. W. Morris are reproduced), we just could not find the spot. We checked Knole Park and every sports field, including that of Sevenoaks School, the football pitch to the east at Seal and the one to the west at Sundridge, all to no avail. Having exhausted all the possibilities suggested to us by the many people we questioned, including the local police, we were on the point of giving up when an anonymous lady said that she recognised the houses as those in Homedean Road (in the Chipstead area). To our amazement, she was absolutely correct, the 'parade ground' being a field beside the post-war A21 bypass, the houses — Darenth Lea, Llechfaen and Deans Gap all surviving virtually unchanged.

The same format was adopted for each whistle stop. This is Tunbridge Wells where Montgomery had had his HQ when commanding XII Corps in 1941. (The house, No. 10 Broadwater Down, still stands, having survived a threat of redevelopment in 1988.) *Above:* **The venue was St Mark's Recreation Ground at the top of Frant Road, the houses in the background being those in Bayham Road.**

It was desirable to acquire additional sea lift, not only for the assault, but also for the subsequent build-up. As I saw the problem, we had to ensure that there would be adequate forces to withstand immediate counter-attacks on D-Day, and we also had to 'build-up' sufficiently rapidly to meet the first major co-ordinated counter-attack which I appreciated might develop on D+4. Once we had established a footing on the Continent, in spite of hostile attempts to hurl us back into the sea, the enemy would concentrate to deliver a properly staged thrust at some selected area. The COSSAC plan envisaged up to five or six mobile enemy divisions being in action against the beach-head by D+3, and it was essential that our own build-up should ensure that we had comparable forces ashore and ready for action on that day, bearing in mind that the assault divisions would by then be very tired and probably depleted.

The problem was whether the naval and air forces would be able to fall in with these revisions to the COSSAC plan, and above all whether the additional craft and shipping could be found to make them possible. Air Chief Marshal Leigh-Mallory agreed to the modifications and, from the point of view of the air forces, there appeared to be no insoluble difficulties. But Admiral Ramsay showed that grave problems confronted the Allied navies in the revised plan. The additional naval resources, assuming provision of craft, would create serious congestion of shipping on the south coast of England, affording a good target for hostile air action or rocket activity; the standard of training of the extra crews required would not be as high as that of the naval forces already organised for the invasion; the wider area of assault would increase the minesweeping commitment, as extra cross-Channel lanes would be required; and an increased naval bombarding commitment would be incurred for neutralising the enemy coast defence batteries. The basic problem was provision of the necessary assault craft to transport the larger invasion force; this would have to be

We discovered that Monty had addressed the troops on what is now a field beyond the present rugby ground. Nos. 33 and 35 Bayham Road unchanged on the left.

By now, the tour was really getting into its stride. This is the Bowater Sports Ground in Woodstock Road, Sittingbourne.

In quick succession, troops stationed at Maidstone, Westgate, Dover and Hastings were all subjected to the Monty treatment. Roy Humphreys, who took the comparison (*below*) for us on the Crabble Sports Field in Dover commented that he could just imagine the command: 'Round me in a half-circle — MOVE!'

obtained from the Pacific, from the Mediterranean, from current production in Britain and the United States, or from a combination of these sources. If the target date could be extended to May 31 (instead of May 1), craft production of an additional month would be available and the extra time would give the opportunity for improving the training of additional assault craft crews. Admiral Ramsay therefore favoured a revised target date.

On examination, it was found that, even with an additional month's production, there would still be insufficient craft for the undertaking and it was thereupon suggested that additional resources should be made available for 'Overlord' from the Mediterranean.

After inspecting the troops (61st Division) at Canterbury, the town so severely damaged in May 1942 as a reprisal for the RAF's 1,000-bomber attack on the German cathedral city of Cologne, Montgomery paid a visit to see the mayor and he is pictured here having just left the Guildhall.

Dating from the 12th century, the Guildhall was fully protected under the Ancient Monument Acts yet, although it had come through the bombing unscathed, Hitler's desire to raze Britain's historic buildings was achieved in 1951 when the local council had it demolished.

The visits to the troops continued but we must break at this point, not only to avoid becoming repetitious, but to look at another aspect of Montgomery's pre-D-Day campaigning. 'After I had been a few weeks in England, the Ministry of Supply asked me to visit factories which were engaged in the production of equipment for the armies. In many cases, such equipment was urgently required for "Overlord" and men and women were working overtime to produce it for us. On the 22nd February, I addressed at Euston Station a representative gathering of railwaymen from all over England. The Secretaries of the Railway Trades Unions were present, all the men's leaders, and, in fact, a selection from every type of railway official. I spoke for 1½ hours, and told them of our problems in what lay ahead and how they could help. I said we now had the war in a very good grip and the bad days were over; we must all rally to the task and finish off the war. When I had finished speaking, the Secretaries of the Trades Union pledged their full support.'

To go back some time, an operation called 'Anvil' had been under consideration in the Mediterranean since the Casablanca Conference, having as its object the mounting of an assault on southern France, which was to link closely with the timing of the invasion of north-west Europe. The 'Anvil' assault was planned on a frontage of three — or at worst two — divisions and a corresponding proportion of available landing ships and craft had been allocated to the central Mediterranean theatre.

The Supreme Commander regarded 'Anvil' as an important contribution to 'Overlord', for it was to contain enemy forces in southern France; but he advised the Combined Chiefs-of-Staff that he regarded 'Overlord' as first priority, and that if insufficient naval resources were available for both operations, he considered 'Anvil' should be postponed or reduced to a one-division assault: to be delivered when enemy weakness justified its implementation.

The major factors affecting the provision of craft for 'Overlord' were thus the question of extending the target date and the postponement or reduction in scope of Operation 'Anvil'.

Above: **'On the 3rd March, I was asked to go to the London Docks, where I addressed some 16,000 dockers, stevedores and lightermen. My theme was the same as to the railwaymen — there is a job to be done and together we will do it.'**

The picture was taken in the Royal Victoria Dock, just inside No. 8 Gate on the north side near the Connaught public house. Inevitably, industrial locations have undergone dramatic change since the war, the London docks, so far up the river, being replaced by containerised facilities elsewhere. And at Birmingham, the subject of an extensive visit to factories on March 9, due to demolitions and redevelopment, we were unable to take meaningful comparisons at either the GEC works at Witton (*below left*) or the Birmingham Railway and Carriage Works at Sandwell (*below right*) and pictures at other locations in the series offered poor recognisable features.

After visiting wounded Eighth Army soldiers in Hallam Hospital the General reviewed a Guard of Honour provided by the 31st and 32nd Warwickshire Home Guard outside the Council House — Birmingham's name for the Lord Mayor's office.

Apart from naval considerations, the advance of the target date to May 31 afforded a longer period for the strategic bombing offensive on Germany; for the effective completion of the programme for reducing the enemy's railway potential; and for destroying the major bridges on his communications in western Europe. Moreover, it appeared likely that weather conditions at the end of May would be more likely to favour the mounting of a large-scale Russian offensive which would assist 'Overlord'; and in the Mediterranean the situation might be sufficiently resolved to exclude the necessity for 'Anvil', in that our forces in Italy might have drawn the available German reserve divisions in southern Europe into that country. The Supreme Commander was averse to any postponement if it could be avoided but, when there appeared to be no alternative, he recommended to the Combined Chiefs-of-Staff that 'Overlord' should be mounted with a target date not later than May 31. The Combined Chiefs-of-Staff agreed to this on February 1, and, at the same time, General Eisenhower made the reservation to them that the exact date of assault be left open pending detailed study of moonlight and tidal conditions prevailing during the first week of June.

The decision to provide extra craft for 'Overlord' at the expense of 'Anvil' was not taken immediately but, eventually, the Combined Chiefs-of-Staff agreed to General Eisenhower's recommendations and confirmed that the additional craft required would be found from the Mediterranean. 'Anvil' was postponed and indeed did not finally take place until August 1944.

'These visits brought me into contact with a large public outside the Army. I used to tell them that we were all one great army, whether soldier on the battle front or worker on the Home Front; their work was just as important as ours. Our combined task was to weld the workers and soldiers into one team, determined to destroy German domination of Europe and of the world.'

Centre: **Montgomery addressed the huge crowd assembled in Victoria Square from a platform which had been erected in front of the Council House.** *Right:* **In 1993, the square was totally remodelled and unveiled by the Princess of Wales. We took the comparison from the peristyle of the concert hall — confusingly referred to as the Town Hall.**

'In my journeying round the country, I was seen by the civil population and received everywhere with great enthusiasm', wrote Montgomery in 1958. 'The people seemed to think I had some magic prescription for victory and that I had been sent to lead them to better things. I sensed danger in this and knew my activities would not be viewed favourably in political circles. Nor were they. I received an intimation that I should "lay off" these visits — to which I paid no attention, beyond replying that I had been asked to undertake them by certain Ministries in Whitehall.'

I have already mentioned that the COSSAC plan assumed an air lift for only two-thirds of an airborne division; this lift was to be used on D-Day for a descent on Caen. It was evident that airborne forces could play an extremely important rôle in the assault, and it seemed unfortunate that such a small lift should be at our disposal when there would be three or four airborne divisions available for operations on D-Day. Extension of the invasion frontage to the base of the Cotentin peninsula resulted in increased commitments for airborne forces, as they were required on the western flank to ensure the capture of the causeways leading across the inundations behind the assault beaches. The Supreme Commander strongly supported the need for additional air lift and, as a result of his recommendations, the availability of transport aircraft and gliders was materially increased. The extension of the target date helped in this matter, for the extra time made it possible to concentrate more aircraft and to train additional crews.

At the conference on January 21, General Eisenhower approved the revisions to the COSSAC plan and recommended their adoption to the Combined Chiefs-of-Staff. As time was already short for completion of all the detailed staff work required for such a great undertaking, he ordered that planning be undertaken at once on the basis of the revised plan.

I am of opinion that the Army Council should instruct General Montgomery to bring to an end his public tours and civic receptions. We are getting very near the great battle, and a bad effect will be produced if it is thought that the General immediately responsible is spending his time at demonstrations which are more appropriate after the victory than before. Let not him that girdeth on his harness boast himself as he that putteth it off. There is a mass of intricate Staff work to be done, and the Army Council, yourself [the Secretary of State for War] *and the CIGS* [Chief of the Imperial General Staff] *are directly responsible for seeing that this is not relegated to second place. If anything were to go seriously wrong and it were found that something had been neglected, the General would come in for heavy criticism.*

WINSTON CHURCHILL, APRIL 18, 1944

Where better to end the tour than Birmingham's Montgomery Street. It was given out at the time that the road was specifically named after him but, in reality, this insignificant little back street in Sparkbrook was just one in an area where many of the streets are named after counties in England and Wales.

While General Montgomery's egocentric ways did not endear him to his contemporaries (Air Vice-Marshal James Robb, the Deputy Chief-of-Staff (Air), being particularly critical of Montgomery's discourtesy in never once visiting Eisenhower at his HQ), nevertheless he remained hugely popular with the ordinary soldier and civilian alike; the confidence he inspired was legendary and Monty soon became every British schoolboys' warrior hero. General Smith, the SHAEF Chief-of-Staff wrote to Montgomery on June 22, 1944 having received from 'a most reliable and intelligent source, a report on attitude and state of mind of American troops: "Confidence in the high command is absolutely without parallel. Literally dozens of embarking troops talked about General Montgomery with actual hero-worship in every inflection. And unanimously what appealed to them — beyond his friendliness, and genuineness, and lack of pomp — was the story (or, for all I know, the myth) that the General 'visited every one of us outfits going over and told us he was more anxious than any of us to get this thing over and get home.' This left a warm and indelible impression." ' ***Above:*** **Yet another facet of Montgomery's inimitable style: a display laid on in Birmingham from March 25 to April 15.**

THE INTER-SERVICE ORGANISATION

Admiral Ramsay, Air Chief Marshal Leigh-Mallory and myself were jointly charged with planning and executing the assault and initial development of the lodgement area. Our respective staffs were closely associated in the production of the detailed plans and directives which guided the planning of our subordinate formations. On February 1, we presented for the Supreme Commander's approval an 'Initial Joint Plan', which provided the basis for planning the operation. Subsequently, the armies, with their associated naval and air force authorities, produced detailed plans of action, and the whole planning period culminated in the 'Presentation of the Plans' exercise, staged in London on April 7, when commanders of the three Services explained their intentions and examination was made of the whole project. Subsequently, the joint Commanders-in-Chief presented their final plans to the Supreme Commander.

My orders provided for an assault on a frontage of two armies, United States First Army on the right, employing two divisions, and British Second Army on the left, with three divisions. This arrangement of forces placed the American troops on the Atlantic flank, as they would ultimately be maintained direct from the United States. In conformity with this organisation, the associated naval forces were organised into the Western Task Force working with US First Army and the Eastern Task Force which was allied to British Second Army. These task forces were in

The Birmingham display comprised the two command vehicles which had been captured in North Africa from the Italians (see *After the Battle* No. 20). For the coming campaign in Europe, Montgomery wanted a suitable vehicle for briefings in which the interior walls could be lined with maps and, in January 1944, a 'map caravan' was ordered from the British Trailer Company, Manchester. ***Above:*** **It was delivered to St Paul's School on April 17.**

turn divided into seven forces, one for each of the assault and follow-up divisions. The Eastern Naval Task Force comprised Forces 'S', 'G' and 'J', with Force 'L' as its follow-up; the Western Naval Task Force had Forces 'O' and 'U' in the assault, and Force 'B' in the follow-up. The lettering of these force designations corresponded (in the assault echelons) to the code-marking of the beach areas they were to attack.

According to the information released at the time, 'six war workers had given up their spare time to build it'. The vehicle resembled a motor-driven horse-box and had been designed by the General personally. The mobile 'office' was part and parcel of Montgomery's system of personal command from a 'tactical' headquarters located well forward in the battle area. TAC HQ consisted of signals, cipher liaison staff, a small operations staff, and defence troops. Main HQ — the central core of the whole HQ organisation — (currently at St Paul's but soon to move to Portsmouth) was where the Chief-of-Staff and senior administrative personnel both lived and worked. Rear HQ included the administrative echelon — the 'A' Branch — under Montgomery's long-time Chief Administrative Officer, Major-General Sir Miles Graham, and the 'Q' Branch (quartermaster).

After the war, Field-Marshal Montgomery claimed the three motor caravans as his personal property, two having been captured in battle and one given to him. While the War Office did not accept this argument, it was agreed that Montgomery could retain them during his lifetime. Four months after his death in March 1976, the vehicles were removed from the barn where they had been stored at his home, Isington Mill, in Hampshire. *Above:* On October 28, 1976, the three caravans were drawn up in front of the Imperial War Museum, London, for their formal handing over by the Ministry of Defence. Left, the BTC map lorry; centre, the caravan captured from Maresciallo Giovanni Messe, commander of the First Italian Army in Tunisia; and, right, the vehicle captured near Benghazi from Generale di Corpo d'Armata Annibale Bergonzoli, commander of XXIII Corps. Today, the three caravans can be seen at the museum's outstation at Duxford airfield.

The transfer to Portsmouth took place on April 28, concurrently with Admiral Ramsay moving into Southwick House, located some five miles north-west of the city centre behind the Ports Down escarpment. The home of the Royal Navy navigation school, HMS *Dryad*, had been earmarked by Admiral Ramsay in January for his headquarters; now the 21st Army Group Main HQ was established in tented accommodation in Place Wood just a few hundred yards to the north. *Left:* Major-General Miles Graham and *right* Major-General C. M. F. White, the Chief Signals Officer.

This picture was fortuitously taken by the US 7th Photo Group on April 21, before the leaves were fully out, so that the tents of both Main and TAC HQs show up between the trees. A tell-tale track has already been worn across the park between Main HQ and the house. The drive to the south-east leads to Eisenhower's Advance CP in Sawyer's Wood (see page 33).

It was General Eisenhower's intention to assume direct command of the land forces on the Continent when the growing build-up of the American forces had led to the deployment of an American army group in the field. No definite period was stipulated for this, but HQ US 12th Army Group were formed in London and prepared to take command of the US First and Third Armies at the appropriate time. Meanwhile, I became responsible for co-ordinating the planning of US 12th Army Group with a view to ensuring that there would be no interruption in the general conduct of operations when it took the field. Within the scope of this co-ordination were included plans made by the 12th Army Group for introducing the US Third Army into the Continent.

In view of my responsibility towards United States forces, I arranged with General Bradley for a proportion of American officers to join the headquarters of 21st Army Group to assist in the detailed planning, to ensure smooth and efficient liaison with the United States formations, to advise on the framing of orders and instructions having in mind the difference between the organisation and staff procedure of the two armies, and to take their share in the staff work of the operation until the American army group became operational. On the General Staff side, the staffs were integrated, but the difference in the administrative systems of the two armies proved so great that it was found preferable to attach a self-contained American administrative echelon to 21st Army Group. The American Brigadier General in charge was appointed deputy to my Chief Administrative Officer (CAO) and the two staffs worked side by side so that their planning marched in step. Under the general co-ordination of 21st Army Group, the US First Army was responsible for its own detailed administrative planning, while longer-term projects were handled by US 12th Army Group. These arrangements proved eminently satisfactory and I would like to pay tribute to the knowledge, efficiency and adaptability of the American officers who served with 21st Army Group staff.

Montgomery's intelligence chief, Brigadier E. T. 'Bill' Williams (in cardigan), with his British and American assistants. Williams' youthful appearance is unmistakable — he shows up in many wartime pictures — and belies his brilliant brain, and Montgomery gave him credit for playing a large part in winning the Battle of Alamein.

Today, nothing remains to indicate to the casual visitor that here, 50 years ago, 21st Army Group finalised its plans for the coming invasion. ***Left:*** **The entrance to the Main HQ in Place Wood and** ***right,*** **the site of TAC HQ. The avenue of trees has gone to be replaced by housing in Boulter Lane (see also page 160).**

(Incidentally, Churchill had set down the diplomatic niceties of the coming operation in a note to the Foreign Secretary (the Rt. Hon. Anthony Eden) in February. 'We "invade" all countries with whom we are at war', wrote Churchill, 'but we "enter" all subjugated lands we wish to "liberate".')

Montgomery believed that close liaison between British and US forces was paramount and, to that end, he integrated American officers into his administrative structure. L–R: Lieutenant C. W. Sandford (American); Major C. D. O'Gowan (British), and Major A. S. Donald (Canadian).

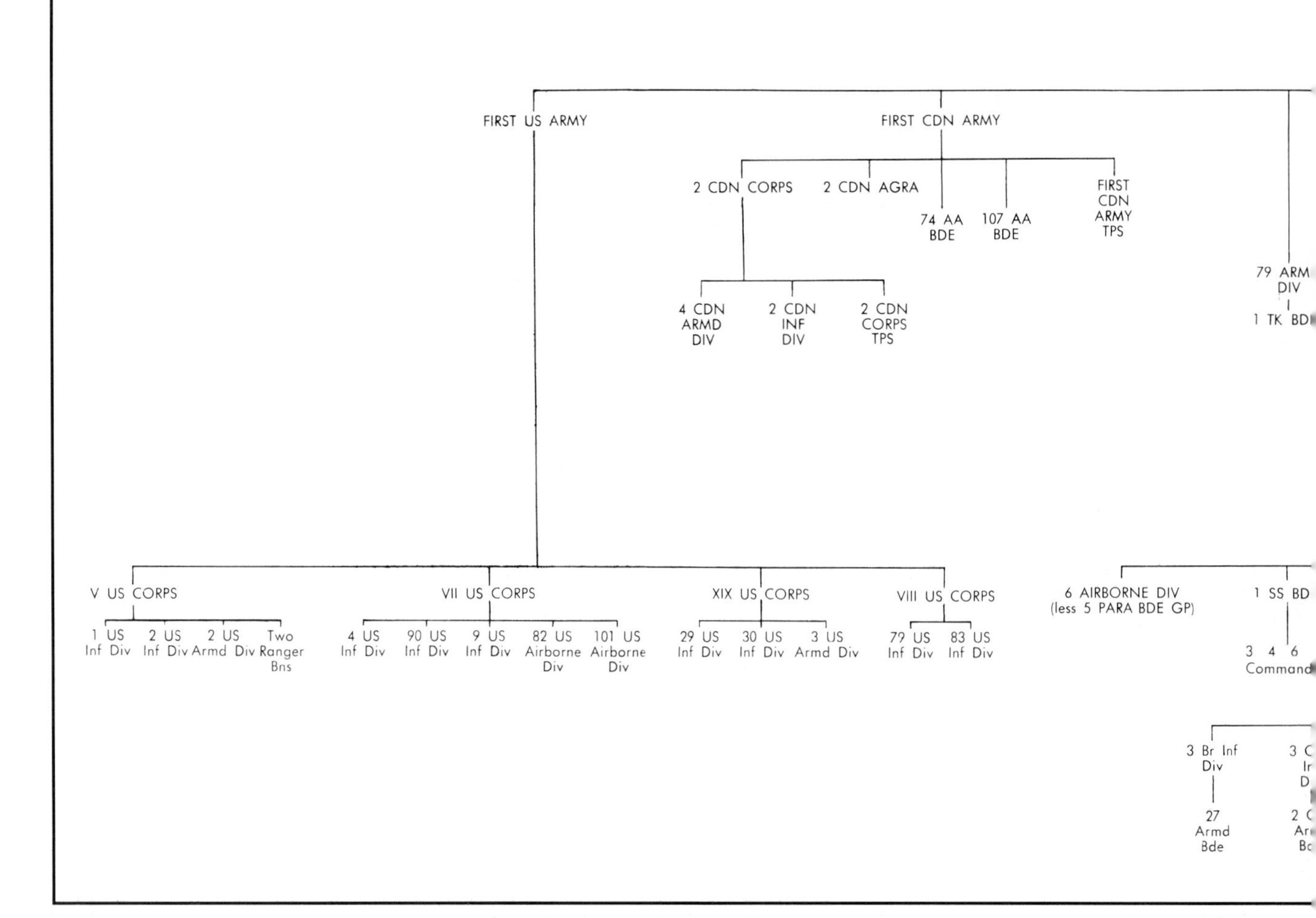

I made a number of changes in 21st Army Group staff proper in order to introduce officers who had already had considerable experience in the field. I brought back from Italy a number of senior staff officers, including my Chief-of-Staff, Major-General Sir Francis de Guingand.

The troops under my operational control comprised 21st Army Group and US First Army (General Omar N. Bradley). The outline order of battle is shown in the adjacent chart, from which it will be seen that 21st Army Group comprised Canadian First Army (Lieutenant-General Henry Crerar), British Second Army (Lieutenant-General Sir Miles Dempsey), the British airborne troops (Lieutenant-General Frederick 'Boy' Browning), and the various Allied contingents. Attached to the US First Army were the American 82nd and 101st Airborne Divisions.

Reference to the order of battle shows that the bulk of forces available for Operation 'Overlord' was lacking in battle experience. These formations had spent a long period energetically training in England, but inevitably some of their notions and doctrines had become theoretical. During the planning period, therefore, I set about the task of putting across to the troops under my command a sound battle technique. This process was facilitated by the fact that I had the 7th Armoured, 50th and 51st Divisions and two armoured brigades who had had considerable service in the Eighth Army; by exchanging officers between these formations and those less experienced I endeavoured to spread our available experience as much as possible. I also held a conference of all general officers in the army group as early as I could arrange it, to explain to them my views on the major points of battle technique. I moreover decided to make certain changes amongst the commanders of formations in England, again with the object of making good as far as possible the inevitable lack of battle experience I found so prevalent.

The process of forging the weapon for the task which lay ahead occupied much of my time right up to D-Day. I was determined to gain the confidence of the fighting troops, and to inspire them with confidence in themselves and in their ability to achieve the task which lay ahead of them. I aimed to build up their morale to the highest possible state so that they would sweep all before them in this great adventure. I travelled throughout England in order to visit each individual formation under my operational control — both British and American.

Lieutenant-General Henry D. G. Crerar was the senior officer at Canadian Military Headquarters in London during 1939-40. In 1940-41, he served as Chief of General Staff, Canada, and later that year became commander of the 2nd Canadian Division Overseas. From 1942 to 1944, he commanded the Canadian I Corps and also the Canadian Corps Mediterranean Area (1943-44). He led the Canadian First Army in 1944-45.

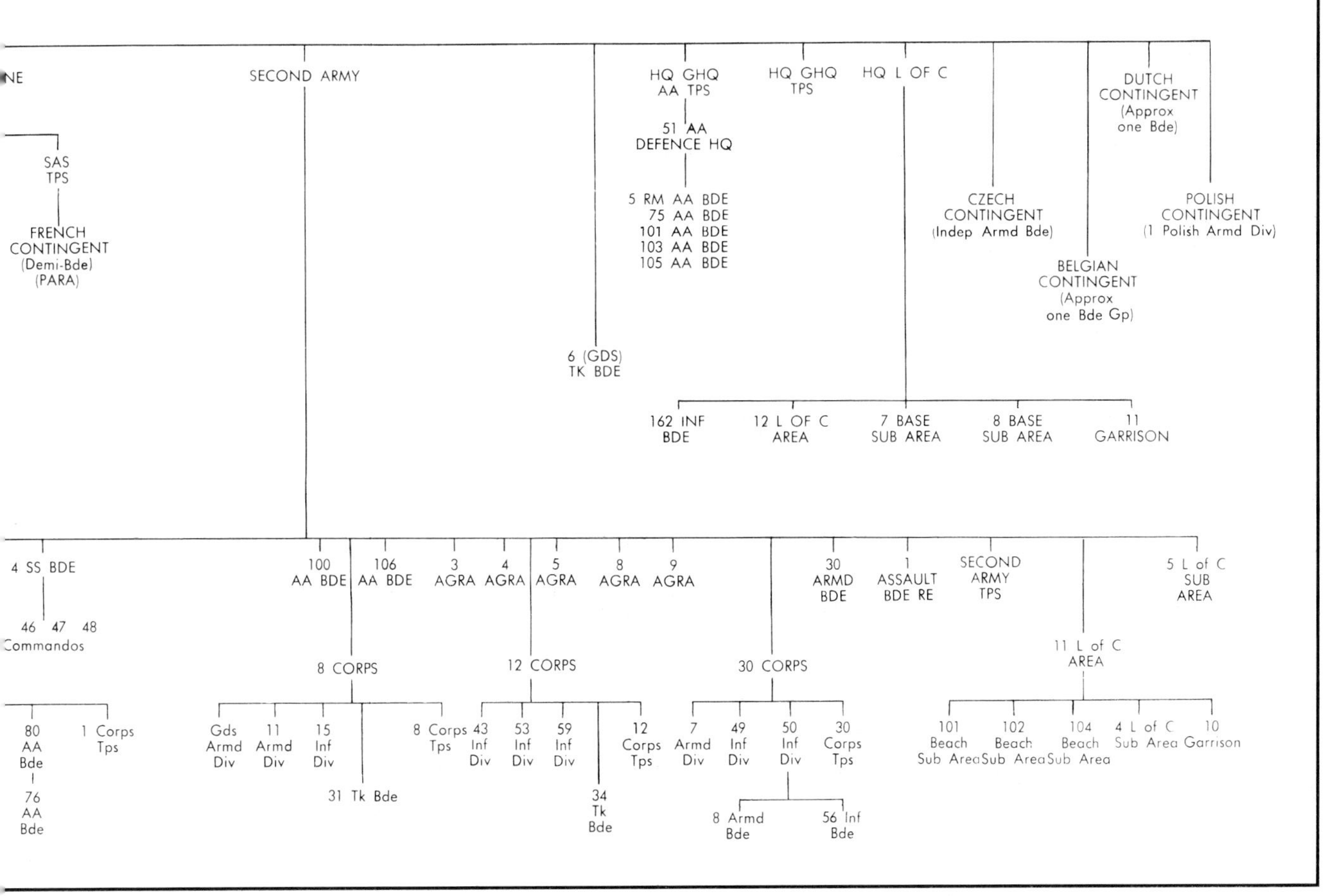

Lieutenant-General Sir Miles Dempsey had commanded the 13th Infantry Brigade in France in 1940, later becoming Brigadier General Staff with the Canadians under General A. G. L. MacNaughton. Shortly after El Alamein, he took command of XIII Corps of the Eighth Army and led it in the Sicilian campaign and in the invasion of Italy. In January 1944, he became commander of the British Second Army.

During the later planning stages, some difficulties arose over the so-called 'levels' of command between the army and air forces authorities. As long as 21st Army Group was responsible for overall direction of the land battle, the appropriate air headquarters with which planning was conducted was Allied Expeditionary Air Forces; but when two army groups were later deployed under SHAEF, Headquarters Second Tactical Air Force was to become our associated air command. Consequently, longer term planning therefore suffered delays because co-ordination with two separate air force authorities was required.

In considering the time available for planning, it was regrettable that the command set-up and appointment of the commanders were so much delayed. The responsibility and importance of the task laid upon the commanders and staff, and the truly formidable amount of detailed work required for such a gigantic undertaking, would imply that no effort should have been spared to ensure that those concerned had time to discharge their functions under reasonable conditions. In the event, by D-Day, when they should have been fit and fresh for the start of the great adventure, in many cases the staffs were bordering on a state of exhaustion.

Lieutenant-General Frederick 'Boy' Browning was transferred from the 24th Guards Brigade in October 1941 to carry out Churchill's orders to form a combined airborne division of parachute and glider troops. His title of GOC Airborne Forces was redesignated GOC I Airborne Corps in August 1944 when he also became deputy commander of the First Allied Airborne Army under Lieutenant General Brereton.

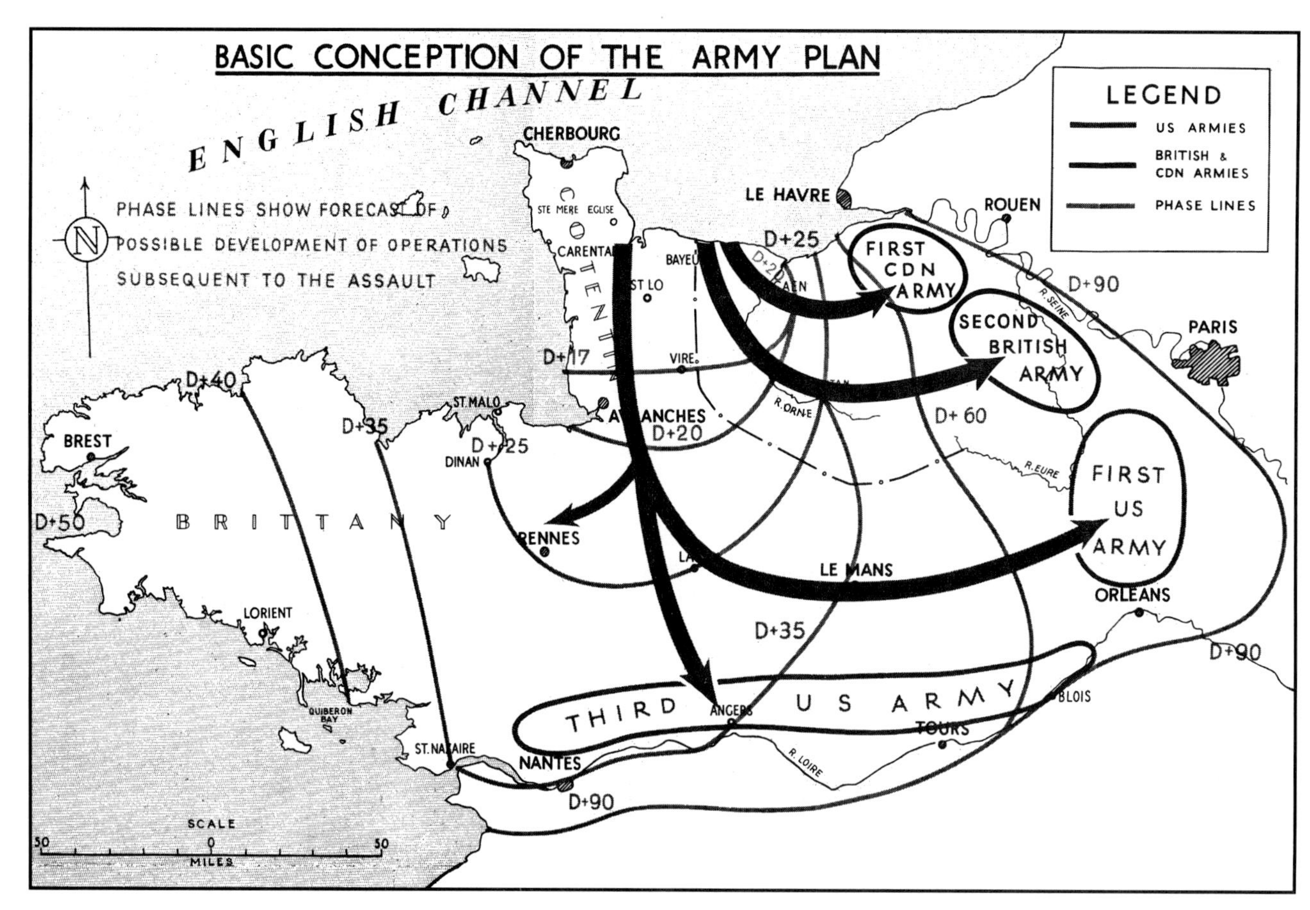

On April 7-8, Exercise 'Thunderclap' took place at St Paul's School so that General Montgomery, Admiral Ramsay, and Air Chief Marshal Leigh-Mallory could present the military, naval, and air plans to an audience comprising the commanders of all the forces involved. The Prime Minister also attended after lunch. One aspect of the briefing, which caused argument, both during and after the war, was the inclusion by Montgomery of this phase line map prepared under the direction of Lieutenant-Colonel Christopher Dawnay, Montgomery's Military Attaché. As de Guingand explained, such maps merely show the optimum progress of development, if everything goes as planned, but 'a phase line does in no way imply a guarantee that we shall reach such and such a position by a certain date'. However, General Bradley did not favour the use of phase lines because he felt that they made planning too rigid and might prevent the exploitation of an unexpected development. Bradley refused to agree to the dates on the lines for the American sector and insisted they be removed.

THE ARMY PLAN

The intention for Operation 'Overlord' was to assault, simultaneously, beaches on the Normandy coast immediately north of the Carentan estuary and between the Carentan estuary and the River Orne, with the object of securing as a base for further operations a lodgement area which was to include airfield sites, the port of Cherbourg and the ports of Brittany.

To achieve this task, I decided upon the plan of the land battle and subsequently explained it myself to the general officers of the field armies in London on April 7.

No photographs exist of the briefing, or the subsequent 'war game' on Saturday, but this shot of a later army commanders' conference shows the then Field-Marshal using a floor map similar to that employed at St Paul's. General Bradley: 'In the assault, two US airborne divisions and two seaborne divisions were to be matched by Dempsey's British force of one airborne and three seaborne divisions. A relief map of Normandy the width of a city street had been spread on the floor. With rare skill, Monty traced his 21st Group plan of maneuver as he tramped about like a giant through Lilliputian France.'

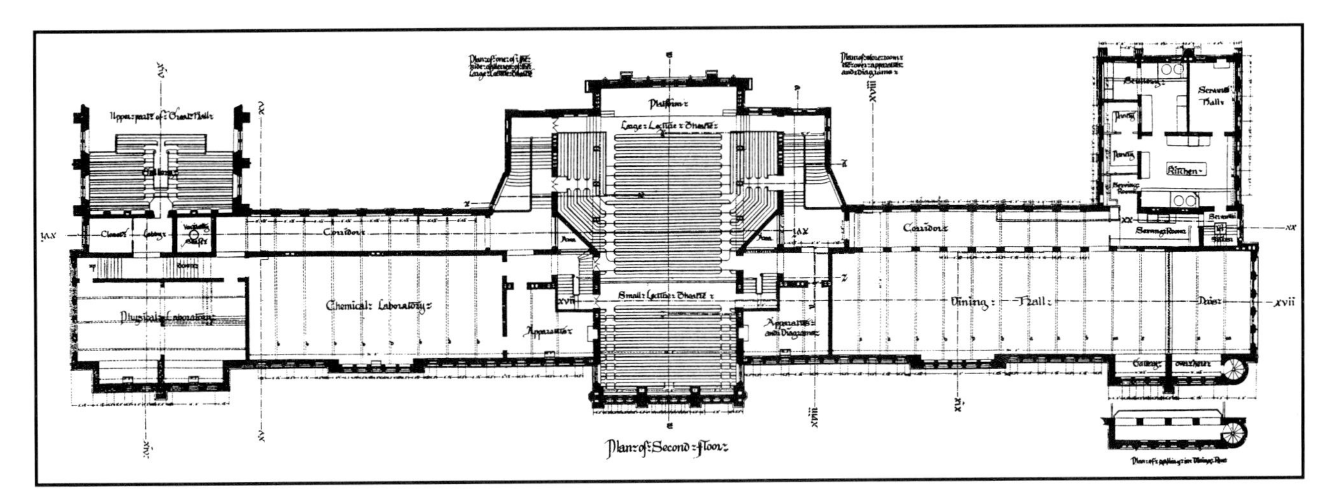

Once ashore and firmly established, my plan was to threaten to break out of the initial bridgehead on the eastern flank — that is, in the Caen sector. I intended by means of this threat to draw the main enemy reserves into that sector, to fight them there and keep them there, using the British and Canadian armies for the purpose. Having got the main enemy reserves committed on the eastern flank, my plan was to make the break-out on the western flank, using for this task the American armies under General Bradley, and to pivot the whole front on Caen. The American break-out thrust was to be delivered southwards down to the Loire and then to be developed eastwards in a wide sweep up to the Seine about Paris. This movement was designed to cut off all the enemy forces south of the Seine, over which river the bridges were to be destroyed by air action.

This strategy was evolved from consideration primarily of the layout of enemy reserve formations in western Europe, the run of rail and road communications leading to Normandy and the immediate task of the operation: which was to secure ports. The capture of the Cotentin and Brittany peninsulas and the opening of the ports located in them meant that we required to make rapid territorial gains in the west; on the eastern flank, acquisition of ground was not so pressing providing the air force requirements for airfield construction could be met. This pointed to the need for breaking out on the American front. If in turn the expansion in the west were to proceed rapidly, we had to draw the enemy weight away from that flank and in this we were greatly assisted by the immense strategic importance of Caen.

The city of Caen was a vital road and rail communication centre through which the main routes from the east and south-east passed. Since the bulk of the enemy mobile reserves was located north of the Seine, they would have to approach Normandy from the east and might be expected to converge on Caen. Hence, if a major threat to the enemy containing forces could be developed and sustained in the Caen sector, his reserves would tend to become initially committed there.

It was to be expected that the enemy would react strongly to an advance on Caen; such a course would indicate to

The 'Presentation of Plans' on that historic Friday was held in the school theatre which originally comprised two rooms: the Upper and Lower or, on this plan, the Small and Large Lecture Theatres. In the picture *below* showing the rear of St Paul's with Gliddon Road in the foreground, the theatre block can be seen in the centre overlooking the playing field.

Montgomery's own explanation of the phase line map was that 'in the planning stages of a major operation, it is customary to issue for the guidance of subordinate commanders and staffs, an estimate of the progress of operations. Such an estimate normally takes the form of a series of "phase lines" drawn on an operational map to indicate the positions to be reached by leading troops at intervals of a few days. The phase line map for the operations was produced in April 1944. I was not altogether happy about this map because the imponderable factors in an operation of the magnitude of 'Overlord' make such forecasting so very academic.'

Fifty years later, the sports field has been lost beneath the buildings of the Hammersmith and West London College.

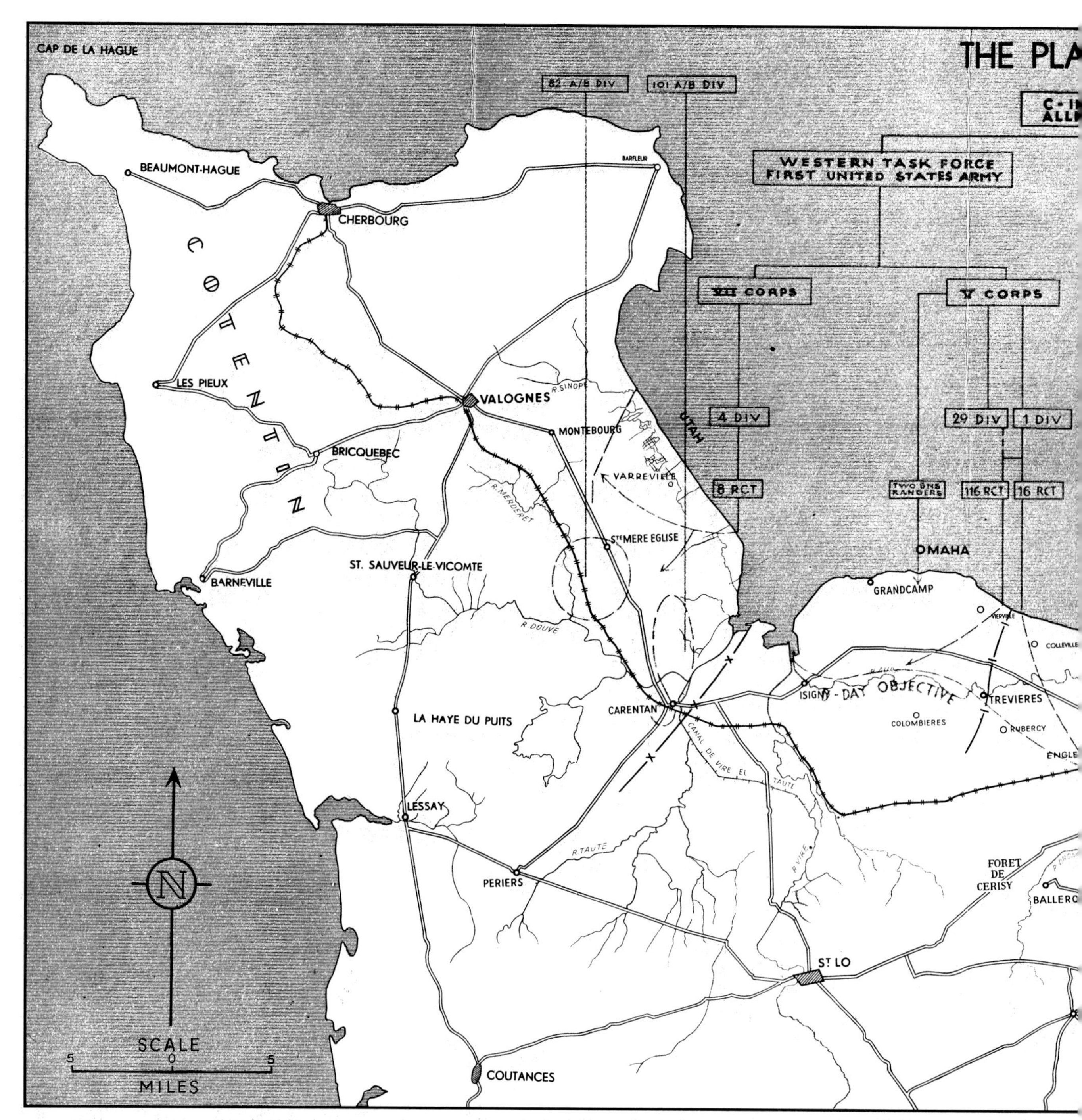

him our intention to break through the Caen bottleneck in order to exploit our armoured resources in the more open country to the south-east. This direction would moreover give us the shortest approach to the Seine ports and Paris.

These arguments convinced me that strong and persistent offensive action in the Caen sector would achieve our object of drawing the enemy mobile reserves on to our eastern flank.

This was my original conception of the manner in which the Battle of Normandy was to be developed. From the start, it formed the basis of all our planning, and was the aim of our operations from the time of the assault to the final victory in Normandy. I never once had cause or reason to alter my plan. In order to understand the Battle of Normandy, it is essential that this fact should be clearly appreciated.

THE ASSAULT

The overall plan of assault was designed to concentrate the full weight of the available resources of all three services in getting the assaulting troops ashore and in assisting them in their task of breaking through the Atlantic Wall.

The US First Army was to assault astride the Carentan estuary with one regimental combat team between Varreville and the estuary (Utah), and two regimental combat teams between Vierville and Colleville (Omaha). The initial tasks were to capture Cherbourg as quickly as possible and to develop operations southwards towards St Lô in conformity with the advance of British Second Army.

The British Second Army assault was to be delivered with five brigades between Asnelles and Ouistreham (Gold, Juno and Sword), with the initial task of developing the bridgehead south of the line St Lô–Caen and south-east of Caen, in order to secure airfield sites and to protect the eastern flank of the First Army while the latter was capturing Cherbourg.

The inter-army boundary made Port-en-Bessin, and the line of the River Drôme to Englesqueville, inclusive to Second Army.

During the night preceding D-Day, while the naval assault forces made the sea passage, the programme of intensive air action against the enemy defences was to begin with operations by RAF Bomber Command, while airborne forces were to be dropped on the flanks of the invasion area. At H-Hour, supported by naval bombardment and air action and by the guns, rockets and mortars of close-support craft, the lead-

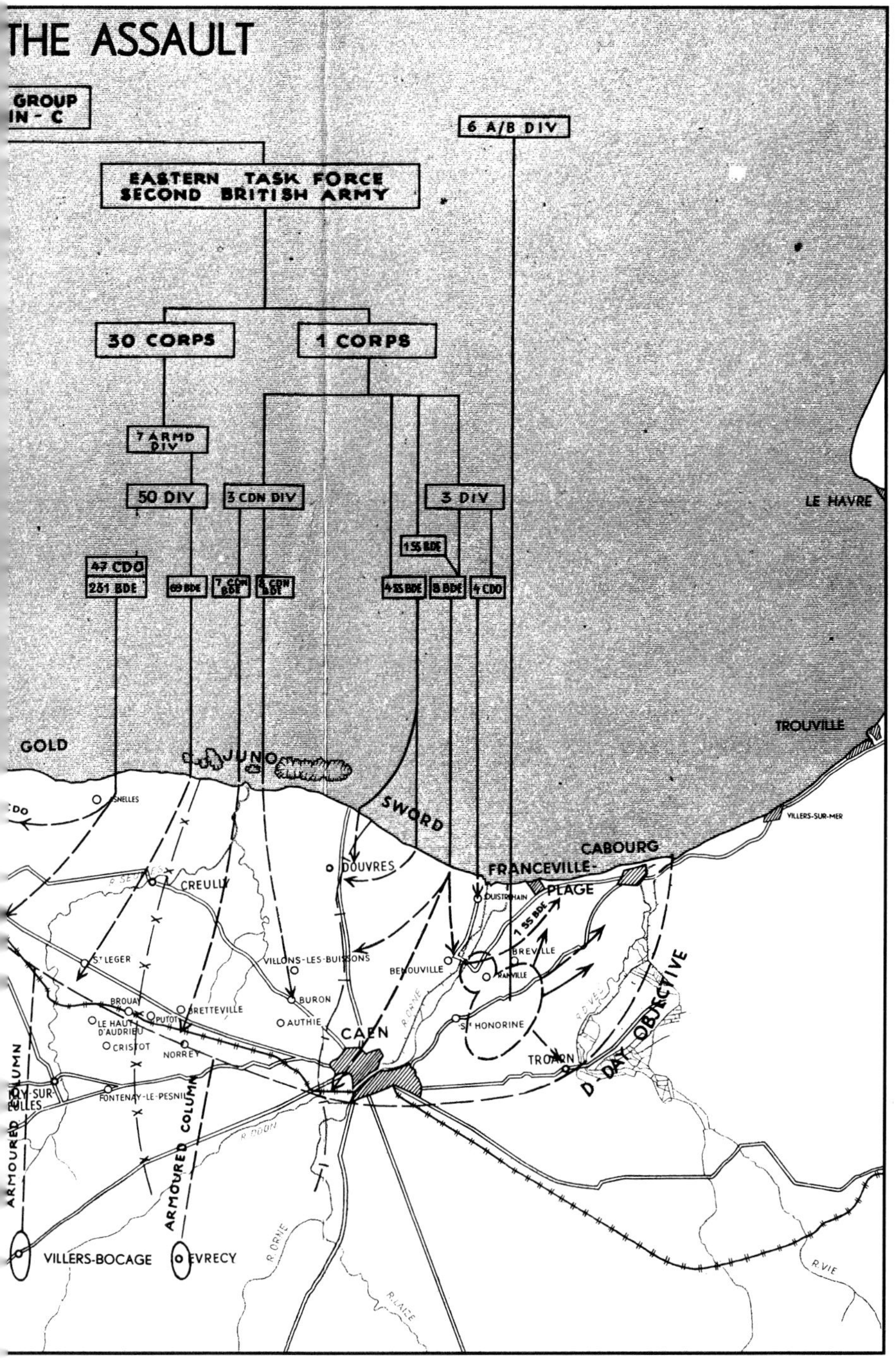

Ever since the war, a heated controversy has also existed over whether the Normandy campaign developed exactly according to Montgomery's master plan. In all his post-war works, Monty consistently claimed that, right from the start, he had intended to pivot at Caen. However, as American historian Carlo d'Este demonstrated in his 1983 book *Decision in Normandy*, Monty's personal notes for the April 7 presentation clearly show that in actual fact he originally intended to pivot, not at Caen, but at Falaise, 20 miles further inland. The hinge at Caen was in fact forced upon him after D-Day, when his failure to quickly capture that city compelled him to improvise a new solution. Montgomery's character was such that, rather than admit that he had had to change his original plan, he chose to alter the plan to fit what actually happened, in order to save the myth of his infallibility. Brigadier David Belchem, head of Montgomery's Operations Staff, claims to have chosen the actual code-names given to the British landing. Gold, Juno and Sword were selected from an old army manual which listed short words easily pronounced, while Belchem says that Major General J. Lawton Collins, the VII Corps commander, chose Utah, and Major General Leonard T. Gerow, Omaha, for V Corps. (See also page 517.)

ing wave of troops was to disembark and force its way ashore.

The total initial lift in the assault and follow-up naval forces was of the order of 130,000 personnel and 20,000 vehicles, all of which were to be landed on the first three tides. In addition to the basic eight assaulting brigades/regimental combat teams, a variety of attached troops were required in the assault including special assault engineers, amphibious tanks, and other detachments which varied for the different beaches according to the specific 'menu' (i.e. composition of the assault wave) decided upon by the subordinate formations. The total forces to be carried in the initial lift consisted of the essential combat elements (with minimum transport) of:

US First Army:
- Three infantry divisions
- Five tank battalions
- Two Ranger battalions
- Corps and Army troops
- Naval and Air Force detachments.

British Second Army:
- Four infantry divisions (less two brigade groups)
- Three assault tank brigades
- One armoured brigade
- Two commando brigades
- Corps and Army troops
- Naval and Air Force detachments.

Priority of air lift was given to American airborne forces owing to the vital tasks of securing the beach exits and facilitating deployment from Utah. Main bodies of both the 82nd and 101st Airborne Divisions were to land in the general area of Ste Mère-Eglise on the night D-1/D, the latter to assist the seaborne assault on the Utah sector and the former to guard the landward flank and prevent the movement of enemy reserves into the Cotentin peninsula. The remaining air lift was allotted to Second Army for the 6th Airborne Division (less one brigade) which was to land before H-Hour east of Caen, with the tasks of seizing the crossings over the Orne at Bénouville and Ranville and, in conjunction with commando troops, of dominating the area to the east of Caen in order to delay the movement of enemy forces towards the town.

American Ranger units were to land in the assault on the west of Omaha and had the task of attacking enemy defences on the east side of the Carentan estuary. One British brigade of two commandos was to link the assaults on the Juno and Sword areas. A second commando brigade was to land behind the assaulting division on Sword and, while one commando dealt with Ouistreham, the remainder of the brigade was to cross the Orne at Bénouville and attack the enemy coast defences east of the river up to Cabourg inclusive.

Prolonged study and numerous experiments had been devoted to the development of the technique of assaulting a defended beach. As a result, various types of specialised military equipment were available by D-Day, including assault engineer tanks, tank-carried bridges for crossing anti-tank ditches, mat-laying tanks for covering soft clay patches on the beaches, ramp tanks over which other vehicles could scale sea-walls, flail tanks for mine clearance, and amphibious assault tanks. These devices were integrated into the specially-trained assault teams which led the invasion forces.

The final review of the 'Overlord' plans on May 15 also took place in the theatre *(right)* at St Paul's. *Above:* This is the entry pass used by Rear-Admiral W. R. Patterson, Flag Officer aboard HMS *Mauritius* of Assault Force 'S'. His opposite number aboard the USS *Tuscaloosa* (Assault Force 'U') was Rear Admiral Morton L. Deyo who later wrote that 'as we took those uncompromisingly hard and narrow seats, the room was hushed and the tension was palpable . . . All in that room were aware of the gravity of the elements to be dealt with.' *Below:* The seating plan for the first two rows.

ACM SIR ARTHUR HARRIS	LT. GEN. ISMAY	FIELD MARSHAL SIR ALAN BROOKE	MARSHAL OF THE RAF SIR CHARLES PORTAL	ADMIRAL STARK	FIRST SEA LORD	PRIME MINISTER	SUPREME COMMANDER	DEPUTY SUPREME COMMANDER	FIELD MARSHAL SMUTS	ADMIRAL RAMSAY	GENERAL MONTGOMERY	ACM SIR T. LEIGH-MALLORY	ADMIRAL CREASY	LT. GEN. GALE	LT. GEN. BRERETON	MAJOR GEN. DE GUINGAND
LT. GEN. GRASETT	ACM SIR SHOLTO DOUGLAS	GEN. SIR H.E. FRANKLYN	LT. GEN. SPAATZ	LT. GEN. PATTON	ADMIRAL KIRK	LT. GEN. BRADLEY	LT. GEN. SMITH	LT. GEN. DEMPSEY	LT. GEN. J.C.H.LEE	LT. GEN. CRERAR	AVM WIGGLESWORTH	LT. GEN. DOOLITTLE	ADMIRAL VIAN	AM SIR A. CONINGHAM	LT. GEN. MORGAN	AVM ROBB

PLANNED DEVELOPMENT OF OPERATIONS

I have already outlined my broad strategic plan for the development of operations designed to secure the lodgement area.

Once the troops were ashore, it was necessary for them to 'crack about'; the need for sustained energy and drive was paramount, as we had to link our beachheads and penetrate quickly inland before the enemy opposition crystallised. I gave orders that the leading formations should bypass major enemy centres of resistance in order to 'peg out claims' inland. I emphasised to commanders on all levels that determined leadership would be necessary to withstand the strain of the first few days, to retain the initiative and to make sure that there would no setbacks.

While I had in my mind the necessity to reach the Seine and the Loire by D+90, the interim estimates of progress could not, I felt, have any great degree of reality. The predictions were particularly complicated by two major divergent requirements. On the one hand, the general strategic plan was to

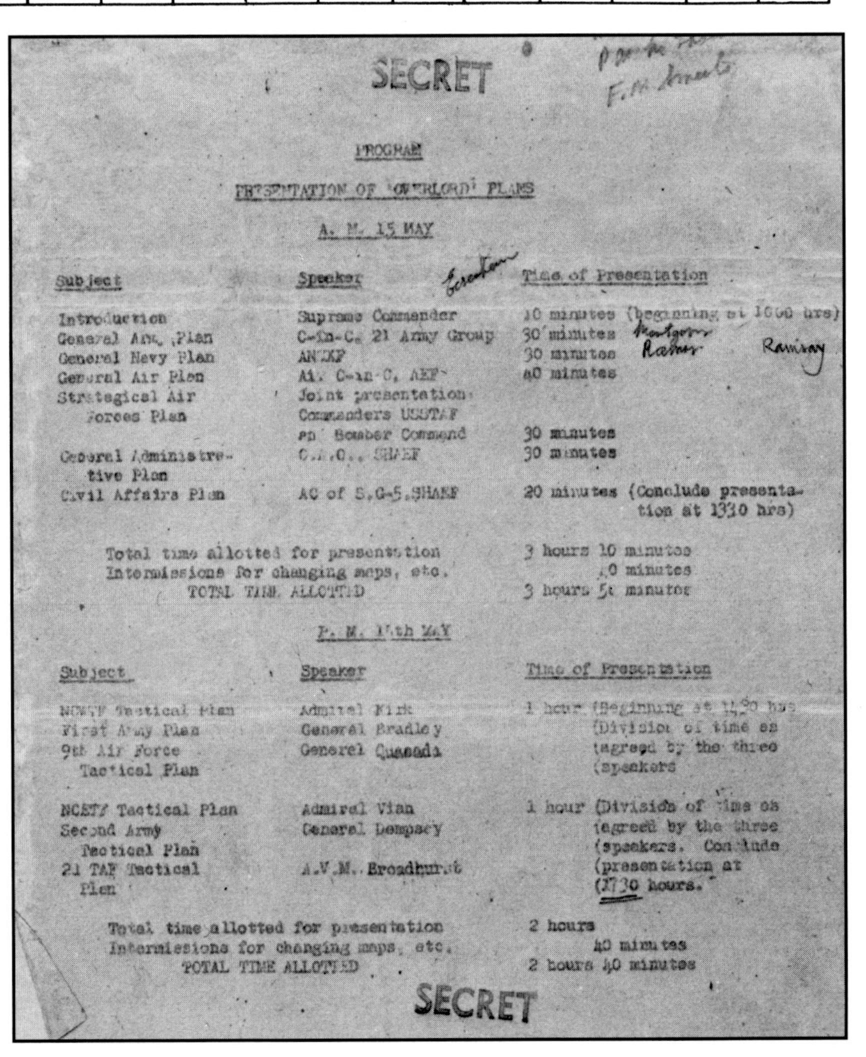

SECRET

PROGRAM

PRESENTATION OF 'OVERLORD' PLANS

A. M. 15 MAY

Subject	Speaker	Time of Presentation
Introduction	Supreme Commander	10 minutes (beginning at 1000 hrs)
General Army Plan	C-in-C, 21 Army Group	30 minutes
General Navy Plan	ANCXF	30 minutes
General Air Plan	Air C-in-C, AEF	40 minutes
Strategical Air Forces Plan	Joint presentation: Commanders USSTAF and Bomber Command	30 minutes
General Administrative Plan	C.A.O., SHAEF	30 minutes
Civil Affairs Plan	AC of S, G-5, SHAEF	20 minutes (Conclude presentation at 1310 hrs)

Total time allotted for presentation — 3 hours 10 minutes
Intermissions for changing maps, etc. — 40 minutes
TOTAL TIME ALLOTTED — 3 hours 50 minutes

P. M. 15th MAY

Subject	Speaker	Time of Presentation
NCWTF Tactical Plan	Admiral Kirk	1 hour (Beginning at 1430 hrs (Division of time as agreed by the three speakers
First Army Plan	General Bradley	
9th Air Force Tactical Plan	General Quesada	
NCETF Tactical Plan	Admiral Vian	1 hour (Division of time as agreed by the three speakers. Conclude presentation at 1730 hours.
Second Army Tactical Plan	General Dempsey	
21 TAF Tactical Plan	A.V.M. Broadhurst	

Total time allotted for presentation — 2 hours
Intermissions for changing maps, etc. — 40 minutes
TOTAL TIME ALLOTTED — 2 hours 40 minutes

SECRET

HM King George VI was also present at this second conference as was the Prime Minister and Field-Marshal Jan Smuts of South Africa, who was in the UK with the other Dominion prime ministers for a two-week conference. To General Bradley, one of the afternoon speakers, it was 'the greatest gathering of Allied brass that I saw in World War II', and even Eisenhower said that 'during the whole war I attended no other conference so packed with rank as this one.'

The Supreme Commander opened the proceedings and, according to Deyo, 'before the warmth of his quiet confidence the mists of doubt dissolved. When he had finished, the tension was gone. Not often has one man been called upon to accept so great a burden of responsibility. But here was one at peace with his soul.' The morning session closed with a short address by the King. According to Lieutenant General Brereton, the speech was 'beautifully done — clear and simple. He talked more like a soldier than a statesman. I was surprised to note the clarity of his speech; his unfortunate impediment of speech was barely perceptible. He talked with his hands crossed behind his back and, once or twice, when he had to pause, you could see his shoulder muscles tense as he fought to maintain his flow of speech.' ***Above:*** **The theatre underwent drastic remodelling in the summer of 1958 when the stage was enlarged, the side seats and galleries removed to provide store rooms, and the centre seating and part of the pine pews in the upper gallery replaced with crimson upholstered chairs. (The large plaque seen on the right, commemorating the event, is now displayed in the Montgomery Room of the new school at Barnes.)**

make the break-out on the western flank pivoting the front on the Caen area, where the bulk of enemy reserves were to be engaged; on the other hand, the Air Forces insisted on the importance of capturing quickly the good airfield country south-east of Caen. Though I have never failed in my operations to exert my utmost endeavour to meet the requirements of the Air Forces, in planning these operations the overriding requirement was to gain territory in the west. For this reason, while accepting an estimate for seizing the open country beyond Caen at a relatively early date after the landing, I had to make it clear that progress in that sector would be dependent on the successful development of the main strategic plan.

SAS ACTIVITIES AND THE FRENCH RESISTANCE GROUPS

Plans were made for ensuring as far as possible the co-operation of the French Resistance movement in our operations. Arms and equipment had been delivered by air to the French over a long period and a network of wireless communications had been set up. Arrangements were made to pass instructions and guidance concerning sabotage to the Resistance leaders and to alert their organisations as soon as the invasion began.

A considerable number of our own Special Air Service troops were dropped in France with sabotage missions designed to delay the movement of enemy reserves. In many cases, these troops linked up with Resistance personnel who afforded them ready assistance.

Having established the exact position where the theatre stood in relation to the new flats which now occupy the site of the school, we returned on Sunday afternoon, May 15, 1994, to take this picture (*left*) in Lily Close. It was here, exactly 50 years before, that Winston Churchill gave the closing address, including his remark: 'I am hardening on this operation.' This has been taken by others to mean that Churchill had been against the cross-Channel operation, but the Prime Minister explained in 1952 that the phrase came from a telegram sent to General Marshall, in March 1944 and that he meant the words 'in the sense of wishing to strike if humanly possible, even if the limiting conditions we laid down are not exactly fulfilled.' ***Right:*** **Unfortunately, nothing of significance remains at the St Paul's site today, save this Emergency Water Supply notice painted on the front gatepost, and no one has seen fit to commemorate the vital part the building played in the 'Overlord' story.**

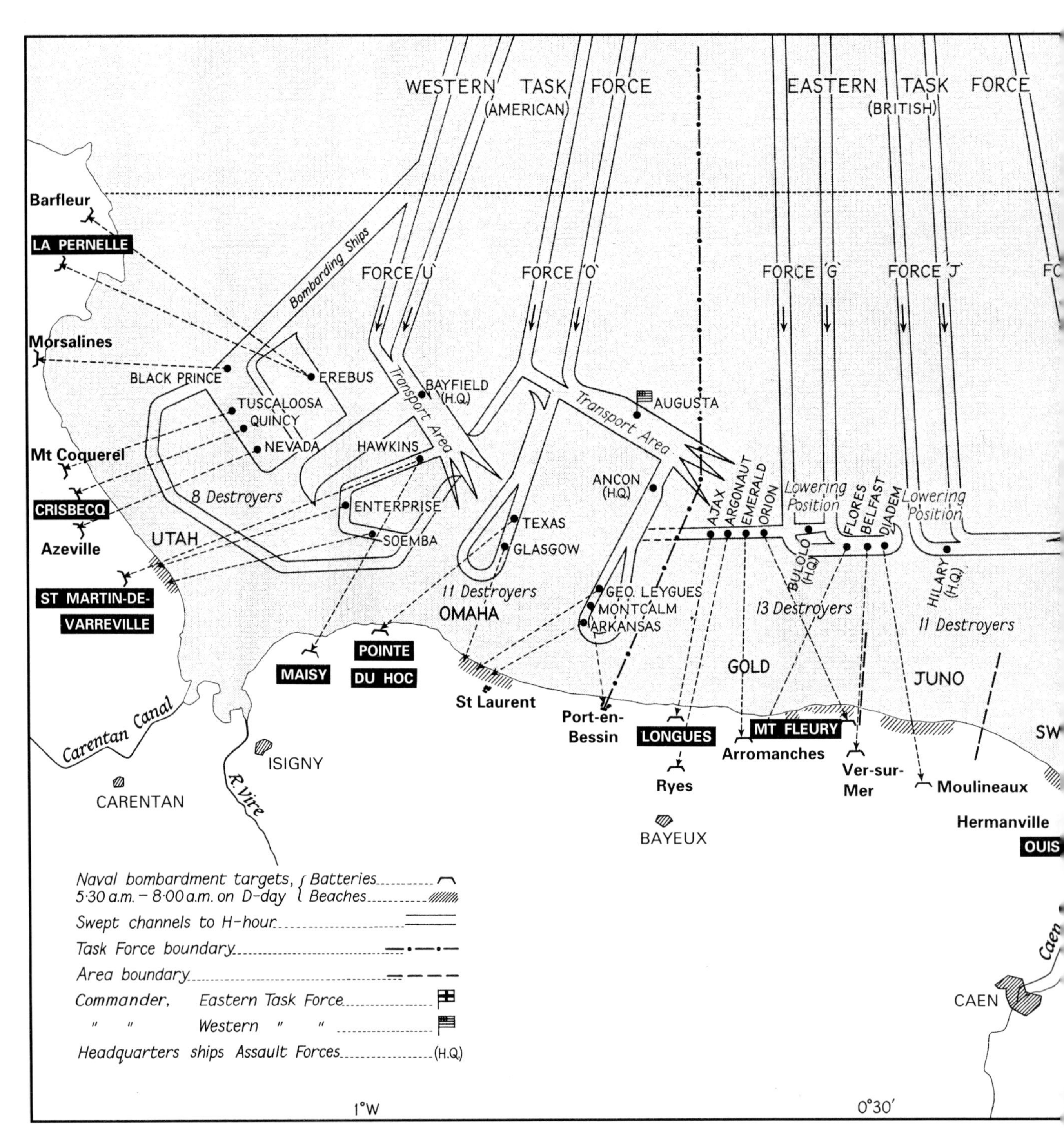

THE JOINT FIRE PLAN

The purpose of the Joint Fire Plan was to allocate tasks to the resources of the three services with the object of assisting the Army to get ashore. The chief requirements were to destroy or neutralise the enemy coastal artillery batteries which might interfere with the approach of the naval convoys or bring fire to bear on the anchorages, and to neutralise the enemy strong points and defended localities that were sited for the immediate defence of our assault beaches.

It has been shown that preliminary air attacks were delivered against enemy coast defence batteries in the preliminary operations prior to D-Day. The Fire Plan proper was to begin on the night preceding the assault, when the heavy bombers of Bomber Command were to attack in great strength the ten most important batteries: the operation was to be timed as late as would be consistent with the return of the aircraft to England by daylight. Following the Bomber Command operations, attacks were planned by medium bombers, using special navigational devices, on a further six coast defence targets; this phase was to begin at civil twilight and at about the same time bombardment was to start from assault craft carrying various types of armament. [Civil twilight, when the sun is still below the horizon, is best described as the time corresponding to the lower limit of daylight for any outdoor activity.]

Shortly afterwards, naval gun-fire directed by spotting aircraft was timed to commence, and, about half-an-hour before H-Hour, the heavy bombers of the Eighth Air Force and medium bombers of the Ninth Air Force were to begin action against coast defence artillery and enemy beach defences and localities. Included in the naval assault forces was a variety of specially-fitted craft carrying 4.7-inch guns, 4-inch mortars, barrages of 5-inch rockets, Centaur tanks fitted with 75 millimetre howitzers, 17-pounder anti-tank guns, as well as ordinary self-propelled field guns of the assaulting divisional artilleries which were to be embarked in Tank Landing Craft and to work as regimental fire units.

The Fire Plan aimed at building up the supporting fire to a tremendous crescendo which would reach its climax at the latest possible moment before the leading troops waded ashore, in order

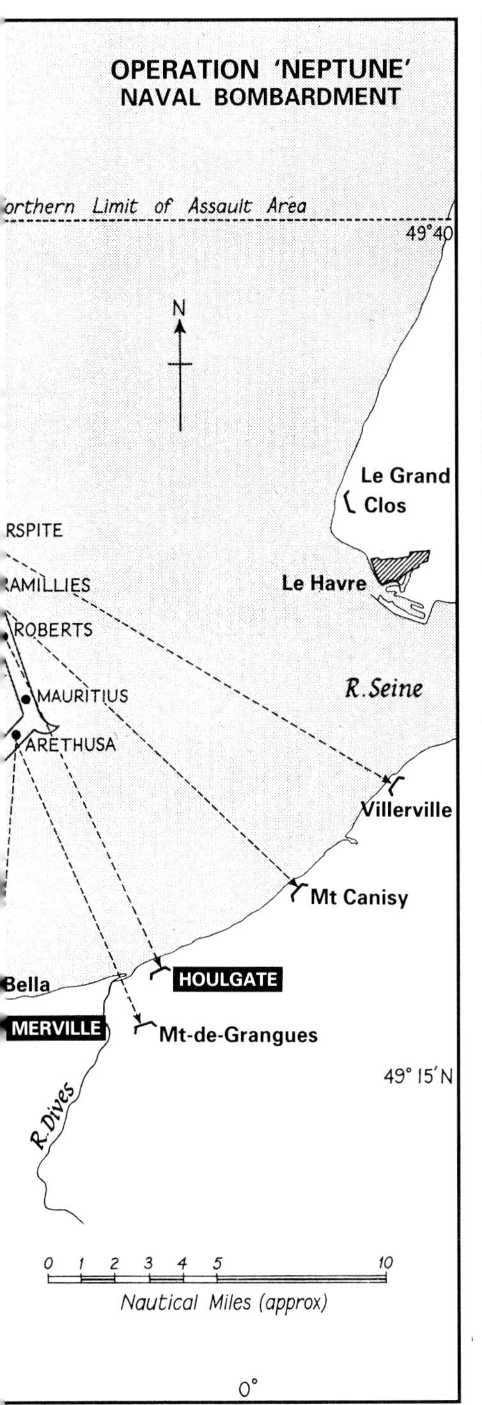

to give the defenders the minimum time to recover before being set upon. The heavy air bombardment was timed to continue on the beach frontages to within ten minutes of H-Hour, and from this time fighters and fighter-bombers were to take up the air offensive, and in particular undertake the task of neutralising the enemy field batteries located inland. Air support tentacles were to accompany the assaulting troops, and fighter-bomber squadrons were to be at hand to answer calls for close support, while the medium and heavy bombers returned to their bases to refuel and rearm in readiness for further missions. No fewer than 171 Allied fighter squadrons were to be employed in the overall assault phase, and in the event the Allied air forces flew some 11,000 sorties on D-Day.

As we have seen, the air forces were very late in getting a decision over the most favourable targets which would best serve 'Overlord', and the commanders of the heavy bombers were reluctant to commit themselves as to the amount of support they could provide. Both Harris and Spaatz were unhappy at being diverted from their established programmes so that the integration of their forces in the Joint Fire Plan came very late in the day. The plan specified: (*a*) The batteries to be bombed, (i) before D-Day, priority being given to those most menacing to the approach of naval forces; (ii) by heavy night bombers, during the night of D–1/D-Day, and (iii) by medium bombers during the early hours of D-Day. (*b*) The batteries to be engaged by naval gunfire to cover the assault. (*c*) The heavy and medium bomber effort available to supplement the naval beach 'drenching' fire and its distribution between the task forces commencing at H-45; about 2,500 tons were to be dropped in the British and some 1,700 tons in the American area. The air effort was also limited by the necessity to bomb targets outside Normandy as part of the cover plan, and for every bomb dropped west of Le Havre, two were dropped on batteries to the north. In the event, ten batteries were selected as being the most threatening and each received an average of 500 tons of bombs. They were Houlgate (*above*), mounting four 155mm guns; Merville (four 100mm); Ouistreham (four 105mm); Mont-Fleury (four 122mm); Longues (four 150mm); Pointe du Hoc (sometimes referred to as St Pierre-du-Mont in official reports — six 155mm); Maisy (four 105mm and six 155mm); St Martin-de-Varreville (four 105mm); Crisbecq (four 210mm), and La Pernelle (three 170mm). (The actual calibres/number of guns was not always correctly known at the time.)

Houlgate battery today. Sometimes referred to as Tournebride, it was armed with four 155mm Kanone 420(f) with a range of 21300 metres. The battery consisted of two concrete casemates and five open gun positions with the garrison quartered in an extensive underground shelter.

The precise date and time for 'Overlord' had still not been settled, and Admiral Ramsay wrote in his diary after the May 15 St Paul's conference that they held a further Supreme Commander's meeting after everything was over to further look at H-Hour in respect of the American beaches. The ideal time, to get full value from the naval and air bombardment, would be about an hour after civil twilight, which is the point at which there is sufficient light for any outdoor activity. In June, this came around 5.15 a.m. and bombing could commence about ten minutes later. Admiral Ramsay had decided that the earliest acceptable date would be June 5, which would give 55 minutes of daylight, and this was put to a meeting held at Widewing on May 8. With June 1 already fixed as a benchmark referred to as Y-Day, Eisenhower decided that D-Day should be Y+4, i.e. June 5. Although there would be an extra 25 minutes of daylight on June 6, this was considered equally acceptable although the 7th was not as good as it gave two hours of daylight before touch down. After that, the tides would not coincide for a fortnight and, if the same moon was required, a delay of a whole month would be necessary. Meanwhile, preparations were well underway in the Southern Command area of England to widen roads and strengthen bridges for the massive convoys which would soon be en route for the embarkation ports. *Above left:* Tree-felling on the A338 south of Salisbury. *Above right:* By 1994, the road at this point beside Longford Castle has been converted into a dual carriageway.

THE SELECTION OF D-DAY AND H-HOUR

The determination of H-Hour, defined as the time at which the leading wave of assault craft should hit the beach, and of D-Day for the assault, was made only after a prolonged and intensive study of the various factors affecting them.

In the first place, it was jointly decided that H-Hour should be in daylight and that there should be moonlight during the preceding night. From the naval point of view, a daylight assault facilitated station-keeping and deployment of the vast armada of ships and craft employed, and also the accurate location of the beaches. Moreover, in order to provide accurate naval gunfire and air bombardment against the enemy defences immediately before H-Hour, a period of daylight was necessary for observation. These advantages were considered to outweigh the drawbacks of allowing the enemy time to engage by observed fire our ships and craft before the assault began, and of making our troops advance to the attack in daylight; we had such preponderance of naval and air resources that we counted on stunning the defenders with the weight of our bombing and shell-fire. The moonlight preceding H-Hour was preferred for facilitating naval movements and the approach of airborne forces.

Having decided on a daylight assault, it was in the Army's interest to fix

Left: Work under way to widen the old Hythe–Southampton road, the B3053, just outside Dibden. *Right:* Fifty years later, John Chester clears the roadside at the same spot beside Locks Farm.

H-Hour as early after first light as possible, so that the defenders would have the minimum time for observation of our movements, and in order to conserve as many hours of daylight as possible for landing the follow-up on the second tide before nightfall. There would be a period before sunrise when aircraft spotting for naval guns, and heavy bombers observing above the target area, would be able to see sufficient for their purpose before the visibility became clear for defenders at sea level. The crux of the problem was to decide upon the minimum time required for effective engagement of shore targets by the naval guns and for delivery of the bomb loads by our air formations; eventually, the period from nautical twilight (the first sign of morning light) to 40 minutes later was accepted as sufficient for our needs.

Tidal conditions had now to be considered. The timing of H-Hour had to be related to the height of the tide for naval reasons and because of the necessity to deal with underwater obstacles which were sited to offer maximum interference at high water and which could not be demolished by sappers unless exposed by the tide.

The obstacles could most easily have been dealt with if the troops had landed at low water, but at low tide the landing craft would have grounded so far from the shore that assaulting infantry would have had to cross a wide stretch of exposed beach before closing with the defences; moreover, the beach surfaces in some cases were so uneven that troops wading ashore from the low tide mark would have dropped into hollows deeper than the height of a man before reaching dry land. Again, it was desirable to have as many hours as possible of rising tide upon which to land the supporting arms and enable the landing craft to retract; but the flow of the tide until about three hours before high water, and from three hours after, was so fast that there would have been insufficient time to discharge the landing craft before they became completely grounded.

A beautiful discovery in the New Forest. The D-Day replacement for the old wooden bridge on the Brockenhurst–Beaulieu road still standing today.

Park your tank here! Parking bays being readied in the market square of the Hampshire town of Wickham, seemingly deserted in May 1944 but a hive of activity 50 years later.

From a consideration of these factors it was decided that the best conditions would obtain if H-Hour were fixed 40 minutes after nautical twilight on a day when at this time the tide was three hours before high water mark. These conditions could not be obtained on all beaches simultaneously, because the flow of the tide up the English Channel resulted in high water occurring in the Utah area about 40 minutes earlier than in the Sword area. This fact, together with the difference in positioning of underwater obstacles on the various beaches, and complications due to the rock outcrop on Juno, led to the decision that a separate H-Hour should be fixed for each beach. This inevitable compromise resulted in the right-hand beaches having the bare minimum period for observed fire prior to the assault, whereas the left-hand beaches had considerably more than had been deemed essential. On the day ultimately selected, H-Hour varied between 0630 hours for the Western Task Force to 0745 hours on the east sector of Juno.

The selection of H-Hour to fill these many requirements restricted the days suitable to three in every fortnight or, with moonlight, to three in every month. I have already explained that, while the target date was set for May 31, the Supreme Commander had specified at the time that tidal and other conditions might cause D-Day to be selected during the first week in June — in fact June 5 was determined as the first of a three-day period suitable for the operation. Elaborate arrangements were made for weather forecasting, and for a machinery of postponement should this become necessary; but it should be noted that, had the weather been unsuitable in the first three-day period, a postponement of at least a fortnight, and more probably a month in order to have moonlight conditions, would have been inevitable.

And everywhere the countryside was full to overflowing of the machinery of war. This ordnance depot 'somewhere in England' was stated on the original caption as being at Ashchurch, Gloucestershire, but several hours of searching and making enquiries in the area drew a blank.

In the end, it was Janet Thompson of the Tewkesbury Library who, by a stroke of luck, established that the depot had been located at Naunton Farm, Toddington, seven miles to the east of Ashchurch. Geoffrey Slatter, the farmer, has lived in the area all his life and described how the equipment was stored over a wide area on the southern slopes of Dumbleton Hill.

THE BUILD-UP

The general principles upon which the build-up of our forces and material was planned were, first, the provision of the maximum number of fighting formations on the Continent in the first few days and, secondly, the introduction into the build-up system as quickly as possible of the maximum degree of flexibility: so that changes in priority of troops, administrative echelons, transport and stores could be made as the situation demanded.

By the end of D-Day it was planned that, including airborne forces, the Allies would have eight divisions ashore together with commando units, Ranger battalions and some 14 tank regiments. By D+6, the total forces would rise to some 13 divisions, exclusive of airborne formations, with five British armoured brigades and a proportionate number of American tank units. Between 23 and 24 basic divisions were due in Normandy by D+20. Comparison with the estimated enemy strength was

Ready for the build up. In 1944, ammunition could be seen stacked alongside country roads, this dump being located in Essex near Littlebury. Picture taken on May 15 by Sergeant Bill Woolridge. We rephotographed the spot on the road leading to Littlebury Green in May 1994.

difficult to make; some types of enemy division were organised on a considerably smaller establishment than our own; some were under conversion from training organisations and were known to be deficient of equipment. Our own build-up, moreover, included a considerable proportion of fighting units classed as corps and army troops and which, therefore, were not apparent in the divisional figures of the build-up table.

Planned build-up tables are inevitably suspect; it was impossible to estimate the delaying effect on the enemy build-up of our air action, or the success our cover plan arrangements would achieve in causing a dispersion of German resources. In our own estimates, the effect of weather on cross-Channel movement and beach working was a major imponderable.

In order to make our build-up plans flexible, a special inter-service staff was organised called 'Build-Up Control' (BUCO). This body was formed, as a result of Mediterranean experience, to organise the loading and despatch of craft and ships from home ports, and was the agency by which changes in priority were effected.

It is of interest to record that in order to fit the assault forces into the available craft and shipping, British divisions were limited to 1,450 vehicles in the initial lift, the corresponding figure for armoured brigades being 320. No formation was to be made up in excess of 75 per cent of its war establishment in transport until after D+14. Similar limitations were imposed on the American units.

An assortment of armour at No. 6 M.T. Group at Slough. This extensive vehicle park lay south of the railway line in an area of the trading estate now completely occupied by industry. On the left are some Humber Scout Cars, fitted for wading and, on the right, a Loyd carrier. Further away are several Sherman Fireflys and Universal carriers and, on the right, an AEC Armoured Command Vehicle.

Arterial bypasses, constructed during the pre-war expansion of the road net around Greater London, provided ideal storage depots as the road could simply be closed and traffic diverted along the original route. *Left:* **The Crawley bypass formed No. 17 Armoured Fighting Vehicle Depot.** *Right:* **The maintenance area is still recognisable.**

ADMINISTRATION

The administrative problem facing the British forces was essentially different from that of the Americans. The operational plan demanded the very rapid development of lines of communication behind the American forces, and the administrative requirements for opening up railways and roads from Cherbourg and the Brittany ports were very large. There was no parallel problem foreseen on the British flank.

The British forces were to be maintained over the beaches until such time as sufficient ports were captured and developed, and it was assumed that beach maintenance could cease on the opening of the Seine ports. In the US sector, it was planned to open Cherbourg and subsequently the main ports of the Brittany peninsula, and in this way to dispense gradually with the necessity for beach working.

Sometime in the spring of 1944, we lads thought Christmas had arrived early. The army appeared and closed off half the [Crawley] bypass, all the southern side. Not only did they put up sentry boxes and a pole barrier at each roundabout access but they also built workshops for the REME. The reason for this activity became apparent when dozens of tanks and armoured vehicles arrived to be double and treble parked on the road, cycle track and grass verge. There was still not enough room so the fields were used also. The fields opposite my home, now called 'The Dingle', were totally filled. It did not take us long to realise one young sentry could hardly supervise several hundred tanks. When we climbed in through the hatch and lowered ourselves inside we were in a wonderland. The first thing to do was to adjust the periscope to keep an eye on the sentry . . . we just looked about us without touching anything. The live shells were there for the gun. The cartridges all in place for the machine guns. A Colt revolver in a real leather holster. A Very pistol and flares.

I was in a Churchill one day and started the turret turning to the left . . . it was fascinating. I found the control and reversed it trying to peer through the periscope at the same time. As it slowly turned back, there he was, the sentry, racing straight towards me. No doubt I left faster than if a member of the Wehrmacht had slipped a grenade through the driver's hatch!

REX WILLIAMS, 1993

The Chertsey bypass, when first planned by the Ministry of Transport, was to run in a wide sweep south of the town. *Left:* **The section which had been completed before the war became a storage site for No. 1 Vehicle Reserve Depot but when the 'bypass' was finally completed (***right***), it became the M3 motorway.**

No. 1 VRD had another site at Laleham on the north-western side of the Queen Mary Reservoir. *Left:* Once, hundreds of Fords, Austins, DUKWs and Diamond Ts lay crammed together; now RMC's Reservoir Aggregates ply their trade.

No. 11 AFV Depot was based in north London at Haringey Stadium on Green Lane where new Universal carriers from Ford Canada were being readied for issue. A Canadian GM Fox Armoured Car can be seen in the background.

A few hundred yards away, Finsbury Park, on Seven Sisters Road, had been taken over to store more vehicles belonging to No. 11 AFV which appears to have held mainly Universal and Loyd carriers.

As we have seen (page 102), 21st Army Group headquarters had by now moved to Portsmouth, centred in the grounds of HMS *Dryad*. *Left:* General Montgomery's personal quarters were situated some two miles away in Broomfield House, Purbrook Heath, and it was here that he was photographed with the Prime Minister on May 19. *Right:* Broomfield House is now the home of Elisabeth and Richard Gale and they kindly agreed to stand in for Monty and the PM on their front drive.

BROOMFIELD HOUSE

On April 28, my headquarters moved to Southwick House in the Portsmouth area, which was to be our operational headquarters on D-Day. My 'A' Mess was established nearby in Broomfield House.

It has been written that I had a row with the Prime Minister shortly before D-Day, and even threatened to resign. This is untrue. I would like to tell the true story. Here it is.

For some time before D-Day, the Prime Minister had not been satisfied that we had the right balance between fighting troops and vehicles for the initial landing on the Normandy beaches. He reckoned there were not enough men with rifles and bayonets, and too many lorries, radio vehicles, and so on. He gave out that he would come to my headquarters near Portsmouth and investigate the matter with my staff. On that, I invited him to dinner to meet my senior staff officers.

He came on May 19. I asked him to come to my study for a short talk before meeting the others. Having got him comfortably seated I said:

'I understand, sir, that you want to discuss with my staff the proportion of soldiers to vehicles landing on the beaches in the first flights. I cannot allow you to do so. My staff advise me and I give the final decision; they then do what I tell them.

'That final decision has been given. In any case, I could never allow you to harass my staff at this time and possibly shake their confidence in me. They have had a terrific job preparing the invasion; that work is now almost completed, and all over England the troops are beginning to move towards the assembly areas, prior to embarkation. You can argue with me but not with my staff. In any case, it is too late to change anything. I consider that what we have done is right; that will be proved on D-Day. If you think it is wrong, that can only mean that you have lost confidence in me.'

A somewhat awkward silence followed these remarks. The PM did not reply at once, and I thought it best to make a move! So I stood up and said that if he would now come into the next room I would introduce him to my staff. He was magnificent. With a twinkle in his eye he said: 'I wasn't allowed to have any discussion with you gentlemen.'

We had a most amusing dinner and I went to bed feeling what a wonderful man he was: too big to stand on his dignity, or not to see when he was on a bad wicket.

Chapter V

On the verge of the greatest Adventure
with which these pages have dealt
I record my confidence that
All will be well
& that
the organization & equipment of the Army
will be worthy of the valour
of the soldiers
& the genius of their chief.

19.v.44 Winston S. Churchill

Churchill's account of his meeting with Montgomery is slightly at variance, yet substantially the same, as that given by Monty (see text), and at no time did Montgomery threaten to resign as has sometimes been said. 'After our talk,' wrote Churchill, 'we went to dinner, at which only eight or nine persons, mostly the General's personal staff, were present. All our proceedings were of a most friendly character, and when that night the General asked me to put something for him in his private book, as I had done before other great battles, I wrote the following: "On the verge of the greatest adventure with which these pages have dealt, I record my confidence that all will be well, and that the organisation and equipment of the Army will be worthy of the valour of the soldiers and the genius of their chief".'

King George came to lunch with me at Broomfield House on May 22, to say good-bye. On the next day, I was to start on my final tour of the armies to address all senior officers and I gave the King a copy of my notes (which I will give in full below) for those talks.

I began my tour the following day. As D-Day was to be on June 5, I had to be back in good time. I was determined to address all officers down to the lieutenant-colonel level, and to get over to them the main issues involved in the tremendous operation on which we were about to embark.

We returned to Broomfield House on Sunday, May 22, 1994 to have the date right for this comparison. In this case, Fizz boisterously joined in the fun. The magnificent cedar tree in the background died about 20 years ago; when Richard Gale cut it down, he found it full of lead — rumoured to have been fired at it in after-dinner target practice.

The King was shown around the TAC HQ caravans which were parked beside the drive. ***Left:*** **The office caravan acquired by Montgomery when he took command of the Eighth Army in North Africa. His predecessor, Lieutenant-General Neil Ritchie (who now commanded a corps in Monty's army group) had captured it from the Italians in February 1941.** ***Above:*** **The King leaves the newly-acquired BTC map lorry.**

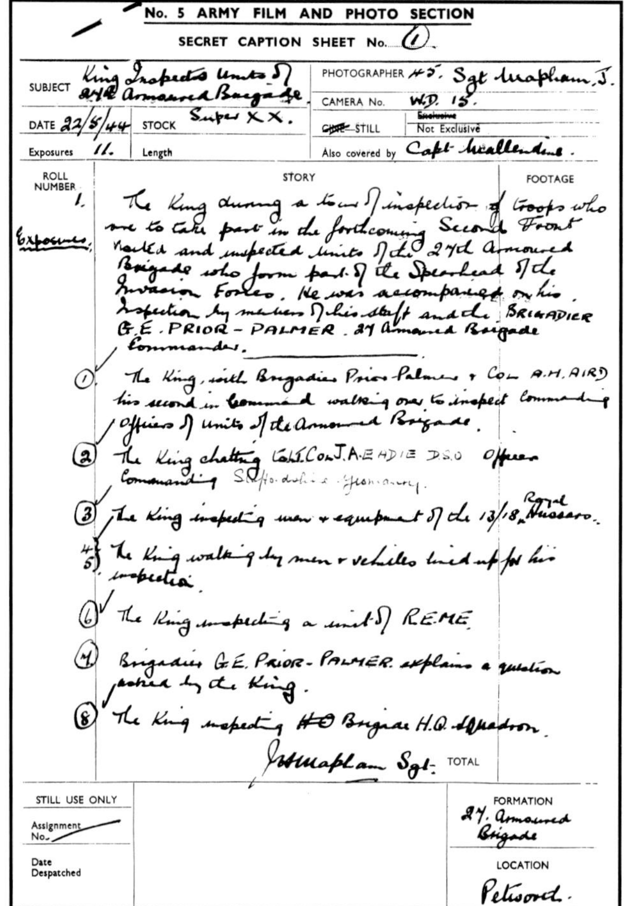

No. 5 ARMY FILM AND PHOTO SECTION

SECRET CAPTION SHEET No. (1).

SUBJECT King Inspects Units of 27th Armoured Brigade.
PHOTOGRAPHER 45. Sgt Mapham. J.
CAMERA No. W.D. 15.
DATE 22/5/44 STOCK Super XX.
~~CINE~~ STILL ~~Exclusive~~ Not Exclusive
Exposures 11. Length
Also covered by Capt. Mcallendine.

ROLL NUMBER | STORY | FOOTAGE

1. Exposures. The King during a tour of inspection of troops who are to take part in the forthcoming Second Front visited and inspected units of the 27th Armoured Brigade who form part of the Spearhead of the Invasion Forces. He was accompanied on his inspection by members of his staff and the BRIGADIER G.E. PRIOR-PALMER. 27 Armoured Brigade Commander.

(1). The King, with Brigadier Prior-Palmer & Col A.H. AIRD his second in Command walking over to inspect Commanding Officers of units of the Armoured Brigade.

(2) The King chatting Lt. Col J.A. EADIE D.S.O Officer Commanding Staffordshire Yeomanry.

(3) The King inspecting men & equipment of the 13/18th Royal Hussars.

4/5) The King walking by men & vehicles lined up for his inspection.

(6) The King inspecting a unit of R.E.M.E.

(7) Brigadier G.E. PRIOR-PALMER explains a question asked by the King.

(8) The King inspecting ~~HQ~~ Brigade H.Q. Squadron.

J. H. Mapham Sgt. TOTAL

STILL USE ONLY
Assignment No.
Date Despatched

FORMATION 27. Armoured Brigade
LOCATION Petworth.

Earlier on May 22, His Majesty had inspected elements of the 27th Armoured Brigade camped in Petworth Park. The visit was photographed by Sergeant Jim Mapham, the man responsible for taking what is arguably the best known of all the D-Day photographs (see page 525), and gives us the ideal opportunity to illustrate something which is not usually seen — the photographer's own 'dope' sheet. These were written up by the cameraman and later used to produce the official captions although wartime censorship would remove details of the unit and location. *Above left:* Exposure 1 with *right* the present day comparison. The park in West Sussex is now open to the public although the storms of the 1980s have felled many of the trees. *Below:* Exposure 2 with exposure 4 (*bottom left*) taken on the level ground near the lake (*bottom right*).

I visited every corps and divisional area, and spoke to audiences of from 500 to 600 officers at a time. On each occasion, it was essential that I should go 'all out'; if one does this properly, energy goes out of you and leaves you tired at the end. It took eight days in all and was an exhausting tour but I am sure it did good and instilled confidence, and that was vital as the day grew near. The notes I used for all the addresses ran as follows:

Before I launch troops into battle, I make a point of speaking personally to all senior officers down to the lieutenant-colonel rank inclusive. In this way, I can get my ideas across and ensure a common line of approach to the problem that lies ahead of us; and at a final talk, like this one, I can emphasise certain essential features, and give you some points to pass on to your men. In fact, I use these occasions in order to influence the armies, to instil confidence, and thus to help win the battle.

Above: **May 19: Montgomery visits the 2nd Battalion, Royal Ulster Rifles, of which he was divisional commander in 1939-40. Here he is welcomed by Lieutenant-Colonel I. C. Harris.** *Below:* **This would have been a difficult place to find but fortunately the photographer, Sergeant Albert Wilkes, quoted a map reference on his dope sheet.**

Although the house is indistinct, Grenville Hall, at Droxford, little changed over five decades, makes for a nice comparison.

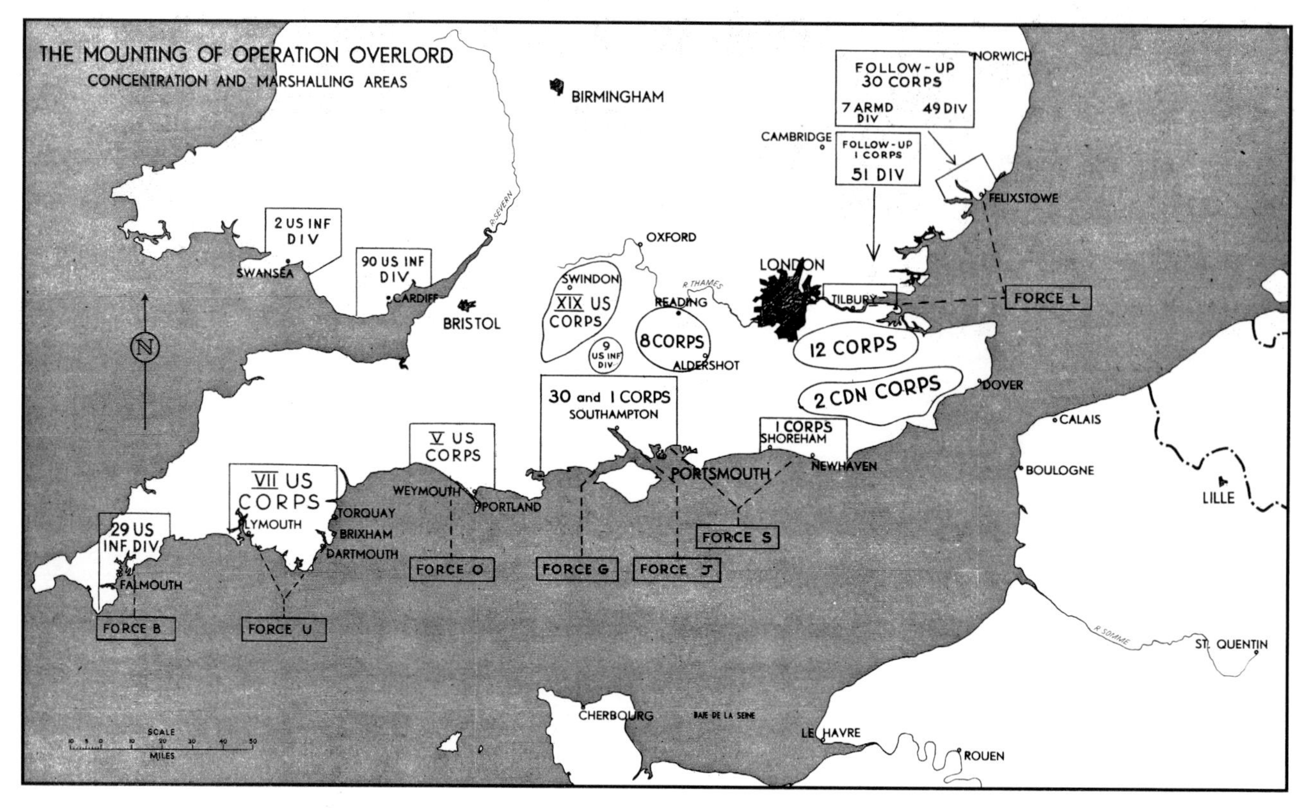

I would like to talk to you today on the following subjects:

(a) The past — very briefly.
(b) The present state of the war.
(c) The future prospects.
(d) The task immediately confronting us.
(e) Basic essentials for success.

The Past

We have been through some very bad times in this war. In our darkest days, we stood alone against the combined might of the Axis powers; we suffered some great shocks and some bad disasters. But we stood firm — on the defensive, but striking blows where we could.

Then America joined us; but that great nation was not immediately ready to strike heavy blows, and required time to develop her strength. The two of us — America and the British Empire — gradually began to fight back. Slowly, but surely and relentlessly, the lost ground was recovered and we began to pass from the defensive to the offensive.

Since that time we have been working throughout on the same strategy. This has been:

(a) To clear the enemy out of Africa.
(b) To knock Italy out of the war, and open the Mediterranean for our shipping.
(c) To bring Turkey into the war.
(d) To defeat Germany, while containing Japan.

That has been the broad strategy of the Allies, and we have stuck to it and never wavered. We are now about to reap the harvest.

Present State of the War

How do we stand today? Of the four basic points in our strategy, the first two are achieved.

(a) The Germans are out of Africa.
(b) Italy is out of the war, and the Mediterranean is open for our shipping.

These are great achievements, of which we may well be proud — and we are.

We failed in the third point. Turkey has not reacted in the way we hoped. But the Allies have done so well in other directions that it has not mattered overmuch; and the day may well come when Turkey will regret her present attitude, and will wish she had come in with the Allies — who are now going to win.

We are now about to embark on the final phase of the fourth point: to defeat Germany; that is the crux of the whole matter.

May 29: 'All vehicles in the armies commanded by Gen. Eisenhower for the forthcoming invasion will carry a white star both on the side and the top to facilitate recognition both from the air and by the land troops'. British Army vehicles have the new insignia added (in this case at an MT depot at Virginia Water, Surrey) before leaving for the marshalling areas nearer the south coast.

May 29: 'Members of the 66th Regiment of the 2nd Armored Division are briefed, at a marshalling area in England'.

After 4½ years of war, the Allies have, by hard fighting on sea, land and in the air, worked themselves into a position where they cannot lose. That is a very good position to reach in any contest; but the good player is never content 'to draw' — he wants to win. And so we must now win, and defeat Germany. And while doing that, we are doing more than contain Japan. That country is now definitely on the defensive and, in the south-west Pacific, the American and Australian forces are gradually working their way towards the Philippines and Formosa, and are killing great numbers of Japanese in the process.

Future Prospects

Germany is now fighting on three fronts: in Russia, in Italy, and in the Balkans. Soon, she will have a fourth front — in western Europe.

She cannot do this, successfully. She has a large number of divisions, but they are all weak and below strength. Everything is in the shop window; there is nothing 'in the kitty'.

Her cities and industries are being devastated by bombing; this will continue on an ever-increasing tempo all this year; by next winter, there will be little left of more important cities.

The Allies have the initiative and Germany is ringed round; she is about to be attacked from Russia, from the Mediterranean front, and from England; and all the time the bombing will go on relentlessly.

A very great deal depends on the success of our operations. If they succeed, I consider that Germany will then begin to crack. They will succeed; and the bombing will go on, every day and all around the clock. Germany will not be able to stand it.

If we do our stuff properly and no mistakes are made, then I believe that Germany will be out of the war this year. And Japan will be finished within six months after we have put Germany out.

Although no location was given with this Signal Corps picture, as the 2nd Armored was part of V Corps, we knew it would have been taken somewhere in the area between Southampton and Weymouth. The terrain looked like Salisbury Plain and as most of it is still a military training area, we contacted the Range Liaison Officer. Fortunately, the Land Warden, Bob Lock, recognised the location as being part of the present Cross-Country Driving Area at Bulford. He took us out to the spot, our comparison being taken from the lower slope of Sidbury Hill looking south towards Dunch Hill.

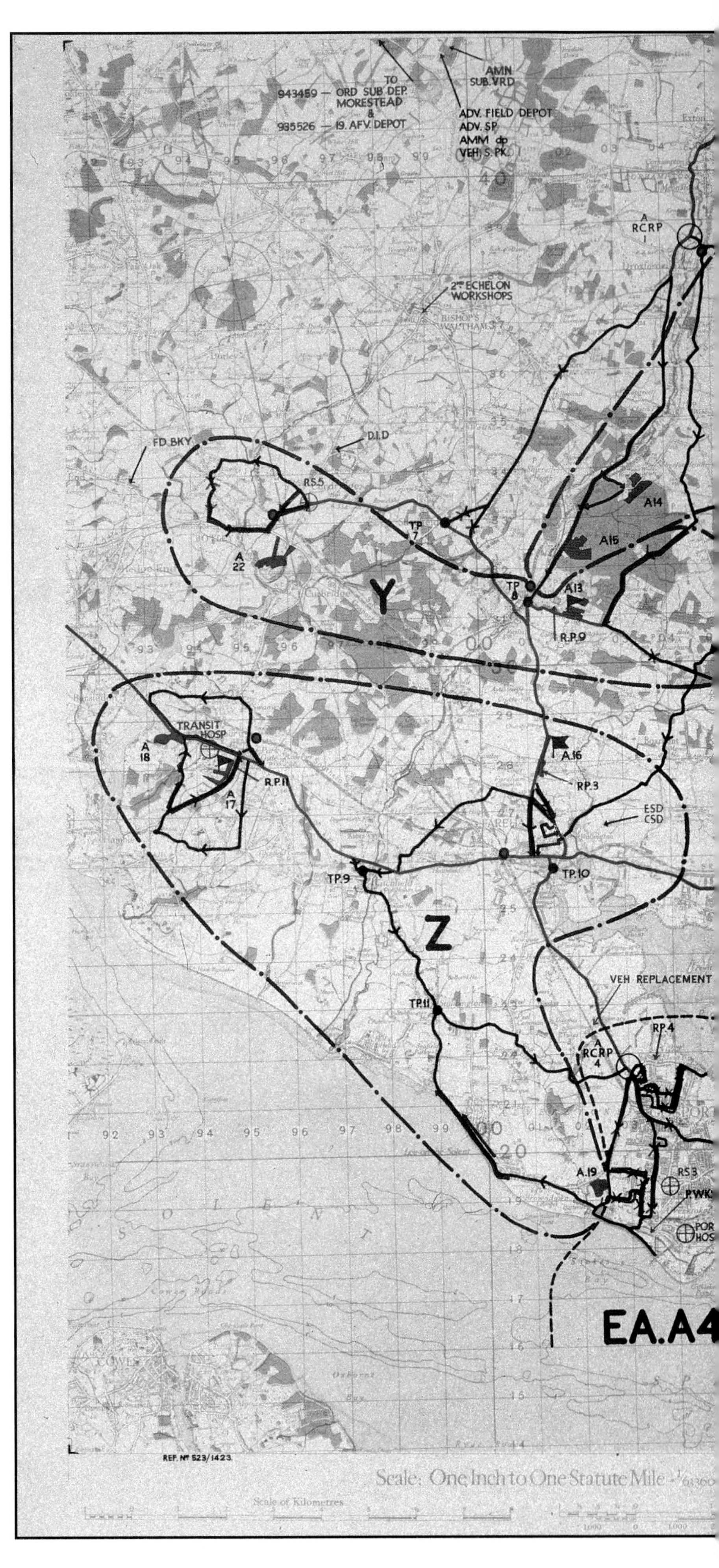

Each port area was divided into separate Embarkation Areas denoted by an alpha-numeric code, in this example of Portsmouth, A3 and A4. Inland, Marshalling Areas, split into individually-lettered Sub-Areas, containing the staging camps and supply depots. Access routes — some one-way — were detailed as were the facilities which would be required after the initial assault: the hospitals and PoW cages. This series of pictures was taken on May 29 at Camp A2. *Above:* Lieutenant Thornton of the Royal Army Pay Corps, issues French money (printed in 1938) to members of the 5th Battalion, King's Liverpool Regiment. *Below:* Lance Corporal Collings of the 5th Royal Inniskilling Dragoon Guards consults the French handbook which was issued to every man taking part in the invasion.

Camp A2 was located in this wood at Emsworth.

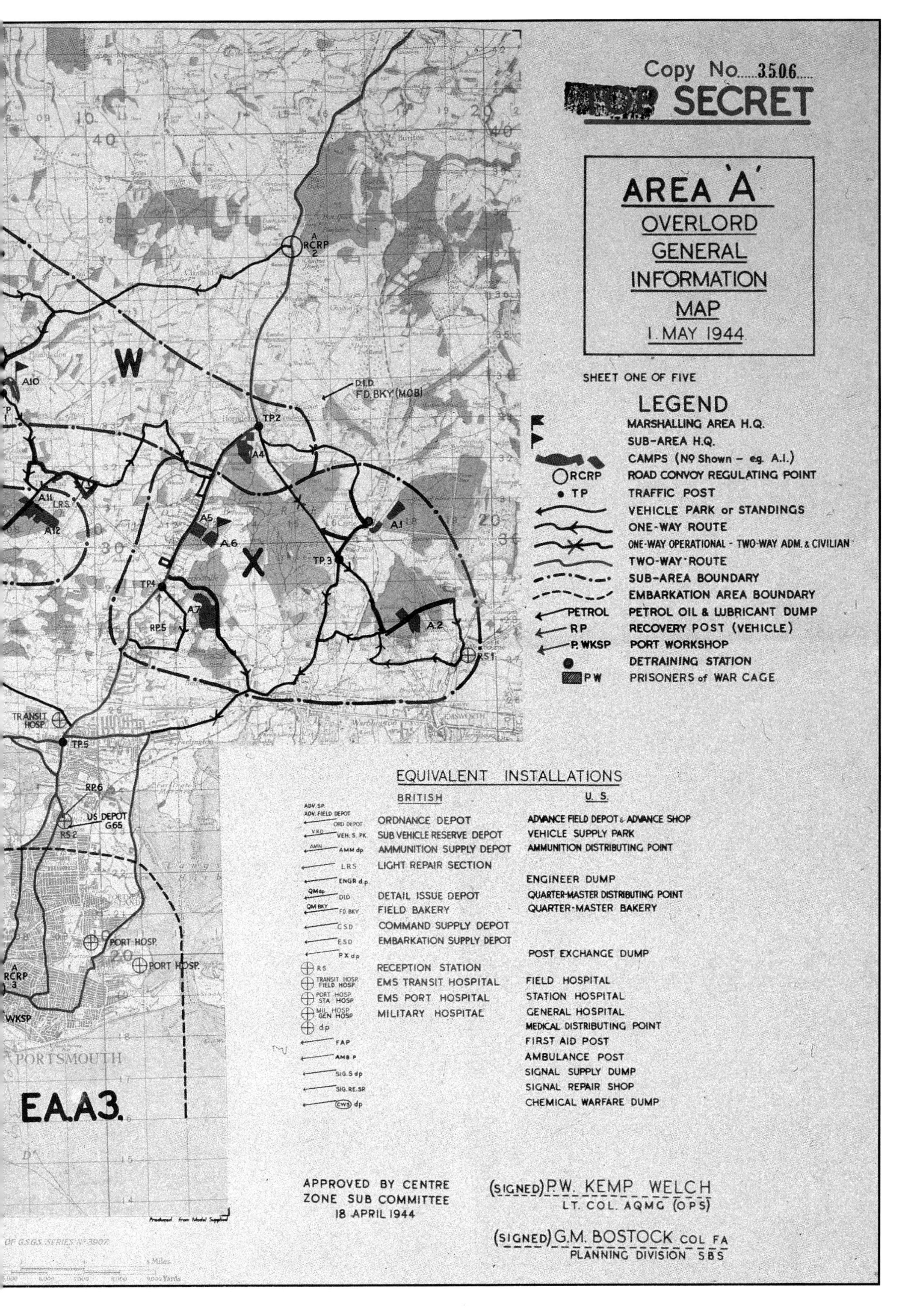

Copy No. 3506
SECRET
AREA 'A'
OVERLORD
GENERAL
INFORMATION
MAP
1. MAY 1944
SHEET ONE OF FIVE
LEGEND
MARSHALLING AREA H.Q.
SUB-AREA H.Q.
CAMPS (Nº Shown – eg. A.1.)
RCRP ROAD CONVOY REGULATING POINT
TP TRAFFIC POST
VEHICLE PARK or STANDINGS
ONE-WAY ROUTE
ONE-WAY OPERATIONAL - TWO-WAY ADM. & CIVILIAN
TWO-WAY ROUTE
SUB-AREA BOUNDARY
EMBARKATION AREA BOUNDARY
PETROL PETROL OIL & LUBRICANT DUMP
RP RECOVERY POST (VEHICLE)
P. WKSP PORT WORKSHOP
DETRAINING STATION
PW PRISONERS of WAR CAGE
W
X
A10
A11
A12
LRS
A4
A5
A6
A7
A1
A2
TP1
TP2
TP3
TP4
TP5
RP5
RP6
A RCRP 2
A RCRP 3
RS1
RS2
D.I.D. FD. BKY (MOB)
TRANSIT HOSP.
US DEPOT G65
PORT HOSP.
PORT HOSP.
WKSP
Clanfield
Buriton
Horndean
Emsworth
Warblington
PORTSMOUTH
EA.A3.
EQUIVALENT INSTALLATIONS
BRITISH
U. S.
ORDNANCE DEPOT
ADVANCE FIELD DEPOT & ADVANCE SHOP
SUB VEHICLE RESERVE DEPOT
VEHICLE SUPPLY PARK
AMMUNITION SUPPLY DEPOT
AMMUNITION DISTRIBUTING POINT
LIGHT REPAIR SECTION
ENGINEER DUMP
DETAIL ISSUE DEPOT
QUARTER-MASTER DISTRIBUTING POINT
FIELD BAKERY
QUARTER-MASTER BAKERY
COMMAND SUPPLY DEPOT
EMBARKATION SUPPLY DEPOT
POST EXCHANGE DUMP
RECEPTION STATION
EMS TRANSIT HOSPITAL
FIELD HOSPITAL
EMS PORT HOSPITAL
STATION HOSPITAL
MILITARY HOSPITAL
GENERAL HOSPITAL
MEDICAL DISTRIBUTING POINT
FIRST AID POST
AMBULANCE POST
SIGNAL SUPPLY DUMP
SIGNAL REPAIR SHOP
CHEMICAL WARFARE DUMP
APPROVED BY CENTRE
ZONE SUB COMMITTEE
18 APRIL 1944
(SIGNED) P.W. KEMP WELCH
LT. COL. AQMG (OPS)
(SIGNED) G.M. BOSTOCK COL FA
PLANNING DIVISION SBS

The sight of the endless convoys of vehicles moving towards the ports is one that those who witnessed it will never forget. Military traffic was so dense that all movements were strictly timed and controlled by military police. These Shermans, unfortunately bearing censored markings, were pictured on the A27 between Traffic Post 5 and 10 on the map on the preceding pages.

Our Immediate Task

But the essential condition is that the Second Front should be a great success. And that brings me to my next point.

When the time comes for us to operate on the Continent, no one will claim that our task will be easy. The enemy is in prepared positions; he has protected his beaches with obstacles; we cannot gain close contact and recce his position carefully, so as to examine the problem and ensure we have the right solution. There are, and there are bound to be, many unknown hazards. He has reserves positioned for counter-attack.

We have a long sea journey, and at the end of it we will have to land on an enemy coast in the face of determined opposition. During all this, there is bound to be a certain loss of cohesion in assaulting units; and even reserves coming ashore will require a little time to collect themselves. The enemy will know every inch of the ground; we shall be operating in a strange country.

But we have certain very great assets, and they are the ones that matter.

We have the initiative; the enemy does not know where, or when, we shall land.

We have great fire-power to support our initial landing, from the sea and from the air.

We have a good and simple plan.

We have well-trained troops, who are spoiling for a fight.

We have available to see us on shore, the whole of the Allied air power in England, and this air power will continue to support our operations and to bomb Germany. Its strength is terrific. There are some 4,500 fighters and fighter-bombers; and about 6,000 bombers of all types. Nothing has ever been seen like it before.

Unknown hazards must have no terrors for us. We have first-class engineers, and every kind of mechanical and special equipment. All we need is a very robust mentality; as difficulties appear, so they must be tackled and stamped on.

What we have to do is to blast our way on shore, and gain ground inland quickly so that we secure a good and firm lodgement area before the enemy has time to bring his reserves into action against us. The violence, speed, and power of our initial assault must carry everything before it.

The enemy reserves will be closely watched from the air; when they sacrifice concealment and begin to move, they will be bombed and shot-up from the air without ceasing, and enemy reserve units will be in poor shape when they reach the battle area.

Fortunately, the distinctive house on the right still survives although hidden by trees in this comparison. North Park lies on the opposite side of the road. The armour is travelling eastwards towards Porchester where presumably it will turn right at TP 5 for Embarkation Area A3.

A picture often used to portray the invasion build up, the original caption does not give any clue as to the location, although it has been given as Paulsgrove, to the north-east of Porchester. We toured the area in vain looking for the terrace on the right. Later, we had to drive along the A32 from Fareham to Gosport (south from TP 10) when suddenly the terrace came into view, virtually unchanged. It is most likely that the convoy was waiting to proceed to the Hardway where a 'hard' had been constructed (see page 181) for two LST berths facing Portsmouth Harbour.

Another very well known pre-D-Day picture is this one taken by a photographer from *The Daily Sketch*. The location was never given and it was not until the City Heritage Services at Southampton appealed to local people to come forward and give oral accounts for the 50th anniversary, that a Mr Bert Bagg came forward.

Basic Essentials for Success

I would like now to give you a few points which I regard as terribly important. Obviously, such points must be few in number, since everything cannot be important. I consider that compliance with the following points is essential for success.

Allied solidarity

We are a great team of allies, British and American. There must be throughout this team a friendly spirit; we must have confidence in each other.

As a British general, I regard it as an honour to serve under American command; General Eisenhower is captain of the team and I am proud to serve under him. And I regard it as a great honour to have American troops serving under my command.

When we visit each other, there should be only one idea; and that is — how can I help the other chap. Let us have no suspicion and no petty jealousy. Let us have, throughout, complete mutual confidence and goodwill, all pulling together as one great team.

Offensive eagerness

This is vital. Once on land and the battle starts, we must be offensive, and more offensive, and ever more offensive as the hours go by. We must call on the soldiers for an all-out effort. Every officer and man must have only one idea, and that is to peg out claims inland, and to penetrate quickly and deeply into enemy territory. After a long sea voyage and a landing followed by fighting, a reaction sets in and officers and men are often inclined to let up and relax. This is fatal; senior officers must prevent it at all costs on D-Day and on the following days. The first few days will be the vital ones; it is in those days that the battle will be won, and it is in those days that it could well be lost. Great energy and 'drive' will be required from all senior officers and commanders.

I consider that once the beaches are in our possession, success will depend largely on our ability to be able to concentrate our armour and push fairly strong armoured columns rapidly inland to secure important ground or communication centres. Such columns will form *firm bases in enemy territory* from which to develop offensive action in all directions. Such action will tend to throw the enemy off his balance and will enable our build-up through the beaches to proceed undisturbed; it will cut the ground from under the armoured counter-attack.

Offensive eagerness is not only necessary in the soldier; it is essential in the officer, and especially in the senior officer and commander. Inaction, and a defensive mentality, are criminal in any officer — however senior.

Enthusiasm

Every officer and man must be enthusiastic for the fight and have the light of battle in his eyes. We must send our soldiers into this encounter completely on their toes; they must be imbued with that infectious optimism that comes from physical well-being and absolute conviction in a great and righteous cause.

In the photo are my grandparents Soloman and Eliza Bagg — he owned the house, No. 185 Hill Lane, on the corner of Hill Lane and Rockleigh Road. My mother Annie is hanging out the clothes. I was at work. The photographer asked to use the back bedroom to take the photo, as far as I know he was a reporter from The Daily Sketch. *The heading of the photograph was 'War Over the Garden Wall' when it was printed.*

The Americans and the Free French were here, all packed up outside the house to go to the embarkation points, it was taken in the early part of 1944. They were very friendly, especially when the sirens went, they were down in the shelter before we were; we were immune to it after 4 years, we didn't worry. We knew it was approaching D-Day but the troops never knew where they were going.

I was born in the house, my father and mother lived there, my grandparents were 82 at the time. My grandfather was a builder, in fact, he was the bricklayer who built the house and then he bought it in 1901. He paid £320 for it. The house is still there today, it hasn't altered much except for some modernisation of the windows.

BERT BAGG, 1994

The 'historic' garden of No. 185 Hill Lane captured on film 50 years later, thanks to the helpfulness of the Conroy family.

As far back as 1940, Southampton had been earmarked as a major base for the invasion of north-western Europe, and in July 1943 the US Army's 14th Port Transportation Corps arrived to organise the shipment of American troops and stores. Designated Embarkation Area C, the area was closed to all visitors as from March 31, 1944 as part of Regulated Order (No.2) which established a ten-mile wide exclusion zone along the coast of southern Britain from the Wash to Land's End. The camps were sealed on May 24 and loading began on May 31. Two-thirds of the British and Canadian force for the initial assault passed through Southampton and, by the end of the war, 3½ million service personnel had used the port. *Above:* Vehicles awaiting shipment to Normandy enter the docks through Gate 10. *Right:* The same view today from the second floor of the Rank Hovis building.

June 1. US forces for the assault phase departed from ports further to the west, V Corps being based in the Dorset area and VII Corps in Devon. This M7, identified in the original caption as belonging to Battery B, 42nd Field Artillery, moves towards the hard at Upper Ferry West at Dartmouth where Hard PC2 could accommodate four LCTs.

BBC reporter Frank Gillard: 'I was frequently at Broomfield House in the early days of June 1944. Having been with Monty in North Africa, Sicily and Italy, he was used to having me around the place. Twice in those days, I took my recording truck to him there. The first occasion was on June 1 to record a special "performance" he gave for me of his famous pre-D-Day address to all officers of the rank of lieutenant-colonel and above. I had emphasised to him that although this material could obviously not be broadcast at the time, it had great archival value and should be preserved on record. He declined to allow my presence at a delivery before an audience, on the grounds that I would be too much of a distraction. Hence this private re-run, just for the BBC. Actually, the records were at once impounded by the War Office on security grounds by the officer seen sitting in the truck. They were kept in the War Office vaults, and it was not until 1947 that they were handed back to us in the BBC for use in a D-Day commemorative programme called *The Story of D-Day*. I am practically certain that the photograph was taken on that occasion — June 1, 1944. Monty considered broadcasting to be what he called "an arm of warfare". He used to say to me that he was the first General in history who could speak directly to his officers and men. He felt that this was an important factor in the building of confidence, and confidence in the leadership was essential to high morale. So as the BBC's man on the spot, I enjoyed a privileged association with him, as the person who could enable him to make his voice very widely heard. I must add that he never used this association to influence my reporting in any way. When he made a recording with me, he always insisted on listening to a playback before we packed up. In the photograph, he is standing in the doorway. I am on his left. The Napoleonic pose has been assumed by my recording engineer. Is it not remarkable that the doorway of Broomfield House is absolutely unchanged after all these years?'

'My second visit to Broomfield House with the recording car in that week was for the purpose of recording Monty's Order of the Day, in which he expressed his total confidence in the success of the forthcoming operations and wished good hunting to all involved. My records show pretty clearly that this recording was made in the late afternoon of June 5. However, in his *Memoirs,* Monty says it happened on the morning of the 6th. I certainly visited him that morning, but not, I think, with the recording car. It is the presence of the officer sitting at the rear of the recording truck which finally convinces me that the correct date for this photograph (*opposite*) is June 1.' (Letter from Frank Gillard to the Editor, June 1994.)

Confidence

I want you, and every soldier to know that I have complete and absolute confidence in the successful outcome of the operations that will shortly begin. With stout hearts, and with enthusiasm for the contest, let us go forward, to victory.

An all-out effort

Everyone must go all out. And, as we enter battle, let us recall the words of a famous soldier, spoken many years ago:

'He either fears his fate too much,
Or his deserts are small,
Who dare not put it to the touch
To win or lose it all.'

Good luck to each one of you. And good hunting on the mainland of Europe.

THE START OF THE GREAT ENTERPRISE

As they started out for the coast of Fortress Europe, my personal message was read out to all troops and with these words, the Allied assaulting divisions were launched into battle.

B. L. Montgomery
General.

21 ARMY GROUP

PERSONAL MESSAGE FROM THE C-in-C

To be read out to all Troops

1. The time has come to deal the enemy a terrific blow in Western Europe.

The blow will be struck by the combined sea, land, and air forces of the Allies—together constituting one great Allied team, under the supreme command of General Eisenhower.

2. On the eve of this great adventure I send my best wishes to every soldier in the Allied team.

To us is given the honour of striking a blow for freedom which will live in history; and in the better days that lie ahead men will speak with pride of our doings. We have a great and a righteous cause.

Let us pray that "The Lord Mighty in Battle" will go forth with our armies, and that His special providence will aid us in the struggle.

3. I want every soldier to know that I have complete confidence in the successful outcome of the operations that we are now about to begin.

With stout hearts, and with enthusiasm for the contest, let us go forward to victory.

4. And, as we enter the battle, let us recall the words of a famous soldier spoken many years ago:—

"He either fears his fate too much,
Or his deserts are small,
Who dare not put it to the touch,
To win or lose it all."

5. Good luck to each one of you. And good hunting on the main land of Europe.

B. L. Montgomery
General
C-in-C 21 Army Group.

5-6-1944.

Left: **Air Marshal Trafford Leigh-Mallory, right, pictured on the third anniversary of the Battle of Britain in September 1943 with Air Chief Marshal Lord Dowding who had led Fighter Command to its victory in 1940. Two months later, Leigh-Mallory was appointed Commander-in-Chief of the Allied Expeditionary Air Force, his promotion to Acting Air Chief Marshal being made on December 5, 1943.** *Bottom:* **Leigh-Mallory's personal office at Bentley Priory has been preserved, yet it is with Dowding and the Battle of Britain that the memorabilia in the room are now associated . . . save that of the German field glasses on their tripod in the corner, reputed to have been brought back from Normandy specially for Leigh-Mallory.**

Air Operations for D-Day

By Air Chief Marshal Sir Trafford Leigh-Mallory

COMMANDER-IN-CHIEF, ALLIED EXPEDITIONARY AIR FORCE

In the Overall Air Plan, I set out the undermentioned principal air tasks for the forces under my command and for the allotted effort of the strategical air forces and Royal Air Force Coastal Command. These tasks were decided upon after discussions with the Supreme Commander and the respective Commanders-in-Chief as to the requirements of the Army and the Navy from the air forces.

(a) To attain and maintain an air situation whereby the German Air Force was rendered incapable of effective interference with Allied operations.

(b) To provide continuous reconnaissance of the enemy's dispositions and movements.

(c) To disrupt enemy communications and channels of reinforcement and supply.

(d) To support the landing and subsequent advances of the Allied armies.

(e) To deliver offensive strikes against enemy naval forces.

(f) To provide air lift for airborne forces.

My plan for the use of air power in direct support of the assault called for the fulfilment of the following principal air tasks:

(a) To protect the cross-Channel movement of the assault forces against enemy air attack, and to assist the Allied naval forces to protect the assault craft and shipping from enemy naval forces.

(b) To prepare the way for the assault by neutralising the coast and beach defences.

(c) To protect the landing beaches and the shipping concentrations from enemy air attack.

(d) To dislocate enemy communications and control during the assault.

The co-ordination of the air plans with those of the other services was achieved by weekly meetings between the other Commanders-in-Chief and myself, together with our respective Chiefs-of-Staff and chief planners, held alternately in the office of the planning centre of each of the three services. Since the United States Army Air Force and the Royal Air Force respectively depended on separate administrative systems, no attempt to combine them was made, except where advantage was clearly to be gained.

PHOTOGRAPHIC RECONNAISSANCE

The photographic reconnaissance units of the Allied air forces were the first to begin active and direct preparation for the invasion of Europe from the West. For more than a year, much vital information was accumulated which contributed very greatly to the ultimate success of the assault. The variety, complexity and, moreover, the detailed accuracy of the information gathered and assiduously collated, was of great importance in the preparatory phase of the operation.

Each particular service had its own requirements and individual problems which only photographic reconnaissance could hope to solve. Then again, within each service, specialised sections relied to a great extent for their information on these sources, e.g. as early as possible after each major bombing attack, damage assessment sorties were flown.

Photographic coverage of the entire coastline from Holland to the Spanish frontier was obtained to gather full details of the coastal defences. Verticals and obliques were taken of beach gradients, beach obstacles, coastal defences

The Air C-in-C meets American pilots in Normandy after the invasion. Leigh-Mallory laid down that the main base for air operations was to remain in the United Kingdom and that the principal administrative units were not to be moved to the Continent until it was clearly advantageous to do so. Of these, photo-reconnaissance was one of the most important, having bases at Benson (RAF) and Mount Farm (USAAF), both in Oxfordshire close to the Allied Central Interpretation Unit at Medmenham.

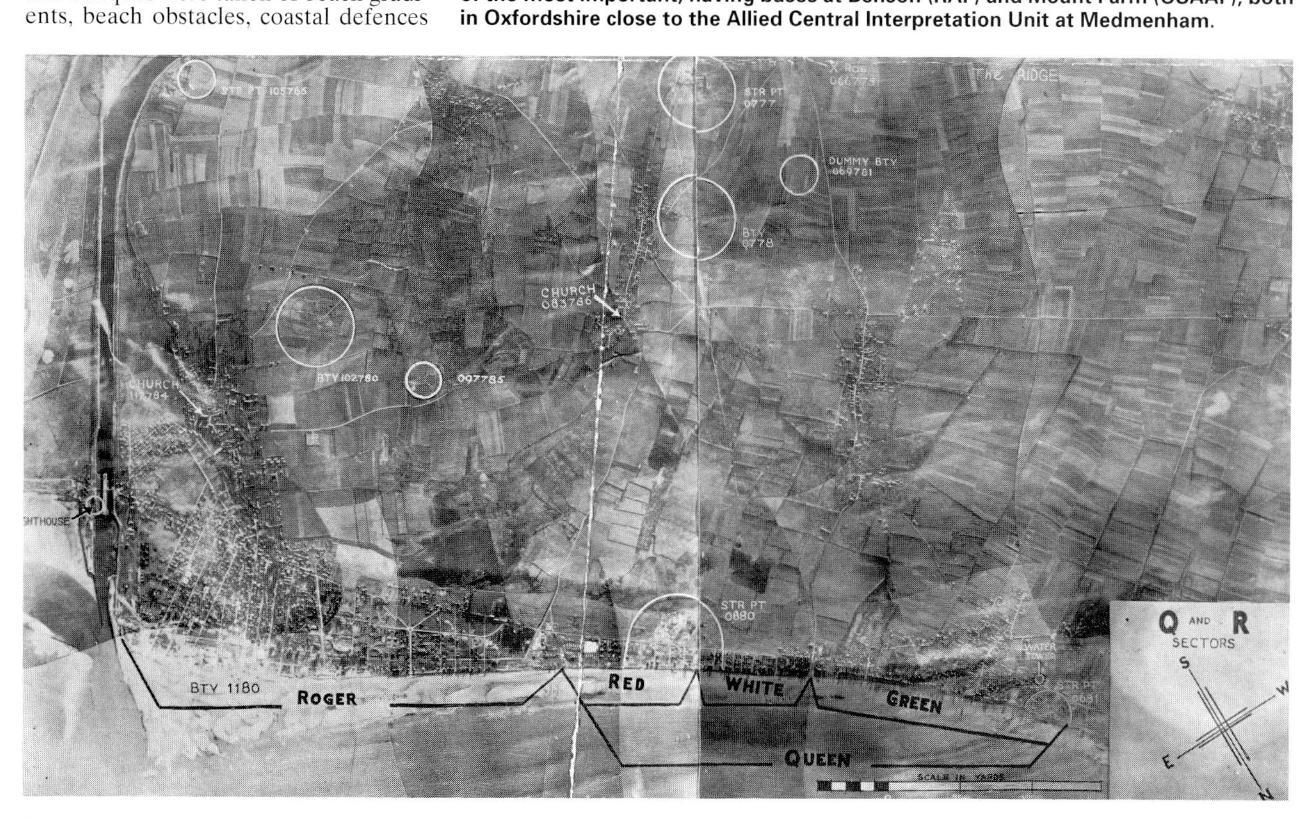

Leigh-Mallory: 'The demands of all three services for photographic cover were very varied and so great in number that it was necessary to set up a controlling body to deal with them. Accordingly, the Central Reconnaissance Committee was established at SHAEF headquarters. This inter-service committee received requests for photographic cover from all services and allocated the task to the most-suitable reconnaissance force. One of the most important functions of this committee was to watch the security aspect of the reconnaissance effort and, by ensuring that this effort was judiciously distributed, conceal from the enemy our special interest in the assault area. The bulk of this invaluable reconnaissance effort was flown by aircraft of AEAF which, in the period from April 1 to June 5 flew no less than 3,215 photographic reconnaissance sorties. Aircraft of other commands, however, including No. 106 Group of RAF Coastal Command and the US Eighth Air Force, operating under the control of RAF Benson, also contributed notably to this work, flying a total of 1,519 sorties during the same period. The excellent co-operation between British and American reconnaissance units in fact enabled the needs of all services to be fully met by D-Day. If we had had to rely, however, entirely on orthodox high-altitude reconnaissance aircraft for this work, not more than a small proportion of these needs could have been met. The weather in western Europe, never very suitable for high-altitude photography, was particularly bad in the early part of the year. There was an urgent need for a medium/low-altitude photographic reconnaissance aircraft to supplement high-altitude reconnaissance. It was decided, therefore, to convert some Mustang fighters into tactical and strategical medium/low-altitude reconnaissance aircraft. They were equipped with oblique cameras, were armed to protect themselves and were fast enough to outpace most German fighters.'

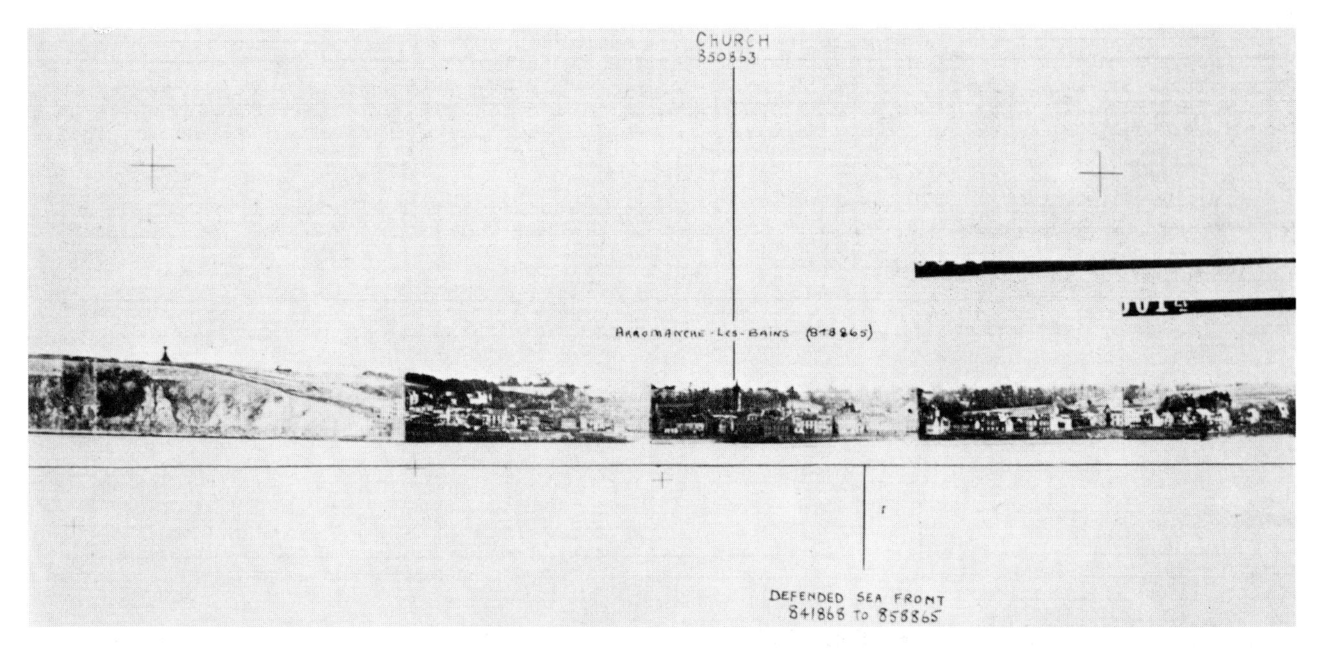

and batteries. Full photographic coverage from Granville to Flushing, both in obliques and verticals, was obtained. This very large coverage also served to hide our special interest in the selected assault beaches.

Obliques were taken at wave top height, three to four miles out from the coast, in order to provide the assault coxswains with a landing craft view of the particular area to be assaulted or likely to be their allotted landing spots. Then, obliques were flown 1,500 yards from the coast at zero feet, to provide platoon assault commanders with recognition landing points. Further obliques were taken, again at 1,500 yards from the shore, but at 2,000 feet to provide, for those who were planning the infantry assault, views of the immediate hinterland.

Inland strips were photographed behind the assault areas, looking southwards, so that infantry commanders could pinpoint themselves after they had advanced. Again, it was necessary to photograph hidden land behind assault areas, so that the infantry commanders would know the type of terrain behind such obstructions as hills or woods.

Bridges over rivers were photographed and special attention was paid to the river banks to enable the engineers to plan the type of construction necessary to supply temporary bridges in the event of the enemy blowing up the regular bridges.

The prospective airfield sites were selected by the engineers after they had studied the vast quantity of reconnaissance photographs available.

Above: **Wave-top obliques were quite crudely montaged and compiled into identification booklets for the Admiralty with the photo strips concertina-folded to produce a pull-out covering one whole section of coastline. Fifteen booklets, lettered A to S, completed the Normandy sector (*below*).**

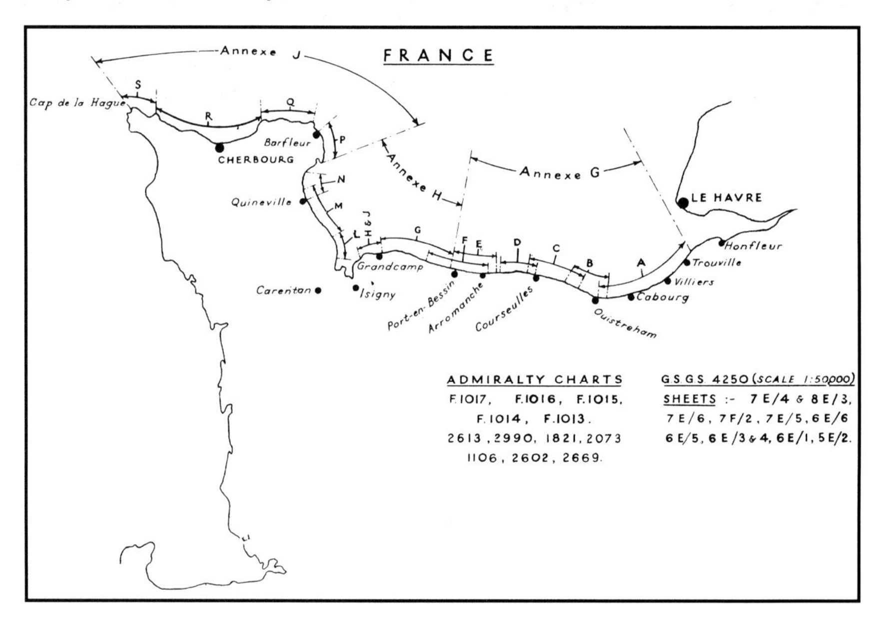

Other obliques were annotated to provide the troops with details of the assault areas and the terrain just beyond the beaches.

Some of the results were beautifully clear — this is the harbour of Courseulles, comprising an avant-port and a wet dock, which could accommodate vessels drawing 13 feet at mean high water. Rommel's beach obstacles show up clearly. However, Leigh-Mallory explained that 'low-altitude reconnaissance, whether visual or photographic, was at all times a hazardous business in view of the risk of being jumped by higher-flying enemy fighters'.

'None the less, early results achieved by Mustangs were very encouraging and eventually a number of reconnaissance squadrons were partly re-equipped with converted Mustangs to supplement their high-altitude aircraft. Their work', wrote Leigh-Mallory in his post-D-Day report, 'proved invaluable and the development of this aircraft for photographic reconnaissance work has been one of the outstanding lessons of the air war.' A good example of a typical Mustang low-level oblique taken by No. 168 Squadron. Recce prints were annotated and captioned for reference purposes.

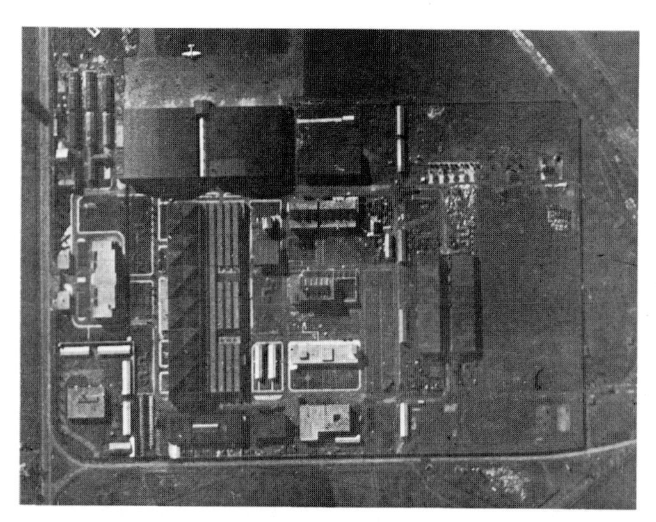

An example of the before and after strike photography beloved of the intelligence officers. The caption stated that 'on the night of 29th-30th April, 1944, RAF bombers attacked the Clermont-Ferrand Aulnat airfield. The next day, USAAF day bombers followed up the attack with a second blow. So accurate was the bombing that out of the many buildings and hangars in the SE corner of the airfield (including the Atelier Industriel de l'Air), only the sick bay was undamaged. Two very large hangars collapsed and nine others were severely damaged. Extensive damage was done to main workshops and offices and 40 smaller buildings stand roofless or totally destroyed. The railway station area and tracks were left pitted with craters. Tarmac and runways were obliterated at many points and about 110 craters were seen in the northern half of the landing ground. At least seven damaged planes were counted nearby.

ESTIMATION OF THE CAPABILITIES OF THE GERMAN AIR FORCE

I was confident that the German Air Force would constitute no serious threat to our operations on land, sea or in the air. However, I could not dismiss the possibility that the enemy was conserving his air forces for a maximum effort against the Allied assault forces. A bombing plan was therefore prepared which aimed at driving German fighters on to bases as far from the battle as were the Allied fighter forces.

As D-Day approached, however, it became necessary to ensure that our measure of air superiority was fully adequate to our needs. Plans had accordingly been made for direct attacks upon the enemy air force, particularly in France and the Low Countries. The effect of these plans was to deny the German Air Force the advantage of disposition which its fighter squadrons would otherwise enjoy as compared with our own in the initial stages of the assault. It was, therefore, necessary to neutralise a considerable number of airfields within a radius of 150 miles of Caen. The primary object of these attacks was to destroy the aircraft repair, maintenance and servicing facilities and thereby cause the maximum interference with the operational ability of the German Air Force.

I planned that these attacks should start at least three weeks before D-Day, and they actually began on May 11. It was necessary to bear in mind in the planning of these attacks that no indication should be given as to the selected area for the Allied landings.

Forty main operational airfields were selected for attack. Twelve were assigned to Bomber Command and the remaining 28 to AEAF and the Eighth Air Force. Fifty-nine other operational bomber bases with important facilities within range of the assault area and ports of embarkation in the United Kingdom were also selected for attack, as opportunity permitted.

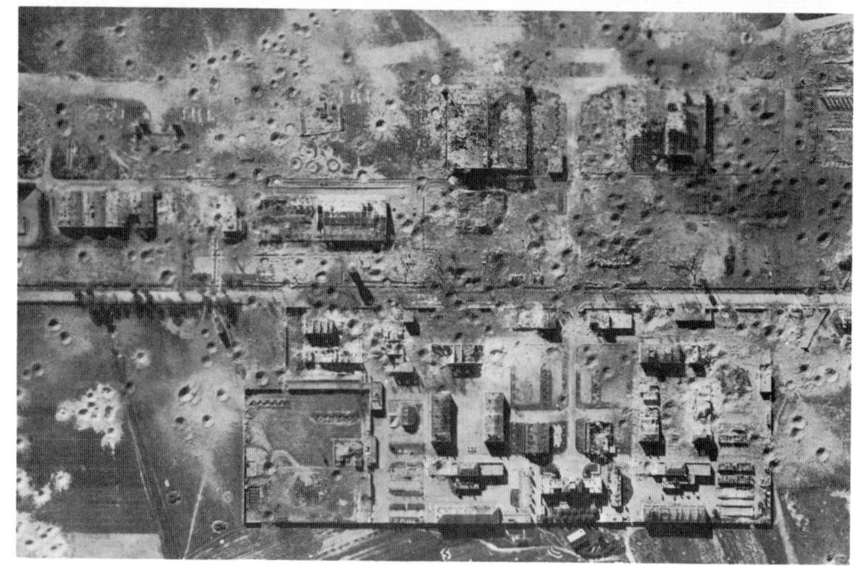

Centre: **On the night of May 7/8, a cameraman from the RAF Film Production Unit took this night flash photograph as 53 Lancasters and 8 Mosquitos of No. 5 Group hit the airfield at Tours (200 kilometres from Normandy).** *Right:* **The post-raid picture.**

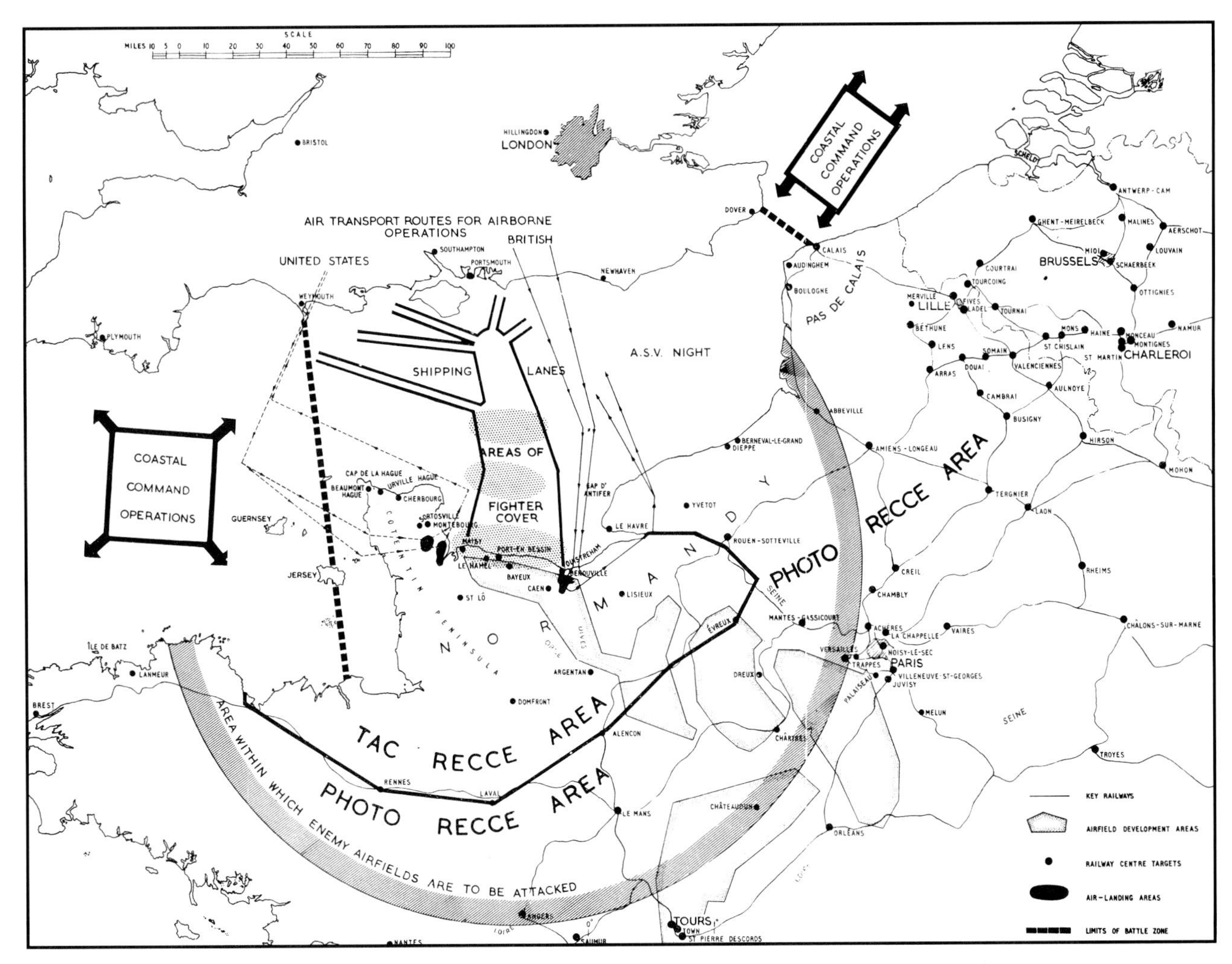

OBJECTS OF PREPARATORY BOMBING

I considered that the primary objective of preparatory bombing should be to impose the greatest possible delay in the movement of the enemy reinforcements and supplies, and to this end, the railway bombing plan was designed. The object of this plan was to produce a lasting and general dislocation of the railway system in use by the enemy. By so doing, the capacity of the system as a whole would be greatly reduced, and the task of dealing with isolated movement once the battle was joined would be made all the easier. Accordingly, the primary targets planned for attack were the railway centres where the most-important servicing and repair facilities of Northern France and the Low Countries were located; the secondary targets were the principal marshalling yards, particularly those which possessed repair facilities. The selection of targets was made difficult in some cases by the necessity of avoiding heavy civilian casualties or damage to historic buildings. Where railway centres were situated in thickly-populated areas (as at Le Bourget, for example), alternative centres were chosen in order to isolate them. A further limitation was imposed by the necessity to pinpoint the attacks on these targets; this demanded visual bombing conditions for day attacks and clear weather during moon periods for night attacks. The possibility of unreliable weather, particularly round about D-Day, was one of the major factors which dictated an early commencement of this plan; in fact, the weather did seriously hamper its execution.

Complementary to the railway plan, a further plan was made, covering the destruction of road and rail bridges. This plan which called for the cutting of the Seine bridges below Paris and the bridges over the Loire below Orleans was put into operation at D–30.

Other preparatory bombing plans included attacks on coastal batteries, enemy naval and military targets and the radar chain. It was necessary to remember when making these plans that the enemy should not be given any indication of the area selected for the assault. The principal effect of this on the preparatory air operations was that at least two attacks were made on each type of target outside of the projected assault area to one attack on a target within that area.

Leigh-Mallory: 'Next to the winning of air superiority, the dislocation of the enemy's lines of communication was the most important task set the Air Force. The basic intention was to force the enemy off the railways, initially within an area of 150 miles from the battle front. There were two broad plans for doing this: one was a short-term policy which involved attacks on certain rail centres during the period immediately before D-Day; the other was a longer-term plan of destroying the potential of the railway system in north-western Europe. The short term policy involved attacks on 17 specially selected rail focal points, plus an extra 7 points as cover. It was claimed for this plan that if the attacks were made immediately before D-Day, the enemy's reinforcements by rail would be adequately delayed. The longer-term plan involved attacks on a large number of repair and maintenance centres designed to reduce the movement potential and the motive power of the railway system, supported by complementary action in cutting railway lines and bridges on the canalized routes nearer D-Day. In March the longer-term plan was accepted.'

THE RAIL PLAN — FEBRUARY 9 - JUNE 5

Force	*Sorties*	*Bombs*
Allied Expeditionary Air Force	8,736	10,125 tons
RAF Bomber Command	8,751	44,744 tons
US Eighth Air Force	4,462	11,648 tons
	21,949	66,517 tons

ALLOCATION OF TARGETS

A total of 80 rail targets of primary importance were scheduled for attack by Allied Expeditionary Air Force, Royal Air Force Bomber Command and the United States Eighth Air Force. These targets were finally allocated as follows:

AEAF	18
RAF Bomber Command	39
US Eighth Air Force	23

By D-Day, of the 80 targets allocated, 51 were categorised as being damaged to such an extent that no further attacks were necessary until vital repairs had been effected; 25 were categorised as having been very severely damaged, but with certain vital installations still intact, necessitating a further attack; the remaining four were categorised as having received little or no damage, and needing a further attack on first priority.

The first of the really heavy and damaging attacks on rail centres was that made by Bomber Command on Trappes on the night of March 6/7.

An immediate interpretation of photographs taken after this attack showed extremely heavy damage throughout the yards, the greatest concentration of craters being in the 'Up' reception sidings. A total of 190 direct hits were scored on tracks, as many as three tracks having, in several cases, been disrupted by one bomb. Numerous derailments and much wreckage were caused by 50 bombs which fell among the lines of rolling stock with which the yard was crowded. All the tracks of the main electrified line between Paris and Chartres which passes through this yard were cut, several of the overhead standards having been hit and, at the east end of the yard, at least five direct hits were scored on the constriction of lines. To the north-east of the target, the engine shed was two-thirds destroyed.

Of the other early attacks carried out in March and early April, some of the most successful were those on Paris/La Chappelle, Charleroi/St Martin, Paris/Juvisy, Laon and Aachen. At each of these centres, the locomotive servicing and maintenance facilities were rendered almost, if not completely, useless and great havoc was wrought in the marshalling yards. At Paris/Noisy-le-Sec, the whole railway complex was almost annihilated. Other damaging attacks in this early period were made on Ottignies, Rouen, Namur, Lens and Tergnier. Nine of these 11 attacks were carried out by Bomber Command.

From the first attacks, the enemy energetically set about endeavouring to make good the damage inflicted, but Trappes was still under repair at the end of April.

As Air Chief Marshal Tedder explained earlier (see pages 85-86), the arguments regarding the sensibilities of the killing of French civilians hampered the full-scale introduction of the rail plan with the final go ahead being delayed until President Roosevelt gave his unequivocal response on May 11. Nevertheless, the bombing of rail targets had been going on during the previous two months beginning with the test raid proposed by the Chief of the Air Staff. The attack on the railway centre at Trappes, just west of Paris, took place on the night of March 6/7 when Nos. 4, 6 and 8 Groups of Bomber Command despatched a total of 261 Halifaxes and 6 Mosquitos. Visibility was good and the subsequent photographs showed enormous damage from the 1,258 tons of bombs dropped.

The success of the Trappes raid, which put the centre out of action for a month, vindicated the soundness of Leigh-Mallory's rail plan. However, civilian casualties (31 killed, 45 injured) in the Le Mans raid the following night led to anti-British slogans appearing on walls in the town, a further 48 people being killed in a follow-up raid on the night of March 13/14. Amiens was hit twice on March 15/16 and 16/17, killing 36 French civilians but the most serious of the March raids was that against Courtrai on the night of March 26/27 when 252 Belgians lost their lives, many being visitors in the town to celebrate that Sunday's religious festival.

Although all air operations carried out against continental targets influenced the end result in some way, Leigh-Mallory fixed April 1 as the commencement of the preparatory phase for the 'Overlord' campaign. The official date for the transfer of the main Bomber Command effort to pre-invasion targets was April 14 although the raids had commenced on the night of April 9/10 when rail yards at Lille and Villeneuve-St Georges (near Paris) were attacked by nearly 500 aircraft. Over 90 civilians were killed at Villeneuve but at Lille, where the Délivrance goods station had been the target, most of the bombs fell in the suburb of Lomme, killing 456 and causing much resentment against the British. Had the effects of this attack been known by the Allied command, it may well have influenced the debate then being waged in Britain; as it was, General Eisenhower was about to depart from his own rail yard — Addison Road Station (*above*) in the West End of London — for a tour of airbases in East Anglia. He boarded his personal train at what is now Olympia station, on the evening of April 10 in the company of the air force commanders — Lieutenant General Spaatz and Lieutenant General Brereton.

Although the journey to the first base, Great Dunmow, could have been done by road in a couple of hours, Commander Butcher, who made the travel arrangements, organised a 'night-day-night trip taking a leisurely route, with long stop-overs at quiet places'. Having reached the first station on Tuesday morning, Butcher recorded in his diary that 'I noticed a crowd gathering and some persons inquired "When would Monty leave the train?" As it was time for Ike and Spaatz to depart, I went aboard and announced to them that they should hurry as the crowd was impatient to see Monty. They chuckled.' *Above:* 'Monty', escorted by Colonel Herbert Thatcher, the CO of the 99th Bomb Wing, which was also based at Great Dunmow and had tactical control of four B-26 groups, and Lieutenant Colonel Sherman Beaty, Executive Officer of the resident 386th Bomb Group, walks from the control tower towards the technical site.

Unfortunately, neither the control tower nor the concrete road leading from the perimeter track to the crew rooms remains. Nevertheless, this is the exact spot determined from plans of the airfield and aerial photographs. The car stands on the peri-track, now reduced to a single-width estate road. We followed in Eisenhower's footsteps exactly 50 years later and took the comparison on April 11, 1994.

However, the intelligence hut does still remain as a farm store, more than likely the place where this picture was taken. Commander Butcher stands in the right background. According to Major General Brereton, 'General Eisenhower examined flak suits, Mae Wests, parachutes, dinghies, and other flying equipment, and was shown strike photos of attacks on rail yards at Creil, Hasselt, and Haine-St Pierre. He sat at the controls of Marauder *Son of Satan*, a 50-mission ship, and congratulated Sgt. Laurence Duthill from Lower Salem, Ohio, on his work. I noticed again that when General Eisenhower did not understand something he never hesitated to ask for details. He watched the group take off for an attack on "Crossbow" [V-weapon] targets, their third attack in 30 hours.' (Unfortunately, Brereton got the target information wrong in his diary; the 386th BG were in fact about to bomb the rail yards at Charleroi.)

We motored to Debden, where the 4th Fighter Group operated. Lunched there and met Colonel Donald J. M. Blakeslee — quite the most colourful airman I have met. He has some 20 planes to his credit and is fudging on his operational hours so he won't be grounded. He appears a born leader. Also met Captain Don S. Gentile, who actually leads Americans in Europe with 23 planes shot down in the air and seven shot up on the ground. He is Italian-American. Both were decorated with DSCs by Ike.

General Spaatz had one of the new modified P-38 (Lightning) planes which have been equipped with a bomb-sight and a place for a bombardier in the plexiglass nose, which has been extended. In air lingo, the new P-38 is called the 'Droop Snoot'. Ike inspected one with great interest. The pilot invited him for a ride. He accepted immediately and had about a ten-minute ride, twisting and diving, his first ride in a fighter.

COMMANDER HARRY C. BUTCHER

The next stop was Debden, a drive of about 20 minutes. After inspecting the guard, Eisenhower was taken to the Group Intelligence Block located in temporary huts to the rear of the control tower. There he listened to Colonel Blakeslee, the brilliant CO of the 4th Fighter Group, going through a mock briefing, followed by the award of the Distinguished Service Cross to Blakeslee and two other officers. However, the ceremony was re-enacted for the cameras outside where an array of fighters (*right*), including a 55th Fighter Group P-38J, had been drawn up.

***Left:* The picture was taken with the second P-51 — a 4th FG machine with a red nose — as a backdrop. Blakeslee watches as Captain Don Gentile, the leading fighter ace of the group, receives his award. Not pictured is Captain Robert Johnson of the 61st Fighter Squadron, 56th Fighter Group, based at Boxted — at the time the leading ace of the Eighth Air Force with 24 victories — who also received the DSC. *Right:* Today, Debden is an army barracks, the current home of the Royal Engineers bomb disposal organisation. Fortunately, one hangar, the correct one for the comparison, still survives.**

After the second award ceremony was over, though the day was overcast, Ike got himself a ride in the Lightning although in Butcher's original diary entry he makes it appear as if the flight took place at the third airfield they visited. (We have transposed the text opposite in its correct order.) After he landed, Eisenhower lunched in the Officers' Mess. Back row, L-R: Lieutenant Colonel Oscar Coen, Major General William Kepner, Lieutenant Colonel Jim Clark, General Eisenhower, Colonel Don Blakeslee, Lieutenant General Carl Spaatz, Captain Don Gentile, Brigadier General Jesse Auton, Lieutenant Joseph Lang. Front row, L-R: Colonel Ronald Fallows, Brigadier General Joseph Curtis, Major Jim Goodson, Lieutenant General James Doolittle, Captain Bob Johnson, Commander Harry Butcher, Captain Alfred Markel and Lieutenant William Rowles. Mr Joe Banks, then the British Permanent Mess Steward at Debden, stands by the window.

At exactly 1.12 p.m., we took the comparison, assisted by Captain Tim Lardner of the RE's Explosive Ordnance Disposal.

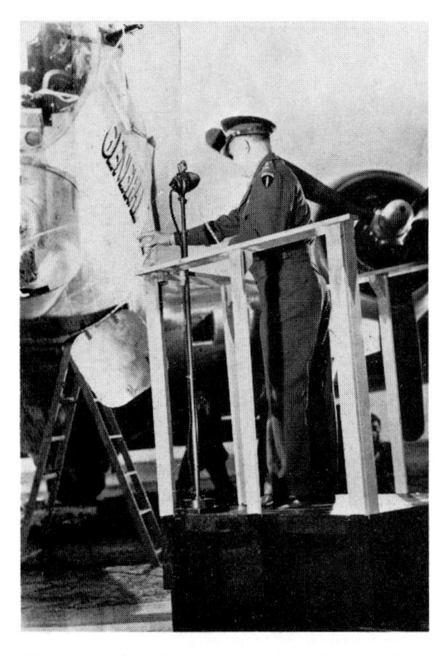

After lunch, the party proceeded further to the west to Station 121, home of the 91st Bomb Group — 'The Ragged Irregulars'.'Next, we stopped at Bassingbourn, from which some 60 B-17s had been airborne for the attack on Germany', recorded Commander Butcher. 'Ike made a thorough inspection of billets, training facilities, and kitchens. As we filed through the kitchen and mess room for the enlisted men, I fell into conversation with a sergeant. I was tagging along and, as usual, worked the other side of the street. He had overheard the mess officer telling Ike what a fine mess he was running and what fine chow the men were getting. My new-found friend, who had battle stars for three campaigns in North Africa, gave me the lowdown. He said the mess stinks, the food is frequently cold, and insisted the mess officer was just putting on a good show. General Ike dedicated a B-17, named *General Ike*. He met all the crew and wished them the best of luck.'

Bassingbourn also now belongs to the army which uses it as a basic training depot. Fortunately, all the buildings of what was one of the permanent RAF stations built between the wars, still remain.

Ike meets the crew of *General Ike*. Smiling on the right is the Group CO, Colonel Claude Putnam. The aircraft, 42-97061, was pictured standing on the grass with hangar No. 1 in the background. It was said to be the first metal-finish aircraft obtained by the 401st Bomb Squadron and, by the war's end, *General Ike* had completed more than 70 missions, often flying as the lead aircraft of the group. It was flown back to the States on July 8, 1945 and was eventually broken up at Kingman Air Force Base in Arizona. As far as the heavy bombers of the Eighth Air Force were concerned, April 11 was an ordinary day with over 900 B-17s and B-24s despatched to targets in Germany as part of its on-going assault on industrial and military targets. The 91st had visited Stettin in the morning, having completed its 240th mission. Three days hence, the Eighth Air Force was to join with RAF Bomber Command in the attack of pre-invasion targets.

During the last days of April and throughout the month of May 1944, the same high degree of success achieved by the early attacks was maintained. A growing paralysis was being extended over the rail networks of the Région Nord, west of a line Paris–Amiens–Boulogne, and south Belgium. In these areas, all the principal routes were, at one time or another, interrupted. Other centres to the east and south of Paris had also been attacked.

In the last week of April, Aulnoye, Villeneuve-St Georges, Achères, Montzen, St Ghislain, Arras and Béthune were all attacked. During May, the heaviest attacks were made on Mantes/Gassicourt, Liège, Ghent, Courtrai, Lille, Hasselt, Louvain, Boulogne, Orléans, Tours, Le Mans, Metz, Mulhouse, Reims, Troyes and Charleroi.

Attacks by heavy and medium bombers on railway centres were maintained up to and after D-Day. From D–7, they were supplemented by attacks designed to cut the lines and halt or destroy such traffic as could still be moved. In these tasks, fighter-bombers played the major part, although the medium and heavy bombers also cooperated. The principal targets in these attacks were bridges, junctions cross-overs and tunnels, as well as locomotives and rolling stock.

Attack on repair depots and facilities was the main method of achieving the desired reduction in traction power. It was accepted that these attacks would, at the same time, damage and destroy locomotives.

I first initiated special large-scale fighter sweeps against trains and locomotives in Northern France and Belgium on May 21. On this day, concentrated efforts were made in certain areas in France, with some attention to connections from Germany and Belgium. Fighters of AEAF and the Eighth Air Force swept over railway tracks covering a very wide area and created havoc among locomotives, passenger trains, goods trains and oil wagons. A total of 504 Thunderbolts, 233 Spitfires, Typhoons and 10 Tempests of AEAF operated throughout the day, claiming 67 locomotives destroyed, 91 locomotives damaged and six locomotives stopped. Eleven other locomotives were attacked with unknown results and numerous trains were attacked and damage inflicted on trucks, carriages, oil wagons, etc.

On this same day, Eighth Air Force Fighter Command sent out 131 Lightnings, 135 Thunderbolts and 287 Mustangs against similar targets in Germany. They claimed 95 locomotives destroyed and 134 locomotives damaged. In addition, one locomotive tender, six goods wagons and three box cars were destroyed, whilst seven goods wagons, seven trains, three rail cars, four box cars and 13 trucks were damaged, and 16 trains set on fire.

From May 22 to D-Day, the AEAF flew 1,388 sorties with the primary purpose of attacking locomotives. In this period, they claimed 157 locomotives destroyed and 82 damaged, as well as numerous trucks.

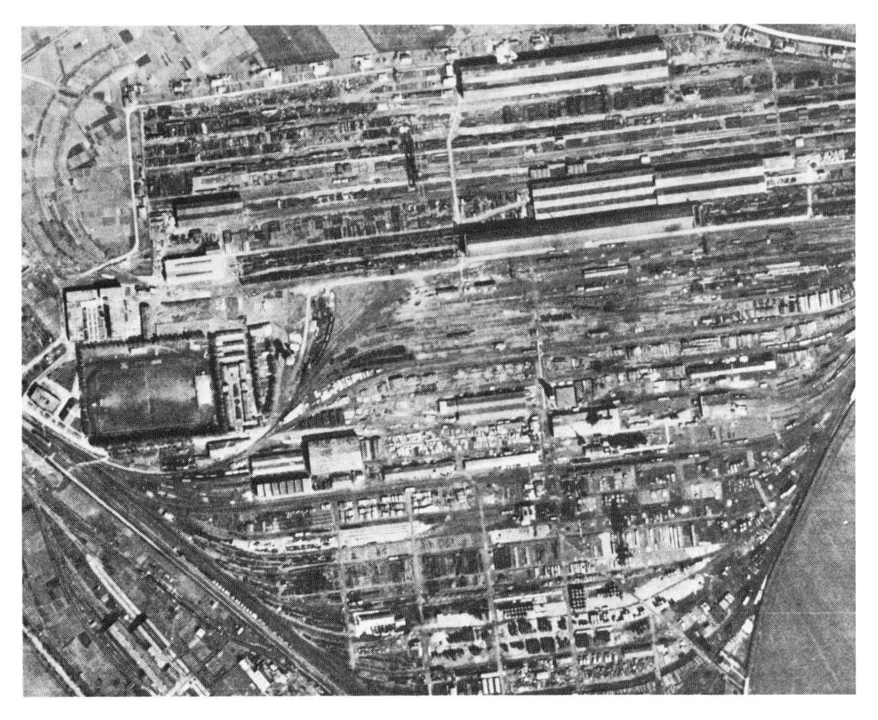

Eisenhower spent the night on his train at Newmarket before returning to London on Wednesday morning. On Monday night, another disastrous attack by RAF Bomber Command had taken place against the railway yards at Ghent, killing 428 Belgians; a week later, 464 French civilians lost their lives when bombing at Noisy-le-Sec (a suburb in north-east Paris) spread over an area six kilometres long by three kilometres wide. ***Above:*** **One of the most important railway targets in the Nord region of SNCF was the main stores and repair depot at Chambly (*above*), north of Paris. It was attacked on the night of April 20/21 but only four out of the 14 Stirlings dropped their bombs using a blind-bombing device.** ***Below:*** **Bomber Command returned to Chambly on the night of May 1/2 and this time 120 aircraft carried out an extremely successful raid with 500 bombs hitting the depot which had been accurately marked. Only five civilians were killed. On several other raids, where the Master Bomber responsible for controlling the bombing felt the target-marking flares were inaccurate, or there was a risk of civilian casualties, the attacks were aborted. The Master Bombers themselves ran a considerable risk of being shot down as they remained flying over the target throughout the raid, and during the operation to the marshalling yards at Le Mans on May 19/20, the Lancasters of the Master Bomber and Deputy Master Bomber, both from No. 7 Squadron, collided over the target. In the main, civilian casualties were kept to the yardstick laid down by the War Cabinet (see page 86), namely 100 to 150 deaths per target, although this figure was exceeded at Malines on May 1/2 (171 killed); Louvain on May 12/13 (160 killed) and at Angers on May 28/29 (254 killed).**

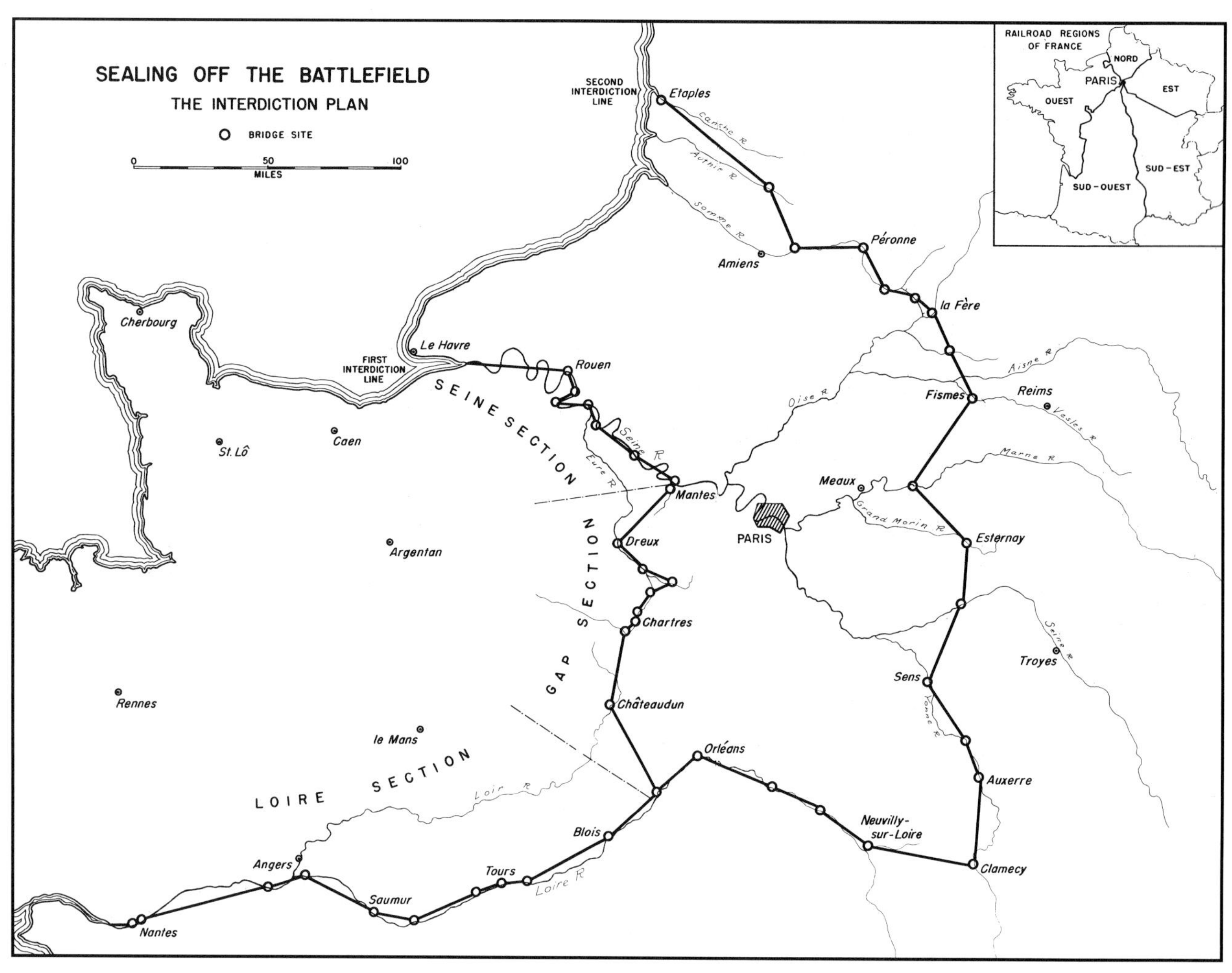

DESTRUCTION OF BRIDGES

As I have already explained, complementary to the plan to destroy, by air attack, the enemy's rail motive power, I planned also to endeavour to destroy all the principal rail and road bridges leading into the assault area. If these were destroyed, not only would the enemy's rate of build-up in that area be further checked and his flow of reinforcements and supplies be further impeded, but also his ability to escape rapidly from the assault area in the event of his being forced to retreat would be very seriously impaired. The implications of the attacks on bridges were, therefore, somewhat wider than those of the other attacks on his communications system. In conjunction with these other attacks, the attacks on bridges were designed to seal off the assault area and so force the enemy to stand and fight, and since he could not easily retreat, any defeat would be decisive.

A bridge is, by nature of its size, very difficult to hit and, by nature of its construction, even more difficult to destroy completely. Calculation suggested that approximately 600 tons of bombs per bridge would be needed if the task were entrusted to heavy bombers. In fact, it was found that an average of 640 tons of bombs per bridge was needed. What was not at first realised was how effectively, and relatively cheaply, the task could be carried out by fighter-bombers. It was learnt from the attacks on bridges by the aircraft of AEAF that

The Seine and Loire rivers provided natural water barriers to the east and south with the section in between, termed the 'Gap Section', covered by the Eure. Because experience in Italy showed that the destruction of bridges required an inordinate effort out of all proportion to the military value of success, such targets had not been included in the original transportation plan. However, 21st Army Group pressed for some experimental attacks to be carried out by medium bombers and fighter-bombers on the Seine bridges. Success was spectacular with only 220 tons of bombs being necessary to destroy one bridge. However, to avoid defining the assault area, bridges over the Loire were not hit until after D-Day. This is Mantes — the easternmost bridge destroyed on the Seine.

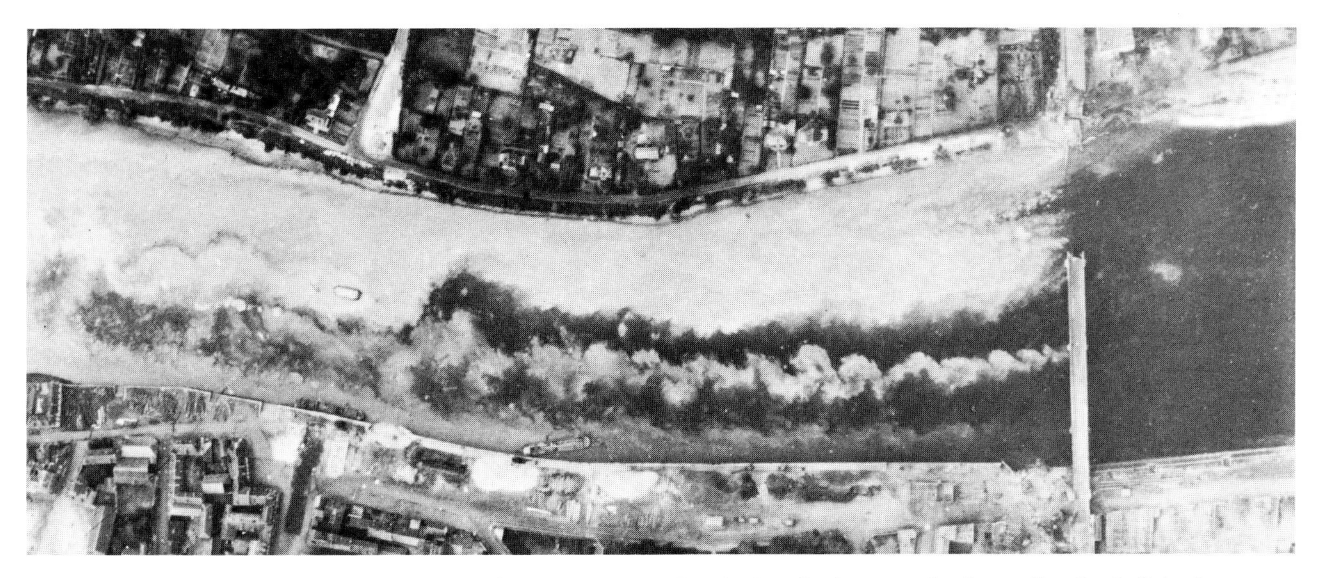

Above: **At Elbeuf, the western bridge, the Pont Guynemer, was destroyed completely, the other, the Pont Jean Jaurès, hit at its northern end. By May 26, all routes over the Seine north of Paris were cut despite German efforts to repair the damage.** *Below:* **For example, two bridges south of Oissel, just south of Rouen, were attacked and damaged on May 10. The Germans decided to repair one for emergency use and by June 6 the railway engineers announced that it was operational. It was bombed again the same day but suffered only light damage so the aircraft returned the following day to finish the job. The attack caused heavy damage, but the German engineers nevertheless set to work to repair the bridge and estimated that they could have it working again by July 2. Allied air forces kept watch and on June 29, when the repairs were almost finished, mounted another attack. This finally completed the destruction and all three superstructures fell into the river.**

a bridge could be destroyed for the expenditure of approximately 100 sorties, that is between 100 and 200 tons of bombs.

In order not to betray a special interest in the 'Neptune' area, attention was paid in the preparatory phase principally to the bridges over the Seine, with some others over the Oise, Meuse and the Albert Canal, leaving to the assault phase the task of attacking bridges south of Paris to Orléans and west along the Loire.

On April 21, the first of a series of attacks against bridges was made by Typhoons. Subsequent attacks were carried out by formations of fighter-bombers which included Thunderbolts, Typhoons and Spitfires and by the medium bombers of the US Ninth Air Force. The early operations were of an experimental nature, the intention being to explore the possibilities of attacks by fighter-bombers and medium bombers against this type of target. The success of the early operations by fighter-bombers surpassed expectations. It is probable that in one or two early attacks, a lucky hit exploded the demolition charges that had been set in place by the Germans and, in such cases, the destruction caused was out of all proportion to the effort expended. Nevertheless, proof was speedily available that fighter-bombers could carry out the task of destroying bridges effectively and relatively cheaply.

The outcome of these attacks was that, on D-Day, 12 railway bridges and the same number of road bridges over the River Seine were rendered impassable. In addition, three railway bridges at Liège and others at Hasselt, Herenthals, Namur, Conflans (Pointe Eifel), Valenciennes, Hirson, Konz-Karthaus (Germany) and Tours, as well as the important highway bridge at Saumur, were also unserviceable.

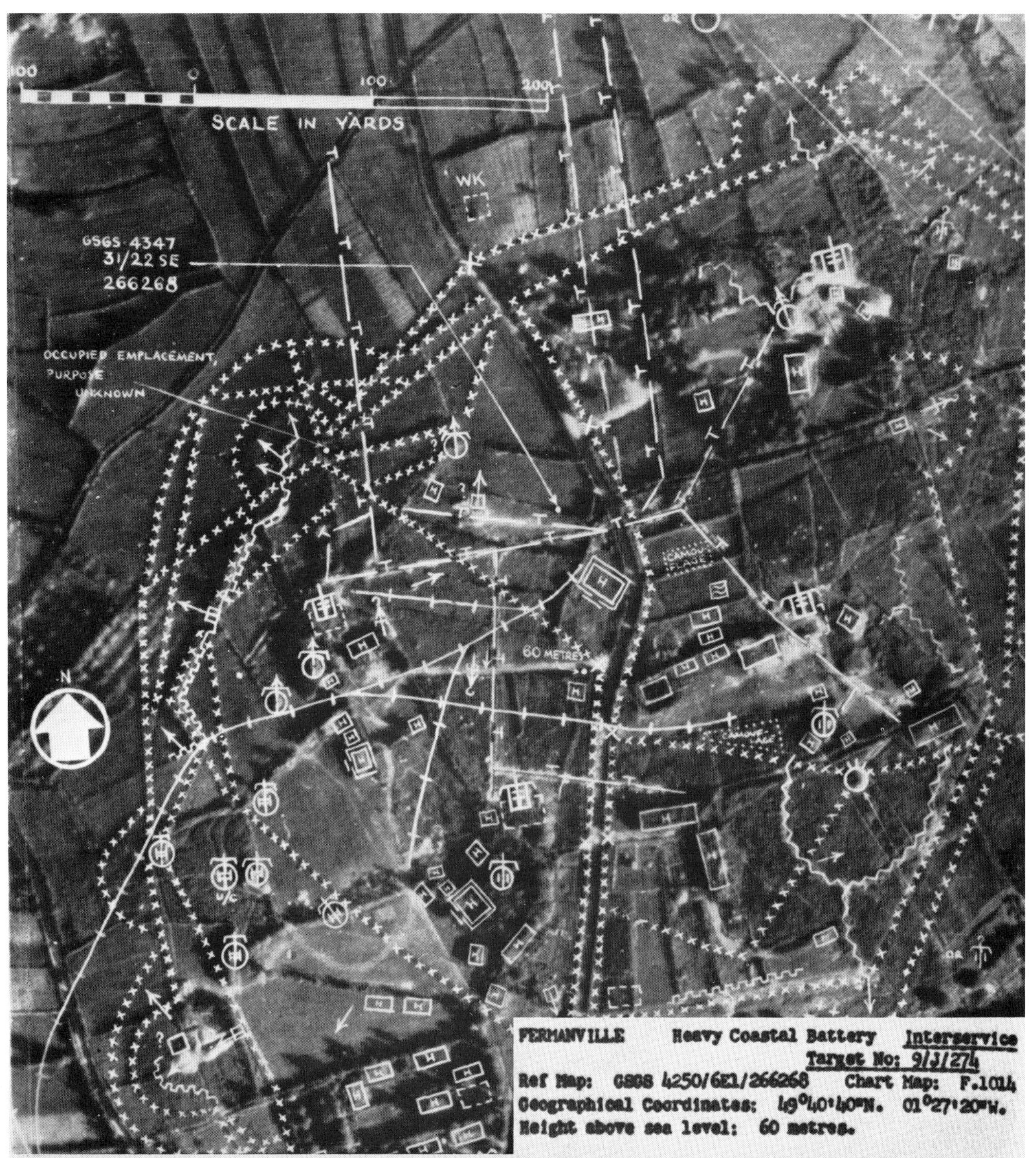

Four 280mm (11 in) guns. Range ?40,000 yards. Weight of shell 660 lbs. Guns in armoured turrets 22 feet by 12 feet, in circular concrete platforms 43 feet in diameter, 160-203 yards apart. Large excavations for shelters are being built behind, and partially enclosing, three of the gun platforms. Arc of fire of each gun is 180°, and if the new shelters are low enough, the guns may be capable of all around fire.

Accommodation: Numerous huts.

Observation Post: At 26332764.

Secondary Armament: Six light AA guns. Also a six-gun heavy AA battery recently installed within the western perimeter of battery: Six 88mm (3.46 in) guns, range 16,200 yards horizontal, 26,250 feet vertical. Rate of fire 15-20 r.p.m. Weight of shell 20 lbs. Guns in circular earthen pits 25 feet in diameter, each with three ammunition bunkers.

All coastal batteries, whether within the assault area or not, had been allocated an individual Interservice Target Number and fully-annotated photo prints were produced of each. This is Target 9/J/274 at Fermanville, 12 kilometres east of Cherbourg. Although Batterie Hamburg, to give it its correct name, actually mounted four guns of 240mm (not 280mm as given in the intelligence summary), it was still one of the most important installations in the Cotentin peninsula. Manned by the Kriegsmarine, it dominated the whole north coast of the peninsula with a range of 26750 metres (28,000 yards).

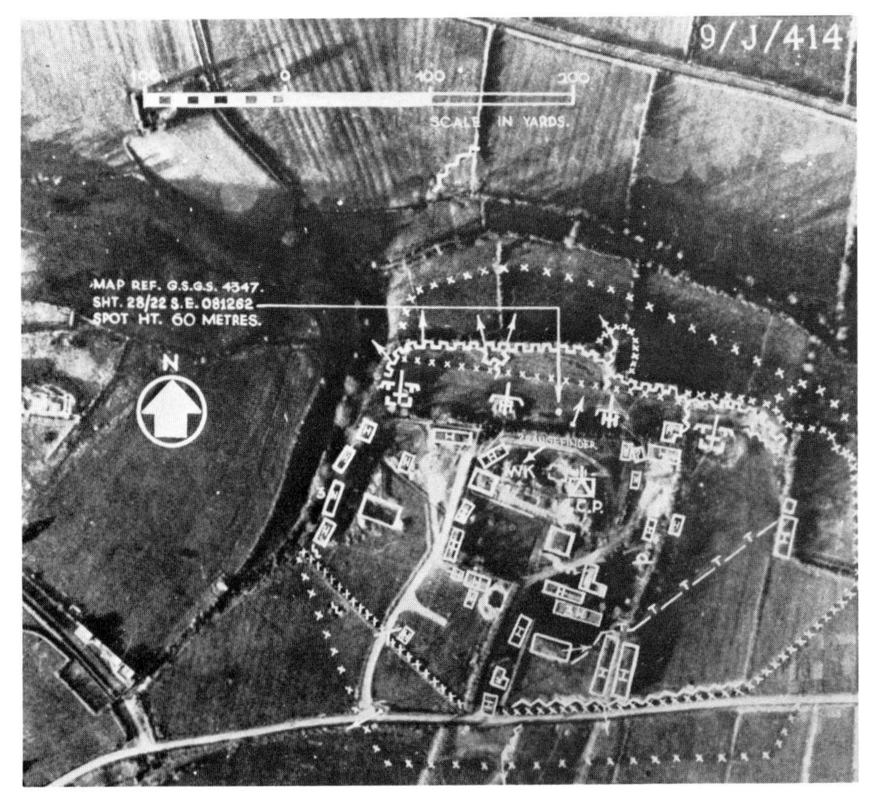

NEUTRALISATION OF COASTAL DEFENCES

These operations had to be commenced well in advance of D-Day as it was essential, as far as possible, to destroy the enemy's capacity to prevent Allied shipping from approaching the assault area and to blind him to that approach.

There were 49 known coastal batteries capable of firing on shipping approaching the assault area. Included in this number were some batteries still under construction. In the conditions that would obtain at the time of the assault, it would clearly be impossible for the naval forces successfully to engage all the coastal batteries. They, therefore, had to be dealt with before the landing and the air forces undertook this task at the request of the Naval and Army commanders.

I did not consider that aerial attacks against batteries whose casemates were completed were likely to be very effective. Fortunately, those batteries in the Cherbourg area were the last to be casemated, and it was possible therefore to attack many of them while they were still incomplete.

To avoid showing particular interest in the assault area, it was planned to attack batteries outside the assault area ranging as far north as Ostend, in the proportion of two outside to one within the area.

Interpretation reports revealed that, in a great many instances, the bombing was more successful than I at first expected; by D-Day, the majority of the coastal batteries within the area had been subjected to damaging attack. Total for the period April 10 to June 5 was 8,765 sorties, 23,094 tons of bombs and 495 × 60lb rocket projectiles.

Of these attacks, one of the most outstanding was that carried out by 64 Lancasters of Bomber Command, with 7 Mosquitos acting as a Pathfinder Force. During this raid on the night of May 28/29, 356 tons of high explosive bombs were dropped on the coastal battery at St Martin-de-Varreville, with excellent results.

Effective attacks were also carried out by aircraft of Bomber Command against the six-gun battery at Morsalines, and by Marauders of the Ninth Air Force on the batteries at Houlgate, Ouistreham and Point de Hoe *(sic)*

Out of 40 sites allotted to AEAF, 37 were attacked, 16 out of 18 in the assault area and 21 out of 22 outside. Of these, nine in the area and 14 outside received hits on one or more emplacements. In all, 48 sites were allotted to Bomber Command, 14 of which were outside. Hits on essential elements were secured on five batteries in the area and nine outside. Of the 52 targets allotted to the Eighth Air Force, 32 of which were in the assault area, only six sites in the area and 16 outside were attacked. Some of the batteries were allotted to two commands.

In addition to the targets listed in the plan, many other coastal defence targets in and out of the area were attacked as targets of opportunity.

Batteries and strong points under construction were regularly photographed to check on the progress of the works. As Leigh-Mallory explains, the Cherbourg batteries were the last to be built and they were bombed before they were completed. *Above:* To SHAEF, this was simply Interservice Target 9/J/414 La Rivière (Querqueville) located eight kilometres west of Cherbourg, but to the Germans it was their Batterie Yorck. The Allies incorrectly assessed its four guns as being of 150mm whereas they were in fact 170mm. Casemating began in February 1944 as it also had at the battery on the height of Castel-Vendon *(below)* further to the west. In this case, the Allies correctly guessed the calibre of the four guns as 150mm, labelling it Interservice Target 9/J/507 and naming it Gruchy after the nearby village.

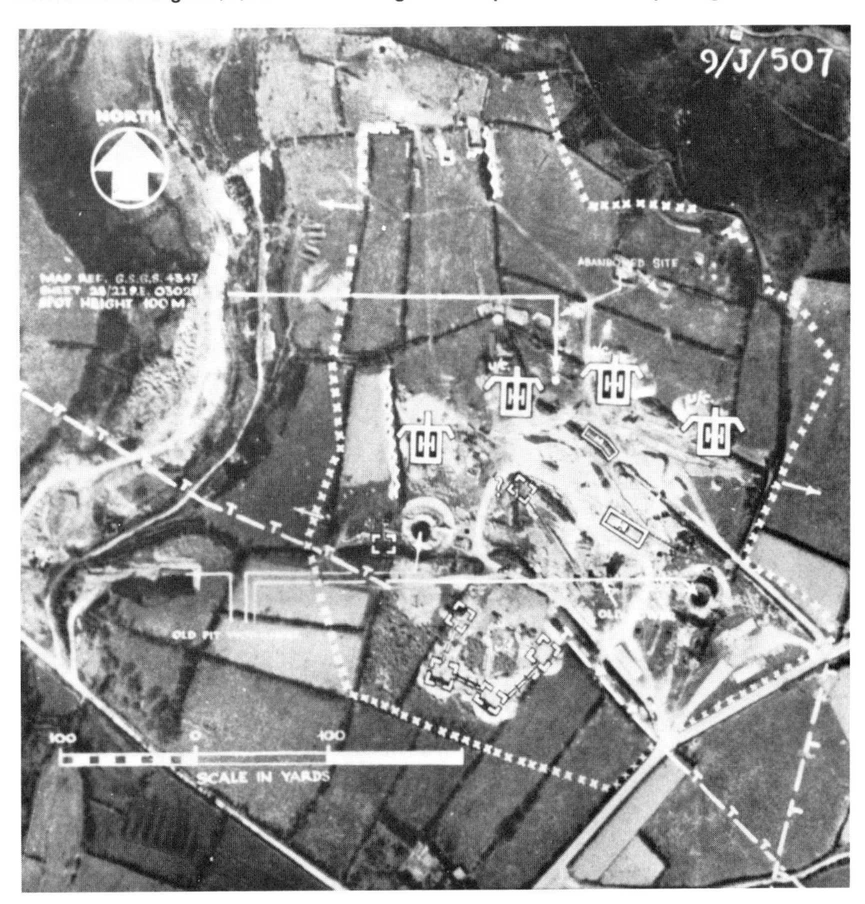

The battery with the largest calibre which posed a threat to the invasion force was the 380mm at Le Grand Clos just north of Le Havre. Depending on the weight of the shell fired, the range was up to 55 kilometres which brought shipping off Sword, Juno and Gold within the danger zone. Casemates were being built for three of the massive 15-inch guns although only one gun had been installed by June. Compare the post-bombing picture *(left)* with the same area today *(right)*.

Another then and now pair of verticals showing the battery at Mont-Canisy, just south-west of Deauville. Manned by Heeres-küstenbatterie 2./1255, it had six former French 155mm guns with a range of 21300 metres. In this picture showing four casemates under construction, Allied intelligence referred to its location as Benerville — the nearest town on the coast.

D-Day target photographed from zero feet: the Freya and Giant Würzburg radar installation at Cap de la Hève, west of Le Havre.

DISRUPTION OF ENEMY RADAR COVER AND W/T FACILITIES

The enemy radar cover on the Western Front was complete from Norway to the Spanish border. This cover was obtained by a chain of coastal stations, each composed of a number of installations. The density of these stations was such that there was a major site, containing an average of three pieces of equipment, every ten miles between Ostend and Cherbourg. This coastal chain was backed by a somewhat less-dense inland system and by numerous mobile installations.

On May 10, a series of attacks was begun against the long-range aircraft reporting stations, and on May 18, on the installations used for night fighter control and the control of coastal guns. On May 25, 42 sites were scheduled for attack. These sites included 106 installations; at D–3, 14 of these sites were confirmed destroyed.

To conserve effort, I then decided, three days before D-Day, to restrict attacks to the 12 most important sites; six were chosen by the naval authorities and six by the air authorities. These 12 sites, containing 39 installations, were all attacked in the three days prior to D-Day.

Up to D-Day, 1,668 sorties were flown by aircraft of AEAF in attacks on radar installations. Typhoons in low-level attacks flew 694 sorties and fired 4,517 × 60lb RPs [rocket projectiles]. Typhoons and Spitfires made 759 dive-bombing sorties, dropping 1,258 × 500lb bombs and light and medium bombers dropped 217 tons of bombs. In addition, the sites and equipment were attacked with many thousands of rounds of cannon and machine gun fire.

These radar targets were very heavily defended by flak and low-level attacks upon them demanded great skill and daring. Pilots of the RAF's Second Tactical Air Force were mainly employed and losses among senior and more-experienced pilots were heavy. There is no doubt, however, that these attacks saved the lives of countless soldiers, sailors and airmen on D-Day. The following details of some of the successful attacks made during the last three days before the assault, show the outstanding results obtained by Typhoon and Spitfire pilots in low-level attacks pressed home to very close range.

Dieppe/Caudecote. This site was attacked by 18 RP Typhoons of No. 198 and No. 609 Squadrons, Second Tactical Air Force, on June 2. 104 × 60lb. RPs were fired, with the result that the 'Hoarding' was destroyed and the 'Freya' and 'Würzburg' installations, used for medium-range aircraft reporting, night fighter control and control of coastal guns, were damaged. One of the Typhoons was destroyed by flak.

Cap d'Antifer. This station was attacked several times. On June 4, 23 Spitfires of Nos. 441, 442 and 443 Squadrons, Second Tactical Air Force, dive-bombed with 23 × 500lb M.C. instantaneous bombs; nine direct hits were scored. The 'Chimney' and one 'Giant Würzburg' were destroyed, and other installations damaged.

Cap de la Hague/Jobourg. This site was attacked by rocket-firing Typhoons of Nos. 174, 175 and 245 Squadrons, Second Tactical Air Force, on June 5. and 200 × 60lb RPs were fired. The 'Hoarding', an installation used for long-range aircraft reporting, was destroyed. Three of the attacking aircraft were destroyed by flak.

In addition to the attacks on the enemy radar stations, attacks were also made on the most important of his navigational beam stations and on certain special W/T stations.

Air-launched rocket projectiles had been developed as anti-ship and anti-AFV weapons of which there were two kinds: a 25lb solid armour-piercing head of 3·44ins in diameter, and a 6-inch 60lb semi-armour-piercing version. It was the latter with its high-explosive head which proved to be a most effective weapon against ground targets, concrete gun emplacements and buildings, etc., and, as is documented in the text, it was used widely in the Normandy campaign. Here, an 'enemy radio installation in northern France' is under attack on D-Day itself.

RADIO COUNTER-MEASURES

On the night of June 5/6, in the opening phase of the assault, counter-measures against such installations as were still active were put into operation. These counter-measures covered five separate and distinct tasks:

(a) a combined naval/air diversion against Cap d'Antifer:
(b) a combined naval/air diversion against Boulogne:
(c) a jamming barrage to cover the airborne forces:
(d) a VHF jamming support for the first three counter-measures:
(e) feints for the airborne forces.

These various components of the counter-measure plan were interdependent and the results can, therefore, best be summarised by giving an indication of the enemy's reactions.

The most important fact concerning this reaction was that the enemy appeared to mistake the diversion towards Cap d'Antifer as a genuine threat; at all events, the enemy opened up, both with searchlights and guns on the imaginary convoy. Further, the VHF jamming support which was flown by a formation of aircraft operating in the Somme area apparently led the enemy to believe that these aircraft were the spearhead of a major bomber force, as he reacted with 24 night fighters, which were active approximately three hours, hunting the 'ghost' bomber stream.

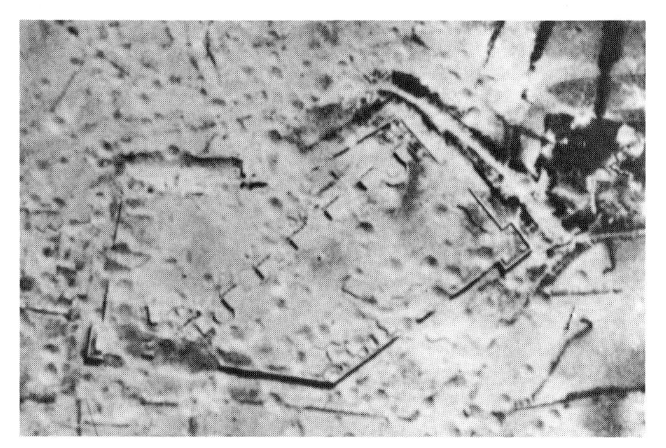

The most far-reaching attack on a W/T centre was that against the headquarters of the German signals intelligence service in north-western France located west of Cherbourg at Urville-Hague (also described as Ferme d'Urville). Although the precise function of the station was not known when it was effectively wiped off the map by a force of nearly a hundred Lancasters from No. 5 Group on the night of June 3/4, Leigh-Mallory believed that its destruction may well have been 'an important contributory factor to the lack of enemy air reaction to the assault'.

The former French Camp Militaire de Mailly lies in open countryside, midway between Reims and Troyes. It had been taken over by German forces in 1940 and had become one of their major tank training areas and armoured storage depots for the Western Front. If it could be destroyed, it would deprive the German panzer forces of important reinforcements, and Bomber Command mounted a major raid against Mailly-le-Camp on the night of May 3/4. Nos. 1 and 5 Groups despatched 346 Lancasters and 14 Mosquitos led by two Mosquito Pathfinders. Their target indicators were accurately placed and backed up by the Lancaster Marker Leader flown by Wing Commander Leonard Cheshire but, when he ordered the main force onto the target, the Main Force Controller could not relay the signal to the waiting Lancasters because of radio difficulties, one set being blocked by an American forces broadcast. The Deputy Controller then took over and the bombs were released accurately on target. This night flash photo shows one of the attacking Lancasters above the towering columns of smoke.

ATTACKS ON MILITARY FACILITIES

As well as preparing the way for the assault forces by attacking the enemy's coastal defences and radar system, it was planned to prepare the way further for the landing by reducing the enemy military potential, both in the assault and rear areas. Certain ammunition and fuel dumps, military camps and headquarters were considered suitable targets for attack, in order to fulfil this purpose.

On the night of May 3/4, Bomber Command attacked in force the tank depot at Mailly-le-Camp. 1,924 tons of bombs were dropped and assessment photographs show the whole target to have been severely damaged. In the mechanical transport section and barracks, 34 out of 47 buildings were totally destroyed. Even more remarkable results were obtained by an attack on an ammunition dump at Châteaudun carried out on the same night. Eight Mosquitos of Bomber Command attacked with approximately 13 tons of bombs. The bombs were dropped very accurately and caused sympathetic detonation throughout the dump. In the resulting explosion, the entire western wing of the depot, containing 90 buildings, was completely destroyed.

The Bourg Leopold military camp in Belgium was heavily attacked on two occasions. On May 11/12, 201 aircraft of Bomber Command dropped 585 tons of bombs on this depot. On the night of May 27/28, a force of 324 aircraft, also from that Command, dropped 1,348 tons of bombs, and photographic reconnaissance revealed very heavy damage throughout the whole area of the camp. Six large buildings and at least 150 personnel huts received direct hits.

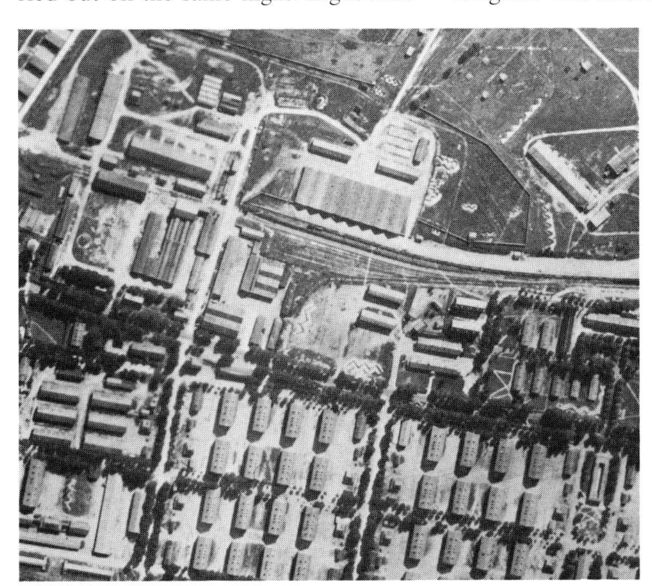

Reports indicated that over 150 buildings had been hit with 100 vehicles and nearly 40 tanks destroyed. Casualties amongst the German personnel numbered 218 killed, mostly NCOs, and 156 injured. However, the cost to Bomber Command was high, with over 11 per cent of the force failing to return — an effective loss of well over 300 crewmen.

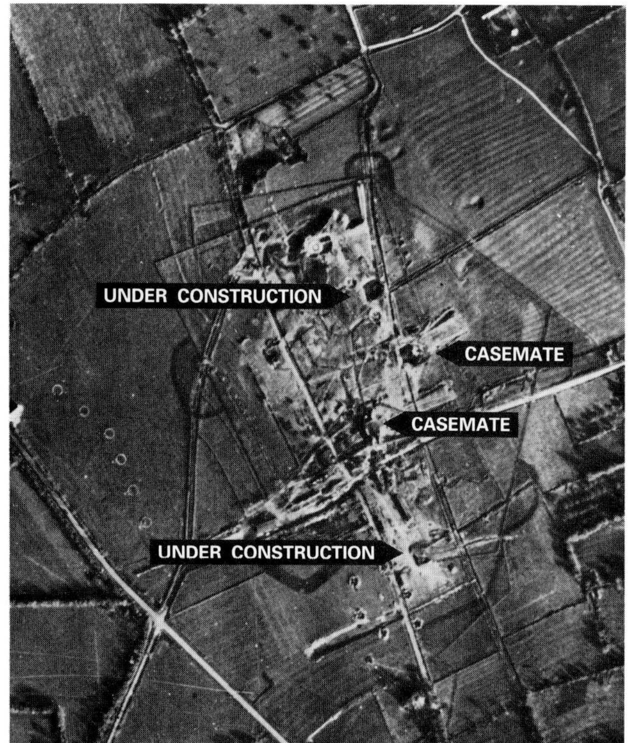

Finally, on the morning of D-Day itself, came the last-minute bombing operations to assist the naval fire plan in the neutralisation of those batteries directly threatening the landing areas. A good example is provided by the attack on Crisbecq which would be able to bring its 210mm guns to bear on Utah. The open gun positions beside the four casemates under construction led the Allies to label it as a six-gun heavy battery although only two concrete casemates had been completed by D-Day.

PROTECTION OF THE CROSS-CHANNEL MOVEMENT

The task of assisting the naval forces to protect the passage of the assault armies from surface and U-Boat attack, was undertaken chiefly by RAF Coastal Command though aircraft of AEAF assisted in this task. On D-Day and D+1, aircraft of Coastal Command flew 353 sorties on anti-shipping and anti-U-Boat patrols. A line of patrols was provided at either end of the Channel. The air protection thus afforded contributed much to the safety of the Allied shipping from both surface and underwater attack by enemy naval forces.

Fifteen squadrons of fighters were allotted the task of protecting the shipping lanes. These squadrons flew 2,015 sorties during the course of D-Day and D+1, the cover being maintained at six-squadron strength throughout this period. Owing to the lack of enemy reaction, I was able later to reduce this cover to a two-squadron force.

NEUTRALISATION OF COASTAL AND BEACH DEFENCES

The task of neutralising as many of the coastal defence positions as possible during the crucial period of the assault was shared by naval and air bombardment. The air bombardment plan called for attacks to commence just before dawn on D-Day.

RAF Bomber Command commenced the bombardment with attacks on ten selected heavy coastal batteries in the assault area: Crisbecq, St Martin-de-Varreville, Ouistreham, Maisy, Mont-Fleury, La Pernelle, St Pierre-du-Mont [Pointe du Hoc], Merville-Franceville, Houlgate, and Longues.

During the hours of darkness preceding the actual assault, a tremendous air bombardment was directed on to the batteries which could not be destroyed within the assault area, aimed at neutralising them during the critical assault period.

As Bomber Command left the assault area, Eighth Air Force heavy bombers took over the bombardment rôle. In the 30 minutes immediately preceding the touchdown hour, 1,365 heavy bombers attacked selected areas in the coastal defences, dropping 2,796 tons of bombs.

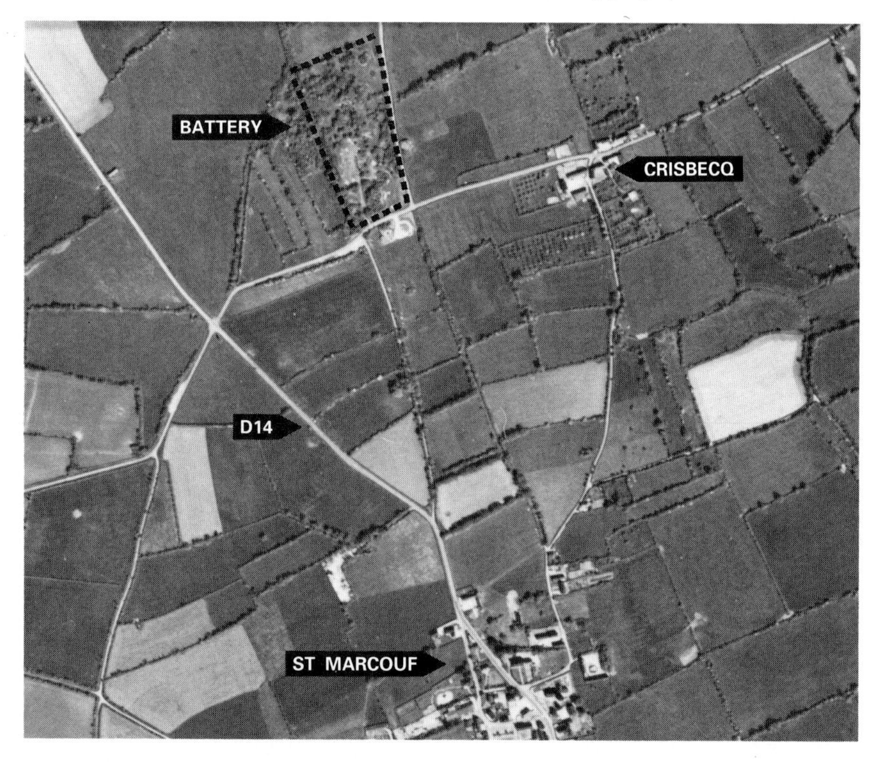

The official German title for the position was Marine-Küstenbatterie Marcouf, after the village of that name just to the south, and the Allied references to Crisbecq have often caused confusion. We shall see it later from ground level; meanwhile, this is the modern air view of the battery site today.

And a final word from Air Chief Marshal Leigh-Mallory: 'Air superiority was the principal pre-requisite for the successful assault of Europe from the west. The winning of air superiority was therefore the cardinal point of air planning. Air operations to ensure that the requisite degree of air superiority had been gained by D-Day were begun in the preliminary phase and continued during the preparatory phase. On D-Day itself, a series of concentrated attacks was made on the German Air Force airfields in the pre-selected area but, as a result of the earlier operations, I was confident that the necessary degree of air ascendancy had been gained some time before D-Day. In the event, the German Air Force was more impotent than I expected.' *Above:* **The majority of fighter aircraft giving close cover over the landing beaches were based in the Tangmere Sector A, and a new Sector Operations Room had been established in February 1944 in the hall of Bishop Otter College at Chichester, a mile west of the airfield. This forward air operations centre controlled 56 squadrons, some based on airfields as far away as Surrey and Berkshire, and General Eisenhower had inspected the facilities on April 20.**

The result of these operations added to the previous air bombardment and, combined with the naval shelling, neutralised wholly or in large part almost all of the shore batteries, and the opposition to the landings was very much less than was expected.

Medium, light and fighter-bombers then took a hand in the attacks on the enemy defensive system by attacking artillery positions further inland and other targets in the coastal defences.

The heavy bombers of the Eighth Air Force operated again later in the day and, although cloud interfered with bombing about midday, necessitating the recall of some missions, a further 1,746 tons of bombs were dropped. In all, the Eighth Air Force flew 2,627 heavy bombers and 1,347 escort and offensive fighter sorties during the day.

PROTECTION OF THE LANDING BEACHES

In addition to the cover given to the cross-Channel movement of the assault forces, I provided a continuous daylight fighter cover of the beach-head areas. Nine squadrons in two forces of six squadrons of low cover and three squadrons of high cover continuously patrolled over the British and American beaches. A reserve of six fighter squadrons on the ground were also kept at readiness to strengthen any point if the enemy came up to challenge.

On D-Day alone, 1,547 sorties were flown on beach-head cover. Night fighters also patrolled continuously during the hours of darkness over the beach-head and shipping lanes; six squadrons of Mosquitos were available for these operations.

I wish to congratulate all units of the Allied Expeditionary Air Force on the magnificent work which has been done in preparation for the invasion. The situation on the eve of the battle has exceeded my highest hopes.

Now, we are faced with the greatest operation of its kind ever undertaken. The Air Forces have a vital part to play and a tremendous undertaking in delaying and disorganising the German armies, as well as defeating the German Air Force.

I have every confidence that you are well up to the great work that lies before you. I am proud to be with you as a member of the team to fight this great battle. I have every confidence in you all, and wish you God Speed and the best of luck in the great task that lies before you.

AIR CHIEF MARSHAL SIR TRAFFORD LEIGH-MALLORY,
JUNE 1944

Shortly after the end of the war, a memorial plaque was unveiled in the old ops room, now sub-divided into two science laboratories.

'England, May 12, 1944. General Eisenhower and Prime Minister Churchill meet with Mackenzie King of Canada, Peter Fraser of New Zealand, Godfrey Huggins of Rhodesia and Jan Smuts of South Africa at an unidentified railroad station.' A picture from US archives but where was it taken?

OK, Let's Go?

By General Dwight D. Eisenhower

After the abandonment of the May target date, the next combination of moon, tide, and time of sunrise that we considered practicable for the attack occurred on June 5, 6, and 7. We wanted to cross the Channel with our convoys at night so that darkness would conceal the strength and direction of our several attacks. We wanted a moon for our airborne assaults. We needed approximately 40 minutes of daylight preceding the ground assault to complete our bombing and preparatory bombardment. We had to attack on a relatively low tide because of beach obstacles which had to be removed while uncovered. These principal factors dictated the general period; but the selection of the actual day would depend upon weather forecasts.

If none of the three days should prove satisfactory from the standpoint of weather, consequences would ensue that were almost terrifying to contemplate. Secrecy would be lost. Assault troops would be unloaded and crowded back into assembly areas enclosed in barbed wire, where their original places would already have been taken by those to follow in subsequent waves. Complicated movement tables would be

It was important that we established the correct location as this picture has sometimes been used to illustrate Churchill's later pre-D-Day visit to Southampton when his train was parked at Droxford. We soon established it was not Droxford station as the fretwork of the canopy there is different. The Prime Minister's tour of inspection of 'Overlord' troops on May 12 began on the Kent coast, with demonstrations at Lydd, and ended a hundred miles away at Ascot in Berkshire where Churchill was joined for dinner by the New Zealand Prime Minister, Peter Fraser, and Eisenhower. Unfortunately, the original station roof at Ascot was replaced after a fire in 1986.

This was the occasion when Churchill demonstrated his one-piece, zip-fastened boiler suit or 'siren suit' for the cameras, one well-known sequence showing him unzipping the front. The caption to this British official picture states: 'General Smuts, Sir Godfrey Huggins, Mr Churchill and Mr Mackenzie King. Mr Churchill is wearing his famous siren suit.' It was taken on the same platform looking in the opposite direction.

OLD BILL: BY BRUCE BAIRNSFATHER
"If yer asks me, mate, that's where Eisenhower's goin' to land, right there!"

Preserving the secret of D-Day was a nerve-racking business. On May 27, *John Bull* published their 'Old Bill' cartoon in which the grand old student of war put his finger exactly on the spot where the Allies would land ten days later. 'Old Bill' was alone among the commentators of the period to have accurately predicted the correct location.

scrapped. Morale would drop. A wait of at least 14 days, possibly 28, would be necessary — a sort of suspended animation involving more than 2,000,000 men! The good weather period available for major campaigning would become still shorter and the enemy's defences would become still stronger! The whole of the United Kingdom would become quickly aware that something had gone wrong and national discouragement there and in the United States could lead to unforeseen results. Finally, always lurking in the background, was the knowledge that the enemy was developing new, and presumably effective, secret weapons on the French coast. What the effect of these would be on our crowded harbours, especially at Plymouth and Portsmouth, we could not even guess.

It was a tense period, made even worse by the fact that the one thing that could give us this disastrous setback was entirely outside our control. Some soldier once said: 'The weather is always neutral.' Nothing could be more untrue. Bad weather is obviously the enemy of the side that seeks to launch projects requiring good weather, or of the side possessing great assets, such as strong air forces, which depend upon good weather for effective operations. If really bad weather should endure permanently, the Nazi would need nothing else to defend the Normandy coast!

'Old Bill' might have been a good guesser, but could the same be said for Leonard Dawe who revealed five of the top secret D-Day code-words in crosswords he compiled for *The Daily Telegraph* in 1944? Dawe was the headmaster of Strand School at Effingham, Surrey, and in his crossword on May 2 (No. 5775), the clue for 17 across was: 'One of the U.S.' — Answer: 'UTAH.' Then on May 22, the clue for 3 down read: 'Red Indian on the Missouri.' — Answer: 'OMAHA.' To pick a classified code-word once could be luck; twice a fluke, but what were the odds against three more words appearing in quick succession? 'OVERLORD' appeared as the answer for the cryptic clue to 11 across on May 27 ('— but some bigwig like this has stolen some of it at times'); 'MULBERRY' as the answer to the 11 across three days later ('This bush is a centre of nursery revolutions') and 'NEPTUNE' for the June 1 clue for 15 across ('Britannia and he hold the same thing'). Dawe was questioned by MI5 but cleared of any deliberate leak as he said he had compiled the crosswords some months earlier. Was it pure chance that he picked those five words or had he heard them, possibly from his brother-in-law who worked at the Admiralty? No one appears to have taken it up with Dawe before he died in 1963, and no reliable explanation has ever been forthcoming, even following discussions between ex-pupils from his school who met at the *Telegraph* offices in June 1990 to unveil a portrait of Dawe.

As we have seen (page 33), an Advance Command Post *(left)* had been set up at Eisenhower's request within easy distance of Naval headquarters at Southwick where daily weather conferences were due to be held starting on May 28. However, the General still had to keep in touch with his own HQ at Bushy Park, and the air headquarters even further away, necessitating a round trip of some 200 miles. Even using motorcycle outriders, it would have been a long, frustrating journey on the A3 during which the Supreme Commander would have been completely incommunicado. Commander Butcher (seen here in the background) says that Eisenhower was to spend nights at the Advance CP to be able to attend the late-night meetings to consider the weather, and then drive back to 'Widewing' during the day. On Thursday, June 1, the SHAEF Public Relations Officer, Colonel R. Ernest Dupuy (based in London at Portland Court), told Eisenhower of the arrangements for press coverage at 'Sharpener' which would be restricted to four reporters, two British and two American. Lieutenant Colonel Thor Smith (right) would be PRO for the Advance CP, assisted by Captain Victor Meluskey as the US censor (rear left), with Major W. R. Carr (to his right). *Right:* The precise location of 'Sharpener' had been lost to history until we carried out an investigation in 1994 (detailed in *After the Battle* No. 84) leading to its discovery in Sawyer's Wood.

Before the actual assault, operational portions of SHAEF and 21st Army Group headquarters were set up at Portsmouth on the south coast. This was the region of our principal embarkation point, and here also the Navy had established a communication system that would keep us in touch, during the early hours of D-Day, with the progress of each element in the great armada.

All southern England was one vast military camp, crowded with soldiers awaiting final word to go, and piled high with supplies and equipment awaiting transport to the far shore of the Chan-

Stanley Birch (Reuters) and Robert Barr (BBC), on Eisenhower's right, Merrill Mueller (NBC) and Edward Roberts (UPI), to his left, were due at 'Sharpener' on Sunday, June 4, but their arrival was cancelled by Eisenhower because too much was going on. The big unresolved problem was political. In September 1943, the French Committee of National Liberation in Algiers had contacted London and Washington to determine the conditions under which the French administration would co-operate with Allied forces in France. However, neither the British nor American governments were prepared to recognise the FCNL, President Roosevelt being particularly antagonistic towards its leader, Général Charles de Gaulle. Roosevelt steadfastly refused to discuss arrangements for the civil government of France prior to the invasion and was instead preparing to install a wholly military administration, only permitting Eisenhower to consult with the FCNL once in France. To compound the problem, it had been decided that the French should not be informed in advance of the preparations for 'Overlord', the ban even extending to Général Pierre Koenig, the London-based commander of the Free French Forces of the Interior whose co-operation was essential before, during and after D-Day! For his part, Général de Gaulle was determined to take control of liberated France. With public opinion in Britain firmly in favour of recognising de Gaulle as the new leader of France, Churchill found himself in an impossible situation. On May 26, the FNCL officially proclaimed itself the provisional Government of the French Republic; the following day, de Gaulle was invited to London. The Général arrived in England on the morning of June 4 to be handed Churchill's invitation to join him on his train which was positioned six miles north of 'Sharpener' in this railway cutting *(left)* just to the south of the little railway station at Droxford, now a private house *(right)*.

'Welcome to these shores!' Churchill's message had begun. 'Very great military events are about to take place. I should be glad if you could come to see me down here in my train, which is close to General Eisenhower's headquarters, bringing with you one or two of your party. General Eisenhower is looking forward to seeing you again and will explain to you the military position which is momentous and imminent. If you could be here by 1.30 p.m., I should be glad to give you déjeuner and we will then repair to General Eisenhower's headquarters.' Anthony Eden, Churchill's Foreign Secretary who was more involved in the politics than anyone else, wrote that 'I arrived in time to walk down the railway line with de Gaulle. The Prime Minister, moved by his sense of history, was on the track to greet the Général with arms outstretched. Unfortunately, de Gaulle did not respond easily to such a mood.' Although the discussions began amicably, by the end of the meal the atmosphere had deteriorated into a shouting match between Churchill and de Gaulle, exacerbated by the fact that the Allied command was going to introduce their own currency to France, something that de Gaulle refused to accept. After being repeatedly pressed to take his case to Washington, de Gaulle exploded. 'Why do you seem to think that I need to submit my candidacy for the authority in France to Roosevelt?' he thundered. After lunch, Churchill and Eden drove with de Gaulle to 'Sharpener' *(left)* where Eisenhower took the Général to his map tent to explain in detail the coming operation. As he was preparing to leave, Eisenhower told him that he was going to broadcast a proclamation to France and he hoped de Gaulle would do the same. This set the Général off again: 'You broadcast a proclamation to the French people? By what right? And what will you tell them?' *Below:* No wonder this party photographed that Sunday outside Eisenhower's office tent (it was panelled inside) look peeved . . . all, that is, save the First Sea Lord, Admiral of the Fleet Sir Andrew Cunningham. L–R (rear): Lieutenant Commander Charles 'Tommy' Thompson, Churchill's ADC; Commander Butcher; Lieutenant-Colonel James Gault, Eisenhower's British aide; Cunningham; Major-General Leslie Hollis, Senior Assistant Secretary to the War Cabinet. Front: Captain Mattie Pinette, Eisenhower's personal secretary; Churchill; and Eisenhower's chauffeuse, Lieutenant Kay Summersby. *Above right:* All that remains at 'Sharpener' today: the tell-tale cinders once crunched by the mighty.

nel. The whole area was cut off from the rest of England. The government had established a deadline, across which no unauthorized person was allowed to go in either direction. Every separate encampment, barrack, vehicle park, and every unit was carefully charted on our master maps. The scheduled movement of each unit had been so worked out that it would reach the embarkation point at the exact time the vessels would be ready to receive it. The southernmost camps where assault troops were assembled were all surrounded by barbed-wire entanglements to prevent any soldier leaving the camp after he had once been briefed as to his part in the attack. The whole mighty host was tense as a coiled spring, and indeed that is exactly what it was — a great human spring, coiled for the moment when its energy should be released and it would vault the English Channel in the greatest amphibious assault ever attempted.

In the end, the Général agreed to make a recording to be broadcast to France although now, overshadowing the problems with de Gaulle, came the worry about the weather. The conferences were scheduled to be held at Admiral Ramsay's 'Overlord' headquarters which lay less than a mile from Eisenhower's camp. (See also page 102.)

But the big question mark always before us was the weather that would prevail during the only period of early June that we could use, the 5th, 6th, and 7th. We met with the Meteorological Committee twice daily, once at 9.30 p.m. in the evening and once at 4 a.m. in the morning. The committee, comprising both British and American personnel, was headed by a dour but canny Scot, Group Captain J. M. Stagg. At these meetings, every bit of evidence was carefully presented, carefully analysed by the experts, and carefully studied by the assembled commanders. With the approach of the critical period, the tension continued to mount as prospects for decent weather became worse and worse.

The final conference for determining the feasibility of attacking on the tentatively-selected day, June 5, was scheduled for 4 a.m. on June 4. However, some of the attacking contingents had already been ordered to sea, because if the entire force was to land on June 5, then some of the important elements stationed in northern parts of the United Kingdom could not wait for final decision on the morning of June 4.

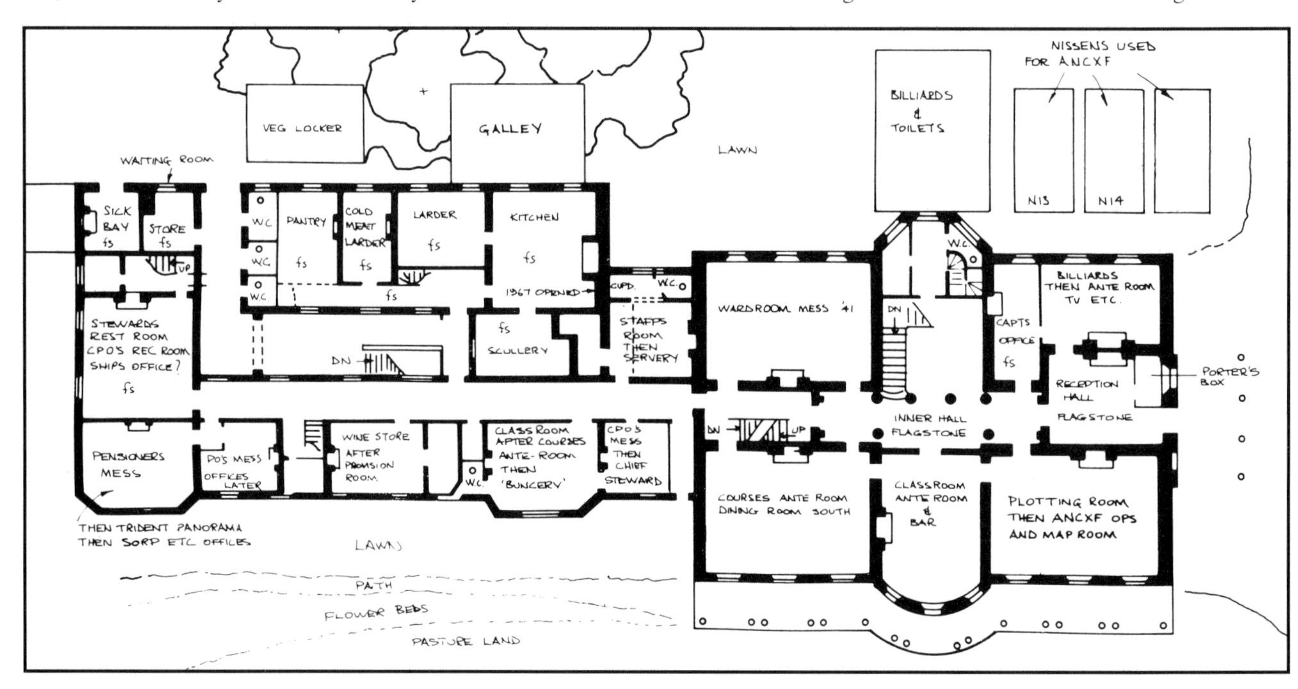

Southwick House had been requisitioned from its pre-war owner, Lieutenant-Colonel Evelyn Thistlethwayte, in 1941 to house the Royal Naval School of Navigation which had been bombed out of its own premises in Portsmouth Dockyard.

Left: **Group Captain John Stagg had been appointed chief meteorologist to SHAEF in November 1943 to co-ordinate 'the meteorological arrangements for disseminating weather information and advice to the naval, army and air forces, US and British, under the Supreme Allied Commander's control'. Each of the forces already had its own forecasters, but Stagg's job was to analyse their predictions and present the overall picture in a succinct form. His deputy was Colonel Donald N. Yates of the USAAF. Stagg travelled to Portsmouth from 'Widewing' on Sunday, May 28, where he and Yates shared office space with Admiral Ramsay's chief weather officer, Instructor Commander John Fleming, in a Nissen hut just behind the house** *(right).*

OVERLORD WEATHER

Meteorological requirements for the Assault

Navy. *Surface winds — not exceeding Force 3 (8-12 mph) on shore, Force 4 (13-18 mph) off shore during D-Day to D+2. (Force 5 bearable in open sea but for limited periods only.)*

No prolonged periods of high winds in the Atlantic causing substantial swell in the Channel.

Visibility — not less than 3 miles.

Air Force. Air Transport

Cloud ceiling at least 2,500 ft to and over target. Visibility 3 miles at least.

Heavy Bombers

Not more than 5/10ths cloud below 5,000 ft, cloud ceiling not below 11,000 ft over target.

Medium and Light Bombers

Cloud ceiling not less than 4,500 ft over target, visibility at least 3 miles.

Fighters and Fighter Bombers

Cloud base not less than 1,000 ft.

Bases. *Cloud not below 1,000 ft.*

Army. Airborne Landings

Surface wind over the target area not to exceed 20 mph and not gusty. Half moonlight at least.

Ground Forces

Ground dry enough to take heavy vehicles off the main roads.

Procedure. *January 1944: Directors of Meteorological Services for Air Ministry: Royal Navy, United States Forces, and Chief Meteorological Officer at SHAEF began joint consultations. They devised a routine procedure each week for issuing a forecast for a period of five days. i.e. for five days ahead.*

First conference February 1944 (from mid-April conferences every day). They found after the first conferences that it was extremely difficult to predict more than 2 or 3 days ahead. During May (when the weather was mainly settled) the experts forecast 18 days on which the weather was suitable for invasion.

GROUP CAPTAIN J. M. STAGG
NOTES ON REPORT TO SCAEF, JUNE 22, 1944

Group Captain Stagg's responsibility cannot be overstated, nor can his difficulty in reconciling the sometimes differing forecasts produced by the Air Ministry Meteorological Office at Dunstable and the main US weather centre at 'Widewing'. Writing after the war, Stagg explained that his first task on being appointed to the job had been 'to try to elicit from COSSAC planners which was the most likely time for "Overlord" and what kind of weather they considered necessary for its success. According to the COSSAC plan, May was the most likely time; it could be later but almost certainly not earlier. An answer to the second part of the question about the kind of weather need for "Overlord" was less easy to come by so the question had to be rephrased to "What are the least favourable conditions in which your forces can operate successfully?"'

The wartime buildings have been replaced by modern office accommodation.

The nerve centre of Admiral Ramsay's headquarters was the operations or map room on the ground floor. This watercolour, ***Headquarters Room*** by Barnett Freedman (1901-58), depicts how the room appeared in June 1944. The painted plywood map on the far wall had been fabricated by a well-known Midlands-based toy firm, Chad Valley, but in order to maintain secrecy of the chosen landing area, the map as ordered covered the whole European coastline from Norway to Spain. Only when it arrived at Southwick House was the correct section mounted in position, the two workmen involved then being confined to HMS *Dryad* until the operation had been launched.

The Final Conferences

Sunday, May 28th. *Meteorological report to Supreme Commander that the 'mainly quiet wind conditions would continue during the coming week'. (Risk of a gale seemed rather small.)*

Monday, May 29th. *Meeting with Supreme Commander etc., at Portsmouth. 1000 hrs. Forecast for the five days up to June 2nd. Mainly quiet wind conditions — not more than Force 4 — except for wind of Force 5 in western Channel on last two days of the period. Variable cloud conditions average 5/10-7/10 but increasing. Risk of deterioration.*

Wednesday, May 31st. 0830 hrs. *ACS/G3 SHAEF (General Bull) was advised that prospects were not favourable for weather after Sunday, June 4th. 'There were indications that the Azores high pressure area was beginning to show signs of weakness; but no evidence yet that the wind would exceed Force 4.'*

Friday, June 2nd, 1000 hrs. *(With Supreme Commander etc.) 'There is now indication that the present relatively quiet weather may end about Tuesday.'*

Winds will be westerly mainly not above Force 4 but Force 5 at times especially in western Channel on Monday 5th, and Tuesday, 6th. Cloud conditions — variable — 7/10-10/10 early morning. Visibility — moderate to good but risk of fog patches.

Friday, June 2nd, 2130 hrs. *No substantial change. Eisenhower enquired whether improvement likely for the 6th or 7th. Reply — NO: in fact danger of Force 5 winds on the 6th. Cloud conditions poor with periods of 10/10 at 1,000 ft.*

Saturday, June 3rd, 0830 hrs. *Bull was advised: no improvement — risk of Force 5 winds now forecast for Monday and even late Sunday. Cloud forecast uncertain — most likely 7/10-10/10 base 1,000 ft.*

Saturday, June 3rd, 2130 hrs. *(Supreme Commander etc.) 'The high pressure area over the Azores is rapidly giving way and a series of depressions across the Atlantic is moving rapidly eastward; these depressions will produce disturbed conditions in the Channel and assault area. Winds will be W-SW, Force 5 on the English coast, Force 3-4 on the French coast from early Sunday until a cold front trough passes. That passage is timed to be sometime on Wednesday, June 7th. From Sunday morning onwards, cloud will be mainly 10/10 with base 500-1,000 ft in the morning hours. Visibility will be mainly 3-4 miles [but] there is a risk of fog spreading from the West up the Channel. After Monday, this risk of fog will decrease. During Wednesday, a front associated with a depression now off Nova Scotia and New England will probably pass through the assault area. Conditions over enemy bases on Monday will, on the whole, be better than over bases in England which were likely to be blanketed with 10/10 cloud at 500-1,000 ft.'*

Nevertheless, Eisenhower commented that the situation seemed slightly better since the previous night but the experts replied that 'the balance has now swung too far to the unfavourable side for it to be quickly counteracted'.

Following the presentation of this information, the assault was provisionally postponed for 24 hours.

GROUP CAPTAIN J. M. STAGG
NOTES ON REPORT TO SCAEF, JUNE 22, 1944

Admiral Ramsay quit Southwick early in September when SHAEF headquarters moved to France. The operations room fell into disuse, its purpose fulfilled, and it was not until the war was over that a decision was made to backdate the symbols on the map to the situation that existed on June 6, 1944 and protect it behind glass. Had he been alive, Admiral Ramsay would have performed the unveiling but he had been killed in a plane crash just outside Paris on January 2, 1945. Instead, the ceremony was carried out by his Chief-of-Staff, Rear-Admiral George Creasy (pointing) on August 7, 1946.

When the commanders assembled on the morning of June 4, the report we received was discouraging. Low clouds, high winds, and formidable wave action were predicted to make landing a most hazardous affair. The meteorologists said that air support would be impossible, naval gun-fire would be inefficient, and even the handling of small boats would be rendered difficult. Admiral Ramsay thought that the mechanics of landing could be handled, but agreed with the estimate of the difficulty in adjusting gun-fire. His position was mainly neutral. General Montgomery, properly concerned with the great disadvantages of delay, believed that we should go. Tedder disagreed.

Weighing all factors, I decided that the attack would have to be postponed. This decision necessitated the immediate dispatch of orders to the vessels and troops already at sea and created some doubt as to whether they could be ready 24 hours later in case the next day should prove favourable for the assault.

The layout of the Ops Room at Southwick House is well portrayed in the painting by Barnett Freedman, Official War Artist. I remember him painting the picture and getting in everyone's way. The Wren Plotting Officer in the foreground is Alison Egerton. The Liaison Officers (RAF, US, Army, etc.) sat with their backs to the wall, facing the wallplot, at small individual tables, squeezed together each with a telephone on his desk.

The large table plot was exactly as in Freedman's picture, in front of the big windows — daylight was taken advantage of but the windows were of course blacked out at dusk. The room became very hot when it was crowded. Officers never removed jackets and the majority smoked. ventilation was minimal.

Present were a Wren Plotting Officer, two Wren plotters, both probably Leading hands, a Junior Naval Staff Officer, probably a full Lieutenant, a Duty Commander, three or four Liaison Officers, not present all the time, and a Wren telephonist (there was a small standing switchboard in the room, awkwardly placed in front of the door).

Furniture was very ordinary, workaday type office tables and chairs. Telephone wires trailed everywhere, coming out of the floor. Signals were decyphered or decoded elsewhere, brought in and added to the appropriate clipboard. People looked in constantly and the room got very crowded.

The plots, wall and table, were 'picture' plots as opposed to 'operations plots'. In other words, the plots at Southwick were a record of information obtained elsewhere. This came through by telephone from other operations rooms along the coasts, which in turn had received the radar reports from the chain of radar stations taking readings from their screens. Years of practice had perfected this system. We used chinagraph pencils on perspex. Our telephone technique and speed of marking were impressive. Ordinarily, the plots would be up-dated at regular, precise intervals, perhaps half-hourly, but during an operation or flap this could be increased to every ten minutes.

RECOLLECTIONS OF AN OPS ROOM OFFICER, APRIL–SEPTEMBER 1944

Seventeen years later to the day, General Eisenhower returned to Southwick House on a pilgrimage to Britain and France. He visited the preserved map room on August 7, 1963 where he was interviewed by Walter Cronkite during the filming of a CBS documentary, *D-Day Plus Twenty Years*, which was being made for transmission the following June. To Eisenhower, it was an 'adventure into nostalgia' and at Southwick he said simply: 'I just want to say thanks.'

Today, the map room doubles as a lecture room, the easy chairs being rowed up in a very similar fashion to how those in the mess, where the weather conferences actually took place, were arranged in June 1944. The final series of meetings to confirm or postpone 'Overlord' began with the one at 9.30 p.m. on Saturday, June 3. Present were the following: General Eisenhower, Air Chief Marshal Tedder, Admiral Ramsay, Air Chief Marshal Leigh-Mallory, General Montgomery, General Smith, Air Vice-Marshal James Robb, Major-General Kenneth Strong (Assistant Chief-of-Staff G-2), Major General Harold R. Bull (Assistant Chief-of-Staff G-3), Rear-Admiral Creasy, Air Vice-Marshal Philip Wigglesworth (Senior Air Staff Officer to Air C-in-C), Major-General de Guingand, Lieutenant-General Sir Humfrey Gale (SHAEF Chief Administrative Officer), and Air Marshal Coningham.

Sunday June 4th, 0415 hrs. *(Supreme Commander etc.) No new evidence — the only small change is that the front which was expected to clear the Channel areas of low clouds 'during Wednesday' is now expected in the first part of Wednesday. Winds will be Force 5 in the Channel from Monday morning onwards: cloud 10/10 at 500-1,000 ft from Sunday-Tuesday. Postponement confirmed.*

Sunday June 4th, 1745 hrs. *Bull was advised that 'there had been a substantial change in the situation since the early morning. It is now likely that there will be a fair interval starting about mid-day today and lasting till about dawn on Tuesday. During this fair interval, and particularly from Monday evening to Tuesday morning, cloud amounts will probably be substantially smaller than given in the forecast this morning: winds will also moderate temporarily, particularly on Monday night and at first on Tuesday. A deterioration will probably set in again during Tuesday; weather on subsequent days will continue unsettled and disturbed.'*

Sunday, June 4th, 2100 hrs. *'Since the statement made before the meeting on Saturday evening, there have been some rapid and unexpected developments in the weather situation over the Atlantic. A front from one of the deep depressions in the NW Atlantic has moved much further south than was expected and is now traversing the Channel areas. It is almost over Portsmouth now and will clear the eastern Channel, at least on the English side, overnight. When that front has passed, there will be an interval of fair conditions which, from evidence we now have, should last at least until dawn on Tuesday.*

'Wind speeds by Monday evening should decrease to Force 3-4 on the French coast and cloud will become mainly less than 5/10 with base 2,000-3,000 ft. After that interval, lasting until Tuesday morning, cloud will probably increase to 8/10-10/10 from the West during Tuesday afternoon and will continue so over Tuesday night.

'Wind will be mainly Force 4 on the English Channel coasts and Force 3-4 on French Channel coasts; in sheltered stretches of the French Channel coast, periods of Force 2-3 could be expected. Wind direction throughout will be westerly.'

In reply to Eisenhower, the experts said: 'Considering the time of the year and the evidence we now have, there is reasonable prospect of the weather slowly improving after Friday if the present trend continues.'

In reply to Tedder, the experts explained that 'pressure systems had formed, deepened and crossed the Atlantic at a rate appropriate to mid-winter'.

In reply to Leigh-Mallory, they said that 'good though not uninterrupted conditions for visual bombing by heavy and medium bombers could be expected from Monday evening till early forenoon on Tuesday'.

Provisional instructions given for assault on Tuesday, June 6th.

GROUP CAPTAIN J. M. STAGG
NOTES ON REPORT TO SCAEF, JUNE 22, 1944

Actually, the manoeuvre of the ships in the Irish Sea proved most difficult by reason of the storm. That they succeeded in gaining ports, refuelling, and readying themselves to resume the movement a day later represented the utmost in seamanship and in brilliant command and staff work.

The conference on the evening of June 4 presented little, if any, added brightness to the picture of the morning, and tension mounted even higher because the inescapable consequences of postponement were almost too bitter to contemplate.

Next to the map room (see plan on page 160) lay the saloon of the old house which served the Navy both as a school classroom and mess. Today, this is the ante-room. The conference room used for the weather meetings is through the doorway in what was Colonel Thistlethwayte's library.

'That large, long room remains vivid in my memory', recalled Group Captain Stagg. 'Though it had the appearance of having been the library of Southwick House, it was, I believe, used as the senior mess room of Admiral Ramsay's ANCXF staff. The tables it contained at other times must have been pushed to the far end; I didn't notice them. The walls that were not curtained were lined with empty bookcases. In the half of the room just inside the door which gave entrance from the hall, easy chairs and couches were arranged informally in two or three roughly parallel arcs across the room, facing towards the wall on the left beyond which was the war room where, on vast wall maps, the disposition and current movements of the "Overlord" forces were displayed. Backing on this wall and facing towards the "stalls" were two or three other chairs, that one of which was the nearest to the door was invariably occupied by the Supreme Commander and the others by his Deputy, Air Chief Marshal Tedder, and his Chief-of-Staff, General Bedell Smith. A table, which I assumed had been placed in front of General Eisenhower's chair, had been pushed out of the way into the far left-hand corner. The Commanders-in-Chief and their deputies occupied the couches or chairs in the front ring facing the Supreme Commander, the Chiefs-of-Staff and Chiefs of Operational Divisions and others sat behind them, sometimes on the arms of chairs. The setting and the atmosphere were completely informal and reminded me of nothing so much as an after-lunchtime meeting of the mess committee in a senior officers' mess in the Royal Air Force.'

Today this is the wardroom, its conversion to a bar totally eliminating its decor as in 1944, the only reminder of those momentous days being the plaque on the end wall, also unveiled by Rear-Admiral Creasy in 1946.

Monday, June 5th, 0415 hrs. *No substantial changes in information given at previous evening's meeting.*

'The fair interval had now begun at Portsmouth and will probably last into the forenoon of Tuesday. During this interval, cloud will be mainly less than 5/10 with base 2,500-3,000 ft. Wind on the beaches in the invasion area will not exceed Force 3 in this interval and will be westerly. Visibility will be good.

'During Tuesday, clouds will very probably increase again, from the West, giving a period of overcast sky with cloud base at about 1,000 ft in the assault area later in the day. These cloud conditions will continue overnight Tuesday-Wednesday. Winds will be westerly Force 4 on the English coast and mainly Force 3 on the French coast.

'Conditions will probably continue unsettled after Tuesday and it is difficult to time further changes . . . The situation even after Wednesday must continue to be regarded as disturbed: a quiet settled spell cannot be expected to start immediately after such an intensely disturbed situation. But the time of year suggests that changes after Wednesday may be expected to be in the direction of improvement rather than renewed and further deterioration to the present intensity.'

Following this presentation, the final and irrevocable decision was made to launch the assault on Tuesday, June 6th.

GROUP CAPTAIN J. M. STAGG
NOTES ON REPORT TO SCAEF, JUNE 22, 1944

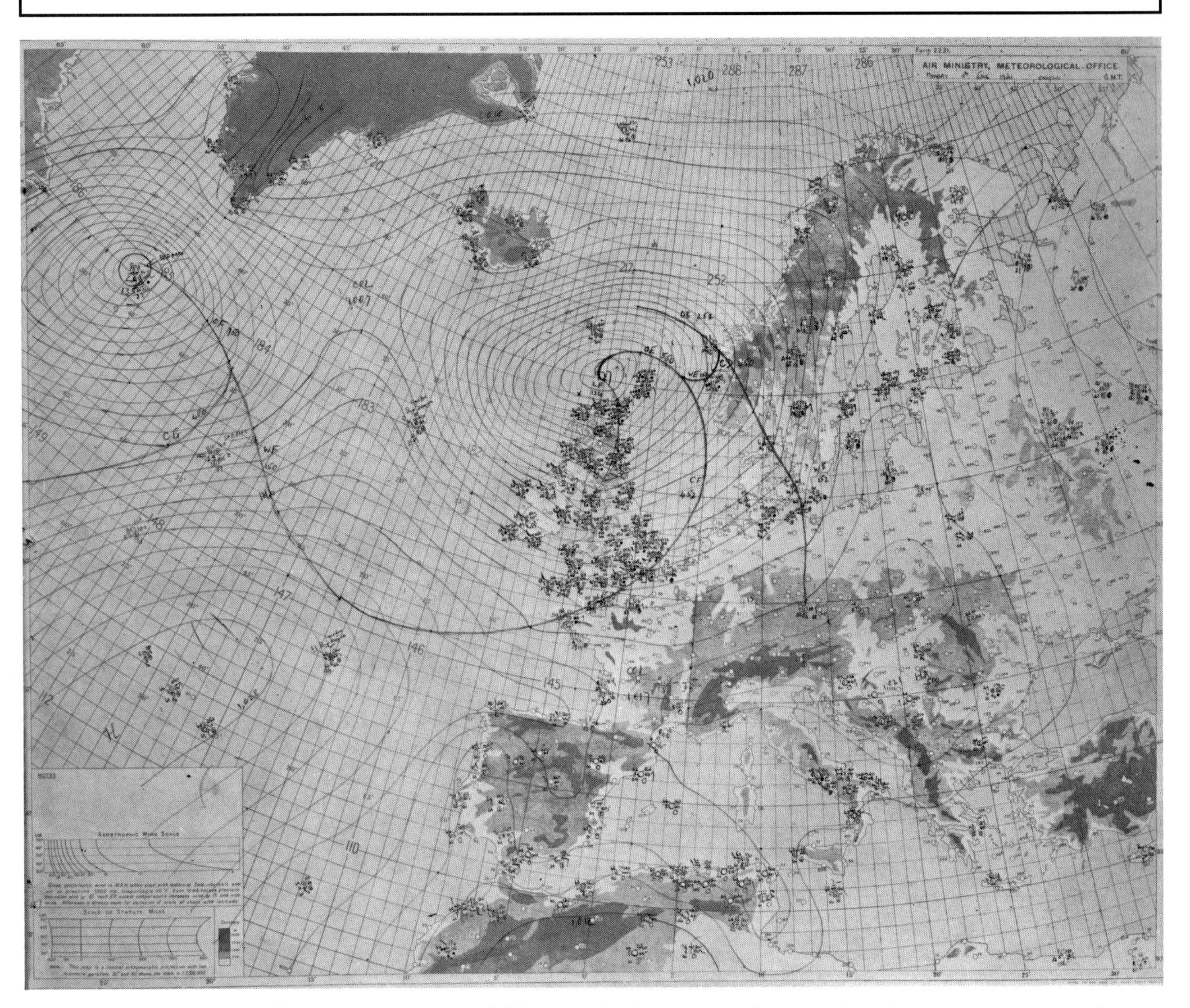

This is the original Air Ministry forecast prepared at 0100 hours on Monday morning. The actual conditions on June 5 were 10/10 cloud with 1,000 ft base over the assault area at 0600 hours and had been so during the night. No airborne operations or medium bomber attacks would have been practicable. Winds on the beaches were Force 4.

At 3.30 a.m. the next morning, our little camp was shaking and shuddering under a wind of almost hurricane proportions and the accompanying rain seemed to be travelling in horizontal streaks. The mile-long trip through muddy roads to the Naval headquarters was anything but a cheerful one, since it seemed impossible that in such conditions there was any reason for even discussing the situation.

When the conference started, the first report given us by Group Captain Stagg and the meteorological staff was that the bad conditions predicted the day before for the coast of France were actually prevailing there and that if we had persisted in the attempt to land on June 5 a major disaster would almost surely have resulted. This they probably told us to inspire more confidence in their next astonishing declaration which was that by the following morning a period of relatively good weather, heretofore completely unexpected, would ensue, lasting probably 36 hours. The long-term prediction was not good but they did give us assurance that this short period of good weather would intervene between the exhaustion of the storm we were then experiencing and the beginning of the next spell of really bad weather.

The prospect was not bright because of the possibility that we might land the first several waves successfully and then find later build-up impracticable, and so have to leave the isolated original attacking forces easy prey to German counter-action. However, the consequences of the delay justified great risk and I quickly announced the decision to

Ramsay *'Admiral Kirk must be told within the next half hour if "Overlord" is to take place on Tuesday. If he is told it is on and his forces sail and are then recalled, they will not be ready again for Wednesday morning; therefore a further postponement would be for 48 hours.'*
Eisenhower *'Conditions are almost ideal up to a point, even if the operations of the heavy air may be held up later. Suppose you (to ANCXF) give orders tonight that Tuesday is on; should we meet again in the morning?'*
Montgomery *'The only decision the weather experts could give at 0400 hours tomorrow would be the position of the next depression.'*
Smith *'Looks to me we've gotten a break we could hardly hope for.'*
Leigh-Mallory *said he thought it would be likely to be only a moderate night and that Bomber Command would have great difficulty in getting their markers down and in doing useful bombing. This brought the response from several members present that 'You are referring to another day, in fact you are a day out.' L-M's statement brought the following response from the Supreme Commander — 'Don't be that pessimistic'.*
Smith *'Our apprehension now concerns spotting for Naval gun-fire and the second mission for the heavies. It's a helluva gamble but this (the decision to go ahead) is the best possible gamble.'*
Tedder *mentioned that it would be a question of making best use of the gaps between the trailing fronts brought along by the series of 'lows'. 'Agree with L-M, the operations of heavies and mediums are going to be chancy.'*
Eisenhower *'We have a great force of fighter-bombers.'* (To Montgomery) *'Do you see any reason for not going on Tuesday?'*
Montgomery *'I would say — Go!'*
Eisenhower *'The alternatives are too chancy. The question, just how long can you hang this operation on the end of a limb and let it hang there. The air will certainly be handicapped.*
Leigh-Mallory *'Hell of a situation if German night bombers can operate and our night fighters cannot get off. At Dieppe . . . '*
Eisenhower *'If you don't give the instructions now, you cannot do it on Tuesday.'*
Tedder (to Leigh-Mallory) *'If the later forecast shows a deterioration earlier (i.e. during Tuesday night), putting on the night bombers at an earlier hour might be considered.'*
Eisenhower *'Well, I'm quite positive we must give the order; the only question is whether we should meet again in the morning.'*
'Well, I don't like it, but there it is.'
'Well boys, there it is, I don't see how we can possibly do anything else.'

SOUTHWICK HOUSE,
2130 HOURS, SUNDAY, JUNE 4, 1944
MEMO BY AIR VICE-MARSHAL JAMES ROBB

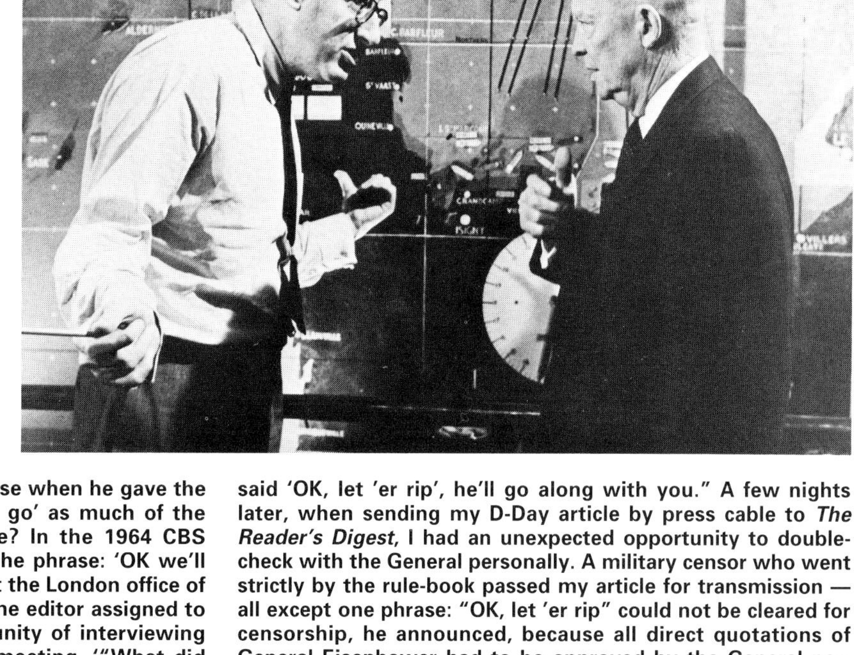

In the text, Eisenhower makes it appear that the 4.15 a.m. conference on Monday morning was the vital one at which the period of 'relatively good weather' was announced, but the records clearly indicate that this news had been given by Stagg the previous evening (see page 164). In fact, the General muddles the two meetings, the decision to launch 'Overlord' having been made by him at 9.45 p.m. on Sunday. Air Vice-Marshal Robb confirms in his signed memo dated June 5 that 'a further meeting was held at 0415 hours, Monday, June 5 but was very brief. The further weather chart was explained and discussed but nothing arose to alter the decision given the previous evening.'

go ahead with the attack on June 6. The time was then 4.15 a.m., June 5. No one present disagreed and there was a definite brightening of faces as, without a further word, each went off to his respective post of duty to flash out to his command the messages that would set the whole host in motion.

So what words did Eisenhower actually use when he gave the final confirmation? Did he say 'OK, let's go' as much of the D-Day literature would have us believe? In the 1964 CBS documentary, Eisenhower said he used the phrase: 'OK we'll go' but it seems he did not. Alan Michie at the London office of *The Reader's Digest* was the only magazine editor assigned to the Advance CP and he had the opportunity of interviewing Admiral Ramsay shortly after the final meeting. '"What did Eisenhower say? What words did he actually use?" I asked him expectantly. "I can't quite remember", admitted the Admiral. "I know it was a short phrase, something typically American." I tried several phrases, "OK, we'll go" among them, but the Admiral rejected them all. "How about 'OK, let 'er rip'?" I queried. Admiral Ramsay smiled. "That sounds like it, but you'll have to get General Eisenhower's agreement." I hurried over to Eisenhower's trailer-tent encampment, placed my problem before Butcher, and appealed to him to ask the General to recall for me his exact words. In a few moments, Butcher came back from the Supreme Commander's "circus wagon". "The General says that if you and Admiral Ramsay agree he said 'OK, let 'er rip', he'll go along with you." A few nights later, when sending my D-Day article by press cable to *The Reader's Digest*, I had an unexpected opportunity to double-check with the General personally. A military censor who went strictly by the rule-book passed my article for transmission — all except one phrase: "OK, let 'er rip" could not be cleared for censorship, he announced, because all direct quotations of General Eisenhower had to be approved by the General personally! In vain I pleaded and argued and stormed that the General *had* approved the quote, and that the entire 6,000-word cabled article hinged on that very phrase. Desperate, I urged him to telephone the General at Telegraph Cottage. It was near midnight, but I hoped that one of his staff might be awake or would not mind too much being waked by the phone. The censor, being a captain, smartly handed the phone to me! To our surprise, General Eisenhower answered the phone himself! After patiently listening to my account of near-frustration, he laughed and assured me that "OK, let 'er rip" was an authorised quote. He also authorised the censor to pass the phrase, and the cable went on its way to New York.'

Operation 'Neptune'

By Admiral Sir Bertram H. Ramsay
ALLIED NAVAL COMMANDER IN CHIEF

From the outset of detailed planning, it was clear that success would be largely dependent upon the ability to exercise close and continuous control of the thousands of ships and craft taking part. This overall control would have to embrace control of loading of all types of shipping and craft, control of convoy sailing, control of tugs, and control of ship repairs. Without it, time would inevitably be lost and the best use could not be made of the great resources given to the operation to establish our forces ashore and then to reinforce them as quickly as possible. As other services and authorities besides the Navy were intimately concerned with many of the problems connected with the rapid reinforcement of the Expeditionary Force, it was found necessary during planning to set up new organisations to control various aspects of the operation during the vital first few weeks in which the tempo of the initial assaults had to be maintained at the highest pitch. TURCO (Turn Round Control Organisation), BUCO (Build-Up Control Organisation), COREP (Control Repair Organisation) and COTUG (Control Tug Organisation) accordingly came into being and were instrumental in the success achieved.

D-Day morning: Eisenhower leaves Admiral Ramsay and enters his Cadillac for the short drive across the park to 'Sharpener'.

More importantly, the sun was shining, as is evident from the strong early morning shadows in these pictures taken on the morning of June 6. Group Captain Stagg had come up to Southwick from 'Sharpener' at 5 a.m. for a shave. There, he bumped into Rear-Admiral Creasy who congratulated him: 'You must feel a tremendous load off your shoulders, Stagg. Anyway, you can feel proud of your forecast.' But, as the extracts reproduced below from his diary show, even after the decision to go had been taken, the next 24 hours had been equally worrying.

Monday, June 5th, 0815: *Up at 7.30 and back to Southwick for breakfast and personal talk with Dunstable before speaking to General Bull. I got Harding just going off duty. He confirmed that no major change in ideas had taken place at Dunstable since 0300 hrs. except that they now thought that Tuesday's warm front may be deferred till Tuesday night.*

0845: *Phoned General Bull and told him we stuck to our story given at 0415: I added that information from France showed that the front which was passing Portsmouth between 2200 and midnight last night was covering the assault area hinterland during most of the night and that 10/10ths low cloud was the accompaniment.*

When we got back to lunch, the sky was 10/10ths, some of it very low, 800-1,000ft it seemed, and wind force up to 5-6. What the mischief was going wrong? I got in touch with Dunstable: Douglas said we must expect 10/10ths late evening and some cloud up to 5/10ths persisting in the target areas. The air unstable with inversion at 7,000ft cumulus spreading out and filling the sky: there would not be much dissipation until dusk but it would break up. I felt slightly assured.

1930 Conference: *Still conflict between Dunstable and 'Widewing'. Krick holds for less than 5/10ths overnight while Pettersen and Douglas hold for continuing cloudiness up to 10/10ths at times interspersed with fair breaks. The SC and Admiral Creasy came into the office before the conference worried about the 10/10ths cloud and high wind (it was still Force 4-5). 'What do you think, Stagg?' said Eisenhower. 'I hold to my forecast, Sir, breaks after dark tonight.' He clapped me on the shoulder and said, 'Good, Stagg, hold to it', and went out smiling.*

2100 Conference: *(It continues 10/10ths with only very slight breaks; the wind has gone down.) A long dreary conference. I was too tired to concentrate: finished at 11 p.m. the upshot was to accept a cloudy picture. But when Yates and I went to see General Bull at the War Room at the Command Post we stuck to our early forecast. Light winds; breaks tonight. We waited in the War Room for news of recce flights. Any reliable reports we got showed the same conditions likely over there. To bed at 1 a.m. still cloudy but calm.*

DIARY OF GROUP CAPTAIN J. M. STAGG
JUNE 1944

Because the assaults were to be carried out on a narrow front, and because British and US forces had to share port facilities in the Isle of Wight area, it was evident that co-ordination of naval plans in some detail would be necessary on my level as the Allied Naval Commander-in-Chief. This was effected smoothly due to the loyal support of both Task Force Commanders, but I am aware that the US naval authorities had to exercise considerable restraint in submitting to a degree of control by superior authority on a level higher than that to which they were accustomed. In their reports, the US naval commanders have commented that in their view my orders extended to too much detail. No argument, however, that has been produced since the operation has led me to change my opinion that full co-ordination in detail was necessary on the highest naval level.

Monty is absent although Major-General G. W. Richards of the Royal Armoured Corps is a good 'double'. (Major-Generals M. E. Dennis, left, and J. D. Inglis.)

BIGOT

TOP SECRET. -5- ONEAST/G.ONE.
20th May, 1944.

FORCE "G" ORDERS FOR OPERATION "NEPTUNE".
(Short Title - ONEAST/G).

NAVAL OBJECT.

24. THE OBJECT OF THE NAVAL FORCE COMMANDER IS THE SAFE AND TIMELY ARRIVAL OF HIS ASSAULT FORCES AT THEIR BEACHES, THE COVER OF THEIR LANDINGS AND SUBSEQUENTLY THE SUPPORT, MAINTENANCE AND RAPID BUILD-UP OF OUR FORCES ASHORE.

METHOD OF EXECUTION.

D-DAY AND H-HOUR.

25. D-day will be the day on which the assault will be carried out. H-hour will be the time at which the first landing craft should hit the beaches. D-day will be communicated by the Allied Naval Commander-in-Chief by signal to those authorities holding his orders (series ON).

TIME OF H-HOUR.

26. H-hour will be related both to morning civil twilight and to the time of local High Water. Thus, if postponement is necessary, H-hour will alter. H-hour on the first suitable day will be about 85 minutes after morning civil twilight and approximately three hours before High Water. This should allow a minimum period of 70 minutes good daylight for observed bombardment before H-hour, and sufficient time for the clearance of beach obstacles before they become submerged.

SIGNALS FOR THE COMMENCEMENT AND POSTPONEMENT OF THE OPERATION.

27. The signal for the commencement of the operation will be made by Naval Commander Force "G" to holders of his orders (ONEAST/G series) in the form:- "Open ONEAST/G. ONEAST/G. ONE paragraph 27, carry out operation NEPTUNE Serial ....".

This serial refers to the number of the serial given in the table below and indicates the date of D-day and the time of H-hour.

Serial.	D Day.	H Hour (Zone-2).
1	June 6	0720
2	" 19	0635
3	" 3	0600
4	" 18	0600
5	" 4	0615
6	" 17	0550

At this point, we must go back for a moment to look at the preparations for Operation 'Neptune'. Earlier, in 1943, the original code-word for the invasion had been 'Torrent', but this was cancelled in an instruction issued by COSSAC HQ on October 13 stating that 'all original "Torrent" documents should be issued under the code-word "Overlord".' The word "Neptune" had been selected by the Prime Minister to denote the 'actual operation within "Overlord"', and a memo stated that 'Neptune' was 'to be used instead of "Overlord" in communications and documents which disclose directly or by inference either of the following: (a) the target area; (b) the precise dates of assault'. As it was considered impractical to scrutinise and mark all earlier 'Overlord' documents with the new code-word 'Neptune', it was instructed that 'all folders and covers which contain such documents should now be stamped on the outside with the word "BIGOT"'. This special security classification had come into being in September 1943 upon the recommendation of the Overlord Security Sub-Committee of the Inter-Services Security Board which had been established by COSSAC the previous month to draft regulations to guard the secrets of the cross-Channel operation. BIGOT documents, like this one which gave the time and place, were limited in circulation and were only seen by specially cleared personnel subject to stringent safeguards.

SECURITY

Complete security was maintained, and it is considered that the very highest satisfaction may be felt that, despite the many hundreds who were for months aware of all the details of the plan, so far as is known there was no leakage. Some anxiety was felt on one or two occasions over individual cases in which orders or maps were distributed or opened contrary to the instructions given, but no harm is believed to have come of these isolated incidents and, when the very large number of documents is considered, it is perhaps remarkable that so few grounds for anxiety existed before full briefing commenced.

One breach of BIGOT security, which resulted in a court-martial, occurred at the US Army Post Office at Sutton Coldfield when 2nd Lieutenant Theodore R. Nuttmann of the US Adjutant General's department disclosed classified information to Lieutenant Robert A. Wahlquist.

3. The competent evidence for the prosecution may be summarized as follows:

Accused, a second lieutenant in the 576th Army Postal Unit, APO 270, on or about 8 May 1944 reported to Captain Pierre B. Aiman, Headquarters XIX Corps, who was custodian of all "bigot" records and files and charged with the dissemination of "bigot" material and the "bigoting" of personnel to be classified "Bigot". Accused had been recommended for "Bigot" classification (R6-7,11). Accused was admitted to the "Bigot" Section and was informed of the required reading material which included certain form letters on "Top-Secret Control Procedure" and "Operation Code Word and Bigot Procedure" (R11). The security regulations, code words, a plan of operations including the landings on hostile shores and the subsequent "follow-up" and "build-up" by the XIX Corps were divulged and explained to him. Locations were pointed out to him on a map in the "bigot" room of the proposed landings, assembly areas, and command posts at such places as Trevieres, Aire and St.Lo in the Cherbourg peninsula in France. Dates of the first landings were given to him. All of this information was "bigot" information and only "bigoted" personnel are entitled to receive it. The need for security was explained to accused. He was then issued a classification and identification card to show his classification as "Bigot-NE" (R7-9,12) (Ex.B).

The date 4 June 1944 was not "bigoted" information nor was the fact that a unit had been notified to be on the alert to move at six hours notice from 4 June 1944 (R8-9).

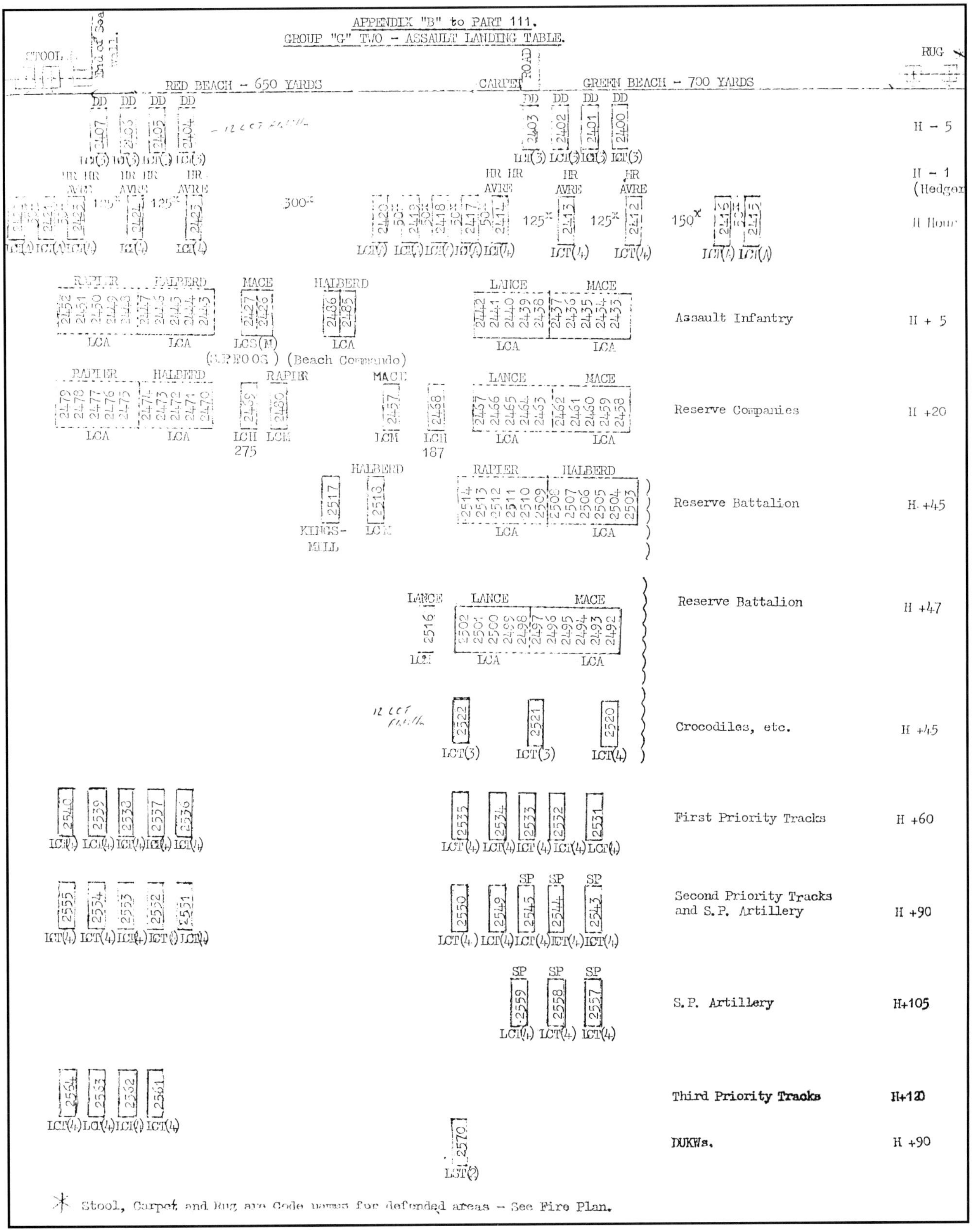

APPENDIX "B" to PART 111.

GROUP "G" TWO – ASSAULT LANDING TABLE.

STOOL* — Edge of Sea Wall — RED BEACH – 650 YARDS — CARPET* — ROAD — GREEN BEACH – 700 YARDS — RUG*

DD DD DD DD — 2407 2406 2405 2404 — LCT(3) LCT(3) LCT(3) LCT(3) — 12 LCT RN/RM — DD DD DD DD — 2403 2402 2401 2400 — LCT(3) LCT(3) LCT(3) LCT(3) — H – 5

HR HR AVRE — HR HR AVRE — HR AVRE — 125ˣ 125ˣ 300ˣ — 2420 2419 2418 2417 2414 — LCT(4) LCT(4) LCT(4) LCT(4) LCT(4) — HR HR AVRE 2413 125ˣ — HR AVRE 2412 125ˣ — HR AVRE 2411 — 150ˣ 2416 2415 — LCT(4) LCT(4) — H – 1 (Hedgerow) — H Hour

RAPIER HALBERD — 2452 2451 2450 2449 2448 2447 2446 2445 2444 2443 — LCA LCA — MACE 2427 2426 LCS(M) — HALBERD 2436 2435 LCA — (SUPF00S) (Beach Commando) — LANCE MACE 2442 2441 2440 2439 2438 2437 2436 2435 2434 2433 — LCA LCA — Assault Infantry — H + 5

RAPIER HALBERD — 2479 2478 2477 2476 2475 2474 2473 2472 2471 2470 — LCA LCA — 2489 LCH 275 — RAPIER 2480 LCM — MACE 2457 LCH — 2458 LCH 187 — LANCE MACE 2467 2466 2465 2464 2463 2462 2461 2460 2459 2458 — LCA LCA — Reserve Companies — H +20

HALBERD — 2517 KINGSMILL — 2518 LCM — RAPIER HALBERD 2514 2513 2512 2511 2510 2509 2508 2507 2506 2505 2504 2503 — LCA LCA — Reserve Battalion — H +45

LANCE 2516 LCM — LANCE MACE 2502 2501 2500 2499 2498 2497 2496 2495 2494 2493 2492 — LCA LCA — Reserve Battalion — H +47

12 LCT RN/RM — 2522 LCT(3) — 2521 LCT(3) — 2520 LCT(4) — Crocodiles, etc. — H +45

2540 2539 2538 2537 2536 — LCT(4) LCT(4) LCT(4) LCT(4) LCT(4) — 2535 2534 2533 2532 2531 — LCT(4) LCT(4) LCT(4) LCT(4) LCT(4) — First Priority Tracks — H +60

2555 2554 2553 2552 2551 — LCT(4) LCT(4) LCT(4) LCT(4) LCT(4) — 2550 2549 SP 2545 SP 2544 SP 2543 — LCT(4) LCT(4) LCT(4) LCT(4) LCT(4) — Second Priority Tracks and S.P. Artillery — H +90

SP 2559 SP 2558 SP 2557 — LCT(4) LCT(4) LCT(4) — S.P. Artillery — H+105

2564 2563 2562 2561 — LCT(4) LCT(4) LCT(4) LCT(4) — Third Priority Tracks — H+120

2570 LST(2) — DUKWs. — H +90

* Stool, Carpet and Rug are Code names for defended areas – See Fire Plan.

The orders directing the movements of the 6,000-odd ships for a complicated operation in confined waters were necessarily very voluminous — some 1,000 pages overall — and Admiral Ramsay was 'gravely concerned at the problems likely to arise in the smaller vessels when, shortly before D-Day, not only his orders but, in addition, the orders of the task force, and lower commanders would be opened'. The contract to produce some 3,000 copies of three sets of orders went to Harrow Printing Press on April 10 and the first copies issued on April 24. As security demanded the latest possible date for opening the sealed orders, 'to avoid consternation and possible outcry from the ships', arrangements were made for the captains of the smaller vessels to receive assistance by briefings after opening the orders. Admiral Ramsay subsequently commented that 'in an operation where a large number of command levels are concerned, it is believed that the orders of the C-in-C should be issued as early as possible, but to do this inevitably means that when issued they are incomplete and incorrect. But it is strongly felt that it is far better to issue orders early and amend them later, rather than to delay until all the details are reasonably firm'. This appendix issued on May 20 from Force 'G' Orders for Operation 'Neptune' (abbreviated title 'ONEAST/G' — 'ON' being the abbreviation for 'Operation Neptune') would also appear to be a typist's nightmare!

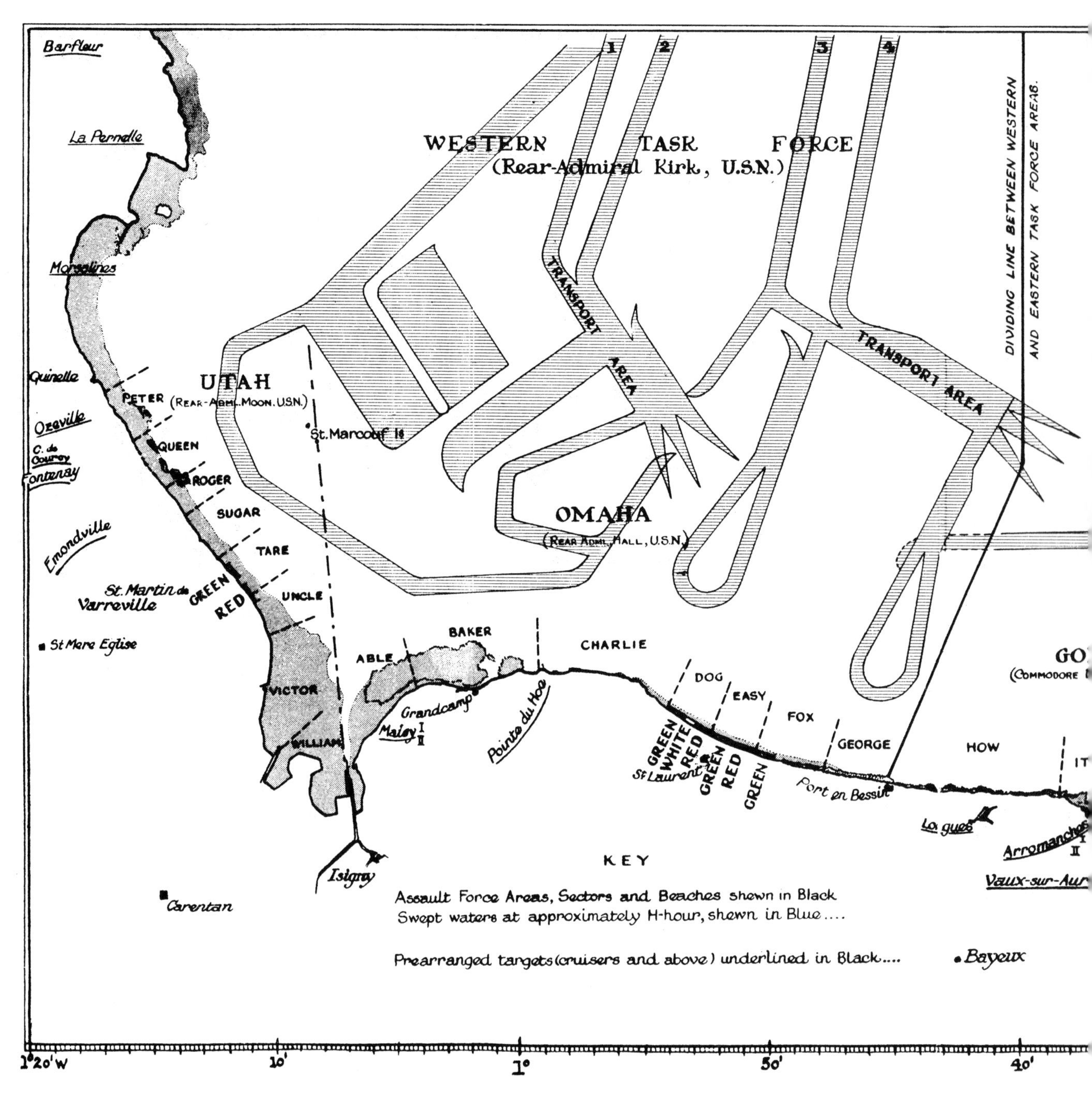

DEVELOPMENT OF THE PLAN

The naval problem that had to be faced can be briefly summarised as, first, the breaking of the strong initial crust of the coast defences by assault together with the landing of the fighting army formations; and, secondly, to commence, and continue without a pause for five or six weeks, their reinforcement at as high a rate as possible. The first required the co-ordination of the movement of thousands of ships and landing craft and aircraft and then of their fire-power, the second, the co-ordination of the activities of hundreds of thousands of men and women of all services, both in the United Kingdom and off the French coast, marshalling, loading, sailing, unloading and returning at least eight ship convoys a day in addition to ten or twelve landing craft groups. Considerations of time and space did not permit the use of any unexpected manoeuvre to confuse the

Monday, February 7, 1944. *It is clear that we must quickly reach finality on the assault phase policy and procedure.*

Thursday, February 10. *Kenneth Edwards, Naval Correspondent of the D.T.* [The Daily Telegraph] *came to see me in regard to my inclusion in his Vol. II of 'Men of Action'* [published in 1945 entitled *Seven Sailors*]. *Found him pleasant and easy to talk to but I doubt if he got much 'copy' out of his visit. After dinner sat with Monty in his room and discussed the technique of the beach assault. He liked my ideas, which differ from the sil*[ent] *assault now in vogue and decided there and then to issue directions to the armies. This is not what I wanted at all as they must be allowed to give their views on what* **they** *want. After task is known we can make a final decision.*

Saturday, February 19. *Heavy air raid during the night. I held a meeting of all US and British Naval Commanders in order to discuss the time of H-Hour. The views expressed were nearly unanimous that it should be as early as possible after dawn allowing sufficient time for effective air and naval bombardment to take place prior to touch-down. Kirk* [Rear Admiral Alan G. Kirk, commander of the Western Task Force] *alone favoured a dark attack but he advanced no convincing reasoning. It was a really useful meeting and achieved a most useful purpose.*

DIARY OF ADMIRAL SIR BERTRAM RAMSAY

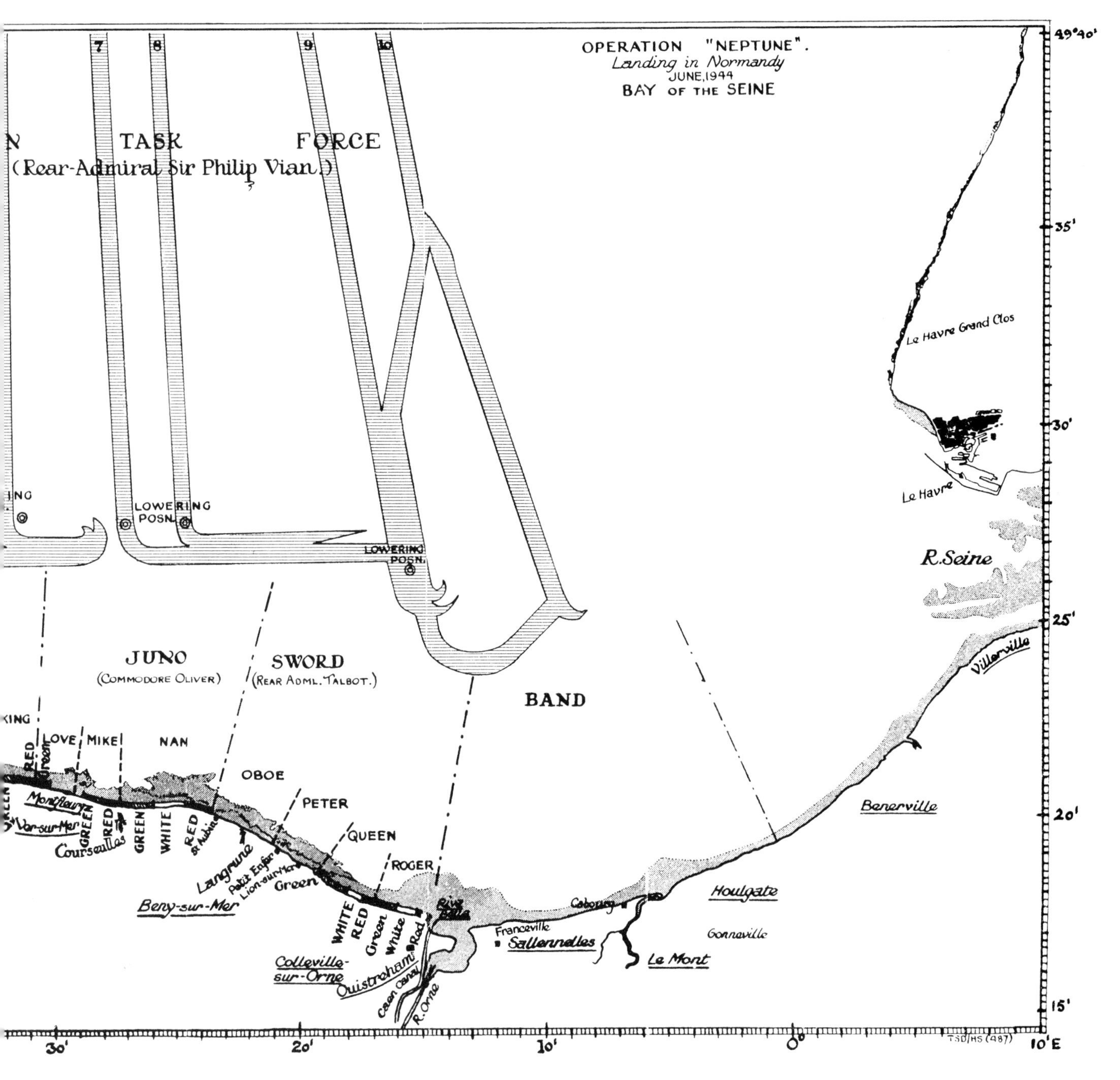

enemy: we had simply to drive ahead in great strength and to ensure that the organisation was as efficient as it could be, as the time factor was all-important.

The one fundamental question on which there had to be early agreement was whether to assault during darkness so as to obtain the greatest measure of surprise on the beaches, or whether to assault after daylight and to rely on the greatly-increased accuracy of air and naval bombardment under these conditions. The decision which was made, to make a daylight landing, was in accord with experience in the Pacific against strong defences, when the assaulting force possessed decisive naval and air superiority, and I am convinced that this is the correct answer under these conditions. When the decision was made, there were no beach obstructions in place on the 'Neptune' beaches. Their later appearance would almost certainly have caused the decision to be revised, had it been originally made in favour of darkness, and it was very fortunate that no change was necessary as all training and, to some extent, development of weapons was affected. It should, however, be noted that there was by no means general agreement as to a daylight attack, and that even after the initial decision had been agreed between the three commanders-in-chief of the Expeditionary Force, at least two vain efforts were made to change it.

The assault area was defined as being bounded on the north by the parallel of Lat. 49°40'N, and on the west, south and east by the shores of the Bay of the Seine. This area was divided into two Task Force areas, the boundary between them running from the root of the Port-en-Bessin western breakwater in an 025° direction to the meridian of Long. 0°40'W and thence along this meridian to Lat. 49°40'N. The Western Task Force area, of which Rear Admiral Alan G. Kirk was the Naval Commander, was divided into two assault force areas: Utah covering the east coast of the Cotentin peninsula to the River Vire, and Omaha from there to the British area. Two Naval assault forces, Force 'U' and Force 'O' respectively, were responsible for all naval operations in these areas. The Eastern Task Force area, commanded by Rear-Admiral Sir Philip Vian, was divided into three: Gold area from Port-en-Bessin to Ver; Juno area from there to a point west of Langrune; and Sword area eastwards to Ouistreham — served by Naval Assault Forces 'G', 'J' and 'S' respectively. (Although Band was designated east of the Orne river, it was not actually used in the assault.) The assault force areas were then sub-divided into lettered sectors according to the phonetic code ('Able', 'Baker', 'Charlie', etc.), the individual beaches in each sector being known as Red, Green, or White Beaches.

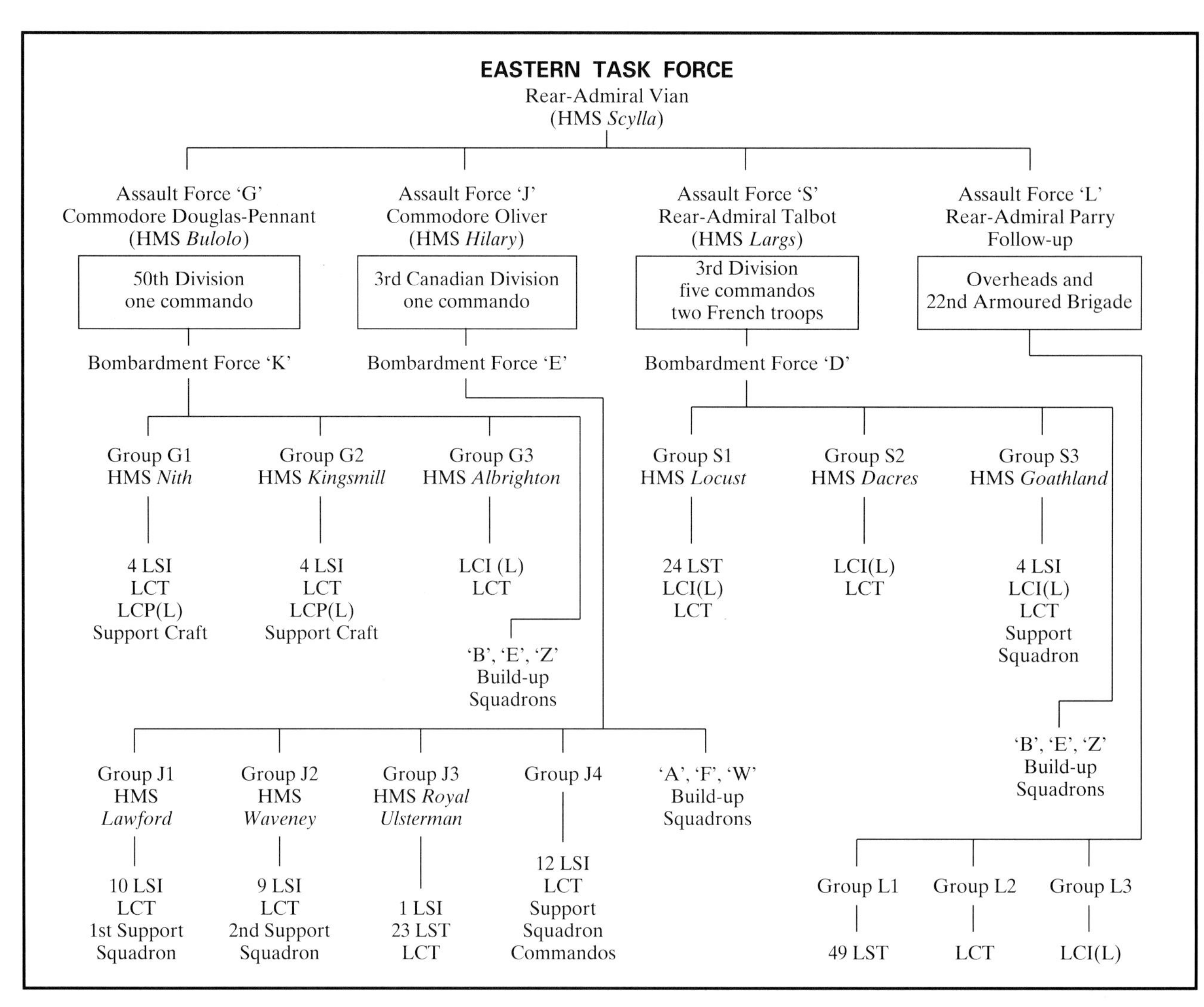

Below left: **Rear-Admiral Sir Philip Vian had served in the First World War and was present at the Battle of Jutland. In February 1940, as captain of the 4th Destroyer Flotilla, he took the *Cossack* into Josing Fjord to rescue 300 British prisoners from the *Altmark*, an exploit from which he became known as 'Vian of the *Cossack*'. He commanded the 15th Cruiser Squadron in the Mediterranean, and in 1943 led one of the three British assault forces landing in Sicily. His assault force was the nucleus of Force 'J' and it returned to Britain to be built up to strength to be able to lift a division. In November 1943, Rear-Admiral Vian was appointed its commander for 'Neptune', Force 'J' being the most experienced of the five assault forces. It was well into its training with the Canadian 3rd Division when, in February 1944, Vian was switched to command the Eastern Task Force.** *Below right:* **HMS *Scylla*, a Dido-class cruiser which had been launched in 1940 and entered service in 1942, served as Admiral Vian's flagship for 'Neptune', and is pictured here in action on June 6. She struck a mine on June 23 while sailing from Juno to Sword, which caused extensive damage although she remained afloat. *Scylla* was towed back to Britain where she was patched up but she was never completely repaired and was scrapped in 1950.**

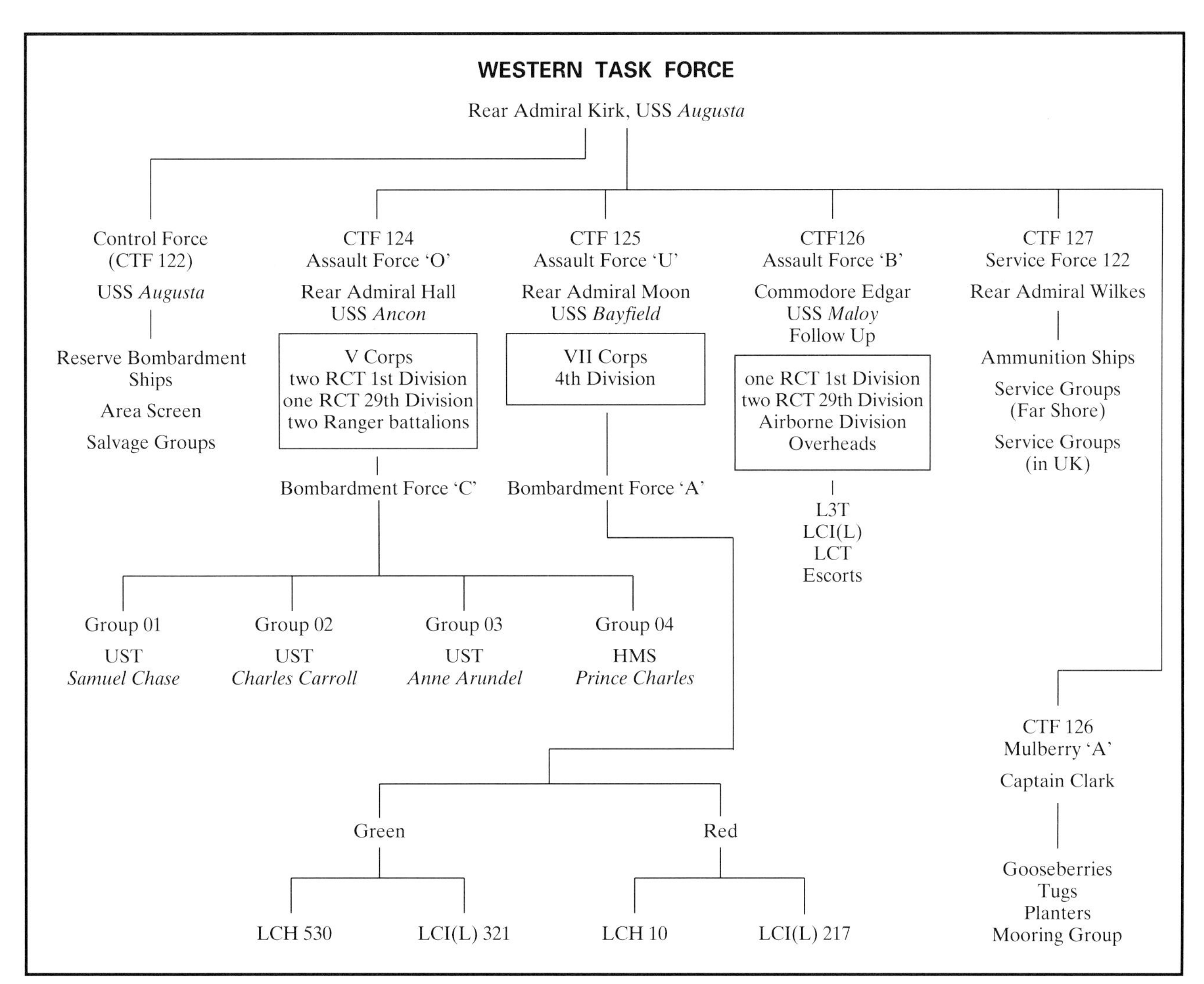

Below left: **Rear Admiral Kirk had been the US naval attaché in London in 1941, and from March to October that year he served in Washington as Chief of Naval Intelligence. This assignment was followed by brief tours on convoy duty in the North Atlantic and in transporting troops to Iceland. In May 1942, he became Chief-of-Staff to Admiral Harold R. Stark, the commander of US Naval Forces in Europe (COMNAVEU), in London. In March 1943, Admiral Kirk was appointed Commander, Amphibious Force, Atlantic Fleet, and helped prepare the forces for the Sicilian operation. He was appointed commander of the Western Task Force for the cross-Channel attack and held operational control of all US naval forces under General Eisenhower except those in the south of France. Later, he became head of the US Naval Mission at SHAEF and was for a short time acting Allied Naval Commander after Admiral Ramsay was killed in January 1945.** *Below right:* **Kirk's flagship was the USS *Augusta*, a Chester-class heavy cruiser launched in 1930 mounting nine 8-inch and twelve 5-inch guns. She had been fitted out with extra accommodation for service as a command ship by extending the forecastle aft to the catapult used for launching the four aircraft carried in the amidships hangars. Kirk is seen here leaving the ship on June 14.**

Initially, 'Overlord' had been conceived with the idea that the Royal Navy would provide all the shipping necessary, save for some landing ships and landing craft which were to come from the US Eighth Fleet in the Mediterranean. In view of the predominance of the British contribution, and also because of a shortage of US naval officers, a fully integrated British/US naval staff was never set up. Consequently, the Royal Navy system of planning, where much control was centralised at the Admiralty, was imposed on the Americans, much to their frustration, and Ramsay and Kirk failed to hit it off. When extra shipping was provided by the US following the addition of the two extra assault areas, Utah and Gold, the Washington Navy Department intimated that they required their own naval representation at SHAEF, regardless of the fact that Admiral Kirk was already responsible for the safe employment of all US ships provided for 'Neptune'. Eisenhower remained loyal to Ramsay, stating that all naval advice must come through him, although he said he would agree to a US officer from Washington being attached to the Allied Naval Command. Ramsay was certain that this arrangement was not what the US naval chiefs had in mind, but by the time Rear Admiral Bernhard Bieri arrived in England (on May 18), it was too late as there was no operational requirement for such an appointment (see page 200) and instead he was attached to the Future Planning Section at SHAEF as a Deputy Chief-of-Staff. The HQ ship for Utah, under Rear Admiral Don P. Moon, was the *Bayfield* *(right)*, an attack transport which could discharge over 1,500 troops via LCVPs, four of which are moored at her stern.

The headquarters ship for Rear Admiral John L. Hall, commanding Force 'O' (Omaha), was the USS *Ancon* which had been built in 1939 specifically to serve as an amphibious force flagship.

Saturday, May 6. *A quiet day on the whole but we are all preoccupied with the H-Hour-cum-obstruction problem and meeting with E.T.F.* [Eastern Task Force] *in forenoon and W.T.F.* [Western Task Force] *in afternoon have been arranged for tomorrow to try and arrive at an agreed naval answer prior to Commanders' meeting on Monday. . . . Received two hysterical letters (official) from Alan Kirk, one on the allocation of salvage craft to W.T.F. and the other on the E-Boat threat to W.T.F. He has quite lost his sense of proportion besides being rather offensively rude. My opinion of him decreases steadily. He is not a big enough man to hold the position he does.*

Sunday, May 7. *A busy day with a meeting . . . at which agreement was readily reached as to the best dates and times for D-Day and H-Hour with regard to latest known conditions. P.M., Kirk, Hall and Moon arrived and we went through the same picture and reached agreement though not before Kirk had behaved with pomp and stupidity and I somewhat lost patience with him. He is forever trying to save face and clear his yard-arm in the event of trouble. A poor fish.*

Monday, May 15. *I spent the day at the big Presentation of Plans at St Paul's. . . . I spoke for thirty minutes and gave the general naval plan, which I think was quite good. . . . Kirk was stupid in his talk with the P.M.* [Prime Minister] *and tried to make out that part of my orders were not clear. He is getting me amazed by his wilful stupidity which, I know, is only face saving.*

DIARY OF ADMIRAL SIR BERTRAM RAMSAY

. . . the British admiral [Ramsay] *had become very testy and very difficult about the American effort.*

My staff and I then ran into a situation that was most difficult. The whole war college system of training for our navy always gave broad directives from the top to the principal commanders, who worked out their plans and submitted them to the topside fellow for approval and then passed it downward. Each fellow then did the details with his staff. Well, the British didn't do that. All the planning was done in Norfolk House by Admiral Ramsay and his staff in the minutest detail. These orders would come to me and would have to be sent down the line. It was really quite a mental adjustment.

My staff officers would from time to time make comments: 'We could do it better this way or that way', and these were never accepted by Admiral Ramsay's staff. In fact, we got some rather tough little comments back, directed at me for allowing these younger officers in their turn to speak out against the voice of the commander-in-chief. It got to be a little touchy, a little bit awkward.

I and my staff found the differences in the British and American approaches to naval command a very complicating feature in dealing with Ramsay and his staff. The Normandy operation, the landing, became in the eyes of the British what they termed a set piece. In other words, no initiative was possible. It was like a fireworks display. You set off a little wick at a certain point and certain things begin to burn, lights go off, and what-not. This was their idea of what this was to be — a somewhat formalised affair.

ADMIRAL ALAN G. KIRK, 1961

Admiral Ramsay devoted part of May 24 and 25 to inspecting the various headquarters ships with HM The King. *Above:* HMS ***Bulolo***, the HQ ship for Force 'G' (Gold) under Commodore Cyril Douglas-Pennant. In February, Ramsay had pressed for her to be brought back from the Mediterranean where she had just been used by the British naval commander at Anzio. (She was an Australian-owned liner built in Glasgow in 1938, converted as an HQ ship for combined operations in 1942.)

Wednesday, May 24. *Spent all morning with The King and his party who came down to inspect the E.T.F. Started at Exbury on Beaulieu river at 0945. Lovely Day. Everything went off very well and H.M. was most friendly and happy. Went on board Bulolo* [headquarters ship for Force 'G'], *Vectis* [stationed at Cowes, headquarters of Force 'J'] *and Largs* [headquarters ship for Force 'S'] *in turn in Solent and Spithead and inspected all the LCAs who passed the HQ ships in excellent formation. Ended up in Scylla for an excellent lunch. Took leave after lunch and went ashore in my new barge. Not a comfortable boat.*

Thursday, May 25. *Left at 0815 for Portland to meet H.M. The King and attend him during his visit to US Force 'U'. Did journey comfortably in 2 hours 20 minutes. H.M. arrived 1040. Kirk, Hall and Wilks* [Rear Admiral John Wilkes, US Flag Officer West] *there to greet him. Visited different types of craft at the hard and then embarked in a PT and did a round of shipping and went on board Ancon. Spent ¾-hour there and then to Augusta to lunch. After lunch H.M. inspected Augusta. All ships very clean and orderly. Left ship at 1445, and Portland at 1510.*

DIARY OF ADMIRAL SIR BERTRAM RAMSAY

Right: HMS ***Largs*** was the former French passenger liner ***Charles Plumier***. She was the flagship of Rear-Admiral Arthur Talbot, commanding Force 'S' (Sword). Another former commercial vessel, ***Hilary***, had been hired from the Booth Steamship Co. in 1940 and was used by Commodore Geoffrey Oliver, commanding Force 'J' (Juno). HMS ***Hilary*** became Rear-Admiral Vian's flagship for the Eastern Task Force on June 24 when ***Scylla*** was put out of action. In official terminology, the vessels were designated Landing Ship Headquarters, the function of the LSHs being to serve as a floating command post. The ships were the nerve centres from which the assault was fought until the military commanders went ashore and operations rooms and communication and radio services were provided, with staff accommodation on the ***Bulolo***, for example, for over 400 personnel of all three services.

The introduction of a Flag Officer (i.e. an officer of admiral rank) as Allied Naval C-in-C to conduct an operation on the scale of 'Neptune' called for careful consideration of the division of responsibilities between him and the respective Commanders-in-Chief of the Nore (Dover area), Plymouth, and Portsmouth Commands within whose stations he was called upon to operate. From the outset, it was Admiral Ramsay's policy to employ existing organisations, where they existed, rather than to institute new ones. Ramsay subsequently remarked that 'some resentment might well have been felt by the Cs-in-C Home Commands, in the Channel, at receiving directions from an authority other than the Admiralty, especially as all three were senior to me. I cannot speak too highly, however, of the unselfish manner in which they accepted the situation'. For Rear Admiral Kirk, the position was even more complicated in that he was responsible to three higher authorities, viz: Admiral Ramsay for planning, training and active operations; for administration and logistics to the commander, US Twelfth Fleet; and for operational matters of interest to the Commander-in-Chief, US Fleet. In addition, when US forces were operating within the limits of a British Home Command, those forces were under the operational control of the C-in-C of that command. Rear Admiral Kirk made 'no comment as to what other organisation might have been possible' but remarked that 'the success of a command based on co-operation does not change the old rule that naval operations are most effective when controlled through a simple and direct chain of command'. As far as 'Neptune' was concerned, the most important of the Home Commands was Portsmouth, under its C-in-C, Admiral Sir Charles Little, who was originally designated as the Allied Naval Commander-in-Chief in May 1943. However, a separate Naval C-in-C was appointed when it was realised that an extra-heavy burden would fall on the Portsmouth Command because of its geographical position. Portsmouth Naval HQ was located at Fort Southwick, built in the 1860s. These pictures were taken when HM The King visited the underground headquarters (UGHQ) excavated 80-100 feet beneath Ports Down.

PRE-D-DAY RECONNAISSANCE

During planning it was necessary to carry out certain reconnaissances in the 'Neptune' area to check the depths of water, both over drying rocks and also in the Mulberry sites, and to examine the nature of the beaches, as geological estimate had reported unfavourably regarding the latter. This reconnaissance was carried out between November 1943 and January 1944, being confined to the dark-moon period in each

Back in January, Admiral Ramsay had paid a visit to Fort Southwick, which also housed Combined Forces Headquarters, to consider using it himself, but he was 'not impressed with the accommodation unless much of that in use by C-in-C Portsmouth could be handed over'. As we have seen, he settled instead on Southwick House, a mile or so to the north, but he still made extensive use of the communications facilities at the UGHQ.

month. Combined Operations Pilotage Parties were employed, using first small personnel landing craft fitted for survey duties (LCP(Sy)), which were towed towards the French coast by MLs (motor launches), and later two-man submarines (X-craft). Their missions were carried out successfully and skilfully, and, so far as is known, only on one occasion was a party sighted by the enemy.

As diversions for these reconnaissances, operations were carried out between the Channel Islands and the Pas-de-Calais (both inclusive). Initially, these operations consisted of small-scale raids, but were later replaced by offshore reconnaissance by LCP (L) — large personnel landing craft — similar to the 'Neptune' reconnaissance. The diversion operations were planned by Combined Operations Headquarters and executed by the appropriate Home Naval Commands.

Three main tunnels running parallel to each other with 12 cross passages provided office space, limited messing facilities and some cabin and dormitory accommodation. In addition, two other tunnels and one cross passage were used as gangways and for emergency off-watch bunk sleeping. There were two main entrances and four emergency exits. Air conditioning was provided through anti-gas filters and the system could, if necessary, be operated as a closed recirculation circuit. Two 2,000-gallon tanks were provided for fresh water, and six weeks supply of victuals was available. At the end of the war, the upper fort was, for a period, used by the RN Signals School, but the UGHQ was sealed off, the intention being that it should remain dormant ready for use in any future emergency. During the 1950s, i.e. between the Korean War (1950-52) and Suez (1956), the Commander-in-Chief Portsmouth, who in February 1952 was appointed to the NATO post of Commander-in-Chief Channel (CINCHAN), decided that to meet his national and NATO responsibilities, he would require a headquarters which could provide better facilities than those available in HM Dockyard at Portsmouth. The choice fell on the UGHQ at Fort Southwick but, in the meantime, it was discovered that the UGHQ had been broken into and considerable damage wrought by local vandals. Repairs took about 12 months. Later, during the Suez crisis, the entire UGHQ was refurbished to an operational state. In 1968-69, after the move of CINCHAN to Northwood, and in the light of the proposed new Naval Home Command Organisation, it became evident that the UGHQ was too big and required extensive modernisation. There was also a problem with water seepage and it would obviously have been extremely imprudent to fit expensive electrical and communications equipment in damp underground tunnels. A further consideration was that the Ministry of Defence fire authorities submitted a report that the UGHQ was a fire hazard. As a result, a new above-ground communications centre was built, and the UGHQ gutted and sealed off in September 1974 ***(above right).***

AVAILABILITY OF LANDING SHIPS AND CRAFT

During planning, there were frequent discussions as to what percentage availability of landing ships and craft should be taken for the operation. The original planning figures of 90 per cent for LST (Landing Ship, Tank) and 85 per cent for LCT (Landing Craft, Tank) and LCI(L) (Landing Craft, Infantry, Large) were challenged by Washington who held that the US Navy could achieve a higher standard of maintenance. British Admiralty opinion, on the other hand, supported these estimates in view of the extremely heavy burden that would be thrown on all the repair facilities on the south coast shortly before the operation.

Experience in the Mediterranean had shown that a greater number of ships and craft always offered for loading for an assault than had been expected, as the incentive of action had a clearly salutary effect on repairs previously deemed essential. While I therefore really expected the planning figures to be exceeded, I was very loath to gamble on this and I only accepted higher figures for US LST of 95 per cent after Rear Admiral Alan G. Kirk (Naval Commander, Western Task Force) had agreed them. In the event, due to the splendid efforts of Rear Admiral John Wilkes, the Commander Landing Craft and Bases, 11th Amphibious Force, and his staff, the record overall figure of 99.3 per cent for all types of US landing ship and landing craft was attained. The similar British figure was 97.6 per cent, and, in my opinion, the very highest credit is due to all concerned in the maintenance and repair organisations of both countries for this achievement, which is the more outstanding when it is remembered that the majority of the assault ships and craft had to be used continuously during months of training before the operation.

Arguably, the most important type of vessel in the 'Neptune' stable was the LST — the tank landing ship — without which the invasion could never have taken place. Indeed, it was the shortage of the Landing Ship, Tank that led to intensive negotiations with Washington in the early weeks of the year. Britain built 45 and Canada 18, but the vast majority came from the United States, and of the 1,500 constructed by the war's end, around 240 were employed in June 1944 to establish a foothold in France. These LSTs were photographed at anchor at Plymouth at the beginning of April. The only number visible is LST 400 which formed part of the Assault Group Red in Force 'U' under its SOAG — the Senior Officer Assault Group — Commander E. W. Wilson.

TRAINING AND REHEARSALS

The training facilities and assault firing areas were originally provided for a three-divisional assault, and the extension of the plan to include five assaulting divisions introduced some difficulties in providing adequate facilities for the two new divisions. But due to the great co-operation shown by all concerned, to the unselfishness of the commanders whose divisions were already nearly trained, and to the initiative and drive of the commanders of the new divisions who had to fit a six months' programme into three, all difficulties were overcome, and on the day the forces for the additional beaches, Gold and Utah, carried out their assaults with the precision of yet another rehearsal.

LSTs could steam at 10 knots loaded with heavy vehicles and their crews to land them without assistance directly onto a beach. Here LST 509, in the foreground, also part of the Red Assault Group, with LST 500 behind (Assault Group Green under its SOAG, Commander A. L. Warburton) and LST 504 in the distance (a Force 'B' follow-up ship), leave Plymouth on April 25 to take part in Exercise 'Tiger', one of several rehearsals held in Britain before the invasion.

With a vast cargo area measuring 288ft x 30ft, LSTs could be described as the world's first mass-produced 'roll-on, roll-off' ferries, the precise load which could be carried — 18 tanks or 30 vehicles or from 500–1,400 tons of stores — depending on the draught acceptable when unloading. Over flat beaches like these in Normandy, an LST could be beached (the bow usually grounded in about 3ft 6in of water) and allowed to dry out to discharge at low water, or she could anchor in deep water and unload into smaller craft under the ramp. *Above left:* To facilitate loading in Britain, over 50 hardened beaches called 'hards' were constructed in south-coast ports to avoid clogging the quays. The concrete 'chocolate-bar' type of segments could only be laid down when the tide was out. This work is being carried out on May 16 on the two-berth Hard G.H. laid down alongside Priory Road at Gosport. *Right:* We were very fortunate to find this picture taken two weeks later showing British 3rd Division vehicles (9th Brigade) being backed aboard LSTs 361 and 324 at the completed hard. Both these vessels sailed with Assault Group S1 (part of Force 'S') with Commander A. B. Alison (the 1st Flotilla commander) and Lieutenant-Commander A. J. Bell, respectively, at the helm. Force 'S', commanded by Rear-Admiral Arthur Talbot, had begun assembling in the Portsmouth area at the beginning of April, having been based in Scotland with headquarters at Inverness since October 1943. Training for the 3rd Division commenced in December, but this was seriously handicapped by the restrictions in its assault training areas; not until the final exercise at the end of March, for example, could close-support fire and the assault be practised at the same beach. Another great difficulty was the stormy winter weather of the Moray Firth, but this Rear-Admiral Talbot subsequently considered 'a blessing in disguise'. Five full-scale exercises were carried out at Burghead which, from a hydrographical point of view, closely resembled that part of Sword which was to be assaulted in Normandy.

The concrete slipway still remains to be seen today opposite Green Lane — in fact it is now a public slipway called 'Hardway'. We have already seen armour en route for this hard on page 129; at the end of our story, we will see it come full circle when this same hard was used to unload the first batch of German prisoners-of-war.

Training facilities had originally been designed and allocated on the basis of the three-divisional assault in the original COSSAC plan. The main exercise area for American troops was at Woolacombe on the north Devon coast where the US assault training area had been established in 1943 close to the Combined Operations Experimental Establishment (COXE) at HMS *Appledore*. This was the motor pool at Woolacombe, pictured from Challscombe Hill above the town.

The sea-front car park now occupies the site where the new mess halls were constructed in October 1943.

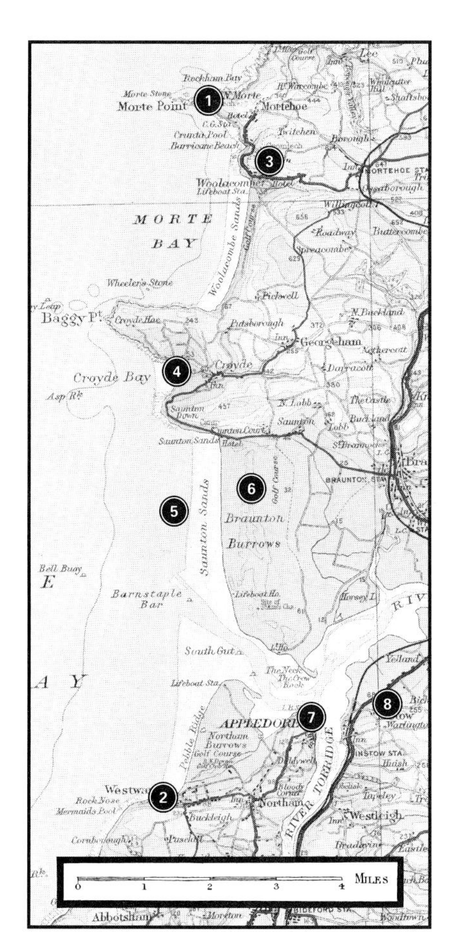

From Morte Point [1] to Westward Ho! [2], a distance of some ten miles, all manner and means of dealing with beach fortifications were tried out and tested on a variety of defences, and the Assault Training Center at Woolacombe can certainly be proud of the part it played as a D-Day proving and training ground. [3] Woolacombe; [4] Croyde Bay; [5] Saunton Sands; [6] Braunton Burrows; [7] Appledore; [8] Instow.

Pillboxes were constructed to simulate those which would be found in Normandy. This could easily be Casemate WN72 on the western shoulder of D-1 exit at the extreme eastern end of Charlie sector on Omaha; in fact, it is Pillbox No. 8 at the southern end of Croyde Bay.

It remains to be seen today almost as if it is still yesterday. Steve Casely had to wait till the tide went out to avoid getting wet feet!

One problem which occupied minds at COXE, which had been established in 1943 to test, develop and evaluate new weapons for 'Overlord', was how to breach the concrete walls which were believed to protect beach exits on the French coast. The 'Great Panjandrum' was the most spectacular project tested on the beach in front of Westward Ho! Having the appearance of a huge cable reel, two ten-foot rocket-powered wheels were joined by a hollow drum containing 4,000lbs of explosive. Like a giant Catherine wheel, the idea was to light the blue touch paper and launch it from the ramp of a landing craft with the rockets powering it up the beach to crash and explode against the wall. However, in spite of numerous tests throughout the autumn and winter of 1943-44, every prototype went awry, usually when a rocket on one side failed, so upsetting the balance. At one of the final tests in January 1944, cameraman Luis Klemantaski caught the action on film as the Great Panjandrum headed straight for him at a speed of over 50 mph, shedding live rockets as it careered up the beach. Understandably, it was one weapon which did not see service on the beaches of Normandy!

A demonstration of more conventional methods of beach obstacle demolition on the range at Braunton Burrows, still an army training area today. *Left:* Steel scaffolding blasted by a Bangalore Torpedo — an explosive pipe inserted beneath an entanglement. Picture taken at Crow Point looking towards Appledore across the estuary of the Torridge/Taw rivers. *Right:* Major Reginald J. B. Page shows the correct way to place a 25lb ammonal charge to destroy a horned scully.

At the same time, HMS *Appledore* was training the men of the Landing Craft Obstacle Clearance Unit (LCOCU) in possibly the most dangerous job of all to be performed on D-Day. Made up of Royal Navy, Royal Marines and Royal Engineers personnel, with nothing more than a frogman's suit for protection, the LCOCU units were to clear the way through the beach obstacles in advance of the assault troops. Armed with parcels of TNT, the men would be the first to land, to be faced with fire from the enemy as well as bombardment from friendly forces. No wonder the men referred to themselves as 'suicide squads'. Rubber dinghies and swimming pool demonstrations belie the task that awaited them in France. 'It was the toughest job we've ever had', said one man later. 'Some of our plans went just as scheduled and others all went screwy. For instance, we were a little late getting in and the water was higher than we expected. We had to work with water up to our necks, sometimes higher. Then there were the snipers. They were nipping us off as I was working with two blokes on a tough bit of element, when suddenly I found myself working alone. My two pals just gurgled and disappeared under water.'

Above: US engineers built several dummy landing craft at Saunton Sands to be used as training simulators. This part of the old Area 2 of the Assault Training Center is now part of the local golf course. *Below left:* Considerable earth moving took place to create the East Green part of the course, the concrete undoubtedly buried beneath this mound. *Below right:* Steve Casely explored the area for us in April 1994 and he found other remains.

The Assault Training Center, commanded by Lieutenant Colonel Paul W. Thompson, began its first training courses in September 1943 and all the regiments of the 4th (Utah) and 29th (Omaha) Divisions underwent some training there, but only the 16th Infantry Regiment out of the 1st Division (also destined for Omaha) as the division had already been battle-tested in North Africa and Sicily. In addition, 2,000 men of the 101st Airborne went through short courses. *Left:* This memorial was presented by Stanley Parkin as a permanent reminder of the vital rôle played by Woolacombe in the invasion. *Right:* Fifty years later, landing craft are still to be seen in the area, usually moored at the army base at Instow.

Small-scale landing exercises were carried out at various beaches, although none of the photographs we acquired gave any indication as to the locations. One nice sequence, which included these two pictures, bore absolutely no clues at all; not even a caption. With hundreds of miles of coastline to search, it was a daunting task, but there is nothing Steve Casely likes more than a challenge, and he agreed to pick up the gauntlet. In spite of the numerous possibilities, within a couple of weeks Steve laconically reported back: 'LCP(R) 599 discharged its GIs onto St Mary's Beach near Brixham with Sharkham Point in the background. British soldiers hold the craft to the beach. LCA 43 follows 599. Both vessels have probably come round Berry Head from Brixham harbour three to four miles away.'

'In this shot, the photographer has scaled the cliff behind the beach (known locally as mudstone) to catch the GIs climbing the steep path carrying a machine gun and mortar. No unit patches or insignia are visible, but possibly these are men from a 1st or 29th Division unit whose task it would be to lead the assault on similar steep cliffs behind Omaha.'

And this was another of Steve's remarkable finds. The original caption to this US Navy picture, recorded as being 'received June 6, 1944', simply stated: 'US Navy Beach Battalion taking part in invasion rehearsal off the coast of England. Charging out of LCVP.' This time, Steve identified the location as East Portlemouth beach with Salcombe in the background, and to prove it he submitted the comparison below. The LCVP (Landing Craft, Vehicle/Personnel, also known as the Higgins Boat, after the New Orleans builder) was the American equivalent of the LCA (Landing Craft, Assault) and could carry a small vehicle in place of an equivalent load of troops. It was similar in appearance to the British LCM (Landing Craft, Mechanised) though shorter. The LCVP could be carried on the deck of a transport or slung from special davits and launched ready loaded. The LCP (Landing Craft, Personnel) seen opposite was the parent of the LCVP. It was designed in the United States, later types (like the one illustrated) having a ramp which technically changed the official nomenclature to LCP(R). However, after 2,600 had been built, it was replaced by the more versatile LCVP with its larger ramp. The LCA, also shown in the picture on the facing page, was the standard assault craft for landing troops. Weighing around ten tons, it was light enough to be slung on the davits of an ordinary passenger ship and could carry 36 men. Driven by twin Ford V8 engines, it had a speed of seven to ten knots. A pair of forward armoured doors led to the ramp which could be lowered on pulleys.

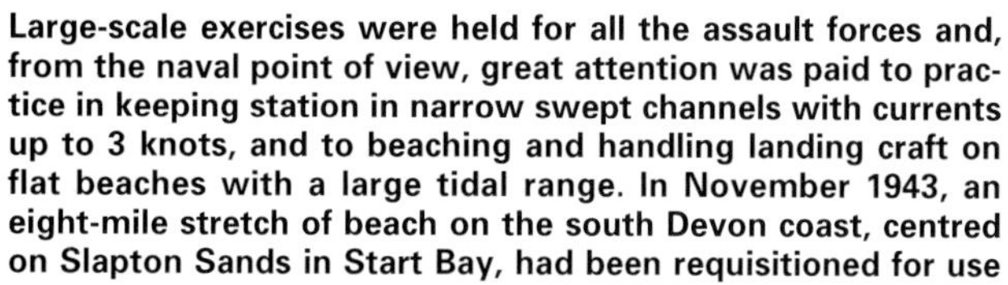

Large-scale exercises were held for all the assault forces and, from the naval point of view, great attention was paid to practice in keeping station in narrow swept channels with currents up to 3 knots, and to beaching and handling landing craft on flat beaches with a large tidal range. In November 1943, an eight-mile stretch of beach on the south Devon coast, centred on Slapton Sands in Start Bay, had been requisitioned for use as an assault landing area for Force 'O'. *Left:* **Here, a variety of assault craft assemble on the River Dart, five miles to the north, for the first exercise, Operation 'Duck', in January 1944. This is Hard P.C.1 which could berth two LSTs. A wooden staging has been built with a gang-plank ramp to assist the boarding of troops.** *Right:* **The Upper or Higher Ferry slipway at Dartmouth still bears traces of the chocolate-box concrete.**

It had always been felt that the enemy might react when large-scale exercises were carried out in the Channel. He did not do so until Exercise 'Tiger', which was the final rehearsal for Force 'U' (Utah), when during the night of April 27/28 three groups of E-Boats penetrated the patrols covering Lyme Bay and delivered a successful attack on the last convoy to sail to the exercise consisting of eight LSTs. Two LSTs were sunk and one was damaged, and there was a regrettably high loss of life. Naval defensive measures on this occasion were undoubtedly on the weak side and this incident underlined the need for every available warship and craft to take part in the opening phases of 'Neptune' when the enemy must be expected to attack our convoys with everything at his disposal.

Operation 'Beaver' followed in March for the more recently-assembled Force 'U', but it turned out such a shambles, with confusion and lack of co-ordination, that a second exercise for the Utah force was set up the following month.

Exercise 'Tiger' was to be a full-scale rehearsal covering assembly, loading, assault and build-up operations. Force 'U' sailed during the night of April 26/27 from Plymouth, Salcombe, Dartmouth, Torquay and Brixham. In order to simulate the long mine-sweeping approach which the force would have to undertake to reach the Bay of the Seine, it followed a circuitous route; first to the northern part of Lyme Bay, then to the southward and finally west to Slapton Sands where, at daybreak on the 27th, the landing was carried out successfully. That evening, the last convoy to simulate the build-up set sail, being due to arrive at Slapton Sands at 7.30 a.m. on the 28th. It consisted of eight LSTs and two pontoons, escorted by the corvette HMS *Azalea*. Unfortunately, the escorting destroyer, HMS *Scimitar*, which had been detailed by Rear Admiral Moon as part of the escort for this convoy, suffered a collision with an LST the night before and failed to sail from Plymouth after her repairs. Shortly after 1 a.m., the convoy was intercepted by S-Boats of the 5. and 9. Schnellboot-Flottille based at Cherbourg and LSTs 507 and 531 were sunk, with LST 289 seriously damaged.

The first round in the invasion of Normandy had been won by the Germans, and Kapitän zur See Rudolf Petersen *(left)*, the Führer der Schnellboote who controlled all such operations in the Channel and North Sea, was rewarded with Oakleaves to his Knight's Cross. It was an amazing victory (fully detailed in *After the Battle* No. 44) and, as LST 289 berthed at Hard P.C.3 *(above)*, Rear Admiral Moon, the Force 'U' commander, was counting the cost: two ships sunk, two ships damaged, with 639 men killed and 89 wounded, of whom two-thirds were army personnel.

Night fell, and our group of three LSTs from Brixham and Torquay joined up with five that had loaded in the port of Plymouth. The convoy proceeded onward, and I turned in early to get some sleep in anticipation of the next morning's practice invasion. I was jarred awake around 1.30 in the morning by the sound of the ship's general alarm.

Upon arriving in the wardroom a few minutes after hearing the general alarm, I heard reports of some shooting outside. I remember talking about the possibility that some gunner on one of the ships in company with LST 507 was shooting at shadows or something equally dubious.

Just after two in the morning, I heard the sound of a tremendous explosion. In quick sequence came the sound of crunching metal, a painful landing on the steel deck with both knees, falling dust and rust.

Later, I learned that a torpedo launched by one of the German E-boats had rammed into the starboard side of the ship, about 30 feet forward of where I was standing, and penetrated into the auxiliary engine room, where it exploded. Since the auxiliary equipment was knocked out, there was no electricity for light, none for water pumps to fight the fires soon raging on board the ship, and none for lowering the landing craft that might provide escape for those of us on board.

As more reports of damage came in, we realized that the center part of LST 507 was an inferno. Consequently, no one could pass from one end of the ship to the other, either topside or below decks.

Since I was stuck at the stern, I decided to search for wounded men and to ensure watertight integrity to whatever degree might be possible. That meant closing all open hatches to prevent water from flooding into dry compartments. I knew that the other officers were busy trying to maneuver the ship, fight fires, and so forth, so I set out to do what I could. The result was one of the most difficult decisions of my life.

As I moved about below decks, I approached a hatch leading into the tank deck, a large open area filled with vehicles and men. As I looked in, I saw only fire — a huge, roaring blast furnace. I tried to enter and to call out to the men inside, but it was futile. Trucks were burning; gasoline was burning; and small arms ammunition was exploding. Worst of all were the agonizing screams for help from the men trapped inside that blazing inferno. But I knew there was no way I — or anyone else — could help them. I knew also that smoke inhalation would soon end their misery, so I closed the hatches into the tank deck and dogged them tightly shut.

LIEUTENANT EUGENE E. ECKSTAM, 1994

The casualty list was three times that which Force 'U' would suffer on Utah on D-Day itself, and Admiral Moon was summoned by Admiral Kirk to appear on his flagship immediately. When Moon arrived on the *Augusta*, he was hauled over the coals by Kirk's Chief-of-Staff, Rear Admiral Arthur Struble. Those that knew Don Moon *(right)* say that he never got over the disaster at Slapton and, three months later, the death toll increased yet further when he shot himself while the *Bayfield* was at Naples, ready for the forthcoming landings in the south of France.

The German victory led to a panic on the Allied side when it was discovered that ten of the officers missing had BIGOT security clearance. Although they would not have known the date of the invasion (even Eisenhower would have got that wrong had he been asked on April 28), the 'Bigots' would have been aware of the location of the landing beaches and would possess much other information of use to the enemy. When it was learned that the German boats had closed the spot where the LSTs had gone down and switched on their searchlights, it followed that they might have taken prisoners (which was, in fact, the case). A vast fishing operation was then set in motion in Lyme Bay to retrieve as many corpses as possible and, although many bodies were never recovered, all ten of the Bigots were found floating in their lifejackets. *Above:* The first casualties from Slapton are buried at Brookwood in Surrey where American forces had established a burial ground alongside their permanent First World War cemetery. The graves were disinterred in 1948 when the remains were either transferred to the permanent cemetery then being laid out at Cambridge, or repatriated to the next of kin in the USA.

RECOMMENDATIONS

(a) Larger escort force, if available.

(b) Insure that vital information on enemy contacts is disseminated quickly.

(c) That a standard procedure and a special circuit be established in each operation for reporting emergencies of a tactical nature; also that collective radio calls be assigned for each group of ships acting as a unit.

(d) All hands should again be cautioned not to look too long at flares or fires, as it cuts down on ability to see objects in the dark.

(e) For short operating periods, carry only sufficient fuel for the operation. This will cut down on burnable material. Unused fuel oil tanks could be filled with water.

(f) Rifles and pistols should be made generally available to fire at E-Boats when they pass close aboard, especially when guns cannot depress sufficiently.

(g) A high-frequency voice circuit used at low power will materially aid operators of isolated units.

(h) Life rafts and lifeboats — where possible they should be made as near ready for lowering as gun-fire requirements and structural limitations permit.

(i) Illumination rockets — a type of rocket suitable for use by slow-moving and large ships like LSTs is recommended for illuminating craft such as E-Boats.

(j) Fire Fighting — that a more adequate means of drawing water to fight fires — and dependent entirely on manual operation — be provided for LSTs and other ships carrying highly inflammable cargo.

(k) Life preservers — from the number of dead bodies observed in the water, it is believed that the kapok jacket is more effective for holding up the head of exhausted swimmers than the CO_2 inflated single belt type.

(l) Heavy shoes — survivors who were questioned stated that heavy shoes were a burden while a man is attempting to remain afloat. It is recommended that where abandoning ship is a possibility personnel wearing heavy shoes be indoctrinated to loosen shoe laces so that shoes may be quickly removed if necessary.

COMMANDER B. J. SKAHILL, USN
LST GROUP 32, FLOTILLA 11, MAY 3, 1944

Although the huge loss of life remained a closely-guarded secret until the war was over, behind the scenes a full investigation was mounted to establish what had gone wrong and who was to blame. A significant factor was the absence of the escorting destroyer and, when Admiral Sir Ralph Leatham, C-in-C Plymouth, extended his profound regrets to Rear Admiral Hall, he admitted that a lack of liaison had delayed detailing a replacement. Admiral Leatham also felt there were strong contributing factors: '(i) the fact that concurrently with the execution of Exercise 'Tiger' many urgent movements, planning and preparations were in progress for Exercise 'Fabius' following closely on its heels. (ii) that a night action with enemy destroyers was fought on 25/26 and plans were being made for another offensive operation on 28th April, thus . . . the capacity of the staff was severely stretched. (iii) the immense recent increase in communications arising largely out of causes (I) and (ii) above, which caused abnormal delays in the distribution of signals. (iv) the late distribution of the exercise orders and incompleteness of some of the sets supplied which gave very little time for their study and digestion by the many officers concerned.' Nevertheless, lessons had been learned and these were soon acted upon.

The final rehearsals for the other four assault forces took place on May 2-6 under the code-name of 'Fabius'. Opportunity was taken to exercise the simultaneous sailing from the Isle of Wight area of the three forces based there and also to try out the arrangements whereby the Allied Naval Commander-in-Chief, Expeditionary Force (ANCXF) would assume control of all operations in the Channel. So far as the naval assault forces were concerned, the exercises were satisfactory, but a freshening south-westerly wind in the afternoon of the first day caused the full programme to be curtailed to avoid damage to landing craft. Enemy reaction to 'Fabius' was negligible, being confined to an aircraft attack on a destroyer in one of the covering forces. That it was not greater, and indeed that our naval preparations proceeded with so little interruption, must be largely attributed to the very high degree of air superiority achieved in the months before D-Day. Enemy air reconnaissance was slight and infrequent.

Exercise 'Fabius' was the final big rehearsal to test all the facets of the invasion plan and it was divided into five separate phases spread over May 2-6. 'Fabius I', held again at Slapton Sands, was for Assault Force 'O'. ***Above:*** **Landing craft circle their mother ship awaiting the signal to come in.** ***Below:*** **An LCT disgorges its complement of headquarters' Jeeps. On the right, vehicles reach the shore via a 'Rhino' ferry, basically a large pontoon propelled by its own separate tug.**

Left: **Troops who will comprise Force 'S', pictured at their camp A6 at Cowplain (in Sub-Area X north of Portsmouth — see map pages 126-127), prepare the inner man before taking part in 'Fabius'.** ***Right:*** **Camp A6 lay down Park Lane in the area now occupied by housing between Cherry Tree and Yew Tree Avenues.**

Above: **The A3 through Cowplain between Traffic Posts 2 and 4 was a designated vehicle park. Here, Bren Gun carriers lie along the eastern side of the road while a Crusader mounting a 40mm Bofors and other vehicles from the 67th Anti-Tank Regiment travel towards Embarkation Area A3.** *Below:* **Troops, unidentified in the original caption, are taken out to their LSI (Landing Ship, Infantry). LSIs were a mixture of vessels ranging from converted passenger liners and cargo vessels to pre-war cross-Channel steamers. Most could carry landing craft on deck or in davits. The start of 'Fabius' was delayed for 24 hours — just like the real landings — because of unfavourable weather conditions, and it finally began at 8 a.m. on May 3. Admiral Ramsay watched the departure of Force 'S' ('Fabius IV') from the *Scylla* at Spithead, en route for their simulated assault against the beach west of Littlehampton.**

Today, the A3 trunk road at this point has been superseded by a motorway bypass, the A3(M), leaving the old road largely for use by local traffic.

Assault Force 'G' ('Fabius II'), comprising troops from the 50th Northumbrian Division, had their 'Gold' beach on Hayling Island (just south of Havant, while 'Juno' beach for Assault Force 'J' ('Fabius III') brought the Canadian 3rd Division ashore just to the east of Bracklesham Bay. *Above:* These vessels are LCIs (Landing Craft, Infantry). Driven by a series of eight diesel engines, the ship-type bows helped give the LCI a reasonable speed of 14 knots. It could carry 200 men and its draught enabled it to beach in water shallow enough for the troops to wade ashore. *Left:* Lieutenant-General Dempsey, left, was on the beach to see how his forces performed, a particular point of interest being the use of the specialised machines in the armoury of the 79th Armoured Division, commanded by Major-General Sir Percy Hobart, right. Hobart had originally served as a Royal Engineer, but transferred to the Tank Corps in 1923 — the year it was granted its Royal 'warrant'. In 1942, he was charged with building up the new 79th Armoured Division (its nucleus being the 27th Armoured Brigade then comprising the 4th/7th Dragoon Guards, 13th/18th Hussars and the 1st East Riding Yeomanry) which, in March 1943, was given the rôle of developing special equipment so that its armour could help overcome the problems of landing on heavily-defended beaches. Two examples are illustrated *below*: an SBG (Small Box Girder) bridge attached to the front of a Churchill for spanning an anti-tank ditch, and matting to provide a reasonably stable surface across the beach. This could be laid either by a Roly Poly AVRE or from a large reel or 'Bobbin' attachment on the front of an AVRE, and was unrolled and pressed down as it drove over it.

ENEMY MISCALCULATIONS

Because the power of manoeuvre at sea was so limited, the need for keeping the enemy uncertain as to our precise objectives was paramount. Characteristic wireless traffic accompanying training and movements of assault forces had to be controlled. Other measures included the berthing of dummy landing craft in Dover and Nore Commands before D-Day and the parking of Phoenix and Whale units (components of the artificial Mulberry harbours) at Selsey and Dungeness. Arrangements were also made with the Admiralty for the large number of commercial ships that were destined for the Thames and ships for loading to sail in later 'Neptune' convoys to wait in Scottish ports until the operation began. Thus the concentration of shipping automatically spread itself throughout the ports of the United Kingdom and, although most congested on the South Coast, it was not confined to that area.

Tactically, a naval diversion employing light craft was carried out in the Straits of Dover to support the air bombardment in this area simultaneously with the main assaults, whilst a similar diversion was made in the neighbourhood of Cap d'Antifer. In both of these, and also off Cape Barfleur, radio counter-measures were employed by aircraft and by the surface craft taking part to give an appearance to enemy radar similar to that presented by the real forces. We now know that these were very successful and were an instrumental factor in enabling our forces to continue for so long towards the enemy coast before their composition could be determined.

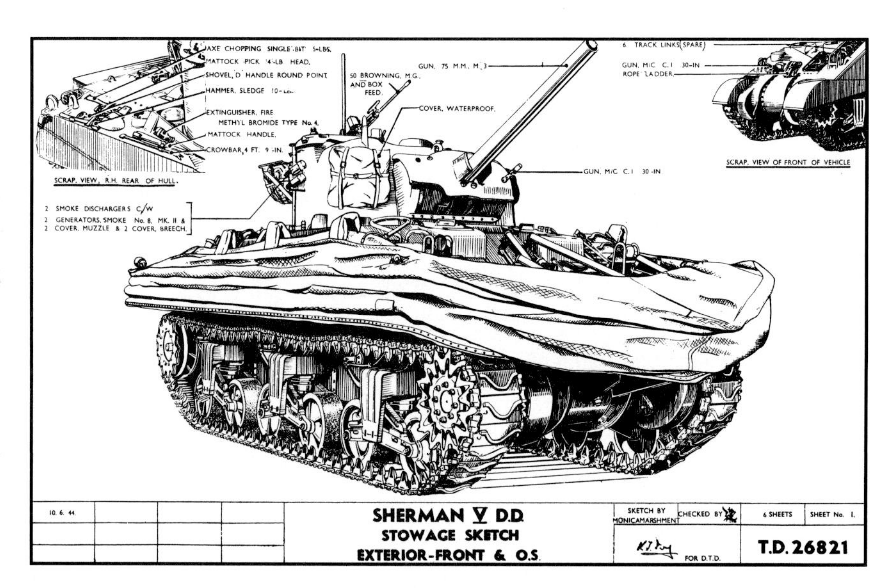

The most famous of all Hobart's 'Funnies' was undoubtedly the Duplex-Drive (DD) swimming tank invented by a brilliant Hungarian engineer, Nicholas Straussler. With adequate displacement, anything can be made to float, even a 30-ton tank, and he proved that the addition of an inflatable canvas skirt could enable a tank to 'swim' ashore, its own power being transmitted to underwater propellers.

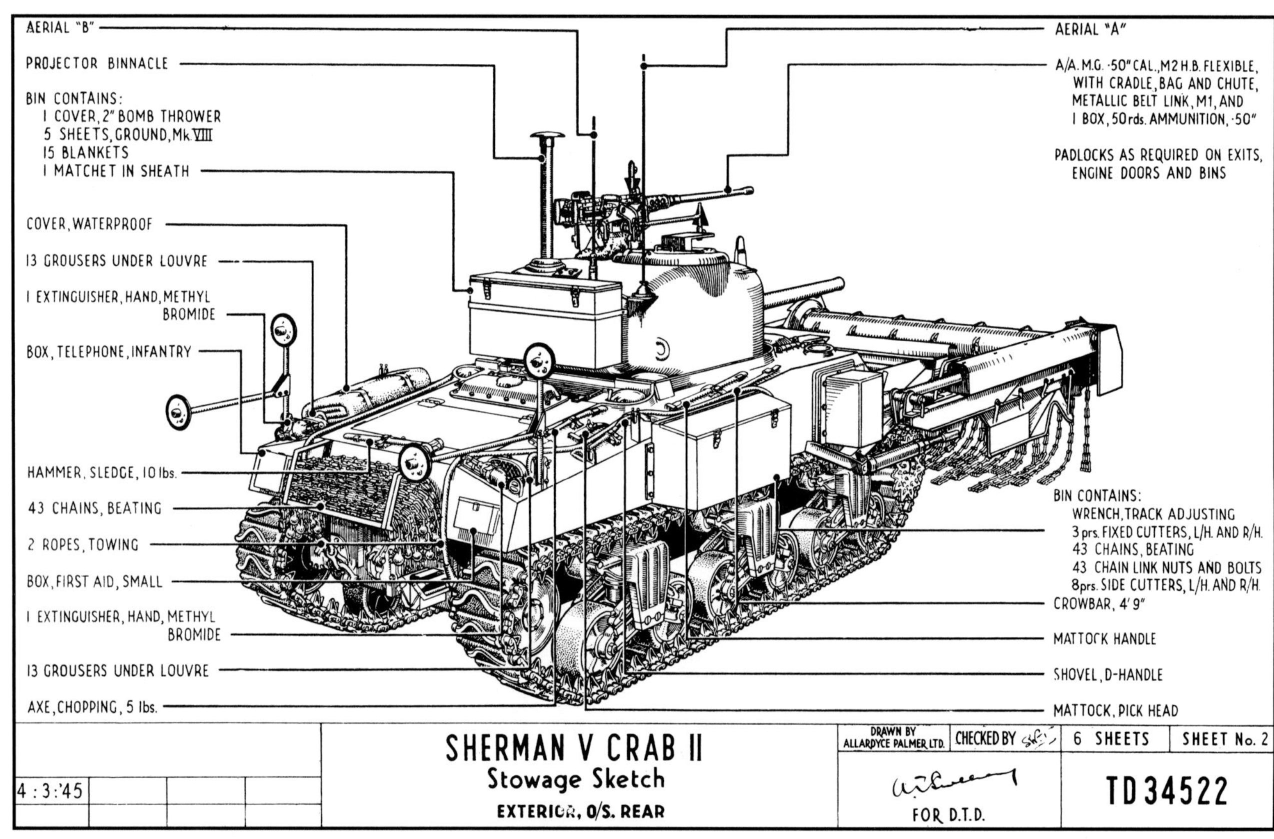

The mine-clearing Flail beat the ground ahead of it with heavy chains to explode mines. The chain was easily replaced.

A series of conversions to the Churchill transformed it into what was called the AVRE — the Armoured Vehicle Royal Engineers. Each tank was provided with attachments to enable special equipment to be added on in a variety of ways like the SBG and the Bobbin. The 'Petard' was the primary weapon on all AVREs, and was used to deal with pillboxes and enemy strong points. It had the ability to lob a 26lb explosive charge over 200 yards from its stubby 12-inch diameter barrel, the only drawback being that it had to be reloaded from outside the turret by 'breaking' the barrel like an air rifle.

A Fascine AVRE had a huge bundle of chestnut paling which could be dropped into an anti-tank ditch. However, this conversion was at the expense of losing all forward vision, the commander having to expose himself on top of the bundle to direct the driver. Carrying the palings on the rear was not advisable as it rested on the exhaust and could catch fire!

Armoured bulldozers, 'Snake' mine-clearers, 'Ark' climbing ramps and 'Crocodile' flame-throwers. Hobart's inventory was extensive and some devices worked better than others. The ingenuity of the British in developing and using such equipment was not matched in this instance by the Americans. Normally noted for their enthusiasm for mechanisation, the United States Army chose not to rely on specialised armour on D-Day, save for the employment of some DD Shermans.

MULBERRY PROJECT

The suggestion that artificial harbours should be constructed in the assault area was, it is believed, first made by Commodore J. Hughes-Hallett, when serving as Chief-of-Staff (X) to Commander-in-Chief, Portsmouth, who suggested the use of sunken ships for this purpose. The original designs for such harbours, which were, however, to be constructed of sunken concrete caissons, were prepared by the War Office. It was apparent soon after

Intelligence on the enemy-held coastline was required for a variety of purposes, not least for the detailed planning for the positioning of the two prefabricated harbours, Mulberry 'A' at Vierville-sur-Mer and Mulberry 'B' at Arromanches-les-Bains. In May and June 1942, listeners to the BBC Home Service heard an appeal for anyone who had photographs, postcards and the like, taken anywhere in Europe or the Far East, to send them to the Admiralty where they would be copied and returned. The scope was deliberately left as wide as possible so as to give no clues to the Germans as to which areas were of particular interest. By 1944, seven million pictures had been received, of which at least 150,000 formed the basis of the Naval Intelligence Division's ground photo library. Many of the pictures were used to illustrate the division's series of geographical handbooks, and publications produced by the Inter-Services Topographic Department. *Above:* This picture sent in shows the sea wall at Arromanches which would have to be breached for access to the harbour.

Piers for Use on Beaches

SECRET

CONDITIONS OF BEACH

Average gradient is 1 in 200 and beaches are open to the south west.

CONDITIONS OF TIDE

2. Range of spring tides is 30 feet and the strength of the tide parallel to the beach is 4 knots at springs.

SCAFFOLDING PIERS

3. A pier to be of use for unloading ships of 20 foot draught would have to be 1 mile in length and 40 foot in height at the seaward end. The present type of scaffolding pier does not exceed 20 foot in height. It is doubtful whether a pier of these large dimensions could be made with scaffolding, but in any case the amount of material required would be prohibitive.

PONTOON PIERS

4. A pontoon pier would have to be similar in length. All floating piers suffer from the disadvantage of having to be securely moored with heavy anchors. Even then they are most vulnerable and will not stand up to a gale of wind. The strength of the tide is so great that the moorings will have to be very large. If large pontoons were moored, 20 yards apart, at least 200 anchors would be required. The sea-ward end of a floating pier must be particularly well moored and the mooring chains form an obstacle to ships coming alongside. Owing to the poor ratio between the weight of a floating pontoons and the weight they can carry, and to their vulnerability to sea wind and tide, they are not favoured in comparison with scaffolding piers on open beaches.

CCO
or Deputy

They must float up & down w the tide. The anchor problem must be mastered. The ships must have a side-flap cut in them and a drawbridge long enough to overreach the moorings of the piers. Don't argue the matter. Let me have the best solution worked out. The difficulties will argue for themselves.

WSC 30.5.42

It was also in May 1942 that consideration was being given by Churchill to a memorandum prepared by Combined Operations on the possible designs for piers to be used for unloading to speed the build-up after an invasion of northern France. Although it was early days — the idea that a sheltered harbour should be created by an artificial breakwater was not proposed until June 1943 — Churchill's notation is now part of the folklore of D-Day: 'Prime Minister to Chief of Combined Operations. "They *must* float up and down with the tide. The anchor problem must be mastered. The ships must have a side-flap cut in them, and a drawbridge long enough to overreach the moorings of the piers. Let me have the best solution worked out. Don't argue the matter. The difficulties will argue for themselves. May 30, 1942."'

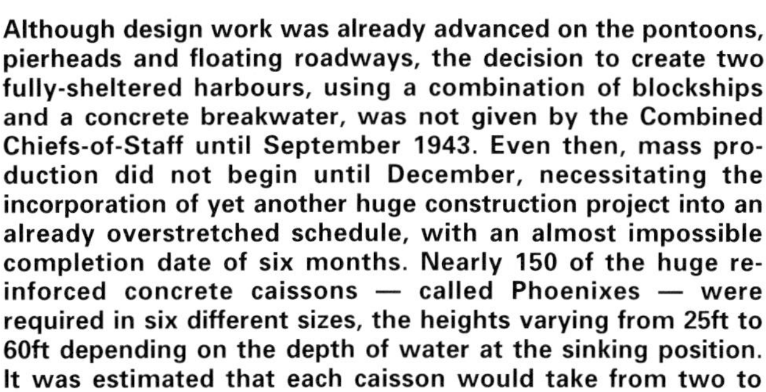

Although design work was already advanced on the pontoons, pierheads and floating roadways, the decision to create two fully-sheltered harbours, using a combination of blockships and a concrete breakwater, was not given by the Combined Chiefs-of-Staff until September 1943. Even then, mass production did not begin until December, necessitating the incorporation of yet another huge construction project into an already overstretched schedule, with an almost impossible completion date of six months. Nearly 150 of the huge reinforced concrete caissons — called Phoenixes — were required in six different sizes, the heights varying from 25ft to 60ft depending on the depth of water at the sinking position. It was estimated that each caisson would take from two to seven months to construct and they would require a total of over 500,000 cubic yards of concrete, 30,000 tons of reinforcing steel and 20,000 tons of timber for the shuttering. Phoenix construction was allocated to six firms or consortiums of consulting engineers: Oscar Faber, Sir Alexander Gibb & Partners, W. T. Halcrow & Partners, Sir Cyril Kirkpatrick, Rendell, Palmer & Tritton, and Robert White & Partners, with a labour force required of nearly 25,000. Two-thirds of the caissons were built on the Thames, the ideal location being dry docks, although these could only accommodate a fraction of the total requirements. ***Left:*** **This is the dry dock at Tilbury.** ***Right:*** **In 1990, it was permanently flooded while the old lock entrance behind is now used as a branch dock.**

taking up my appointment that much greater naval supervision of the preparations and an experienced naval staff to conduct the operation were necessary and I asked the Admiralty to appoint Rear-Admiral W. G. Tennant, to take charge of this matter. From the outset, Admiral Tennant was uncertain of the ability of the concrete Phoenix units to withstand even a moderate gale; and their placing had been estimated under the most favourable conditions to take at least 14 days. It was on his suggestion that 70 obsolete ships were prepared as block ships, which could be placed in two or three days and thereby speedily provide some shelter over the 40 miles of beaches before the Phoenix breakwaters could be built. His foresight was proved in the gale that blew from June 19 to 22, as these blockships alone gave some shelter to the hundreds of landing craft and barges on a lee shore and greatly reduced the number that was damaged, as well as making it possible to continue unloading on a small scale.

The construction of the units for the Mulberries was an undertaking of considerable magnitude and, coming at a time when all efforts were already centred on the preparations for 'Neptune', proved difficult to complete to schedule. As the completion fell behind, the difficulties were accentuated by the shortage of tugs, as a regular phased programme was essential if all units

Two of London's 'wet' docks, the East India north of the river and the South Dock ***(left)*** **in the Surrey Commercial Docks, were dammed and then pumped out. Rubble was then dumped on the bottom around the edges to create a base on which the concrete could be poured. However, because these docks had always held water, two of the walls subsequently collapsed. These B1 type caissons are four of the eight built there by Mowlems under Sir Cyril Kirkpatrick's supervision.** ***Right:*** **The whole area of the Surrey Docks has seen dramatic change in recent years, but the 'cut' through which the caissons were taken to the Greenland Dock on the right can still be identified.**

were to be moved into their assembly positions before D-Day. Vigorous and continued representations for more and more tugs for 'Neptune' were made, both in the United Kingdom and to the USA and, although there was still not a sufficiency to meet the full towing programme by D-Day, the Mulberry units were in the main ready and in their assembly areas, thanks to the initiative and resource displayed by Admiral Tennant and his staff.

In conception and execution these harbour shelters were unique. The damage wrought by the June gale to Mulberry A, which necessitated the abandonment of the completion of this harbour, does not detract in any way from the value of the idea, for, had it been constructed similarly to Mulberry B, there is reason to suppose that it might have survived to the same extent.

Additional construction sites were found by the novel idea of digging a pit on open land beside the river in which caissons could be built. The river bank was then cut away to allow water to flood the excavation so that the partially-completed caisson could be floated out at high tide. Eight sites were chosen along the Thames at Barking, Erith and Grays. The basins were used several times by sealing the entrances with steel piling. This A1-type — the largest — has just emerged from Erith Basin where Nutalls and Costains built eight caissons under Oscar Faber.

TYPES OF CAISSON

Type	*No. reqd*	*Height*	*Length*		*Breadth at w/l*		*Displacement*	*Draught*	
		ft	*ft*	*in.*	*ft*	*in.*	*tons*	*ft*	*in.*
A1	60	60	204	–	56	3	6,044	20	3
A2	11	50	204	–	56	3	4,773	16	4
B1	25	40	203	6	44	–	3,275	14	0
B2	24	35	203	6	44	–	2,861	12	5
C1	17	30	203	6	32	–	2,420	14	3
D1	10	25	174	3	27	9	1,672	13	0

The Phoenix basin still remains at the edge of Erith Marshes. In the background, the Ford Motor Company works at Dagenham.

The fourth method of building the caissons — used for all the B2 types — was to lay them down on the sea-shore and then launch them like a ship down a slipway. Three sites were selected near Southampton at Stokes Bay and Stone Point on the Solent, and Langstone near Portsmouth. ***Above left:*** **Preparing the ground at Stokes Bay in the autumn of 1943.** ***Above right:*** **Now the location of the Stokes Bay Sailing Club, until recently the concrete foundations could still be seen on the foreshore.**

Above: **The last of the Phoenix units to leave London passes through the King George V Dock entrance lock. It had been intended to tow the caissons to suitable parking areas along the south coast, but this idea had to be abandoned for lack of moorings. Instead, the caissons had to be sunk off the coast near Dungeness and Selsey Bill with the idea of refloating them just before D-Day.** *Below:* **A new bridge and the London City Airport transform the view 50 years on.**

ADMINISTRATION OF FERRY CRAFT

Previous operations had shown the great difficulties in administering the craft of the ferry service during the first few weeks before naval shore facilities had been properly established. The problem in 'Neptune' was greater than ever before, 1,500 craft and barges and 15,000 personnel having to be provided for, but, although there were individual failures and resulting hardship, reports show that in general the measures taken proved successful in maintaining the morale and efficiency of officers and men who perforce had to work long hours for days on end.

SALVAGE, REPAIR AND FUELLING ORGANISATIONS OFF BEACHES

As the plan envisaged the use of the beaches for a period of three months, it was evident that provision would have to be made on a scale hitherto unknown for the salvage, repair, fuelling and watering of the great number of ships and craft that would be damaged or that would require fuel or water off the enemy coast. A considerable salvage fleet had to be assembled and special ships and landing barges were fitted for repair work and others to carry fuel and water. Naval parties were trained to assist in craft repairs ashore and were attached to the assault forces. Owing to the widespread damage caused by the four days' gale, the salvage repair organisation was tested far beyond anything contemplated and, although it seemed at one time that it would be unable to compete, yet in the end it may be said to have triumphed, assisted as it had to be by additional resources from the United Kingdom.

Refloating the caissons turned out to be easier said than done. It developed into a major problem with inadequate arrangements having been made for pumping them out, and some caissons becoming 'glued' to the sea bottom by suction. Even worse, was the shortage of tugs, at least 130 being required to tow all the various parts of the Mulberries to France. In the end, extra vessels were provided from the United States, and the North Atlantic was robbed of its rescue vessels. Even so, the target date of D+14 for full operation of the prefabricated ports had to be put back by seven days. (We will return to the Mulberry story in a later chapter.)

To try to solve Admiral Ramsay's worry over the possible reaction from ship's captains when they saw the bulk of the operational orders, on Wednesday, May 24, a message was sent by the Admiralty to reassure them that, although they would find the orders very voluminous, only a small part would directly concern their vessel, and any queries would be cleared up during briefing. All holders were then directed to open their sealed orders at precisely 2330 hours the following day. Three days later, a further signal was sent out naming June 5 as D-Day and specifying the five different H-Hours for the respective assault forces. As of that Sunday (May 28), all personnel were sealed in their ships with all outside contact forbidden. *Above:* GIs of the 4th Division march through Torquay on June 3. They are most probably part of the first Regimental Combat Team (RCT, the US equivalent of a brigade group) destined to lead the assault on Utah. Their route appears to be lined by military police, no doubt enforcing the stringent security measures to avoid any contact between troops and civilians.

Steve Casely, a stickler for accuracy, arranged to take the comparison from the balcony of Room 104 of the Queen's Hotel on Victoria Parade.

METEOROLOGICAL

Early in planning, it was appreciated that the decision which the Supreme Commander would have to make to launch the operation would be one of the most difficult and far-reaching of the whole war. Not only was good weather necessary for the assaults, but also for the period immediately following them, to ensure a good start for the build-up. The meteorologists were doubtful of their ability to forecast the weather more than 48 hours ahead for certain, which was barely sufficient to cover the hour of the assaults, as Force 'U' from Devonshire had to sail 36 hours before H-Hour. To assist the forecasts, two additional US and two British warships were stationed in the Atlantic to transmit weather reports for some days before D-Day. For security, this procedure was also adopted before exercise 'Fabius' and this, in addition, served to practise the meteorological team concerned in making their deductions.

Monday, May 22. *Attended Commanders' meeting at Widewings. Discussed arrangements for meeting to decide issue of instructions for D-Day and that next Monday's meeting would be* [at Southwick House] *at 1000. Further meetings at the same place but earlier on 1st June et seq. Lunched there with Bieri* [Rear-Admiral Bernhard Bieri, Deputy Chief-of-Staff (US) — see page 176] *and discussed his work but with no very clear conception of it. Time alone will show how he can best employ himself.*

Went to London to Club and to shop, leaving at 1500 and arriving [at Southwick House] *1700. Very busy evening with too numerous papers up to 2330. Stark getting very busy now getting ships to escort US forces. Whereas formerly Washington would give me nothing, now they are nervous and are giving ships with both hands.*

Tuesday, May 23. *A long and arduous day. Spent nearly all morning in conference with Vian, Oliver and Creasy with experts including Prof Bernal* [Professor J. D. Bernal, Scientific Adviser to Combined Operations Headquarters] *on the subject of the reefs off J Beaches necessitating 3ft more water than originally planned. This entirely mucking up H-Hour. Could find no satisfactory conclusion except to wildly stagger S with J and G and all with W.T.F. The result on the assault is to make it much more chancy. We now await confirmation of the figures. I had to send Creasy home for a couple of days as he was looking and feeling pretty done in. Most awkward at this moment. Had an intense afternoon and slaved without any let up and am feeling the need of a rest myself.*

DIARY OF ADMIRAL SIR BERTRAM RAMSAY

A month before D-Day, the increasing number of underwater beach obstacles necessitated a reconsideration of the timing of H-Hour. Understandably, the Army wanted a simultaneous landing all along the coast, but now aerial reconnaissance showed what appeared to be rocks off the Juno area. The only way the Canadians could be given sufficient depth of water to cross them safely was to delay H-Hour, but US forces wanted the first waves to touch down at low water. The compromise was to stagger H-Hour from 6.30 a.m. for Force 'U' in the west to 7.45 a.m. for Force 'S', even though this would negate any idea of surprise for the Eastern Task Force. Subsequently it was discovered that the 'rocks' were strands of seaweed!

Loading began on Wednesday, May 31, but as the troops of Force 'U' had the furthest distance to sail from their ports of Torquay, Brixham, Dartmouth and Plymouth East, the ships had to be ready to assemble on June 3. *Above:* 'Der Fuehrer's Express', a quadruple ·50-calibre AA half-track belonging to Assault Group Green, scheduled to land on Tare Green Beach, backs down Hard P.C.2 at Dartmouth on June 1. LST 47 was part of Lieutenant J. E. Chadwick's Unit No. 1, but LST 346 on the east side of the river belonged to Unit No. 2 of Assault Group Red (Uncle Red Beach). *Right:* Today, this is the western slipway of the Upper Ferry although the wartime four-berth hard was angled to point down the river. *Below:* More vehicles of Assault Group Red join their LSTs at Breakwater Hard at Brixham, these particular vessels also being part of Unit No. 2 under Commodore S. B. Purdie.

MINING

Sea mining was carried on continuously by the Admiralty and by Bomber Command, but for some months before 'Neptune' the mining programme was planned to afford direct assistance to the operation both as regards location and timing of each lay. Considerable success is known to have been achieved by mines laid during this period under Plan 'Maple', which was really an integral part of Operation 'Neptune'.

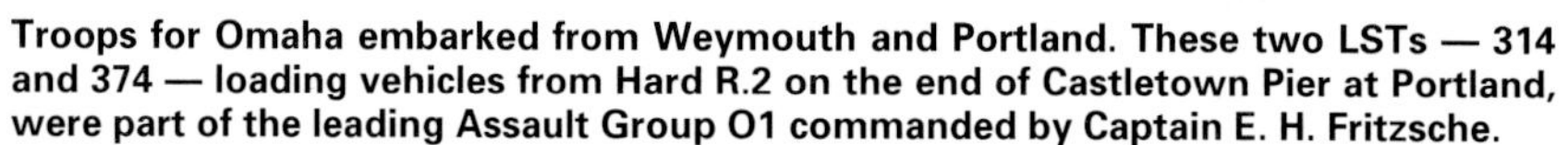

Troops for Omaha embarked from Weymouth and Portland. These two LSTs — 314 and 374 — loading vehicles from Hard R.2 on the end of Castletown Pier at Portland, were part of the leading Assault Group O1 commanded by Captain E. H. Fritzsche.

When we visited Portland to take the comparison, we were amazed to find two Mulberry caissons still 'parked' just off the end of the pier — especially as they did not appear in the 1944 photo. However, after making several enquiries, we were told that the two Phoenixes were 'overs' not needed in Normandy and that they had been brought to Portland and sunk in the harbour as an additional breakwater. Both appear to be in pristine condition as they are sheltered from the worst of the weather.

Left: **This assortment of half-tracks mounting both 37mm and twin ·50 machine guns are, according to the original caption, from 'an armoured unit with their pet crow, Oscar. A few hours later, the men, material and Oscar moved to strike the first blow of the last act of the greatest conflict in history'. Technically, the vehicles are M15A1 Combination Gun Motor Carriages although the one with the push-bike on the back would appear to be an ordinary M2.** *Right:* **Now, Hard R.3 is part of HMS** ***Osprey*****, the helicopter base, although perhaps it should be renamed HMS** ***Crow*** **in memory of Oscar!**

INCREASING ENEMY NAVAL ACTIVITY

Although the enemy were slow to react to our much-publicised invasion preparations from the end of April onwards, enemy naval activity in the Channel did increase. On April 29, in an engagement between two Canadian destroyers, who were covering a minelaying operation off Ile de Bas, one of our destroyers and one of the enemy's were sunk. Throughout the month of May, enemy E-Boat activity in the central Channel increased, and it was apparent that more E-Boats were being moved to Cherbourg and Le Havre. Our destroyers and light coastal forces operated by Commanders-in-Chief, Portsmouth and Plymouth, were, however, able to keep the enemy in check and to inflict casualties on him.

The first enemy U-Boat was reported in the western Channel on May 20, which necessitated a change in the dispositions of our covering forces. The Admiralty had some weeks earlier announced their intention of allotting four A/U Support Groups to Commander-in-Chief, Plymouth, to operate in the western Channel and to co-operate with Coastal Command in sealing this approach to the 'Neptune' convoy routes. The Air Officer Commanding-in-Chief, Coastal Command, Air Chief Marshal Sir W. Sholto Douglas, had similarly made new dispositions to be effective some weeks before D-Day in anticipation of the movement of the U-Boat battle to the Channel. Coastal Command threw themselves into the preparations for 'Neptune' with as much enthusiasm as any unit in the Allied Expeditionary Force, and I personally and the whole Naval Expeditionary Force are deeply indebted to them for the efficiency of the measures they adopted, which was reflected by the very small scale of U-Boat attack that eventuated.

No weapon that the enemy might have employed before D-Day against our forces caused me more anxiety than the potentialities of minelaying. Mines were employed defensively on a considerable scale in the Bay of the Seine during the months prior to D-Day and

Keep fit and communion at Weymouth — strange bedfellows for these men of the 116th Regimental Combat Team (29th Division). LCI 92 on the right was to suffer a spectacular fate on Dog White Beach on June 6 when an underwater explosion set off her fuel tanks. At 1200 hours on Thursday, June 1, Admiral Ramsay officially assumed operational command of all the 'Neptune' forces and general control of operations in the Channel, and the first sailings of warships for the assault area took place the following day (Bombardment Force 'D' from the Clyde bound for Sword). Also, two midget submarines, *X.20* and *X.23*, which were to mark Juno and Sword, began their tow from Portsmouth so as to be at their release point early on the 3rd.

Father (Major) Edward J. Waters conducts the service while Sergeant Herman Wall of the 165th Signal Photographic Company took the pictures. He crossed over to France with the men and we will see more of his work later on.

Next to sail on the 3rd were the Western Task Force bombarding forces ('A' for Utah and 'C' for Omaha) which sailed from Belfast, and Bombarding Force 'E' (Juno) and 'K' (Gold) from the Clyde. Force 'G' embarked from Southampton — these LCTs are massed alongside Berth 101. The picture was taken from the two-berth LST Hard S.1.

caused the naval plan largely to be framed round the requirements for sweeping our forces through the enemy's minefields. In the six weeks before D-Day, the enemy also considerably intensified his minelaying off the south coast of England, using aircraft on a scale which had not been attempted for over two years and introducing two new types of mine. This minelaying was confined to moonless periods. Had D-Day been in such a period, it is doubtful whether the Portsmouth channels could have been cleared in time. As it was, no interruption was caused to the rehearsals nor to the assembly of our forces and it is considered that the enemy missed a great opportunity in not still further extending this form of attack. That he did not attempt more was yet another result of the air superiority we achieved before D-Day. Towards the end of May, some aircraft minelaying was combined with night air bombing attacks on a light scale on south coast ports, but very few casualties were caused to ships and personnel.

Left: **This is the long wharf facing the River Test (Berths 101-109) with the caisson of the King George V dry dock on the left. (Because of its similarity with the Normandie Dock at St Nazaire, it was here that No. 2 Commando had rehearsed 'the greatest raid of all' in March 1942.)** *Right:* **Without a ship to stand on, the comparison is from a slightly different angle.**

Force 'J' troops left from Portsmouth and also from Southampton where Gilbert Milne, the Canadian war photographer, pictured the 9th Brigade embarking with their two-wheeled transport. The LCIs are drawn up on Hard S.3. As we have seen, at 0415 on Sunday, June 4, D-Day was postponed for 24 hours. This delay was telephoned from Southwick House to the Admiralty and the Commanders-in-Chief, Home Commands, and a general signal despatched to all forces at 0515.

D-DAY AND H-HOUR

No single question was more often discussed during planning than that of H-Hour. As H-Hour was linked to tidal conditions, D-Day was dependent on it. Until obstructions appeared on the assault beaches, the argument was largely confined to the determination of the ideal balance between a sufficiency of light for aimed air and naval bombardment and the minimum daylight approach, taking into consideration the number of days to which postponement in the case of bad weather would he acceptable in view of the different tidal conditions on later days. But as beach obstructions in some numbers were erected on the beaches, the need to deal with these dryshod, and therefore to land below them, overcame all previous arguments, and H-Hour and D-Day were finally largely determined by the position of these obstacles.

As on the western (US) beaches, the obstructions were known to be in place further down the beach than on the eastern (British) beaches and as in Force 'J's sector (Juno) near low water there were some rocks which would be a danger to the assault craft, it was finally necessary to select five different H-Hours, ranging over a period of one hour and 25 minutes. Anxiety was felt on two counts, first that the earlier H-Hours in the US sector, coupled with their requirements to arrive in the transport area earlier relative to H-Hour than the British, might prejudice surprise in the west before it was lost in the east, and second, that so many H-Hours might confuse some or many of the ships and craft taking part. In the event, the lack of alertness of the enemy obviated the first, and good briefing prevented the second.

Owing to the need to take account of the latest photographic reconnaissance showing the exact positions of the obstacles, the final decision as to D-Day and H-Hour was not made until May 17 when June 5 was selected, with postponement acceptable to June 6 and 7.

Unfortunately, a new block of luxury flats now stands on the site of the wartime slipway on Town Quay, hence this angled shot from its western end.

Convoys at sea were ordered to reverse course, the blockships from Scotland being diverted to Poole Bay. However, Convoy U2A, which had sailed from the Salcombe area at 1653 the previous afternoon, failed to respond to the postponement signal. By now, she had been joined by other vessels from Dartmouth and Portland, forming a very large convoy of 138 vessels including 128 of the unwieldy tank landing craft. Four hours after the signal had gone out, the convoy was still steaming its course towards France and was then 25 miles south of St Catherine's Point, the southernmost tip of the Isle of Wight. Two destroyers were sent at full speed by the C-in-C Plymouth to try to catch the convoy, and the C-in-C Portsmouth despatched a Walrus aircraft, which reported at 0948 that all the vessels had turned northwards. These LCIs of Force 'J' were pictured in Ocean Dock on the eve of D-Day.

WEATHER IMMEDIATELY BEFORE D-DAY: 24-HOUR POSTPONEMENT

The Supreme Commander held the first meeting to discuss the weather forecast for D-Day on June 1. The outlook was not very good and it deteriorated further during the next three days. At the meeting held on June 3, Eisenhower decided to allow the movements of the forces to commence, despite the unfavourable outlook, in view of the many advantages in launching the operation on the first possible day. But at the next meeting at 0415 on June 4, it was clear that conditions the next day would not be acceptable and a postponement of 24 hours was ordered. By this time, all of Force 'U' from Devonshire and a proportion of Force 'O' (Omaha) from Portland were at sea, and ships and craft had to reverse their course and return to harbour. Instructions for this eventuality were included in the operation orders and worked smoothly, except in the case of Force U2A, a large, slow assault force composed of 128 LCTs with their escort, which failed to receive the signal ordering the postponement. By 0900, this force was about 25 miles south of St Catherine's Point and still steering south. Two destroyers and a Walrus aircraft had to be sent at full speed to turn it round. Had this not been done, it is possible that the force would shortly have been detected by the enemy's radar and this would undoubtedly have resulted in his increased vigilance for the next few days.

The craft of Force 'U' had a bad time punching into a head sea on their return westwards and, although the whole force was ordered into Weymouth Bay, a number of craft never managed to enter it. Considerable anxiety was felt throughout June 4 both as to the need of a further postponement with all its resulting loss of efficiency of craft and assault troops, and whether Force 'U' would be in a fit state to go forward again early the next morning should the decision be made to go on with the operation. At one time, it was thought that Force 'U' would have to return to Devonshire to reform, but, when it was pointed out that this would almost certainly result in the postponement of the operation to the next moon period, Rear Admiral Kirk, with characteristic verve, announced his readiness to proceed.

THE PASSAGE

When the assault forces again sailed early on June 5, the weather was still largely unfavourable for landing craft, but more suitable conditions had been forecast for the early hours of June 6. Wind was WSW Force 5 veering to WNW decreasing in force at times but with strong gusts; waves were five to six feet in mid-Channel. These conditions made the passage difficult, and considerable discomfort was experienced by the troops embarked in LCT and LCI(L). Although some of the minor landing craft which were due to arrive p.m. on D-Day had to put back to harbour, and others were delayed, the assault forces all drove on and almost without exception arrived off their beaches to time. The performance of the leading groups of Force 'U' was particularly praiseworthy, since, as has been stated, some of these failed to enter harbour on the postponement, and by H-Hour their commanding officers had been on their bridges continuously for about 70 hours. Out of the 128 LCT in Group U2A, only seven failed to take part in the assault, and this figure took account of engine failures as well as the stress of the weather.

To ensure the correct positioning of the northern ends of the ten approach channels that were to be swept across the known enemy minefields, ten FH 830 buoys had been laid by three HDML (Harbour Defence Motor Launches) of Force 'J' during the night May 31/June 1. The buoys were timed to transmit between the hours of 1400 and 2200 on six successive days, commencing on June 4. At 1800 on June 5, ten HDML took up position to point these buoys for the assault forces, and all reports show that this method was wholly satisfactory. A large number of ships was fitted with receivers to obtain positions from the Gee and Decca radio navigational systems, both of which worked fully according to expectations, and navigation was never regarded as a serious problem. The above additional measures were taken to guard against effective jamming by the enemy p.m. on D–1 should surprise have been lost.

Fifty years later, we climbed the same crane to match the shot. In the background, the famous South Western Hotel.

Portsmouth, Newhaven and Shoreham were the loading points for Force 'S'. These troops are about to embark from South Parade Pier, Southsea.

ACHIEVEMENT OF SURPRISE

There was an air of unreality during the passage of the assault forces across the Channel. The achievement of strategical surprise was always hoped for in 'Neptune' but was by no means certain, whereas that of tactical surprise had always seemed extremely unlikely. As our forces approached the French coast without a murmur from the enemy or from their own radio, the realisation that once again almost complete tactical surprise had been achieved slowly dawned. This astonishing feat cannot be explained by any single factor and must be attributed in part to all of the following: the miscalculations of the enemy; the high degree of air superiority attained by our air forces, which drastically reduced the enemy's air reconnaissance; the bad weather which caused the enemy to withdraw his E-Boat patrols to Cherbourg and, finally, the radio counter-measures employed by our forces, which, coupled with the diversions against the Pas-de-Calais and Cap d'Antifer, left the enemy in doubt as to the points at which we would land even when he had become aware that the invasion was in progress. Although the unfavourable weather caused difficulties and damage to craft off the beaches later, the advantages gained by surprise were so striking that the decision to go on despite the weather was amply justified. A postponement of one more day, e.g. till June 7, would, in the event, have proved disastrous owing to the conditions of sea off the beaches. The problems arising out of a postponement of 12 to 14 days to the next suitable period were too appalling even to contemplate.

On Saturday, Admiral Ramsay went down to the hards with Rear-Admiral Talbot of Force 'S' to see how the loading was going. He was not pleased. LCTs were being overloaded 'which was the fault of the Army whose one idea was to cram as many vehicles and as much into each vehicle as possible'.

ORGANISATION OF THE EXPEDITIONARY FORCE

Force	Assembly Ports	Assault Beaches
	Western Task Force (American)	
Assault Force 'U'	Torquay, Brixham, Dartmouth and Salcombe	Tare Green Uncle Red
Assault Force 'O'	Weymouth, Portland and Poole	Dog Green, White & Red Easy Green and Red, Fox Green
Follow-up Force 'B'	Plymouth, Falmouth, Helford river and Fowey	US area
First Build-up Divisions	Bristol Channel ports	—
	Eastern Task Force (British)	
Assault Force 'G'	Southampton, Solent and Spithead	Jig Green King Green and Red
Assault Force 'J'	Southampton, Solent and Spithead	Mike Green and Red Nan Green, White & Red
Assault Force 'S'	Portsmouth, Spithead, Newhaven and Shoreham	Queen White and Red
Follow-up Force 'L'	The Nore and Harwich	British area
First Build-up Divisions	Thames	—

Almost by way of confirmation of what Admiral Ramsay had witnessed, on June 4, a US tank landing craft, which had broken down, capsized and sank off Portland. No casualties were reported, but she was believed to have been carrying 12 vehicles and 70 men instead of 11 vehicles and 55 men. This picture of an LCT of Force 'S' was taken on June 3 from the Gosport side of the harbour looking towards Old Portsmouth by another renowned D-Day photographer, Sergeant Jimmy Mapham, who went with these men of the British 3rd Division to Queen Beach. It is certainly a very interesting picture with lots to look at. The board with 213 gives the Landing Table Index Number — this was in fact LCT 610.

MINESWEEPING DURING THE APPROACH

The sweeping of ten approach channels for the assault forces represented the largest single minesweeping operation that had yet been undertaken in war. The provision of the necessary minesweeping flotillas had only been achieved by drawing upon some which had little opportunity for practice, and, when my operation orders were written, it was realised that the successful completion of the minesweeping tasks would demand a high degree of skill from all concerned. Subsequently, the late appearance of beach obstacles on the assault beaches further complicated the problem, as the alteration in the time of H-Hour relative to high water that resulted meant that it would now be necessary for all flotillas to change sweeps during passage to avoid sweeping with an unfavourable tide. Some flotillas had no opportunity to rehearse this manoeuvre at all, as it was not decided on until after Exercise 'Fabius', and the fact that all successfully achieved it is considered most satisfactory.

Sweeping was carried out in all cases according to plan, despite stronger tidal streams than had been allowed for and the unfavourable weather, which made very difficult the operation of the Mark 5 sweeps by MLs, and the minesweepers approached the French coast without interference. The early arrival of the Western Task Force flotillas had been a cause of some anxiety during planning but, because surprise was in the event achieved, it had no unfortunate result. The senior officers of the flotillas concerned expressed surprise in their reports that although the enemy coast at Cape Barfleur was sighted as early as 2000 on June 5, no batteries opened fire at them and the operation proceeded unopposed; in this connection, it may be noted that minesweepers switched on radio counter-measures at 2130.

We are looking from where the old chain bridge grounded towards HMS *Vernon* with the dome of Portsmouth Cathedral on the right — another Steve Casely shot.

Steve's crowning glory was to find this location for us back in 1985. The Signal Corps' caption says that 'the GIs, armed with equipment, are on their way to the hards and landing craft at Tor Bay, England, 3 June, 1944'. Both Torbay, the town, and Tor Bay itself lie on the western side of Lyme Bay, north of Slapton, but we searched in vain. We looked all along the Dart, as the water in the background appears more like a river than the sea, but still to no avail. The 29th shoulder patch should have been the clue as the 'Blue and Grey' division belonged to Force 'B', the follow-up part of the Western Task Force. Their departure ports were Plymouth and Falmouth, the latter being some 100 miles west of Tor Bay. Well, Steve motored down to Cornwall and there, at Helford Passage above the River Helford, he found the correct spot, virtually unchanged.

Plymouth West was the other loading point for Force 'B'. Waiting to catch the Torpoint Ferry: *above* **1944-style;** *right* **in 1994.**

NAVAL BOMBARDMENT

It had been planned that ships should be ready to open fire at their pre-arranged targets either from the time when the assault convoys came within range of them or from the time when it was light enough for the enemy to spot his fall of shot visually, whichever was

Below left: **The area still bears its scars from the air raids of 1941 as the troops queue up in Fore Street for their turn to enter the boats.** *Below right:* **Now, this is the assembly point for the ferry, but the King's Arms on the far corner still stands.**

The men are ferried out in LCVPs to the waiting LCIs. Anchored in the right background is USS *Augusta*, flagship for the Western Task Force.

the later, but that, if possible, fire should be withheld until it was light enough for air observation. In the event, this proved possible with the exception of one or two ships in the Western Task Force, which found it necessary to open blind fire against certain batteries whose fire was more accurate than was the general case.

Right: Commodore C. D. Edgar was the force commander. These are more of his ships loading at the Barn Pool hard. *Below:* Although the hards below Mount Edgcumbe have been dismantled, odd squares of 'chocolate' still remain.

All the years of waiting, all the months of planning, all the weeks of training, all the hours of deliberation and argument . . .

As Bombarding Force 'D' arrived in position on the eastern flank at 0515, a half-hearted attack was made by four enemy E-Boats and some armed trawlers which had come out of Le Havre. The enemy were seen indistinctly against the land and were almost immediately obscured by the pre-arranged smoke-screen laid by our aircraft, from behind which they fired torpedoes. The heavy ships managed to comb the torpedo tracks but the Norwegian destroyer *Svenner* was hit and sunk. One enemy trawler was sunk and one damaged, and the attack was not renewed. The danger to friendly forces of smoke laid to a pre-arranged plan was plainly exemplified.

The fire from enemy batteries, which was never severe, was directed initially against bombarding ships only, and was largely ineffective. This is considered to have been due to the combined success of the pre-D-Day bombing programme, the heavy air bombardment in the early hours of D-Day, and the measures taken to prevent the enemy from ranging and spotting, and it demonstrates that duels between ships and coastal batteries are in certain eventualities feasible provided such precautions are taken. It must be remembered, however, that the scale of coast defence in the assault area was the lowest on this part of the coast and the results would have been very different, for instance, in the Pas-de-Calais. Much of the success of naval bombardment must be attributed to the work of the single-seater fighter spotters, who carried out their tasks tirelessly and gallantly. Communications between bombarding ships and spotting aircraft suffered a number of failures at the start owing mainly to the novel nature of the technique, but they improved rapidly with successive waves of aircraft.

Warships and gun support craft took part in the drenching of beach defences immediately prior to the assault. This fire appeared accurate, and was of sufficient weight to neutralise and demoralise the defenders, except on Omaha Beach where the total failure of the day heavy bombers, due to low cloud base, contributed to the much stiffer opposition than was found elsewhere. Of the support craft, the LCG(L) — the large landing craft equipped with guns — deserves special mention. This craft, which achieved only partial success in the Mediterranean due to lack of training and shortcomings in its equipment, was particularly effective and further demonstrated the value in assault of high-velocity guns at close range.

. . . now came to fruition: 'A landing was made this morning on the coast of France by troops of the Allied Expeditionary Force . . .'

THE ASSAULTS

The choice of the lowering positions had been a matter of considerable discussion, the conflicting factors of being outside the range of the enemy's shore batteries and south of the known mined area having to be balanced. The Eastern Task Force finally chose their lowering positions about 7 to 8 miles off-shore, whilst the Western Task Force decided to place them further to seaward, 10 to 11¼ miles out. In the rough weather that obtained when the assault forces arrived in the lowering positions, the longer passage inshore for the assault craft from the Western Task Force appeared to add appreciably to their difficulties.

To mark the approaches to the beaches for Forces 'S' and 'J' (Sword and Juno), two X-craft were employed as it was very important that Force 'S' should not be too far to the eastward, and the coast in Force 'J's sector was not distinctive in outline. These craft had sailed on the night of June 2/3, being towed for part of the passage. Each submarine received at 0100 on June 5 a message that the assault had been postponed 24 hours, and, in spite of the difficulties of navigation for a craft of very slow diving speed in a cross-tidal stream, they had maintained their positions off the enemy coast until daylight on June 6 when they flashed lights to seaward from the surface in their correct positions as a guide to the oncoming assault craft. It is considered that great skill and endurance was shown by the crews of *X.20* and *X.23*. Their reports of proceedings, which were a masterpiece of understatement, read like the deck log of a surface ship in peacetime, and not of a very small and vulnerable submarine carrying out a hazardous operation in time of war.

Weather conditions off the assault beaches immediately before H-Hour were as follows:

Wind — Westnorthwest — Force 4.

Sea — Moderate — waves 3/4 feet.

Sky — Fair to cloudy with cloud increasing.

These unfavourable conditions interfered to some extent with the release of the assault craft and also with the launching of DD tanks, but nevertheless the majority of the leading waves of the assaults touched down at the right place and at approximately the right time throughout the length of the front.

It is to be our privilege to take part in the greatest amphibious operation in history — a necessary preliminary to the opening of the Western Front in Europe which, in conjunction with the great Russian advance, will crush the fighting power of Germany.

This is the opportunity which we have long awaited and which must be seized and pursued with relentless determination; the hopes and prayers of the free world and of the enslaved peoples of Europe will be with us, and we cannot fail them.

Our task in conjunction with the Merchant Navies of the United Nations, and supported by the Allied Air Forces, is to carry the Allied Expeditionary Force to the Continent, to establish it there in a secure bridgehead and to build it up and maintain it at a rate which will outmatch that of the enemy.

Let no one underestimate the magnitude of this task.

The Germans are desperate and will resist fiercely until we outmanoeuvre and outfight them, which we can and we will do. To everyone of you will be given the opportunity to show by his determination and resource that dauntless spirit of resolution which individually strengthens and inspires, and which collectively is irresistible.

I count on every man to do his utmost to ensure the success of this great enterprise which is the climax of the European War.

Good luck to you all, and God Speed.

ADMIRAL SIR BERTRAM RAMSAY, JUNE 1944

6th Airborne Division

By Major-General Richard Gale

Inspection of the 6th Airborne Division by HM King George VI, Queen Elizabeth, and the 18-year-old Princess Elizabeth, on Salisbury Plain on May 19, 1944. Brigadier James Hill, the CO of the 3rd Parachute Brigade, stands on the right with the divisional commander, General Richard Gale, behind.

I well remember with what mixed feelings on February 17, 1944, I heard of the proposals for the part we were to play in Operation 'Overlord'. The 6th Airborne Division was to be under the command of I Corps and to operate east of the River Orne, its rôle being to cover the left flank of the British invasion.

The left flank of the British seaborne assault was bounded by the double water obstacle consisting of the Canal de Caen and the River Orne. The ground to the east of the River Orne, though not high, was sufficiently dominating to overlook the left flank of the British assault. It was not desirable to extend the seaborne landings to the beaches east of the Orne in order to capture this ground, as the sea approaches to these would have come under the fire of the heavy defences of Le Havre. The river and the canal were obstacles of no mean order, and an attack over these would have been a costly and most undesirable operation. The quickest and surest way of seizing the dominating features east of the Orne was, therefore, by means of an airborne assault

Major-General Richard Gale *(left)* had his headquarters at Syrencot House, near Milston on the Plain, the house still owned by the army, but empty in 1994.

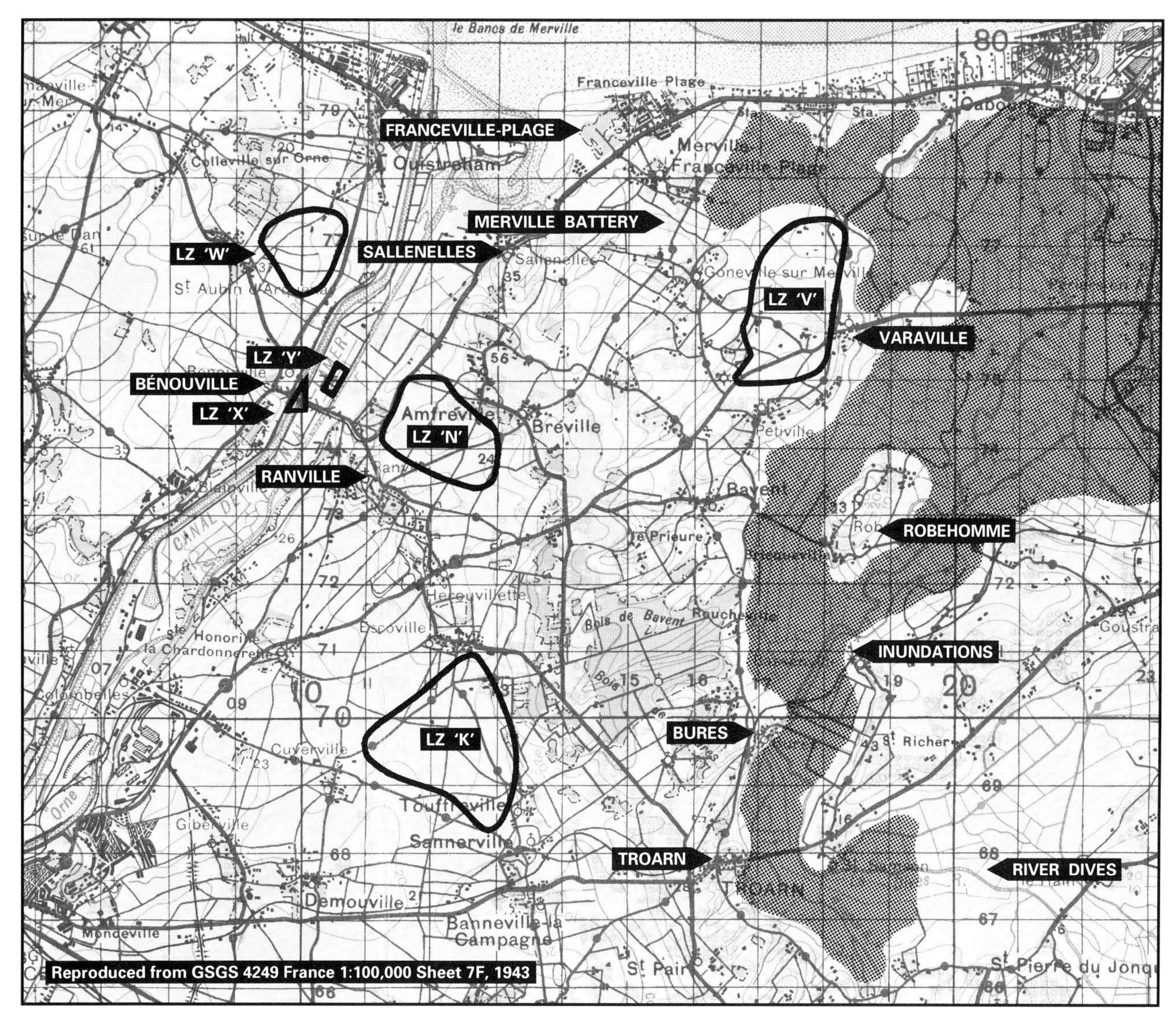

Our first task in order of priority was to seize intact the bridges over the Canal de Caen and the River Orne at Bénouville and Ranville, and to secure a bridgehead of sufficient depth to ensure that these could be held. The defence must have depth: the bridgehead must be sufficiently far out to have the necessary resilience to stand up against any local success which any well-delivered enemy attack might have.

Secondly, in the north of the area in which we were to be landed, there was an important coastal battery. This was located on the high ground at Merville. It was so situated that it could fire on the beaches, as well as on the sea approaches to them, on which the I Corps assault divisions were to land. Our task was to seize and silence this battery before the assault craft came within its range. The sea assault was to be at dawn, and nothing could have been more awful to contemplate than the havoc this battery might wreak on the assault craft as they slowly forged their way in to the shore. It was, of course, hoped that bombing might reduce the battery; but it was by no means certain that bombing alone could achieve this. The actual guns were in enormous reinforced concrete casemates, and nothing but a direct hit from one of the heaviest bombs would knock them out. That meant that each gun in turn would have to be hit. One raid would never achieve this; and prolonged bombing of the battery would be the best way of indicating to the Germans the left flank of the Allied invasion. The whole of the northern coast of France was studded with such batteries. A similar treatment of the others as a bluff would use too much of our bomber effort which was required for a multitude of other tasks. For these reasons, a direct assault on the battery by airborne troops was necessary.

Thirdly, the road approaches from Le Havre and the River Seine crossed the valley of the River Dives some five to seven miles to the east of the Orne. If the bridges over this river could be destroyed, a certain delay would be imposed on any German reinforcements coming from this direction. The third task allotted to the division was, therefore, the destruction of the bridges over the River Dives at Varaville, Robehomme, Bures and Troarn.

Next, but without prejudice to the other tasks, we were instructed to interfere with, and delay as much as possible, the movement of any enemy reinforcements from the east towards Caen.

Finally, the seaside towns of Sallenelles and Franceville-Plage were to be seized and as much as possible of the coastal strip between these places and Cabourg on the mouth of the River Dives was to be cleared of the enemy. For this last task, I was to have Lord Lovat's 1st Special Service Commando Brigade under my command.

The tasks were in all conscience varied and formidable enough. In fact, they involved our first seizing and then dominating an area of some 24 square miles, for which task I should have one division plus a brigade of commandos.

Complete photographic cover of the whole area was available and from this we could glean details as to topography, cultivation and enemy works in the area. The intelligence staff studied and annotated these photographs and we pored over them. From these, and the already very complete maps we had, we made a large model of the whole area.

These investigations showed very clearly that two excellent dropping or landing zones (DZ or LZ) existed within the area in which we were to fight. It further showed that these zones were free from defence works. We could, therefore, land fairly large forces of parachutists or glider-borne troops in close proximity to their task.

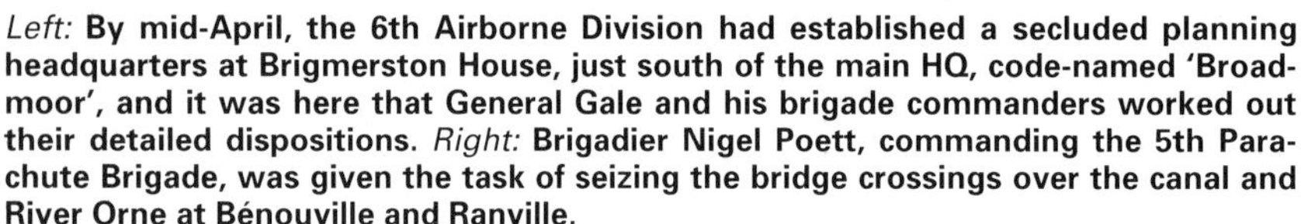

Left: **By mid-April, the 6th Airborne Division had established a secluded planning headquarters at Brigmerston House, just south of the main HQ, code-named 'Broadmoor', and it was here that General Gale and his brigade commanders worked out their detailed dispositions.** *Right:* **Brigadier Nigel Poett, commanding the 5th Parachute Brigade, was given the task of seizing the bridge crossings over the canal and River Orne at Bénouville and Ranville.**

However, the photographs showed us that the battery at Merville was sited in very enclosed country. Approach to it in the dark would thus be difficult as the chances of our troops missing the way would be considerable. A direct advance down any main road would be folly, and the thickness of the country precluded a parachute drop anywhere near the battery. In addition to a deep moat, it was surrounded by a thick and well-constructed wire obstacle which was heavily mined. Preliminary softening by bombing and surprise were our only assets. The battery looked like being our most-unpleasant task.

To seize and secure the bridges over the canal and the river would take one brigade. This task I allotted to the 5th Parachute Brigade under Brigadier Nigel Poett.

Having captured the bridges intact, the problem would then be to hold them. Initially, there must be a bridgehead on both the western and eastern banks. When the seaborne assault division reached Bénouville we would be relieved of the responsibility for that in the west. That on the east would, however, remain our task.

The model brought out certain facts very clearly, far more so than did the map. Looking to the south, the bridges form the apex of a triangle, one arm of which, the River Orne, runs south-west. The other arm, running south-east, is the line of villages and orchards from the bridges through Ranville to Hérouvillette. The river, of course, gave a considerable degree of security on that flank. The tow path and river run much lower than the rest of the country and, as might be expected, was studded with trees and orchards. A drive up this by enemy infantry and tanks would be a very restricted affair and should not be difficult to stop.

To seize the ridge from Sallenelles to Troarn, silence the battery at Merville and to blow the four bridges over the River Dives would take one brigade. This task I decided to allot to the 3rd Parachute Brigade under Brigadier James Hill.

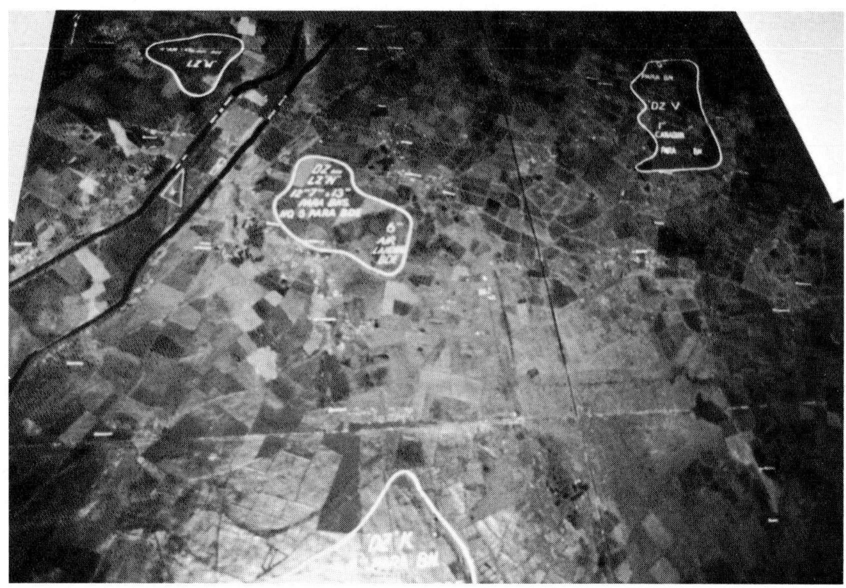

Left: **Brigadier James Hill had as his primary task 'to ensure that the battery 800 yards south of Merville is silenced by 30 minutes before dawn'. It was pointed out in his orders that 'no other commitment must jeopardise success in this enterprise' and that 'while your attitude of mind must be that you cannot contemplate failure in the direct assault, you must be prepared to have to deal with the battery by naval gunfire'. Major G. A. C. Lacoste, the divisional GSO2 (Int), proposed that a large panoramic model** *(below)* **should be made covering the 6th Airborne objectives, and this was constructed at 'Broadmoor' by two Royal Engineers draughtsmen, Corporal 'Taffy' Jones and Lance Corporal Jack Forrest, aided by Lance Corporal Ellis of the RASC. Today, the model can be seen at the Airborne Museum at Aldershot.**

Both Poett's and Hill's brigades, I reckoned, could hold their gains against immediate counter-attack. But greater depth would have to be given to the bridgehead at Ranville; the northern end of the ridge and the sea coast beyond would require further troops; and I must, however small, have some reserve in hand.

The immediate requirement of deepening the bridgehead would be achieved by the advent of the 6th Airlanding Brigade under Brigadier the Hon. Hugh Kindersley on the afternoon of D-Day.

Our force was obviously not sufficient to allow us to control the sea coast east of the Orne, and I very much doubted the wisdom of attacking and mopping this area up. It would, I felt, use up an indefinite number of troops and would take time. I felt, too, that by holding the Sallenelles–Troarn ridge, I really would be freezing out all but the smallest detachments along the coast, and these could be liquidated later when and as it was necessary or desirable to do so. The real battle lay inland and to the south; that was the area on which the eye must be kept, for disaster there would be fatal.

Nevertheless, it was plain that, if the situation permitted, the occupation of the coastal strip would hold obvious advantages. This task, as well as that of strengthening my northern flank, I allotted to the 1st Special Service Brigade of commandos under the spirited leadership of Brigadier Lord Lovat. They were to be among the first troops to land in the assault on Ouistreham and, having cleared that place up, were to join us across the bridges. Their arrival was hoped for by 1 p.m. on D-Day.

As a result of the experiences in the Sicily airborne landings, I was determined that first we must land pathfinder troops of the 22nd Independent Parachute Company, to put out 'aids' for the mass of aircraft that were to follow to 'home' on.

It will be remembered that a task of first priority was the capture intact of the two bridges over the Canal de Caen and the River Orne. I was convinced that once the Germans realised that airborne landings had taken place they would be prepared everywhere. They would certainly be prepared on the bridges which we knew were manned; and they would be ready, immediately they looked like being attacked, to blow them. We knew that virtually all the enemy would have to do would be to press a button or move a switch and up would go these bridges. There is always or nearly always a slip between the cup and the lip: orders are vague . . . there is uncertainty . . . has the moment arrived or should one wait? Who is the individual actually responsible both for working the switch and for ordering the bridges to be blown? These questions are age-old and on the doubts that might exist in some German mind or minds at the critical moment I based the plan. But a moment or two was all that I knew we would get. The assault on the bridges must, therefore, come like a bolt from the blue.

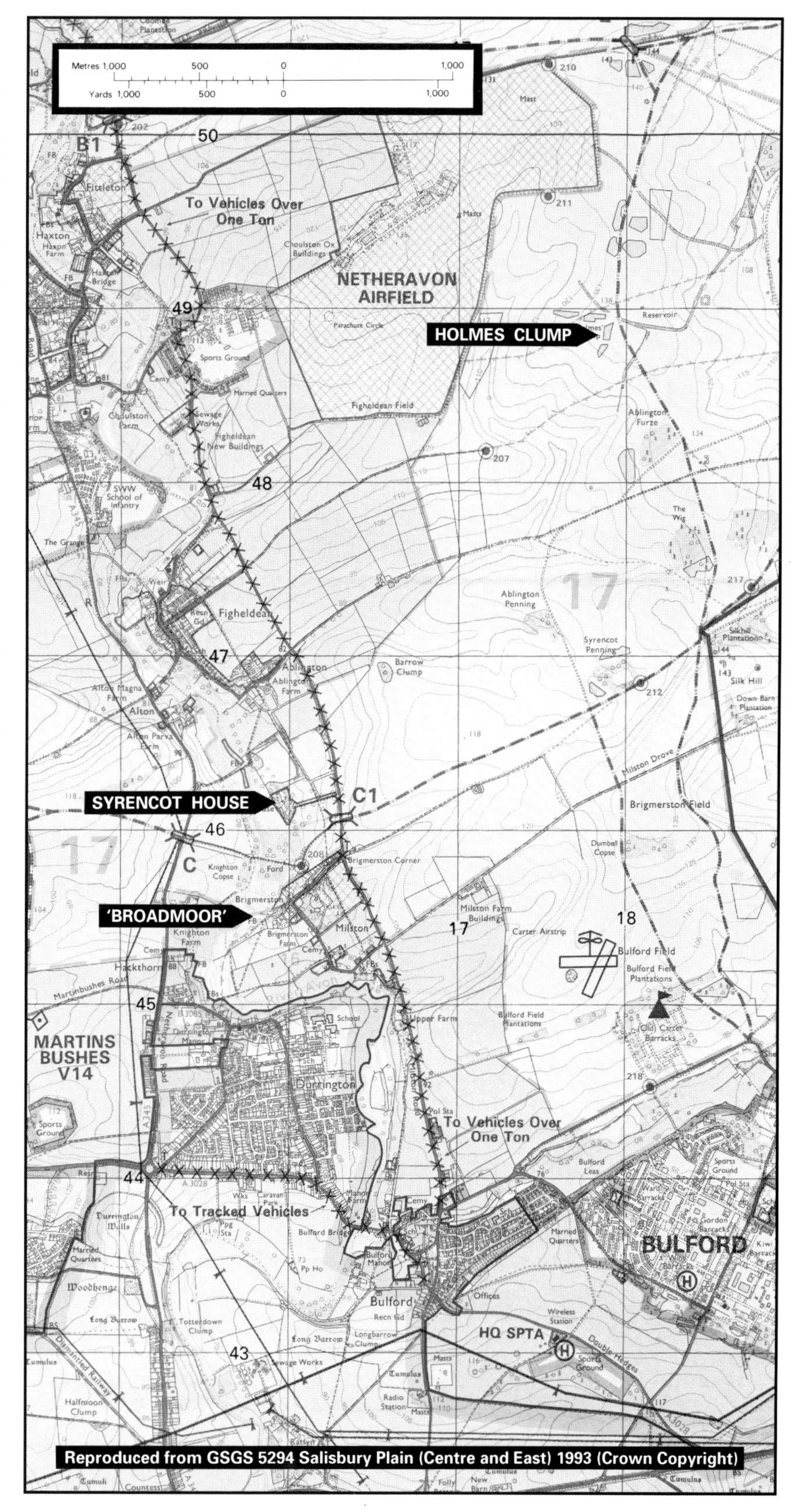

British airborne exercises for D-Day were centred on this area of Salisbury Plain north of Bulford, the inspection depicted on page 214 taking place at 177446. Apart from General Gale's headquarters at Syrencot House and the 'Broadmoor' planning HQ, a joint war room had been established at Netheravon with officers of the RAF's No. 38 Group, which had the responsibility of carrying the division to France. The airfield itself was used for glider training and two areas were marked out on its surface to represent Landing Zones 'X' and 'Y' for the coup de main pilots from the Glider Pilot Regiment to practise their pinpoint landings beside the bridges. When the pilots became proficient, a more difficult LZ, restricted by trees, was laid out just east of the airfield at Holmes Clump. After landing, the gliders would then be pulled back onto the airfield for the next attempt.

The Horsa was the mainstay of the British glider force — it could carry 28 including the pilot and co-pilot.

Planning for D-Day started at the beginning of 1944. No. 2 Wing of the Glider Pilot Regiment (formerly the 1st Battalion, GPR) had returned from Sicily, much depleted and in need of further training. No. 1 Wing (previously the 2nd Battalion, GPR) had been formed in the United Kingdom and I found myself in command of B Squadron stationed at Brize Norton.

The task of the regiment was for 1,500 glider pilots to be trained and exercised in mass landings on a scale never tried before and in time for what was to be, from an airman's point of view, the most complicated operation of all time. There were three types of gliders: the Horsa, Hamilcar and Hadrian (or Waco).

The Horsa, which was the main glider used in the operation by the British forces, was of timber construction and designed to carry a load of three tons. Originally, this was to consist of 26 fully-armed troops, but it was soon realised that the Horsa was of more use carrying weapons such as an anti-tank gun and Jeep or a light field gun or similar loads. Unloading on the battlefield, under fire, was a problem which was solved by making the tail unit detachable by a series of quick release bolts. (I can assure anyone that they were far from being 'quick'!) The story is told of the over-zealous passengers who, in order to expedite the unloading, started to undo the bolts and cut the control cables before landing! Fortunately, they were stopped just in time!

A large loading door was provided on the front port side although the use of the door as a platform was restricted to unloading when any damage would be of little consequence. Instead, a purpose-built ramp was used to manoeuvre large loads and it was a remarkable stroke of luck that a Jeep could just be manhandled around the corner of the door. However, on the battlefield no time could be lost and a band of Cordtex explosive, called a surcingle, was fitted around the rear fuselage to sever the rear end. An alternative modification involved quick-release nuts to enable the tail to be removed. Just over 1,000 Horsas were available for use on D-Day.

The much larger Hamilcar had a nose-entry door enabling Bren gun carriers or light tanks to be driven straight out within seconds of landing. Alternatively, it could carry 40 troops. However, only 70 Hamilcars were available.

The Hamilcar was a massive glider, also of wooden construction, designed to carry a load of seven tons, for example a light tank or Bren carrier, a 25-pdr gun, or similar loads. It had to be towed by a Halifax with specially-boosted engines. The Hadrian or Waco was an American glider of steel tube and canvas construction, but would only carry a gun or a Jeep but not both which meant that the two gliders must land together. The gliders were towed by Albemarles, Halifaxes, Stirlings and Dakotas.

The glider pilot was a volunteer from any branch of the army and was trained to fly light aircraft at the same flying training schools as the RAF and was then converted onto gliders. Not only had he to be a fully-qualified pilot but, once on the ground, he had to fight alongside the troops he was carrying which meant he had to be a jack-of-all-trades able to fire any gun, drive any vehicle, operate a wireless and to use his initiative to the full. On the RAF station where he was based, he crewed up with the tug crew who were to tow him and, as far as possible, carried out all training together with them so that on the operation they were an integrated team.

During the build-up to D-Day, I was involved in the many exercises held to practise landing large numbers of gliders in a mass operation. This culminated on April 23 when 185 gliders landed by daylight in a single mass formation at three airfields: Southrop, Brize Norton and Harwell. (It was necessary to use airfields as landing zones in order to be able to retrieve and fly the gliders back to base.) Finally, we landed 100 gliders by moonlight at Netheravon. I well remember the occasion as I was flying with Colonel George Chatterton, the Commander Glider Pilots, as my co-pilot. For some reason, the ground staff had put out the landing 'T' at 180 degrees to the direction we had all been briefed to land. Half the gliders followed their briefing instructions and half followed the 'T'. The result: gliders approaching from all directions in moonlight. The Colonel was appalled and his language was memorable, but we landed safely and surprisingly so did all the others with no casualties and with only three gliders damaged. Our training had obviously borne fruit.

As D-Day drew near, I was asked by Colonel Chatterton to pick three crews for a most important task which was to land a total of six gliders (B Squadron to provide three of them) in a small field, by moonlight, without any landing aids, released silently from 6,000 feet some distance from the field. At the time, we did not know what the objective was but we commenced training on spot landings by moonlight. Unfortunately, our Albemarle tugs were not powerful enough to take a fully-loaded glider to the required height in the time allowed so, regretfully, my crews had to be transferred to Tarrant Rushton where the Halifax tugs were stationed and where the remainder were training.

The Waco CG4A was a small US-built glider which could carry 15 men or a Jeep or artillery piece. When in British service, it was called the Hadrian although the 140-odd employed on D-Day were all American operated.

Shortly afterwards, I was asked to select three crews for a most hazardous operation. Colonel Chatterton told me they must be volunteers but, when I asked for volunteers, the whole squadron stepped forward so I had the invidious task of making a selection. I picked three of my very best pilots for their flying ability and initiative.

The task was for the three gliders to land on a heavily-defended battery of guns commanding the British Sword Beach, which had to be silenced before the landing from the sea commenced. We did not know the location of the battery until three days before the operation — it was the Merville battery — which was to be carried out by the 9th Parachute Battalion under Lieutenant-Colonel Terence Otway.

Landing aids were to be provided in the form of a radio beacon called 'Eureka' placed on the landing area by a parachutist and a receiver known as 'Rebecca' placed in a glider. I flew several trials with this equipment using dark goggles to simulate a night landing and found it quite efficient.

For the operation, three brand-new gliders were to be provided fitted with the Rebecca and also a parachute arrester gear which would reduce the speed of the glider once it touched the ground. Two days before the operation, six new gliders arrived at the airfield — three fitted with Rebecca and three others with parachute arrester gear! Someone had blundered — panic! Eventually, three gliders were produced with the correct equipment but while two were brand-new, the third was obviously not. There was no time to flight test them and I had to get the pilots to draw lots as to who should fly the ropy one. Sadly, Staff Sergeant Arnold Baldwin drew the short straw. On take-off, he found his glider almost unmanageable as it had been rigged incorrectly, with the result that when the combination went into cloud the tow broke and Baldwin had to make a forced landing at RAF Odiham.

The remaining two gliders reached the objective but the ground Eureka (which had a self-destruct charge should it fall into enemy hands) unfortunately blew up when the parachutist carrying it had a heavy landing. So with no landing aids and in cloud, rain and smoke, and being fired at from the ground, the tug pilots circled the area to find the objective and, although both gliders made heavy landings, they were able to take part in the battle in which the 9th Battalion eventually silenced the guns.

Above: **Final briefing for Glider Pilot Regiment crews at Harwell on June 5 in what is now the Project Department** *(below)* **of United Kingdom Nirex Ltd, the company responsible for providing and managing a repository for the disposal of Britain's radioactive waste products.**

For the D-Day landings, I supplied 17 crews of the 72 required for the final part of Operation 'Tonga' which was the night landing behind the beaches in areas which had been covered with anti-landing poles. These had to be demolished by the sappers before the gliders landed. For the main daylight landing on D-Day itself, I provided 42 crews out of the 256 gliders which were briefed to land. The remainder of my squadron, including myself, were held in readiness to carry the 1st Airborne Division to be landed a few days later to the east of Caen to completely enclose the city, but this operation never took place.

MAJOR IAN TOLER, 1994

An eve of D-Day pep talk from the General who gave the 6th Airborne Division its rousing motto: 'Go to it!' Captain Bill Malandine, the ex-Fleet Street photographer who covered the final hours at Harwell, failed to date his dope sheet for several of his shots, but this picture is believed to have been taken on June 4. Several of the men are members of the 2nd Battalion of the Oxford and Buckinghamshire Light Infantry, and of other battalions of the 6th Airlanding Brigade and of the Parachute Regiment. Nos. 38 and 46 Groups, RAF, were providing 15 squadrons (423 aircraft) for the air lift to Normandy apart from the gliders (see page 250). In addition, 10,000 equipment containers would be dropped. Navigation would initially be by 'Gee', with LZ and DZ identification by the 'Rebecca' homing device onto 'Eureka' radio beacons set out on the ground by personnel of the 22nd Independent Parachute Company.

A 'stick' of parachutists covers a considerable area: under operational conditions 20 men we could expect to cover over 1,000 yards. The concentration of such a 'stick' in the dark and on unknown ground would take time. Immediate surprise was the essence of the bridge problem. If three gliders can be landed slap on the objective, a concentration of 75 fully armed men is immediately achieved.

It was thus for these very good reasons that I decided on two coup de main assaults each by three gliders on each of the two bridges. On account of the necessity for complete surprise, this must coincide with the drops of the Independent Parachute Company and not follow them. The coup de main party must in fact be one of the first incidents of the invasion and so must be prepared to come in without any navigational aids.

The Independent Parachute Company must have time to put out their aids and set up all their equipment and so, not until half an hour after their arrival, and that of the coup de main glider parties, could the two parachute brigades fly in. The 5th Brigade under Brigadier Poett was to land north of Ranville and secure a close bridgehead both west of the canal at Bénouville and east of the Orne at Ranville. The glider coup de main troops were, of course, placed under Poett's command.

The 3rd Parachute Brigade under Brigadier Hill was to land on two widely-separated zones, one in the north near Varaville for the battalions detailed for the Merville battery and the Le Mesnil crossroads, and the other on the open ground south of Escoville with the task of seizing the road junction south-east of this village. This brigade was responsible for the blowing of four bridges over the Dives as well as for investing the country along the whole extent of the ridge.

THE FLIGHT PLAN FOR D-DAY

***(a)* 0020 hours**

Pathfinders on all DZs — two Albemarles to each DZ.

Coup de Main party — three Horsa gliders on each bridge towed by three Halifaxes of No. 644 Squadron and three Halifaxes of No. 298 Squadron.

Advance parties of 3rd and 5th Parachute Brigades — 16 Albemarles of Nos. 295 and 570 Squadrons for 3rd Parachute Brigade, and five Albemarles of Nos. 296 and 297 Squadrons for 5th Parachute Brigade.

***(b)* 0050 hours**

Main body of 3rd and 5th Parachute Brigades. 3rd Parachute Brigade to be dropped by 108 Dakotas of No. 46 Group and to use 17 Horsas towed by Dakotas and Albemarles of both groups for heavy equipment. 5th Parachute Brigade to be dropped by 131 aircraft, Dakotas and Stirlings, of both groups.

***(c)* 0320 hours**

Divisional Headquarters including HQ RA, HQ RE, HQ RASC, FOO [Forward Observation Officer] *and FOB* [Forward Observation Bombardment] *parties and 4th Airlanding Anti-Tank Battery, RA, to be landed in 65 Horsas and four Hamilcars.*

***(d)* 0430 hours**

Three Horsa gliders towed by Albemarles of No. 297 Squadron to land for a direct assault on the Merville coastal battery.

***(e)* 2100 hours**

Headquarters, 6th Airlanding Brigade; 2nd Battalion Oxfordshire & Buckinghamshire Light Infantry, less one company and two platoons; 1st Battalion Royal Ulster Rifles; 211th Light Battery, RA., and the Armoured Reconnaissance Regiment; A Company, 12th Battalion Devonshire Regiment; 195th Airlanding Field Ambulance; 3rd Airlanding Anti-Tank Battery, RA; 716th Light Company, RASC. The total lift for this party was to consist of 226 Horsas and 30 Hamilcars towed by ten squadrons of No. 38 Group and four squadrons of No. 46 Group.

In spite of the imprecise dating of Captain Malandine's photography, his shots provide us with some evocative images, even if some of them are staged. ***Left:*** **The awkward stance struck by Lieutenant Bob Midwood as he briefs the pathfinders of the 22nd Independent Parachute Company is typical of a posed 'Fleet Street' picture.** ***Right:*** **Now kitted up, Bob Midwood, right, synchronises watches with Lieutenants Bobby La Tour, Don Wells and John Vischer.**

Immediately following this, on the northern area just above Ranville, I was to bring in gliders my fighting divisional headquarters, artillery headquarters, anti-tank guns and signals. This would use up all the aircraft available for the first wave.

The next problem was the timing of the fly-in of the second wave. Aircraft had to get back; be gone over for damage by flak; and pilots would have to be re-briefed. It was impossible to say accurately what losses there would be and quite impossible to know which aircraft would either return or not return, or which would be unserviceable. It was, therefore, reckoned that it would be unwise to plan on the arrival of the 6th Airlanding Brigade, and the remainder of the guns, etc., before the afternoon of D-Day.

The first to take off were the coup de main and the Independent Parachute Company. All the men had their faces blackened so that they should not show up in the dark. This advance guard left us with our heartfelt prayers and our blessings. The invasion had begun.

Thumbs up! Another staged press picture, this time of the 6th Airlanding Brigade packed together somewhat unnaturally in a Horsa passenger door.

In this pair of pictures, obviously taken several hours apart, the 'star' in both is Albemarle V1740 of No. 295 Squadron. This aircraft was actually the very first pathfinder plane to take off from Harwell at 2303 hours, piloted by Squadron Leader Merrick and with Air Vice-Marshal Leslie N. Hollinghurst and ten paratroops of the 22nd Independent Company on board. It is also a good illustration of the hastily applied one-foot-wide white bands which were added to wings and fuselages for easy identification of Allied aircraft. Paint and brushes were issued after the camps were sealed, and all RAF and USAAF station personnel had to apply the stripes to more than 10,000 aircraft. (This particular Albemarle survived the war only to be broken up in December 1945 at No. 83 Maintenance Unit at RAF Woolsington — now Newcastle Airport.)

Just before 2 a.m., General Gale embarked in Horsa (Chalk No. 70), his parting gift from the Harwell station CO, Group Captain W. E. Surplice: a tin of syrup for his first breakfast in France.

That night, the moon shone. The sky was clear as one by one the great aircraft, boosting up their engines, roared down the runways. Next to go were the two parachute brigades and the engineers accompanying them. Then our turn came. My glider number was 70. I was accompanied by Tom Haughton, my ADC; David Baird, my GSO2(Ops); my personal escort; my signaller and my driver; and Rifleman Grey, Tom's batman. Also in the glider were my Jeep with wireless set and two motor cycles. There were 12 of us in all. Before us lay an hour-and-a-half's flight. We were to land just north of Ranville in the area captured by Nigel Poett and his brigade. We hoped that the sappers would have cleared away sufficient of the stakes to give us a reasonably safe landing zone.

The morning of Monday 5 June passed quietly. Very few people as yet knew that this was now definitely D–1. But at lunchtime, the whispered word ran round among the operational officers, 'Final briefing at five o'clock!'

There were three briefings, each taking an hour, for three separate but co-ordinated operations, and I listened to them all with rapt intent.

The Station Commander, Group Captain Surplice, opened the proceedings in each case by reading orders of the day from the Supreme Commander, General Eisenhower, and the Commander-in-Chief, Air Marshal Sir Trafford Leigh-Mallory. Then, having explained the general layout of the seaborne assault, he asked General Gale to describe the part that his division was to play.

The briefing over, we returned to the mess. After dinner, a few of us gathered round a very special bottle of wine that I had brought down for the occasion and together we drank to the success of this great venture.

It was now ten o'clock and Group Captain Surplice had very kindly suggested that, if I accompanied him, I would see the take-off to the best advantage. First, we made the complete tour of the airfield in his car; everything was in order; there was no necessity for any flap or a single last-minute instruction. Then, we went to the watch tower, to within a few yards of which each aircraft would taxi up before receiving the signal to go.

Midnight came, but somehow we did not think of it as the beginning of the long-awaited D-Day. That had already started hours ago for us. A number of us rendezvoused at General Gale's glider. There was no awkwardness in that last three-quarters of an hour. The General had just returned from a last visit to his men before they left their camp. He had drunk good English beer with them, and they were still cheering him as they came on to the airfield.

I had noticed that chalked on the side of the glider was the name of an English king — Richard the First. That meant, I knew, simply that Richard Gale was to be the first British General to land in France for many hours, but the unintended parallel with the Great Crusader struck me most forcibly.

The last scene before the General emplaned was one of those simple, kindly jests in which the British delight. A few mornings before, the General had exclaimed with joy on finding that there was golden syrup for breakfast: 'By Jove, I love golden syrup, and I haven't seen any for years!' Upon which he proceeded to tuck heartily into it. So now, our smiling Group Captain, who had been his official host, formally presented him with a tin to take with him to France. I contributed a pound of airtight, tinned Charbonnel & Walker chocolates.

DENNIS WHEATLEY, 1980

From Salisbury Plain to Ranville bridge. Other than these few straggly bushes, nothing remains to mark the LZ at Holmes Clump where Staff Sergeant Roy Howard *(right)* and the other coup de main pilots practised their pinpoint landings. Netheravon airfield can be seen in the background. Picture taken looking west.

On April 21, 1944, my second pilot, Staff Sergeant Fred Baacke, and I were told to start some special training. Apart from gathering that it had something to do with D-Day, we did not otherwise have the slightest idea at that stage of what we were ultimately to be required to do.

The training started in daylight with a 6,000-foot tow from Brize Norton to Netheravon where a very small area had been marked out with white tape. 'Now we want you to get in there', we were told. This went quite well and we repeated it several times until it was decided that our Albemarle tugs did not have sufficient power for the 6,000-foot climb with a full load and we were transferred to Tarrant Rushton and to Halifax II tugs.

For the next phase, a formation of trees close to the east side of Netheravon airfield had been selected and two small fields, side by side, were created. Each day, the six chosen glider crews, three from B Squadron and three from E Squadron, were towed from Tarrant on the same height and course and pull-off point to simulate the operation's requirements, of which we still knew nothing. Three gliders would land in each of these two very small fields. RAF ground crews were there each day to somehow get the Horsas back onto the airfield and service them, which meant that we could only do one landing each day.

The operation required that the three gliders which were to attack the river bridge had to shed their 6,000 feet as quickly as possible, whereas the three gliders attacking the canal bridge were to carry out a longer and more orthodox approach. Our three gliders had only about half the distance to fly although from the same height of 6,000 feet and, in order to lose so much unwanted height in sufficient time, we would have to apply full flap as soon as we released. This would make navigation extremely difficult, but it had been decided by those formulating this brilliant and audacious plan that the height was necessary to deceive the Germans into thinking that it was a bombing raid. As soon as we cast off, the Halifax tugs were to continue straight on to drop bombs on Caen.

By this time, we were training at night. We had a few lights on the ground but, as our landings became more precise, these were eventually removed and we were told to do spot-on landings in these small fields with no lights or aids of any kind. At first, I thought that it could not be done but, after one or two hairy missions, we found that it could.

On May 28, we met our 'load' of Major John Howard and his Oxfordshire and Buckinghamshire Light Infantry and, in my case, Lieutenant Dennis Fox and his men. There followed the most intensive briefing on the military side of the operation, greatly aided by an elaborate sand-table. This showed every detail of the terrain with all the trees and of course the river and canal with its bridges, but we did not know where it actually was until about two days before D-Day.

At 9 p.m. on June 5, we assembled on the runway and loaded our troops under Lieutenant Fox. As No. 6 glider, Fred and I were last off and we staggered into the air with a very heavy load at approximately 10.55 p.m. (Double BST). Later, I was to suspect that every man probably took a few more grenades here, and extra rounds of ammunition there, because the weight proved to be greater than we had allowed.

We crossed the coast near Worthing and set a direct course for Normandy. About three miles from the French coast, the tug navigator gave us a compass check and told us we were on course. Because of the very steep descent angle of a Horsa with full flap (about 45 degrees), our standard P4 compass would have become inoperative, so it was supplemented with a gyro direction indicator. What we were required to do had never been done before, nor to the best of my knowledge was ever required again in the subsequent airborne landings of Arnhem and the Rhine, namely to navigate various courses on a 45-degree angle of descent, dropping at the rate of 2,000 feet per minute in the dark and without aids of any kind.

'Good luck. Cast off when you like', came the tug navigator's message through the wire in our tow-rope. Whether I liked it or not was at this stage academic. The culmination of all my training, and indeed of the short 21 years of my life had reached a point of no return and I cast off immediately.

I reduced speed and applied full flap but, to my horror, I found that I could not get the speed below 90 mph even with the stick fully back. That extra weight was going to ruin all our calculations. I turned my head to the right towards the door between the cockpit and my load and shouted: 'Mr Fox, Sir! Two men from the front to the back — quickly!' This manoeuvre corrected our trim and the Horsa was under proper control again.

As well as the gyro-compass, Fred had been supplied with a special light strapped to his hand so as not to spoil my night vision which in the next few precious minutes was going to be so vital for all of us. So far we had seen nothing, not even the coastline over which we had released. Suddenly, bright as day, we were illuminated by a German parachute flare. Thankfully, we entered a cloud and when we emerged all was dark again.

But we were falling like a brick and steering a course at the same time of 212 degrees, to be held for 90 seconds as Fred checked the map and his stop-watch. This covered the first two miles and we turned again onto 268 degrees which we held for 2 minutes 30 seconds covering a further 3.3 miles. Still not seeing anything of the ground but continuing our half-way-to-the-vertical dive with only the hiss of the slipstream to be heard among all the now silent men, we turned on our third course of 212 degrees for the final run in.

Six Horsa gliders (Chalk Nos. 91–96) carrying six platoons of D Company of the Ox & Bucks, with a detachment of sappers from No. 2 Platoon of No. 249 Field Company, Royal Engineers, towed by Halifaxes from Nos. 298 and 644 Squadrons, lifted off from Tarrant Rushton airfield in Dorset at one-minute intervals beginning at 2256 hours. Just over 75 minutes later, the gliders cast off for touchdown around 0020 — the spearhead of the entire Allied air armada. Staff Sergeant Roy Howard brought his glider (Chalk 96) to rest on LZ 'Y' within yards of the bridge over the River Orne, enabling No. 6 Platoon, commanded by Lieutenant Dennis Fox, to quickly secure the bridge.

We were now at 1,200 feet and there below us the canal and river lay like silver, instantly recognisable. Orchards and woods lay as darker patches on a dark and foreign soil. 'It's alright now Fred. I can see where we are', I said. I thought that it all looked so exactly like the sand-table that I had the strange feeling that I had been there before.

I took off the flaps for a moment to slow our headlong descent and to ensure we had sufficient height. I put them back on as we shot towards the line of trees over which I just had to scrape. We then deployed the parachute brake specially fitted to the rear of the glider in order to shorten our landing run to the minimum to avoid overshoot and being crushed as we hit the embankment which I knew lay at the end of our field. Up with the nose and there came the heavy rumble of the main wheels as we touched down a few minutes after midnight close to the river bridge. 'You are in the right place, Sir', I shouted to Lieutenant Fox who seemed both happy and surprised at the same time as, with a drumming and crash of army boots along the floor of the glider, he and his men disappeared into the night to shoot up the Germans guarding the bridge.

It was up to Fred and me to unload the rest of the stores but now we received a shock as we climbed out through the door of the glider into the field. Where were the other gliders? We had been No. 6 and should have been the third to land in our field. Yet, apart from a herd of cows which had panicked in front of us as we landed, we were quite alone. Alone in front of the whole invasion force which was not to land on the beaches six miles away until daybreak, and ahead of the main parachute drop by half an hour.

It was only much later that we learned that No. 5 had undershot by some 400 yards, whilst No. 4, due to its tug navigator's error, was ten miles away with its load busy capturing a bridge on the wrong river. However, realising the error, they were later able to orientate themselves and fight their way through the night to liaise at our bridge — an astonishing feat of skill and determination in itself.

STAFF SERGEANT ROY HOWARD, 1994

Of the other two gliders destined for this bridge, Chalk 95 landed 400 yards away in the field to the north of the LZ, and Chalk 94 seven miles to the east, having been cast off incorrectly over the River Dives.

Back in April, as part of Exercise 'Mush', the main 6th Airborne rehearsal, the bridge assault was carried out at Lechlade in Gloucestershire, where the A417 crosses the River Thames via St John's Bridge *(right)*. All six platoons took part, including the sappers, in the night attack against the bridge, which was 'guarded' by Polish troops. In the mêlée which followed, the umpires declared that one platoon had misidentified another in the darkness, and that the bridge had been blown in their faces. However, the Poles refused to give up and continued fighting. Although the exercise showed up weaknesses, it also proved the viability of the mission: that if the gliders landed close to the target, it had every chance of success.

Much more practice was necessary, preferably against a target which closely resembled the two bridges to be captured in Normandy, and Major John Howard, the commander of D Company, needed to find a similar location in Britain where two bridges on the same road crossed a canal and river in quick succession. An almost perfect match was found on the southern outskirts of Exeter where the A38 bypass crossed first the River Exe via the Countess Wear Bridge and then passed over the Exeter Canal on a swing bridge. Howard immediately took the area over and moved his men to Devon. For a week, they practised assaulting the two bridges by day and by night, explosions and gun-fire keeping residents awake as every possible scenario was enacted. Howard wanted his men to be ready for any eventuality: gliders landing in the wrong place; only one landing; an assault crossing of the canal in canvas boats; possible diversions, etc. Almost more important than the capture of the canal bridge was to put the pillbox at its eastern end out of action, for it was there that the key was located to the demolition charges — information which had been relayed to Britain via the Resistance from the nearby café owner, Georges Gondrée. (The bascule bridge immediately behind the swing bridge is a post-war addition.)

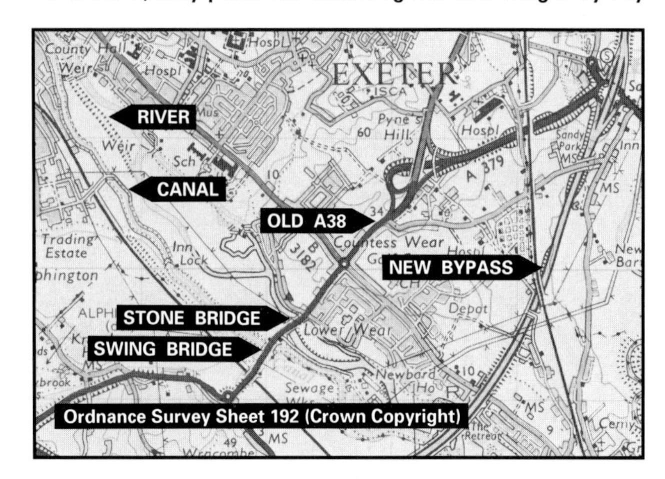

In July 1994, a plaque was mounted alongside the bridges to record the important part they played in the operation.

Landing Zone 'X' lay on the eastern bank of the river just south of Bénouville Bridge. A pond at the northern end of the LZ, clearly visible in this post-war aerial, was a hazard, and on May 30 evidence showed up in reconnaissance photographs that holes were being dug for the erection of posts to prevent glider landings.

Just after midnight, the six gliders carrying the coup de main party of one company of the 52nd Foot (Ox & Bucks Light Infantry) , under the command of Major R. J. Howard, were released and five of them came in to land at their appointed places near the bridges. The leading glider for the canal bridge, piloted by Staff Sergeant J. H. Wallwork, Glider Pilot Regiment, and carrying Major Howard, came in with perfect accuracy and pulled up only 20 yards from the bridge itself with its nose well into the wire of the defences. The other two gliders for this bridge were only a few feet away. The night at this hour was fine and, although the moon was overcast, visibility was between and 30 and 40 yards.

Lieutenant H. D. Brotheridge's platoon were in the first glider. They worked their way to the road at the east end of bridge, then, led by Brotheridge, assaulted across it to the far bank. The few minutes needed to get on to the road were sufficient to rouse the defences across the river and the charge was met by machine gun fire. There was no hesitation however and, although Brotheridge was unfortunately killed, the enemy defences were rapidly overcome.

The second platoon, commanded by Lieutenant D. J. Wood, were out almost simultaneously. They made for the defences on the east bank. The suddenness of the attack took the Germans

Three men from the first glider (Chalk 91), piloted by Staff Sergeant Jim Wallwork, carrying No. 1 Platoon under Lieutenant Herbert 'Den' Brotheridge, were detailed to rush the pillbox and put it out of action with grenades. Meanwhile, the remainder of the platoon, led by Brotheridge, was to dash across the bridge. Lieutenant David Wood's platoon in the second glider (Chalk 92), flown by Staff Sergeant Oliver Boland, was to attack the trenches, machine gun and the anti-tank gun along the eastern bank, while No. 3 Platoon under Lieutenant 'Sandy' Smith in the third glider (Chalk 93), piloted by Staff Sergeant Geoffrey Barkway, was to reinforce the bridge party. However, every platoon was trained to cover the duties of any of the others.

Leigh-Mallory called the landing the finest feat of airmanship in the entire war, and Sergeant Jimmy Christie's picture, taken on June 7, says it all. Remains of the gliders could still be seen in July 1946 but local people cleared away what remained, salvaging any useful items like the seats. Thirty years later, in June 1977, in order to perpetuate the memory, General Gale unveiled three markers indicating the position occupied by the cockpit of each glider.

completely by surprise. Wood's men were soon over the wire and, using grenades and Sten guns, had cleared the pillbox and trenches. A few Germans escaped and were seen running off in a northerly direction.

The third platoon, under Lieutenant R. A. A. Smith, crossed the bridge some five minutes after Brotheridge and reinforced the position on the far bank.

The two platoons which had landed near the river bridge met little opposition and soon secured their objective.

Meanwhile, the sappers had been examining both bridges for demolition charges. It was found that, although the bridges had been prepared for demolition, the charges had not been placed. We later found out that these charges were kept in a house near the canal

Following the penchant of the military for giving bridges names, the canal bridge was officially Euston 1 and the river bridge Euston 2. However, within days of its capture, the lifting bridge had been renamed after the winged horse insignia of British airborne forces, and it was to Pegasus Bridge that a film crew came in August 1961 to re-create the action *(left)* for the epic *The Longest Day*. *Right:* L–R: Darryl F. Zanuck, producer; Peter Lawford who portrayed Lord Lovat, commander of the 1st Special Service Brigade; Irina Demich, actress; the real Lord Lovat; Richard Todd, actor and 6th Airborne veteran (see *After the Battle* No. 5) who played Major Howard; and, right, John Howard himself, one of the film's military consultants.

From the 1940s to the 1990s, this was a scene little changed. Pegasus Bridge became a shrine for returning veterans and battlefield pilgrims, the only concession to 'progress' being the replacement of the roadway decking with steel mesh.

Above: **Sergeant Christie of the Army Film and Photographic Unit (AFPU) went in with the 6th Airborne and he took both these pictures on June 7; possibly he stood on the ladder being used by the signals engineer in the foreground to take the picture at the top of the page.** *Below:* **Robert Voskuil photographed the scene 50 years later as the crowds prepare for the return of the Red Berets on June 6, 1994 . . . but something seems wrong.**

bridge. We had, it would seem, over-estimated the German preparedness here.

Howard's small force then consolidated their position, forming a compact bridgehead west of the canal bridge and east of the river bridge. Here, they waited for the arrival of the 7th Parachute Battalion who were to relieve them and enlarge the bridgehead to the west.

Meanwhile, as the glider landings took place, the pathfinder aircraft carrying the Independent Parachute Company with an advance group of parachutists from the 5th Parachute Brigade dropped their 'sticks' north of Ranville. Poett's aircraft, piloted by Wing Commander McMonnien, came in with perfect accuracy. The two 'sticks' of the Independent Parachute Company were landed just to the east and, with little time available, were forced to put out their navigational signals and apparatus where they were. This inaccuracy resulted in the main body also being dropped more to the east than had been intended, but this had no serious results. The four 'sticks' of the 7th and 13th Parachute Battalions, to whom had been allotted the task of protecting the dropping and landing zones, although

Shortly before the anniversary in June 1990, the authorities in Caen announced plans to replace the old bridge, which dated from the 1930s, with a modern wider structure to cater for the increased weight of commercial traffic heading for the port at Ouistreham. The news was received with dismay by the many thousands for whom Pegasus Bridge symbolised the very essence of the bravery and sacrifice of D-Day — much like the Menin Gate in Belgium did for an earlier generation. Nevertheless, in spite of furious protests on both sides of the Channel, the bridge was dismantled in November 1993, the replacement being erected in April 1994. To all those who cared, the timing, just weeks before the 50th anniversary of its capture, added insult to injury. As far as the designer of the new structure was concerned, he could not understand what all the fuss was about: after all, he said, the new bridge was exactly the same as the old one, just a little wider and longer!

A further loss was the 3.7cm anti-tank gun in its Tobruk gun pit on the river bank at the south-eastern corner of the bridge. ***Left:*** **This is how it appeared soon after the war with the Café Gondrée, also now known as the Pegasus Café, on the opposite side of the canal.** ***Right:*** **Taken 25 years later, the scene virtually unchanged, the gun a magnet for all boys — big and small — visiting the bridge.**

dropped correctly, were very scattered and took a long time to rally.

Members of these early 'sticks' obtained a unique impression of the coup de main party's assault. The gliders were still coming in as the men of the Independent Parachute Company jumped. Anti-aircraft shells and tracer bullets were pouring into the sky, and soon illuminating flares and machine gun fire showed that the German defences were rapidly awakening. For a few minutes after the first glider touched down, the fire was quite intense. Then, almost as rapidly, it died down.

Almost immediately, the success signal was sounded by Howard on his whistle. This was a most stirring sound to Nigel Poett and his advanced headquarters party, who jumped in the leading aircraft with the Independent Parachute Company. With their spirits high, they rushed to the bridges.

Half an hour after the first landings north of Ranville, the main body of parachutists of the 5th Brigade arrived, the roar of a 131 aircraft soon deadened other sounds. In spite of the guiding signals being slightly too far to the east, the drop was made with good accuracy. It was found, not unnaturally, that in general the 'sticks' covered more ground than had been usual in training. This was mainly due to the difficulty that the heavily-laden men experienced in managing their bags, in which they carried their equipment, in aircraft which were taking evasive action. These long 'sticks' resulted in a very wide dispersion on the dropping area and consequent delay in the concentration of the battalions. The total casualties in this brigade drop amounted to 16 killed and 82 wounded, while the number missing in the brigade after rallying was completed was 432.

While the rallying of the main body of Poett's troops was in progress, enemy patrols had begun to probe at the bridgehead held by Howard's small force. No serious attack took place, but the patrols increased in strength and a few tracked vehicles appeared. It seemed to the defenders that something more serious was brewing up. It was, therefore, with considerable relief that those on the bridges saw the leading elements of the 7th Parachute Battalion approach.

The vital pillbox on the far side of the road, from where the demolition charges were controlled, and which Major Howard took over as his command post, also still remained to be seen at the base of the house on the right which had been built over the top of it.

Twenty-five years on, the river bank on the eastern side is cut back. By the time this picture was taken in November 1993, the concrete gun emplacement had completely disappeared, the house having already been demolished some time earlier.

Another shock in the run up to the 50th anniversary was the news in March 1994 that the Café Gondrée had been closed by order of the French authorities. Known before the war as the Buvette du Tramway, the café was the first building in France to be liberated, and Georges Gondrée dug up 99 bottles of champagne he had buried in his garden to hide them from the Germans to celebrate. Thereafter, the café became a home from home for thousands of ex-Servicemen, M. Gondrée continuing to offer them free champagne, a tradition continued by his wife, Terese, after his death in 1969. She is seen *above* in 1944 holding her four-year-old daughter, Arlette, and *right* with General Gale in 1969.

Lieutenant-Colonel Geoffrey Pine-Coffin, commanding the 7th Parachute Battalion, realised the importance of coming quickly to the assistance of the coup de main party. He therefore left his rendezvous for the bridges without waiting for the complete concentration of his battalion. At this time, the containers carrying his heavy weapons had not been found and his wireless was also missing. The battalion passed through Howard's force and succeeded in securing their objectives on the west bank which included Le Port and Bénouville where they established their outposts.

Over the years, the bar became festooned with memorabilia given to the Gondrée family, the Pegasus Bridge Café retaining a special place in the hearts of veterans and visitors alike. However, when Terese died shortly after the 40th anniversary, things began to go horribly wrong. Ownership had devolved to her three daughters, Arlette and Georgette, who were sheltering in the cellar with their parents on the night of June 5/6, and their younger sister, Françoise, born later in 1944. A museum had been established in the café garden in 1974, but after their mother's death, the sisters fell out as to how the business should be run. Arlette and Georgette wanted to carry on as before but Françoise disagreed. The resulting squabble turned nasty and in 1989 a court forced a sale under French inheritance law. Meanwhile, the lease had run out and the café was closed down by the local maritime authority who owned the land. The café was put up for auction in September but the matter was not resolved until December when Arlette made her final successful bid of £160,000, the money being raised partly with the help of donations from the Normandy Veterans' Association and two British newspapers. The café reopened in 1989, only to fall foul of a further dispute with the local authority operating the museum. Pressure was then brought to bear on Arlette to sell the land on which the museum stood, non-renewal of her lease leading to enforced closures of the café in 1993 and 1994.

June 6, 1994. Arlette puts a brave face on her tribulations as the Café Gondrée soldiers on.

Above: **This picture is said to show the glider in which General Gale landed at about 0330 hours although it does not bear the distinctive '70' seen in the pictures on page 223. Sergeant Christie had gone back to LZ 'N' on June 15 — possibly the chalk had washed off by then although marks** *(below)* **were still visible in some of the other pictures he took that day.**

In the glider, we all wore Mae Wests, and, taking our places, we all fastened ourselves in and waited for the jerk as the tug took the strain on the tow-rope. Soon it came and we could feel ourselves hurtling down the smooth tarmac. Then we were airborne and once again we heard the familiar whistle as the air rushed by and we glided higher and higher into the dark night.

I suppose all men have different reactions on these occasions. I went to sleep and slept soundly for the best part of an hour. I was woken up by a considerable bumping. We had run into a small local storm in the Channel. Major Billy Griffiths, the pilot, was having a ticklish time and the glider was all over the place.

Between glider and tug there is an intercommunication line, so that the two pilots can talk to one another. In this bumping we received, the intercommunication line broke; the problem of cast-off would have to be solved by judgement. Griffiths merely said, 'The intercom has bust'.

It was only a few minutes after that that he said, 'We will be crossing the French coast shortly'. We were flying at about 5,000 feet and we soon knew the coast was under us, for we were met by a stream of flak. It was weird to see this roaring up in great golden chains past the windows of the glider, some of it being apparently between us and the tug aircraft. Looking out, I could see the canal and the river through the clouds, for the moon was by now fairly well overcast and the clear crisp moonlight we had hoped for was not there. Nevertheless here we were.

In a few moments, Griffiths said, 'We are over the landing zone now and will be cast off at any moment'. Almost as soon as he had said this, we were. The whistling sound and the roar of the engines suddenly died down: no longer were we bumping about, but gliding along on a gloriously steady course.

Round we turned, circling lower and lower; soon the pilot turned round to tell us to link up as we were just about to land. We all linked up by putting our arms round the man next to us. We were also, as I have said, strapped in. In case of a crash, this procedure would help us to take the shock.

I shall never forget the sound as we rushed down in our final steep dive, then we suddenly flattened out, and soon with a bump, bump, bump, we landed on an extremely rough stubble field. Over the field we sped and then with a bang we hit a low embankment. The forward undercarriage wheel stove up through the floor, the glider spun round on its nose in a small circle and, as one wing hit one of those infernal stakes, we drew up to a standstill. We opened the door. Outside all was quiet. About us now the other gliders were coming in, crashing and screeching as they applied their brakes. It was a glorious moment.

In the distance from the direction of the bridges, we could now hear bursts of machine gun fire. Except for the arrival of more and more gliders, all around us seemed to be still. It was eerie. Had Ranville been cleared of the enemy? Were the bridges taken, were they intact and safely in our hands? How was Terence Otway and his gallant battalion faring at the Merville battery? We could still hear intermittent fire from the direction of the bridges.

Whilst they were attempting to unload the glider, the passing moments seemed like hours. It was still dark and this unloading was proving to be more difficult than we had anticipated. The crash we had had, though not serious, resulted in the nose being really well dug into the ground and the problem of getting the Jeep out was defeating us. Eventually, we had to give it up: and so on foot we set out for Ranville.

MAJOR-GENERAL RICHARD GALE, 1948

The northern end of LZ 'N' looking east from the Orne river. The landing zone ended at the line of the road running towards the camera from Amfréville. Of the 89 gliders (excluding the six coup de main and three Merville assault gliders) which landed the first night, 52 put down on the correct LZ; 20 were further away, and 17 were missing. Of the latter, three landed in the UK and one came down in the sea but the personnel of all four were able to rejoin later. The area outlined on the right is depicted in the low-level oblique. These pictures were taken after the second wave of 250-odd gliders had landed on the evening of D-Day and, although it does not look like it, there were four separate strips prepared by 591st Parachute Squadron: A1 next and parallel to the road, with B2 beyond, both 1,000 yards by 60 yards, with C3 and D4 beyond.

While these events had been taking place, the 13th Battalion and the 591st Parachute Squadron, RE, on the other side of the river, had made good progress in the tasks assigned them. The covering parties to protect the preparation of the glider landing strips were established by a company under Major J. F. Cramphorn, and the obstructing poles were cut with explosives by the sappers and removed by men of Cramphorn's company. The strips were soon ready to receive the gliders of Advanced Divisional Headquarters.

Above: **Sergeant George Laws, a cine cameraman who landed with No. 4 Commando (see pages 540-560) took this still picture. LZ 'N' later became a battleground when German forces counter-attacked on June 10, the gliders themselves being used as cover for the advance against Le Mariquet.**

Lieutenant-Colonel P. J. Luard, commanding the 13th Parachute Battalion, himself supervised the mopping up of Ranville. According to the French, the normal enemy garrison of the village had been approximately one company from the 21. Panzer-Division, chiefly billeted round the château. During the night, the bulk of this company were away from their billets, but a number of defensive posts on the north side of the town, overlooking the dropping zone were held, and miscellaneous parties of the enemy were in various houses in the village. The area was finally mopped up by about 4 a.m. at little or no cost.

The 12th Parachute Battalion had a greater distance to cover than the other battalions and by 2.30 a.m. barely 50 per cent of the men had reported. Their OC, Lieutenant-Colonel A. P. Johnson, however, decided to move off without further delay to the south of Ranville. His move was made without enemy interference and the battalion was in position by 4 a.m., covering the southern approaches to the village.

Above: **This Horsa has been pulled up short by the wall which runs parallel to the D514 between Ranville and Sallenelles.** *Below:* **The glider was actually 50 yards from the road at a place called La Haute Ecarde on the western end of LZ 'N'. In the background, Lord Lovat's 1st Special Service Brigade HQ.**

Below: **Today the line of trees has gone, this view being taken by Robert Voskuil looking south-east across the deserted LZ on the morning of June 6, 1994.**

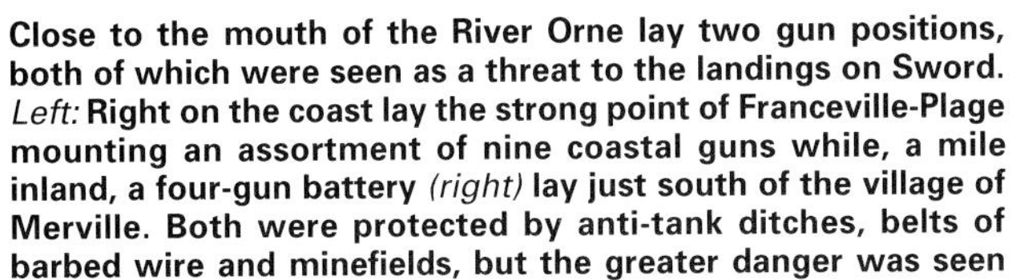

Close to the mouth of the River Orne lay two gun positions, both of which were seen as a threat to the landings on Sword. *Left:* Right on the coast lay the strong point of Franceville-Plage mounting an assortment of nine coastal guns while, a mile inland, a four-gun battery *(right)* lay just south of the village of Merville. Both were protected by anti-tank ditches, belts of barbed wire and minefields, but the greater danger was seen to be the latter battery, whose guns were believed to be of 5.7-inch calibre which could easily dominate the eastern British beach. Although it had been allocated as a naval target in the Joint Fire Plan (see pages 112-113), it was preferable that it be captured and put out of action before the seaborne landings began — a tough task which would have to be completed in just 4½ hours.

The casemates of both batteries survive today although no trace of the anti-tank ditches shows up from the air.

Rommel paid a brief visit to Merville on March 6 where he was shown round by the battery commander, Hauptmann Karl-Heinrich Wolter (left, wearing helmet), of Artillerie-Regiment 1716, at which time casemates Nos. 3 and 4 were still under construction. The actual armament consisted of four Czechoslovakian 10cm 14/19 field howitzers on wheels, made by Skoda, a far cry from the 6-inch fixed coastal guns anticipated by Allied intelligence. With them in the picture is General der Artillerie Erich Marcks (behind Rommel's left shoulder) whom we last saw on page 56. On the night of May 19/20, an attack on the battery was carried out by 63 aircraft of Bomber Command and, although the night was hazy, a direct hit on the Mairie (in the centre of the photo), used as the officers' mess, killed 18 including Major Wolter and his French girl friend.

By now, the great seaborne assault on the beaches had begun. We had heard the shattering air attack on Ouistreham and the roar of the rockets which preceded the direct assault. We had not heard any firing from the direction of the battery at Merville. I tried not to be anxious about Lieutenant-Colonel Terence Otway and his 9th Parachute Battalion; but it was not easy. I knew the proposition he was up against and I knew his determination. All I could really rely upon was this characteristic and the element of surprise. Little did I guess of the extent of his difficulties. We had so far had no contact with James Hill and his 3rd Brigade on the ridge. By 7 a.m., most of my headquarters had assembled, but Bobby Bray, my GSO1, had not shown up, neither had any in his glider. I left my headquarters in David Baird's capable charge and went off to see how things were on the bridges and how Pine-Coffin was faring on the west bank of the Orne.

Poett picked me up on the way and also Hugh Kindersley. The latter had come in with us ahead of his brigade, which was not due in until the evening, in order that he should be thoroughly in the picture by the time his troops arrived. All was well when we got to the bridges, but the signs of the hand-to-hand fighting that had taken place there earlier in the morning were apparent. On the road was an upturned German staff car which I subsequently heard had run into the fighting. On the far side, I could see the smashed-up gliders, right up against the wire near the bridge. They looked an awful mess and yet only one person out of over 70 soldiers of the 52nd Foot who flew in on that hazardous task was killed as a direct result of these crash-landings. On the rising ground beyond the canal bridge at Bénouville, there was a lot of machine gun, mortar and odd rifle fire going on.

Four days later, General Marcks returned to inspect the damage with the new battery commander, Leutnant Steiner. The party is walking on the access road to the battery; this house, although badly damaged in the bombing, still survives.

The actual casemates were unscathed, although a near miss on the corner of casemate No. 1 ***(above)*** **fractured the edge of the roof on this corner.**

The concrete is still cracked today, letting in water which proved a problem when this casemate was converted into a museum 40 years later.

Things were in fact getting sticky. The Germans put in a sharp counter-attack which Pine-Coffin's men dealt with. It was a nasty moment, however, because his battalion was sadly under strength.

Whilst the fighting in the vicinity of Bénouville was in progress, there occurred one of those unreal silly things that happen. Down the canal came two German naval coastal craft of the trawler type. Blissfully ignorant of what had happened inland, they were setting out for the naval basin at Caen to escape from the hot-bed at Ouistreham. The troops let them get really close up and then opened fire. When it was too late, the Germans saw the trap they had fallen into and tried to turn round. This was fatal. They ran aground and were captured virtually without a fight.

To the 9th Battalion had fallen the most dangerous mission of all, the destruction of the coastal battery near Merville. The battalion was under the command of Lieutenant-Colonel T. B. H. Otway, Royal Ulster Rifles. Otway received his orders on April 2 and had therefore only two months to rehearse the operation for which he was allowed carte blanche. A spot in England at West Woodhay near Newbury, where conditions were very similar to those subsequently encountered in Normandy, was chosen. It was good agricultural land in full production, but Otway obtained the use of it in 48 hours, though to do so permission had to be obtained from no less than seven different ministries in Whitehall, a record which should surely stand to the credit of the Parachute Regiment. Here in a week the sappers built a scale model of the battery, its shape and dimensions being known to them from the air photographs available. Tubular scaffolding took the place of the guns. Not only was the actual objective itself reproduced, so also were the approaches to it. Four mechanical excavators and six large bulldozers, brought on tank transporters from as far away as Liverpool and Plymouth, worked night and day, 'the hours of darkness being illuminated by the headlights of vehicles'.

Rehearsals by day and night were frequent. Most were conducted with live ammunition, and continued until every one of the 35 officers and 600 other ranks composing the battalion knew exactly what his part was and how to play it. On May 31, the battalion was moved to Broadwell and briefed. The briefing lasted five days, and every man attending was required to submit to his immediate superior his own sketch, drawn from memory, of the position he was to occupy. In addition to the assault by the 9th Battalion, three gliders carrying volunteers from 9th Battalion and 591st Parachute Squadron, Royal Engineers, were to crash-land on the top of the battery, regarding which a large amount of information had been collected.

LIEUTENANT-COLONEL T. B. H. OTWAY
(as told to Lieutenant Hilary St George Saunders)

Below: **'Merville' in Berkshire. In April 1944, a spot some four miles south-east of Hungerford was sealed off for a battle training area. An exact replica of the gun position was constructed in a field south of Upper Green so that the troops involved could practise the assault on the battery. The excavations carried out to duplicate the German positions show up clearly in this aerial shot taken in September 1945** ***(below right).***

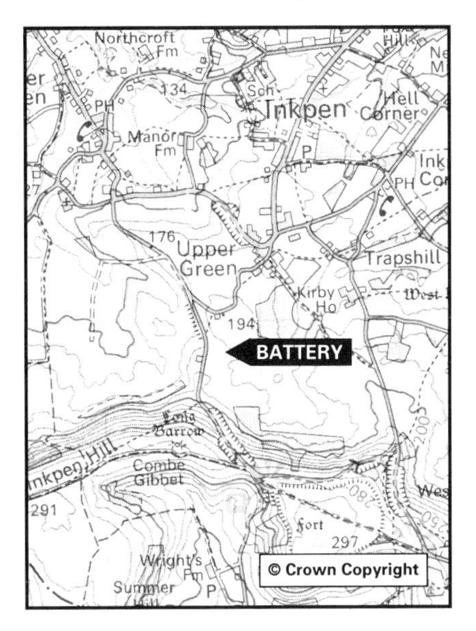

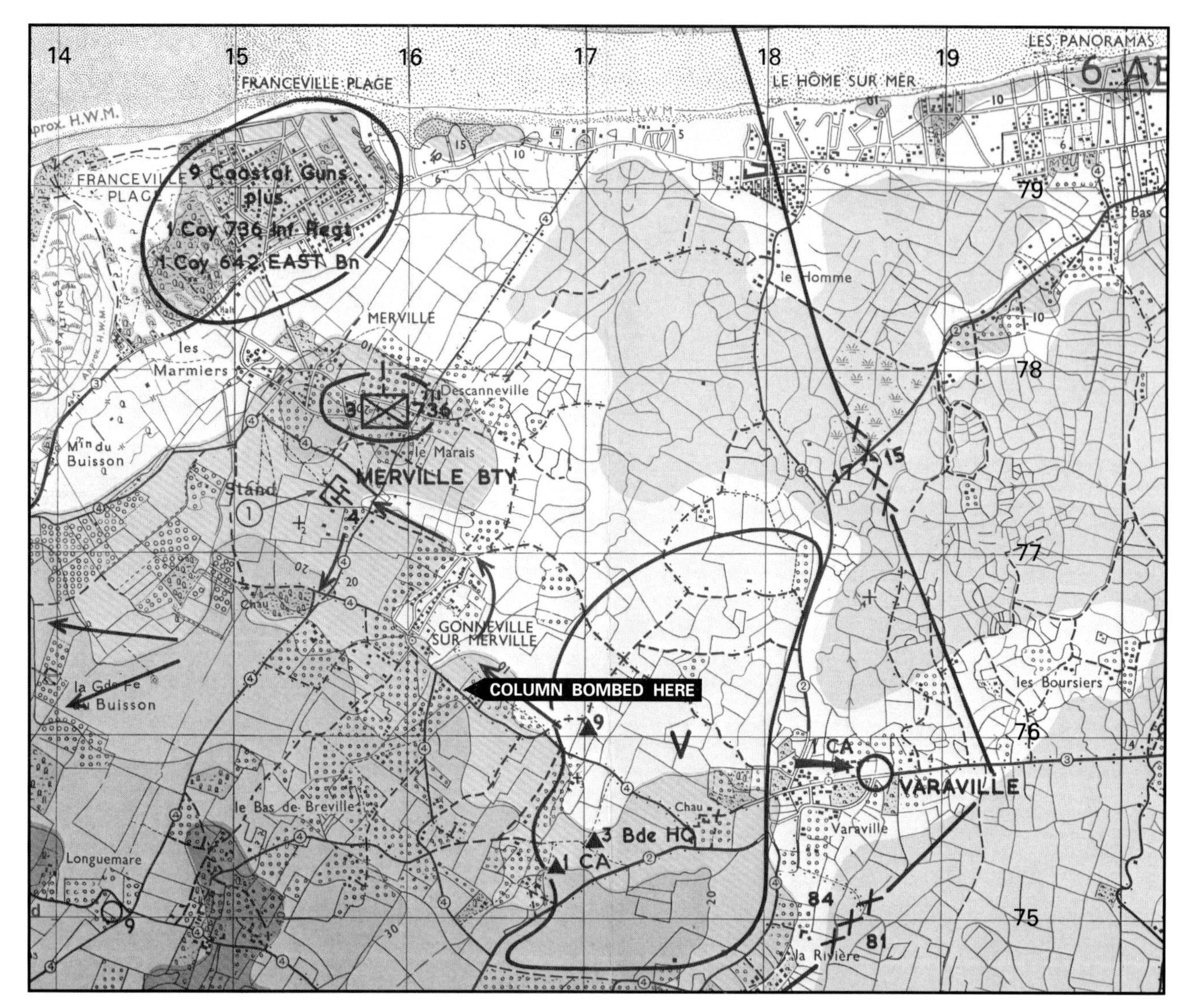

Whilst still in England, Brigadier James Hill, on whose shoulders the responsibility for neutralising the Merville battery had fallen, when addressing his officers the day before the operation, declared: 'Gentlemen, in spite of your excellent training and orders, do not be daunted if chaos reigns. It undoubtedly will.' It was a prophecy which would prove to be only too true. On paper, the plan looked straightforward: 700 men would drop on DZ 'V', form up, march to the battery just over two kilometres away, and attack it with a numerical superiority of over 3:1. The official 6th Airborne Division after action report tells a somewhat different tale: 'The Bn dropped at 0050 hrs over an enormous area. They moved off from the RV at 0250 hrs only 150 strong and having only 1 MG. No mortars, no special stores; no RE or Fd Amb personnel and no mine detectors. The gliderborne element had failed to arrive; and whilst on route to the bty posn it was ascertained that the preliminary hy bomber attack on the bty had completely missed its objective.'

On my return to my headquarters, I was beginning to receive reports of James Hill and the 3rd Parachute Brigade. Terence Otway and the 9th Battalion had done their task at the Merville battery. Their story is really an epic.

The battalion had dropped at approximately 1 a.m. but they were very scattered. Terence Otway knew the importance of time. So, just before 3 a.m., he decided he must move off to his task in spite of the fact that he only had three companies mustering about 50 men in each. His total battalion at that time was not much more than 150 strong. They had not got their special assault stores; they had no engineer or field ambulance personnel; they had no mine detectors; and the glider-borne element of their assault had not arrived.

Whilst on their advance to the battery position, they learned from their reconnaissance parties, which had gone on

The target pictured in the early 1970s in its 'natural' state before being opened as a museum. We are looking at the casemates from where the track from the west crossed the anti-tank ditch. Once Lieutenant-Colonel Otway had assembled his small but resolute force, they prepared to attack the battery from the rear, coming under fire from machine guns outside the perimeter. At this point, one of the three assault gliders that were to crash-land on top of the battery with 50 troopers of the 9th Battalion and eight sappers of the 591st Squadron, RE, arrived overhead having been hit by AA fire, coming down some 200 yards from Otway's position.

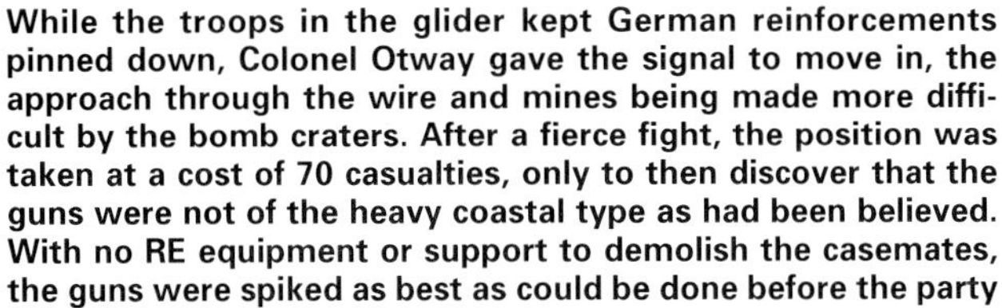

While the troops in the glider kept German reinforcements pinned down, Colonel Otway gave the signal to move in, the approach through the wire and mines being made more difficult by the bomb craters. After a fierce fight, the position was taken at a cost of 70 casualties, only to then discover that the guns were not of the heavy coastal type as had been believed. With no RE equipment or support to demolish the casemates, the guns were spiked as best as could be done before the party withdrew to move on to its second task, the seizure of the high ground near Le Plein. Later, the Germans reoccupied the battery which they then held until it was abandoned on August 17. *Left:* Some 38 years later, a detachment from 10 Field Squadron, RE, arrived to begin clearing casemate No. 1 of the accumulated rubbish to fulfil the plans of the Airborne Assault Normandy Trust to turn it into a museum *(right)* which was established on June 6, 1982.

As I oriented myself, it appeared that I had been dropped with my stick bang in the middle of the River Dives. However, what the Germans had done in anticipation was to flood the valley of the Dives. I had tea-bags sewn into the top of my battledress trousers, so while I was trying to get out of this lake I was just making cold tea! The way we got out was that we each had six-foot ropes with a wooden handle at each end for tying things up. As we met up with others, we linked up with these toggle ropes because if you went into a deep ditch and you weren't tied to someone, you drowned, and there were many drowned that night. After a four-hour struggle, we got out, more or less on the edge of our DZ. The Canadians reported that they had captured the DZ and the German command post so, as far as I could tell, all was going well. I realised I had to get back to my brigade headquarters as soon as I could, but I thought the vital thing was to find out what success the 9th Battalion had had with the battery. By now, I had collected 42 very wet stragglers, and we set off down a track. It was a very mixed party from different battalions, including two naval ratings and an Alsatian messenger dog. It was about twenty to seven in the morning, when all hell broke loose! Then suddenly I heard a noise and I shouted to the chaps to get down. Unfortunately, our little lane had high hedges on both sides and no ditches. I threw myself on top of Lieutenant Peters, and realised that we'd been caught in pattern bombing from low-flying aircraft, and it was horrible. When, thank God, they'd gone, I raised myself on my arms and looked around. This little lane was clouded with dust and dirt and stank of cordite and death. Then I saw a leg in the middle of the road. I knew I had been hit, but when I took another look I saw it had a brown boot on, and I knew it wasn't mine. The only chap in the brigade who got away with wearing brown boots was the mortar officer of the 9th Battalion, Lieutenant Peters, and I was lying right on top of him and he was dead. His leg had been severed from his body, yet I was alive. I had been saved because I had a towel and a spare pair of pants in the bottom of my jumping smock, but my water bottle had shattered and I had lost most of my left backside. From that column the only two people who could get on their feet were my brigade defence platoon commander and myself. I then had a problem as a commander. There I was surrounded by 30 or so dying or very badly wounded men. Should I stay with them or what? The answer was, of course, no. We were fighting a battle and we had to get on. We gave jabs to all of them with their own morphia. Then we collected the morphia from the dead and distributed it amongst the living. As we moved off, those men, who were all to die, gave us a cheer. That moment will stay with me forever.

BRIGADIER JAMES HILL, 1990

ahead, that the preliminary heavy bombing attack on the battery had apparently missed its objective. This bombing had, moreover, fallen uncomfortably near the reconnaissance party. The little party cut gaps in the outer wire fences and penetrated the German minefield. They lay down on the edge of the inner belt of wire observing the enemy posts and fixing exactly the German positions. They were there joined by the tape-laying parties, but only half of the latter arrived and their tapes were missing. They marked the approaches for the assault by digging heel marks in the ground. In spite of these handicaps, this weak, unsupported battalion penetrated the minefields and outer wire defences in the face of heavy fire and finally assaulted and overran the battery position, capturing 22 prisoners. At the close of this action, the battalion was only 80 strong.

Drop Zone 'V' was situated dangerously close to the valley of the River Dives which the Germans had flooded (see map page 215), and many men were drowned. And even then there were other dangers like that which befell Brigadier Hill on this stretch of road near Gonneville (see map *opposite* and also *After the Battle* No. 74).

The flooding on the eastern flank was a double-edged sword, for it also restricted German access to the bridgehead to four routes: the GC27 to Varaville; GC224 to Robehomme; a railway bridge at Bures; and the main N815 through Troarn (see map page 215). Plans were therefore made for all four routes to be cut to isolate the battlefield and prevent the enemy from bringing up reinforcements from the east. The 3rd Parachute Squadron, under Major J. C. A. 'Tim' Roseveare of the Royal Engineers, was tasked with the demolition of six bridges in all and the mining of two roads. No. 3 Troop, under command of the 1st Canadian Parachute Battalion, were to land on DZ 'V', explosive and other equipment being brought in by glider, and blow the masonry bridge at Varaville *(left)* and the girder bridge *(right)* and nearby culvert at Robehomme. However, the men dropped mostly in the flooded area to the east, and Lieutenant Inman was only able to assemble 12 sappers who then made their way with difficulty across a network of ditches to the first bridge at Varaville. There they met with Lieutenant Baillie so, leaving him 200lbs of explosives and five men to carry out the demolition, Lieutenant Inman's party set off across flooded fields to Robehomme. Reaching the bridge, they found that Sergeant Poole, who had dropped nearby, had already successfully cut it with 30lbs of explosives obtained from Canadian troops in the vicinity.

On completion of this task, the battalion moved off to seize the high ground at the northern end of the ridge. Their objective was the high ground in the vicinity of Le Plein. Whilst they were approaching, they were warned by the French that over 200 of the enemy were entrenched in the area. It was now getting light and the commanding officer could see where the main opposition was centred. An attack was put in which from sheer lack of numbers was not successful. The enemy, who turned out eventually to be Russians forced to fight under German officers, told us later that they had been informed by the Germans that if they fell into Allied hands they would be shot as traitors. Be that as it may, they fought hard and stubbornly. This situation was not liquidated until the afternoon when Lovat's men arrived and cleared Le Plein and the whole northern end of the ridge of the Germans once and for all.

James Hill and his headquarters, with about 50 per cent of the Canadian 1st Parachute Battalion under Lieutenant-Colonel G. F. P. Bradbrooke, had by now established themselves at Le Mesnil. The 8th Battalion, under Lieutenant-Colonel Alastair Pearson, had entered Troarn and had a firm base established near the road junction south-east of Escoville.

The four bridges over the River Dives had all been successfully blown.

At Bures, two bridges had to be destroyed: a light steel girder road bridge and a more substantial girder railway bridge. Further south, at Troarn on the N815 highway — a vital east-west route to Caen — a five-span masonry arch bridge lay at the bottom of a steep road leading up to the town.

We rallied as many 8 Para Bn and 3 Para Sqn men as possible and kept them moving down to a track junction 123734. There I contacted Captain Juckes, and we reorganised. Our position was confirmed by a signpost at the crossroads at 121732 [see map page 215]. *On taking stock, we appeared to have a recce boat, a Mk II camouflet set, 4/500 lb of plastic explosive and 45 General Wade charges besides an adequate number of accessories, beehives etc., and the HQ link 68 set and one 18 set. We had only six trolleys, however, sufficient anyway to carry out some form of demolition on our three bridges. About 40 sappers and NCOs were present.*

In the absence of any 8 Para Bn officers, it proved rather difficult to persuade the 8 Bn other ranks to take the lead even under sapper officers, so eventually the point section consisted of Captain Juckes, myself and a few stout-hearted sappers who were not hauling the trolleys. As we moved off to the accompaniment of mortar and MMG fire, a Jeep and trailer with medical stores joined the party. The time was about 0230 hours. The route followed was Hérouvillette–Escoville–road junction 140703. The march, which was fortunately unopposed, was a feat of endurance by the sappers hauling the heavily-laden trolleys. Many were limping with DZ injuries, but they all pulled their weight on the trying gradient up to the road junction.

On reaching the road junction at about 0400 hours, we redistributed the stores amongst the transport available. All the medical stores were unloaded in the timber yard, and all General Wade charges were loaded on the Jeep and trailer. All plastic explosive and the camouflet set were loaded on the trolleys, and I ordered Captain Juckes to proceed at once with the main body of the sappers to attack his bridges; and I took Lieutenant Breese and seven NCOs and sappers with me in the Jeep and trailer to attack the Troarn bridge.

We set off down the road at a moderate pace with everyone ready with a Bren or one of our several Stens for any trouble. Just before the level crossing, we ran slap into a barbed wire knife rest road-block. One Boche fired a shot and then went off. It took 20 minutes hard work with wire cutters before the Jeep was freed. We then proceeded on, leaving behind, it transpired later, Sapper Moon.

MAJOR J. C. A. ROSEVEARE, 1946

Major Roseveare: 'Two scouts were sent ahead to the crossroad 160676. As they arrived, a Boche soldier cycled across complete with rifle. On being dragged from his bicycle, he protested volubly, and we made the mistake of silencing him with a Sten instead of a knife. Troarn was now getting roused, so we lost no time and everyone jumped aboard. As the total load was about 3,000lbs, we only made about 35 mph. At the corner 163678, the fun started, as there seemed to be a Boche in every doorway shooting like mad. However, the boys got to work with their Stens and Sapper Peachey did good work as rear gunner with the Bren. What saved the day was the steep hill down the main street. As the speed rose rapidly, we careered from side to side as the heavy trailer was swinging violently, and we were chased out of the town by an MG34 which fired tracer just over our heads.' *Right:* The main street at Troarn looking down the hill towards the bridge.

'On arrival at the bridge, which was not held, we found Sapper Peachey and his Bren were missing. Thirty-nine General Wade charges were immediately placed across the centre span, a Cordtex lead was connected up, and the charges fired. The demolition was completely successful — the whole centre span being demolished, giving a gap of 15 to 20 feet.'

Meanwhile, Captain Tim Juckes had led his party through the Bois de Bures and reached his bridges unopposed at about 0630 hours. Lieutenant John Shave with one section set to on the bridge over the track south of the village *(left)* while Lieutenant Alan Forster took another party to the railway bridge *(right)*. While they were preparing the demolitions, the main body of the 8th Parachute Battalion, some 100 strong, arrived with two Jeeps and trailers loaded with explosives. Both bridges were successfully blown around 0930 hours. An attempt was then made to extract a Jeep and 6-pdr gun from a glider which had crashed in the river near the railway bridge.

It was then decided that the gap in the Troarn bridge ought to be widened, and Captain Juckes was detailed to lead a party with a Jeep and trailer loaded with 40 General Wades — semi-circular, shaped charges containing 25lbs of explosive (officially a Charge, Demolition No. 2 Mk I) designed specifically for the destruction of bridges. At Troarn, the troops came under fire and a small battle ensued, in which one German was killed and five made prisoner. At the bridge, charges were laid across the next span to that already destroyed, the explosion increasing the gap to 35–40 feet as the pier was almost totally destroyed by the second explosion.

Unfortunately, it is difficult to give balanced pictorial coverage of the various airborne forces operating under General Gale as some units are not represented at all. Also, few photographs of Canadian paratroopers appear to have been taken. It is not normally the policy of *After the Battle* to include a picture without giving an accurate location and with this one from Canadian archives there are few clues, it merely being described as having been taken 'outside house, somewhere in Normandy, circa June 8'. An alternative caption reads: '6 A/B Div area: Canadian paras at farm aid station'.

By now, it was about 10 a.m. and this was the situation as I knew it then. Holding the bridges over the canal and the river was the 7th Battalion, fairly well pinned to the ground in a close-in bridgehead just to the north of Bénouville. In the southern outskirts of Ranville, known as Le Bas de Ranville, holding foxhole positions which they had dug in, was the 12th Battalion. They were on a reverse slope and well concealed from the front; ideal positions from which to deal with any enemy who topped the crest about 1,000 yards to their front. Unless supported by heavy covering fire accurately directed on the 12th, which at this stage could be discounted, any attempt to cross the open ground towards Ranville would be severely punished. The 12th's right flank rested on the river where there was more cover.

The eastern outskirts of Ranville and the village of Hérouvillette were thinly held by the 13th Battalion. Facing south, I had, therefore, two battalions at the time not mustering more than about 800 men between them and deployed on a front of nearly 4,000 yards. In this area I had, in addition, a dozen well-sited anti-tank guns. The troops' tails were well up and the ground was favourable to the defence.

Along the wooded ridge to the east were the 9th Battalion in the north, very weak after their battle at the battery, the Canadians at Le Mesnil in what strength I could only guess, and in the southern half of the Bois de Bavent, south-east of Escoville, the 8th Battalion. Up to this time, I had no artillery of my own and no artillery support from the sea assault divisions, who were quite busy enough fighting their own battle in the area of the beaches and the ground just inland. In the extreme north I had a call on naval gunfire, but this would not reach much beyond Le Plein. It would, I knew, be several hours before I could expect to get any artillery support from west of the Orne and, at the rate things seemed to be going, that certainly not before the morrow. My only reserve was in Ranville: about 60 men of the Independent Parachute Company.

In my appreciation of the German reactions to the invasion, I had always considered the most likely course that he would pursue would be to launch a series of small, but rather violent, immediate counter-attacks. These would be executed by the troops in the immediate vicinity of our landings. And so it had planned out. Later, there would be the more serious counter-attack, ordered by the higher formation, and executed by the local reserves in the area. This latter form of attack we had not anticipated being launched much before the late morning.

The airborne battlefield today. This montage from a 1991 sortie covers an area roughly ten kilometres square — more or less the central part of the map on page 215. Since 1944, villages have expanded; the old railway from Dozulé to Caen (on which the bridge at Bures lay) dismantled, while the new A13 autoroute, built in the mid-1970s, cuts a swathe across the south-eastern corner.

LE PLEIN
LZ 'V'
AMFRÉVILLE
BRÉVILLE
LZ 'N'
HEROUVILLETTE
BOIS DE BAVENT
ESCOVILLE
BOIS DE BURES
AUTOROUTE
LZ 'K'
TOUFFREVILLE
DISMANTLED RAILWAY
BRIDGE
SANNERVILLE
TROARN

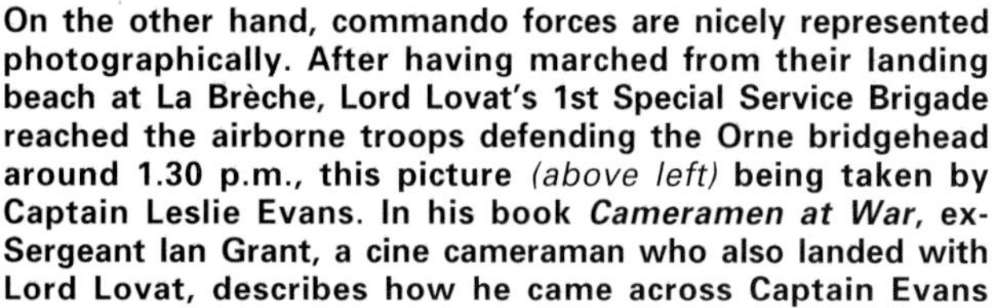

On the other hand, commando forces are nicely represented photographically. After having marched from their landing beach at La Brèche, Lord Lovat's 1st Special Service Brigade reached the airborne troops defending the Orne bridgehead around 1.30 p.m., this picture *(above left)* being taken by Captain Leslie Evans. In his book *Cameramen at War*, ex-Sergeant Ian Grant, a cine cameraman who also landed with Lord Lovat, describes how he came across Captain Evans 'sitting in a ditch with a medical orderly doing something to his face, a stray piece of shrapnel had hit him [and] knocked him out'. Grant says that he handed him his exposed film as Evans was going to go back to a first-aid station. If Grant's chronology is correct, Evans must have returned to take these pictures later once the commandos had reached Bénouville as Jean Paul Pallud established the location *(right)* some 200 metres west of the bridge on the D514.

At the moment, the two most dangerous approaches into the bridgehead area seemed to me to be that from Caen up the west bank to Bénouville, and that from Colombelles up the east bank to Ranville. Had the advance of the 3rd Infantry Division, the beach-assault division, gone according to plan, I should by now have been relieved of anxiety on the west bank. They had been expected to reach the bridges by 9 a.m., that is approximately two hours after their landing on the beaches. I had realised, of course, that this must only be a very rough estimate.

Centre: **Evans also took this shot 150 metres closer to the bridge, and in May 1994 the *Sunday Mirror* found the actual commando, Cyril Harding, now living in Barry, South Glamorgan. Recalling June 6, 1944, when he landed at Colleville, Cyril said that 'You could hear desperate shouts of "Stretcher bearers . . . Medics . . . Medics over here". But we couldn't stop for the wounded. We had to get to the coast road, and inland across the fields, which were strewn with dead cattle and horses, their bodies ripped to shreds by the shrapnel.' Remembering the photograph, Cyril explained that 'we were passing by and they came out smiling, holding out a bottle of apple brandy. I'd never tasted anything like it, it was wonderful. Afterwards, I didn't care if the Germans sent a panzer division against me. I could have taken them on single-handed! When I woke up, I had a mouthful of water and felt drunk again. But perhaps it was the kindness of that family — maybe I got drunk on that.'**
Left: **In the company of a *Sunday Mirror* reporter, he went back to the same house, now occupied by the Bedel family, and they were delighted to open another bottle of Calvados. Cyril took a sip and once again his stomach turned to fire. 'That's the stuff', Cyril said. 'Mind you, 50 years is a hell of a long time to wait for a refill.'**

Ian Grant says that he caught up with the commandos as they marched to the Bénouville bridge: 'Lord Lovat was a little behind schedule but he was determined to give the Airborne a little show. He summoned his personal piper, Bill Millin, to go to the head of the column and told him, "just blow, man, anything at all but make it a rousing march". Bill Millin did as he was told, pumped the bag under one arm and the commandos swung onto the bridge approach, the bagpipes snarling out *Blue Bonnets over the Border*. This was great stuff for my camera and I raced ahead getting as many different angles as I could — Lovat marching as on parade, the fantastic sight of Millin's red cheeks bulging behind the bagpipes, the red and green berets mixed up together, the crashed glider so close to the bridge, civilians waving from the nearby café — and over it all came the sound of enemy fire from the woods. Strangely, nobody gave a damn and nobody appeared to be hit — maybe the German gunners were so astonished by this crazy sight, their thumbs and fingers just froze over the triggers and the firing went as wild as the scene.' Bill Millin's piping of the commandos over the bridge has become part of the folklore of D-Day, particularly after the release of *The Longest Day*, but, unfortunately, it is just not true. Lord Lovat explains in his memoirs, published in 1978, that 'I ran across [the canal bridge] with piper Millin and a handful of fighting men. There was a fair amount of mortaring and a machine gun up the water pinging bullets off the steel struts, but no one noticed and brave fellows from the gliders were cheering from their fox-holes at the other end.' Lord Lovat confirmed that he ordered playing to stop 100 yards from Bénouville bridge and that 'no piper played on the first occasion while crossing the canal'. However, when they reached the river bridge *(above)* 400 yards ahead, 'Bill Millin struck into a march and played us across the water'. Thus legends are born. Even if Ian Grant muddled the bridges, we could trace neither his film nor a dope sheet at the Imperial War Museum, now the repository for all AFPU material.

To summarise: we were very thin on the ground, but we had done what we set out to do and we all believed that we could hold what we had gained. By nightfall we should be reinforced by the Airlanding Brigade and soon the 3rd Division would be up on our right flank.

I will now attempt to trace the fighting as it developed during the day, firstly west of the bridges and then in and around Ranville, for it was in these areas that our greatest dangers lay.

Pine-Coffin's dispositions worked well. During the day, the battalion withstood eight separate counter-attacks in about company strength and sometimes supported by a small number of tanks. In addition, continual attempts were made by small parties of the enemy to infiltrate between his localities. Owing to the lack of wireless and this frequent enemy infiltration, the situation very naturally was often obscure and caused Pine-Coffin a good deal of anxiety.

The first respite for the 7th Battalion came about noon, when in the distance the sound of pipes could be heard. This was to be the signal from Brigadier Lord Lovat that his commandos of the 1st Special Service Brigade were approaching. It was to be answered by a bugle from the 7th if the way to the bridges was clear. In the noise of the fighting, the bugle could not be heard. Lovat's men by-passed the enemy and the first meeting between the seaborne and the airborne troops occurred about 1.30 p.m. That first sound of the pipes meant much to the 7th: it was a stirring moment for those who heard it. It meant that success had been achieved on the beaches and that relief was imminent. A grim battle had been fought for close on 12 hours and the sight of the green berets was tonic which invigorated the troops. The commandos were greeted with cheers and handshakes, a heartily-deserved tribute to their fine performance in getting through some five hours ahead of any other seaborne troops. They crossed the bridges on their allotted task to the east.

No pictures exist of Bill Millin at the bridge in 1944, but fortunately both he and his bagpipes have returned several times since the war. *Left:* **This picture was taken in 1985, his pipes now being displayed in the Pegasus Museum.** *Right:* **The Orne bridge had always been overshadowed by Pegasus Bridge, but on the 45th anniversary the balance was redressed.**

Responding to a suggestion put forward by a Dutch couple, Rook and Nel van Asperen, to Major Ian Toler, president of the Glider Pilots' Association, unveiled a memorial on June 6, 1989, naming it 'Horsa Bridge'. As he commented later, 'people think that because of the name "Pegasus" paratroops captured the bridges but both were taken by glider pilots and the army!'

And the prisoners come in. Captain Evans also photographed this column of prisoners but gave no location. Robert Voskuil explored the area carefully in June 1994 and chanced upon this corner on Rue du Four-à-Chaux, Ranville.

Above: **Late on June 6, some 30 kilometres away to the south-east, a German war photographer pictured some of the first British prisoners captured during the night. These 6th Airborne paratroopers have been brought in by the Hitlerjugend soldiers of the 12. SS-Panzer-Division to St Pierre-sur-Dives where they were marched to the local school and held in the courtyard.** *Below:* **Brana Radovic matched the shot of the prisoners passing the church but when Frank Gleeson recognised himself as the para in the beret to the left of the panzergrenadier, he returned to the village** *(right)* **to have his picture taken on the same spot.**

The arrival of the commandos did not, therefore, end the troubles of the 7th, and the enemy counter-attacks continued until 8 p.m. During the latter part of the afternoon, the company in the southern part of Bénouville bore the brunt of the fighting and the battalion counter-attack force had to be put in to relieve the pressure on them.

By the evening, the leading elements of the 3rd Division made contact with Pine-Coffin's men. At 6.30 p.m., the 2nd Battalion, the Royal Warwickshire Regiment, of the 185th Infantry Brigade, arrived at the bridges. The take-over involved an attack to relieve the forward company of parachutists and allow the evacuation of their casualties, and the position was not finally handed over till midnight.

This ended a great day for the 7th Parachute Battalion. They had fulfilled their task. They had held the west bridgehead and had had 21 hours' continuous and hard fighting. The men were tired but well satisfied and proud of their achievements. Casualties had amounted to 60 killed and wounded.

It was, however, the Ranville front that really worried me. If we had succeeded in blowing the bridges over the Dives between ourselves and the enemy reserves in the Le Havre area, we need not expect serious trouble for a little

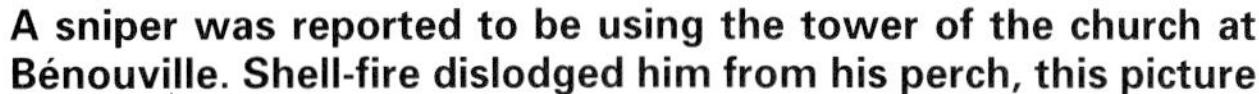

A sniper was reported to be using the tower of the church at Bénouville. Shell-fire dislodged him from his perch, this picture being taken on June 10 by Sergeant Jimmy Mapham, who had landed on Queen sector.

while from the east. At this stage also, it seemed most unlikely that the troops manning the coast defences to the north, would turn south on us: for the fear of an extension of our landing eastwards must surely pin these troops to their ground. It was, therefore, from the south that I was vulnerable.

Ranville was fairly quiet until about 11 a.m. It was at that hour that we came in for mortaring. The mortaring was heavy, and with it was mixed up high-velocity shells which seemed to me to come from west of the canal, probably the high ground north of Caen. It quickly became apparent that a properly-mounted attack was being developed against us, and, as I had anticipated, from the south. This attack was delivered by Panzergrenadier-Regiment 125, with self-propelled guns and tanks, and was launched against the 12th Battalion. This well-supported attack was delivered with skill and determination, but Johnson, an astoundingly gallant leader, held his positions. The Germans did not succeed in breaking in along this line of the river bank and they were severely handled by the 12th in the open. Although one of their tanks actually got into the outskirts of Ranville, the Germans had to withdraw and their casualties were heavy. By 1 p.m., Ranville was clear and the battle died down.

One episode in the fighting outside Ranville stood out. A young captain, John Sim, with a handful of men was holding a position along the line of a hedge. He was attacked by German infantry supported by two self-propelled guns. One of these guns he knocked out. The other, locating his position, lowered its muzzle and at point-blank range shot up his men one by one. Sim held his ground until finally he and only three men were left. Eventually, the gun withdrew, having had enough, leaving this gallant and depleted party the victors.

The 12th Battalion had had a bad time and they were considerably under strength; if the Germans developed a second attack of similar strength and vigour, I doubted their ability, with the best will in the world, to stand up to it. I had by now also put in the Independent Parachute Company and had nothing in hand. The bridgehead was my major responsibility: this must be held. For this reason, on the arrival of the 1st Special Service Brigade, I then diverted Lieutenant-Colonel Derek Mills-Roberts, commanding No. 6 Commando, the leading commando, to the Ranville area. No. 3 and No. 45 (Royal Marine) Commandos came through and proceeded to the north where they secured the ground between Sallenelles and Amfréville and relieved the weak 9th at Le Plein.

But the Germans had had enough; they did not attack again that day. By the evening, things were quiet. It had been a strenuous few hours and anxious; but the battle had gone as we had anticipated and we all felt confident. All objectives had been captured and, what was more important, held.

Left: **Graves of men from No. 3 Commando at Amfréville, photographed by Sergeant Christie on June 15.** *Above:* **Jean Paul Pallud discovered that the temporary graveyard had been located in the walled garden to the Château d'Amfréville located on the western edge of the village. Sergeant Christie probably took his picture from the steps at the rear or a window to get the elevation but the building has since been demolished and the garden walls are crumbling.**

Above: **Meanwhile, preparations were being made for the second lift bringing in the 6th Airlanding Brigade (less one battalion), the Airborne Armoured Recce Regiment, the 211th Light and 3rd Anti-Tank Batteries, RA, and the 195th Field Ambulance.**

The closing incident for this great day was the fly-in of the 6th Airlanding Brigade. It was a sight I shall never forget. Of a sudden, the dull roar of aircraft could be heard. Then they came, hundreds of aircraft and gliders: the sky was filled with them. We could see the tug aircraft cast off their gliders, and down in great spirals the latter came to the landing zone. Most of the stakes had by now been cleared. The landing took place on both sides of the river and canal. It is impossible to say with what relief we watched this reinforcement arrive.

The German reaction was quick. He mortared our headquarters, the village of Ranville, and attempted to mortar the landing zone. His fire was inaccurate and ineffectual, but unfortunately at my headquarters, poor Jack Norris, my artillery commander, received a terrible throat wound. None of us thought that he could possibly survive, but he did. His loss to us out there was great. Jerry Lacoste, my intelligence officer, was also hit. One of my provost men standing just behind me was killed. On the landing zones, however, we were lucky and only one 6-pdr anti-tank gun was hit. This received a direct hit as it was driving off the landing zone on to the road and it and its Jeep were burned out.

Above: **Captain Bill Malandine was still at Harwell ready to photograph the take-off in the early evening, the landing being scheduled for 2100 hours on LZs 'N' and 'W'.** *Below:* **Today, only parts of the old runway survive, Harwell now being owned by the Atomic Energy Authority and used as a research establishment.**

The evening lift from Tarrant Rushton was notable for its employment of 30 of the large Hamilcar gliders.

We held the high, wooded ridge from Hauger to Bures, so that the Germans had no direct observation on this ground. The landing zone we used west of the Orne was just to the north of Ouistreham. This also was not under observation and could not have been suspected by the Germans, for their reaction on this bank was negligible.

There has been a little confusion of thought about the success of glider landings in this operation. Facts, I think, will speak for themselves. Of the six gliders detailed for the coup de main assault on the bridges, four were dead on. Of the 92 others that set out that night, 58 were either dead on their appointed landing places or within 3,000 yards of them, some 17 landed over two miles away and 17 were missing, four of which had forced landings in the United Kingdom. Of the 256 gliders landed on the evening of D-Day, 246 landed safely on the correct landing zones. Counting anything over two miles away or missing as being a failure, approximately 88 per cent of the total glider landings were successful.

Although we have already seen some of Sergeant Christie's photos, he went in with the Airlanding Brigade and probably took the picture on the bottom of the opposite page, although it is not officially credited to him. *Left:* **His named sequence begins with this shot from the cockpit of one of the 220-odd Horsas which also took part.** *Above:* **As soon as he was down, Christie pictured these Hamilcars about to land.**

His hurried third exposure: 'As they landed, glider troops made their way to their appointed positions as quickly as possible. Other gliders can be seen in the distance.'

A corner of LZ 'N', these fields being just south-west of Amfréville. The large glider on the right is one of the Hamilcars — the same one is visible on the extreme right of the picture at the top of page 233.

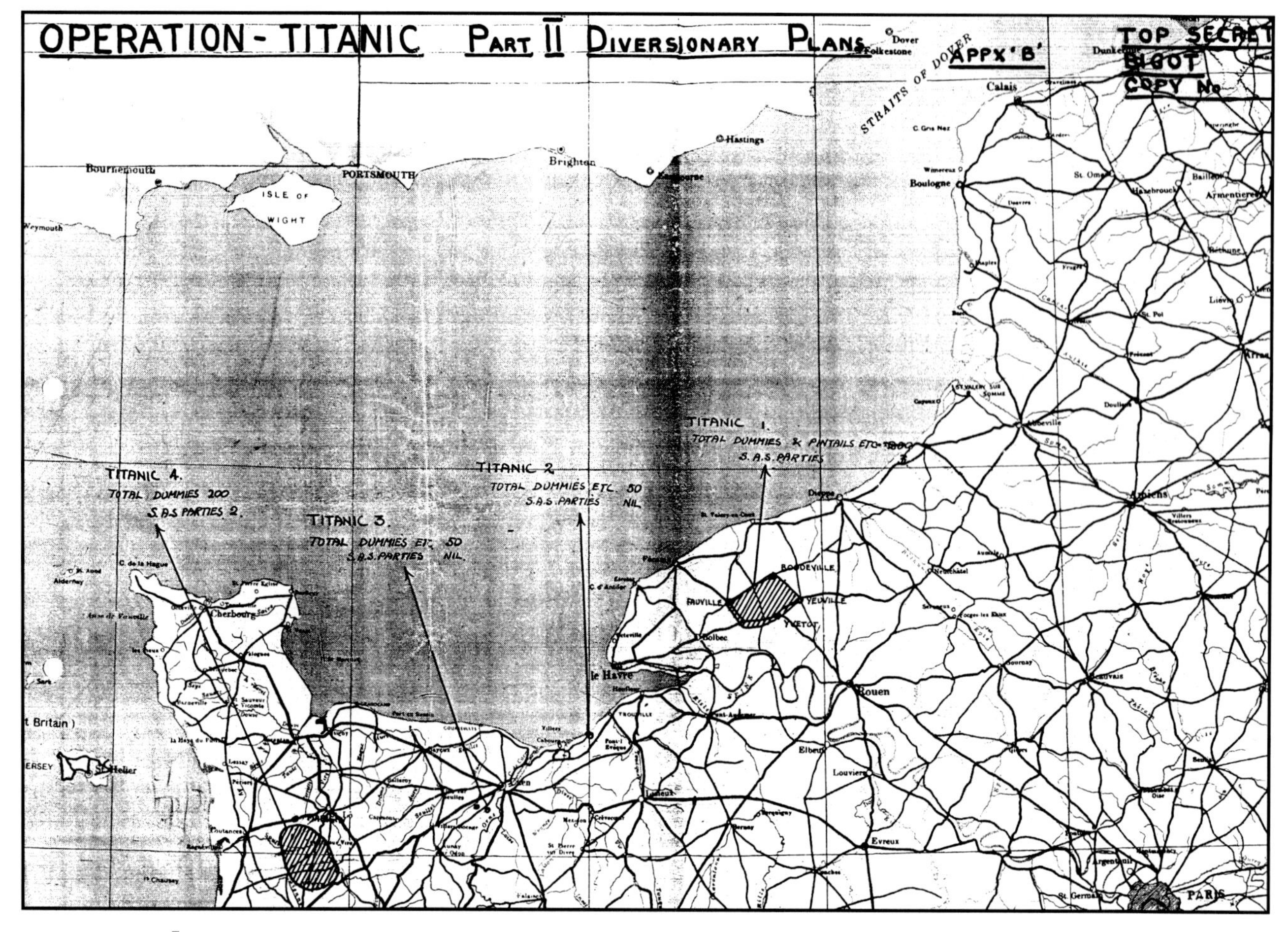

Special Duty Operations

By Brigadier Roderick McLeod
COMMANDER, SPECIAL AIR SERVICE BRIGADE

With the end of the campaign in North Africa, Special Air Service (SAS) units changed the character of their operations to suit the new theatre. The concept of using small parties behind the lines had been accepted and it was decided to make considerable use of such forces for the invasion of France. The SAS units from the Mediterranean were moved back to England and a brigade was formed based on about 1,000 British SAS troops to whom were added 1,000 Free French parachutists and about 250 Belgian parachutists. I, who had been until then the deputy commander of a parachute brigade, was placed in command of this heterogeneous collection and told to organise and train it for 'Overlord'.

This was an assignment that required more than usual tact since half the British had fought with the Eighth Army (1st SAS Regiment) and half with the First Army (2nd SAS Regiment), and they did not speak to each other. Half the French were Gaullists and half had a Vichy background and not only did not speak to each other, but they actively fought [The 3rd SAS Regiment was formed from the 3ème Bataillon d'Infanterie de l'Air (BIA) — later renamed Régiment de Chasseurs Parachutistes (RCP) — and the 4th SAS Regiment from the 4ème BIA which later became the 2ème RCP]. The Belgians were mainly recruited in Canada and some spoke no Flemish. In fact, they were much the best behaved and easiest to deal with.

AIR LIFT, Nos. 38 AND 46 GROUPS, RAF

		Aircraft						*Gliders*		
Operation	*Mission*	*Despatched*	*Effective*	*Abortive*	*Missing*	*Destroyed*	*Damaged*	*Despatched*	*Released at DZ*	*Lost before DZ*
'Tonga'	6th Airborne Division, night June 5/6	373	359	14	9	–	7	98	80	18
'Mallard'	6th Airlanding Brigade, evening D-Day	257	247	10	2	6	21	257	247	10
'Rob Roy I'	Resupply, night June 6/7	50	47	3	9	–	19	–	–	–
'Rob Roy II'	Resupply, night June 7/8	6	6	–	–	–	–	–	–	–
'Rob Roy III'	Resupply, night June 8/9	12	5	7	–	–	–	–	–	–
'Rob Roy IV'	Resupply, night June 9/10	15	15	–	–	–	1	–	–	–
'Sunflower I'	SAS recce parties, night June 5/6	2	2	–	–	–	–	–	–	–
'Sunflower II'	SAS base parties	2	1	1	–	–	–	–	–	–
'Cooney'	FFL SAS rail-cut ops, night June 7/8	9	9	–	–	–	–	–	–	–
'Sunflower III'	SAS reinforcement for ops, night June 9/10	6	6	–	–	–	–	–	–	–
'Sunflower IV'	Further SAS operations, night June10/11	10	8	2	–	–	–	–	–	–
		742	705	37	20	6	48	355	327	28

Simultaneously with the airlift for the 6th Airborne Division to Normandy, No. 38 Group flew in the first SAS parties.

Top: **Operation 'Titanic' as first planned involved parties from both the 1st and 2nd Special Air Service Regiments.**

DIVERSIONARY PLANS

NJO/OO/2GI/33

Introduction

1. The object of this paper is to tabulate the various cover diversionary operations which form an integral part of Operation NEPTUNE.

SEA DIVERSIONS

2. The sea diversionary operations as under will be carried out by naval forces supported by aircraft dropping window on night of D minus 1/D-Day.

Operation Bigdrum

3. The object of this diversion is to engage the enemy RADAR stations in the NORTH of the CHERBOURG PENINSULA and to distract the enemy batteries in that area. This diversionary operation will be carried out by a small force of MLs.

Operation Taxable

4. The object of this diversion is to give greater breadth to the assault forces and to show our intention of landing NORTH of the SEINE. This diversion will be linked with an airborne diversion (see para 6 below).

Operation Glimmer

5. Plans will be made in order to carry out a similar diversion to TAXABLE in the PAS DE CALAIS area should enemy mining permit and the enemy situation prove desirable. Of the possible areas of attack it is considered that the BOULOGNE area will be the most effective.

AIRBORNE DIVERSIONS

OPERATION TITANIC

Operation Titanic I

6. The simulation of the dropping of one airborne division NORTH of the SEINE.

(a) *OBJECT.* To retain enemy forces NORTH of the SEINE and to draw the enemy reserves SOUTH of the SEINE to the NORTH.

Operation Titanic II

7. (a) *OBJECT.* To delay local reserves immediately EAST of the River DIVES from moving WESTWARDS.

(b) *METHOD.* 50 dummy paratroops and a proportionate number of pintails and 'noise' will be dropped in the area of BOIS DE VILLERS 3080 at about H minus 4 hrs 40 mins.

Operation Titanic III

8. (a) *OBJECT.* To draw a proportion of local counter-attack troops to the SOUTH-WEST of CAEN.

(b) *METHOD.* A total of 50 dummy paratroops and a proportionate number of pintails and 'noise' will be dropped in the following areas.

(i) MALTOT 9862.

(ii) Wood NORTH of BARON 9462.

This dropping will be coincident with that of 6 Airborne Div.

Operation Titanic IV

9. (a) *OBJECT.* To draw the enemy counter-attack forces in the area of ST LO to the WEST.

(b) *METHOD.* A total of 200 dummy paratroops and a proportionate number of pintails and 'noise' will be dropped in the MARIGNY area.

This dropping to be coincident with that of 101 US Airborne Div.

(c) Two parties of SAS will be in the dropping zones by H minus 4 hrs 40 mins and will create minor damage to culverts and will attack dispatch riders, lone vehicles, etc., allowing individual enemy to escape and thus confirm by personal contact the rumour of paratroop dropping.

The task given to these special forces was to impose the maximum delay on the movement of German reinforcements to Normandy, and thereafter to assist in the arming and training of the Maquis and to harass the Germans. Although primarily a British formation which had been raised and trained as part of the British Army, its tasks were allocated by SHAEF.

The Allied air forces had already destroyed most of the bridges over the Seine and the Loire, which obviously delayed movement from the east and south, but there was no convenient river line cutting Brittany off from the rest of France. Therefore, the first task of the SAS was in this area.

On the night of June 5/6, SAS reconnaissance parties of the Forces Françaises Libres were dropped 'blind' into the départements of Morbihan and Côtes-du-Nord preparatory to setting up two Maquis support bases. The same night, two British SAS officers with an accompanying Jedburgh team dropped to an SOE reception in the Vienne to pave the way for an independent SAS base. Finally, A and B Squadrons of the 1st SAS Regiment each provided an

SAS BRIGADE OPERATION INSTRUCTION No. 11 (as amended 24 May, 1944)

REF MAP 1:250,000 GSGS 2738
Copy No. 8

TOP SECRET
24 May, 1944
HQ SAS Tps/TSB/5/G

GENERAL

1. Pending results of representation to 21 Army Group by Corps Commander it must be assumed that SAS Troops commitments in cover plan as described to you verbally will stand.

2. Commitments are as under:

(a) 2 SAS will find three parties each of three men to drop in area YERVILLE M0841 – DOUDEVILLE L0048 – FAUVILLE L8542 – YVETOT L9637. Codename — TITANIC I *[this operation deleted May 24]*.

(b) 1 SAS will find two parties each for three men to drop in area MARIGNY T3962, codename TITANIC IV.

INFORMATION

3. All Intelligence to hand at the present is attached at Appendix A, with details of further information already requested.

4. Details of dummies and simulators to be dropped are attached at Appendix B.

5. Parties will be dropped 1 minute before dummy parachutists on separate DZs, on timings as under:

TITANIC IV — H – 5 hrs.

6. Payload of aircraft carrying SAS parties will be made up with containers packed with ballast and packing materials.

INTENTION

7. SAS parties will augment deception to dropping of dummy parachutists by ensuring that the presence of troops on the ground is known to the enemy.

METHOD

8. One aircraft will be allotted to TITANIC IV and will carry all parties detailed for that operation.

9. On landing they will remove the ballast, but leave packing materials, from any container they may find, in order that if the enemy find the empty containers [he] will assume that weapons and troops have been dropped.

10. They will then do anything in their power to make their presence felt, e.g. setting Hawkins mines on roads, shooting DRs, holding up solitary staff cars, etc.

11. On completion of these tasks, they will hide up. It is hoped to make special arrangements for evacuation by sea, preliminary details of which are forwarded under separate cover.

INTERCOMMUNICATION

12. Parties will be equipped with MCR1 receivers.

13. A special broadcast will be arranged for these parties, and in order that they may be notified of any alteration of arrangements for evacuation it is essential that they should be capable of working one-time letter pad.

(signed) R. W. McLEOD, Brigadier,
Commander, SAS Troops

The one-third scale dummy parachutists produced by the Littlewoods factory in Carrickfergus, along with 'Window' were essential to the success of 'Titanic'. They were developed in parallel by the Central Landing Establishment in England and 'A' Force in Egypt in 1942 (and first used operationally in September of that year over Siwa oasis in support of SAS and LRDG operations). Twenty-two Stirling IIIs of Nos. 90 and 149 Squadrons and eight Halifax B Mk II of No. 138 (SD) and four Halifax B Mk IV of No. 161 (SD) Squadrons dropped at least 537 of these dummies, together with 66 Pintail bombs and 66 rifle-fire simulators between 0040 and 0214 hours on June 5/6. No. 90 Squadron lost aircraft 'M' and 'C' with 14 crewmen killed, three PoW casualties, and one man unaccounted for whose fate is unknown to this day. One crewman later managed to escape by jumping from a train on July 23. Curiously enough, the next time these devices were deployed was in April 1945 on the French SAS Operation 'Amherst' dropping into Holland.

officer and two men to 'lend verisimilitude' to the diversionary Operation 'Titanic IV'. Once the bases were established, a series of railway demolitions were to be carried out by parties dropped in for the purpose, withdrawing to the bases upon completion of their tasks. When mounted on June 7/8, 9/10 and 10/11, both the French and British operations were successful, although not without casualties. Within a few days, 'Dingson' in the south near Vannes was 'besieged' by French Gendarmerie and FFI. The entire police force and Maquis of this part of Brittany turned up, demanding arms and to be led against the Germans, and it was only with the greatest difficulty that they were persuaded to disperse until weapons could be brought in for them.

[On June 12, the 'Samwest' base area in Forêt de Duault under Capitaine Le Blond was attacked by 13 truckloads of enemy rear-area security troops who

APPENDIX A' TO SAS BRIGADE OPERATION INSTRUCTION No. 11 DATED 19 MAY 44
(as amended 24 May, 1944)

OPERATION TITANIC IV — ENEMY DISPOSITIONS
Ref Maps GSGS 4250 (1:50,000) sheets 6F1 to 6F4.

Static Troops

1. No static troops are normally in the area except at PERIERS 2772, the HQ of 243 Inf Div which holds the West coast of the COTENTIN peninsula, and at ST LO 4963 which is the HQ of 81 Corps and contains various administrative units.

Mobile Troops

2. 352 Inf Div, which has a counter-attack rôle against the western Normandy beaches, is in the area AMIGNY 4367 — (an inf regt) — BALLEROY 6869 - VILLERS 8257 - CANISY 4359, with its HQ in the last-named town.

3. 30 Mobile Bde is in the area COUTANCES 2356 – ST LO – CERENCES 2342 (name omitted on map), with a Bn at each of these three towns. The Bde's exact composition is uncertain but it consists of mounted and cyclist recce units, one of whose main tasks is the rounding up of paratroops. Details are being obtained, but it is emphasised that all present dispositions are likely to change between now and the time of the operation. All that is certain is that on D-Day the towns in the area will be full of troops at a high state of readiness; some of these troops may already, at the time of dropping, be on the move towards the beaches. A vigorous reaction to TITANIC IV is probable; formed units could easily be on the DZ within 1½ hrs and motor cycle or cavalry patrols should be reconnoitring it within half an hour of the landing.

Installations

4. No fixed defences are reported.

Petrol dumps are reported at 479638, 415565 and 422538. MT parks are reported at CANISY and CARANTILLY 3858.

A WT station is at 459695.

5. Air cover forwarded today (message I 113). Plot follows.

Civilians

6. As in other farming areas near the coast, all civilians not engaged in food production are likely to have been evacuated before D-Day. The remainder will be under strict curfew, lasting perhaps 23 hours out of 24, when operations begin. The Germans can only enforce this curfew permanently in the villages they occupy, but may organise extensive searches of other farms and villages if they suspect paratroops to be in hiding. The degree of help to be expected from civilians is not therefore as high as usual.

7. Further details requested:
trace of coast defences.
check of interior defence line.

APPENDIX B TO SAS BRIGADE OPERATION INSTRUCTION No. 11 DATED 19 MAY 44

1. Allocation of Aircraft and loads:
TITANIC I and IV 6 Aircraft each carrying:
39 dummies
12 Pintail Bombs
14 Rifle fire simulators Mk II
7 MG simulators (or rifle fire simulators if the MG simulators are not produced in time).
2. Description of the various equipments are as under:

A. DUMMY PARATROOP
A model man made of sand-bags, approx 1/3rd the size of a normal man. Parachute to same scale.

B. PINTAIL BOMB
A small bomb containing a Verey light cartridge. It is released at the same time as the dummies, falls to the ground at a speed greater than that of the dummies, and discharges a Verey light.
This serves three purposes:
i. Attracts enemy's attention to the area of the dummies' drop.
ii. Illuminates the dummies in the air.
iii. Makes it appear that there is a reception party on the ground signalling to the dummy dropping a/c.

C. SIMULATORS
These are mechanisms attached to the back of the dummies with a timed delay which is initiated when the dummy leaves the a/c. After the dummies have struck the ground the simulators begin to explode.
They are made to represent rifle and LMG fire, and have a duration of approx five minutes.

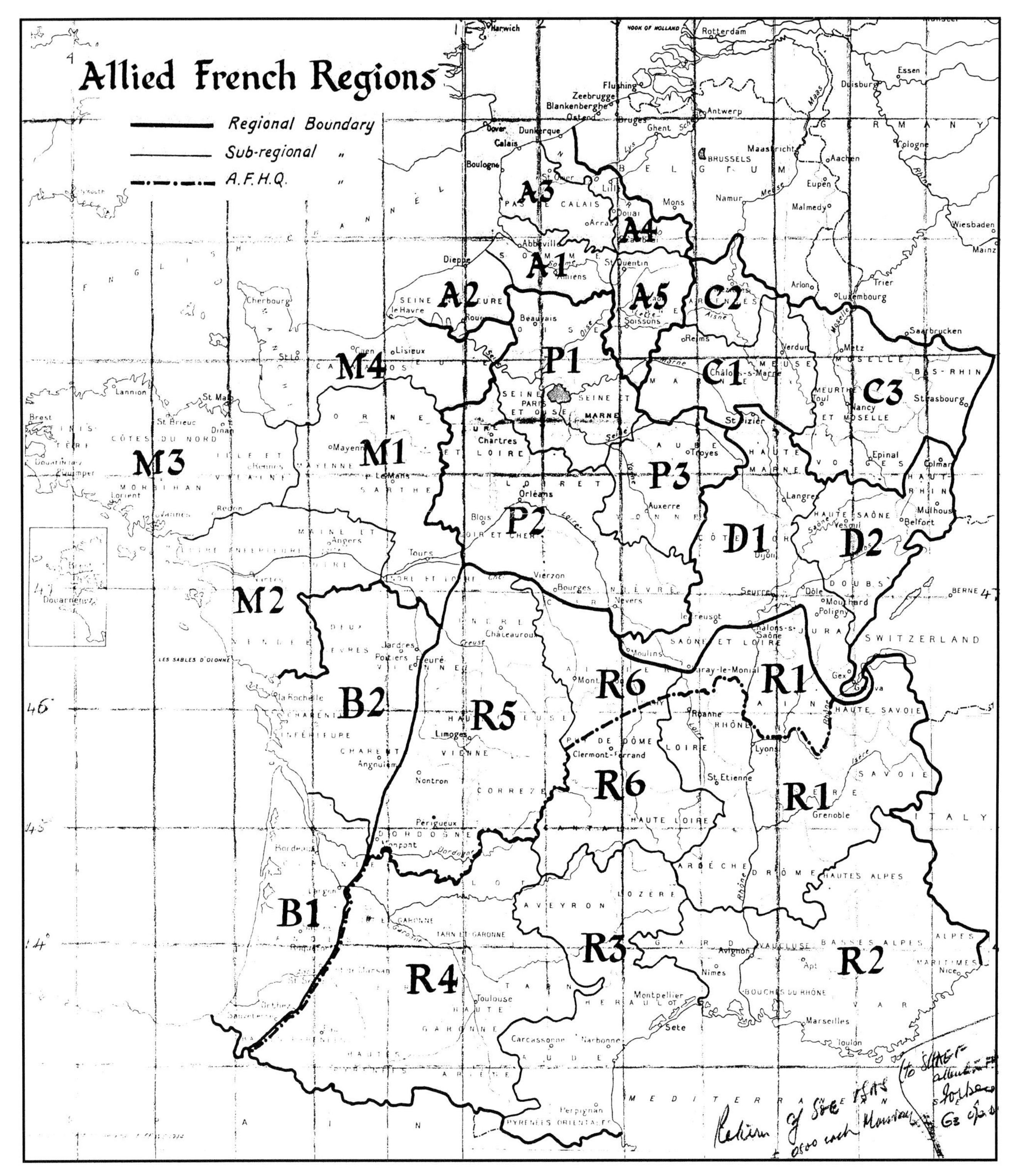

For operational purposes, Special Forces and Forces Françaises de l'Intérieur divided France into military regions. From June 6 to 13, Jedburgh teams with male first names went in from the UK to arm and assist the Maquis in B2, M3, P3 and R5 whilst the 'R' regions received an OSS Operational Group and Jedburgh teams with chemical names from North Africa. Inter-Allied Mission 'Isaac' under SOE's 'République Française' section head went in to co-ordinate the Maquis in D1, P2 and P3. Mixed in with the deception devices were the six men of the 1st SAS Regiment, who planned to drop from Halifax B Mk II 'NF-M' of No. 138 (SD) Squadron near Marigny on a DZ selected from aerial photography (Operation 'Titanic IV'). They actually dropped two kilometres north-west of this spot at 0020 hours, ten minutes ahead of schedule, due to malfunctioning drop command lights in the aircraft. Lieutenant N. H. Poole, the mission commander, tripped over his leg-bag, somersaulted, and was knocked unconscious exiting the aircraft. Lieutenant F. J. Fowles dropped wide and all heavy equipment in the containers was lost. With both officers missing, Troopers Dawson, Saunders, Hurst and Merryweather laid and blew 20 Lewes bombs in an area covering 500 square yards at 0300 hours and retired to cover. Little activity apart from a bicycle patrol on the main Carentan road was seen and the party was subsequently reunited by the Maquis. All six men were later captured by men of 3. Fallschirmjäger-Division near the village of Raids on July 10 whilst trying to filter through the German forward areas. The cumulative effect of all 'Titanic' operations was to divert Kampfgruppe Meyer of Grenadier-Regiment 915, the reserve of Generalleutnant Dietrich Kraiss's 352. Infanterie-Division, away from Omaha and Gold beaches and the DZs of the 101st Airborne Division in the first critical hours of the invasion. All six men survived the war, including a second period of captivity for Trooper A. Merryweather on a later Special Air Service operation.

STRATEGIC DEPLOYMENT OF SPECIAL FORCES IN SUPPORT OF OPERATION 'OVERLORD'

Compiled by David List with David Buxton

Insertion date	*Operation, airfield and sortie duration*	*Operation/payload*	*Squadron aircraft type/ identification*	*Occurrence*
June 5/6	'Sunflower I' Fairford 2223-0310	'Dingson 1': 1 FO/7 FOR, 4ème BIA 1 SOE 'F' Section guide Samwest 1: 1 FO/8 FOR, 4ème BIA	620 (GT) Sqn Stirling IV F	Dropped 0056 and 0115 hours into Region M3. 'Dingson' lost one dead and three men PoW in firefight with enemy in area of DZ.
June 5/6	'Sunflower I' Fairford (ex Keevil) 2304-0320	'Samwest 1'/'Dingson 1': 1 FO/8 FOR, 2 Sqn, 4ème BIA 1 FO/8 FOR, 1 Sqn, 4ème BIA	299 Sqn Stirling IV F	Dropped 0138 and 0106 hours into Region M3. (Teams had been duplicated and cross-loaded to guard against compromise).
June 5/6	'Politician' Tempsford 2307-0457	'Bulbasket 1': 2 BO, B Sqn, 1 SAS; Jedburgh Team 'Hugh' (1 BO/1 FO/1 FOR) +10 containers & 3 packages	161 (SD) Sqn Halifax B Mk V MA-T	Dropped 'blind' at 0137 into Region M1 as no reception lights from SOE 'F' Section réseau 'Shipwright'. Limoges-Vierzon railway cut in 54 places by the Maquis.
June 6/7	'Gondolier 9' Tempsford 2300-0455	'Houndsworth 1': 2 BO, A Sqn, 1 SAS; Jedburgh Team 'Harry' (1 BO/2 FO) +3 packages	161 (SD) Sqn Hudson III MA-R	Intended to 'blind' drop into Region P2 to SOE 'F' Section réseau 'Gondolier'. DZ not located so dropped near Rouvray.
June 7/8	'Sunflower II' Fairford 2220-0434	'Bulbasket 2': Each aircraft 1 BO/8 BOR, B Sqn, 1 SAS +9 containers	620 (GT) Sqn Stirling IV F, J	F' dropped troops at 0152 and 0158 hours into Region R5 to 'Bulbasket' reception. 'J' aborted as no lights seen at 0058 hours.
June 7/8	'Cooney' Brize Norton (Some ex Harwell) 2230-0331	'Cooney': 58 FAR, 4ème BIA split into sixteen operational parties of 3 men and two parties of 5 men all from the same troop. Individual composition of parties by rank and allocation to aircraft not preserved accurately in British records.	295 (GT) Sqn Albemarle I H, U 297 (GT) Sqn 570 Sqn Albemarle I/II G, T P, M 296 (GT) Sqn Albemarle II/V O, F, Y	All 'Cooney' drops were 'blind' on 17 DZs selected from aerial photography and map study as nearest to intended rail-cuts in area St Brieuc-Dinan-Redon-Pontivy. First drop was at 0037 hours on 47° 47' N 01° 53.5' W and last at 0135 hours on 48° 27.5' N 02° 21.5' W. The final DZ was occupied by the enemy who killed two men and captured four. One man escaped to complete his party's mission alone although he died later at 'Samwest'.
June 8/9	'Banc' 'Beck' Blida, North Africa 2200-0540	Jedburgh Team 'Quinine' and Jedburgh Team 'Veganin': each (1 BO/1 FO/1 BOR) +15 containers & 8 packages	624 (SD) Sqn Halifax B Mk II 1a M, ?	Dropped on DZ 'Chenier' (south-west of Aurillac) and DZ 'Tarsis', near Grenoble to SOE 'RF Section's 'Droite' & 'F's 'Jockey' réseaux. 'Veganin' BOR killed in drop.
June 8/9	'Emily' Blida, North Africa 2220-0505	OSS Operational Group 'Helium' (2 USAO/13 USAEM) +10 containers & 2 packages	624 (SD) Sqn Halifax B Mk II 1a H	Dropped 0153-0215 hours on DZ 'Chenier', 'Droite's' permanent depot ground. Tasked to cut principal by-pass railways east of main line Montauban-Cahors-Brive.
	Adverse weather over United Kingdom bases prevented drops 'Houndsworth 2' and 'Bulbasket 3' taking place on this night.			
June 9/10	'Ravine' Blida, North Africa 2235-0625	Jedburgh Team 'Ammonia' (1 USAO/1 FO/1 USAEM) +15 containers & 8 packages	624 (SD) Sqn Halifax B Mk II 1a S	Dropped on DZ 'Umtata' (44° 55' 32" N 01° 17' 19" E) to SOE 'F' Section réseau 'Wheelwright' tasked to cut the main enemy lines of communication in the Dordogne departement.
June 9/10	'Sunflower III' Fairford 0026-0426	'Samwest 3': 16 FAR, 4ème BIA; 'Wash' Mission (1 RAFGLO, SAS Brigade) +7 containers 14 FAR, 4ème BIA; Jedburgh Team 'Frederick'(1 BO/1 FO/1 USAEM) +7 containers	620 (GT) Sqn Stirling IV E, T	Dropped on DZ near Forêt de Duault to 'Samwest' reception at 0245 hours. One NCO died when a grenade in his rucksack exploded when it hit the ground. Grenades also detonated in two other rucksacks without further casualties.
June 9/10	'Sunflower III' Fairford ex Keevil 0035-0357	'Samwest 2': 1 FO/16 FOR, 4ème BIA +9 containers	196 Sqn Stirling IV D	Party delayed from previous night dropped on DZ 3km south-west of Forêt de Duault to 'Samwest' reception.
June 9/10	'Sunflower III' Fairford ex Keevil 0045-0415 Fairford 0049-0436	'Dingson 2': 47 FAR, 4ème BIA; Jedburgh Team 'George' (1 USAO/2 FO) +23 containers	299 Sqn Stirling IV F, O 620 (GT) Sqn Stirling IV Q	Dropped 0215 hours on DZ 'La Baleine' near village of St Marcel to 'Dingson' sponsored reception. Some casualties caused when rucksacks exploded on hitting the ground. Explosions probably caused by pins being jolted out of primed grenades.
June 10/11	'Sunflower IV' Fairford 2320-0319 Fairford ex Keevil 2345-0344	'Dingson 3': CO, 4ème BIA/ 16 FOR, 4ème BIA +14 containers 1 FO/16 FOR, 4ème BIA +unknown number of containers 1 FO/16 FOR, 4ème BIA +unknown number of containers	299 Sqn Stirling IV B, R 196 Sqn Stirling IV G	'R' dropped after 0200 hours on DZ 'La Baleine' near village of St Marcel to 'Dingson' sponsored reception. 'Dingson' then in contact with 'five full strength Resistance battalions, regularly organised'. 'B' and 'G' returned to base with troops due to adverse weather conditions.
June 10/11	'Sunflower IV' Fairford 2230-0356	'Houndsworth 2': OC, A Sqn/ 4 BOR, 1 SAS; 2 Ptl, F Sqn, 'Phantom' (1 BO/4 BOR); SOE 'RF' Section Mission 'Isaac' (1 BO/1 BOR) +4 containers & 3 panniers 1 BO/8 BOR, A Sqn, 1 SAS, 1 FOR, 3ème BIA	620 (GT) Sqn Stirling IV B, S	'B' dropped troops at 0135 hours near Lormes 40 km from the intended DZ. 'S' dropped at 0210 hours on Fétigny 40 km from DZ. All sticks linked up and called in 'Houndsworth 4' to prepare for rail cuts on Operation 'Toby 1' (Lyon-Chalon-sur Saône-Dijon-Paris),'Toby 2' (Le Creusot- Nevers) and 'Toby 3' (general action against the enemy line of communications Paris-Orléans area).
June 10/11	'Sunflower IV' Fairford 2308-0500	Lot 4 and Lot 2: each aircraft two sticks: 1 BO/3 BOR; 4 BOR, B Sqn, 1 SAS	620 (GT) Sqn Stirling IV L, H	Four sticks dropped 'blind' into Region R5. Second stick dropped on enemy-occupied village of Airvault with one man captured.
June 10/11	'Sunflower IV' Fairford 2350-0339	'Samwest 4' (second attempt): 50 FAR, 4ème BIA +39 containers & 1 parcel	620 (GT) Sqn Stirling IV C, G, W	Party delayed from previous night dropped 2 km wide of the 'Samwest' reception on their DZ 3km south-west of Forêt de Duault.

Notes:

3ème BIA: 3ème Bataillon d'Infanterie de l'Air, or (3 French Para or 3 SAS)
4ème BIA: 4ème Bataillon d'Infanterie de l'Air, or (4 French Para or 4 SAS)
GT: General Transport SD: Special Duty
RF: République Française
BO/BOR: British Officer/British Other Rank
FO/FOR/FAR: French Officer/French Other Rank/French All Ranks
RAFGLO: Royal Air Force Ground Liaison Officer

USAO/USAEM: United States of America Officer/United States of America Enlisted Man
Containers: Type III and C could each carry 182kg/400lb of stores when fully loaded and required four men to carry them. 120 Containers gave arms and ammunition for 500 men. Type H broke down into five individually portable drums.
Panniers: Standard British Army wicker-work design which could carry 136kg/300lb of stores when fully loaded. Usually used for indivisible loads which could not be fitted into a container.

used flame-throwers to set the woods alight. Initial casualties were four SAS killed and seven wounded plus five dead and 12 wounded Maquis and civilians for loss of an estimated 45 killed and 100 enemy wounded. SAS and Maquis exfiltrated from 1530 hours to a new SAS sub-base, 'Grog' south-west of Pontivy sponsored by men from 'Dingson'. The 'Samwest' area, like 'Dingson' itself when attacked on June 18, was subsequently subjected to savage reprisals conducted by Ostbataillon (White Russians) with numerous atrocities committed against the local populace and wounded SAS prisoners.]

During the next two months, the Germans in the area were continually harassed by the French SAS troops, and by the Maquis who had been armed and organised. Armed Jeeps were flown in by gliders during August and, by the time the break-out occurred, the whole of Brittany was seething, and German forces were largely confined to the main ports of Brest and Lorient.

When discussing the operations of the US Third Army in Brittany, the Supreme Commander's report to the Combined Chiefs-of-Staff said that: 'Special mention must be made of the great assistance given us by the French Forces of the Interior in the task of reducing Brittany. The overt resistance forces in this area had been built up since June around a corps of Special Air Service troops of the French 4th Parachute Battalion *(sic)* to a total strength of some 30,000 men. As the Allied columns advanced, these French forces ambushed the retreating enemy, attacked isolated groups and strong-points, and protected British troops from destruction. When our armor had swept past them, they were given the task of clearing up the localities where pockets of Germans remained, and of keeping open the Allied lines of communication. They also provided our troops with invaluable assistance in supplying information of the enemy's dispositions and intentions. Not least in importance, they had, by their ceaseless harassing activities, surrounded the Germans with a terrible atmosphere of danger and hatred which ate into the confidence of the leaders and the courage of the soldiers.'

The 4ème Bataillon Infanterie de l'Air, known to the British as 4 French Para or 4 SAS, and B Squadron of 1st SAS Regiment, paid a high price for this generous letter of thanks. Most of the men from the 'Dingson' reconnaissance parties were shot on capture in July by a Feldgendarmerietrupp. The 2ème RCP as a whole lost 22 officers and 145 other ranks killed, wounded and missing from their operations in Brittany. Of the men who dropped on 'Bulbasket' 1 and 2, only two came home. 'Bulbasket' at full strength had 55 all ranks; 31 of them when captured were executed by LXXX. Armeekorps Radfahrschwadron (bicycle squadron) in accordance with Hitler's 'Kommandobefehl' of October 18, 1942 and June 25, 1944, in the Bois de Guron near Rom, Département de Des-Sèvres on July 7.

Operation 'Houndsworth's base set-up team and the men of Mission 'Isaac' pose before Stirling IV 'S' at Fairford on the evening of June 10 either side of Sergeant H. Thompson, their RAF despatcher for Operation 'Sunflower IV'. Taken with his Army issue camera by Lieutenant Johnny Wiseman also of the 1st SAS Regiment (who was to follow them into France on June 22), the men have been identified as, left to right; Rifleman Ken Ralli of 'Phantom', Troopers Babbington and Furness of 1st SAS, Lieutenant 'Tom' Moore, Private Jeff Brinton, Corporal Arthur 'Chippy' Wood and Trooper George Harris all of 'Phantom': At far right 'Telemetre' or Lieutenant-Colonel 'J. L. Hastings' alongside the tall figure of Major Bill Fraser, OC A Squadron, 1st SAS Regiment, one of David Stirling's original 'L' Detachment officers and still wearing his sand-coloured beret despite orders to adopt the red beret of airborne forces on return to the UK. 'Hastings' was actually Lieutenant-Colonel James Hutchison, head of 'RF' Section, SOE, and is apparently wearing one of their 'striptease' agent suits. For Mission 'Isaac', he had taken a new name and had his face altered by plastic surgery as his real name, face and position in SOE were known to the SD. The SAS and SOE officers and all the 'Phantom' men named here were all decorated for their part in the liberation of France.

TOP SECRET

C-1543

Supreme Headquarters
ALLIED EXPEDITIONARY FORCE
Office of the Supreme Commander

TOP SECRET

SHAEF/17240/2/4/Ops (C)
GCT 370.2-4/Ops (C)

25 September 1944

Dear McLeod:

I wish to send my congratulations to all ranks of the Special Air Service Brigade on the contribution which they have made to the success of the operations of the Allied Expeditionary Force.

The ruthlessness with which the enemy have attacked Special Air Service troops has been an indication of the injury which you were able to cause to the GERMAN armed forces both by your own efforts and by the information which you gave of GERMAN dispositions and movements.

Many Special Air Service troops are still behind the enemy lines; others are being reformed for new tasks. To all of them, I say "Well done, and good luck!"

Yours, Sincerely

Dwight D. Eisenhower

Brigadier R. W. McLeod,
Commander, Special Air
Service Brigade.

D-Day's First Fatal Casualty

By Father Alberic Stacpoole, OSB

The grave of Lance-Corporal Edward Hull in North Hinksey cemetery at Oxford sparked off Father Alberic's quest to establish D-Day's first casualty. His letter, published in *The Daily Telegraph* in June 1994, led your Editor to further explore other possibilities . . . leading to the naming of the first British casualty in Normandy: Lance-Corporal Fred Greenhalgh.

On June 4, 1994, half a century on from the day in question, a letter appeared in *The Daily Telegraph* which caused some interest, particularly among veterans of the Parachute Regiment, as it suggested that a member of 9th Battalion, The Parachute Regiment, whose D-Day task was to destroy the Merville Battery, had been first to lose his life.

There are problems in trying to determine who was the first casualty, one of them being where to draw the line of initiation, i.e. when should one perceive Operation 'Overlord' as having begun? British and American parachutists landed in France minutes after midnight on June 5/6: certainly no seaborne troops landed till several hours later. In my view, the only practical criterion is to select from those designated to land on D-Day itself, and put on battle alert to do so.

My interest arose from the fact that I was a regular officer from 1951, volunteering for a three-year tour (as all officers did then, from their regiments) with 2nd Battalion, The Parachute Regiment during 1954-57 which included the Suez operation. In 1960, I became a monk of Ampleforth, and that took me to a degree course, then an appointment at our St Benet's Hall in Oxford. I was wont to cycle out to the military cemetery at North Hinksey on the western outskirts of Oxford, to pray a little on days of military remembrance, and there I found the war grave (No. 167 in Plot I/1) with the heart-warming Parachute Regiment badge chiselled on it. This grave read thus: '6465258 L/Cpl E. T. Hull Parachute Regiment 6 June 1944 aged 25'. How so was such a grave here, not in Normandy, I mused?

I wrote to the Editor of *Pegasus Journal* in Aldershot and what I have gleaned from there and elsewhere is this. Lance-Corporal Edward Hull was the son of John and Esther Hull; he was in A Company of the 9th Battalion, destined for the operation against the Merville Battery, his platoon commander being Lieutenant Hugh Pond. Among three gliders to be flown in after the parachute drop with a total of 58 men, only Pond's glider reached the target area — and even that was hit as it landed.

The 9th Parachute Battalion had been alerted to set off on the evening of June 4, postponed to June 5. The main element, the parachutists, took off from Broadwell that evening; the glider element having left Broadwell in the morning for Brize Norton. Former Sergeant Doug Woodcraft remembers that a company orderly was accidentally shot at Broadwell airfield while carrying instructions to those emplaning for Normandy; a thoughtless moment with a loaded rifle.

Lieutenant-Colonel (later General Sir) Napier Crookenden, who later succeeded Terence Otway as CO of 9 Para, has written in his book *Dropzone Normandy* (Ian Allan 1976): 'A firearm accident wounded L/Cpl Hull of A Coy, glider assault party, so that he died soon after'. What is not clear is whether Lance-Corporal Hull accidentally wounded himself, or if another soldier accidentally shot him. He was taken to the 107th General Hospital in Oxford and his platoon commander, with the battalion padre, managed an exceedingly rare permission to leave their battle-sealed camp to visit the injured man as he was dying. Hugh Pond recorded that Hull was in tears because he would miss D-Day. Pond and the padre were convinced that what had happened was wholly an accident. Pond wrote: 'He was a good-looking boy and a good soldier'.

On D-Day, as his companions were caught up in fierce fighting, Lance-Corporal Edward Hull died in his hospital bed and, in that rather complicated sense, he therefore has claim to be one of D-Day's first casualties even though he lies at peace in Oxford.

A similar incident also occurred on the evening of D–1 at one of the American airborne bases: Spanhoe, five miles north-east of Corby in Northamptonshire. As the paratroops of the 505th Parachute Infantry Regiment of the 82nd Airborne Division were emplaning, a Gammon grenade carried by one of the men in Headquarters Company, 1st Battalion, exploded killing Private First Class Robert L. Leakey, Private Pete Vah and Corporal Kenneth A. Vaught. Every member of the stick was wounded (save Corporal Melvin J. Fryer), and Private Eddie O. Meelberg died later that night, i.e. on June 6. The dates of death for Private Leakey, Private Vah and Corporal Vaught are all recorded as June 5, undoubtedly marking them as the earliest accidental casualties. Both Robert Leakey and Kenneth Vaught remain buried in Britain at the American Military Cemetery at Madingley, Cambridgeshire, Leakey in Grave 26 of Plot E, Row 6 and Vaught right behind in Row 5. The remains of Pete Vah and Eddie Meelberg were sent back to the States (Ohio and Minnesota respectively).

Two of the first American D-Day casualties still buried in the United Kingdom: Pfc Robert Leakey and Corporal Kenneth Vaught, killed while emplaning at Spanhoe airfield, now at rest in the American Military Cemetery just outside Cambridge.

The pathfinders of the 101st Airborne Division, jumping between 0.16 and 0.45 a.m., led the assault on the Cherbourg peninsula. (Those of the 82nd did not begin their drop until 1.15 a.m.) There, the overall picture is muddy as so many men dropped unseen by their fellows but a report was prepared by Captain Frank Lillyman (see page 298) for Major General Maxwell Taylor dated July 1, 1944. In it he refers to 2nd Lieutenant Charles Faith's pathfinder stick (3rd Battalion, 501st Parachute Infantry Regiment) and says that one (unnamed) enlisted man was killed before he could get out of his parachute harness.

George E. Koskimaki, the tireless 101st author and historian (see also page 296), researched this incident with Lillyman in the 1960s and, in Lieutenant Faith's stick which was dropped on DZ 'C' at 0.25 a.m., Private Stanley Suwarsky came down in a tree and was machine-gunned before he could get free of his harness. 'However, it all depends on the time the planes of the various pathfinder teams dropped their sticks', writes George. 'I have been told by fellows of his unit (Base Stick, 501st) that Pfc Harold E. Sellers was dead before he landed, and, according to his friends, Private Donald J. McDougall (also part of Suwarsky's stick) is reported to have drowned. Another possibility is Sergeant Thayer U. Carlton of the 3rd Battalion Stick of the 506th.'

However, records show that both Seller's and Carlton's sticks were dropped on DZ 'D' at about 0.45 a.m., so their deaths appear to have occurred later than those of Suwarsky and McDougall. Only Private Suwarsky and Pfc Sellers are buried in Normandy today, both in Plot F of the American Cemetery at St Laurent (Suwarsky in Grave 16, Row 15, and Sellers in Grave 38, Row 13). McDougall was returned to the US after the war and today lies buried in Golden Gate National Cemetery in California.

At sea, the first casualty of Operation 'Neptune' occurred on the 5th when the minesweeper USS *Osprey* of the 7th Minesweeping Squadron (Force 'U') hit a mine at 6 p.m. and sank at 7.30 p.m. while under tow. There were six casualties, all missing.

In Normandy, the first US casualty of D-Day is most probably Private Stanley Suwarsky, buried in the cemetery at St Laurent.

The 53rd (Worcestershire) Airlanding Light Regiment, RA, of the 6th Airborne Division provided a Forward Observation Group, under Major The Hon. Charles Russell, to land by glider in advance of the main airborne force to get into a position where, by radio, they could act as fire controllers for the naval bombardment supporting 6th Airborne. The precise circumstances of Bombardier Henry Hall's death are obscure (his death certificate merely states that he was 'killed in action') but, to qualify for the unique date of death inscribed on his headstone in Ranville Churchyard, it must have occurred before midnight, i.e. during the flight across the Channel.

However, we know that Private William Richardson was fatally wounded while airborne by flak as he was about to jump from his Dakota, so he may well be the first Allied soldier to be killed *over* Normandy. His body was brought back to Britain and buried near to the airfield from which he had taken off.

Among the very first Allied troops to land in Normandy were two Special Air Service parties, comprising an officer and two men in each, who were dropped at 0.20 a.m. near Marigny as one of the small elements of the 'Fortitude' deception operation in Operation 'Titanic IV' (see map page 250). The first SAS casualty would appear to be Caporal Emile Bouétard who had been dropped with eight others at 1 a.m. on June 6 near St Jean Brévelay some 20 kilometres north of Vannes in Brittany. Around 3 a.m., the party was engaged by the Germans and surrounded. Caporal Bouétard had been wounded and was promptly despatched by his captors. The SAS Memorial at Plumelec, just east of St Jean, lists the names of 77 'parachutistes français' including that of Caporal Emile Bouétard.

During the actual flight to Normandy, Private William Richardson, a paratrooper with the 8th Battalion, The Parachute Regiment, was flying in a Dakota which had left from Blakehill Farm airfield, north-west of Swindon, and as the aircraft approached the DZ, it was hit by flak. Richardson was standing in the doorway ready to jump when he was hit and he died in the Dakota which subsequently brought his body back to the UK. He was buried in Grave 278 in Watchfield Military Cemetery which lies east of the chapelyard of St Thomas' Watchfield in Berkshire.

Within minutes of the 101st Airborne pathfinders dropping, the gliders of the coup de main party of Operation 'Deadstick' made their landings close to the bridges over the River Orne and Caen Canal. Although Lieutenant Herbert 'Den' Brotheridge of 'D' Company, The Oxfordshire and Buckinghamshire Light Infantry, has been accepted as the first man killed in the face of the enemy as he ran across the canal bridge at Bénouville minutes after the landing at 0016, he died some 30 minutes later from his wound. He fell in the road opposite the Café Gondrée, shot in the neck, and was carried to a first-aid post which had been established in a small lane about 150 yards east of the bridge. Today, he lies in Grave 43 in Ranville Churchyard.

Lance-Corporal Fred Greenhalgh in Glider No. 3 (Lieutenant 'Sandy' Smith's platoon) had been thrown out as the Horsa finished its run and broke in two, and he was drowned in the pond, the only casualty of the actual landing. He now lies buried in Grave 4 of Row C in Plot 5 in La Délivrande War Cemetery, and he is undoubtedly the first British casualty in Normandy.

Although the French plaque beside his grave in Ranville Churchyard states that Lieutenant Herbert Brotheridge was the 'first English soldier killed', that is not strictly true.

Although Lieutenant 'Den' Brotheridge was the first British soldier to be killed on the ground in the face of the enemy (see page 227), the soldier who was thrown out and drowned as the gliders came to a standstill was undoubtedly the first Briton to die in Normandy. In all the literature of the period, he has never been identified and it appears that no one has cared enough to find out who he was. In our attempt to give him a name, we came across this shot *(above)* in a cine film taken by Sergeant Ken Hodges of the RAF ground film unit on July 28, 1944. These four graves lie at the eastern end of Bènouville (Pegasus) Bridge at grid reference 100747 with the glider, in which the unnamed man was killed, in the background. The Commonwealth War Graves Commission kindly provided the matching Graves Concentration Report for this location *(below)*, listing the names of the four dead. Lance-Corporal Greenhalgh was in Staff Sergeant Barkway's glider (Chalk No. 93) which broke open over the pond, and Greenhalgh was the only occupant recorded as being killed. However, an unknown hand has altered his date of death to June 7, which is the date presently inscribed on his headstone in La Délivrande War Cemetery *(right)*.

There is no simple answer to the question as to who was D-Day's first fatal casualty; it all depends on the criteria one chooses to adopt. Some may well say: does it matter anyway, as the sacrifice is no different to that of all those who lost their lives on D-Day. That total has never reliably been determined, the best estimate being 2,500 killed on the first day (see also page 620) — a remarkably low figure for what Churchill rightly called 'the most difficult and complicated operation that has ever taken place'.

GRAVES CONCENTRATION REPORT FORM

has
The following have been concentrated here :-

CAL. 24E. 9

(Name of Cemetery) La Delivrande British Cemetery

(Full Map Reference) Sheet 7E/5 Scale 1/50000 027.803

Nationality: BRITISH

(2) Regt. or Corps	(3) Army No.	(4) Name & Initials	(5) Rank	(6) Date of Death	(7) K/A, D/W or Died	(8) Plot	(9) Row	(10) Grave	(11) Date of Reburial	Previous location of grave: Place & Map Ref.		Repo Numb.
R.A. ~~4 Commando~~	118467	Wilson P.M.M.	Lieut	6/6/44	K/A	V	C	2	12 Feb 45	Ranville 1/50000	7F/2 100.747	21 AGp/ CAL 2-2104
R.W.F. 6 Commando	4206553	Charity A.	Fus.	"	"	V	C	3	"	"	"	CAL 2-757 "
Ox. & Bucks (Airborne)	3449663	Greenhalgh F.	L/Cpl	7.6.44	"	V	C	4	"	"	"	CAL "
SCOTS. GUARDS. 3 Commando	2697390	Campbell L.	Gdsm	6.6.44	"	V	C	5	"	"	"	CAL 2-757

82nd Airborne Division

By Major General Matthew B. Ridgway

Matthew Bunker Ridgway was commissioned in April 1917, serving in a variety of postings in China, Nicaragua, the Panama Canal Zone and the Philippines. In September 1939, he was with the War Plans Division in Washington, becoming commanding general of the 82nd Infantry Division in June 1942.

In the last long light of the clear June day, weighted down with my battle gear, I climbed heavily up the little ladder of the plane that was to take me to France. In the doorway, I turned for one last look at the sweep of the English Midlands, now grown soft and green with spring. All around me, the dusty aircraft of the 52nd Troop Carrier Command were taking on their cargoes of fighting men — 6,000 booted, burdened paratroopers of my 82nd Division. For many of them, this was an old story, for they had jumped to battle in Sicily and in Italy. For me, it was a new adventure. I was no stranger to combat nor to jumping. I had jumped in training; and, in Sicily and Italy, seen battle on the ground; I had been with them when the fighting was the hottest. But I had never yet shared with them the very special dangers that are a combat paratrooper's particular lot — the quick leap out of the plane into the buffeting prop-wash, the slow float down, hanging helpless in the harness, the drop into the darkness where armed enemies wait behind every bush and tree.

All this was new to me, and I had prepared myself to face it, as all men must steel their own souls to face new and unknown dangers. In the long days of training, as I readied this veteran fighting force for its greatest testing, there had been no time for introspection, for troubling thoughts of what fate might hold in store for me. But in the darkness after you have gone to bed, when you are not the commander, with stars on your shoulders, but just one man, alone with your God in the dark, your thoughts inevitably turn inward, and out of whatever resources of the spirit you possess, you prepare yourself as best you may for whatever tests may lie ahead.

I cannot speak for other men, but for me in such moments there has always been great comfort in the story of the anguish of Our Lord in the Garden of Gethsemane. And in all humbleness, without in any way seeking to compare His trials to mine, I have felt that if He could face with calmness of soul the great suffering He knew was to be His fate, then I surely could endure any lesser ordeal of the flesh or spirit that might be awaiting me.

There were other thoughts, inspired by poetry and the Scriptures, which gave me strength and comfort. Sometimes, at night, it was almost as if I could hear the assurance that God the Father gave to another soldier, named Joshua: 'I will not fail thee nor forsake thee'. And in my wallet was a picture, stained and faded, of a Scottish soldier's monument that stands in Edinburgh. The soldier sits, head up, rifle across his knees, as if for a moment there had come a lull in battle. Carved in the stone beneath him is an inscription which long ago, unconsciously perhaps, I wove into the fabric of my own philosophy: 'If it be Life that waits, I shall live forever unconquered; if Death, I shall die at last, strong in my pride and free.'

Knowing that, indeed, it might be death that awaited me, in the last moments before I left my quarters for the take-off fields I had sat down to say my last good-bys, to try to express something of the deep pride I felt in the men with whom I now was to go into battle. On the bottom of my own photograph, knowing that somebody would find it if I did not come back, I wrote these lines:

'To the members of the 82nd Airborne Division, with everlasting affection and appreciation of life shared with them in the service of our country. May their incomparable courage, fidelity, soldierly conduct and fighting spirit ever keep for this Division a place second to none in our Army.'

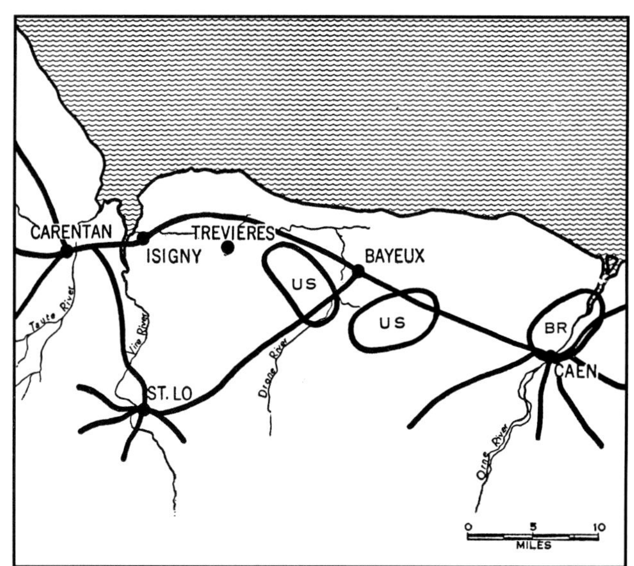

The 82nd Infantry Division, with its sobriquet 'All American', had fought in the First World War and it was reactivated in April 1942 under Brigadier General Omar Bradley. At the time, the creation of an American airborne division was actively under discussion at the Provisional Parachute Group, headed by Brigadier General William Lee who had as his Plans and Training Officer a young paratrooper, James Gavin *(left)*. Two months after Ridgway had taken command of the 82nd, it was redesignated an airborne division, being initially assigned two new parachute regiments, the 504th, and 505th of which Gavin became the commanding officer. After baptismal operations in Sicily and Italy, in October 1943 Gavin was promoted Assistant Division Commander of the 82nd with the rank of brigadier general, and sent to London the following month as General Ridgway's Executive Officer, to participate in the planning of 'Overlord' which, at that stage, was still being pursued as a three-division operation. There were two American airborne divisions available, the 82nd and the 101st. 'The first and major Normandy mission for the airborne troops was a vital one', wrote Gavin in 1947. 'They were to block the German reserves that would attempt to reinforce the defending coastal units. The next airborne force mission was to attack the coastal defenses from the rear. The drop-zones and landing zones *(right)* were suitable, the flak to be expected was not too bad, and the rest of the plan looked feasible enough. But it was obvious that the 21st Panzer Division, which was within ten miles of Caen, would be especially difficult to handle in such good tank country. Clearly, if the airborne troops were to block the hostile reserves, the place to do it was around Caen and Bayeux and in the corridor between them. But airborne troops would be at a great disadvantage in such country. I knew by then that I would participate in the airborne assault and I remembered our experiences with the Hermann Göring Panzer Division in Sicily. I was especially aware of the difficulties we would probably have in fighting off the German armor and so I took a rather dim view of the entire plan.'

It was no masterpiece of literary composition, I know, but it expressed my feelings. And as I took my place in the plane in the hard bucket seat, and buckled my seat belt tight around me, I felt a great serenity. All that I knew to do had been done, and I was ready to accept whatever was to come. From then on, there was no backward glancing to happy days gone by, no inner tremors brought on by fearful imaginings of what might lie ahead. My soul was at peace, my heart was light, my spirits almost gay.

The mood of the men around me seemed equally tranquil as we lifted up, engines roaring, to join the great sky train that was on its way to France. I looked at my watch. It was 10 p.m., June 5, 1944. D-Day –1. For men of the 82nd, the battle for Normandy had begun.

'After I had left the conference,' Gavin recalled, 'somebody pointed out to me that in Major F. O. Miksche's book, *Paratroops* [published in 1943], he had suggested a plan for the use of parachute troops in this same Normandy area — a plan exactly like the one just agreed upon. Well, undoubtedly the Germans had read Miksche too. Later, I was present at a conference at the headquarters of General Bradley in Bryanston Square in London. At this meeting, Bradley showed a particular interest in widening the D-Day assault front to include a landing north of the Vire estuary and, in the event, such plan was adopted, using the airborne troops to assist the landings and cut off the Peninsula, the prompt seizure of the port of Cherbourg being one of the missions of First Army which needed to be blocked off speedily. The country between Carentan and Lessay, in contrast to that between Caen and Bayeux, was excellent anti-tank country. There were very few areas of any size in which tanks could maneuver with any freedom. And there were plenty of drop and landing zones. The mission appeared to be a natural.'

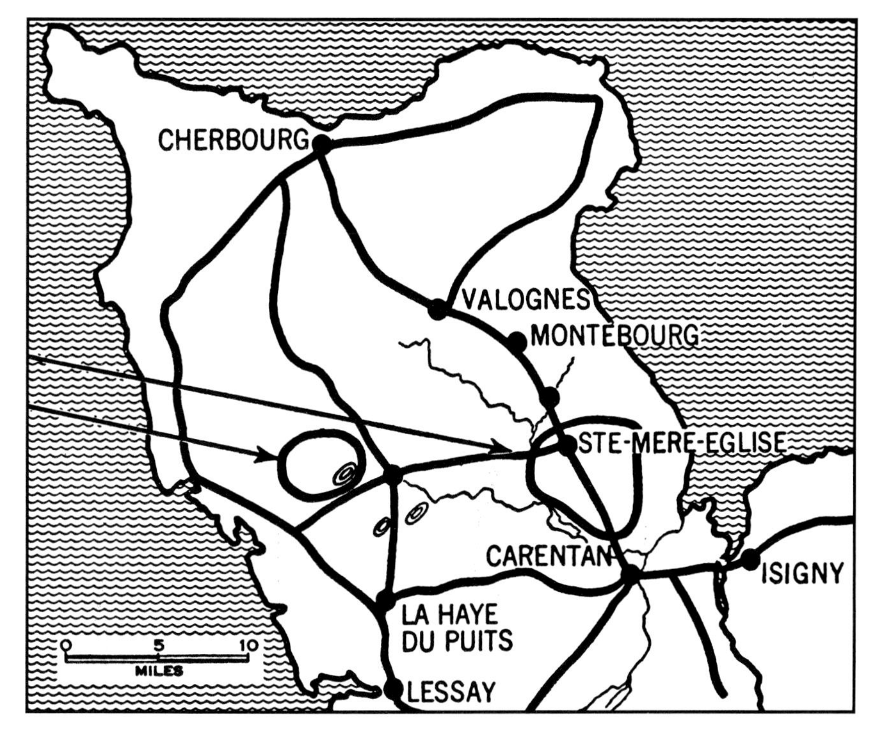

'The plan we finally arrived at was the one toward which all preparations, reconnaissance, and planning were pointed for the next six months', explained Gavin. 'It called for the drop of the 101st north of Carentan. This division was to block the movement of German reserves, seize the western ends of the causeways leading from the assault beaches inland, and also crossings of the Merderet river in preparation for an advance to the west. The 82nd was to land west of St Sauveur-le-Vicomte *(right)* and capture that town and the bridge over the Douve river nearby to block all movement north of the Prairies Marécageuses and block all roads to the coast. We memorized the terrain, the drop areas and the road nets, and we memorized all plans and orders so that no man would have to take a marked paper into combat. Time and again, we held night reorganization and assembly problems. In these, we made use of all the assembly aids that had been improvised since the highly confused night fighting in Sicily. And we held war games on sand tables for all units and squads of every outfit until every man knew not only his own mission but that of his probable neighbors in combat.'

It might be interesting at this time to describe how an airborne division is committed to battle, compared to a standard unit in the Army. The infantry unit goes into battle with its communications and its command structure at its best. The radios are all functioning, the command chain is intact. The commander knows where all his people are, and what's happening to them, and he can exercise an excellent degree of control. The exact opposite is true of an airborne division. When its people hit the ground, they are individuals, and a two-star general and a Pfc are on exactly the same basis. You have no communications whatsoever for some little time, particularly when you have jumped at night. You don't know where you are. You don't know who's around you, friend or foe. Little by little, stage by stage, you have to assemble — to 'roll up the stick', as the paratroopers say.

This is a fairly simple thing in theory. The first men out of the plane note its general heading in relation to the ground. When they hit and chuck out of their harness, they start moving along the track of the plane. The last men out back-track along the path the plane has followed. Somewhere toward the middle they come together. But this takes time. Under the best of conditions, the men in one battalion will be strung out along a path 1,000 yards long and 300 yards wide. Along their route, enemy gunners may block their way until they can be killed. In Normandy, the assembling was further complicated by the fact that the fields were compartments, separated each from the other by the high thick hedges.

The first objective, of course, is to get a battalion together, for the battalion is the basic fighting unit. I went in with the 2nd Battalion of the 505th, commanded by Lieutenant Colonel Ben

'As D-Day neared, we studied intensively the air photos of the operational areas and, typical of the anti-airborne measures we detected, was the German preparation of Hill 110, a clear unwooded height rising 110 meters above the surrounding hedgerows about 5,000 yards west of St Sauveur-le-Vicomte. Finally, about three weeks before D-Day, small black specks in a regular geometric pattern began to show up all over the hill. They continued to grow in number until the entire hill was covered with them. After several days of worry over Hill 110, the tell-tale shadows of the 'Rommelspargel' began to appear although it was impossible to say whether they were connected with wires. Also in mid-May, the German High Command sent in the 91st Infantry Division and located it generally, as well as we were able to determine at the time, in the vicinity of St Sauveur-le-Vicomte. The situation did not look too promising then for the 82nd. Indeed, it looked so unpromising that it was decided to change our landing areas and, a week before our movement to the departure airfields, the drop-zones of all elements of the 82nd Airborne Division were moved about ten miles further east.'

As originally conceived in 1942, an American airborne division comprised one paratrooper and two glider regiments totalling some 8,500 men, but by 1944 the three paratrooper/one glider regiment composition reduced this to 7,500 officers and men. Before D-Day, the two battalions of the 401st Glider Infantry Regiment were hived off to add a third battalion to the 325th Glider Infantry Regiment of the 82nd, and one to the 327th of the 101st Airborne Division. For 'Overlord', the division was split into three echelons: Force 'A' — the parachute troops; Force 'B' — the glider troops; and Force 'C' which was to arrive by sea. The revised plan called for the 505th Parachute Infantry Regiment (landing on DZ 'O') to capture Ste Mère-Eglise and the bridges to the west at La Fière and Chef-du-Pont. The 507th (DZ 'T') was to seize bridges over the Merderet river, while the third regiment, the 508th, arriving on DZ 'N', was to establish defensive positions west of the river.

Vandervoort, one of the bravest, toughest battle commanders I ever knew. He broke an ankle in the jump, but the paramedics who had jumped with us rigged him up a stirrup crutch and cut him a stick for a cane, and he led his battalion, limping but game, throughout the entire campaign.

We flew in a V of Vs, like a gigantic spearhead without a shaft. England was on double daylight saving time, and it was still full light, but eastward, over the Channel, the skies were darkening. Two hours later, night had fallen, and below us we could see glints of yellow flame from the German anti-aircraft guns on the Channel Islands. We watched them curiously and without fear, as a high-flying duck may watch a hunter, knowing that we were too high and far away for their fire to reach us. In the plane, the men sat quietly, deep in their own thoughts. They joked a little and broke, now and then, into ribald laughter. Nervousness and tension, and the cold that blasted through the open door, had its effect upon us all. Now and then, a paratrooper would rise, lumber heavily to the little bathroom in the tail of the plane, find he could not push through the narrow doorway in his bulky gear, and come back, mumbling his profane opinion of the designers of the C-47 airplane. Soon, the crew chief passed a bucket around, but this did not entirely solve our problem. A man strapped and buckled into full combat gear finds it extremely difficult to reach certain essential portions of his anatomy, and his efforts are not made easier by the fact that his comrades are watching him, jeering derisively and offering gratuitous advice.

Wing to wing, the big planes snuggled close in their tight formation, we crossed to the coast of France. I was sitting straight across the aisle from the doorless exit. Even at 1,500 feet, I could tell the Channel was rough, for we passed over a small patrol craft — one of the check-points for our navigators — and the light it displayed for us was bobbing like a cork in a mill-race. No lights showed on the land, but, in the

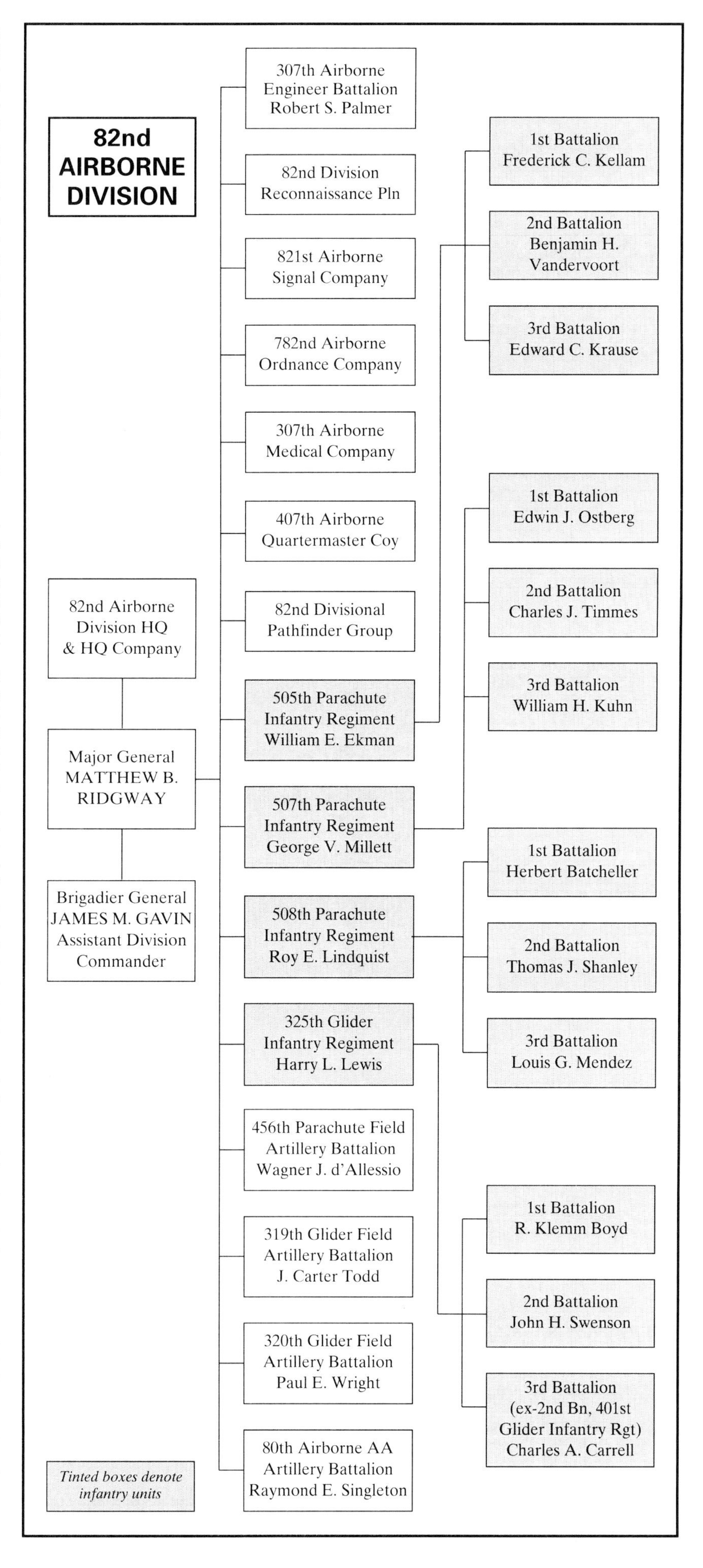

In his personal account, Brigadier General Gavin fails to emphasise the seriousness of the last-minute change of plan, and tends to gloss over the fact that several months' planning had now to be redone in little over a week. The decision to move the 82nd to a completely new area is simply described by him as 'sliding the regimental drop-zones the necessary number of miles to the east'. Gavin said that 'we left unchanged the relative location of the drop-zones, consequently no change had to be made in the assignment of units to take-off airfields and troop carrier units'. *Above:* Gavin, himself (right), took off from Cottesmore (see *Airfields of the Ninth Then and Now*).

pale glow of a rising moon, I could clearly see each farm and field below. And I remember thinking how peaceful the land looked, each house and hedgerow, path and little stream bathed in the silver of the moonlight. And I felt that if it were not for the noise of the engines we could hear the farm dogs baying, and the sound of the barnyard roosters crowing for midnight.

A few minutes inland, we suddenly went into cloud, thick and turbulent. I had been looking out the doorway, watching with a profound sense of satisfaction the close-ordered flight of that great sky caravan that stretched as far as the eye could see. All at once, they were blotted out. Not a wing light showed. The plane began to yaw and plunge, and in my mind's eye I could see the other pilots, fighting to hold course, knowing how great was the danger of a collision in the air.

You could read concern on the grim, set faces of the men in my plane as they turned to peer out of the windows, looking for the wink of the little lavender lights on the wing-tips of the adjoining planes. Not even our own wing lights showed in that thick murk. It was all up to the pilots now. There was nothing I could do, and I did it. I pulled my seat belt tighter and sat back and closed my eyes, taking comfort from the words of Hal Clark, Commanding General of the Troop Carrier Wing, whose planes transported us.

'Matt,' he had told me before the take-off, 'come hell or high wind, my boys will put you there, right on the button.'

The cloud and rough air lasted only a few minutes, though it seemed far longer. As suddenly as we had entered the storm, we broke free. All at once, there was the moon again, and clear skies, and the sharp outlines of the land below, the little fields and hedgerows. But nowhere in the sky, in my field of vision, could I see another plane.

It was too late now to worry about that. Beside the door, a red light glowed. Four minutes left. Down the line of bucket seats, the No. 4 man in the stick stood up. It was Captain Peter Schouvaloff, brother-in-law of Fëdor Chaliapin, the opera singer. He was a get-rich-quick paratrooper, as I was, a man who had had no formal jump training. I was taking him along as a language officer for he spoke both German and Russian, and we knew that in the Cotentin peninsula which we were to seize, the Germans were using captured Russians as combat troops.

A brilliant linguist, he was also something of a clown. Standing up, wearing a look of mock bewilderment on his face, he held up the hook on his static line — the life-line of the parachutist which jerks his canopy from its pack as he dives clear of the plane.

'Pray tell me,' said Schouvaloff, in his thick accent, 'what does one do with this strange device?'

That broke the tension. A great roar of laughter rose from the silent men who were standing now, hooked up and ready to go.

'Are we downhearted', somebody yelled.

'HELL NO!' came back the answering roar.

A bell rang loudly, a green light glowed. The jumpmaster, crouched in the door, went out with a yell — 'Let's go!' With a paratrooper breathing hard on my neck, I leaped out after him.

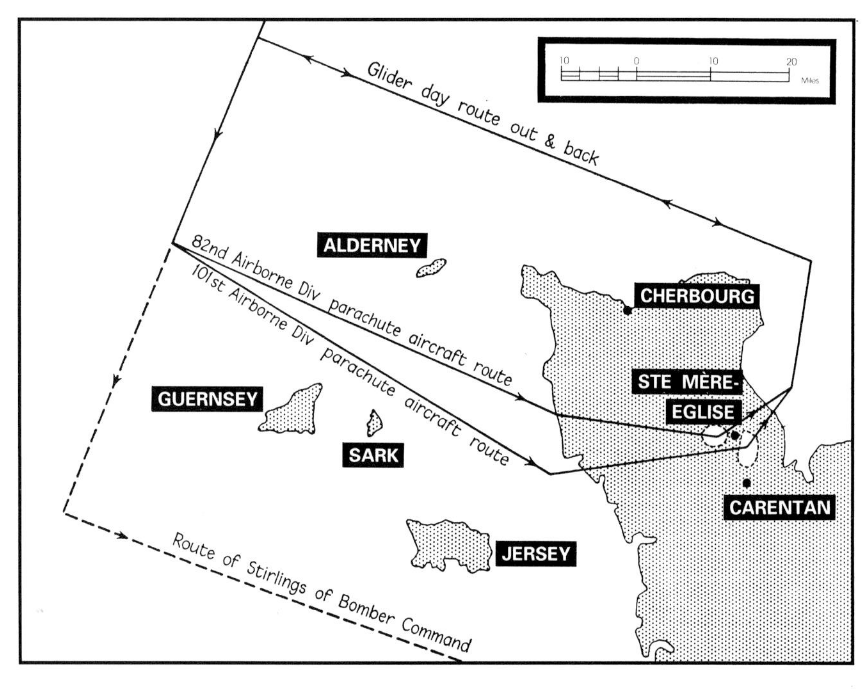

In ideal conditions, a 'serial' of C-47s (36 to 45 aircraft) flying the tight V-formation favoured by IX Troop Carrier Command, could deliver a battalion of paratroops in an area 1,000 yards long by 300 yards wide in about two minutes. However, at night, with a following wind, the route across the Cherbourg peninsula from west to east left very little safety margin, and the timing from when the aircraft crossed the west coast was critical if men were not to be unloaded over the sea. Then there was the risk from flak and small-arms fire against the slow, lumbering transports flying at the optimum height for parachuting of 600 feet, and Air Chief Marshal Leigh-Mallory believed that casualties could run as high as 50 per cent. Also, unlike the large fields available in the British 6th Airborne sector, the small fields in the hedgerow country of the peninsula severely restricted glider operations. Even though Leigh-Mallory insisted on landings being made at dusk and dawn to minimise the risk, he still estimated that losses could reach 75 to 80 per cent.

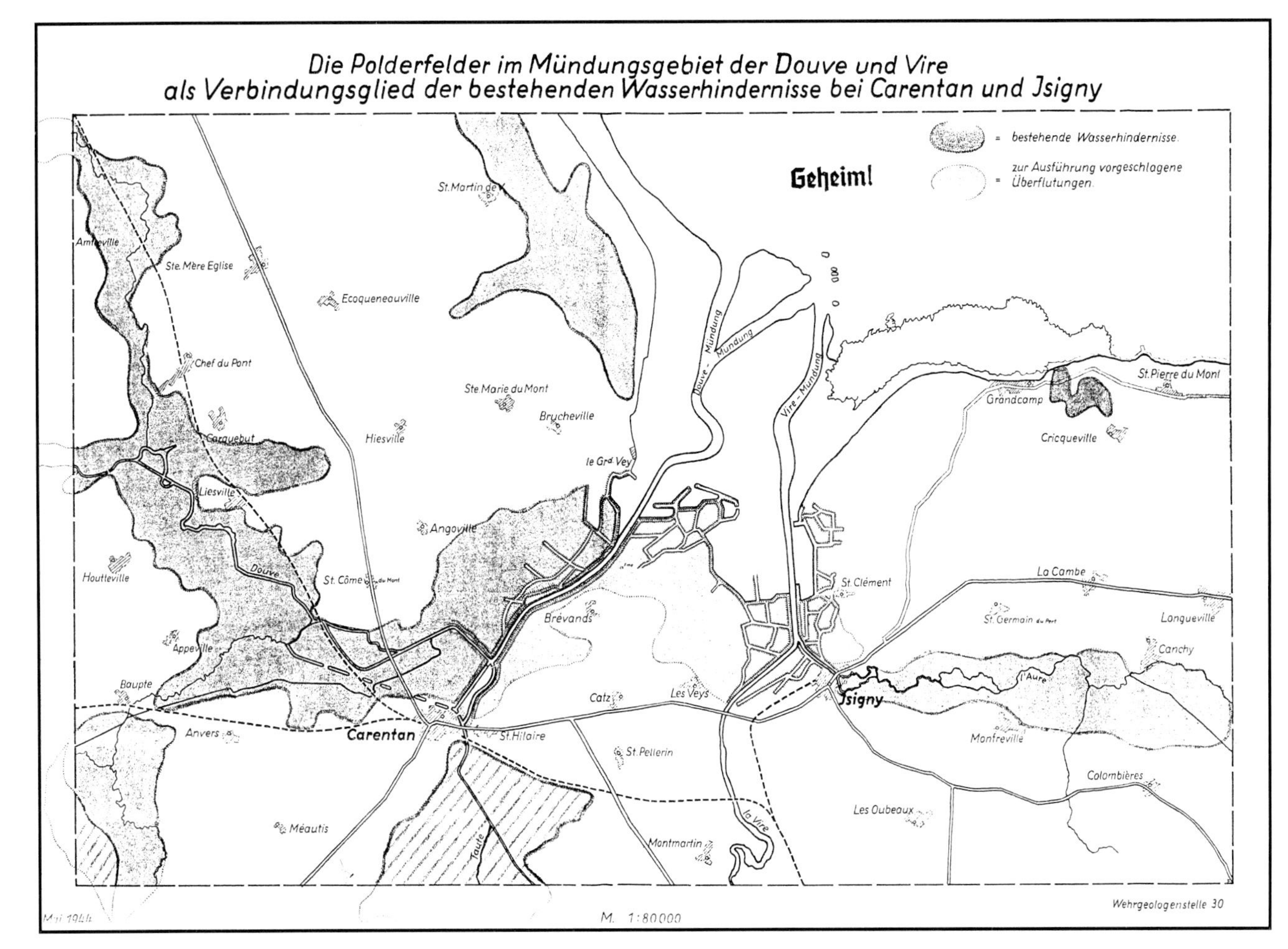

However, there was also another danger, clearly demonstrated by this secret German plan. Apart from a large area which had been deliberately flooded behind the coast, all rivers in the area had been allowed to inundate their valleys, not only restricting the drop-zones, but making any overshoots death traps for the heavily laden paratroopers, most of whom were carrying their equivalent weight in equipment and spare ammunition. Orders for the switch in the 82nd's drop-zones were still being drafted when, on May 27, Leigh-Mallory voiced his fears over the whole American airborne operation which, he said, could result in the virtual destruction of the two US airborne divisions. The following day, VII Corps issued its orders to now drop the 82nd astride the Merderet river. On May 29, in Eisenhower's absence, Air Chief Marshal Tedder presided over a Supreme Commander's conference at which Leigh-Mallory stated that the drop was impossible, while Major-General de Guingand (in Montgomery's absence) reiterated that it was essential. Although Leigh-Mallory was overruled, he pursued his point over the head of Tedder directly to Eisenhower, who had by now moved to Portsmouth.

On May 30, [Leigh-Mallory] came to me to protest once more against what he termed the 'futile slaughter' of two fine divisions. He believed that the combination of unsuitable landing grounds and anticipated resistance was too great a hazard to overcome. Leigh-Mallory was, of course, earnestly sincere. He was noted for personal courage and was merely giving me, as was his duty, his frank convictions.

It would be difficult to conceive of a more soul-racking problem. If my technical expert was correct, then the planned operation was worse than stubborn folly, because even at the enormous cost predicted we could not gain the principal object of the drop. Moreover, if he was right, it appeared that the attack on Utah was probably hopeless, and this meant that the whole operation suddenly acquired a degree of risk, even foolhardiness, that presaged a gigantic failure, possibly Allied defeat in Europe.

To protect him in case his advice was disregarded, I instructed the air commander to put his recommendations in a letter and informed him he would have my answer within a few hours. I took the problem to no one else. Professional advice and counsel could do no more.

I went to my tent alone and sat down to think. Over and over I reviewed each step, somewhat in the sequence set down here, but more thoroughly and exhaustively. I realised, of course, that if I deliberately disregarded the advice of my technical expert on the subject, and his predictions should prove accurate, then I would carry to my grave the unbearable burden of a conscience justly accusing me of the stupid, blind sacrifice of thousands of the flower of our youth. Outweighing any personal burden, however, was the possibility that if he were right the effect of the disaster would be far more than local: it would be likely to spread to the entire force.

If I should cancel the airborne operation, then I had either to cancel the attack on Utah or I would condemn the assaulting forces there to even greater probability of disaster than was predicted for the airborne divisions.

If I should cancel the Utah attack I would so badly disarrange elaborate plans as to diminish chances for success elsewhere and to make later maintenances perhaps impossible. Moreover, in long and calm consideration of the whole great scheme, we had agreed that the Utah attack was an essential factor in prospects for success. To abandon it really meant to abandon a plan in which I had held implicit confidence for more than two years.

I telephoned him that the attack would go as planned and that I would confirm this at once in writing. When, later, the attack was successful, he was the first to call me to voice his delight and to express his regret that he had found it necessary to add to my personal burdens during the final tense days before D-Day.

GENERAL DWIGHT D. EISENHOWER, 1948

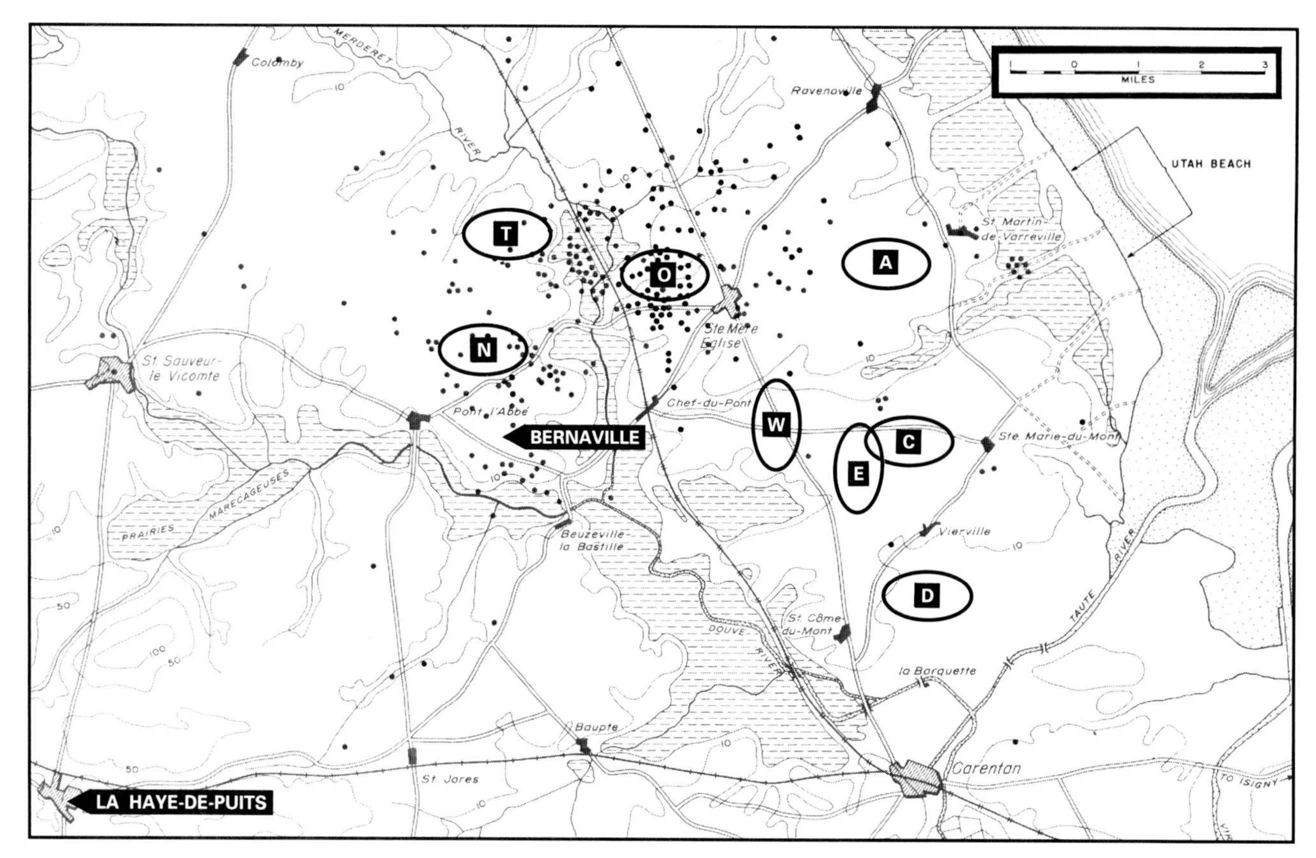

During planning, drop-zones look straightforward although basically they are no more than lines on a map. In reality, at night everything depended on the DZ being marked accurately on the ground with light beacons set up in advance of the arrival of the main force by pathfinders. Ideally, their battery-powered Holophane lights were set out in a 'T', a different colour for each DZ, with the taillight flashing the letter of the drop-zone in Morse. Like those of the 101st, the 82nd's pathfinders took off from North Witham some 30 minutes ahead of the main paratroop force but, out of all the six drop-zones (three for each division), only the teams for DZ 'O' and DZ 'T' were dropped correctly, the others missing their target by over a mile. From their airfields in central England, the route for the 82nd (Operation 'Boston') was about 100 miles longer than that of the 101st who would drop first on DZs 'A', 'C' and 'D' in Operation 'Albany'. Navigation over the sea was assisted by marker vessels but when the force of over 370 C-47s crossed the coast, thick cloud obscured the ground. The formations began to break up, pilots taking evasive action from flak, some opening the throttles to 150 knots at which speed the opening shock of the 'chutes would tear loose equipment from the jumpers. Each dot on the map represents one 82nd 'stick', i.e. one plane-load of paratroops, at least 20 sticks not shown coming down up to 25 miles away. ('E' and 'W' were glider landing zones.)

The shock of the opening was no worse than usual. I glanced up to see the most comforting of all sights, the spread of my canopy, round and bulging, full of air. Below me, off to the left, for a split second I could see the canopy of the jumpmaster hanging, seemingly motionless, in the dark. Then I was alone in the sky. I saw neither man nor parachute, though I knew that all around me troopers and bundles of heavy battle gear were floating swiftly down. In the stillness of the fall, I could hear far above me the roar of the engines as the following planes sped on to their drop-zones.

All at once, the ground was very near, and I flexed my knees for the shock of the landing. Weighted with his heavy battle gear, a combat paratrooper lands hard. He may strike swinging forward, or sideways, or backward, and he absorbs the shock by doing a tumbler's roll, loose-jointed, with springy knees.

I was lucky. There was no wind and I came down straight, into a nice, soft, grassy field. I rolled, spilled the air from my chute, slid out of my harness, and looked around. As I hit, I grabbed for my pistol, for on the advice of the men

The recent arrival of the 91. Luftlande-Division at La Haye-du-Puits was one of the reasons for the late alteration to the 82nd drop-zones; thus it was ironic that one of the division's earliest successes was against its commander, Generalleutnant Wilhelm Falley, whose headquarters (*left,* visited by Rommel on page 56) lay on the edge of DZ 'N'. *Right:* Although shuttered and empty, Château de Bernaville appeared virtually unchanged when pictured by Steve Casely in June 1994.

Because adverse weather ruled out the possibility of an Allied landing, Generaloberst Dollmann, the commander of 7. Armee, relaxed the alert and summoned his senior officers to a map exercise planned for the morning of June 6 at Rennes ***(right).*** **Although the precise venue for the meeting remains unconfirmed, it was most probably to be held in the German Kommandantur on Place Hoche. When first reports were received of the airborne landings, the commanders were immediately roused from their hotels to begin the long drive back to their HQs.**

who had jumped in Sicily, I had got nearly all the division equipped with .45 automatics. In your first moments on the ground, trussed in your tight harness, you are almost helpless. You can't possibly get to a rifle or a carbine, and if somebody is after your scalp in these first seconds, you are in bad shape. But in the tussle to free myself from the harness, I had dropped the pistol, and as I stooped to grope for it in the grass, fussing and fuming inwardly, but trying to be as quiet as possible, out of the corner of my eye I saw something moving. I challenged 'Flash', straining to hear the countersign, 'Thunder'.

As Generalleutnant Falley reached Bernaville, his car approached this house at the very moment when Lieutenant Malcom D. Brannen, the commander of HQ Company of the 3rd Battalion of the 508th, was asking the owner for directions. Brannen had landed nearby and had joined up with four of his men when the German staff car approached down this lane. The paratroopers instinctively opened fire and the car crashed into the side of the house. The officer who had sat in the back was still alive but, as he reached for his pistol, Brannen shot him.

Sometime after Brannen and his party had left the scene, Corporal Jack W. Schlegel, also of HQ Company, together with three other paratroopers, came across the bullet-riddled car with the body of the General and his two staff officers lying in the road. Inside the car lay a briefcase and a rolled-up package which, when opened, revealed a large swastika flag — Falley's Reich Service Flag. *Above:* In 1974, Jack Schlegel (kneeling on the left) took the flag back to Picauville, making a nice comparison with the shot *(left)* of Falley with Rommel on May 17, 1944. Schlegel hid the flag in a barn, but recovered it before he returned to England. Thirty years later, he brought it back to Normandy and donated it to the museum at Ste Mère-Eglise.

No answer came, and as I knelt, still fumbling in the grass, I recognised in the dim moonlight the bulky outline of a cow. I could have kissed her. The presence of a cow in this field meant that it was not mined, nor staked with 'Rommel's asparagus'. In the days before the invasion, our intelligence agencies had received disquieting word about these fields. They were, we had been told, studded with sharp wooden stakes that would impale a paratrooper and rip the belly out of a glider. Wires connected the stakes, rigged up to mines, and a man striking a stake would set off a chain of explosions. The presence of the cow meant that this field, at least, was free of these traps, and, if this one was, perhaps the adjoining fields were also clear.

I found the pistol and started creeping toward the shadows of the nearest hedgerow. Pale as the moonlight was, I felt conspicuous out there in the middle of that field, expecting at any moment to get a burst of small-arms fire. But at least if no friends were visible, neither were any foes, and I felt a great exhilaration at being here alone in the dark on this greatest of adventures.

As I moved cautiously toward the hedge, again I saw a movement in the shadows. I challenged and this time the proper response came back instantly. As I drew nearer, I saw a man lying on the ground in the shadows, his back against the bank on which the tall hedge grew.

'Who are you?' I said.

'Captain Follmer', a voice came back. I could hardly believe what I heard. In

With Generalleutnant Falley dead and Generalleutnant von Schlieben of 709. Infanterie-Division still on the road between Rennes and his headquarters at Chiffrevast near Valognes, it was a bad start for the German command in the 82nd's area. Also, although the drop had gone wildly awry, to the Germans it seemed that paratroops were everywhere. General Ridgway, who had intended to land by glider, changed his mind just before D-Day and instead parachuted with the 505th. When the loading accident destroyed one of the headquarters' aircraft at Spanhoe (see page 257), a spare C-47 was found to keep regimental HQ and the HQ company intact at nine aircraft. It was the 505th's mission to capture Ste Mère-Eglise — specifically that of the 3rd Battalion under Lieutenant Colonel Edward C. Krause — a task which they had achieved before dawn. In the picture *above* we are looking south.

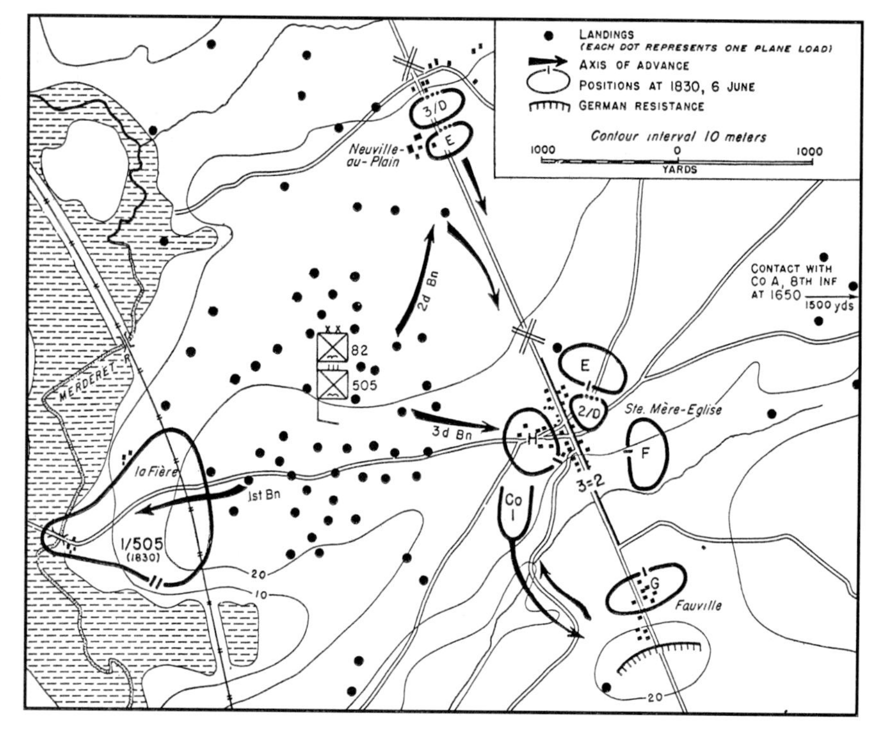

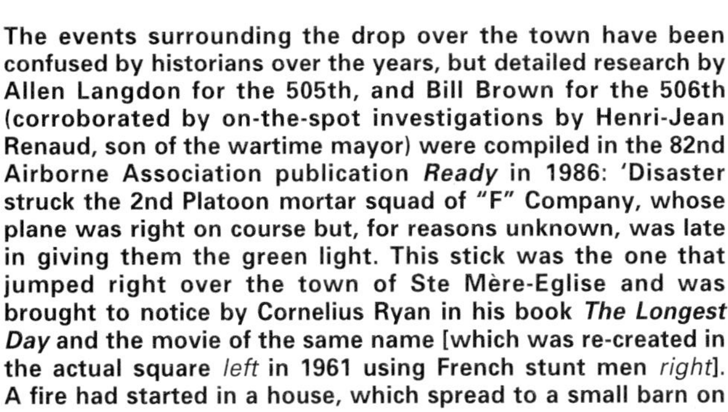

The events surrounding the drop over the town have been confused by historians over the years, but detailed research by Allen Langdon for the 505th, and Bill Brown for the 506th (corroborated by on-the-spot investigations by Henri-Jean Renaud, son of the wartime mayor) were compiled in the 82nd Airborne Association publication ***Ready*** in 1986: 'Disaster struck the 2nd Platoon mortar squad of "F" Company, whose plane was right on course but, for reasons unknown, was late in giving them the green light. This stick was the one that jumped right over the town of Ste Mère-Eglise and was brought to notice by Cornelius Ryan in his book ***The Longest Day*** and the movie of the same name [which was re-created in the actual square *left* in 1961 using French stunt men *right*]. A fire had started in a house, which spread to a small barn on the south side of the church square, and the townspeople had been called out by the mayor, Alexandre Renaud, to fight it. A small German guard had also been called out to oversee this infraction of the curfew. At approximately 0115 hours, about 30 minutes before the 2nd Battalion, 505, began to jump, two sticks from the 506th Parachute Infantry Regiment (101st Division) dropped across the town and at least a dozen more planes from the 2nd Battalion of that regiment dropped their sticks on the outskirts of it, mostly on the east side. At least four of these troopers were killed by the German guard, but others, wounded and unwounded, made their escape. In any event, it was into the midst of a now fully alerted German garrison that the "F" Company, 505, squad had the bad luck to drop about 30 minutes later.'

The inclusion of pictures taken during the making of Darryl Zanuck's feature film is only justified because he restaged it where the events portrayed actually occurred. Zanuck was no stranger to war as he had served as a Signal Corps cameraman/producer although his first film, *At the Front in North Africa* (1943), was compared unfavourably with its British equivalent, *Desert Victory* (1943), because of its lack of action. In the light of subsequent events, it was ironic that during the war Zanuck had to faithfully observe a US War Department directive that prohibited the inclusion of any staged footage, something which the British had no qualms about, as many of the 'action' sequences in *Desert Victory* were filmed at Pinewood!

'Six or seven members of this stick, Lieutenant Harold O. Cadish, Sergeant John Ray, Privates First Class Charles F. Blankenship and Alfred J. Van Holsbeck, Privates H. T. Bryant, Jr, and Ladislaw Tlapa, and possibly Private First Class Penrose D. Shearer were killed either in the air or immediately upon landing. The most remarkable thing about this stick is the number that landed in such a small area, as eleven of them were within little more than 200 yards of each other. Lieutenant Cadish (who was killed by machine gun fire while in the air), Bryant, and Tlapa, came down on the main road just south of the church square. Private First Class Clifford A. Maughn, jumping No. 2 behind Cadish, landed in the back yard of a house just at the corner of the square, and was taken prisoner and held for a time by a German officer living in the house. Sergeant Ray was apparently the only one to land in the square itself and he was shot by one of the guards, but before he died he managed to kill the German who shot him. Private Ernest R. Blanchard, Van Holsbeck, Blankenship and Shearer (if he died there) landed just to the south of the church square among some tall trees and where the house and barn [seen *left* in 1973] were still smouldering. Blankenship apparently had the misfortune to fall into the burnt-out barn, and Blanchard and at least two of the others hung in the trees. Blanchard saved himself by quickly cutting his way out of his harness and making a hasty exit into the darkness. At least one of the others was killed where he (or they) hung. (Blankenship's partially-burned body was positively identified later in the day by Lieutenant Jack P. Carroll of "F" Company. Some histories have reported that a "Private White" also landed in the fire, but there is no record of a Private White being killed or missing in action in Normandy and, indeed, the other members of the stick were later accounted for.) Lastly, Private John M. Steele and Private Kenneth E. Russell hit the church itself. Steele, hit in the left foot by flak on the way down, drifted into the church steeple where he hung for an hour or so before being rescued by the Germans and taken prisoner. He made his escape a few days later, however. Private Russell also hit the church and his 'chute hung up on a lower part of the roof. He had a moment's scare when a German ran towards him and Steele, but then Sergeant Ray landed between them and, as noted, killed the German and died himself. Russell was then able to cut his way out of his 'chute, drop to the ground, and eventually make his way out of the town.' *Right:* June 1994 and once again a paratrooper hangs suspended from the church.

No pictures were taken of airborne operations in France that night and subsequent shots have meagre captions. *Left:* Although this photo gives all the appearance of Hollywood cavalry riding to the rescue, it does show genuine 'action' of 82nd 'mounted' paratroopers on patrol in the town, which was taken at 4.30 a.m. after some 40 Germans had been captured or killed. *Right:* Fifty years later, almost to the hour, Ste Mère-Eglise virtually deserted early on June 6, 1994.

A present-day 82nd Airborne trooper stands in for his counterpart of yesteryear — definitely a posed shot by Steve Casely!

the fighting in Sicily, as I had moved out through no man's land, hunting my paratroopers who had dropped inland in front of the troops that were coming in by sea over the beaches, the first man I had found was Captain Willard Follmer. He was sitting under an olive tree, nursing an ankle he had injured badly in the jump. And here, a year later, out of 6,000 men, again my first encounter was with Follmer.

'Well, Follmer,' I asked, 'what's wrong this time?'

'General, I think I've broken my back.'

'Well,' I said, 'I guess you hope to God you never see *me* again.'

By now, all over the countryside around us, the Germans were beginning to rouse and shoot. The finest fireworks display I ever saw was going on all around me. Rockets and tracers were streaking through the air, and big explosions were going off everywhere. Now and then, glancing up, I could see more C-47s going over, as the formation that had been scattered by the storm got back on course again. Low as they were, they were merely dark shadows against the sky, for a blacked-out plane is very difficult for a man on the ground to see. Even a paratrooper, coming down under a white canopy, is hardly visible until he hits the ground.

All through the night, by twos and threes, the men in Vandervoort's battalion assembled. They came in slowly, for the clouds over the coast had scattered the formations widely. Many men had dropped in the middle of German concentrations and had been killed or captured. By daylight, though, Vandervoort had enough of his battalion together to move out, hunting the enemy, and in the adjacent fields the fragments of two regiments — the 507th and 508th — were assembled, so that by mid-morning we were able to put up some semblance of a division action.

My own little command group of 11 officers and men set up division headquarters in an apple orchard, on almost the exact spot we had planned to be before we left England. Hal Clark's boys had not failed us. They had put us down on the button.

Above: **Officially dated June 12, this picture is believed to have been taken on the 8th when civilians returned after the threat of a German counter-attack had receded following the elimination of assaults against the town from the north and south (see map page 268). Madame Dijon on the Rue de Verdun — the church tower is just visible in the left background.** *Below:* **Today, Ste Mère-Eglise has a bypass and the N13 now crosses the road at this point via a bridge. Comparison by Jean Paul Pallud.**

Left: **Private J. Bishop of the 82nd Airborne Military Police Platoon on point duty at the dangerous crossroads with the original N13. This undated US Navy picture was taken looking back down the D15 towards the overpass.**

The Germans were all around us, of course, sometimes within 500 yards of my CP, but in the fierce and confused fighting that was going on all about, they did not launch the strong attack that could have wiped out our eggshell perimeter defense.

This was in large part due to the dispersion of the paratroopers. Whereever they landed, they began to cut every communication line they could find, and soon the German commanders had no more contact with their units than we had with ours. When the commander of the German 91. Luftlande-Division, Generalleutnant Wilhelm Falley, found himself cut off from the elements of his command, he did the only thing left to do. He got in a staff car and went out to see for himself what the hell had gone on in this wild night of confused shooting. He never found out. Just at daylight, a patrol of paratroopers stopped his car and killed him as he reached for his pistol. The lieutenant commanding the patrol, Malcolm D. Brannen of the 508th, told me the story with great glee.

'Well,' I said, 'in our present situation, killing division commanders does not strike me as being particularly hilarious. But I congratulate you. I'm glad it was a German division commander you got.'

For a while, had I thought about it, the chances were probably fair that I

Bishop appears not to be too overworked, although, without a date to place these pictures, we have no idea how far away the front is. The signs on the left read 'Checkpoint CP' and 'Straight on for collection point' — that is north towards Montebourg. It was some two miles up the N13 that Lieutenant Colonel Benjamin H. Vandervoort (the commanding officer of the 505th's 2nd Battalion who had been promoted at Cottesmore) established a blocking position through Neuville-au-Plain and Baudienville to halt any German attack from the north. Vandervoort had broken his ankle on landing but continued to command his battalion (à la John Wayne in the film) from an ammunition cart and on crutches. Company D, comprising 42 men under Lieutenant Turner B. Turnbull with normal infantry weapons plus extra bazookas, Browning automatic rifles and two anti-tank guns, held an enemy column, which outnumbered them five to one, at bay for eight hours.

Some time later, army engineers arrived to string up signal wire on the burnt-out hairdresser's shop.

Above: **Dated June 12 and released on June 17, this picture is described as showing 'the advance guard of an American convoy in France making use of a captured German tracked motorcycle'. 'Krads' were a very popular mode of transport with airborne troops although this particular convoy is 'advancing' south *into* the town, the same stretch of road being visible on the aerial shot on page 268.** *Below:* **Just off the picture on the right is the town hall and the 'Zero' kilometre marker stone of the Liberty Highway (Voie de la Liberté) which marks the route of the US advance across France.**

would suffer the same fate my German counterpart had met. We had nothing but hand weapons with which to defend ourselves: rifles, pistols, grenades, and light 2.36-inch bazookas. The guns we desperately needed, the 57mm guns that could stop a tank, were to come in with the glider serials that were to bring 4,000 more men into the zone beginning with daylight. They came just as the first streaks of day began to show in the east, but the morning mist rising from the marshy land hung low over the hedgerows, and many a glider was smashed on landing. The fragmentary news that was coming in was both good and bad. By daylight, the division's first objective, the town of Ste Mère-Eglise, was in our hands, and was never lost thereafter.

Liberation may have come to France — but only at a price. A moment of sorrow frozen in time by a US Navy photographer.

Shell-fire on June 7 lost Madame Eugène Jouan her husband; and daughter Julienne a father.

The first of the division's heavy equipment and reinforcements were due to arrive from Ramsbury in 52 Waco gliders on DZ 'O' — used for the para-drop — at 0407 hours i.e. just before civil twilight (see page 114). Fifteen gliders in Operation 'Detroit' were lost before reaching the LZ, many of the others coming to grief in the small fields with their high hedgerows. In all, there were four separate glider missions in support of the 82nd (see table page 309). This picture shows the 82nd's Landing Zone 'W' to the south of Ste Mère-Eglise at Les Forges, looking north beyond the crossroads of the N13 and D70.

The news from the gliders was less cheering. Twenty-four landed, and nearly all were badly smashed up. Some went into the trees that topped the hedgerows. Others went down in swampy places, where men sank armpit deep into the muck as they tried to bring out the heavy radios and the antitank guns.

Soon, we learned what we had lost in the way of key personnel. My Chief-of-Staff, Ralph P. 'Doc' Eaton, and about half the forward echelon of my staff, had come in with the gliders. The Chief-of-Staff was wounded; the G-4, Bennie A. Zinn, was shot through the bridge of the nose and had to be evacuated. The ordnance officer, Joshua A. Finkel, and the surgeon, Wolcott L. Etienne, were either hurt in glider crashes or wounded soon after they hit the ground and had to be evacuated. In the action of the night before, the commander of the engineer battalion, Robert S. Palmer, and one of the infantry regimental commanders, George V. Millett of the 507th, had been taken prisoner.

When Operation 'Elmira' went in on the evening of D-Day, LZ 'W' was still partly in enemy hands so last-minute attempts were made to divert the 176 gliders — 36 Wacos and 140 Horsas — to LZ 'O'. However, approaching this time from the east over Utah, the pilots first came upon the 101st Landing Zone 'E', initially still being marked with panels and smoke, causing even more confusion. The worst 82nd accident occurred near Holdy, a small hamlet just west of Ste Marie-du-Mont, where a Horsa (dubbed by US glider pilots 'The Flying Morgue' due to of its tendency to break up during hard landings) crashed and turned turtle on the western edge of DZ 'C' about 200 yards from the aid station of the 1st Battalion of the 506th Parachute Infantry Regiment. Eighteen dead and 14 seriously injured glider troops were extricated from the wreckage.

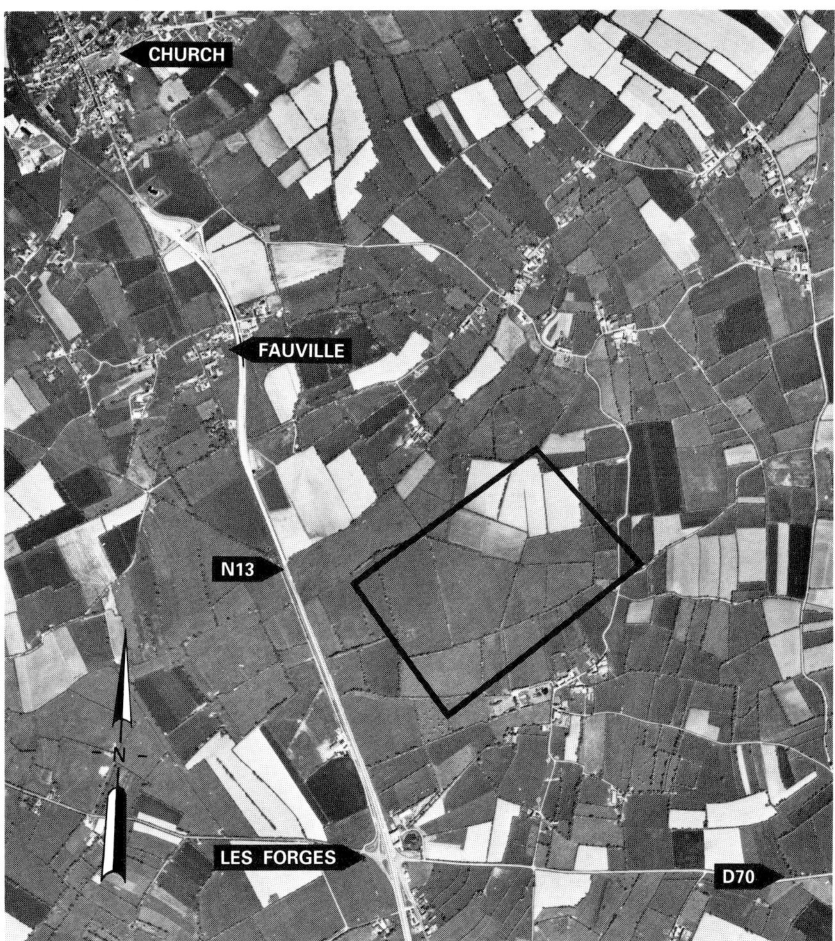

Above: **Officially undated, this picture reproduced from the October 1947 'American Forces in Action' series *Utah Beach to Cherbourg* was probably taken after all the glider operations had ceased. Crashes are arrowed on the original. The area is outlined on a present-day vertical *(right)*, the cover shown being larger to indicate the relationship of Ste Mère-Eglise with the landing zone. It was at Fauville (now bypassed by the upgraded N13) that Companies G and H of the 3rd Battalion (Lieutenant Colonel Krause) held the southern perimeter of the town (see map page 268) and where a German attack was broken up by Company I mounting a flank attack.**

In addition to our personnel losses, we were sadly handicapped in our communications. We couldn't get in touch with anybody — neither the troops that were supposed to be coming in over the beaches by now, nor with anybody back in England, nor with anybody afloat.

In short, we were in the typical situation for which you must be prepared when an airborne division goes into battle. So I shuffled the surviving staff officers about as best I could until some sort of effective command structure was set up. The G-3, Bob Wienecke, took over as Acting Chief-of-Staff. The signal officer, Bill Moorman, took on the additional duties of the wounded G-4. In a little while — a matter of two or three hours — the CP was a going concern. For 36 hours, though, we had no means of knowing how well or badly

Having taken Ste Mère-Eglise, the second mission of the 82nd was to establish defensive positions west of the flooded Merderet river but, more importantly, to capture the two bridge crossings at Chef-du-Pont and La Fière. At the latter place, because of the flooding of the river valley, the approach from the east could only be made along the raised causeway leading to the bridge. In normal circumstances such a position could be easily defended but, in this case, paratroops were also closing on the bridge from the DZs to the west. During the morning, Colonel Roy Lindquist of the 508th arrived at La Fière to take charge of the mixed bag of troops assembled on the eastern side — around 400 men from all three regiments. The attacks went in at noon and successfully reached the far bank to join with a patrol from the 2nd Battalion of the 507th. With 80 men across, and more due to follow, the advance party moved off to the west, leaving the bridge in the hands of 12 men. However, the Germans quickly counter-attacked with tanks and the bridge was recaptured, the survivors swimming back to the east bank under fire. Unfortunately, we have not found any contemporary pictures of the bridge (or that at Chef-du-Pont which was captured). This picture, taken 50 years later, shows the bridge from the eastern bank.

we were faring. The Germans were boasting on the radio that they had destroyed the 82nd Airborne, a claim we were in no position at the moment to debate. As a matter of fact, we learned later, the 82nd had landed on top of, and had destroyed, the 91. Luftlande-Division, which had been moved into this area only two weeks before in anticipation of a parachute attack.

These are merely the highlights of the happenings of the first hours. It is difficult to remember in specific detail the sequence of events. Shortly after I landed, Don Faith, my aide, who had jumped in the same stick with me, loomed up out of the darkness, and with the first light, Sergeant Casey, my bodyguard and 'shotgun man', found me. Dawn came gray and misty, and with it a great hunger. So I climbed up on the ten-foot bank of a high hedgerow at the edge of the field, and broke out a K-ration — one of the three-day supply we carried.

As I ate, I could hear, amid the general rattle and crack of small-arms fire that was going on all around, the sound of heavy firing from the direction of Ste Mère-Eglise, a quarter mile to the east. I went down there to find, to my great satisfaction, that the Germans were pulling out and the town was in our hands. Walking through the battered streets where only paratroopers were moving now, I looked at my watch. It was a few minutes before 8 a.m. on D-Day morning.

There in the town, I found my Artillery Commander, Andy March, slightly scratched and bruised but in good shape. His glider had landed in the top of a tree.

Throughout that first day, I was constantly on the move, from the little CP in an apple orchard near the pasture where I had landed, to the points where the hottest fighting was going on. The Germans, well knowing the value of the causeway crossings that led inland across the swamps from the beach-head, were putting up scattered but fierce resistance against our stubborn advance toward the first of these, the causeway over the Merderet at a hamlet called La Fière. There was little I could do during that first day toward exercising division control. I could only be where the fighting seemed the hottest, to exercise whatever personal influence I could on the battalion commanders as they drove on toward the causeways.

The battle to recapture the bridge at La Fière lasted four days and the bridgehead was not finally consolidated until the 90th Division took over the attack on June 10. Today, this marker on a nearby hillside recalls the exploits of the 82nd in the area.

I had no transportation, of course, and back and forth, back and forth, all day I made that journey from my CP toward the Merderet. No sooner would I return to the apple orchard than a messenger from the 'front' would come panting up to announce that all hell had broken loose in a new spot, and I would have to trudge back down there again.

I was in fine physical shape, but never in all my life have I been so weary as I was at the end of that first day in Normandy. Just before midnight, tottering on my feet as was many another soldier who had fought there on that day, I rolled up in a cargo chute and lay down for the first sleep I'd had in 48 hours. I crawled into a ditch, for the town of Ste Mère-Eglise was only a short distance away, and all that night German airplanes were overhead, dropping 500lb bombs, and German artillery was shelling the city heavily.

By the end of the first day, the organised strength of the 82nd could only be measured in hundreds, and by noon on June 8 the division could still only report 2,100 effectives — less than a third the strength it started out with. In fact, the first estimate sent to VII Corps put total casualties at 4,000 and, even though this included many paratroopers scattered far and wide who would later report in, revised calculations in August still showed D-Day losses at 1,259. Records of airborne operations in the peninsula are very sketchy and few of the hundreds of individual fire-fights which must have taken place in the early days were documented. Even General Ridgway's own account is flawed. His memoirs speak of 'someone' waking him during the night of D+1, something that greatly surprised General Gavin when he read it, as that 'someone' had been him!

Far in the night, I was roused by someone shaking me. It was a messenger from one of the battalions fighting toward the river crossing. The Germans, he said, were counter-attacking in strength across the causeway.

I couldn't see what in the hell I could do about that, single-handed. So I sent back word that the battalion was to hold if it could. If this was impossible, then it could pull back. Then I turned over and went back to sleep. It held.

I woke with the first light, sore and stiff but refreshed, filled my helmet with hot water, and started to shave, with one of these little injector razors with a rotating head that a paratrooper likes because it is small, all in one piece, and takes up not much more room than a pencil. I had got a leather-cased field telephone in by this time, and when I was about half through shaving, it rang — a battalion down by the river reporting on the night's activities. When I put down my phone and reached for my razor again, it was gone. Some SOB had stolen it.

Throughout that day, as more and more men, scattered in the drop, coalesced into their fighting units, we drove hard against the Germans. Radios, dug from the wreckage of the gliders in the swamps, began to function, and the communication set-up was greatly improved. The battle began to take on some form and organisation — though it still in no way resembled what Field-Marshal Montgomery liked to refer to as a 'tidy' battlefield.

I had hardly fallen asleep when someone shook me and told me General Ridgway wanted to see me. This was unlike General Ridgway; he always went forward to see his officers in combat rather than take them away from their tactical commands. I checked again; there was no question about the accuracy of the message. I had not been back that way, but his Command Post should have been near the road to Ste Mère-Eglise. I took Captain Hugo Olson with me, and we started along the road. It was as light as day in the full moonlight, and we walked in the shadows, one on each side of the road. I felt bone weary, having been up for two nights and a day. In addition to the physical exhaustion, combat itself, with its tension and excitement, takes a great deal out of you.

After several miles of walking, I came on the Command Post off to the left of the road. I went to the Operations Center, which was in a tent, and asked for General Ridgway. They pointed out that he was asleep in a small ditch off to the side. I went over and shook his shoulder and woke him up. He didn't seem too happy about it and said he had nothing for me and didn't need me. No doubt a zealous staff officer, thinking it might be a good way to get a first-hand report on the situation along the Merderet river, had sent the message in the name of General Ridgway, and by the time I arrived, the message had been forgotten or the staff officer who sent it was fast asleep.

BRIGADIER GENERAL JAMES M. GAVIN, 1978

The contemporary picture *(top)* to this comparison is indicative of the confusion during the first days. The original caption to this still, taken from a clip of cine film believed shot on June 8, identifies 'an American paratrooper patrol' moving 'cautiously through a French churchyard, taking cover from a stone wall in St Marcouf'. William G. Lord II, the author of the 508th Regimental History, says that one of the Headquarters Company's aircraft dropped its stick, including Captains Abraham and Johnson and Tech. 5 McCloud, nine kilometres south of Cherbourg. This is believed to be that party as it fought its way back to the 508th.

This follow-on shot is captioned by Major Roland G. Ruppenthal (who was responsible for compiling *Utah Beach to Cherbourg*) as 'men of the 22nd Infantry [of the US 4th Division which came ashore on Utah] moving cautiously through the village [St Marcouf] on 8 June when the drive on Crisbecq was resumed.' However, the men's blackened faces, baggy pants, gauze arm-flags and trench knives on ankles all clearly point to their being paratroopers.

The tide began to turn in our favour along about dawn of the third day. Elements of the 82nd made contact with patrols of the 4th Division which had come in from the sea over Utah Beach. Not long afterward, the Assistant Division Commander, Ted Roosevelt, strolled into my CP to offer to us all the help, in guns and ammunition, that we would need. It was almost the last time I was ever to see this gallant officer, a warm, close friend ever since his days as Governor of the Philippines when I, as a young captain, was his military adviser. A few weeks later, he was dead — not of enemy action, though he always walked where the fire was hottest, as if the bullet that could kill him had not been made — but of a heart attack (see page 411). I had one other brief, heart-warming meeting with Ted on the roadside just after Cherbourg was taken. No braver man ever lived.

An airborne outfit in the early days of its commitment to battle fights as light infantry. For heavy fire support, and often for re-supply, it must depend on the conventional divisions. Once we had made contact with the 4th Division, and had the help of its artillery, we could get on apace with our basic mission. That mission was simply this: to seize and hold the causeways leading inland from Utah Beach, and the stream crossings over the Merderet and Douve rivers. With these bridges and defiles in enemy hands, our troops on the beach could be pinned down and decimated by artillery fire. As soon as the 82nd, and the 101st, its companion division which had jumped near Carentan, had cleared these routes over the marshes, and had sealed off the beach area by seizing key road junctions and communication centers, the assault troops of VII Corps, coming in over Utah Beach, could plunge inland, swing right, and clear the peninsula all the way to the great port of Cherbourg.

The strongest opponent of the plan was General Eisenhower's Air Commander-in-Chief, Air Chief Marshal Sir Trafford Leigh-Mallory. Though a man of great personal bravery and boldness, Leigh-Mallory felt that the drop of two airborne divisions in this area would result only in the 'futile slaughter' of these two great fighting units. He based

Jean Paul Pallud took the comparisons, this shot showing the northern end of the village. The road on the left is the D14. Although these men are 82nd, unfortunately few pictures were taken of them in action in the early days. Better coverage comes mid-month when the division, by then backed by tanks and artillery and fighting more as an infantry unit, pushed out of its tenuous bridgehead over the Merderet.

A little later, the same 508th group under Captain Johnson (right, with binoculars) was pictured resting in front of the village church of Ravenoville, three kilometres down the road from St Marcouf. By this time, their parent regiment had still not fully assembled. On D-Day, one lone platoon had established a tenuous toehold across the Merderet at Chef-du-Pont (some 11 kilometres south-west of where Johnson's group now was); about two companies under Lieutenant Colonel Thomas J. B. Shanley of the 2nd Battalion had occupied and dug in on Hill 30, a tactically important knoll on the west bank of the river. Though isolated, Shanley's force had been drawing enemy troops away from the fight for the two Merderet bridgeheads. They were not to be relieved by the main 82nd force from La Fière until D+4.

his arguments, in part, on the presence of enemy night fighter planes, which, he said, would get in among the slow-flying transport craft and knock them from the sky like hawks attacking a flight of ducks. The planes that might escape the fighters, he insisted, would be blown from the skies by automatic weapons' fire when they dropped to 600 feet to launch their paratroopers.

Both General Bradley and I argued strongly that these were risks that we would have to take. The drop was a great gamble, we admitted. The whole great operation was a desperate gamble. In the end, General Eisenhower accepted our point of view.

To the great credit of Leigh-Mallory, when it became known back in England that the two divisions had landed without great loss, he went immediately to General Eisenhower. No one could be more distressed than he about adding to the Supreme Commander's burdens in arguing against this operation before it was launched, he said, and nobody could be happier than he that his prediction had been wrong and General Eisenhower's decision right.

Though the disaster en route that had been predicted did not take place, the fighting on the ground soon proved to be as fierce and bloody as even the most pessimistic of us had anticipated. The hardest fighting took place on the causeways. These causeways were elevated roadways across the deep marshes, narrow two-track roads with an 18-inch shoulder on either side, sloping down to muddy water that was over a man's head. As we crossed the first of these, we learned why, in the first days' fighting, many a paratrooper had never showed up to join his unit. Bodies lay in the water still in their harness. They had hit in the marshes and had drowned before they could free themselves of their chutes and their heavy combat gear.

The place of a commander is where he anticipates the crisis of action is going to be, and it was obvious to me that these causeway crossings were the spots of greatest hazard. Each time, therefore, before we attempted the crossing, I would go down, preferably at dark, by day if I had to, personally to reconnoiter each crossing before I sent any element of my division across.

There were four of these crossings and by far the toughest was the causeway across the wide and sluggish Merderet at La Fière. Here, the road came down and made a right-angle turn through a low cut in the hills about 20 or 30 feet high. It then emerged onto a perfectly open, straight road that stretched 500 or 600 yards across the swamp. The Germans naturally concentrated their fire on our end of the defile, and it was the hottest sector I saw throughout the war. We lost a lot of men there and I think the final assault on June 9 unquestionably would have failed if all the commanders from division to battalion had not been there in person to shove the troops across.

We weren't going after that crossing cold, of course. We had artillery support by then, from the battalions of the 4th Division. We had a battalion of 105mm self-propelled howitzers, a battalion of 155mm howitzers, a platoon of tanks, and every .50-caliber machine gun we could lay hands on. We massed them all there on the river lip, and, for ten minutes before the crossing, we poured shells into the German positions on the far side. It was a tremendous spectacle — the crash of the guns blended into one great blasting roar of terrific noise, and the smoke and dust and haze soon grew so thick you could hardly see six feet in front of you.

The original picture is uncaptioned as to location, but Steve Casely had a stroke of luck while covering the American airborne area for this book: 'I was driving up the D14 just behind the coast when I came across this shot in the main street of Ravenoville', reported Steve. 'As you can see, all is initially the same as in '44 except that there are new wooden palings and the wall has now been rendered. The guys in the comparison run an airborne relics shop on the opposite side of the road and they were ecstatic. I was pretty pleased myself as I really wanted to find this one.'

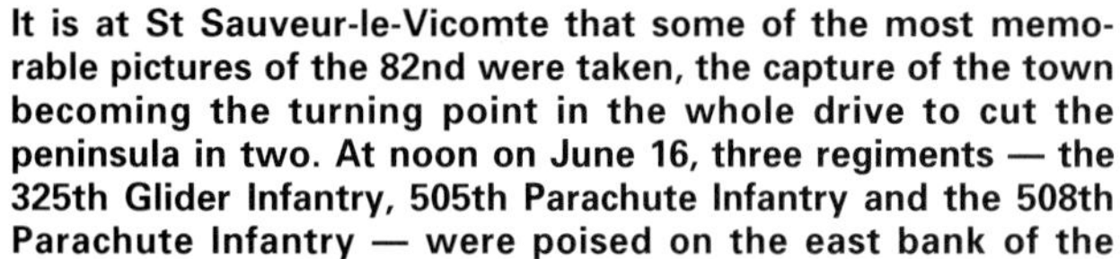

It is at St Sauveur-le-Vicomte that some of the most memorable pictures of the 82nd were taken, the capture of the town becoming the turning point in the whole drive to cut the peninsula in two. At noon on June 16, three regiments — the 325th Glider Infantry, 505th Parachute Infantry and the 508th Parachute Infantry — were poised on the east bank of the Douve overlooking the town. When the Germans were seen to be withdrawing, General Ridgway sought permission from VII Corps HQ to immediately exploit the situation and cross the river and establish a bridgehead. ***Left:*** **Grit, guts and resolute determination exemplify Lieutenant Colonel Vandervoort, still on his crutches amid the ruins of Rue du Vieux Château.**

We really poured the fire across, and we were getting plenty in return. I lay up on the crest to the right of the crossing, alongside one of the tanks, whose gun was banging away with a noise to split the head. Off to the left, the automatic weapons were going like the hammers of hell, and to the rear our heavier artillery was firing, the shells passing directly overhead.

I lay there watching, peering through the haze and smoke, as the first men came down to the crossing, shoulders hunched, leaning forward as if they were moving against a heavy wind. Some of them began to go down, and the others hesitated. Then they turned and started back, instinctively recoiling from the sheer blasting shock of the concentrated enemy fire. I jumped up and ran down there. The men were milling around in the cut. Jim Gavin, my Assistant Division Commander, whom I had put in charge of this operation, was there, with the regimental CO, Colonel Harry L. Lewis of the 325th Glider Infantry, and the battalion commanders. And there in the cut at the head of the causeway, we grabbed these men, turned them around, pushed, shoved, even led them by hand until we got them started across.

We got across all right in spite of fairly heavy casualties, and cleared the far end of the causeway, so that the 9th Division, which was to take up the attack on the other side, could pass through. The division commander, General Manton Eddy, told me a few hours later that he'd never seen so many dead Germans anywhere. I agreed with him. I hadn't either. And I think that fight was as hot a single battle as any US troops had, at any time, during the war in Europe.

After that one, my aide told me, laughing, that back at headquarters they were referring to me as 'The Causeway

Vandervoort had continued to lead the 505th despite his broken ankle. His Jeep stands amidst his men on Rue du Vieux Château.

chance to rest and lick our wounds — 'lie down to bleed a while, then rise to fight again' — in Mr Shakespeare's phrase, but these hours of inaction were brief. We were passed through once by the 90th Division, but they ran into heavy resistance and took a pretty severe mauling, so we were put back into the line immediately, to take over from the 90th and continue with the attack. Then the 8th Division passed through us, and we had a somewhat similar experience. When we were finally withdrawn on July 8, 46 out of every 100 infantrymen had been killed or so severely wounded they had to be evacuated to England. Many others had suffered minor wounds which they ignored to keep on fighting. The dead numbered 1,282, and 2,373 had suffered serious wounds. We had gone into battle with four regimental and 12 battalion commanders. In the course of the fight, 15 of these infantry leaders had been killed, wounded or captured. I doubt very much that any major unit during the war suffered heavier casualties and kept on fighting.

By nightfall, engineers had bridged the river and elements of the division were firmly established more than a mile beyond the town. The capture of St Sauveur marked the high point in the 82nd's sojourn in Normandy. *Above:* **Before the division was withdrawn on July 11, General Bradley decorated several officers and men including Brigadier General Gavin, left, awarded the Distinguished Service Cross. Lieutenant Colonel Krause, second left, and Lieutenant Colonel Vandervoort (who by now had his ankle out of plaster and needed only a walking stick) were also awarded DSCs for extraordinary heroism in the capture and defence of Ste Mère-Eglise.**

Kid'. I didn't see anything particularly humorous in the title, for I saw too many fine youngsters killed at those swamp and river crossings. The fire was always hot along those exposed stretches of straight road. I remember one night I stepped out from behind a farmhouse to the edge of the macadam highway, and saw lights winking in the dark at my feet. I said to the officer with me:

'That's the first time I've seen fireflies around here. Wonder why we haven't seen them before.'

'Fireflies, hell', he said. 'Those aren't fireflies. They're machine gun bullets ricocheting off the road.'

For 33 days, the division was in continuous action in the peninsula. From time to time, we thought we'd have a

Centre: **The impromptu award ceremony was held in the farm courtyard of the Château Brocqueboeuf which lies two miles north-east of La Haye-du-Puits amid the wooded hills of La Poterie ridge where the 82nd fought its last action in Normandy on July 3-7. Vandervoort continued in command of the 505th, parachuting into Holland in September 1944, but was seriously wounded in January 1945 during the Battle of the Bulge.**

101st Airborne Division

By Major General Maxwell D. Taylor

Brigadier General Maxwell D. Taylor escorts the Prime Minister and General Eisenhower on an inspection of the 101st Airborne Division in the company of the Assistant Division Commander, Brigadier General Don F. Pratt, and Churchill's aide-de-camp, Flag Lieutenant C. R. 'Tommy' Thompson.

Shortly alter the 82nd Division moved to England, I became the beneficiary of a stroke of good fortune with a most unfortunate cause. In February, General Bill Lee, the idolised commander of the 101st Airborne Division, suffered a severe heart attack which ended his active service and resulted in his evacuation to the United States. Thanks largely to the intervention of Generals Bradley and Ridgway, I was chosen to replace him and took command of the division on March 14 at its headquarters in Newbury, Berkshire.

General Lee had brought the division into south-west England during the fall of 1943 where a fourth regiment, the 501st Parachute Infantry, joined it in January. By the time I arrived, intensive unit training and staff planning for D-Day had been going on for several

The parade took place on Court Oak Farm just east of Welford airfield on March 23, 1944. We revisited the farm with members of the Ridgeway Military and Aviation Research Group to restage the action on the precise spot exactly 50 years later.

L–R: Farmer Alan Baylis takes on Churchill's rôle with Bill King (Taylor); Nigel Dawe (Eisenhower); Roger Day (Pratt), and John Stephens as Thompson — not to be confused with Detective Sergeant Bill Thompson, Churchill's bodyguard.

Since it was created in August 1942 by splitting the 82nd Infantry Division into two, the 101st Airborne Division had been commanded by Major General William C. 'Bill' Lee *(above)* who had brought the division to Britain in the autumn of 1943. General Lee had Brigadier General Pratt as his Assistant Division Commander but after Lee was incapacitated by a heart attack on February 5, it was Brigadier General Taylor, former Artillery Commander of the 82nd Airborne Division, who was brought in to take command of the 101st. The introduction of an officer from the rival division, over the head of the division's own Assistant Commander who might have expected to be promoted to the position, may well have coloured the VIP inspection on March 23.

months in preparation for the coming operation. Under General Lee's leadership, an unusual division was being shaped to do unusual things, and it was a cruel stroke of fortune which deprived him of the privilege of leading it into battle.

By D-Day, Taylor had been promoted to Major General, a second star being in accordance with his position as a division commander.

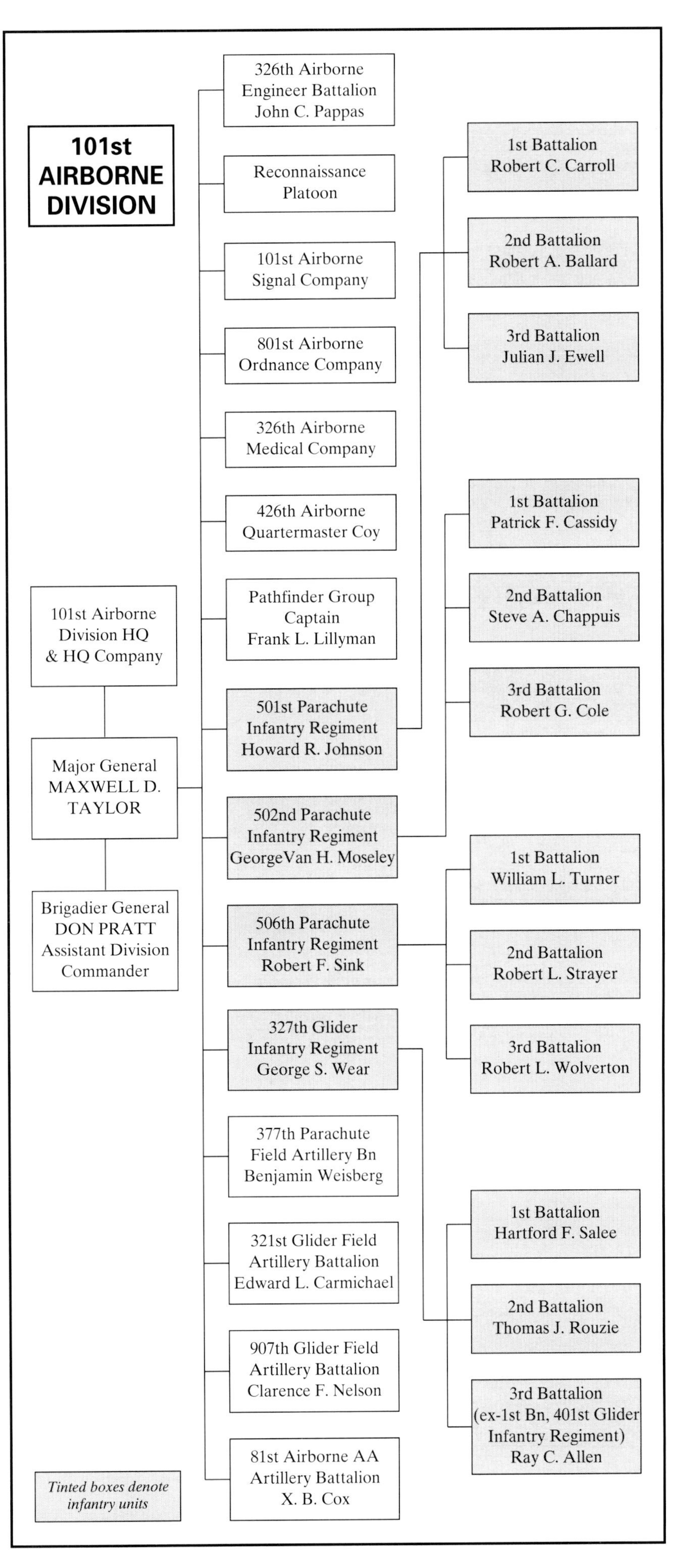

Although I knew that there was some disappointment that Lee's successor had not been chosen from within the 101st, I was received warmly upon arrival. If there were any heartburns among senior officers, they were never visible, but my pleasure in receiving the command was tempered by the knowledge of the highly-qualified men over whom I had been advanced. In a perfect world, it would have gone to the Division Artillery Commander, Brigadier General Anthony McAuliffe, of later Bastogne fame, and I would have been left to take my chances in the 82nd.

There were many things to do to catch up with the requirements of the new job. I had to become acquainted with my officers, particularly the regimental and battalion commanders who would bear the brunt of the coming battle. There was the need to supervise the training programs and verify their quality and realism. In this task, I had the assistance of many able officers: Tony McAuliffe, Brigadier General Don F. Pratt, the Assistant Division Commander; Colonel G. J. Higgins, the Chief-of-Staff; and Lieutenant Colonel Raymond D. Millener, the Assistant Chief-of-Staff for Operations. Also, I had to represent the division at the many planning sessions at higher headquarters in and around London, and adjust the division plans to the changing decisions of the higher commanders.

The 101st was deployed around Newbury in Berkshire with its headquarters at Greenham Lodge on the western edge of the airfield at Greenham Common. Fifty years later, the former HQ stands empty and deserted, its future uncertain.

SECRET

SECRET

VISIT BY V. I. P.

23 March 1944
101st AIRBORNE DIVISION

Major General William C. Lee, Commanding (sick in hospital)
Brigadier General Maxwell D. Taylor, Acting Division Commander
Brigadier General Don C. Pratt, Assistant Division Commander

MAP POINT NUMBER	TIME	PLACE	ACTIVITY	UNIT	UNIT COMMANDER
1	1448	NEWBURY RACE COURSE	Special train arrives		
1	1615	NEWBURY RACE COURSE	Detrain		
2	1635-1650		Inspection of Guard of Honor	101st AB Div (-)	Brig-Gen Pratt
3	1650-1725		Inspection of parked gliders, loading and unloading. Witness landing and assembly of personnel and equipment carried in two Horsas and two Wacos. Inspection of small AB units and equipment.		
4	1725-1740		Witness parachute jump	506th Para Inf Regt 377th Para FA Bn	Col Sink Lt. Col Weisberg
5	1740-1755		Tour of jump area. Visit to Regimental Command Post. Talk to personnel who have just completed jump		
6	1815	NEWBURY RACE COURSE	Entrain		

SECRET

SECRET

At the time of the inspection on March 23, Brigadier General Taylor was still only the Acting Division Commander, confirmation of his position coming when a heartbroken General Lee was officially relieved of command and transferred to the United States for further hospital treatment. This is the original timetable for the afternoon's events which enabled us to take our comparisons at the exact time, allowing, of course, for the fact that Britain was then on Double British Summer Time.

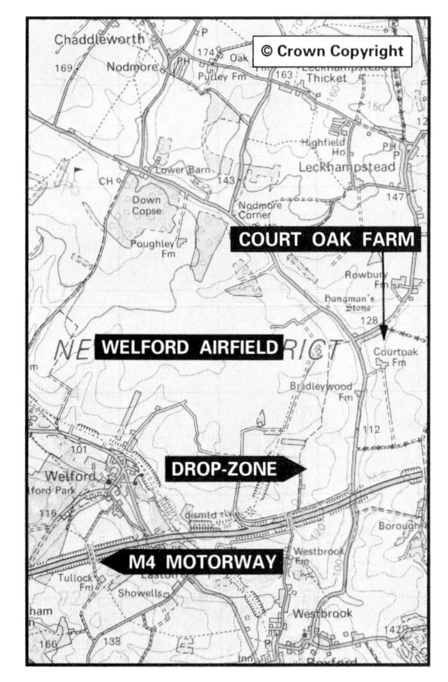

Some time in March 1944, Jack Baylis, who owned Court Oak Farm, was approached by the base commander of Welford asking if they could have the use of his large field on the eastern edge of the airfield for a day. The Americans told Jack that they could not tell him what they wanted it for, and that he must not mention it to anyone, but that he should let his son have the day off school as he would have the chance of seeing something he would always remember. Since the mid-1950s, Welford has been used by the United States Air Forces as an aviation ordnance depot, its surface now covered by storage bunkers and bomb revetments.

I was most fortunate in being under two senior officers for whom I had the greatest respect, Lieutenant General J. Lawton Collins, commanding the VII Corps and General Omar Bradley, commanding the First Army. Collins had been brought from the Pacific, where he had commanded the 25th Infantry Division at Guadalcanal and had won the nickname of 'Lightning Joe', to provide experienced leadership to the corps which would make the initial landing on Utah Beach. As a major, he had been one of my instructors at the Army War College where he had impressed the class with his clarity of thought and expression, as well as by the evidence he gave of being a profound student of the art and science of war.

General Bradley I had first known as a major at West Point when I was a cadet. It was his departure from command of the 82nd Infantry Division in 1942 which set in motion the chain of events which carried me from Washington to England by way of the Mediterranean. As a corps commander in Sicily, Bradley had confirmed his peacetime reputation for leadership and now was about to lead the US Army forces into Normandy alongside Montgomery's British divisions.

Naturally, we had many visitors during the final weeks of our preparations, the most notable being Prime Minister Churchill accompanied by General Eisenhower at the end of March. The division put on a demonstration parachute jump for the visitors in the afternoon, and the Prime Minister and Eisenhower reciprocated with a dinner on board their special train for the American division commanders stationed in that part of England. Churchill was just getting up from a nap when we arrived at the train, and he appeared tired and a bit grumpy. However, drinks were soon passed, and he seized upon a large glass of cognac. Soon the color was back in his jowls and the sparkle in his eyes. He began to reminisce about the Boer War, and by the time dinner was served, he had us in the midst of World War I. He remained in superb form throughout the evening, keeping us early-rising soldiers well beyond our normal bedtime. But it was a grand evening for the visitors

Below left: **Churchill, having just arrived at Court Oak Farm in one of the motor cars parked on the edge of the field, is introduced to Don Pratt.** *Below right:* **Roger Day stands in for the Assistant Division Commander, wearing the helmet once worn by Sergeant Gilbert Morton of HQ Company, 3rd Battalion of the 506th, who was billeted with his aunt in nearby Ramsbury. When Morton returned from Normandy, he gave his dented helmet to the family with the words: 'This is something for you to remember me by'. Now it is Roger's most treasured possession.**

Above: **Eight-year-old Alan Baylis stands with his father and brother Colin, aged four, in the hedge just to the left of the trooper pulling the hand-cart. These men are from the 101st's glider infantry, either the 327th Regiment or the 401st, whose 1st Battalion had now become the 3rd Battalion of the 327th.** *Right:* **Thanks for the memory!**

although, I suspect, rather hard on General Eisenhower who had to bear up under many such long evenings of conviviality. However, one of the notable observations during the evening was the evidence of a warm informal relationship between Churchill and Eisenhower, an asset of priceless value for the Allied cause during the war.

Left: **British officers from the 6th Airborne Division were attached to the 101st on exchange duty to observe US operational procedures.** *Right:* **From the flag, this group is identified as part of the 327th Glider Infantry Regiment, officers being identifiable by either a single bar on their helmets for lieutenants, or a double bar for captains. 'I thank God you are here,' Churchill told them, 'and from the bottom of my heart I wish you good fortune and success.'**

After the inspection came the mass drop which Churchill, Eisenhower and the other officers watched from the VIP stand, the C-47s being provided by the 435th Troop Carrier Group based at Welford. One of the men on parade that day was Private Donald R. Burgett who later recalled his impressions of the day in his book *Currahee*. 'We were told that two battalions would have to make a jump and one battalion would have to stand inspection for the visiting officials. A coin was tossed and the 1st Battalion came out on top. We would stay on the ground while the 2nd and 3rd made the jump, which was witnessed by Churchill. We felt a great respect for this man and we were honoured to be in his presence. The jump was a great success except for that one equipment 'chute which had a "streamer" and pile-drived into the ground.'

The main 101st dress rehearsal, Exercise 'Eagle', was held from May 9–12 with a scenario set out north of Hungerford and Newbury which would closely resemble the division's task in Normandy, which was primarily to capture the causeways leading inland from Utah. Although the exercise was claimed as successful, 28 aircraft returned to their departure airfields without having dropped their paratroops and, of those that jumped, over 400 suffered injuries of one kind or another. In addition, eight sticks were released directly over Ramsbury village, some nine miles from the DZ. For the real drop, the troops were to depart from Exeter, Greenham Common, Membury, Merryfield, North Witham, Upottery and Welford. In the run-up to D-Day, another VIP visitor was Air Chief Marshal Leigh-Mallory whose fears for the coming operation we have already discussed. From these pictures, taken at two of the airfields to be used by the two US divisions' glider-borne elements, it appears that both his routine and that of the cameraman (neither his name nor the date is given in the official captioning) was exactly the same in both cases.

Above: **Aldermaston, home of the 434th Troop Carrier Group from where the 101st pre-dawn 52-glider lift was to take off.** *Below:* **Comparison kindly taken for us by the Atomic Weapons Research Establishment, which now occupies the airfield.**

In its final form, the invasion plan called for the parachute elements of the 101st Airborne Division, some 6,600 men, to land under cover of darkness preceding the seaborne assault and to seize the exits of four causeways leading inland from Utah Beach for use by the 4th Infantry Division which spearheaded the landing forces. We were given this mission because of the anticipated difficulties of the landing forces in moving inland across the extensive inundations just behind the beach, which the Germans had created and then covered by minefields. In so doing, they had limited the exits from the three-mile beach to four roads elevated on causeways that constituted easily-defended defiles through which our troops must pass. Hence, the primary mission of the parachutists of the 101st on landing was to seize and defend the inland exits of these defiles. Thereafter, we were to regroup our forces to the south, seize the town of Carentan, the communications centre at the base of the Cherbourg peninsula, and protect the south flank of the VII Corps as its units landed and turned north to take Cherbourg.

Left: **This is Ramsbury (an 82nd Airborne base), home of the 437th, at the beginning of June, where the control tower has since been demolished.**

Exeter, early evening, June 5. Platoons of the 506th Parachute Infantry Regiment move out to the waiting C-47s of the 440th Troop Carrier Group. The aircraft directly behind the Jeep on the peri-track can be identified as belonging to the 98th Troop Carrier Squadron by its '8Y' coding. Picture taken by the Group's official photographer, Joseph Hudson.

Our parachute troops were to land on three drop-zones and the gliders on one, located three to four miles behind the beach. Parachute pathfinder teams carrying lights and radar beacons for guiding in the planes were to drop shortly ahead of the main body and mark the landing areas. Theirs was the unenviable task of dropping in darkness into enemy-infested territory and announcing their own presence to the Germans by turning on their lights and beacon signals. These pathfinders were among the real heroes of D-Day.

With the invasion set for June 5, I began on May 28 to make the rounds of the 17 marshalling areas scattered over Wales and southern England where my troops were sealed up and receiving their final instructions. Standing on the top of a Jeep, I addressed every unit in the division, trying to communicate to the men my feeling of the historic significance of the drama in which we were to be key actors, and the pride we would feel someday in telling our children and grandchildren that we had been in Normandy on D-Day. Henry V had said it much better on St Crispin's Day, but I was encouraged by the bright-eyed attention of the men and their visible eagerness to get on with the hazardous business which seemed to hold no terrors for them.

Above: After the war, the airfield reverted to its pre-war status as Exeter Airport, the same taxiway to what is now Hangar No. 3 having been widened to cater for today's aircraft like this Fokker F-27. *Below:* Looking back towards the control tower (in the background on the right). Troops leaving from Exeter were the 3rd Battalion of the 506th and two platoons of the 326th Engineers. This and the following pictures taken by Signal Corps photographer Nehez.

Above: **Unfortunately the SHAEF censor has crudely scratched out the shoulder patches and helmet insignia on the negatives of this series, but these men have been identified by post-war historians as Headquarters Company of the 3rd Battalion. They are receiving a briefing from their jumpmaster, First Lieutenant Alex Bobuck.** *Right:* **Bobuck checks the load strapped on this signaller who is carrying two pigeon cases. Homing pigeons were considered a reliable means of communication with messages carried in small capsules attached to the bird's leg. Note also how the paint has run from the hastily-applied invasion stripes on the fuselage of the aircraft.**

My soldiers were always like that throughout the war — an unfailing tonic for senior officers condemned to spend most of their time in planning and making the decisions upon which the lives of these men depended. In my experience, the history books that depicted the rôle of the general as being that of galvanising his men into action were all wrong. I found more often than not that I went up to the front lines not to urge on the troops but to escape the worries of the command post where all battle noises sounded like the doings of the enemy and where it was easy for the commander to give way to dire imaginings. A visit to the men of the 101st under fire never failed to send me back to the command post, assured that the situation was well in hand, and that there was no cause for worry.

Meanwhile, General Eisenhower, as the soldiers would say, was sweating out the decision of the date of D-Day in company with those augurs of a modern commander, the meteorologists. The landing had been set for June 5, but the weather had become so unfavourable that, after hearing all the evidence and listening to all those qualified to advise, Eisenhower postponed it 24 hours to

Colonel Robert L. Wolverton inspects the gear of Captain Stanley E. Morgan, the surgeon of his 3rd Battalion of the 506th.

June 6. A coded message indicating the change reached our division headquarters early on June 4.

The delay was a disappointment because we were all set to go and this meant a break in the momentum. For me, it presented an unusual problem — what to do with a day with no work scheduled. This enforced idleness proved almost my undoing. Among the visitors from London to see us off was an old friend, Colonel Frank Reed, familiarly known as 'Froggie'. As we had played a great deal of squash racquets together in former years, I suggested a game on an air force court at a nearby field. When we got into action, I was surprised to discover that 'Froggie' knew a lot more about the English version of squash than I did and was about to give me a first-class licking, something I had not anticipated. Making a maximum effort to stave off defeat, I suddenly pulled a leg tendon with an audible pop, and I was obliged to stop. Though I escaped the ignominy of defeat through default, the price was high. By evening I could hardly walk, and when I finally parachuted into Normandy the following morning, I instinctively pulled up my game leg and landed with all my weight on the other. It didn't break, but it was a torture to walk for the first week in France, ample time to curse myself for this self-inflicted wound and 'Froggie' for his surprising skill with the squash racquet.

Glider infantry at Greenham Common on June 6. Although the inclusion of this picture at this point is out of strict chronological sequence, as the 82nd Division glider lift from Greenham did not depart until the early evening of D-Day in order to arrive in Normandy at dusk, it is an important picture as it serves to illustrate the location of the 502nd Parachute Infantry's 'Tent City' just off the southern perimeter of the airfield. This is actually an entrance to the administrative area, the picture being taken looking a little south of west with the spire of Newtown church just visible above the trees. The Jeep bears the markings of the 88th Troop Carrier Squadron, one of the four squadrons comprising the 438th Troop Carrier Group.

Still under US tenure, the airfield was massively enlarged after the war with new buildings stretching right across the site where the tents were erected. Nevertheless, we carefully plotted their position in relation to the existing layout and Bill King even brought his Jeep up to complete the comparison.

When the landings were postponed, Eisenhower cancelled the press conference scheduled for Sunday (June 4) at 'Sharpener' (see page 158). After lunch on Monday, with the decision to go having been confirmed early that morning, the four accredited press representatives were briefed by Eisenhower. Commander Butcher wrote in his diary that 'the nonchalance with which he announced that we were attacking in the morning, and the feigned nonchalance with which the reporters absorbed it, was a study in suppressed emotion which would interest any psychologist'. The reporters were invited to accompany Eisenhower that evening on his farewell visit to the 101st and Lieutenant Lee Moore, with a sergeant, was detailed as photographer. Unfortunately, no pictures were taken at 'Sharpener' before the party departed, this photo *(left)*, although appropriate, being taken in July on the same occasion as that on page 158. They left the camp around 6 p.m., with Kay Summersby *(right)* driving the lead Cadillac containing Eisenhower and his British aide, Lieutenant-Colonel James 'Jim' Gault. In the second car were Butcher, Lieutenant Colonel Smith, the SHAEF PR chief, Stanley Birch (Reuters), and Moore with his assistant. Bringing up the rear were 'Red' Mueller of NBC, Robert Barr for the BBC, and Ned Roberts of UP.

Many other visitors filled our headquarters by the end of June 5. The most important one was Ike himself who, with several of his staff, was our guest for an early dinner at our headquarters' mess. After dinner, we drove to several nearby airfields where our parachutists, many in Indian war-paint and with freakish haircuts, were getting into their equipment. Paraphrasing Wellington's feelings about his peninsular troops, General Eisenhower whispered to me that they might not scare the Germans, but they would certainly scare him. He went from plane to plane talking to the men in that wonderfully-friendly, man-to-man way which was one of the strengths of his personality, and the men glowed with pride that the Supreme Commander himself had come to see them off. When the round of visits was over, still in the daylight of the English double summer time, he shook hands, wished me luck, and returned to the manor house at the Greenham Common airfield which served as the division command post.

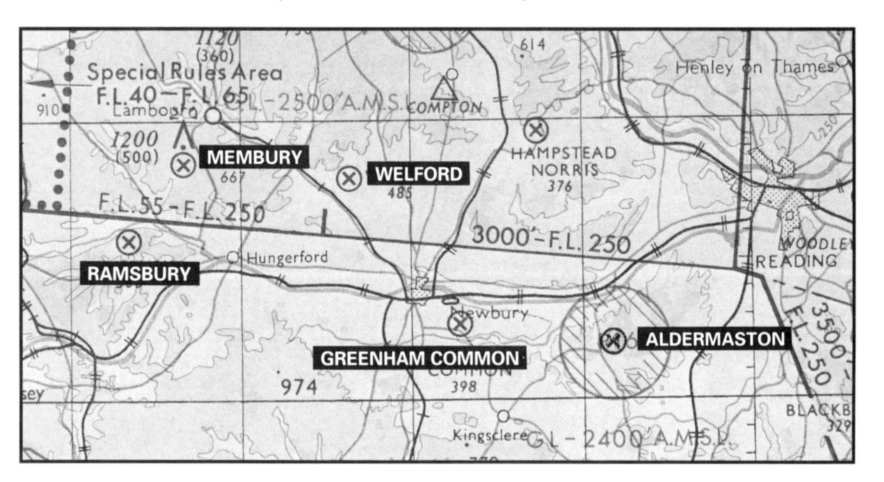

Most probably using the A333 as far as Basingstoke and then the A34 north to Newbury, even with two motorcycle outriders the journey still took the best part of 90 minutes. Kay Summersby said they visited three bases; Leonard Dry, who drove one of the other vehicles, believes it was five, but photos were only taken at two. Arriving at Greenham, Wally Strobel of E Company of the 502nd Parachute Infantry recalls a shout going up when Eisenhower pulled up but, he says, 'we were more interested in Ike's driver. I went down company street near the Tent City (see previous page) and met Ike coming up, so I never did get to see her!'

Cine film was also shot of the visit, the sequence beginning as Ike steps over the wire 'sealing' in the troops in Tent City.

The formal inspection *(left)* soon leads to an informal walk-about *(right)* as Ike is escorted by Colonel George Van Horn Moseley of the 502nd. Following is the regiment's Executive Officer, Lieutenant Colonel 'Mike' Michaelis. Butcher is recognisable in his US Navy uniform, Gault in British Army service dress, and Smith in the field jacket and garrison side hat.

The General held a press conference that morning to brief the pool journalists who would cover the invasion. From then on, the pace was unrelenting.

At six that evening, he stopped everything. He had something important to do, something that turned out to be the most memorable event of the whole war for me. My little blue diary holds this entry: 6.30 p.m., start trip to visit Airborne troops in the Newbury area. Gen. Taylor. Visited 3 airfields. Morale of troops very high. Watched some of them take off. Wonderful sight.

This conveys no idea of the drama of that evening. The night before D-Day, we dropped everything to make the long drive to Newbury and visit the 101st Airborne. They would be the first troops to land in Normandy behind the enemy lines. Some would be towed over in huge gliders that would settle down quietly in the darkness with their cargoes of young fighting men. Others would parachute down into this heavily fortified area. Ike's last task on the eve of D-Day was to wish these men well.

There was no military pomp about his visit. His flag was not flying from the radiator of the car, and he had told me to cover the four stars on the red plate. We drove up to each of the airfields, and Ike got out and just started walking among the men. When they realised who it was, the word went from group to group like the wind blowing across a meadow, and then everyone went crazy. The roar was unbelievable. They cheered and whistled and shouted, 'Good old Ike!'

There they were, these young paratroopers in their bulky combat kits with their faces blackened so that they would be invisible in the dark of the French midnight. Anything that could not be carried in their pockets was strapped on their backs or to their arms and legs. Many of them had packages of cigarettes strapped to their thighs. They looked so young and so brave. I stood by the car and watched as the General walked among them with his military aide a few paces behind him. He went from group to group and shook hands with as many men as he could. He spoke a few words to every man as he shook his hand, and he looked the man in the eye as he wished him success. 'It's very hard really to look a soldier in the eye,' he told me later, 'when you fear that you are sending him to his death.'

KAY SUMMERSBY, 1976

Little does Mike Michaelis (second left in the picture *above*) know that within a few hours he will have to take command of the regiment when Moseley (left in the photo *below*) breaks his leg on landing. Watched closely by his American and British aides, Eisenhower talks to Private Tom Beszouska of F Company, 2nd Battalion of the 502nd, but unfortunately the corporal in the picture below has not been identified. The strips of white cloth were being worn as recognition symbols.

Above: **Possibly Lieutenant Moore's most famous picture — some have even argued the most evocative image of all the D-Day photography. Speaking to Lieutenant Wallace C. Strobel — the one who wanted to see Ike's attractive driver — Eisenhower is officially captioned as calling for 'Full victory — nothing else'. Strobel has said that Ike in actual fact asked him where he was from and, when he replied 'Saginaw, Michigan', Ike declared: 'I've been there and liked it. Good fishing there!'** *Left:* **In June 1990, Eisenhower's son John visited Greenham Common as part of the Journey to Victory celebrations to mark the centenary year of his father's birth. Ken Mason, who took the picture, posed David Eisenhower beside exhibits parked on the taxiway; we went one better** *(below)* **and put Bill King and security guard Mel Field on the exact spot in Tent City. We established the correct location by carefully overlaying wartime aerial photography of the airfield with the post-war layout and even got the time right —** ***exactly*** **50 years later.**

Kay Summersby wrote that they visited three airfields and that General Maxwell Taylor had been the last to leave. She said that Ike had walked him to his plane and shook hands with him before they all went over to the headquarters building of the 101st to watch the take-off. However, Bill King's records indicate that Eisenhower visited *four* of the five airfields in the Newbury area which were the departure points for the 101st. After visiting Greenham Common, Eisenhower went on to Aldermaston to see Brigadier General Pratt (who was departing in a Waco) before doubling back to see General Taylor off at Welford. He then drove to Membury. Eisenhower probably meant to take in the fifth airfield at Ramsbury but by then he was running short of time so he returned straight to Greenham to catch the take-off. Kay compresses these events and gives the impression that the 101st's commanding officer left from Greenham which was not the case. The poor quality of the two pictures taken at Welford suggests that they were illegally taken by a trooper, all cameras having been banned in operational orders shortly before D-Day. Maxwell Taylor is recognisable in the garrison cap.

From the roof, he watched the airborne squadrons form, straighten out in column, and head for the Channel and Normandy.

Once the visitors had gone, the jumpmaster of my stick of parachutists, Major Laurence Legere, helped me into my parachute and suspended from me all the paraphernalia which made parachutists into pack mules: emergency parachute, pistol, jump knife, handgrenades, field rations, canteen, first aid kit, gas mask, maps, and a leg bag in which I had prudently stored a bottle of Irish whiskey. When everything was in place, a brawny sergeant proceeded to tighten the straps of my parachute to the point that breath came hard, reminding me that the tighter the straps the less the shock of opening when I left the plane.

During the normal course of events, Welford is totally out of bounds to visitors but, when three coach-loads of 101st veterans were given the opportunity of viewing their old base during the 50th anniversary, we joined them on a unique occasion. We even obtained special permission to take General Taylor's personal radioman, George Koskimaki, out onto the airfield in a Jeep to picture him at his point of departure on the evening of June 5, 1944.

Eisenhower returned to Greenham Common which was not only the location of the headquarters of the 101st but also of the 53rd Troop Carrier Wing, reaching the airfield around 11 p.m. However, in Eisenhower's post-war account, ***Crusade in Europe,*** he compresses the whole evening, giving the impression that only one location was visited: 'A late evening visit on the 5th took me to the camp of the US 101st Airborne Division, one of the units whose participation had been so severely questioned by the air commander. I found the men in fine fettle, many of them joshingly admonishing me that I had no cause for worry since the 101st was on the job and everything would be taken care of in fine shape. I stayed with them until the last of them were in the air, somewhere about midnight.'

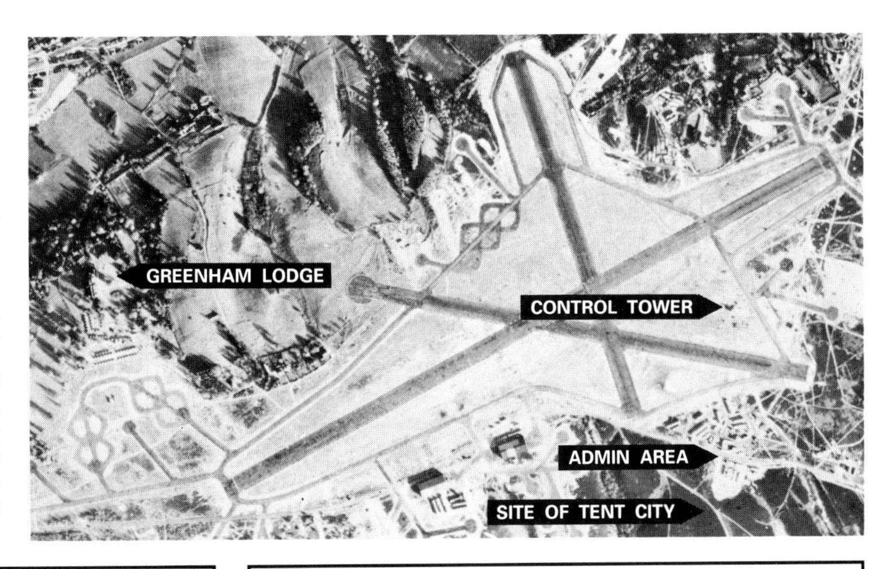

The good weather promised by the meteorologists had arrived, and all the time that Ike had been talking to the paratroopers there was the most spectacular sunset — deep glowing colours stretching across the sky. As it faded and the light started to go, the men began to embark. General Maxwell Taylor was the last to leave. Ike walked him to his plane and shook hands with him, and then we went over to the headquarters building of the 101st and climbed up to the roof.

The planes were taking off, roaring down the runways and climbing, climbing. Soon there were hundreds circling above us. By this time, it was dark and the moon had come up. It was a full moon, so brilliant that it cast shadows. The planes, wheeling like some immense flock of birds, blotted it out from time to time. It was such a gigantic moment! My heart was pounding, and I was practically crying. I knew I had never seen anything like it before and never would see anything like it again. We stayed on the roof for a long time watching the planes. Ike stood there with his hands in his pockets, his face tipped toward the sky. The planes kept circling, and then they began tailing off and headed toward Normandy. We sighed. A lot of those men, men whom Ike had just been walking with, shaking hands with, were going to their deaths.

The General turned and left the roof without saying a word to anyone. I hurried after him, but then I stopped. He was walking very slowly, his head bent. I could not intrude. He needed to be alone. Before he got into the car, he turned to me and said, 'Well, it's on. No one can stop it now.' There were tears in his eyes. We were silent as we drove back along the moonlit road to the trailer in the woods at Southwick.

KAY SUMMERSBY, 1976

SUPREME HEADQUARTERS
ALLIED EXPEDITIONARY FORCE

Soldiers, Sailors and Airmen of the Allied Expeditionary Force!

You are about to embark upon the Great Crusade, toward which we have striven these many months. The eyes of the world are upon you. The hopes and prayers of liberty-loving people everywhere march with you. In company with our brave Allies and brothers-in-arms on other Fronts, you will bring about the destruction of the German war machine, the elimination of Nazi tyranny over the oppressed peoples of Europe, and security for ourselves in a free world.

Your task will not be an easy one. Your enemy is well trained, well equipped and battle-hardened. He will fight savagely.

But this is the year 1944! Much has happened since the Nazi triumphs of 1940-41. The United Nations have inflicted upon the Germans great defeats, in open battle, man-to-man. Our air offensive has seriously reduced their strength in the air and their capacity to wage war on the ground. Our Home Fronts have given us an overwhelming superiority in weapons and munitions of war, and placed at our disposal great reserves of trained fighting men. The tide has turned! The free men of the world are marching together to Victory!

I have full confidence in your courage, devotion to duty and skill in battle. We will accept nothing less than full Victory!

Good Luck! And let us all beseech the blessing of Almighty God upon this great and noble undertaking.

Dwight Eisenhower

Kay Summersby states that the departure was viewed from the roof of the 101st headquarters — a rather vague description as it could hardly be the sloping roof of Greenham Lodge — while the history of the 438th Troop Carrier Group describes the location as being Wing HQ.

Left: The logical vantage point was the balcony of the control tower (on the right); unfortunately it now no longer stands *(right).*

As with the 82nd Airborne Division, the pathfinders of the 101st departed from North Witham. They would be the very first American troops to land in France and the Base Stick *(right)* from the 502nd Parachute Infantry Regiment, bound for DZ 'A', was to be the very first to jump. Captain Frank Lillyman, the commander of the 101st Provisional Pathfinder Company (not present when this group picture was taken), intended to be the first man out at 1220 hours. His C-47 arrived over the DZ ten minutes early, but the pilot overshot and had to go round again. The delay led to the jumping order being changed and, although Lillyman later claimed to be first, and is given as such in many published accounts, he was actually second or third. First man through the door was Pfc. John G. McFarlen (back row, third from left) and, as he said later, 'unless Captain Lillyman found a way to beat me to the ground, I was the first to land'.

The parachutists in a plane, about a dozen in number, constituted a 'stick' which was under the supervision of the jumpmaster, always a picked man and an experienced parachutist. For the moment, he was an autocrat with unchallenged authority somewhat like that of the skipper of a ship. Regardless of the rank of the members of his stick, he was responsible for them for the duration of the flight and could give whatever orders were necessary to carry out his duties. Larry Legere, four years out of West Point, performed that rôle for our stick, checking our equipment, reminding us of exit procedures, and getting us into the proper bucket seat. My fellow passengers included my aide, personal bodyguards, several communications personnel, and Robert Reuben, a Reuters correspondent. Lieutenant Colonel Frank McNees, CO of the 435th Troop Carrier Group, one of the most experienced pilots of the Troop Carrier Command, was our pilot, and I had every confidence that, if anyone could, he would get our plane to the drop-zone.

Promptly at 11 p.m., our plane placed itself at the head of the squadron departing from the field. McNees gunned the engines, we hurtled down the runway, and we were off on what was to be, for most of us, our greatest adventure. To me, it was a moment of relief to be off after so many months of laborious preparation. I was content in the feeling that I could think of nothing which we had left undone to assure success. Now it only remained to go into action in the spirit of the verse of Montrose which Montgomery had quoted to the Allied commanders at their last conference:

He either fears his fate too much
Or his deserts are small,
That dares not put it to the touch
To gain or lose it all.

Our parachute planes circled in the dusk over England for more than an hour as the successive squadrons rose from the airfields to join the airborne caravan which now included not only the planes of the 101st but also those of the 82nd arriving from their fields in central England. In all, there were over 800 transport planes in the formation as it turned toward France, carrying about 13,000 parachutists of the two divisions.

By the time my plane reached the Channel, it was dark with a faint moon showing. We were flying very low in a tight V of Vs formation to keep below the vision of the German radars on the French coast. As I stood in the open door of the plane, I felt that I could touch the sparkling waves of the Channel so close below. The men were strangely quiet, some seeming to doze on their hard metal seats in spite of the load of their equipment. They, too, seemed to have left their cares behind.

As well as North Witham and the bases in the Newbury area, the 101st also departed from three airfields in the West Country: Exeter, Upottery and Merryfield. These pictures show the CO of the 441st Troop Carrier Group, Colonel Theodore G. Kershaw and his crew *(left)* who piloted the lead aircraft out of Merryfield.

Our route was across the Channel from Portsmouth to an air corridor between the islands of Guernsey and Jersey on the west and the Cherbourg peninsula on the east which then turned eastward across the base of the peninsula to our drop-zones. As we came abreast of the Channel Islands, from my post in the door I could see a great grey wall to the south-east where the Cherbourg peninsula should be. It was unexpected fog, the enemy of the airman, which was to be the first disrupting factor in our well-laid plans.

The air column, still flying in orderly formation at low altitude, made its final turn eastward and headed into the fog bank. It was very thick at first, so thick that I could not see the planes flying on our wing-tips. Almost immediately, the formation began to break up as the flank planes, fearing collision, veered to the right and left and some increased their altitudes. But there was little time for worry about the fog in our plane. The hook-up signal came on quickly and Legere had us in the aisle attaching the static lines of our parachutes to the overhead wire which would trip the opening device on our chutes as we jumped. We checked our equipment and stood in file, each crowding against the man in front to ensure a rapid exit when the time came. I was almost riding on the back of Legere who was to lead the stick out the door.

Soon, the fog became broken, and we could see patches of ground from time to time as we flashed over the Merderet river; by the time we entered the landing area, it was almost completely clear of fog. It was a thrilling sight to see: the sky ablaze with rockets, burning aircraft on the ground, and anti-aircraft fire rising on all sides. The green light flashed — the signal to jump — and out we went shouting 'Bill Lee!' in honour of our former division commander instead of 'Geronimo!', the traditional war-cry of the American parachutists.

As the plane roared away, I was left floating to earth in a comparative quiet, broken only by occasional bursts of small-arms fire on the ground. Since we had jumped at about 500 feet, to shorten the time during which we would be floating ducks for enemy marksmen, there was little time to try to select a point of landing. At the last moment, a gust of air caused me to drift away from my comrades of the stick and only by a mighty tug on the shroud lines did I manage to escape becoming entangled in the top of a tall tree. Then I came down with a bang in a small Norman field enclosed by one of the famous hedgerows which compartmented the countryside. In most places, these hedges consisted of rows of trees planted on earthen banks which, in combination with the trees, presented formidable obstacles to military operations of all sorts. Many a parachutist that morning found himself suspended from one of those tall trees, from which he could only hope to lower himself by a rope before a German rifleman found him.

At last on the soil of Normandy, I began to struggle out of my parachute, expecting that some of my men would appear to help me. But looking around I saw not a single soldier, only a circle of curious Norman cows who eyed me, disapprovingly I thought, as if resenting this intrusion into their pasture. I was still attempting to extricate myself from my 'chute when a German machine pistol opened up in the next field with the tell-tale sound of a ripping seat of pants which energised me to frantic struggles to free myself. In the wet morning grass, it was a terrible job to unbuckle the many snaps, and I finally gave up and used my parachute knife to cut my way out. Then, reluctantly abandoning my leg bag and its contents, I started out, pistol in one hand and identification cricket in the other, to find my troops — a lonely division commander who had lost or at least mislaid his division.

Moving in the shadow of the hedgerow, I became aware of the smell of freshly-turned earth and soon came upon some newly-dug trenches, a warning that the Germans were probably nearby and to proceed with caution. This I did, creeping in the shadows along the hedgerow to the end of the field. There, I heard someone just around the corner of the hedge and veered toward the sound ready to shoot. But then there was the welcome sound

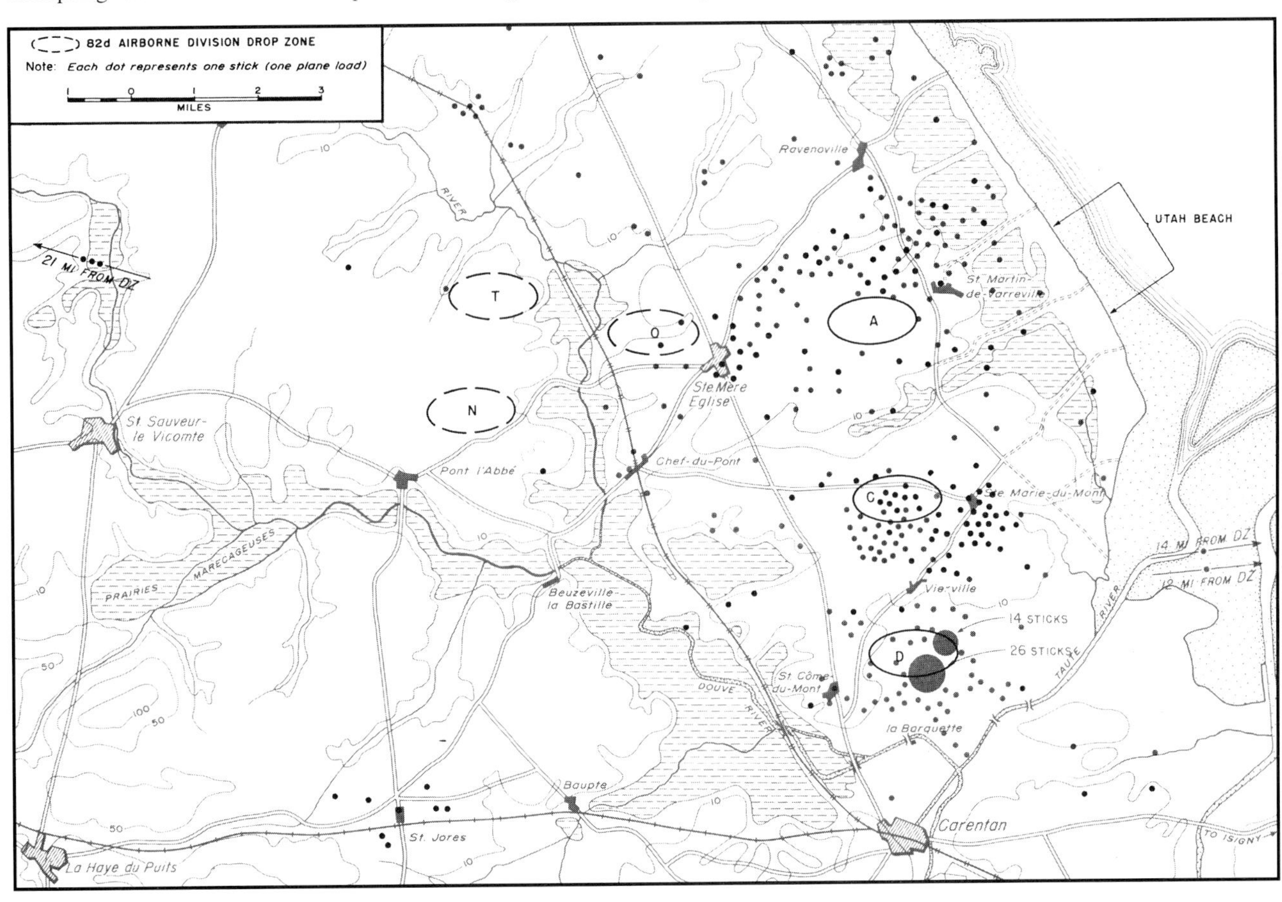

The drop of the 101st Airborne Division was equally as widespread as the 82nd, covering an area of some 15 miles by 25 miles and, out of the 6,600 men who came in by air, only 1,100 were effective on D-Day. At least 35 sticks dropped beyond the area depicted, some up to 20 miles from their designated DZ. (Compare with the 82nd map on page 266.)

Hundreds of American paratroopers were quickly captured and taken to St Lô where they were held in the French cavalry depot which lay between the cemetery and the Place du Champ de Mars, just north of St Croix Church. This area has now been completely redeveloped and all the old buildings demolished, making a present-day comparison meaningless.

of a cricket to which I quickly responded in kind and jumped around the corner. There in the dim moonlight was the first American soldier to greet me, a sight of martial beauty as he stood bareheaded, rifle in hand, bayonet fixed, and apparently ready for anything. We embraced in silence and took off together to round up others of our comrades who were beginning to appear.

As the night was only about five hours long in that latitude, there was just about one hour left in which to assemble the troops who had landed in the vicinity. Three battalions of parachute infantry should have arrived in the area before me, but it was apparent that the drop had been badly scattered and that only a few members of these battalions had reached their destinations. However, I soon ran into Tony McAuliffe, Gerry Higgins, and Julian Ewell, the commander of the 3rd Battalion of the 501st Parachute Infantry which had been scheduled for this drop zone. Together we beat the nearby fields until daylight by which time we had assembled about 90 soldiers, the odd remnants of various units and services. They ranged in rank from general to private and in skills from radio operators, cooks, clerks, and military police to riflemen, engineers, artillerymen, and Reuben, the war correspondent. We were long on officers but short on combat troops, particularly infantry, a fact that has led me to comment later that 'never were so few led by so many'.

Despite the long hours spent in England poring over the maps of this part of Normandy, I was not sure exactly where we were until the first morning light. Then I recognised to the northeast the church steeple of Ste Marie-du-Mont which indicated that we were approximately on the intended dropzone of the division headquarters. However, we had only a sprinkling of the troops assigned to the critical mission of securing the southern causeways of Utah Beach.

Now beginning to appreciate the wide dispersion of the troops — about 80 per cent of our parachutists had landed in a rectangle 27 by 15 miles — I decided to send Colonel Thomas Sherburne of the Division Artillery with a small detachment westward to Hiesville where we had planned to set up the division command post, while I moved with the remainder of the troops to take over the mission of seizing the exit of the southernmost of the causeways. I put Ewell in command of the column with orders to move on Pouppeville, occupy and hold it until the leading troops of the 4th Division could pass over the causeway. Then, McAuliffe, Higgins and I attached ourselves to the column to supervise the job.

As we turned eastward, we came on the first farmhouse in our path. The members of the family were battened down inside as the war swept over and around them, but responded when we pounded on the front door. I spoke to the farmer and asked him the location of the nearest German troops which he identified as Ste Marie-du-Mont. Then I inquired about the poles set up in one of his fields to serve as an obstacle. In England before our departure, we had been very much intrigued by this poling of fields which had taken place throughout Normandy, thinking that from the pattern of the poles we could deduce something of the German plan of defence. But to the hour of our take-off

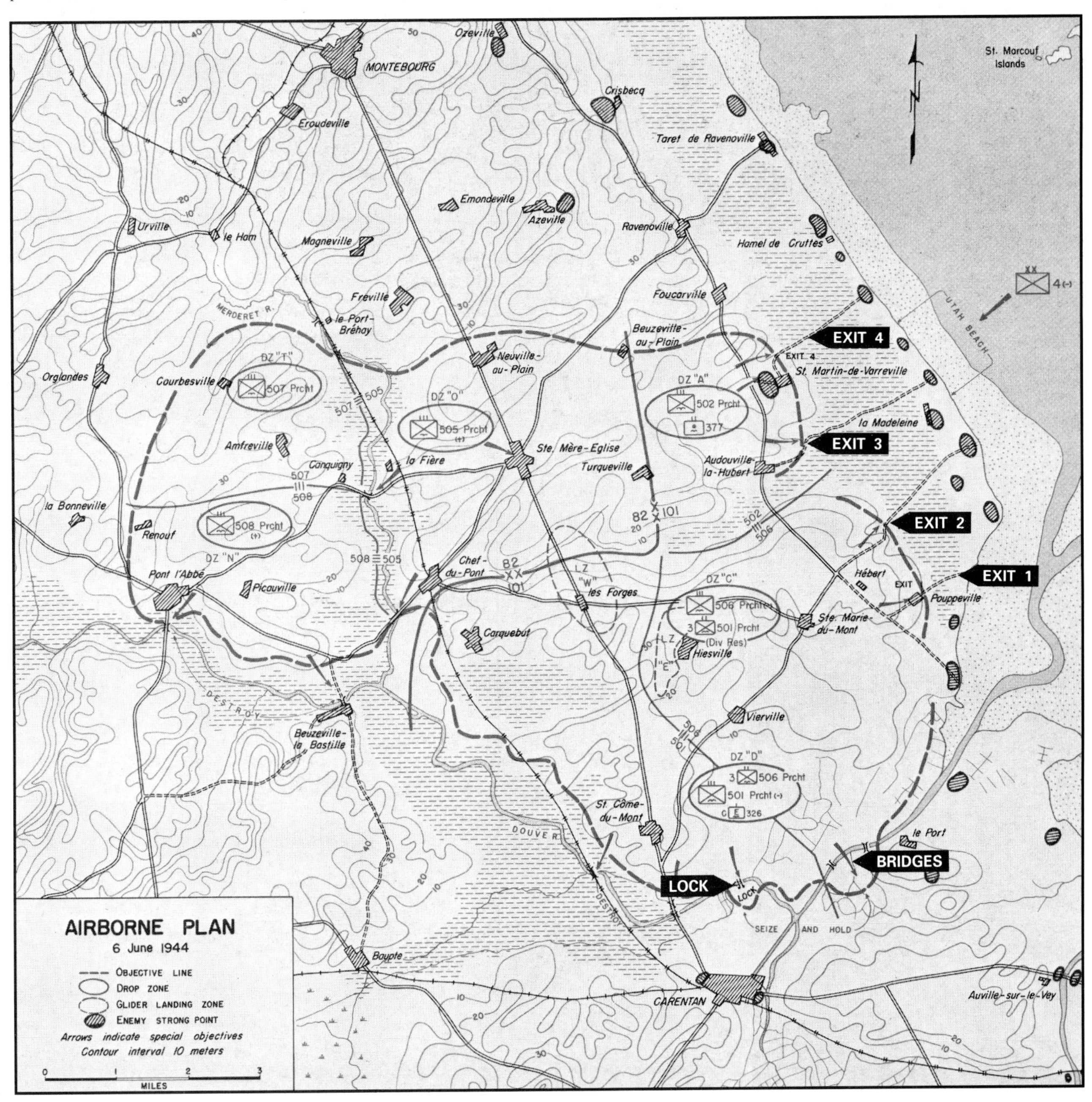

As planned, the 502nd Parachute Infantry was to drop on DZ 'A', destroy the coastal battery at St Martin-de-Varreville and capture the western ends of the two northern beach exits, Exits 3 and 4, and join up with the 82nd Airborne Division landing further to the west. In the event, when captured, the battery at St Martin revealed that it did not contain any guns at all and the two northern exits were found to be clear by a small force, mainly comprising the 1st Battalion of the 502nd under Lieutenant Colonel Patrick F. Cassidy. The capture of the two southern beach exits — which proved to be the more important due to the fact that the seaborne attack came ashore further to the south on the wrong beach — was the responsibility of the 506th under Colonel Robert F. Sink, its 1st and 2nd Battalions dropping on DZ 'C'. However, 30 minutes before H-Hour, a small force of some 40 men from another regiment, the 501st, had already assembled to try to clear Pouppeville at the inland end of Exit 1. They were held up all morning by resistance in the village, but troops of the 2nd Battalion of the 8th Infantry (Lieutenant Colonel Carlton O. MacNeely) advancing from Utah made contact with the airborne force about noon. As far as Exit 2 was concerned, the 2nd Battalion of the 506th, detailed for the capture, mis-landed near DZ 'A' and by the time it had fought its way to Houdienville, troops advancing from the beach had already passed through the village. Finally, it was the task of the 3rd Battalion of the 506th to land on DZ 'D' and capture two bridges over the River Douve at Le Port and establish a bridgehead on the southern bank. This was achieved by a small force of some 50 men but increasing German pressure forced them to withdraw to the northern bank during the day. The last 101st objective was to capture the lock at La Barquette, which the Germans had obstructed to create the flooded areas along the Douve and Merderet rivers, and also to blow the bridges between St Côme-du-Mont and Carentan to prevent the enemy advancing up the main road which acted as a causeway through the inundations. The lock was successfully taken by a miscellaneous force assembled by Colonel Howard R. Johnson, the CO of the 501st, but strong German forces prevented the capture of the bridges.

Ste Marie-du-Mont lies on the eastern edge of DZ 'C' in the heart of the division's operational area. With its peculiar domed-steeple church in the central market square, it bears a similar meaning for the 101st as Ste Mère-Eglise does to the 82nd. Paratroopers dropped in and around the village, one of the earliest fire-fights taking place here beside the village pump when its recess was used by an unnamed American to pick off members of the German garrison. Later that morning, a western-style shoot-out between an American and a German by the war memorial saw both men fall wounded from the other's fire. This picture was taken in June 1974 looking towards the beach-head with Exit 2 crammed with transport from the very first Military Vehicle Conservation Group tour to Normandy.

we had perceived no plan or method in the poling operations. Now I had a farmer who could explain it.

So I asked him why he had poled one of his fields and not the other of his small farm. His reply showed the folly of assuming rationality in human behaviour. 'The Germans told us farmers to pole all our fields by June 15. My cow never liked that west field so I poled it first.' In this case, the whim of a French cow was the controlling factor, not the plans of the German General Staff. As I was about to go, the farmer asked me to wait a moment, went back into the house and returned with a clip of World War I rifle ammunition. He gave it to me with the injunction 'Allez me tuer un Boche'. ('Go kill me a German.')

Above: **This picture, taken in front of the pump, is believed to show men of the 1st Battalion of the 506th. The girl in the centre, half turned away from the camera, is Andrée Desselier who later married a 101st trooper, Frank Polosky, her wedding dress being fashioned from his reserve parachute.**

It was now after daylight as we pushed eastward. The landing on Utah Beach had begun, and we were the privileged spectators of the greatest military show of history. The sea was filled with landing craft, the air with fighters and bombers. Bombs were falling on both the Utah and Omaha Beach defences and our Navy had opened up on shore targets with heavy guns. Fired with high velocity on a flat trajectory, their shells would hit the beach and then ricochet inland emitting bloodcurdling screams as they passed overhead. Resisting a temptation to stand and watch the show, we continued across country toward the beach in a column of two's with patrols out to the front and flank, picking up a few more men as we went.

We made our first contact with the Germans as we neared Pouppeville

Below: **The GC70 (Chemin de Grande Commune 70) has become the Chemin Départemental 70 (D70) but it still leads to Les Forges in 82nd Airborne country and the post-war Airborne Museum.**

where our column halted on the outskirts while Ewell organised his attack on the town. The resistance was light, but it was a time-consuming task to clear out each house and eliminate the snipers. While we senior officers observing the operation controlled with difficulty our impatience to get into the act, Ewell went about his business with professional thoroughness and mopped up the village by about noon. In so doing, we captured some 40 prisoners and suffered about 20 casualties. One of these was Larry Legere who received a severe hip wound which resulted in his evacuation for long hospitalisation in the United States.

These 101st paratroops of the 3rd Battalion of the 502nd are moving out of the village due west along the GC70 (today the D70) on D+2 to defend the Blosville-Houesville area against a possible German counter-attack. These particular men are from Company H — Tech. 5 Robert Marois on the left facing Signal Corps cameraman Kaye.

Reference with the aerial photograph opposite will show that the troopers were photographed crossing the square with the town hall (since refaced) in the left background and the church behind the trees on the right.

Left: **Some time later, a US Navy photographer pictured the square with the war memorial on the right.** *Right:* **One of a number of plaques, set up in the town to commemorate the events of June 6, has now been mounted on the pump.**

Left: **Another plaque — this time on the gatepost of the Lecaudey farm** *(centre)* **at nearby Hiesville — records its use by General Taylor as his command post. The group of farm buildings had already been earmarked for the 101st headquarters back in Britain, this picture** *(right)* **having been taken on June 15 showing the first organised distribution of aid there to the civilian population in this part of Normandy. In the foreground, members of the Léonard family evacuated from Le Ham near Valognes.**

Left: **A few hundred yards north of the CP, the Château Colombière had been requisitioned by the 326th Airborne Medical Company for their field hospital. However, it had to be evacuated after the Luftwaffe bombed it just before midnight on D+3, killing five patients and six medical personnel.** *Right:* **It was rebuilt after the war in a somewhat more modest style.**

Shortly after the occupation of Pouppeville, we could hear the firing of the troops of the 4th Division approaching from the beach. To avoid the possibility of a collision of the two forces, I sent a patrol to meet them and inform them of the situation around Pouppeville. Very soon, the advance guard of the 8th Infantry appeared to the cheers of our parachutists. It was an historic moment, the long-planned junction of the air and seaborne assaults on Hitler's Fortress Europe. Utilising the communications of the 4th Division, I conveyed the welcome news to General Bradley.

Left: **Major General Taylor pictured in his personal Jeep at his command post.** *Right:* **When Steve Casely arrived at the Lecaudey farm in June 1994 to match the shot, he met Captain Adolph Gueymard who had commanded Battery B of the 81st Anti-Aircraft Artillery Battalion and had witnessed the death of the Assistant Division Commander, Brigadier General Pratt who had left Aldermaston for Normandy in the initial 101st glider lift (Operation 'Chicago'), at 0119 hours on D-Day.**

Pratt rode into battle sitting in his Jeep inside his Waco *(left)* named ***Fighting Falcon No. 2.*** Captain Gueymard (later Major) explained that the General was sitting on a parachute which raised him in his seat so that when the glider crash-landed in this field on Landing Zone 'E', his helmet hit an overhead strut and broke his neck. Gueymard, who landed 50 yards behind Pratt's glider, was instrumental in having this memorial *(right)* erected 250 metres west of the crash site.

Our mission finished in this part of the field, I turned our little column around and started inland for the division command post at Hiesville. It was hard going not because of the enemy but because of the condition of my legs as the result of the pre-D-Day squash game. Just east of Hiesville, we ran into Colonel Robert Sink, commanding the 506th Parachute Infantry, who during the morning had had a hot fight in the vicinity and had captured a German field artillery battery of which he was very proud, explaining that henceforth he would have his own regimental artillery. He warned us, however, that there were lots of 'hostiles' nearby and that we should be prepared for anything.

Hiesville was merely a group of farmhouses which we had chosen as our command post from a map in England because of its central location in relation to our division missions. When we reached it in the late afternoon, Colonel Sherburne had the command post in operation, radio contact established with a few subordinate units, and its defence organised against a surprise German attack. He had quartered most of the elements of the command post in a farmhouse which was surrounded by a high stone wall constructed so solidly as to constitute a formidable redoubt. Once arrived and divested of impedimenta, I set to work with Higgins to evaluate the situation of the division as we approached the end of the 'Longest Day'.

The situation was far from clear in most parts of the division sector. The causeways were secured and the 4th Division was having no difficulty in landing; that was the most encouraging news. However, unit reports received at Hiesville accounted for only about 2,000 of the 6,600 parachutists who had jumped that morning and these were intermingled in groups of various sizes, many including men from the neighbouring 82nd. In the course of the day, the men had shown remarkable initiative in forming small task forces under the officers or non-commissioned officers who happened to be present and then heading for the nearest division objective, as we had done at Poupeville. Much equipment had been lost in the drop, including virtually all of our parachute artillery. Two small glider detachments had landed, one in the morning with the parachutists, the other at the end of the day. They had brought in important heavy equipment including a long-range radio capable of communicating with England, anti-aircraft and anti-tank weapons, and medical equipment. But we had paid a heavy price in the loss of Don Pratt, the Assistant Division Commander, who was killed in the crash of his glider in the morning landing.

The quartermaster sections of both airborne divisions established separate temporary cemeteries, the 82nd selecting a site at Blosville, and the 101st a field at Hiesville. Chaplain Francis L. Sampson of the 501st Parachute Infantry Regiment is pictured giving absolution to the dead about to be buried in graves dug by German prisoner labour. The Hiesville cemetery was soon closed and the bodies transferred to two cemeteries laid out by VII Corps at Ste Mère-Eglise. After he war, the families of American servicemen were given the choice of having the remains reinterred in a permanent overseas war cemetery, or returned to the United States for burial in either a national or private cemetery as designated by the next of kin. *Right:* **Brigadier General Pratt now lies in Arlington National Cemetery in Washington.**

In due course, Pratt was replaced by the divisional Chief-of-Staff, Brigadier General Gerald J. Higgins, but now we must turn our attention to the northern flank where Exits 3 and 4 had been found undefended (see page 301). Road blocks were set up around Foucarville to stop any attacks against the beach-head from the north, this picture being captioned as having been taken at St Marcouf on June 8. Although the shoulder patches are censored out in the officially-released print, other versions show the Screaming Eagle insignia yet it was not until Michel De Trez published *At the Point of No Return* in 1994 that the picture could be correctly identified and put into context. Michel reproduced the whole roll of illicitly-taken photographs by Private Forrest Guth of the 2nd Battalion of the 506th. 'Gody' Guth and several members of Company E had come down six miles north of their designated DZ 'C' and had ended up at Ravenoville, mid-way between Foucarville and St Marcouf.

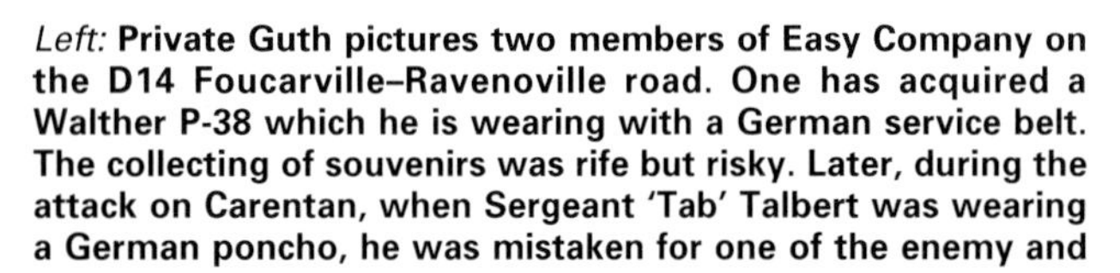
Left: Private Guth pictures two members of Easy Company on the D14 Foucarville–Ravenoville road. One has acquired a Walther P-38 which he is wearing with a German service belt. The collecting of souvenirs was rife but risky. Later, during the attack on Carentan, when Sergeant 'Tab' Talbert was wearing a German poncho, he was mistaken for one of the enemy and bayoneted in the chest by one of his own men! *Right:* In June 1994, *After the Battle* reader Phillip Bradley travelled to France from New South Wales, Australia and, as part of his own 50th anniversary trip to Normandy, followed in Guth's footsteps, matching the photographs while reading the account of the action at Ravenoville in Donald Burgett's *Currahee*.

This was an area occupied by stray elements of both divisions and, as the men began to move down the hedgerows, they joined up with about 30 others of the 506th, the 377th Parachute Field Artillery, and some from the 82nd, all under Major John P. Stopka, the XO of the 3rd Battalion of the 502nd, to mount an attack on Ravenoville. Some 200 yards south of the village, they came on the Marmion Farm just opposite the junction with the D15 to Ste Mère-Eglise. *Left:* The trooper on the left is trying to attract enemy fire by waving a cloth on his rifle. *Right:* Phillip found the farm almost unchanged.

The upper windows of the farm overlooked the beach and it took some time to winkle out German snipers from the first floor. Having captured the farm complex, the rush for souvenirs began. *Left:* Forrest Guth sports a German helmet rather too small for him, while *right* a captured Renault UE tractor and cargo trailer was to prove useful in the subsequent attack on the last German troops holding out in the church in the south-eastern corner of the village.

If the news was good from the beach, there was little known about the situation to the north or to the south. The 82nd was heavily engaged to our west where it had encountered considerable German strength. I had immediately available at the end of D-Day only about 1,000 troops under Colonel Sink. So there was little to do as night fell other than to direct Sink to move south at daylight with all the men he could collect, establish contact with our units along the Douve, and take over our second mission, that of covering the south flank of the VII Corps and its divisions moving north towards Cherbourg.

It took us three days to assemble our scattered parachutists, bring the 327th Glider Infantry from the beach where it had arrived by ship to a position on our left flank, and clear out patches of resistance north of the Douve. During these days, my principal concern was a German counter-attack, which I expected nightly after D-Day, but except for sporadic small-scale bombings there was no enemy reaction to disturb us.

A Nazi flag was one trophy they discovered and a succession of paratroopers were photographed holding it. *Left:* Private Francis J. Mellett and Forrest Guth hold it out for the camera.

Right: In November 1994, Michel De Trez travelled to the USA to picture the same flag which 'Gody' Guth had retained since that day in 1944.

Pfc Wilbur H. Shanklin of Headquarters Company of the 506th Parachute Infantry holds a prisoner at gun-point, in a rather posed-looking picture taken at Turqueville, some two miles south-east of Ste Mère-Eglise. Although not in any of the paratrooper dropping zones, several sticks of the 101st Airborne, mostly of the 502nd and 506th Parachute Infantry, came down in the vicinity of the village. Shanklin can be seen to be typical of the American paratrooper warrior in the Cotentin. Apart from his M1 rifle with bayonet, hand-grenades and M3 fighting knife (with his name written on his ankle scabbard), he has armed himself with a machete, a German bayonet and two German 'potato-masher' hand-grenades. He has also acquired a German canteen bottle. Close scrutiny shows that he is wearing the identification cricket — issued only to the 101st and not to the 82nd — tied to his left shoulder loop. (One 'click' from this spring-steel toy snapper was to be answered by two 'clicks'.) His prisoner very probably belongs to the Georgische Infanterie-Bataillon 795. Composed of Georgian soldiers pressed into Wehrmacht service and now part of Infanterie-Regiment 739 of the 709. Infanterie-Division, it was deployed around the village of Turqueville. On D-Day, they formed a pocket of enemy resistance along the ridge from Turqueville across the N13 to Fauville, thereby preventing the seaborne forces from linking up with the 82nd Airborne at Ste Mère-Eglise. After putting up a stiff fight and withstanding several attempts to dislodge them, the Georgians were finally talked into surrender on the morning of D+1.

Karel Margry matched the picture at the crossroads of the D67 and D129 just outside Turqueville.

The 101st was to be reinforced by just two glider lifts, Operations 'Chicago' and 'Keokuk', and the 82nd, operating further inland, was scheduled to receive four (see table). All the gliders for both divisions left from the same seven airfields in southern England: Aldermaston, Greenham Common, Membury, Merryfield, Ramsbury, Upottery and Welford. The CG-4A Wacos were used in the early morning landings, with Horsas *(above)*, being added later in daylight when it was assumed that the larger glider would stand less chance of crashing. Altogether, 294 Wacos and 222 Horsas were despatched, each towed by a single C-47, like this one taking off from Greenham Common on the evening of D-Day with part of the 80th Airborne Anti-Aircraft Battalion for the 82nd. This was the operation which screwed up so badly: destined for LZ 'W', it was switched to DZ 'O' in a last-minute change which so confused the troop carrier pilots that many released their charges over LZ 'E'.

Greenham Common 50 years later. The houses of Bury's Bank on the left still stand hidden by trees but the airfield is now closed and awaiting disposal, the USAF having withdrawn the 501st Tactical Missile Wing in 1992. The empty Tomahawk cruise missile shelters lie behind the camera position.

AIR LIFT, US IXth TROOP CARRIER COMMAND

		Aircraft					*Gliders*			
							Horsas		*Wacos*	
Operation	*Mission*	*Despatched*	*Effective*	*Abortive*	*Destroyed/ missing*	*Damaged*	*Despatched*	*Abortive*	*Despatched*	*Abortive*
'Albany'	101st paratroops, night June 5/6	443#	436	2	13	81	–	–	–	–
'Boston'	82nd paratroops, night June 5/6	378#	377	1	8	115	–	–	–	–
'Chicago'	101st gliders, dawn D-Day	52	51	1	1	7	–	–	52	1
'Detroit'	82nd gliders, dawn D-Day	52	52	–	1	38	–	–	52	1
'Keokuk'	101st gliders, dusk D-Day	32	32	–	–	1	32	–	–	–
'Elmira'	82nd gliders, dusk D-Day	177*	175	2	5	92	140	2	36	–
'Galveston'	82nd gliders, dawn D+1	102	100	2	–	26	20	2	84	2
'Hackensack'	82nd gliders, dawn D+1	101+	101	–	–	11	30	–	70	–
'Freeport'	82nd resupply, morning D+1	208	153	55	11	94	–	–	–	–
'Memphis'	101st resupply, morning D+1	119	117	2	3	35	–	–	–	–
		1664	1594	65	42	500	222	4	294	4

including pathfinder planes (11 for the 101st, 9 for the 82nd) * including one paratroop plane + including a pathfinder plane without troops

(Source: Dr John C. Warren: *Airborne Operations in World War II, European Theater* (USAF Historical Division, 1956))

Left: Having now rejoined their unit, Messrs Guth, Mellett, Morris, West, Talbert and Smith pause on their way south to have their photo taken in the square in Ste Marie with three infantrymen of the 4th Division who have come ashore at Utah. *Right:* Fifty years later, Forrest Guth returns to find the monument restored.

The priority in the American sector was to effect the link-up between the two beach-heads, the critical towns being Isigny for V Corps driving west from Omaha and Carentan for VII Corps in the neck of the Cotentin peninsula. The latter mission initially fell to the 101st Airborne Division already engaged along the southern flank of the Utah sector. Having taken St Côme-du-Mont on June 8, plans were made to launch the assault on Carentan. This picture graphically illustrates the problem faced by the attacking force and also the ease with which a defender could hold up the advance. All the low-lying ground north-west of the town was flooded, with only the railway line to Cherbourg above water. However, the Germans had anticipated an assault along the tracks and had blown a gap in the embankment. At this point, we are looking north with the hamlet of Le Bougamet in the foreground, the photo being taken shortly before D-Day.

We launched a pincer attack against Carentan on the night of June 9/10, the 327th Glider Regiment under Colonel Joseph H. Harper making an unopposed crossing of the Douve near its mouth while the 502nd Parachute Infantry attacked southward astride the Cherbourg-Carentan highway. The advance here was severely constricted by the causeway formed by the road which created a defile covered by fire from German trenches to the south. Here occurred the only authentic bayonet charge to which I can testify in the course of a war in which the bayonet was used far more frequently against ration cans than against the enemy. The charge was led by Lieutenant Colonel Robert G. Cole, the CO of the 3rd Battalion of the 502nd, against the German position blocking the exit from the Douve river causeway. Cole, who received the Medal of Honor for his gallantry, was later killed in action in Holland.

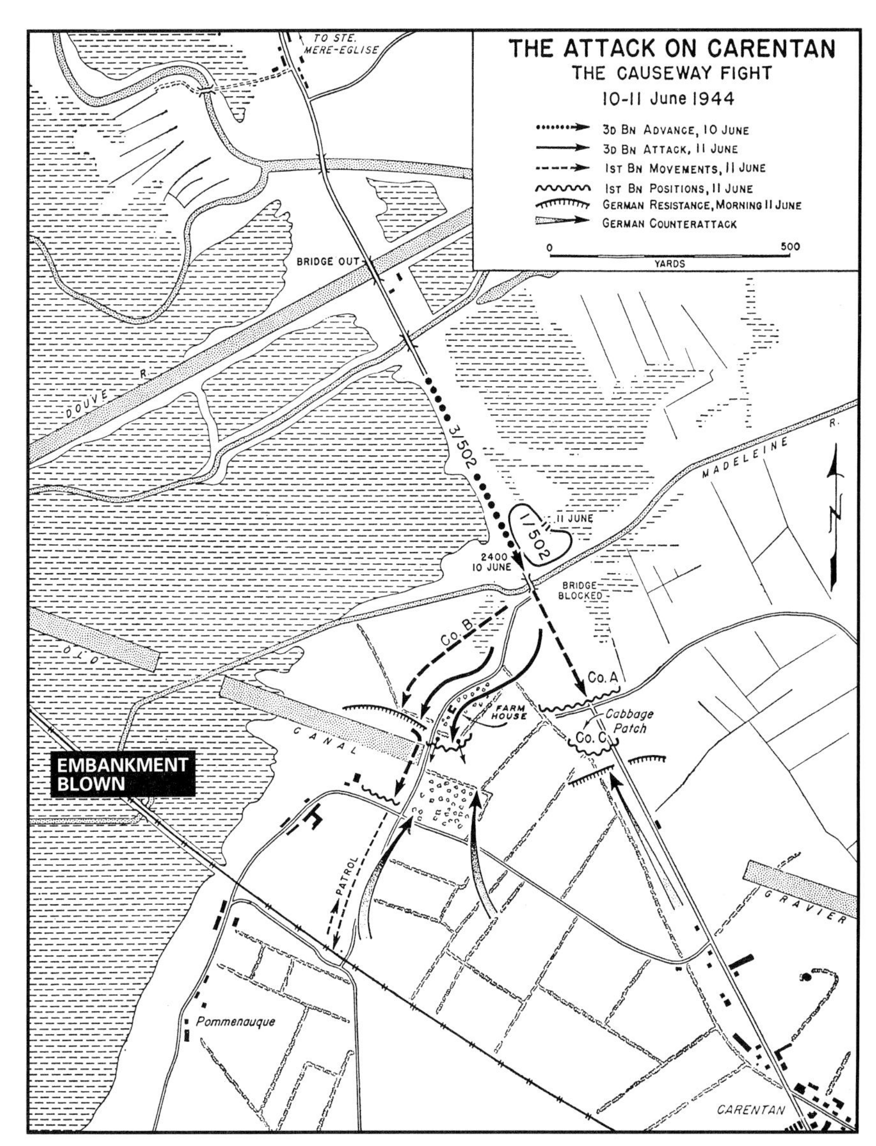

With the railway embankment denied them, the only other approach route lay along the N13 — dubbed by the Americans 'the causeway'. Once the advance had crossed the bridge over the River Madeleine (Bridge No. 4), the attack could fan out but, before that, troops on the causeway would be exposed to fire from each flank and also straight up the road from the town. The plan shows the opening moves by the 3rd Battalion of the 502nd, an attack which led to its commanding officer, Colonel Robert G. Cole, and Major Stopka, his XO, mounting a bayonet charge on the farmhouse at 0615 on the morning of June 11. Of the 250 men who should have followed the two officers, only about 70 did so, Colonel Cole's action earning him the Congressional Medal of Honor.

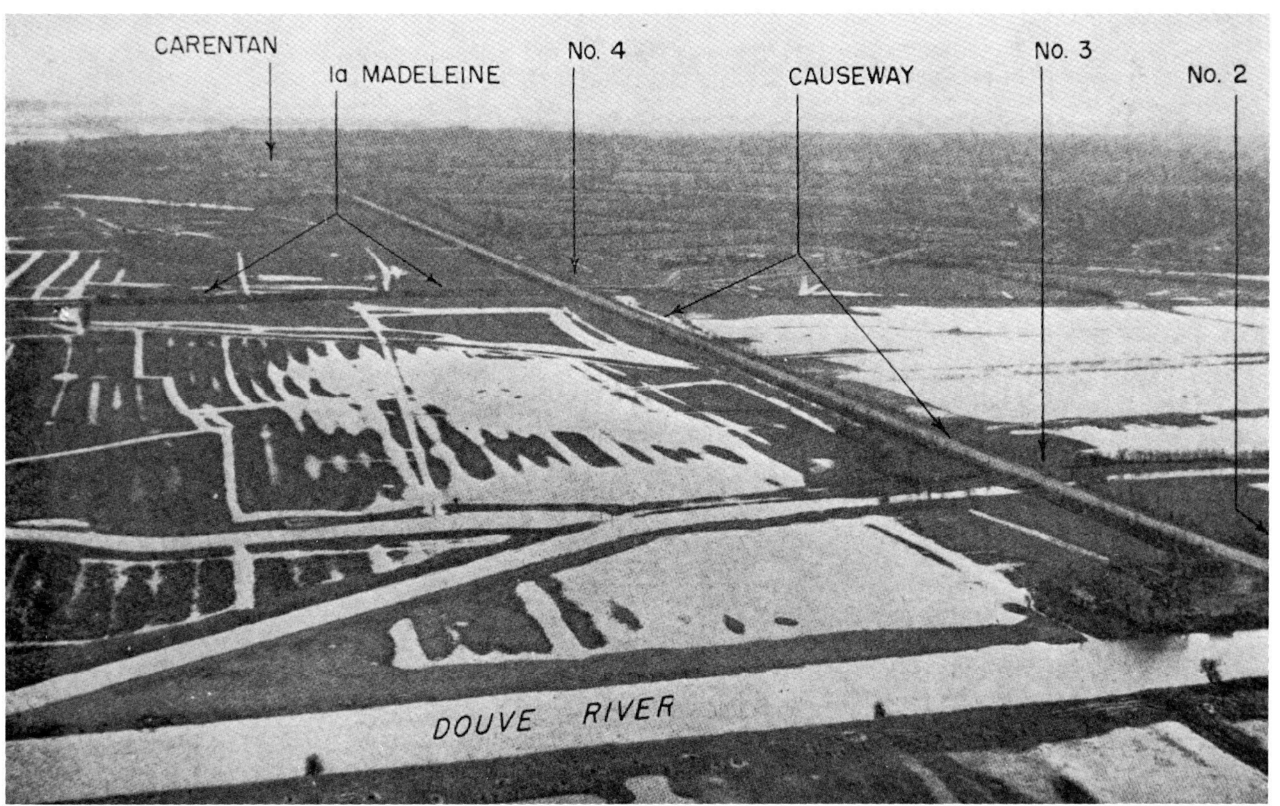

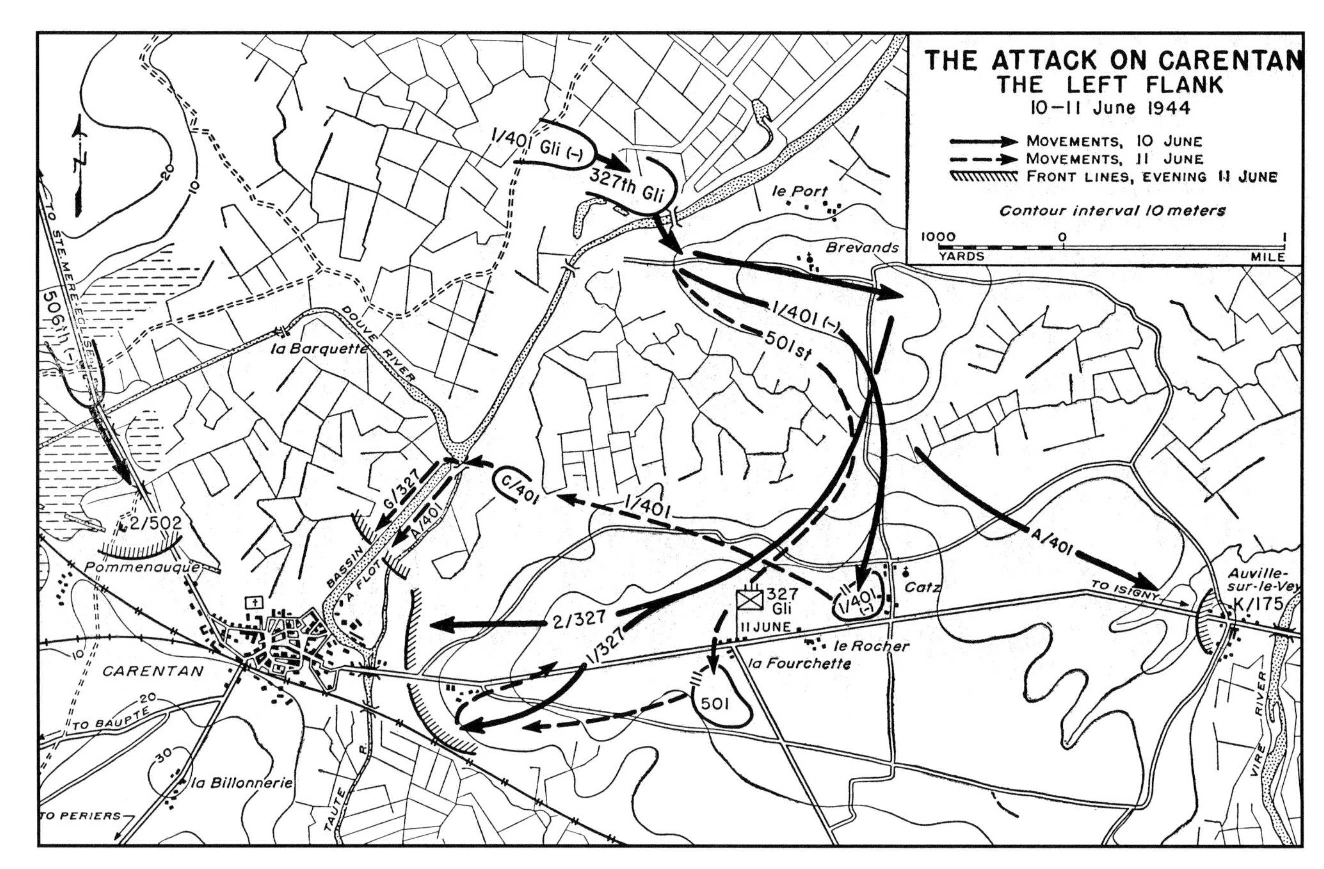

Meanwhile, the 327th Glider Infantry Regiment had crossed the Douve river out to the east of the city and were launching an enveloping movement on the left flank. The first contact with troops from Omaha took place on the afternoon of June 10 when Company A of its 3rd Battalion (the old 1st Battalion of the 401st) met forces from the 175th Infantry Regiment at Auville-sur-le-Vey.

The 502nd by this time was under Lieutenant Colonel John H. 'Mike' Michaelis who assumed command of the regiment when its colonel, George Moseley, broke his leg in the D-Day jump. Moseley was a veteran parachutist who had worked without stint to prepare his regiment for Normandy. It was an odd quirk of fortune that this experienced jumper should have been a casualty while Millener, my Assistant Chief-of-Staff for Operations, made the first jump of his career on D-Day without injury. It was hard to tell Moseley that he must give up his regiment and return to England. I found him on D+1 being pushed about in a wheelbarrow while he directed his troops with a cane. It took my personal order to get him to the aid station on the beach.

General Taylor was not pleased with Colonel Wear's performance commanding the 327th Glider Infantry Regiment, and he was replaced on the afternoon of June 10 by Lieutenant Colonel Joseph H. Harper, the commander of the split-up 401st Glider Infantry, who had been acting as beachmaster at Utah Beach for the 101st seaborne tail, for the final assault on Carentan. During the night of June 11/12, the town was subjected to a heavy bombardment from artillery and naval guns before the 327th moved in from the north-east to link with the 2nd Battalion of the 506th driving up the N171 *(left)* from the south-west. *Above:* Carentan has undergone drastic change in recent years, the old N171 being downgraded to the D971 and Rue Holgate blocked off where it used to cross the railway via a level crossing.

Rommel had perceived the danger should Carentan fall, for it was not only the link between the two US beach-heads, but also the key to an American drive west to cut the base of the peninsula. Defence of the city was in the hands of Major Friedrich-August Freiherr von der Heydte commanding Fallschirmjäger-Regiment 6. On the morning of D-Day, he had come forward from his command post near Périers to see the situation for himself — thus the battle for the city was largely fought between opposing airborne troops. By June 11, von der Heydte claimed he was running desperately short of ammunition and, acting on his own initiative, he decided to pull out and set up a new line to the south-west of the city. The regiment evacuated Carentan on the afternoon of the 11th, making the American bombardment that night somewhat superfluous, and the assault by the 101st early the next morning something of an anti-climax. Von der Heydte was later accused of suffering a temporary mental and physical breakdown and he only escaped court-martial because of his past record.

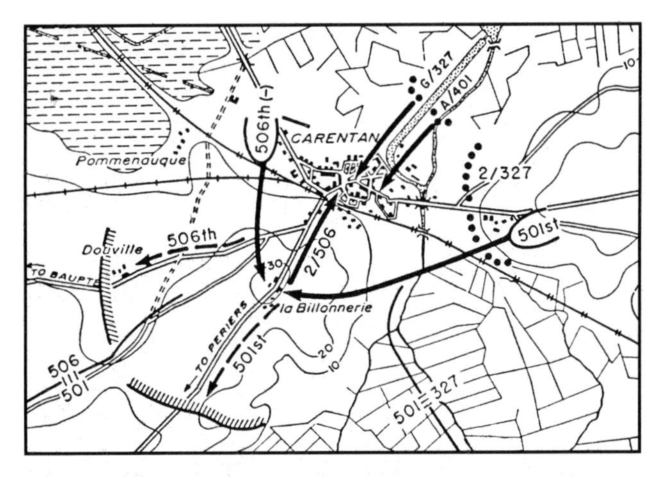

The battle for Carentan lasted for three days during which I was constantly scuttling in my Jeep from one flank of the division to the other. The pincers formed by our two flanks came together on June 12 in Carentan, which I entered from the east with Bud Harper's glider troops. On June 13, we received the delayed counter-attack which I had been expecting; it was mounted by the 17. SS-Panzergrenadier-Division and Fallschirmjäger-Regiment 6 against our troops on the south-west outskirts of Carentan. As an airborne division was very weak in anti-tank weapons, we might have had considerable difficulty in beating off the attack had not General Bradley, unsolicited, sent us the reinforcement of a combat command of the 2nd Armored Division commanded by Colonel John H. Collier. Our hard-pressed infantry welcomed the tanks with cheers, patted their steel hulls, then plunged after them down the hedgerows in pursuit of

With buildings still burning from the overnight bombardment, airborne troops are pictured on the Rue Holgate on the morning of the 12th. This is the junction of the Périers road (now the D971) and the D903 to Baupte and La Haye-du-Puits.

Move 'em out! Now the paratroops proceed south to prepare for a possible German counter-attack .

Approaching the level crossing, at least some of these men can be identified from their helmet markings as 327th Glider Infantry. The same building down the street on the right can be seen in the picture on page 312. The counter-attack came on the morning of June 13 from the south-west along both the Périers and Baupte roads. Supported by armour from the 17. SS-Panzergrenadier-Division, the Germans pushed the Americans back to within 500 yards of the city, and not until tanks from the 2nd Armored Division were called forward to assist the hard-pressed 506th was the attack halted.

Left: Now the flags can come out as the first French city is liberated. This Jeep, travelling east along Carentan's main street, belongs to the ubiquitous 1st Battalion of the 401st.

Right: The Rue de l'Isle, no longer the N13, has been upstaged by a new bypass, the Boulevard de Verdun, which leads to the appropriately-named Rue de la 101^{e} Airborne.

Although a victory had been won, unfortunately the fighting had been marred by excesses committed by both sides, there being many accounts of German prisoners being shot out of hand, and of Americans being mutilated and killed after capture. (We examine this further in Volume 2.) Also, regimental commanders on both sides had been found wanting. ***Above:*** **On the evening of June 20, the 101st Airborne Division held a ceremony in the Place de la République to decorate its regimental commanders with the Silver Star. The third highest American award after the Medal of Honor and Distinguished Service Cross was given to Colonel Johnson (501st); Lieutenant Colonel Michaelis (who had taken over the 502nd from Colonel Moseley); Colonel Sink (506th) and Colonel Harper. 'Bud' Harper had been the regimental commander of the 401st Glider Infantry since it was raised in 1942, and he had been incensed when it was split up to add the extra battalions to the 325th and 327th, so he must have been more than pleased to now be back in charge.**

the Germans flushed from their shelters by the tanks. By the end of the day, the German threat was completely dissipated, and the division organised a defensive position covering Carentan which it held during the ensuing weeks while the American divisions from Utah Beach occupied the peninsula and port of Cherbourg to the north.

The battle for Carentan ended our part of the serious fighting in Normandy as we were withdrawn to England following the capture of Cherbourg and before the Allied breakout from the beach-head. In the campaign, our casualties totalled some 3,800 men, approximately one-third of the men who reached Normandy. It was a heavy price to pay but far below what had been estimated in the planning phase in England.

For the senior airborne commanders, the campaign held many lessons. The feasibility of large-scale airborne operations had been verified although the scattered drop of the parachutists was renewed evidence of the need for greater accuracy of Air Force navigation in darkness. Until such accuracy was clearly demonstrated, I was convinced that parachute commanders would have to expect dispersion and should make provision for it in their planning. If a mission required the strength of one battalion on the spot to carry it out at night, planners should assign it about three times that number to compensate for the probable dispersion.

Overshadowing the airborne lessons of the Normandy landings was the revalidation of the wonder-working effects of concentrated power used with surprise, mass, and mobility in accomplishing great military purposes. The Allies achieved these effects through a willingness to put it all 'to the touch' and in so doing won it all. The fate of Hitler's Reich was sealed in the course of just one week's fighting, in which time Fortress Europe was breached and the Allied armies were firmly established on the Continent.

Abbreviated Index

FOR FULL INDEX SEE VOLUME 2

Note: page numbers in *italics* refer to illustrations